The River That Flows Uphill

Ever seen a river flow uphill? Go down to the bottom of the Grand Canyon and stand on the shore, downstream of one of those big rapids on the Colorado River. A grand sweep of water flows back upstream.

Evolution, too, seems like a river that flows uphill, hoisting itself by its own bootstraps to ever-fancier innovations. The attainment of DNA, of cells, of sex, of brains—they're the waterfalls of the uphill river, ascent amid turbulence.

The most recent and puzzling of the uphill waterfalls, language and consciousness, may just be a spare-time use of some brain circuits occasionally needed in ridiculous quantities for throwing accurately, much enhanced by our ancestors' survival on the ice-age frontiers. That may be how we got our musical skills too, just another innovative use of those same mostly idle sequencing cells.

New uses for old things—that means that some skills are unearned gifts. They arrive without instruction manuals. We're still trying to figure out our storytelling consciousness, perhaps bootstrapping ourselves up to yet another serendipitous surprise as we explore that beneficent bonus. I've always liked the way that Tom Robbins phrased it: "Our great human adventure is the evolution of consciousness. We are in this life to enlarge the soul and light up the brain."

The River
That Flows Uphill

A Journey from the Big Bang to the Big Brain

WILLIAM H. CALVIN

SIERRA CLUB BOOKS
San Francisco

The Sierra Club, founded in 1892 by John Muir, has devoted itself to the study and protection of the earth's scenic and ecological resources—mountains, wetlands, woodlands, wild shores and rivers, deserts and plains. The publishing program of the Sierra Club offers books to the public as a nonprofit educational service in the hope that they may enlarge the public's understanding of the Club's basic concerns. The point of view expressed in each book, however, does not necessarily represent that of the Club. The Sierra Club has some sixty chapters coast to coast, in Canada, Hawaii, and Alaska. For information about how you may participate in its programs to preserve wilderness and the quality of life, please address inquiries to Sierra Club, 730 Polk Street, San Francisco, CA 94109.

This edition is reprinted by arrangement with Macmillan Publishing Company, a division of Macmillan, Inc.

Library of Congress Cataloging-in-Publication Data

Calvin, William H., 1939–
    The river that flows uphill.

    Bibliography: p. 491
    Includes index.
    1. Neurobiology—Philosophy. 2. Brain—Evolution.
3. Human evolution. I. Title.
QP356.C35 1987   575   87-381
ISBN 0-87156-719-9 (pbk.)

Acknowledgment is made to the following for permission to reproduce copyrighted material from the sources named:
Wallace Stevens poetry at Mile 29 and Mile 71, from *The Palm at the End of the Mind: Selected Poems and a Play* by Wallace Stevens, edited by Holly Stevens. Copyright 1967, 1969, 1971 by Holly Stevens. Reprinted by permission of Random House, Inc., and Alfred A. Knopf, Inc.
Annie Dillard excerpt at Mile 160, from *Living by Fiction* by Annie Dillard, pp. 180–185 with deletions. Copyright 1982 by Annie Dillard. Reprinted by permission of the author and Harper & Row.
Jorge Luis Borges poetry at Mile 225, from "A New Refutation of Time" in *A Personal Anthology* by Jorge Luis Borges. Copyright 1967 by Grove Press, Inc. Reprinted by permission of Grove Press, Inc.
Wildlife sketches at Mile 109 and Mile 134, from *Mammals of the Grand Canyon* by Donald F. Hofmeister. Copyright 1971 by Donald F. Hofmeister. Reprinted by permission of the University of Illinois Press.

Cover design by Paul Bacon

Printed in the United States of America on recycled acid-free paper

10 9 8 7 6 5 4

In memory of my father,
FRED HOWARD CALVIN
(1909–1979)
who would have enjoyed this trip.

Contents

Illustrations

Preface

Theorists as diverse as Freud, Skinner, Marx, and Mao have argued that it simply is not possible to pull oneself up by one's bootstraps, moral or otherwise, if the historical, social, genetic, and economic conditions in one's world are not just right. Other thinkers have tried to show that it is in fact possible to do justice to our intuitions about purpose, free choice, and moral responsibility within a mechanistic framework.

OWEN J. FLANAGAN, JR.
The Science of the Mind, 1984

When we hear that Archimedes claimed, given a lever and a place to stand, he could even move the earth, we smile. There is no possible place to stand.

The right footing also seems to be the problem when trying to pull yourself up by your own bootstraps. Yet bootstrapping exists, to our surprise, and ever bigger brains are but one example. Charles Darwin discovered where we stand while pulling ourselves up. His great contribution was to propose a plausible mechanism to allow the simpler forms of life to bootstrap themselves up to more intricate and sophisticated forms. Since 1838, when Darwin had his inspiration about natural selection editing the random variations seen in all species, there has emerged one example after another of evolutionary bootstrapping. These extend all the way from the Big Bang to the Big Brain.

Order, even intelligence, can fortuitously arise out of chaos via what Jacob Bronowski liked to call stratified stability. When we someday build a computer or superhuman smarter than we are but lacking our destructive tendencies, we will be carrying on the bootstrapping tradition.

Such is the stuff of sagas. It seems only fitting to tell this evolutionary tale while visiting the greatest evolutionary spectacle on earth—the mile-deep Grand Canyon of the Colorado River, with its stratified rock layers going down to when bacteria ruled the earth, its fossils recording the post-Cambrian explosion of life forms of increasing complexity, its ruins re-

vealing Stone Age human history. And because its wilderness setting so epitomizes the lives experienced by our ancestors, it acquaints us with those uncivilized circumstances for which evolution shaped us, helps put us back in touch with those roots we find so hard to evoke or articulate.

Only fitting, perhaps, but to attempt to narrate even an ordinary saga or spectacle is to feel inadequate to the task. Yet most scientists—certainly my fellow neurophysiologists—get used to feeling inadequate in the face of the richness and complexity of nature. We comfort ourselves with the knowledge that limited approximations to the truth can be useful, educational, and heuristic—in the way that Newton's relativistically inadequate description of falling apples paved the way for Einstein. And we are finally beginning to provide approximate answers for two age-old questions: *How were humans created?* And *What is the nature of mind?* The new insights from anthropology, evolutionary biology, and neurobiology provide the opportunity to build up from below with a knowledge of the building blocks. Descartes, and until recently most other thinkers as well, was forced to work from the top down, starting with that primal intuition, *Cogito ergo sum,* and trying to guess the underlying nature of the brain.

Few scientists are fortunate enough to stumble upon such a natural framework in which broad scientific concepts can be developed for the unaided general reader. As writers since the time of Homer have rediscovered, however, the journal of a journey can carry the reader along; as scientists since Galileo have known, conversations between imaginary characters can communicate new ideas. This book purports to be a river diary reporting on a series of conversations between scientists and nonscientists during a two-week journey floating down the Colorado River through the bottom of the Grand Canyon. The talk ranges over ecology and the self-organizing stages in the evolution of intelligent life, as the travelers speculate about the recent evolutionary emergence of language and consciousness. Except for casting topics into conversations on the river and inventing a few characters (the real people have surnames given, though I tend to put words in their mouths too), it is nonfiction. While the scientific summarizations given here are among those currently used by scientists to explain their own fields to outsiders, I would caution the reader that some of these "simplified truths" will have shorter lives than others. So consider this a draft, an unfinished book, surely in need of constant revision.

W.H.C.
Seattle
Spring 1986

The River That Flows Uphill

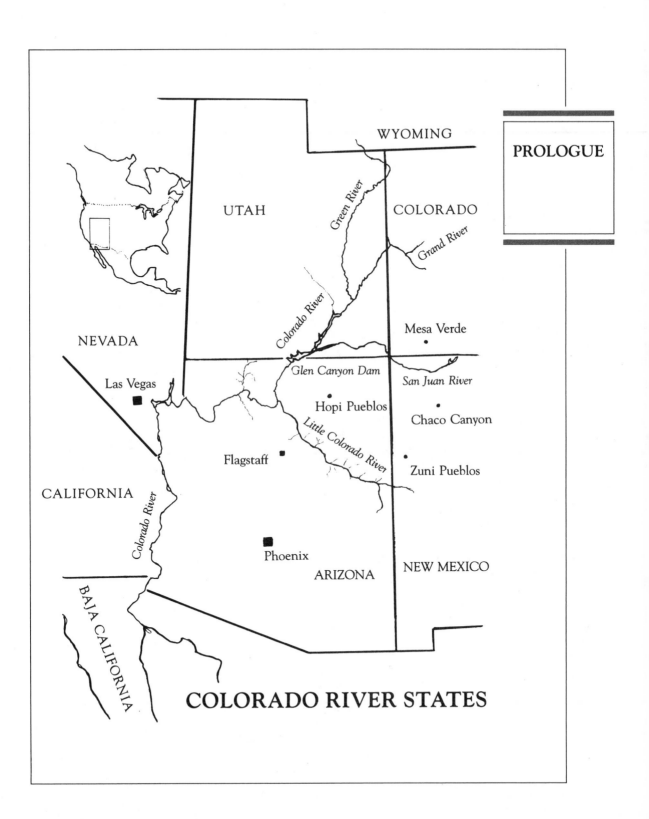

WYOMING

UTAH

COLORADO

Green River

Grand River

NEVADA

Colorado River

Mesa Verde

Las Vegas

Glen Canyon Dam

San Juan River

Hopi Pueblos

Chaco Canyon

Little Colorado River

Flagstaff

Zuni Pueblos

CALIFORNIA

Colorado River

Phoenix

NEW MEXICO

ARIZONA

BAJA CALIFORNIA

COLORADO RIVER STATES

Navajo Reservation
Day 1, about 2:00 A.M.

Man without writing cannot long retain his history in his head. His intelligence permits him to grasp some kind of succession of generations; but without writing, the tale of the past rapidly degenerates into fumbling myth and fable. Man's greatest epic, his four long battles with the advancing ice of the great continental glaciers, has vanished from human memory without a trace. Our illiterate fathers disappeared and with them, in a few scant generations, died one of the great stories of all time.

The anthropologist
Loren Eiseley (1907–1977)

He who calls what has vanished back again into being, enjoys a bliss like that of creating.

The historian
Barthold Niebuhr
(1776–1831)

WHERE DO WE COME FROM, we humans? Darwin called this "the great subject." Even five-year-old children sometimes ask this question.

That we ask such a question at all is a testament to human consciousness. I somehow doubt that the desert animals around here, including the two bats cruising overhead, spend much time contemplating their origin and destiny. We humans love to spin "what-if" scenarios stringing together various concepts from our memories. With them, we attempt to explain the past and forecast the future. However, our consciousness can only be as good as the mental images we conjure up. And memories are surprisingly fragile.

The Navajo Indians of Arizona, on whose desert reservation I am now nursing a cup of coffee in the moonlight, wandered down here from Alaska and northwestern Canada only 500 years ago, hunting and gathering along the way. They arrived just in time for the sixteenth century Spanish explorers to "discover" them. Their grandchildren were undoubtedly entertained with stories of the old country and the journey, just as my grandfather Leebrick told me of coming west in a covered wagon from Virginia to Missouri in 1882. Yet, only twenty generations of grandparents later, the Navajo have now forgotten all about their ancient home in the Yukon.

The Navajo are not unusual in such forgetfulness. For most people in most times, there has probably been little notion of history: they think that the world has always been pretty much like it is now. Except, of course, for a Creation; unfortunately, there are hundreds of creation stories around the world and there is very little consensus.

Writing changed that status quo. It gives the societies that possess it a window into the past, though a narrow one. It enabled the Jews to know, seventy generations after their dispersal, that they once constituted an ancient nation in the Middle East. In the part of the world where agriculture first blossomed, historical records go back 200 generations in some places; empires and other plagues can be seen to come and go. Once the idea of a changing world developed, contemporary clues took on new meaning. In the nineteenth century, the notion that there had been an ice age arose when geologists tried to explain boulders that had been transported long distances from their origins, the strange shapes of some valleys and the parallel scrape marks on their bedrock. They endured scathing skepticism when they reluctantly proposed that mile-high sheets of ice had moved down the valleys and covered up much of northern Europe, Asia, and North America. "No common sense," critics complained.

But the geologists were right. There may, in fact, have been several dozen ice ages.

Now we can reconstruct the past in various ways. The French and Spanish cave paintings give us a glimpse of life 1,100 generations ago at the height of the last ice age. The remaining preagricultural societies help give us a picture of what life might have been like 400 generations ago, after the ice melted but before settled agriculture got started. For the present-day Inuit (Eskimos), the last ice age hasn't ended; their traditional life styles help us imagine how our ancestors might have existed on the ice age frontiers where skillful hunting was necessary to get through the winter.

Science is now recovering the lost facts about human origins, sketching in dates, places, and anatomical changes via the stones and bones that survive. While only a limited view of prehistoric cultures, science has radically revised our preconceptions. The brain has been rapidly enlarging for about 100,000 generations, 99.6 percent of whom lived a hunting-and-gathering way of life before agriculture, civilization, and science came along. We are today using that brain for things entirely different than the tasks that shaped its evolution.

We have found that our roots reach back to a world of which little can be seen today. To understand ourselves—our pleasures, fears, abilities, and consciousness—we must understand what shaped us: our ancestors' way of life and the challenges they faced.

Though it might be a coincidence, the human brain has been enlarging ever since some crazy fluctuations in the earth's climate started to occur about 2 to 3 million years ago. After many millions of years of a cooling and drying trend, the earth began to build up ice in its northern latitudes, covering as much as 30 percent of the land surface; this was an unusual development because the earth has been without polar ice caps for 99 percent of its history. About every 100,000 years, some of the accumulated ice melts off; then the drift back to ice resumes. This has been going on for several dozen cycles, each icy period pushing the more highly selected frontier population back into competition with tropical populations, each warm period providing an opportunity for the survivors on the frontiers to gradually enjoy a baby boom, then fading into another squeeze-and-expand cycle.

During this peculiar 2 to 3 million-year period since the climate began to fluctuate, one species' brain underwent what was, by the standards of evolutionary biology, an extraordinarily rapid growth. For some reason—and the rapidity suggests that it was a compelling one—our brains more than tripled in size. That's

3.6 times larger than the brain that sufficed for the other apes during the same time period. Why?

THAT'S PERHAPS THE KEY QUESTION, and it has emerged after millennia of humans sitting out at night under the stars, wondering what life is all about, from whence we came. The "great subject" is what stirs my thoughts tonight, sitting here above the Colorado River in the moonlight, perched on a great slab of sandstone in the desert and warming my hands on a coffee cup. The nearly-full moon is about to set in the southwest and, so close to the mountainous horizon, it appears huge and yellow to me, dominating all else.

Yet a few minutes after touching the mountains, the moon is gone. The stars come out. The hour is late enough on this summer night that some of the winter constellations can be seen rising in the eastern sky.

Many minds, stimulated by similar sights, have pondered our origins but pure thought cannot make much progress. Modern humans have many more facts and concepts to aid their contemplation, and we better understand the nature of consciousness itself, why and how we think.

We have arrived at the refined version of the question, "What caused brains to enlarge, to distinguish humans from apes?" only because a few intermediate things happened to aid our thinking, such as writing and science. Writing made possible the accumulation of facts over the generations. A settled life allowed techniques to progress.

Facts and techniques aid human consciousness in its attempts to make up stories: we take mental images from past and present, string them together with various future possibilities, and wind up with "what if" scenarios. We then "think it over," trying to see what might go wrong with a plan—and so we discard most such plans before ever acting, thanks to our quality judgments. We make choices, and live with them.

This ability to simulate the real world inside our heads gives us an enormous advantage, both keeping us out of trouble and allowing us insights which lead to new ways of doing things. To call them plans is to emphasize only one of their uses; I just call them scenarios. We imagine doing something, see how it plays. We like to make up stories, see how they sound.

Science, too, accumulates facts and techniques, but by making consciousness into a group activity, refines it even more. A scientist struggles to comprehend the facts and ideas about some concept, thinks up a scenario or equation that seems to account for most of the known facts, and publishes this theory for everyone to see, and then we all (originator included) attempt to poke holes in it. In so doing, we evolve a better explanation. This back-and-forth fitting procedure (similar to a carpenter hanging a door), rather than the usual textbook nonsense about precise logical deduction, is what the "scientific method" is all about. Creating a scenario may be best done inside a single head; trying to find exceptions to the scenario is surely best done by many heads.

Pondering this, I can see that the time is coming—and soon—for a comprehensive biological theory of human origins. Only in this last generation have most of the known facts about human prehistory emerged. During the same twenty-five years, our knowledge of animal and human brains has also expanded enormously: we understand more about how mental images are formed, more about the fragility of our memories and how they can fool us, more about our feelings, more about how our brains influence the health of the rest of our bodies. We neurophysiologists can now even conceive mental images about the inner workings of the human brain itself—and even construct scenarios for how the brain makes up scenarios. A lot has happened. In very fundamental ways it affects how we think of ourselves—and on an everyday basis, not just when we find ourselves contemplating the moon setting behind mountains on a starlit night, as the moonlight dims and the Milky Way begins to emerge from the darkening sky.

We still don't know why those evolutionary changes occurred, but we're getting close to providing a detailed scenario that would seem to answer that crucial question about brain size—and a few related ones as well. Various experts now know enough to make some educated guesses about how humans happened, to spin some scenarios that fit the facts—if one can get them to talk about it.

It usually takes a special setting to get scientists to speculate, off the record, about what isn't yet certain. A long river trip through the Grand Canyon is just the sort of setting in which it might happen. On the river and around the campfire, inundated by the evolutionary stories told by the Grand Canyon itself, will be a good place to discuss these tentative scientific versions of the old creation myths.

Our new [anthropological] origin beliefs are in fact surrogate myths, that are themselves part science, part myth. . . . People clearly want to be free to choose their evolutionary origin stories. Bear this in mind as you read this and other accounts of human evolution.

The archaeologist
GLYNN LLYWELYN ISAAC
(1937–1985)

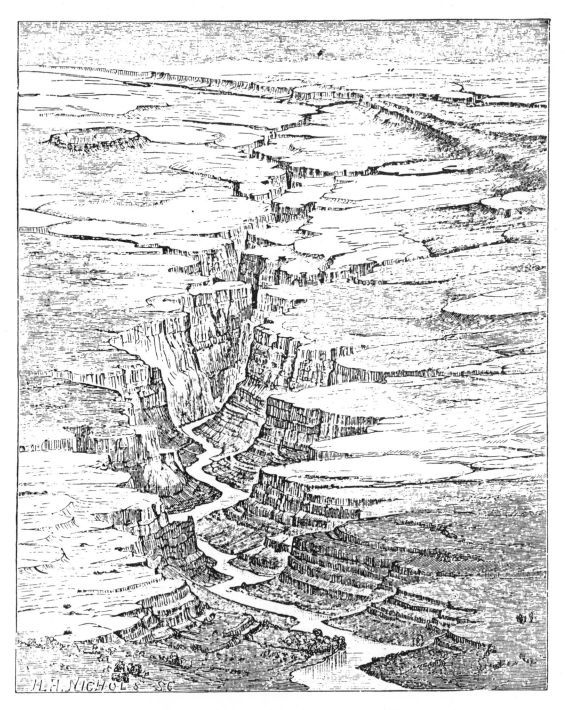

MARBLE PLATFORM

SEEN FROM ATOP THE EAST KAIBAB MONOCLINE

H. H. Nichol's drawing from John Wesley Powell's book on his 1869–1872
Explorations of the Marble and Grand Canyons of the Colorado River.

THE HIGHWAY EMERGES from a narrow cut in the pastel rocks of the painted desert. From the edge of the cliff, the view opens out and down. Far below the flat desert of the Marble Platform stretches out toward the southwest as far as I can see, with the shadows of early morning seeming to elongate it. The Grand Canyon, the greatest evolutionary spectacle on our planet, is on that distant horizon.

Some distance upriver from the Grand Canyon, the Colorado River begins its descent through the layers of our biological history. This happens in a narrow canyon, somewhere just below where I am now.

Hiking away from the road into the mountainous desert, I felt the fresh breezes of dawn touch my face. As I approached the precipice, the view opened to the north, revealing a majestic horseshoe of cliffs, the cornucopia out of which the flat Marble Platform seems to flow.

I am now sharing the viewpoint with four birds preoccupied with their early morning chatter, quite oblivious of me writing in my river diary. The morning sun is shining on the cliffs across the way. The shadow line of the new day starts to creep across the Marble Platform toward me as the earth slowly rotates, taking me with it.

Morning in the painted desert: the incredible red-orange and blue-gray of the rocks, enhanced by the special warm light of the sunrise, the spotlighting, and the shadows. The best time of day, worth the all-night journey to get here on time.

The Colorado River, which carved the Grand Canyon, is out there somewhere in the middle of the horseshoe, heading down toward its most grandiose achievement to make a few more minor alterations in the Canyon's sculpture. The Colorado is not a small river but one of the largest in North America. Yet even from this grand viewpoint there is no river to be seen.

Back up the road, I glimpsed the river by moonlight, heading this way. Yet the Marble Platform seems devoid of rivers, as well as of the trees, sheep, cattle, fences, cultivated fields, houses, towns, and everything else that tends to grow up around rivers. If I sit so that the edge of the cliff obscures my view of its lone highway, the Marble Platform and its surroundings look like a scene from a planet unscarred by humans. Were it not for all the cactus and birds near me on this cliff, I'd say that the view was of a planet untouched by life.

I see only natural scars: the surface of the Marble Platform is interrupted by giant, ragged-edged cracks that descend down into the planet. One crack is the Marble Canyon of the Colorado River, predecessor to its Grand Canyon; the others are the side canyons that lead down to the river, carved by the runoffs of

Marble Platform Overlook
Day 1, Sunrise

the occasional summer thunderstorms. The river is hidden from this vantage point because it has dug itself a very deep trench during the last 30 million years.

The limestone of the Marble Platform was laid down about 250 million years ago, near the end of the Paleozoic era. The land masses and sea floors were then rearranging themselves into just one big continent, Pangaea, surrounded by one big ocean, Panthalassa. The rock underfoot up here on the overlook was formed about 200 million years ago, early in the dinosaur days of the Mesozoic, when Pangaea was beginning to break up into what became our present set of smaller continents, but before they'd yet wandered very far. As I stood up, I accidentally kicked loose a Mesozoic rock, which promptly fell down toward the Paleozoic. I heard it ricochet down through the ages.

NOT ONLY IS THE RIVER HIDDEN, but even the cracks disappear when I descend the Echo Cliffs Monocline and drive along the Platform.

Untouched by life? I can now see that the Platform has a scattering of desert scrubs, but even the local bedrock has been made by life itself. Limestone forms at the bottom of the ocean when the little floating animals die and their calcium-containing bodies sink to rest. And even the other half of the calcium carbonate in limestone was largely contributed by life: the carbon dioxide, CO_2, breathed out by animals may, if not recycled by plants, make its way into forming this nice hard rock. Limestone isn't so much an inanimate object, like the lava pushed up from the depths of the earth, as it is ex-animate.

The road ahead rises and falls a little as it works its way around some of the minor hills in what, from up atop the cliff, looked like a flat surface. Another misapprehension exposed. I find that looking up from the road is very distracting, since I am surrounded by the horseshoe of cliffs, their layers a pale pastel rainbow of colors dominated by reds and browns. There is no hint of the dramatic in the desert floor. Then, at the bottom of one of those little dips in the roadway, the highway swings to the left around some rocks—and right before me appears an enormous crack in the earth, as wide as a superhighway corridor. There is nothing subtle about the way the Canyon greets visitors.

To the early Spanish explorers coming up from the south, confronting the Canyon must have been a tremendous shock, since they were not forewarned by the almost aerial view of the cracks that I glimpsed from atop the cliffs. Some conquistador's horse probably stopped so suddenly at the sight of this gaping hole that the rider was in danger of pitching forward over the poor animal's head. Once the riders collected themselves and ventured on foot to the edge, they would have seen that there is water in the midst of this desert; indeed, quite an amazing amount of water: probably the largest river they'd ever seen. But getting down to the water is like descending the outside of the Statue of Liberty from the torch to the waters of New York harbor. Then there is the little problem of getting back up again. Such is an explorer's life. Fortunately, I know the easy way down to the water. It's at the base of the horseshoe, a mere 7 kilometers upriver from here, at the old nineteenth-century river crossing place called Lee's Ferry. It is about the only easy way down to the river in the entire state of Arizona. All the long float trips down the river must cast off from that one beach.

Lee's Ferry: the only beginning. Just as we count time from the beginning of the universe, so is Lee's Ferry the place from which all distances along the Colorado River are reckoned. Indeed, when they ran out of fancy Spanish, Hindu, and local Indian names for all the subcanyons of the Grand Canyon, they just gave names such as 75 Mile Creek and 220 Mile Canyon, using the distance downriver from Lee's Ferry to describe the place.

The ferryboat was replaced in 1928 by the Navajo Bridge. This two-lane arch bridge looks like an antique. It peaks up in the middle just like the earliest iron arch bridges in England. It is an exaggeration to say that it looks like a pair of hands folded in prayer, meeting above the river, but the hinge in the middle of the span is designed to allow it to rise up higher when the afternoon heat expands the steel.

To the properly observant, the bridge could serve as a giant Texas-sized thermometer: the hotter it gets, the more peaked it looks. One drives slightly uphill to the middle, crosses the peak, and drives down the other side. But I stop, straddling the peak. I turn off the motor. Silence. It's not my natural perversity that makes me halt, merely the view. The signs prohibit stopping, but I have yet to see another vehicle on the highway at this hour.

It is as if I were the only person on this world, a visitor exploring a strange and beautiful planet, seeing occasional relics of an ancient civilization and its primitive technology, listening to the sounds of its winds and birds, smelling its natural odors without the overlay of civilization's everyday pollution. There is a breeze flowing upriver, brushing past me as I lean over the old railing. A pleasant breeze, indeed.

Thirty stories below is the Colorado River. The canyon is about as wide as it is high. A box canyon. The precipitous walls seem brown; the river appears a dark mint green in this shadowed light. Along both sides of the river, clumps of greenery grow on the occasional sand beaches.

Rivers rarely flow in a straight line for very far, given their tendencies to meander, but for a kilometer or more in each direction from the bridge, I can see along the crack until the river bends out of sight. The water is flowing much more quickly than I would have guessed. Something splashes near the left shore, and I look carefully for more activity. Beaver? Rocks falling? Fish jumping? But it isn't repeated.

That's a different world down there. Many birds fly over the river, undoubtedly collecting insects. Sometimes the swallows (or are they swifts?) ascend halfway up a canyon wall to disappear into a hole, probably to feed a hungry family. Up here on the bridge, one is a spectator, a passer-by in the manner of an airplane passenger examining the terrain below. I've come closer to the river than when I was up on the cliff, but I'm still detached. Literally, above it all. Only the breeze, the smells, and the faint sounds of the river below serve to make me feel a part of the river environment.

Such distancing often happens today. Our civilization takes us far away from the elementary sounds and experiences of our hunting and gathering ancestors, leaves us out of touch with our ancient preagricultural roots. Evolution shaped us from prehumans to humans over at least 100,000 generations; the 400 or fewer generations that we've spent away from the hunting and gathering life style probably hasn't changed our gene pool very much. Our deep roots are to ice-age tribes; although we seem extraordinarily flexible and adaptable, our civilized behaviors are inevitably an overlay, a frosting that may sometimes be spread too thin if it is not well anchored in classic ice-age behavior patterns. Getting away to the wilderness occasionally can be a way of watering those roots, firming up the connection to the overlying high culture, preventing dislocations.

The sun has finally peeked over the top of Echo Cliffs. The shadow line has reached the canyon. Scattered clouds tower over the cliffs, backlit by the rising sun. Mountain sunrises and desert sunrises have always been my favorites. And this is mountainous desert. By the time the sun is overhead today, a group of us should be floating down the river beneath this spot. And probably looking up at this bridge. Tourists will wave at us. The Navajo Bridge will be about the last we'll see of civilization's monuments for two weeks. There are no roads reaching the river for 225 miles, no fences, no billboards. It's a wilderness, totally unlike the Grand Canyon glimpsed by millions of tourists from up on top, behind crowded railings.

The best we can do—if we want a journey backward in time,

to see the mileposts in the evolution of intelligent beings, to take a voyage to the origins of life itself, if we want to try to piece it all together—is to take ourselves to the bottom of the Grand Canyon. There we will find rocks of great age, we will find fossils, we will find the dwellings of Stone Age peoples. We will find the land much as our ancestors experienced it, during all those untold generations when prehumans were being shaped into humans. The dimly remembered world from which we somehow took flight.

Such a journey requires some time. The best way is to float down the Colorado River, taking several weeks to investigate the rapids by boat, the side canyons on foot, the waterfalls by inundation. With, of course, the right companions.

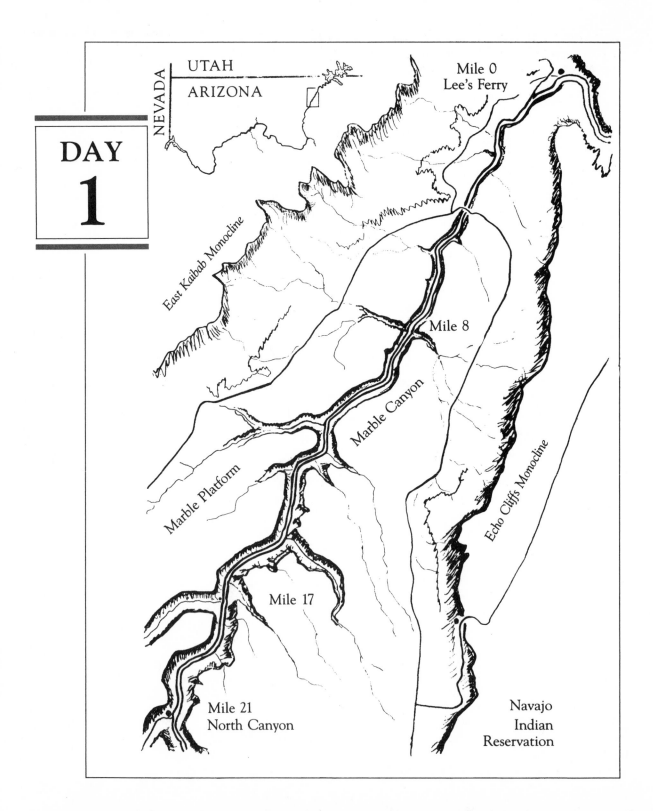

WE CAST OFF from Lee's Ferry onto the Colorado River about noon. Floating away from civilization, it was only a matter of minutes before the collection of park rangers, well-wishers, trucks, buses, outfitters, and motorboats disappeared behind the first bend in the river. Gone. Just like that.

What was left was the incredible view. This is indeed painted desert country. Not for their edibility are the lower rockwalls called the Chocolate Cliffs. The dark red ones above them are the Vermillion Cliffs and, somewhere unseen over the horizon, are Kodachrome Basin and Rainbow Plateau. Reds and oranges and browns occur in various combinations, often streaked with iridescent metallic colors. Different shale layers are colored blue, purple, green, pink, gray, maroon, and brown.

This panorama forms a horseshoe encircling the view back upriver. The river takes such a sharp S-shaped bend just before Lee's Ferry that one can hardly see its canyon. Looking upriver seems a dead-end. The Colorado River thus appears to come out of nowhere, arising fully fledged from the base of the cliffs.

Setting off the red cliffs from the racing green water is a white high-water line bordering the river, much like the lines that delimit other highways. All of this contrasts with the greenery along the Colorado's shoreline, the super-green of the willows and tamarisk. People who haven't experienced the grandeur of the Canyon often refuse to believe a picture of it—they assume the intense colors are some trick of photography. You just have to see it for yourself.

The Colorado moves along at a good clip, generating a welcome breeze. We often don't row but just float along. To keep up with us, someone would have to jog at a good pace along the shoreline. Ashore we were uncomfortable in the hot, still air as we waited for the last of the packing to be done and the last calls to be made from the lone telephone booth with its eavesdropping lizards. Lizards are advanced animals that have the good sense to take shelter from the midday sun.

Now we have the breeze. The windwaves pitter-patter against the bottom of our boat as we pass the confluence with the Paria River. The Paria comes down from Utah, draining the waters of Bryce Canyon into the Colorado.

I EXPLORED THE PARIA'S CANYON this morning while waiting for everyone else to arrive. In most places, the Paria (which rhymes with "Maria") is a muddy creek almost narrow enough for me to jump across, though I wouldn't want to be caught in its narrow canyon during a flash flood. By comparison, the Colorado is a torrent, as wide as a six-lane highway. The Paria's muddy waters slide in along the right bank of the

MILE 0
Lee's Ferry

Tell me to what
  you pay attention
and I will tell you
  who you are.

José Ortega y Gasset

Colorado, mixing like cream poured slowly into a dark mint tea.

There were lots of lizards along the banks of the Paria, jerking their tails about, scurrying among the rocks carried down by the Paria in its more forceful moments. Many of the lizards seem to wear collars, a dark ring encircling their necks. Surely they are therefore Black Collared Lizards. But no, I find that they are Yellow-backed Spiny Lizards. So says the river-runner's blue bible, Larry Stevens' invaluable waterproof book *The Colorado River in Grand Canyon: A Comprehensive Guide to its Natural and Human History*. Authors who have been published in hardcover, paperback, and book club versions now have a new ambition: to see a waterproof edition of their works, truly durable.

All of the Colorado boatmen I've met are knowledgeable and versatile, but Larry Stevens carries things to extremes: he's artist, author, publisher, photographer, biologist, boatman all rolled into one. Mr. Renaissance Man. But, what with his Ph.D. thesis research keeping him too busy, he's not on the river this summer. Happily, another biologist-boatman, Alan Williams, is on this crew—he caught me up on the progress of his thesis research while we were loading the boats. An ecologist, he studies how cottonwood trees wage psychological warfare on attacking aphids. They make 10 percent of their leaves so attractive to aphids that the tiny insects will fight each other to the death for a standing-room-only spot on a tasty leaf, thus minimizing the damage to the other 90 percent of the leaves. And if you think that's wild, another ecologist showed that an attacked willow tree releases a "war cry" odor that alerts the downwind willows to the invaders so they can mobilize their tasty defenses in advance. And I used to think that plants were stupid. I doubt that even lizards are that socially-minded.

The lizards are doing pushups. They run around, then they stop and do pushups for awhile. Not only do their heads bob up and down, but their whole bodies with it. This happens when two lizards meet. A lizard will blow itself up to look bigger than it really is, then knock off a snappy set of stiff-body pushups that would make an army drill instructor proud. The second lizard responds with a similar act of its own. The two lizards then go their own ways, back to the serious business of finding food and mates while the sun shines, before darkness (or too much sun) forces them into quiescence.

Lizards are distant cousins of ours. We shared a common ancestor with them about the time the base of the local cliffs was laid down. The earliest reptiles date back to 340 million years ago, offshoots of amphibians like frogs who were less firmly committed to life on land. The mammals started their own act soon afterward.

THIS BOAT is carrying us down through the ages, the rocks on the left bank getting older by the minute. Indeed, by millions of years each minute. Our vehicle is an inflatable descendant of a dory, crossed with a life raft. Racetrack-shaped like the classic life raft, it is the length of a full-size car and has two inflated crosspieces dividing the boat into three compartments. The rubber (actually neoprene) is stressed to elevate the two ends somewhat, a bow being helpful when crashing into waves, two bows being better than one where rapids may spin the boat around. Two passengers sit forward, two aft, and the boatman with his oars takes the elevated perch in the middle. A rectangular aluminum frame outlines the middle compartment, holding the oarlocks. We carry all of our provisions for the 14-day journey. The boatmen are all pros; the rapids of the Colorado River are the premier white water of North America, no place for amateurs to practice.

In back of us is a great natural amphitheater, a panorama of varicolored cliffs. The blue sky is scattered with fluffy white cumulus. Soon we float into the Canyon proper, with walls rising up out of the river to enclose us, first on the left bank and eventually on the right as well. The rocks in the walls are about 245 million years old, Paleozoic limestone left over from an ancient seabed. They contain fossils of fish and reptiles, but they're a little too ancient to contain evidence of the dinosaurs. The Mesozoic layers from maybe 220 million years ago, which used to sit atop the canyon walls, were eroded away long ago. But the dinosaur layers are still to be found in the Vermillion Cliffs behind Lee's Ferry. And the birds are somewhere above all that, starting at about 200 million years ago. The fossil birds, that is—the present-day descendants of those Mesozoic birds are flapping all around us, catching insects.

The canyon walls keep rising at a prodigious rate. We were on the river for less than an hour before we saw the peaked bridge spanning the gorge, thirty stories up. It provided a momentary bit of shade in midriver, then we floated clear of its shadow. We didn't even look back to say goodbye to this last vestige of the familiar.

MILE 4
Navajo Bridge

There is something
touching and heroic
About the early Mesozoic.
                    CLARENCE DAY

SURPRISE—in the shallows we saw a great blue heron lumbering along with its swiveling gait. That bird could have served as the artist's model for the winged dinosaur; it was almost as tall as one of us, standing perched atop a rock. Then it flew away gracefully, in slow motion, not as ungainly as one somehow imagines a pterodactyl to have been. At least the heron has feathers. They do improve flying, judging from the aerial acrobatics of the swifts and swallows that flit around our boats, skimming along the wavetops in search of insects. We spent some time craning our necks to look up high on the canyon walls, trying to spot the swallow nests in little cracks in the rocks.

There are also big, glossy-black ravens perched on some rocks nearby. Unlike the smaller crows, ravens have shaggy throat feathers, similar to the ones on the tips of their wings. They argue with one another, sounding *cr-r-ruck* in annoyance. Ravens are much larger than crows, more the size of seagulls. The boatman in the neighboring boat has apparently told a raven story, because several of the neurobiologists have started to respond with their own stories about smart birds.

I once heard of a nature-film producer up in Seattle who had observed some of the northwest crows that frequent the beaches practicing an ingenuous form of shell-cracking at a ferry dock. Clams protect themselves against predators by a muscle that holds the half-shells firmly closed. I suppose that one could use a pry bar, but the crows have instead found a way of simply shattering the shells. Before the ferry would arrive, the crows would fly in carrying some clams extracted from the nearby beach at low tide. The Great Clam Airlift! They would then line up the clams on the pavement, right in the path of the cars coming off the ferry. Not surprisingly, the departing cars ran over the clams. After the cars passed, the crows would swoop down to eat the innards. Crows have rather large brains; even though they themselves are about the same body weight as an adult rat, their brains are five times larger.

Gulls are also clever at opening shells: they have been known to carry shells aloft and drop them on a rocky area. In this way, gravity becomes a simple but effective tool. If a shell doesn't crack when first dropped, the gull will pick it up and carry it aloft again, repeating this dozens of times until getting to the food inside. While it obviously works best if there are rocks below, I've also seen gulls repeatedly drop shells on an ordinary sand beach at low tide; the impact on hard, wet sand eventually seems to work, after a few round-trips.

It isn't just coastal birds that have the shell-cracking idea, either. The Egyptian vulture does it in the African savannas, carrying ostrich eggs aloft and then dropping them. If the egg is too large to carry, the vulture has another scheme: it carries a rock aloft and bombs the egg. This was observed in the middle of the nineteenth century, long before humans re-invented bombing.

Ravens bomb too. Scientists who were inspecting a raven nest halfway up a cliff face were being "mobbed" by the frantic parents. Then some rocks came falling down. The scientists at first wondered if they were just loose rocks, knocked free by the unhappy parents. But, when they retrieved the rocks, they found a telltale ring of organic matter which demonstrated that the ravens must have pried half-buried rocks out of the ground atop the cliff and then dropped them; the bombing was no accident.

We neurobiologists enjoy talking science, especially about our specialty: how brains work. It isn't a workaday subject, to be left behind on vacation, but more like a hobby in which we continually indulge ourselves. Some of us specialize in humans, others in monkeys, and quite a few study the primitive brains of various invertebrates. Some have medical school backgrounds, others zoological or anthropological or psychological. This mix should help us to understand the foundations on which brains are built, as together we have quite an evolutionary perspective. The Grand Canyon, of course, inundates us with evolution. It's in the walls surrounding us, layer upon layer. And the layers are still growing, higher and higher.

"Some of Darwin's finches in the Galapagos Islands use tools, you know," Dan Hartline volunteered. He's an old friend from Hawaii, another neurobiologist. "The finches down there are all probably the descendants of just one species of finch, blown west from South America. All it takes is one animal blown far out to sea to start colonizing an island chain."

"One animal is going to get pretty lonely—doesn't it take two animals blown to the same island?" someone asked.

"All it takes is one pregnant female," Dan replied, "and a little incest. Pretty soon, there were lots of the species. And then that first species subdivided into a whole series of new species, each with a different beak shape corresponding to the food they eat. Some have thick beaks for seed-cracking, others have long skinny beaks, handy for poking into cracks in a tree trunk and catching the insects that live down there. As we say in the business, the finches have diversified.

"The Tool-Using Finch doesn't have a particularly long beak," he continued, "and certainly doesn't have the long tongue that a woodpecker uses to probe inside the hole. But he still gets the insects. He finds a twig or a cactus spine and holds it in his beak, pokes it down the hole, and the insects start crawling all over the stick. He pulls the stick out and eats the insects. Now

I think that's pretty clever—that's just like chimpanzees, fishing for termites by poking a stick into a termite nest."

Islands are a great place for seeing evolution in action. Hawaii, for example, is filled with tiny fruit flies. The islands themselves aren't very old, but in that time the flies have diversified even more massively than Darwin's finches.

"But aren't there lots of problems with evolutionary explanations like that?" someone asked from the neighboring boat. "From what I read in the papers, Darwin was wrong."

"It'd be very surprising if he wasn't wrong about something, considering the massive detail of his writings," I answered. "But Darwin was amazingly correct, considering that no one knew about genes in 1858, and none of population biology had been done yet. What he didn't guess was the detailed mechanism of how the genes changed to create a new species out of an old one. But you've got to distinguish between *if* evolution has taken place, and the details of how and where and when it took place."

"Evolution is a very straightforward conclusion, drawn from two observations," Dan Hartline explained. "First, every individual has a parent or two. So far as we know, that has always been true—linking us to the past in an unbroken chain. Second, for each and every species, there was a time when it didn't exist. Together, these two things tell you that evolution has taken place, modifying some ancestors of a different species into the species' present-day form."

All this was obvious and widely known even before Darwin's time. There are other "explanations" but they are—literally—unnatural. "For example," I added, "there are birds all around us here on the river. But there are no bird fossils in those walls of the canyon—those rock layers are too old, laid down when the fishes and amphibians were still the dominant forms of animal life and the reptiles were recent inventions. But if you go up north in Utah, where I was yesterday," I said, pointing back upriver, "you'll find layers of the earth from much more recent times which haven't been eroded away yet. And they'll contain fossils of what look like modified primitive reptiles—birds, as well as dinosaurs. Go further north, up into Wyoming, and you can even find some bones of the early primates. So, while birds didn't exist before 200 million years ago, surely the first birds had parents too, dinosaurs that didn't quite fly."

"Dan, pardon my ignorance," someone volunteered, "but did you say that an individual could have only one parent? I guess that in high school biology, I pretty much thought that it took two."

"Maybe you were fixated on sex at the time," someone else kidded.

"There is a tendency to confuse sex with reproduction," smiled Dan. "But having two sexes happened only in the last third of our biological history. And the old-fashioned ways—such as budding-off and spores—still work in many species."

"You mean clones?"

"That's still another way, though I dislike the word these days, ever since the popular press got hold of it and created newspaper-selling headlines about how Hitler could have been cloned."

"So who first invented flying?" asked Dan Richard, sitting up front in our boat. We have two Dans. This one's a lawyer, a legal counsel to the governor of California. "I fly sailplanes, and I've always wondered how flying got started. Were the flies the first to fly?"

"Probably," I responded, "though not the usual two-winged flies that you swat. They're a streamlined version of more traditional four-winged insects, having suppressed the genes that make the second pair of wings just as the chickens have suppressed the genes that make teeth. But flying itself goes a long ways back. It's been re-invented so many times that it makes you wonder if even the insects were the first. There were flying dinosaurs, such as the pterodactyls, although their reptilian ancestors probably didn't fly. The birds did it with feathers rather than just skin on their wings. Among the mammals, the bats used skin on their forelimbs to make a wing."

"And all sorts of other mammals can glide between trees," Abby noted, "using folds of loose skin that they stretch out tight by sticking out all four legs, making a kind of parachute."

"Did you know that besides the gliding squirrels and the flying fish, there's even a gliding snake?", volunteered Dan Richard. "I saw it on television. Down in the tropics there is a snake that eats insects that live up high in a tree. He climbs the tree with the aid of scale-like protrusions on his underside. When he has picked one tree clean, there's this little problem of backing down to the ground and climbing another tree. So instead he casts off, flattens his body into a ribbon like a boomerang, and glides between trees. There's even a parachuting spider."

"Jumping between trees is basically a behavioral invention," noted Dan Hartline. "Behavior precedes form, as Konrad Lorenz once said. Only later does anatomy get modified to make the behavior less dangerous and more efficient. So those animals with extra body skin on their legs are able to glide better, suffer fewer injuries, eat more insects, leave behind more flabby-skinned offspring than their competitors. That's natural selection—there are just lots of variants within a species, and some succeed better than others."

"It seems only common sense to us now," I commented. "But it took many decades after evolution itself was well known for someone to stumble upon this selective survival as a mechanism for evolving new species. Variations, then editing. One of Darwin's contemporaries said something like 'How extremely stupid not to have thought of that' before!"

MILE 8
Badger Rapid

THE LONG RUN IS POSSIBLE only if we consistently take care of the short run. And so our talk of evolution ceased in favor of paying attention to a consuming interest downriver.

Sue stepped atop her seat, as lithe and loose as a ballet dancer just finished with her warmup. Captain of the ship, she had just gotten the four of us wedged tight into our corners of the rubber raft. (I couldn't help but compare her casual manner upon arising with that of a commuter getting up to leave a bus at the next stop. Then I remembered that she was the driver.) She was, I supposed, not planning to abandon us but merely standing up to get a better view down into the boiling white water of the rapid, toward which we were drifting with the current. Sue guided us by an occasional stroke on the oars.

The water of the Colorado River was deceptively calm—the way it always is, upstream from waterfalls. Like a reservoir above a dam. But, I reassured myself, Badger Rapid is not yet a waterfall. One must be quantitative about waterfalls, after all— Badger rates a mere 7 on the Grand Canyon's scale (10 is a barely navigable monster rapid; I suppose that 11 would therefore rate as a waterfall). Beyond the lip of the rapid, where the flat river seemed simply to end, great eruptions of white water were being thrown into the air, as if the rapid were advertising its virility, like a gorilla thumping its chest.

Strangely, each great splash was soundless—drowned out, I supposed, by the sustained roar of the rest of the rapid. The splashes were just white flashes against the reddish-brown background of the Canyon walls, first here, then there. Like lightning when you're too far away to hear the thunder. But those splashes are, ahem, close. And getting closer. Were we going through that?

As we drifted toward the rapid, Sue gave us a quick safety lecture. Life-jackets are very nice when you need them, but the major goal is to keep yourself inside the boat. "Crouch down in one corner of your compartment," she said. "As the floor of the boat rises and falls with the waves, pump your legs, just as if you were skiing. Wedge yourself into a corner, and keep your feet under your body. And keep a secure grip on your two handholds. Always two."

Her lecture completed, Sue sat back down again just as casually as she had stood up, routinely fastened her lifejacket a little tighter, and checked her belt knife ("Don't get entangled with a rope if we flip over," she'd said only minutes before). She pushed on one oar and then the other, rowing us over to the exact spot where she wanted to enter the rapid, never taking her eyes away from the white water ahead. I think she likes running rapids.

THE WATER WAS SO CALM that we felt a bit silly, wedged into our corners and hanging on with whitened knuckles. Then we slid over the smooth lip of the rapid and into the first gentle, rolling wave of the tongue. Pleasant, but I'm not fooled. When we finally reached the tip of the tongue, a viciously cold lateral wave splashed over the right side of the boat, eliciting yells from those slapped by it. Even when one expects it, a bucket of cold water is still a bucket of cold water. After that brief introduction, everything happened so quickly that we had no time to think about what we were doing.

The boat bent up in the middle as its bow climbed a wave, exhibiting a flexibility that we hadn't suspected. Over the crest of the wave and the boat arched its back just as radically the other way. A rubber roller-coaster. Aided by several swift strokes on the oars, Sue slid us sideways around another standing wave that ended in a boiling white "hole." We had successfully cleared the hole when still another small wave appeared out of nowhere and threw several buckets worth of cold river over the stern compartment. Two more big waves followed. Everyone was yelling, involuntarily or with perverse pleasure.

The river spun us around, sending us careening downriver stern first. The rubber floor of the boat seemed to have a life of its own, dropping slack and then popping up into the compartment with some force. As if we were skiing an endless field of moguls, our legs pumped like pistons, keeping us wedged into our chosen corners.

Then the twisting and turning was over, the ups and downs gradually moderated, and we were left with just the cold water dripping off our amazed faces. We saw a swirling back-eddy alongside, where the water was gracefully sweeping back upriver. Pulling hard against the currents, Sue rowed us over into the eddy—whereupon we reversed course and were carried back upriver.

What is she up to now? Is she going to run it *again*? Not that we had any time to marvel at all this. Per instructions, we were all bent over, bailing buckets of water out of the bilges. We scarcely managed to see the incredible Marble Canyon scenery for a few minutes.

Take care to get what you like
or you will be forced
to like what you get.
Where there is no ventilation,
fresh air is declared
unwholesome.

GEORGE BERNARD SHAW

SUE SAID that she normally stayed out of the back eddies, but that we had to provide emergency towing and pickup services for the other boats in case they got into trouble. (Ah, but who covered us?) Which was one reason why we had to bail the water out of the bilges as soon as possible. A boat that's overloaded with water is no fun to row and doesn't make a particularly swift rescue vehicle. Hint, hint. So we tried to get the last teaspoon of river out of the bilges. Sue runs a tight ship.

From our new vantage point, we got to watch the other six boats come through. We could barely hear their passengers yelling above the roar of the rapid. A boat would disappear into a trough and then surprise us by suddenly reappearing on a different side of a wave than we had expected. Most boats got a lot wetter than we did. The last boat through hit a wave wrong, briefly lost control, and slid down into a fury of boiling waves. When it finally sped past us, looking somewhat low in the water, all four passengers were bailing furiously. Sue pulled us out of the back-eddy with a series of strong strokes and we finally caught the main current to follow them down the river.

Susan Bassett, our boatman and an ex-Harvard Medical School secretary, is called "Subie" by the other boatmen. She is tall and slender, with large expressive eyes that don't miss a thing. As we were renewing our acquaintance, I remembered the first river trip I took with her, down the Middle Fork of the Salmon River up in Idaho. At the time she wore a baseball cap with the letters "SUE B." on the front (the first river crew on which she rowed had another Sue). I suspect that the cap is long since deceased, but everyone still calls her Subie. I took my first big course on brains at Harvard Med when she worked in the Dean's Office there, and I strongly suspect that she was the helpful secretary who somehow found a spare microscope for me to borrow. We meet again in the strangest places.

AN ESCALATOR FOR BIRDS? It certainly looks like it. Some of the birds are circling around above the left bank, rising higher and higher on each revolution. Dan Richard spotted it, that being one way that glider pilots spot thermals—just look for the birds utilizing them.

Abby, upon seeing this, told us about what she'd seen yesterday down at an ancient cliff-dwelling, Betatakin. "We got down in this canyon with the park ranger about nine in the morning, just when the sun was starting to illuminate the cliff-dwellings set back in this enormous alcove in the cliffs. But out in front of Betatakin, circling in the air, must have been three-dozen big birds. Probably turkey vultures."

"They were riding a thermal up out of the canyon?" asked Dan Richard.

Abby nodded. "That's what the ranger said. They just started circling lazily, and soon they were halfway up. A little longer, and they were up out of the canyon. Then they started flapping away with that distance-covering wingbeat of theirs. Pretty soon they were out of sight. By the time we'd hiked further down the canyon to the ruins, they were all up the escalator and gone. Off to work."

Hot air rises. And birds know it. Or at least the birds that can discover it are a lot more efficient, get more babies to grow up, and so populate the world with smarter birds.

THE ARGUMENT FOR A GRAND DESIGN usually says something to the effect that fancy anatomy is too sophisticated to have arisen by chance, that it goes against common sense to say otherwise. Architecture requires an architect, and so forth.

The argument against design usually substitutes Darwinian natural selection, saying that all our abilities have been shaped by gradual adaptations, such as the loose skin that gliding squirrels use. In this adaptationist view, success in one endeavor allows the genes that promote success to produce a relatively larger share of the next generation. Even small differences in survival and reproduction count when compound interest operates over thousands of generations. And so Darwin's finches arise, a whole family of birds, each specialized for a particular food or two. What can happen in a newly colonized island in only a few millennia may take longer to happen back on the mainland, but the basic process is the same. It's probably how all species have arisen, including us.

Abby was not convinced by this approach to evolution. "You know, what bothers me about this standard evolutionary story are not the usual things, like the eye—how could such a perfect optical instrument arise by chance, surely it bespeaks the guiding hand of a Creator—because I buy adaptation for useful traits." She took off her big straw hat and brushed back her blond hair. "But there are just too many things around in which our talents seem greatly in excess of anything our environment demands."

She leaned forward, then continued with a sweeping gesture. "Take music, for example. What on earth is the survival advantage of being able to follow, let alone compose, Bach's *Goldberg Variations*? Sure, a little love of music might have helped social cohesion, a little dancing to music might have eased social tensions. But I don't believe for a minute that prehuman primates held rock concerts and that this made them better warriors or

Evolution is fact, not theory. . . . Birds evolve from nonbirds, humans evolve from nonhumans.

The geneticist
RICHARD C. LEWONTIN, 1981

Everything is what it is because it got that way.

The biologist
D'ARCY THOMPSON,
On Growth and Form, 1917

more peaceful citizens. And even if they did, how did it select for the fancy musical abilities like harmony? Four-part inventions? Adaptation arguments just won't work for music."

No, we conceded. Try as we could, we couldn't think of any reason that our considerable musical abilities—far in excess of the frenzied chimpanzee rain dance—could have aided evolution enough to help a prehuman survive better.

But, we pointed out, some things in evolution are sidesteps in which an anatomical feature turns out to have additional, unexpected uses besides the one for which natural selection shaped it. Maybe music is another sidestep.

"So what was the original talent from which music emerged?" asked Abby, pursuing her point.

A good question. "Maybe language? They are both timed sequences of sounds," answered someone I didn't know. I liked that answer.

"But don't abilities such as music," continued Abby, "make you wonder if there isn't some higher principle shaping life, some goal to evolution?"

No, we biologists replied. That's not to say we're sure there isn't, but our agnosticism is an occupational hazard of our profession. We cannot assume the existence of a guiding principle because it would discourage us from seeking simpler explanations. It would paint us into a corner. We'll just have to see if we can come up with a scenario for the invention of music via a sidestep from some adaptive improvement in another skill.

"And what about laughter, what is its evolutionary utility?" Abby added. Here we go. "The chimps and monkeys may romp and tickle, but they don't laugh or seem to have a real sense of humor. And laughter is almost an involuntary reflex, not what you expect for higher cerebral activity. So how did natural selection produce that?"

Sigh. I'll add it to the list. Explanations needed: Music, humor, and now laughter. We have a whole two weeks in which to think about them.

Subie calls our attention to Ten Mile Rock, a big pillar of rock on the right bank, a few stories high. Once upon a time, it fell off the face of the cliff above. Somehow it didn't topple over upon crashing into the riverbank. Not your usual balancing rock, like the one we saw driving up the road from Navajo Bridge to Lee's Ferry. Those are formed by erosion, eating away a softer layer that underlies harder stuff.

I liked the way several people responded to Abby's point about the involvement of "something else" in evolution. They said that doing science is rather like piecing together a jigsaw puzzle, trying to make the big picture emerge from all the little fragments.

So far, the big picture looks like a tree. A single big tree, not a lot of little ones.

Just as there were no birds before 200 million years ago, so there were no large-brained primates until the last several million years. We don't know if the prehuman fossils we find are direct ancestors of ours or just cousins on a slightly different branch of the tree. But the shape of the rest of the underlying tree is abundantly clear to anyone who examines the facts. And it isn't a collection of independent creations every now and then.

We're apes. Apes come off the primate branch. Primates are rooted in the mammals. The mammals and the birds evolved from the reptiles. About the time that the canyon surrounding us was laid down, the reptiles evolved from amphibians. Earlier, the amphibians evolved from fish, which evolved from primitive chordates, which evolved from an invertebrate rather like the sea-squirt. The invertebrates, and all other multicelled organisms, evolved from a single cell type called a eukaryote—or, as I call it, Supercell. Supercells are the main trunk of the evolutionary tree, the one from which several dozen major branches have arisen.

Supercell took a long time to evolve from Simplecell, the bacterium. Bacteria have been around for about 75 percent of the earth's existence, three times as long as Supercell. In fact, Supercell's constituents, such as mitochondria, look as if they may have been hitchhikers, independently living organisms that were taken in and put to work. Supercell looks to be a great committee effort, self-organized from bacterial components, co-evolving together. The bacterium in its many forms evolved from some ancestor, probably the outcome of some competition in the early oceans between various forms of self-replicating chemical systems using a common genetic code. The bacterium's machinery for making proteins will even construct human proteins—such as the growth hormone that dwarfs lack—if you snip the genetic instructions for making these proteins out of the DNA of a human cell and insert them into the bacterium, thus neatly demonstrating that we still use the same protein-building system that was around during the earth's childhood.

We can even imagine how chemicals floating around in shallow waters self-organized themselves during the earth's infancy into primitive bacterial cells that had the amazing ability to make copies of themselves. We can guess how the genetic coding instructions might have evolved, those necklace-like blueprints that tell the cell how to construct another living cell. We know how the carbon-based chemicals that make up living organisms can have arisen before life itself, since we can see them being synthesized in many different laboratory experiments mimicking the conditions that existed on the early earth. And how carbon and all the other elements heavier than hydrogen and helium were constructed in the dense centers of collapsing stars. And something of how the Big Bang evolved from pure energy to form stars of hydrogen and helium.

The whole chain of events has taken about 15,000 million years, while our peculiarly large brains have only evolved in the last 2 million years. The puzzle has been pieced together, largely by the last few generations of humans, using science to build on the cultural edifice of many thousands of generations. There is no need to postulate a miracle at any stage. It's just like doing a jigsaw puzzle: whenever you think that there is no piece that can possibly fill a blank space, you don't just throw up your hands and insist that only a miracle will solve the problem. You keep looking, and eventually you find something that links together the parts of the puzzle.

Yet the magnificent façade of science is not a completed jigsaw puzzle, not now. Perhaps there will someday be a piece that won't fit, a space that won't fill. Still, the critics who now and then cry "unproved" (rather than "unfinished") are shortsighted if they cannot tell that the picture contained in the incomplete puzzle is a single giant tree. One need not have lines connecting every generation with the immediately preceding one to see that the big picture is one big tree, and not a forest of little trees independently created *de novo* every now and then.

The theory of evolution isn't like a Euclidian theorem describing geometry that must be "proven"—it's a historical synthesis that explains major features of the past in an economical way, a way that makes correct predictions. It's a well-tested theory that ties together the entire edifice of biology, from molecules to humans. But it's not complete yet, and its implications aren't always clear.

[Miracles rest simply] upon our perceptions being made finer, so that for a moment our eyes can see and our ears can hear what there is about us always.

WILLA CATHER, *Death Comes to the Archbishop,* 1927

□   □   □

SOAP CREEK RAPID has come and gone. We're still wet, though the water is now out of the bilges. Soap Creek's rated a 5, though some people have gotten into real trouble here. Subie points out an inscription, carved into a rock in 1889, telling of the death of F.M. Brown—and Peter Hansbrough, who carved it, was himself drowned five days later. While fatalities do occur on the Colorado, they're pretty rare these days due to better boats and better boatmen, thanks to a century of experience passed on from one generation of river-runners to the next. For example, now one rows rapids facing into them, rather than backwards in the traditional rowboat style. Funny how it helps to look where you're going. Such improvements make cultural evolution work a lot faster than biological evolution—which might have to wait for a variant that did things backwards.

Lacking foresight, evolution is simply opportunistic, retaining those features that were available when opportunity knocked, forming a patchwork of makeshifts. We too are imperfect, products of the unique set of challenges posed during the ice ages after our ancestors got started with a brain the size of a gorilla's. Somehow, evolution enlarged that brain threefold and created a unique set of inborn skills for making tools, throwing spears, and speaking sentences. It even created the capacity for music and poetry. And humor. Somehow.

We are all sitting at a cosmic poker game in which the house has an infinite supply of chips. Neither we nor our genes can ever really win, since we can never cash in our chips and go home. . . . There is nothing but the game, and since it has been going on for a long time, only the best players are left. It is an existential game, the only one in town, and all we can do is to stay in as long as possible. We are all playing, so perhaps we may as well enjoy it. Certainly we should understand it.

   The sociobiologist DAVID BARASH, *The Whisperings Within,* 1979

□   □   □

ANCIENT REPTILE TRACKS are to be found over on the left bank somewhere, but we don't have time to stop. Besides, we're busy bailing again. Sheer Wall Rapid only drops the river level down a story or less, but we just happened to get a big wave over the stern, right where I am sitting. An old guidebook says that Sheer Wall is rated a 7, but the blue bible indicates that modern boatmen only rate it a 2. *Sic transit gloria.*

   The reptile tracks are in the Coconino sandstone, the Sahara-Desert-like layer that emerged from the river back about where the bridge spans the canyon. Here, it's high above the waterline now. Curiously, no reptile fossils have been found in it, just tracks. I was going to say that maybe the vultures and hawks ate them all, but the only flying animals back 270 million years ago were the insects. The river certainly does focus us on time, immense stretches of time.

MILE 17
House Rock Rapid

THE RIVER HAD BEEN GETTING SLOWER. And wider. Subie was having to row more. And then there was the sound of an airplane roaring somewhere—except that it didn't disappear into the distance as airplane sounds are wont to do. It just slowly got louder. Subie smiled at our attempts to locate the airplane and said that House Rock was just around the corner. House Rock Rapid, an 8, is an even larger fraction of a waterfall than Badger.

About the time that we started to worry about our cameras getting soaked, Subie told us not to bother stowing them away in our ammo cans yet, because we were first stopping above House Rock Rapid to have a look at the rapid from shore. She beached our boat on a broad sandy beach on the right shore, and we all climbed out.

Subie and the other boatmen all went bounding through the field of boulders to their favorite lookout place. The rest of us, still clad in orange lifejackets, wandered down the beach to inspect it up close. For most of a city block, the river was a series of big waves. There were a few giant crests but mostly smooth ups and downs, many as tall as a person. Here and there, great holes of white water could be seen where the river poured over a steep rock face in the manner of a waterfall, carrying a lot of air underwater with it; this plunging turbulence is what the boatmen call a "hole."

But the big waves stood still, like hills and valleys usually do. Even those of us who understood why found this amazing. In the ocean, waves move forward but the water doesn't—the energy is just transferred forward, as in a tightly-packed row of billiard balls hitting one another wham-wham-wham, with only the last ball in line actually moving very far. In a rapid, waves are stationary but the water moves. Standing waves, literally, just like Pythagoras discovered 2,500 years ago when analyzing musical chords. They do splash around a little, not being completely stationary, just to make things more interesting for the boatmen. And, of course, the amount of water coming down the river makes a big difference in where the waves and holes are located in the rapid.

Unfortunately, the water level of the Colorado is now under the control of technicians at the Glen Canyon Dam, Dan Richard explains. And not just seasonally—since about 1980, they have adjusted the water release every hour according to how many air-conditioners are turned on in Phoenix, engaging in what is called peaking power generation. Without so much as an environmental impact statement (which the government was legally required to file, according to our lawyer), the Colorado is now flooded daily with large artificial tides, rising and falling with the business day. Release twice as much water several hours later and the standing waves are drowned by high water. To the people who built and run the dam, the Canyon is an inconsequential sluiceway. And all those beautiful canyons upriver of Glen Canyon Dam, with names like Music Temple and Tapestry Wall, are now illuminated only by a pale green light. And the reddish brown silt, which for millions of years gave the river its rich color, is now filling the drowned canyons. This is not your usual benign flood-control dam. High-rise hydroelectric dams don't prevent floods so much as they create them.

THE BOATMEN were in a hurry and waved us all back to the boats in short order. We wanted to get started before the rush of water arrived, from when the air-conditioners were turned on this morning.

Subie's boat was again to be the first to take on the rapid, and she rowed upriver with a strong backstroke to position our boat in the center of the river channel. She again specified exactly which handholds were safe and which were to be avoided. "Don't grab the blue line around the outside of the boat, unless you're swimming for some reason and need something to grab. And you don't want to get wrapped up with a rope, or get your leg wedged in a crack. If the boat flips over, you *want* to be thrown clear and not trapped underneath." In the life jacket, Subie explains, "you'll go bobbing down the river just like an orange cork, getting a unique cork's-eye view of the white water. And someone'll row over and pick you up." Reassured, we faced the rapid—visible now only as a lot of splashing water beyond the smooth surface of our backed-up lake.

"Oh yes," Subie added, "if I yell HIGH-SIDE, I want you to throw your weight to the high side of the boat. That's in case one side of the boat gets submerged in a wave." Just as in sailboats, one high-sides to counterbalance. In a hurry.

Subie, complaining earlier about someone tracking sand into the bottom of the boat, had said "Oh, well, we're taking her to the boat wash." Running House Rock Rapid was indeed like being in a washing machine, first a wave from one direction, then from another, overlapping the first. Again and again, as if giants were shuffling a deck of watery cards. And when we bailed the boat, out went the sand too.

We got cooled off again. The water temperature is cold, about 9° Celsius (also known as about 48° Fahrenheit in certain insular parts of the world, namely the United States, most everyone else having officially gone metric). The river water doesn't come from the surface of Lake Powell, the dam intakes being well below the surface to avoid sucking in all the floating trash from the boaters, and the sun's rays don't warm up the water very much down at those depths.

BACK TO THE BIRDS. We know they evolved from the reptiles but, aside from a half-dozen specimens of a small dinosaur called *Archaeopteryx* whose forelimbs suggest wings, the intermediate species have not been identified very well. The key evolutionary problem with birds, however, has been in figuring out how they got started on their flying careers. Standard reasoning, based on Darwin's natural selection, usually leads people to think in terms of "adaptation"—that each successful little stage of anatomical change is rewarded with more descendants in the continuing battle for the survival of the fittest. And if the next stage proves still more useful, it is further rewarded, and so on.

Feathers are all very nice for flight, but one needs a lot of them before they do any good at all. A few feathers on the limbs of a running dinosaur would hardly induce liftoff, to recall Stephen Jay Gould's lovely phrase. So how did the reptile develop ever greater numbers of feathers, to build up to the threshold for flight? Evolution has no foresight, in the manner of human consciousness—it cannot just plan ahead for something useful in the future, such as when the unexplained "#" and "*" buttons were included in pushbutton telephones decades ago, anticipating the future expansion of special services (and causing millions of parents to have to admit, when inevitably asked "What's that for?", that they didn't know).

Even if we knew that there was another ice age coming, we couldn't prepare for it by growing more and more body hair with each generation until we became hairy again. Evolution selects useful features, but based on *present-day* needs. If you don't have them when they're needed—well, it's just someone else's turn.

Which, of course, suggests that feathers were initially useful for something besides flying. Indeed, feathers are useful for the same reason as body hair: thermal insulation against the cold. I'm sure that someday we will discover a feathered dinosaur; maybe we'll get lucky while out searching for the footprints of running dinosaurs, and find a place where one of them stumbled and fell. If it left a nice imprint in a hardening mud flat, it might reveal an abundant plumage on an otherwise reptilian body.

The archaeologists studying the prehuman footprints found at Laetoli in Tanzania, where hardening volcanic ash preserved the footprints left by some upright-walking hominids 3.7 million years ago, presumably have the same hope: to find where someone slipped and fell, or sat and rested. Then we could see how much body hair they had, whether they were wearing clothing or perhaps carrying a basket, and the like. The record of the past is terribly biased by the fact that hard evidence (literally hard: bones, stone tools, pottery fragments) survives better than wooden spears, carrying baskets, and characteristic behaviors. Yet the soft evidence would, in the case of humans, tell much more of the story.

BOULDER NARROWS, this spot is called. It is narrow enough to make this the deepest place on the river for the next 110 miles. And there is a big slab of limestone sitting in the middle of the river, forcing the boats to detour one way or the other.

There is some driftwood atop the boulder, left there by the great flood of 1957, one of the last big spring runoffs before the dam was built. Since the dam gates were closed in 1963, most of the driftwood has been trapped in Lake Powell. River parties don't collect driftwood anymore for bonfires, since what is left is the home of birds and rodents.

FEATHERS MIGHT HAVE AIDED THE SURVIVAL, in temperate climates, of those who had them, keeping those feathered few somewhat warmer during cold nights and colder winters. And the more feathers the better—provided that the dinosaurs had a good way of cooling off when they needed to. But, of course, all they needed to do to control their blood temperature was allow some extra blood to circulate through the feathers while moving, like water through an automobile's radiator. A nice system, and we can surmise that natural selection suitably rewarded the genes that inadvertently invented it.

Nature, of course, is always trying out variations on a good thing. The variants that find a use—such as downy insulation—are likely to be retained by Darwinian natural selection. But someday, such as when there were enough wing feathers, they might become useful for something else—say, for gliding quickly down a hill while chasing prey. Or for jumping up into the air to bat down a passing insect. From such mundane beginnings may have come the graceful flight of birds.

Evolution rarely proceeds in a straight line from A to B, probably because there are no goals to evolution. Evolution is always finding new uses for old things; this innovative use is the primary basis for how animals have become smarter and more versatile. Bootstrapping can happen when we least expect it, a new combination of anatomy and behavioral skills suddenly exhibiting unexpected properties that allow for a quantum leap in capabilities. Was this the route for the invention for music? And laughter? But as a sidestep from what. . .?

Evolution's tempo is a lot like the river's course through the Grand Canyon. There are long, quiet stretches of flat water where nothing much changes. Then there are exciting periods of great turbulence, such as House Rock Rapid, which are followed by an intermediate stretch where currents swirl around, finding a new dynamic equilibrium, becoming quiet again. Most animal species don't change much for millions of years. When they do change, it is during one of those turbulent periods, when they are tested, when they sink or swim. What emerges is sometimes a new species, retaining those features which were handy. The evolutionary theorists think of this scenario as a *punctuated equilibrium*. Myself, I think of it as being like my favorite river: the Colorado River going down the Grand Canyon Staircase.

THESE BOATS DON'T SINK EASILY. I just saw a boat, being rowed temporarily by an energetic passenger, impale itself on a rock hidden just below the surface of the river. Such rocks are easy to avoid, since the swirling waters nearby give them away, but the boatman wasn't supervising carefully on such an easy-looking stretch of river. Abby saw the boat about to run over the hidden rock and yelled "Feet up!" loudly. The two passengers in the front lifted their feet quickly as they saw the rubber floor of the boat rising up, and the boat began to slowly pivot around this point, carried around by the river currents. Then it slid free of the obstruction uneventfully, or so it seemed.

Later, when no amount of bailing could reduce the foot-deep bilgewater, the boatman leaned far over the bow and felt underneath the boat. He came up muttering "Yep, big triangular hole." Pivoting atop a sharp rock works just like a drill. It's just a hole in the floor; the boat won't sink (unlike a rowboat, the flotation comes from the air-filled compartments). At least the front pontoons were spared. There are, in any event, close to a dozen separate compartments for air, and it's pretty hard to hole more than two at a time. A nice design.

The boatman decided that repairs could wait until we made camp. That boat took a lot more rowing than the rest, hauling along all that water in the bilges. Penance. One passenger was transferred to our boat to lighten the load. So, though we survived Badger and House Rock, the only damage was done by a minor rock in a quiet stretch of river.

EMERGENT PRINCIPLES are things not predicted by a reductionist taking-things-apart approach—things where the whole really does turn out to be different than the sum of the parts.

Not just greater, but often qualitatively different—such as bird flight, emerging willy-nilly from enough thermal underwear.

Most nonscientists don't know very many examples of emergence, other than snowflake crystals. And most scientists know only several examples within their own specialty. Without analogies, it is indeed hard to imagine us humans happening without design—and so one is led to suspect some sort of cosmic principle, if not the guiding hand of a Creator, shaping evolution towards complexity. And us.

Evolutionary theorists usually have seen enough examples of emergence to have faith that, as in the case of natural selection shaping the eye, adaptation and emergent "sidestepping" will be sufficient to explain the overall trend of evolution toward intelligent animals. Including ourselves. But as I said before, we can't be insistent about this expectation in the same way as when we relate the fact of evolution itself—our working hypothesis about emergence is, for us, an occupational hazard of being researchers.

PATCHING THE BOAT turned out to be easier than I thought. But then I had imagined a surgical sewing job of whale-sized proportions. I had forgotten about the nautical equivalent of duct tape. The simple repair procedure? First unpack the boat and remove the tubular frame. Then tilt the boat up on one side, propping it up on the beach in a near-vertical position, using an oar or two stuck in the sand. Next, just as when patching an inner tube, rough up the surface around the tear in the floor. These boats carry a repair kit that consists primarily of odd-sized sheets of neoprene, some sandpaper, and a can of contact cement. I pushed on the inside while Alan smeared on some cement and applied a patch from the outside. Then we traded places and he applied another patch to the inside. And except for repacking, which Alan is saving until morning, that was it—a whole lot easier than fixing a tire. I can see that this is my kind of boat.

As we were resting in camp after our long day's labors, sampling the contents of the little aluminum cans kept cool in the bilges, the wind came up. The sky clouded over and then it really began to blow. The fine particles of sand (this stuff is sometimes called "blowsand" for just this reason) began to billow in great clouds across the camp and out over the river. There were sand dunes forming before our very eyes, but we were not inclined to watch as the fine sand kept getting into our eyes. Bandanas came out and were draped around the edges of sunglasses, hats were held to shelter faces from the wind, and we all headed

MILE 21
North Canyon Camp
First Campsite

uphill. The easterly wind was blowing down out of the side canyon, so we all gathered on the upriver ledges of Supai around
the corner, huddled against the force of the sand gusts. Still we
were sandblasted. Sandstorms, it is said, do not last forever. Mike
Marsteller, one of the other boatmen, said it was one of the two
or three worst sandstorms he'd ever experienced in 500 days in
the Canyon.

THE SUPAI LAYERS in which we took refuge vary enormously, probably because the climate changed more frequently
in some periods of the earth's history and gave rise to thinner
layers than those deposited during longer periods. Near camp,
we found thin layers of Supai sandstone. Ten stories up, another ten stories of steep cliff begins with thicker layers of more
recent Supai. Then atop that is the crumbly Hermit shale forming a 45° slope, topped by the cliff-like Coconino and Toroweap sandstones and the Kaibab limestones. Cliff-forming means
hard stuff.

Five layers have arisen around us in only 21 miles of river,
and we hear that the Redwall Limestone will start just downriver from here. We also hear the next section of river is named
"The Roaring Twenties" and that we should wear our raingear
tomorrow morning if we don't want to get a little cold. There
are nine rapids in ten miles.

Cold, with it this hot? But when I go to wash the sand and
grime off in the river, I am reminded that the river is beer temperature. My wet bandana comes away from my face coated with
fine sand particles; it feels good to get the sand off. I even got
a nap before dinner.

SITTING ALONG the river after dinner, the storm having disappeared, we heard the clanking sound of breaking and falling
rock.

The boatmen all started to jump and shout, exuberantly running around trying to get a better view of the rockfall. In all
their years in the canyon, some had never witnessed an actual
spontaneous incident in the continuing erosion of the Grand
Canyon. They cheered on the rocks when they tumbled into
sight across the river and plunged in, with big splashes: "Ker-
plunk, ker-plunk." We watched the final trickle of small rocks,
trailing along behind the big rocks, with a feeling that we might
never see it again. Few of the millions of visitors to the Grand
Canyon each year ever get to see it as anything other than a
static colossus—a frozen, finished sculpture. Now we, at least,
know better.

Erosion made the Grand Canyon. Rocks falling downhill,

shattering into smaller rocks along the way, is the most obvious aspect of erosion. What goes up (via lava upwelling and the mountain-building uplifts that occur as seafloor spreading causes continental plates to come together and push their colliding edges into the sky) must eventually come down. Aiding gravity in this matter are water, wind, and ice. For example, the water that gets into cracks in rocks at higher elevations is likely to freeze in winter, forcing the halves of the rock further apart just as surely as a wedge splits firewood. So watch out in the spring-time for a lot of fresh rockfalls.

Then, a half hour after the rockfall, we got another sur-prise—the river changed color! Chameleons, maybe, but a river? Starting in the middle of the channel, a reddish-brown tongue intruded into the otherwise mint green waters of the Colorado. Then the tongue widened as we watched, soon filling most of the river except for the shallows along the shoreline. (Why a tongue? Water flows faster in midriver because the shorelines slow down the flow.)

Evidently that sandstorm was a side effect of a big rainstorm up north. This red color, Subie tells us, is what the Colorado River used to look like most of the time, before the dam created that big silt trap called Lake Powell. Now the Colorado turns red only when a side canyon floods somewhere within the park. But where? The Paria doesn't run red, Subie points out, so the water was probably dumped into Soap Creek, Tanner Wash (which created Sheer Wall Rapid), or Rider Canyon (which donated House Rock Rapid), those being the only possible sources of so much red silt. So, thanks to this little bit of detective rea-soning, we know that we missed seeing a flash flood in a side canyon by only about a dozen miles or less.

There seem to be no end of unusual events today. At this rate, we'll see a comet or a supernova tonight.

I ALWAYS SLEEP BADLY the first night out, and so after tossing and turning in my sleeping bag for half an hour, I finally got up and made my way back down to the river where a few people remained, talking quietly. The skies had cleared and I could actually see my way by starlight and a bit of moonlight reflected from the far canyon wall.

Like many others, I had been somewhat skeptical about the boatmens' plea to avoid the use of flashlights on aesthetic grounds (light spots flashing across the canyon walls, as someone turns around, seem inevitable no matter how carefully one tries to re-strict a flashlight beam to the path). We thought we'd stumble around our dark camp bumping into rocks and trees. But it ac-tually works, I could see the whole camp; if I'd used a flashlight,

I'd have seen only the swath cut by the beam. I also would have lost my dark-adaptation and so would have had difficulty spotting the fainter stars for the next half hour. They were indeed hard to spot, what with the moon shining from behind the western canyon wall. Being at the bottom of a narrow canyon, we see only a narrow swath of sky. It rather focuses the attention.

As I looked up at the sky for clusters of familiar stars, I knew that I was a real amateur compared to our ancestors who carefully studied the night sky. The names of many constellations, such as the Big Bear (Latinized as Ursa Major), have come down to us from the time before writing was invented 5,000 years ago. Our ancestors had a good mental image of a bear, and they could fit seven stars to it.

However, they had a rather limited mental image of their family tree—restricted to several generations, mostly people they'd seen sometime in their lives. Passing on information for which there is no reminder in the environment, such as a real bear, is not easy (which is the reason why most of us can't name our eight great-grandparents, either—and why the Navajo forgot the Yukon). A skill, cultural artifact, or ritual helps carry information along through the generations, but only with the inevitable modifications that eventually change things radically after a dozen generations. As culture changed, the constellation Ursa Major came to be called the "Big Dipper" in some parts of the world, and to anyone who has used a ladle, it's hard to see a bear there anymore. Most of us, alas, see more punchbowl ladles than bears.

Living in a city, one seldom sees the stars at all. That leads to a certain insular perspective: at night in the Canyon, I realize that I'm sitting on a planet, almost feeling it turning as I see new stars suddenly appear from behind the high canyon wall on the east side of the river. Here we don't have to struggle to see through all that distorting haze near the horizon; instead, the stars pop out when we study the top of a cliff. The Milky Way spans the top of the canyon walls. Our very own galaxy, seen edge-on. A few-hundred-billion stars, plus our Sun. Plus the black holes and dark matter of sundry sorts. We passed around the birdwatching binoculars in the starlight.

NOT ALL "STARS" are sharp points of light; some are rather fuzzy. And it isn't just poor optics, as an adjacent star may appear quite sharp. The German philosopher Immanuel Kant, back 200 years ago, correctly interpreted the fuzzy stars as "island universes" of millions of stars well beyond the confines of our own galaxy, the Milky Way. Today we use the word "universe" to include all galaxies, just as we have expanded the definition of the word "galaxy" beyond its original Greek meaning of "milky way."

There are two galaxies that circle our own Milky Way, rather like the moon orbiting the earth. They are close enough to appear too large to be passed off as mere fuzzy stars. From the southern hemisphere, they appear as luminous clouds to the naked eye. The sixteenth-century Spanish explorer Ferdinand Magellan was the first to tell Europe of these great fuzzy patches of light and they have been known there as the Magellanic Clouds ever since. There are actually about 20 galaxies in our part of space, known as the Local Group (which is 3 million light years in diameter). Then for almost 50 million light years, space is virtually empty—before arriving at a particularly rich collection of about a thousand galaxies known as the Virgo Cluster. And there are lots more galaxies than just those.

All those galaxies are still fleeing the Big Bang, that cosmic point of origin that marked the beginning of the universe as we know it. The Big Bang occurred 12,000 to 17,000 million years ago. Call it 15 billion years ago for the sake of convenience (at least until they recalibrate the Hubble constant again, that great astrophysical fudge factor that relates redshift to distance).

IN THE BEGINNING, there was no matter. Everything was radiation—the stuff that constitutes light and radio waves alike. Radiation comes in packets called photons: radio waves, infrared and ultraviolet light, and X-rays and gamma rays, they're all photons just as red light is. The only difference is the amount of energy stored in the packet: lots in X-rays but not so much in infrared photons. Red photons are your average sort of photon—around here, during the day.

Out of such packets of radiation, matter was created (just remember E equals mc^2, which tells how energy and mass are interconvertible). Two photons of light colliding in the dense packing of the early universe (another way of saying it was very hot) can produce protons and neutrons. In the first microsecond of the lifetime of the universe (one-millionth of a second), it was simply too hot for anything else to exist for long. Particles were converted back into photons almost as fast as photons were converted into particles. But by the time that a millisecond (one-thousandth of a second) had gone by, the universe had expanded and cooled enough for lighter-weight elementary particles, such as electrons, to form from light and survive.

Actually, the story should be told in terms of quarks, the building blocks of protons, neutrons, electrons and, in fact, everything in the universe. Quark? When the physicist Murray

The world began with what it is now the fashion to call the "Big Bang". . . it could not, of course, have been a bang of any sort, with no atmosphere to conduct waves of sound, and no ears. It was something else, occurring in the most absolute silence we can imagine. It was the Great Light.

LEWIS THOMAS
Late Night Thoughts on Listening to Mahler's Ninth Symphony, 1983

Gell-Mann postulated these building blocks in 1960, he wanted a neutral term to describe them, with no physical connotations—and so he picked a made-up word from that masterpiece of make-believe, *Finnegans Wake*. It has been noted by literary killjoys that James Joyce was living in German-speaking Zurich at the time he wrote about quarks. And quark, in German, means "cottage cheese." But that's not a bad analogy: the "quark soup" of the earliest moments of the universe may be conveniently envisaged as slightly lumpy. Mostly light, but with little bits of matter forming within it.

With more expansion and a thinner "soup," photons quit colliding with each other except on rare occasions. And the particles in the infant universe began to cluster together long enough to assume new identities. Between three minutes and a million years of age, the universe's elementary particles began to form clusters as the electrical attractions between positive protons and negative electrons brought them together. When an electron and a proton stick very close together, the combination is called a neutron. Or an electron might begin to circle a proton at a great distance; this particular combination is called an atom of hydrogen. This looser clustering was an important event because the neutral hydrogen atom is less likely to capture passing photons than a separate electron and a separate proton.

At approximately 3,000° Kelvin (that's about as hot as a lightbulb filament), as much matter is converted into photons as photons are converted into matter. As the universe expanded further, however, the balance shifted. This happened when the universe was about a thousand times smaller than at present. At that point, some photons escaped absorption and scattering by electrons—indeed, they escaped the fireball forever. We can still see these "fossil" photons. They are cosmic, arriving from every direction in space (except for those blocked by the moon), a fact which suggests that the universe "inflated" at that point rather than scattering as in an explosion. The fossil photons' wavelength has also changed. They were originally released at a temperature of about 3,000° Kelvin but they have been severely red-shifted by gravity; from originally having wavelengths like visible light, they've shifted down into microwaves.

Redshifts are the archetype of monetary inflation, shrinking the energy content of the photon and thus shifting its color, just as if when the buying power of a dollar bill shrank, its color somehow gradually shifted from green to yellow to red. These fossil photons are the afterglow of the infancy of the universe, shrinking as their potential energy instead builds up. Should the universe begin to collapse someday, the potential energy will be restored to the photon, shifting its wavelength toward the blue end of the light spectrum. To date, no one has seen any signs of a blue shift.

It's one thing to travel down a giant crack in the earth and see the remains of ancient life fossilized in the rock. But to see light left over from the early universe, fossilized as microwaves! This escaped radiation, still rattling around the universe, marks the time at which hydrogen atoms were first formed, the fireball of the expanding universe finally became transparent, and light was no longer trapped in it.

One of the neurobiologists on our trip, a former physicist, told us the story of the discovery of the fossil photons. The scientists who detected the 3° Kelvin microwave photons coming in from all directions in space were, of course, quite concerned about false readings, particularly as some pigeons had adopted their horn-shaped antenna. Particularly when dealing with signals near the noise level of the receivers and amplifiers, one has to keep in mind that perhaps the "signals" are nothing but garbage fooling you. The astrophysicists claim that, when contemplating the data, one of the researchers said: "Either we've seen a pile of pigeon-shit or the creation of the universe." The former possibility has now been eliminated; the observations have been repeated many times in many places, with even better equipment and fewer birds. You can even see them on a home TV set—just tune to an empty channel and look at the "snow." About one percent of the little "snow particles" are generated by cosmic photons left over from the early universe becoming transparent.

Most of the original energy of the universe is now packaged as particles—mass dominates the universe, though it may be converted back into photons whenever some sort of transaction takes place and there are some leftovers. Most of the mass is still in the form of hydrogen atoms. If, however, the binding force between protons and neutrons were only a few percent stronger, hydrogen would be unstable; as the physicist Freeman Dyson once pointed out, that means that stars like our sun couldn't exist. And there would be no water, a serious matter indeed to river-runners.

Hydrogen, it turns out, is the building block of the universe because of what happens to hydrogen atoms when a lot of them coalesce to form a star. All stars were initially great quantities of hydrogen held together by gravity. Hydrogen has two "heavy" isotopes, deuterium and tritium; their nuclei have a neutron or two in addition to the usual proton of the hydrogen atom. Being neutral in charge, these extra neutrons attract no additional electrons into orbit. But when these heavy hydrogen atoms collide with each other at the 10 to 12 million degree temperatures found in the interiors of stars, their nuclei may fuse, yielding a new nucleus with a 2 + 2 configuration: two neutral neutrons and two positive protons. This doubly-charged nucleus naturally attracts two negative electrons into distant orbit. This "doubled deuterium" is an atom of helium, and the process by which it is formed is called fusion.

Some extra energy—I call it spare change—is given off in the process, because the energy needed to hold together a helium nucleus is slightly less than the sum of that for the heavy hydrogen nuclei (it's somewhat the same problem as trying to divide up $100 three equal ways—you're going to need some coins in addition to currency, and it still won't come out all equal). This excess binding energy appears as photons of light. In fact, photons such as this—after an eight-minute-and-twenty-second trip through space—have inflicted more than one case of sunburn today. And that spare change also heated up the rocks on which we sat to watch the stars.

Twinkle, twinkle little star,
I don't wonder what you are
For by spectroscopic ken
I know that you are hydrogen.
ANONYMOUS

We have mimicked the fusion furnace of stars here on earth. It is called a thermonuclear reaction (though, in fact, little of the energy released by a hydrogen bomb is from fusion: the great energy release of an H-bomb really occurs because the fusion enables more of the uranium or plutonium of the atomic bomb, which served as the trigger for the hydrogen, to be split). $E = mc^2$ means that it takes only 1 gram of matter (a small coin weighs about 2 or 3 grams) to release as much energy as there was in one of the atomic bombs dropped in World War II. Someday, controllable fusion (without a "dirty" fission trigger) will become a source of really cheap and clean energy that could make coal burners and hydroelectric dams obsolete, along with the present nuclear fission plants and their waste disposal problems (instead, we'll have to worry about thermal pollution!). At least, notes Dan Richard, there will be no Organization of Petroleum Exporting Countries to control their fuel, seawater.

HEAVIER ELEMENTS LIKE CARBON, with its 6 protons and (usually) 6 neutrons, were not created in the Big Bang. And carbon is the prime building block of life, so something else had to happen in between the early universe and the evolution of life. The early universe expanded (and thereby cooled) so fast that, by the time enough protons and neutrons were around, it was too cool for building nuclei heavier than helium. Nor are heavy elements created by fusion in ordinary stars like our sun, whose packing density remains too thin for heavy elements to begin forming. It really requires a lot of cramming together to make a heavy element's nucleus. To make most elements requires the death of a star—a supernova.

A supernova doesn't last very long, but for days or weeks it may be so much brighter than an ordinary star that it can be seen in the middle of the day, a bright point of light in the blue sky. Our sun, it is said, can never become a supernova. It isn't big enough. A supernova is created from a star somewhat larger than our sun. After about 10 percent of its hydrogen has been converted into helium, the star becomes unstable and eventually collapses into a small, dense ball of matter (thus began the cliché, "The bigger they are, the harder they fall"). As the star collapses, particles in it move fast enough (another way of saying that the temperature is hot enough) so that when helium nuclei collide, they can fuse to make carbon, oxygen, and indeed all of the ninety heavier elements. Such fusions, of course, release even more nuclear binding energy than the hydrogen-to-helium conversion, the excess again appearing as light. And so the supernova flashes into existence, lighting up the night sky and soon the daytime sky with the spare change from the pressure cooker that is creating heavy elements in the collapsing star.

It is supernovae that allow matter to evolve, that permit simple atoms to become heavier atoms whose additional electrons in orbit allow the more complex kinds of chemistry needed for life. The evolution of life can occur only after the evolution of heavier matter. Had, however, the Newtonian gravitational force constant been slightly different, all stars would instead become either blue giants or red dwarfs, either too hot or too cool for most scenarios allowing the evolution of life.

Now carbon and oxygen are the stuff on which the chemistry of life depends. And with the exception of a few created here on earth in bomb tests, every one of the carbon atoms in our bodies and every bit of oxygen we breathe got their start in a supernova. They were flung out into space by the explosive collapse of the star, and later assembled into a planet. And into us. A dramatist would say that stars have died that we might live.

No more than 6,000 to 7,000 million years ago, there was a supernova nearby. Matter flung out from it eventually, under gravitational attraction, began to cluster. Some of the hydrogen collapsed to such a density that the hydrogen-to-helium conversion was ignited and our sun was born. That was about 5,000 million years ago. At roughly the same time, other particles of cosmic dust from "our" supernova and others coalesced into a giant disk of swirling dust, spiraling around the sun. Eddies formed here and there, just as in the river, and an eddy within the spiral disk was probably the focus for the gravitational collapse of some dust into a compact ball. A planet. While some planets developed hot interiors, none ignited. One of these planets, third from the sun in distance, is the earth; it went into business about 4,600 million years back.

The star of Bethlehem was the supernova of 6 B.C. recorded by the Chinese astronomers (a monk counted incorrectly back in the Middle Ages, when tallying up the elapsed years since the birth of Christ). If we had stayed up long enough for Orion to rise in the eastern sky, we might have seen the nearby Crab Nebula, the galaxy that was the site of a big supernova back in the year A.D. 1054. It was so bright that the new star could be seen during the daytime for weeks. But someone estimated that Orion wouldn't rise until after four in the morning, and that it would be sunrise before it was high enough in the sky to clear the eastern canyon wall.

We gave up before that. No comets, no supernova, but a half-a-dozen shooting stars as meteors tracked up the night sky. Still, not a bad day.

I DECIDED TO SLEEP on a rock ledge, something of a shallow cave, because that was the best refuge in the sandstorm. And it beat putting up a tent. Dan Hartline and I squeezed ourselves into a shallow cave where a chunk of the canyon wall has disappeared. It's really more of a ledge, with a roof over it. Sitting up in bed is out of the question.

It took a long time to get to sleep. And then, out of the blue, someone turned the lights on. As suddenly, I thought, as if someone were turning on the bedroom lights in the middle of the night. Surely it wasn't sunrise yet.

It was the *moon*, shining into our cave. I'd been in the shadows up until a moment before. It took me several minutes to figure out how to deal with this novel situation. Finally I put my sunglasses on. And tried to get back to sleep. Moonglasses?

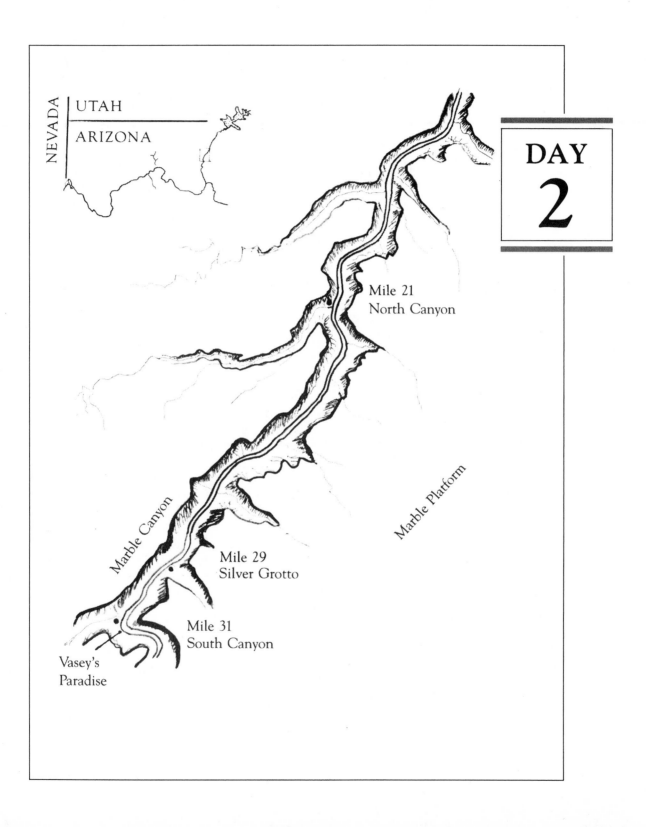

NEVADA

UTAH

ARIZONA

DAY
2

Mile 21
North Canyon

Marble Platform

Marble Canyon

Mile 29
Silver Grotto

Mile 31
South Canyon

Vasey's
Paradise

MILE 21
North Canyon Camp

MORNING ARRIVES, BEARING COFFEE. Sorry, but I mix my metaphors at this hour. "If you'll hold out your cup, I'll pour you some coffee." A voice.

I blinked in the dim daylight and tried to focus on a bearded face peering up over the ledge. Another dream.

"Hey, Bill. Want some coffee?" the voice repeated after a short interval. There was a very large, campfire-blackened coffeepot associated with the beard. Emitting steam. And a familiar odor. Morning?

I propped myself up on an elbow and finally located my Sierra cup. I was both half-asleep and puzzled by the dim light. "*Sunglasses?*" I muttered, snatching them off. Then I held out the cup.

"Breakfast line's a-forming down there," said Alan, making conversation in case I might fall asleep again.

Dan was already out of his sleeping bag, nursing a cup of steaming coffee, looking only slightly more awake. Then Alan bounded away over the rocks connecting our ledge to the camp, holding a heavy coffeepot aloft with one hand like the Olympic torch, in that maddening free-form ballet affected by the boatmen.

Silence. The bottoms of our cups revealed a few coffee grounds. Dan's seemed to have a small piece of eggshell. The boatmen's recipe for coffee sometimes includes a raw egg, handy for getting the floating coffee grounds to sink.

We descended into camp on stiff legs, wobbling awkwardly across the rocky stretch that Alan had just bounded across.

We were, ahem, late for breakfast. As were some of the other galaxy watchers. Everyone else was on seconds already. Pancakes. Between bites, Dan and I agreed that our cave was much hotter than the camp below. Thinking about it, we realized that the afternoon sun really heats up the surface rocks and that they hold that heat all night. I think we'll try the edge of the river next time; veteran river types assure us that there is nearly always some breeze by the water.

I DON'T BELIEVE this place. We're hiking up North Canyon this morning, carved in the Supai sandstone behind our campsite. There are thousands of layers of Supai sandstone little more than an inch thick, and so the trail up the canyon has a series of little steps and, when a number of layers have been broken away together, big steps. There was recently a creek flowing down this canyon, as there are a number of pools of stagnant water which we walk around. Then there are steep jumbles of boulders blocking the path, rocks from the high cliffs carried down by a flash flood; they would have added to the rapid below if they'd been carried as far as the river. We climb up them, a knee here and an elbow there, sometimes gaining a handhold from a convenient tree growing in a crack. We meet up with dry waterfalls, where a resistant ledge of Supai forms a lip over which the creek sometimes pours. It is too high to climb, but there is a path around it to the right.

And the greenery—it was pretty at Lee's Ferry and along the river, but back here in the narrowing side canyon, the greenery is completely surrounded by red rock and so appears even greener than green. Good old color contrast, the reason why they stick blue labels on yellow bananas, to enhance the yellow. Well, here the red enhances the green. The view is truly spectacular. There are also some flying mammals flitting about—probably brown bats who didn't get enough to eat during the night. Maybe the sandstorm was hard on the insect population.

The canyon walls are closing in as we hike higher. We circle some more pools, seeing our reflections superimposed on those of the red walls behind us. Then we hear the waterfall. And, as we round another little sculpted pool, there is the grotto. Little water is falling, but the graceful beauty of this place, carved by thousands of years of rushing water, leaves us breathless. The waterfall looks like a flower, almost an orchid with its tongue extending downward toward the luminous pool at its base. The colors—well, the red shades into pastels and, as the water channel is approached, into silver and subtle grays through which the blue-and-white water flows peacefully. There is the grace of an Oriental painting to this scene. Some of us wade up the pool to the gentle waterfall, to see if it is real.

Returning, I decide that I can get the best view from an elevated perch. So I begin climbing the Supai sandstone layers up a steep slope on the left wall of the saddle-like pass we're standing in. Eventually I perch upright in a crack in the Supai, with a nice view of the sculpture. And with a view down the canyon toward the river. The little pool that we skirted just before arriving at the waterfall's pool now reflects the canyon wall beyond, deepening the red and orange colors. A willow tree is gracefully draped, arching over the little pool. Looking up to the distant Supai sandstone being reflected in the pool, I see a zone of fractured rock leading steeply up the wall of the side canyon. Like the saddle opening out into the grotto, it is probably a flexure, where great subterranean forces have twisted the Supai layers, the twists later exposed by erosion. So the orderly layers of Supai sandstone are broken by this flow of collapsing layers, only to again resume their order. The colors are red-orange, shading into pastels, at least in this morning light.

Then there is the problem of getting down, camera in hand.

Going up, I just edged up the crack, but heading down is another matter, and I hesitate to just stride downhill, not trusting the traction of my still-wet shoes. So I sit down a lot, and finally make it to the bottom. I could have just run down and then up the other side while slowing down, reversing and coming back, but I'm not that nimble-footed. I hear, however, that one of the boatmen loves to do exactly that for exercise. Jimmy, apparently, gets restless and runs up this canyon early in the morning by himself, does a series of back-and-forth runs across this U-shaped saddle (running up even higher than I carefully climbed) before reversing to run back down, and then runs back down the trail to the river. All before breakfast. Undoubtedly in his sandals. The boatman telling me all this claimed that Jimmy gets irascible if he doesn't get enough exercise.

No one, fortunately, was in any hurry to leave this place.

RIVER CORRIDOR CROSS SECTION

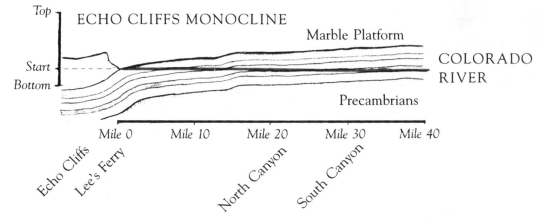

WE'VE BEEN GETTING quite an introduction to the layers of the earth. As we float down the river, they rise up out of the water, Phoenix-like. First we see a little of the new layer at the waterline; ten minutes later, it's taller than we are. It's like having a mountain range grow up around us. From the rim, of course, it looks different, more like a sunken mountain range—the Paiute Indians called the Canyon "Kaibab," the "mountain-lying-down."

The Colorado Plateau may have been uplifted by lava welling up from the depths of the earth, pushing up the earth's surface like a blister. The river cut down through this domed layer-cake like a meandering knife. Imagine a cake pan in the oven with a wavy, serrated knife suspended above it, the blade is just off-center and tilted slightly downhill. As the hot cake rises up around the knife, a canyon is formed to one side of the dome's peak (the North Rim). In the case of the Colorado Plateau, the cake was cold and already layered when lava and continental drift helped push it up. And it rose anywhere from 1,500 to 4,000 meters (5,000 to 13,000 feet).

Starting back about the end of the Mesozoic (and the dinosaurs), there was a 20-million-year-long episode of rock-buckling and mountain uplifting called the Laramide Orogeny (no relation to orgy, someone explained—orogeny is Greek for "mountain birth"). This produced all sorts of buckling and folding of the earth, not to mention the Rocky Mountains. The Colorado Plateau itself was not unduly squashed except for some spectacular wrinkles such as the Waterpocket Fold up in Utah. Then, starting 20 million years ago, after things were quiet for awhile, the Miocene period saw the whole American Southwest stretched and torn apart.

While the river runs downhill, as rivers prefer to do, it seems an even steeper descent because of the doming. At Lee's Ferry, we were at an altitude of 940 meters (3,107 feet) above sea level, standing on Kaibab Limestone. Only 70 river miles downstream from Lee's Ferry, the layers have been pushed up more than one mile; the Kaibab also forms the top of the North Rim, at an elevation of 2,640 meters (8,800 feet). The plateau ascends 1,700 meters, the river descends about 140 meters in that 70-mile distance—so it seems as if you're going downhill at a much faster rate than you really are. The doming presumably happened gradually, more slowly than the rate at which the river's erosion could cut through the layers; usually, rivers go around mountains rather than through them.

Rock layers bent and folded? Yes indeed. They sometimes fracture, of course, and form cracks called fault lines. And when they slip and slide in those cracks, we feel earthquakes. There are several fault lines just downriver from here, and we'll see some really big ones later in the trip.

For now, though, back to the Kaibab Limestone. Not far below the Paria confluence, another, grayer layer could be seen in the ledge just above river level. Soon it too had grown tall; now it's far above us. This Toroweap is a thin-layered limestone with some silty layers mixed into it.

Then, still further downstream, emerged a white sandstone, the Coconino. This layer formed from ancient sand dunes when it was above sea level; it then sank and later, about 250 million years ago, the Toroweap limestone was deposited, compressing

MILE 28 CROSS SECTION

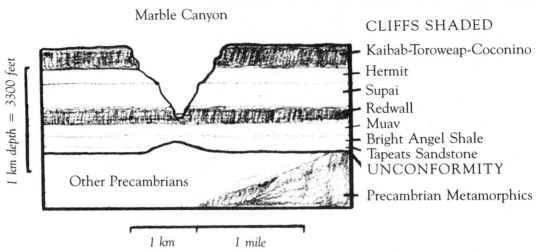

Marble Canyon

CLIFFS SHADED

— Kaibab-Toroweap-Coconino
— Hermit
— Supai
— Redwall
— Muav
— Bright Angel Shale
— Tapeats Sandstone
UNCONFORMITY
— Precambrian Metamorphics

1 km depth = 3300 feet

Other Precambrians

1 km　　1 mile

the sand and cementing it together into sandstone. Sandstone forms more quickly than limestone, a meter being laid down in a mere 1,700 years by the wind, as compared to the 8,000 years it takes for the same thickness of limestone to be deposited underwater by little animals dying.

And then we got into the Hermit and Supai layers. The Hermit is a colorful, fine-bedded shale deposited along an ancient floodplain, while the Supai is a reddish, chunky layer of sandstone and siltstone. Siltstones and shale come from river deltas. When a river fans out, it slows down. And when it slows down, the dirt particles suspended in the water settle out, building up to about a meter thick within 3,300 years. The red color signifies that a lot of iron oxide, more familiarly known as rust, was carried by that ancient river, probably from the erosion of an inland mountain.

So these layers tell us that an ancient, rust-containing river delta that existed here was covered by sand dunes as the climate changed and dried up this area. The area then sank for some reason and became an ocean floor burial ground for microscopic animals. Then, much later, it arose to become land again. Most erosion takes place on land, and indeed there is very little left atop the Kaibab around here. We saw those more recent layers yesterday in the horseshoe behind Lee's Ferry. At Zion National Park up in Utah, one can see 300 stories of more recent layers—the bottom of Zion Canyon is the same Kaibab Limestone that forms the top layers of the Grand Canyon. But down here, those more recent layers atop the Kaibab have been eroded away by wind and rain. If this land sank again, the new layers formed atop the local Kaibab would conceal a 250-million-year gap of missing layers. There would be fish fossils and then, in the layer atop that, modern animals—maybe even a hapless sailor or two. The geologists call such a discontinuity an "unconformity." The Canyon has many of them, but we usually cannot spot them.

"Just try adding up the expected depth of the Grand Canyon," Alan noted, "as if a meter depth formed every 8,000 years, and you'll see that a lot of it must be missing. In fact, more than 95 percent of it. We're just sampling the history."

All this, just in the five layers of rock we face on the shadowed eastern wall of the Canyon. Five layers emerged yesterday in a mere eleven miles; if things kept going at that rate, we'd run out of layers in another day or two. And be halfway to China soon afterwards. I assume the number of new layers per hour will not continue at its present rate.

NORTH CANYON RAPID was just downstream of our campsite. It is a rapid of which many rivers would be proud. On the Grand Canyon scale, it rates a 5, at least until the next flash flood moves those boulders down into the river. And sculpts the grotto a little more.

Planning ahead, we're all wearing raingear for the next 10 miles of rapids. The Marble Canyon is still in shadow since it runs north-south and the sun is still in the east. It must only be nine o'clock or so, yet it seems as we've had a half-day's adventures already.

The Redwall layer rises quickly out of the river, or so it seems. Actually one has to watch carefully to spot the first little bit of it several miles below North Canyon. It appears on the left shore in the midst of a talus slope (talus, in this context, does not mean the iron man in Spenser's *Faerie Queene*, nor the ankle bone in anatomy; in geologists' and hikers' vocabularies, talus is short for "a big pile of big rocks" fallen from above, the gravel of the giants). The talus covers up the Redwall for a while, then there is a Redwall section a half-story high standing there, like a section of stage backdrop. Then the rapids hit; this stretch of river is called the "Roaring Twenties" for a reason. So we were busy watching the rapids, or watching the bottom of the boat while bailing afterwards. Our boatman today is J.B. (also known as Jim Irving); he tried to get a lot of water into the boat, and even poured a 20-liter bucket of water over his seat and the silver-colored storage boxes, so that we could bail yesterday's sandstorm out of the boat. I spent a lot of time jumping up and down on the floor of the boat to stir up the sand before scooping with the bailer bucket.

At first, we didn't notice that the cliffs, which had grown several stories tall along the riverbanks, were no longer the familiar Supai. The red-orange color and regular layers are quite different from the Supai's chocolate-red and chunky appearance. We suddenly realized that we were quickly getting deeper into the Redwall.

Almost immediately, we started seeing caves along both shores. They weren't from the river's carving but rather from erosion by underground water, trickling down from the North Rim snowmelts. Redwall tends to be sufficiently resistant that it channels groundwater sideways, making an underground lake. Where it pools is called the "water table." The moist limestone may form caves here and there where the Redwall is less resistant. Although some caves have almost round entrances, most have elongated horizontal openings—little ledges with roofs. But we don't see much evidence of the seepage. As we roared through Cave Springs Rapid at Mile 25, I looked around for springs flowing out of the canyon walls but saw little sign of the greenery that is the tipoff of seepage, much less a flowing spring near the river. Then I had to bail again.

"Is the patch holding tight?" I shouted over to Alan's boat.

"How could we possibly know—with another rapid throwing water in just when we finish bailing?" replied Laura Sirota.

RIVER MILES OR RIVER KILOMETERS? Someone suggested that river miles should be made metric, but that would be like moving the milestones on an old Roman road to correspond with modern measurement. And while 10 river miles are usually 16 kilometers long, mapmakers don't re-measure every time a new meander is cut or a sandbar is washed away, lengthening or shortening the river a little. So it's all approximate anyway. Still, although there aren't markers along the river calling off the passing miles, the guidebooks have them marked on the maps and aerial photos. They wouldn't be hard to change to metric, but map names like 140 Mile Canyon would also have to be corrected all over the Grand Canyon, not just along the river corridor. And someone points out that we'd have to rename all the stretches of river like the Roaring Twenties and the Photogenic Fifties that incorporate mileage in their names, making them the Euphoric Eighties or some such name in metric. Ah, well, America needs one relic of the English system of measurement just for historical perspective—we'll let it be the Grand

Canyon river mileage. Generous of us, I know, but we're enjoying ourselves immensely.

DESERT VARNISH is a dark stain that appears on the Supai and Redwall layers. We've been noticing it as we float along. It looks like a black stain spilled down the face of the red rock, the sort of thing one sees on the outside of a paint can. Someone compares the sight to a painting, causing a cynic to comment that the painter had something in common with the one who did his house, leaving those black drip marks everywhere.

The drip marks occur because of dew and rain at night, or so the story goes. When the surface of the rock is wet, the water seeps down into the rock a little way, following the fine cracks. In this fashion it covers an enormous amount of surface area. The water also dissolves some of the minerals in the rock, such as manganese and iron. When the sun comes along the next day and warms the rock, the water on the surface evaporates and the water in the cracks wicks back up toward the surface, carrying the dissolved minerals along with it. When the water finally evaporates, the minerals are left on the rock's surface. There they oxidize into what we see as black varnish. Lichens like the moisture too, adding to the texture of the surface.

This cycle repeats itself after every rain, every dew. Gradually, a layer of oxide builds up where water has been draining before it evaporates. Thus the similarity to drip marks on the outside of a paint can.

There is no desert varnish on the Kaibab or Toroweap layers; they seem not to have the right stuff.

The scenery continues to be spectacular, even more impressive than yesterday because the Canyon is getting deeper. It's a good thing that I brought along waterproof geologists' notebooks in which to write this diary. They conveniently fit inside my hat, one of the drier places so far. I seem to remember that Abraham Lincoln carried a whole file cabinet worth of papers inside his stovepipe hat.

Back to bailing.

THOUGH IT IS CALLED SHINUMO WASH on the maps, this place is most notable for the exquisite grotto—Silver Grotto—that lies just a short distance up the way. It takes more than a casual hike to reach it because the going is, shall we say, "interesting." The boatmen tell us that we're in for something more like a climb, slide, and swim.

First to the serious business—lunch. A boatman fills up two

MILE 29
Silver Grotto

great cooler jugs with river water (it's clear again, the red silt disappeared overnight), and measures out a few drops of liquid bleach into each. One is set aside as the water supply, but people are asked to wait a while for the chlorine to work. The other cooler jug gets an added ingredient—a big can of lemonade mix is dumped in and stirred around. Both jugs are set atop overturned bailer buckets. In the meantime, two folding tables have been erected and a plastic tablecloth spread out, and cutting boards laid down after being washed in the soap bucket (two more buckets of river water serve as a hand wash and rinse). Then the boatmen slice up tomatoes, onions, lettuce, cheese, and a few other things. Everyone awaits the official announcement, and then one has a choice: the long make-your-own-sandwich line or the short express line for fans of peanut-butter-and-jelly sandwiches (today we also have leftover pancakes from breakfast, on which one can spread jam). You can, of course, do one after the other, so I stand in the long line munching on a pancake sandwich. Seconds continue for some time, and there are cookies for dessert, even apples and oranges.

Lunch is a leisurely affair, and bird-watching is popular here. Eventually most of us head over to the cliff. Not everyone goes on every hike; people often elect to stay behind and lounge around the riverside. This hike in particular is advertised as "not for everyone" due to the climb—and then several obligatory swims; indeed, most river trips don't stop at Silver Grotto. And because of the swimming, most people who do make the trip leave their cameras behind. However, my little palm-sized camera fits under my hat if I loosen the chin strap, so I plan to swim with my head above water.

The cliff is less than two stories high. We wouldn't have to climb it at all if the river were higher; we could step directly from the boat onto the tongue of the dry waterfall. At ordinary river levels, one has to ascend the cliff on the upriver side, about like trying to climb into an upstairs window, but with lots of natural handholds here and there.

It is a slow but relatively safe process, aided by spectators below pointing out the next grip or foothold, and, when one gets close to the top, by the strong arm of a boatman to help one make the last step. I discovered a little problem with my camera-carrying method: it is very disorienting to have your head weigh more than usual when climbing; it felt funny every time I bent my neck to look for another handhold. It probably wouldn't have bothered Abe Lincoln, but I'm not in practice. I finally slid off my hat with one free hand, while midway up the rock face, and dropped both hat and camera down to Dan Hartline, who was waiting on the beach below.

Climbers arriving at the top of the cliff are greeted by several giant agave "century plants" which tower over everyone. I looked back down. Dan had stuck my camera in his pocket, the usual sensible place to carry it, and was wearing my hat as he effortlessly climbed the cliff.

Next, we hiked along a narrow ledge at the top of the cliff, leading into the canyon. The ledge got narrower and narrower, and we finally came to a lovely view of a pool several stories below. And a smooth, steep descent path to reach the pool. Someone has thoughtfully installed a permanent bolt anchor for a climbing rope here, and all one needs do to descend is to back oneself down the slope, letting out rope, aided by suggestions of "stand up straighter" or "lean back further into the rope, it'll hold you."

Once at the bottom, I re-installed my camera inside my hat and pulled the chin strap tight. Then we started wading our way up the pool; when the bottom dropped away, we swam a dozen strokes until we could get our footing at the end of the narrowing canyon. The next obstacle the canyon posed was a slick, one-story-high "V" groove which we climbed by wedging our bodies across the gap and wiggling sideways with our shoulder blades. At the top of the "V" groove we pushed off into a longer, deeper pool. Then, dripping wet, we climbed a series of thin Redwall ledges.

Hard work, but it's spectacular. A bandshell-like cave rises above us in the Redwall. For about one story up from the flat floor, all is white, gray, and black horizontal stripes; the bandshell above is red, with some little vertical black stripes from desert varnish, and some touches of green from hardy desert plants that have found a cranny to root in—one of them a maidenhair fern which cascades down a short distance. There is a small pool on the floor, and one story above it is an opening, into which a waterfall occasionally pours, though not today. Through the U-shaped opening I can see that the canyon takes a jog to the left, white walls opening into a large cave in which some dark greenery hangs. The white walls just beyond the opening have some faint red stripes. Above them is a dark gray wall with giant vertical red stripes, some obviously mud. Crowning the bandshell is Redwall colored by a deep red wash. But this highest red layer—just to complement the contrasting horizontal black, gray, and white stripes of the lower walls of the bandshell, and the vertical red stripes of the white and gray backgrounds inside the opening—is vertically striped with black desert varnish. It is quite a sight to behold as one arrives, dripping with water and sweat and perhaps feeling "it-better-be-worth-it after all-I've-gone-through." This is the Silver Grotto.

Most of us sit comfortably on ledges—on one or another of those black and white and gray layers—around the edge of the bandshell. But an adventuresome few climb up into the U-shaped opening via a path from the left with foot- and handholds here and there. One hiker loses his balance and slides a half story down an unobstructed path into the deep pool below, swims to shore, and tries again. Those who make it disappear within.

There is not too much more to see, the climbers report on their return to the top of the waterfall, just the cave and a steep groove left by another waterfall which there is no hope of climbing. Sounds nice to me—maybe they're just saying that so we won't feel bad. The climbers stand at the opening atop the ancient waterfall like orchestra conductors surveying the size of the audience (which is their nonchalant way of contemplating the path back down—getting down is always harder than the ascent). Most abandon the idea of the path. Then they sit down and prepare themselves for the plunge into the pool. There are suggestions from the audience that they take the plunge.

A big frog is spotted climbing up the wall that rises out of the pool, resting comfortably between hops on unbelievable inclines. It is heading up toward the opening in a flanking move—John DuBois suggests that it's an "attack frog" coming to get the trespassers. To the cheering of the audience, the climbers slip and slide down into the frigid pool, swim ashore, then hurriedly haul themselves out so that they can run around the floor to warm up. The frog takes no notice of their passing.

We are in no hurry. The boatmen, once convinced that we're too tired to try to imitate them, demonstrate that with enough speed, one can actually run around the wall above the pool. They race around, halfway up between the pool and the opening. It is indeed a banked turn, just as on a racecourse. A slow-motion movie would suggest that the boatmen had defied gravity, jogging at a 30° angle from the vertical. One after another, the boatmen zip around the horseshoe turn. None goes too slow, none slips. Good old centripetal force presses them into the wall, making their floppy sandals grip better. That's cheating, we shout—try going slower. But they know better. Then they run into the left approach but keep going upward, their speed actually carrying them up into the opening. We suggest they get down with a running start as well, but the course won't work in reverse.

The frog ignores them too. I sometimes think that frogs can't see people, that we don't exist in their world of flies and other frogs.

What a lovely spot for a concert. We understand that on one trip a year, a string quartet hauls their old instruments along in waterproof cases (the cello is the big problem—the boatmen haul it up and float it across the pools on an air mattress), and give concerts along the river. The grotto at the end of the North Canyon hike would be a nice site too. Silver Grotto is perfect for music making. Today we have to imagine the music. There are special places in a desert—broad swatches of red and black color with delicate green decoration, church-like acoustics, and an unearthly light—and this is one of them.

Heading back down, there is a stunning view of the meandering path followed by the flash floods that have polished this silvery gray channel, beyond which we catch a glimpse of the Colorado River flowing along at an unseemingly hasty clip. Its backdrop is twenty stories of steep Redwall cliff on the far side of the river, capped by chocolate-red Supai chunks. The light from the Redwall is reflected in the pools we must swim through, and here and there a swimmer starts out, rippling the smooth orange waters. A magical place.

THE SWALLOWS SEEM TO WORK HARD for their living, gliding along just a hand's-breadth above the surface of the water in search of insects. I haven't even seen any insects, but the birds seem to find them. The swallows have to eat enough to support all that wing flapping. Between the swifts and swallows during the day and the bats during the night, there are few flying insects left to pester us. There are no mosquitos, not one, though high water may bring some. Perhaps we should train bats to follow us around back home.

Not unlike the bats, the violet-green swallows have a distinctive way of flapping their wings. Facing upwind in a mild breeze, they seem to stand still while they jack themselves straight up into the air, almost as if they were climbing an invisible ladder. When they are several stories high, they fold their wings, drop their noses and go into a stall, turn in the direction they want to go, extend their wings slightly into a swept-back V, then dive down with wings fully extended as they speed along the surface of the river, flapping vigorously again as they lose speed. Then they flap their way up to a child's height and dive for another minor sweep or two before climbing that tall ladder again. If they miss a choice morsel, they will turn into the wind, flap their way up a story or so while allowing themselves to be swept backwards, then dive again over the same spot on the river. In quieter moments, we hear their song, "Chit-chit-chit-wheet-wheet."

I wonder if they're any more likely to notice us than the frog up at Silver Grotto? Or is the swallow's world divided up into birds, food, probably cats, and "all others"?

The man replied,
"Things as they are,
Are changed upon
the blue guitar."
WALLACE STEVENS
The Man with the Blue Guitar,
1937

MILE 30
Giotto's Tower

FLYING CATS? I've been teasing Dan Richard that even cats can fly. By parachute. Not as naturally as the spiders do, but at least all in the interests of ecology.

The Royal Air Force and the World Health Organization once parachuted domestic cats into remote villages in Borneo in which all the local cats had died, allowing a population explosion of rats (which are potential carriers of all sorts of nasty diseases such as typhus, leprosy, and plague). And why did all the native cats die? From the insecticide DDT, sprayed to eradicate malaria-carrying mosquitos (as many as 90 percent of the people suffered from malaria).

This is a sobering story that we professors tell biology classes to illustrate the importance of a food chain and its ecological interrelations. The mosquitos in the story were controlled by spraying the insides of village huts with DDT. Malaria was indeed eradicated. All seemed well until the thatched roofs of the huts began to collapse on their occupants. It seems that the thatch was being eaten by the larvae of a moth that was normally present in the hut roofs—but never before in such numbers. Apparently they'd undergone a population explosion. The moth's predator, a parasitic wasp, had also been killed off by the DDT, but the wasp larvae had had the sense not to eat DDT.

But still, what is the loss of a few thatched roofs compared to eradicating malaria? But there were further consequences—the DDT was eaten by cockroaches, though not in great enough quantities, alas, to kill them. A little clue: DDT isn't broken down and excreted very well—once it's in, it can't get out. It just builds up. Not enough, however, to kill very many cockroaches.

Next, the DDT-laden cockroaches were eaten by the friendly neighborhood geckos, those lizards that walk across ceilings with their suction cup feet. Now a gecko has to eat a lot of cockroaches to make a living, and the DDT from the cockroaches accumulated in the bodies of the geckos until it reached concentrations an order of magnitude higher than in the cockroaches. But still not enough to kill the geckos.

The trouble was that a village cat ate lots of geckos in addition to an occasional rat. Hundreds of cats were therefore accumulating the DDT ingested by millions of cockroaches. And while the DDT concentrations were never high enough to kill very many cockroaches or geckos, they finally did become concentrated one order of magnitude too high—and killed the cats. And saved the rats. And helped spread the other nasty diseases.

"Operation Cat Drop" eventually restored the cat population and eased the threat of plague. Ignorance is expensive. Just knowing that mosquitos spread malaria and that DDT kills mosquitos isn't sufficient—you've got to understand what else will eat DDT, even in sublethal doses, and so on up the food chain.

The whole system's the thing. It is called ecology. Our agricultural/medical/industrial society is dumping all sorts of new chemicals into the environment, with little knowledge of what they'll do. The remedy—if any—isn't usually as simple as parachuting cats.

LIKE THE OTHER LIMESTONES such as the Kaibab top layer, Redwall is really a light creamy gray color. The red coloring is just a wash, an overlay from the Hermit and Supai layers atop the Redwall—those former river deltas with all the rusty silt in them from ancient mountains. The red iron oxide washes down over the Redwall limestone, coating it with the lovely red so familiar to Grand Canyon visitors as they concentrate on the tallest steep cliffs inside the Canyon. We're privileged to see the original gray color wherever a stream has washed away the red coating, or wherever a slab of Redwall has recently fallen away, exposing the underlying colors. Therefore, we can spot sites of recent rockfall just by the patches of pale color amidst the red. In a while, the dripping rust will color these red too, healing the wound.

Where the red has been washed away by the spring floods of the untamed Colorado, the underlying color in this stretch of canyon alternates between a light and a dark gray. Standing by the river is a slab of fallen Redwall limestone, standing vertically like Ten Mile Rock did yesterday. It has alternating dark gray and white horizontal bands, but no red. It is squared off, almost as if a stonemason had been at work. Someone is reminded of the black-and-white banded architecture of Giotto's Tower in Florence, and of his church in Siena, and I agree. A little bit of fourteenth-century Italy, here in the bottom of the Grand Canyon. Art imitates nature—but sight unseen?

WE PASSED A LOVELY CAMP on the right shore. As we zipped by, I thought that it was too bad we couldn't stop. But we stopped there after all; it's just that the nice place to park at this campsite is downstream of the rapid. And so J.B. ran the rapid, then caught the back-eddy. We rode it back up to camp. Disorienting, this river flowing uphill occasionally.

No sooner are the boats tied up than shouts of "Bag line!" are heard. The black rubber bags containing our gear are tossed by a boatman to the first person on the shore, who passes them along in bucket-brigade fashion. A pile of black bags forms back in the center of camp. As one boat is emptied, a new bag line forms at the next boat. And then everyone is free until dinner,

MILE 31
South Canyon
Second Campsite

free for bathing, napping, or exploring. We explore the camp, picking out nice sites to spread a sleeping bag. They are every-where.

CLIMBING UP A CRACK in a three-story cliff of Redwall, I find a platform of eroding rock and debris from higher layers that didn't make it as far as the river. The platform extends for a mile along the right bank, and was home to the Anasazi. These Native Americans of a thousand years ago probably grew beans, corn, and squash in nearby South Canyon. And surely on the sand bars of the river, down where our tents are taking root. I wondered aloud about how many of our campsites are, in fact, old Indian camps. Probably most, said Subie.

The foundations and walls for a few small buildings remain up here; they probably built down near the river too, but floods have since erased the evidence. The northernmost ruin has a clever design, with a baffle protecting the front door, a wall keeping the north winds of winter from blowing into the room. The Anasazi must have been small, because someone as tall as I am would never have fit inside the one room except diago-nally. Even assuming the short stature that poor diets cause, there would have been comfortable sleeping room for no more than two persons. Broken pottery and stone tools are laid out near each ruin; we pick them up and examine them carefully. As compared to tourists generally, river-runners and hikers rarely walk off with souvenirs. If this were the South Rim they'd be gone in a day—not so much a matter of lesser virtue as of sheer numbers of visitors. Three million people come to see the Grand Canyon in some years, and 98 percent never get more than a few steps below the rim. Only one-half of one percent run the river, most during the April-to-October season.

At the junction of two paths was a large rock slab covered with desert varnish. At first I passed it by without a glance. Later I found that it had been decorated with quite a number of pet-roglyphs. These are like painted pictographs, except that they are pecked into the rock face. No one knows whether the An-asazi used this method because they didn't have enough colorful material for painting pictographs, or because they knew that de-signs etched into the rock would better survive the desert var-nishing.

Many of the traditional Anasazi forms can be discerned on the slab, including near-replicas of the famous pair of spirals (one large, numbering seven turns, and one half-size with three turns) found at Chaco Canyon over in New Mexico which the an-cient inhabitants used to track the 18.6-year lunar cycle, the equinoxes, and summer solstice. The spirals here couldn't have been used the same way, as there is nothing to create a shadow as at Chaco, but I presume the spirals were widely copied as magical symbols, decorating many local walls and rock slabs around the Colorado Plateau.

Another six stories up are a number of caves in the cliffs overlooking this three-story-high living platform, and the teenagers have been exploring them. The trail leads to a narrow crawl space. Jeremy DuBois tells me that from it one can peer out of a hole to see far down a cliff into South Canyon below. Once, unfortunately, someone fell to his death from that hole, Alan tells me; mishaps involving river passengers (as opposed to ill-prepared hikers coming down from the rim) are fairly uncommon, particularly on the oar-powered trips on which there is an experienced boatman for every three or four passengers.

I can see where the local Giotto's Tower came from: the entire Redwall cliff across the river is one alternating light and dark gray layer after another for over thirty stories up from the river, each layer about as far apart as the rungs of a ladder. The red Supai coating seems to have been washed away from an enormous expanse of flat cliff, perhaps by groundwater seeping out of the walls at some other time of the year (it's dry now). There are also vertical cracks evidently made by water seepage and the white layers often bridge the gap where the darker layers above and below them have been eaten away, suggesting that the white layers are harder stuff, purer limestone. As a result, the cracks look like ladders, but they lead nowhere.

On this side of the river, the late afternoon bathers are out. There is a deep but protected channel leading upriver out of South Canyon, a nice place for a quick dip. We've all collected a coating of algae from our swims back at Silver Grotto. We wash off, but no one stays in the frigid water for very long.

HOMINIDS GOT THE WANDERLUST about 1.5 million years ago. This topic came up after dinner when we got to talking about the Anasazi and the other natives of the Americas. Someone brought up the Bering Sea land bridge, and off we went.

Hominoids are the apes and the hominids. Hominids are us, our ancestors, and our cousins back to the time that we split off from the chimpanzees about 7 million years ago. Prior to 1.5 million years ago, the hominids apparently stayed put in Africa. *Homo erectus*, with its partly enlarged brain, spread out of Africa into Asia and later Europe. *Homo sapiens* was around by 100,000 years ago. Australia (which was joined with New Guinea during ice ages, when the drop in sea level connected them) and the Americas, however, seem to have waited a long time for human habitation. Only at about 50,000 years ago do traces of *Homo sapiens* appear in Australia. Perhaps boats were invented then, allowing the water barriers between the earth's land masses to be surmounted, though the Mediterranean islands were not inhabited until 13,000 years ago, the traditional time assigned to the invention of boats.

Anthropologists now think that water is not the barrier it was once thought to be. One can, after all, even walk on water in special circumstances. Traditionally, the peopling of the Americas has been attributed to the substantial lowering of sea level (by about thirty stories) by the last ice age, when the ancient pioneers could walk across the Bering Strait from Asia to Alaska. However, as Alaskan anthropologists note, anyone who thinks that the Bering Strait is a barrier simply hasn't been around during the wintertime. (They slyly suggest that the textbook myth about the Bering Strait is a fiction created for the summer tourists). Just as the Lapps conduct migrations across the ice-covered Baltic Sea between Sweden and Finland, so could anyone have strolled across the Bering Strait during the winter, ice age or not. The barrier would be getting from coastal Alaska down south to the main body of the continent; during an ice age, that's rough. Crashing surf and rugged headlands keep one from hiking down the coast. Glaciers kept anyone from using inland routes. About 13,000 to 14,000 years ago, as the most recent ice age was starting to melt off, a corridor opened from the Yukon down to Edmonton, Alberta, and so travel would have become much easier starting then. Certainly there are a number of Alaskan species of mammals, such as the grizzly bear, which suddenly make an appearance down south after that date.

Still, though, travelers could have come to the Americas before the last ice age got started or during it—if they had come by boat, anywhere along the coastline of North, Central, and South America, from Africa, Asia, or Europe. Any time they could have gotten the boats and brave sailors together. Present evidence suggests that this happened only in the days of modern-type *Homo sapiens sapiens*; Neanderthals had probably disappeared before the peopling of the Americas. The ages of properly excavated archaeological sites go back to 31,000 years ago in Brazil, 21,000 years in the eastern United States, and 14,000 years ago in Chile, although there are scattered claims of even older finds.

One of the California neurobiologists noted that there is a large human skull, arguably dated to the last ice age, that washed out of the cliff above the surfing beach at Del Mar, just north of San Diego; some archaeologists are trying, so the local joke goes, to locate his surfboard for tree-ring dating.

There is evidence that only a few small groups made it to the Americas, and that each then had a population explosion. All of the South American natives seem to fall into one group. The Inuit (Eskimos) and the Athapascans (Navajos, Utes, Apaches, and many of the west coast "Indians," as well as the groups between the Yukon and Lake Athabasca) constitute another. The rest of the North American Indians comprise a third group, though for most purposes they can be identified with the South American Indians. The groups are based not on cultural similarities but on genetically coded traits, such as blood types, and are constantly being revised as new genes are analyzed. However, it is evident that, except for the late-arriving group of Eskimos and Athapascans, the natives of the Americas aren't especially related to the peoples of northeastern Asia on the other side of the "Bering land bridge." Most Indian skull shapes are quite similar to the types found in China before the Classic Mongoloid type invaded China from the north about 15,000 years ago; the oldest Eskimo and Athapascan skulls are clearly Classic Mongoloid and more recent.

In the Southwest, there were paleo-Indians around hunting with Clovis point arrowheads 11,000 years ago (these characteristic arrowheads, found widely across North America, were named after the find at Clovis, New Mexico). Hereabouts, the archaic Indians periodically visited the Canyon about 4,000 years ago. In Stanton's cave—the big hole in the Redwall that we can see downstream in the fading daylight—they left figurines made of willow branches. It wasn't until about A.D. 900, however, that they stayed in the Canyon long enough to bother building habitations, at least ones sturdy enough for the archaeologists to detect after a millennium.

The Indians had been around the Southwest long before that, irrigating crops at Mesa Verde by A.D. 600. They may have been distant relatives of the Meso-American Indians, who were building cities down in the Yucatan peninsula of Mexico by that time. The Anasazi, as the ancient Indians who lived around here are called, were hunter-gatherers who settled down; but not before they got some of their ideas about check dams, irrigation, stars, and agriculture from the Mayan civilizations down south, who were into empires in a big way by A.D. 600.

The old-yet-young aspect makes the Americas extraordinarily interesting to anthropologists. We can stand here at South Canyon and see thousand-year-old relics of a Stone Age people—including "soft" artifacts like baskets and sandals—without all of the overlay of subsequent Bronze and Iron Age peoples, without the Greeks and then the Romans having built temples atop the site. Here one can study the fluctuations of climate in the thick and thin tree rings of long-surviving trees, see what the vicissitudes of rainfall did to the Anasazi population numbers, get some feeling for what it was like to live in a marginal situation out on the fringes of the main population, where every bit of cleverness counted. The Grand Canyon's Anasazi are an anthropologist's dream, giving an uncluttered view of a people not unlike those who were once on the cutting edge of human evolution.

□   □   □

We have lived upon this land from days beyond history's records, far past any living memory, deep into the time of legend. The story of my people and the story of this place are one single story. No man can think of us without thinking of this place. We are always joined together.

AN ANASAZI DESCENDANT, member of the Taos Pueblo in New
Mexico, 20th century

□   □   □

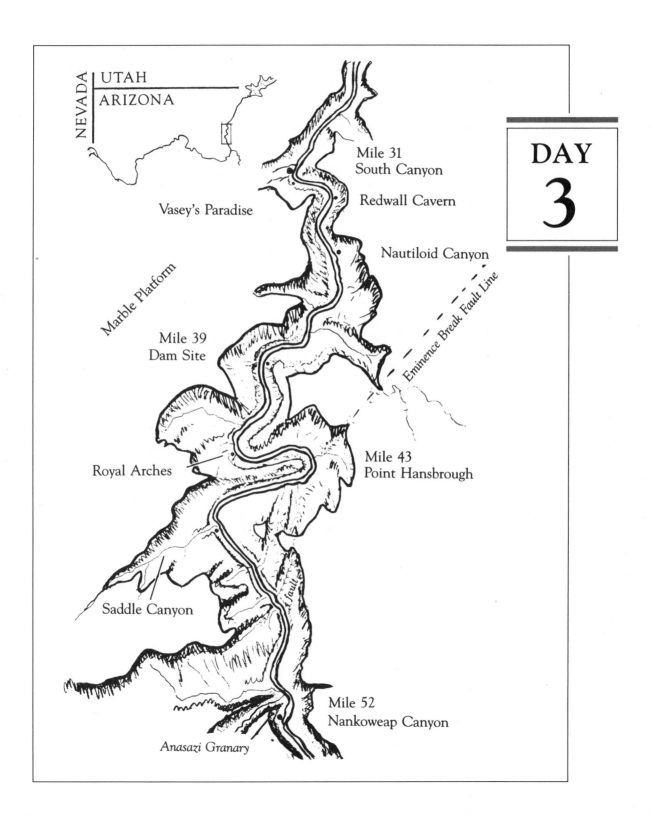

NEVADA UTAH ARIZONA

Mile 31
South Canyon

Redwall Cavern

Vasey's Paradise

Nautiloid Canyon

Marble Platform

Eminence Break Fault Line

Mile 39
Dam Site

Royal Arches

Mile 43
Point Hansbrough

Fault

Saddle Canyon

Mile 52
Nankoweap Canyon

Anasazi Granary

DAY

3

MILE 31
South Canyon

THE SUNRISE FIRST ILLUMINATED the high and distant canyon wall, and then crept down slowly to catch the lower, and closer, ridge lines. It was all a beautiful red-orange in the morning light as I watched from my sleeping bag. When the light reached the wet greenery, the sparkles started. I couldn't imagine what was causing them, so I got up to get a better view.

Down the river, less than half a mile from South Canyon, are two great, sparkling banks of greenery descending from about four stories up the canyon wall. Through the binoculars passed to me by several other people attracted by the sight, I surveyed the waterfalls that the greenery had invaded. Out of the right canyon wall a fair-sized creek flows amidst the ferns and ivy. The river takes a sharp left turn at that point, so one can see only part of the second bank of greenery, which is Vasey's Paradise.

The sun also shines into Stanton's Cave, the large opening halfway between the campsite and Vasey's. As we watched, the whole hanging creek became an intense, wet green, contrasting with its red backdrop. Across the river, the left bank was still cloaked in shadow, its thirty stories of alternating light and dark gray bands a monument of a more subtle sort.

It is a quiet morning in camp, with most of the boatmen sitting in their boats alone, combing their hair, brushing their teeth, reading, or mending a shirt. These professional river-runners learn to make time, for these boats are their home for six months, longer than their houses back in Flag (which seems to be the local name for Flagstaff, about 225 kilometers north of Phoenix), which they visit for three or four days at a time between trips.

The Canyon is quiet, almost. The birds are seen more than heard at this hour, the swallows (and an occasional swift) fly in patterns, cruising along the wavetops, then soaring back up, powering through a nongliding turn with that characteristic flapping of the wings which they share with the bats, then coming around again for another pass. The sounds of the water, fluting noises as the river passes over a submerged rock near shore, mix with the pitter-patter of the windwaves against the undersides of the moored boats, drumming up a beat.

And, of course, ever present is the roar of the nearby rapid. When one is near a minor rapid, it is a constant white noise, a backdrop of "wheee-ee-ee." One sees the waves occasionally rising to an episodic splash, but doesn't hear this culmination as an additional clap, instead hearing only the white roar of the whole river flowing through the rapid. In a symmetrical rapid like Badger, with canyons on both sides that create a V-shaped gravel bar, the rapid starts as a tongue of flat water flanked by narrowing courses of white water. At the tip of the V, the flat water gives way to white water as well. The tail of the rapid is a flurry of choppy waves, sometimes culminating in a series of standing waves.

We had a raven come visit us at breakfast. It cruised past the boats, then perched atop a nearby rock to survey the scene with cocked head. He wants us to hurry up and leave, not being by nature a particularly patient bird. The boatmen tell more raven stories, some along the lines of "they're too smart for their own good." Ravens seem to enjoy practical jokes, mockery, and petty thievery—as if they were bored, too smart for their role in life.

The sight of the glittering greenery downriver continues to distract even the most experienced river-runners among us. The boats are now being packed up, and most of us are idly admiring the view. Camp routine in the morning has us up at first light, though there is no announcement or alarm; everyone just falls into it. Most of us are up by about 6 A.M., though almost no one is wearing a watch anymore. The first boatman up puts several pots of water on to boil (we carry a quiet three-burner propane stove plus a charcoal enclosure for baking and grilling). Within half an hour, coffee or tea can be had; usually there are several people standing there waiting for the floating coffee grounds to settle, the sign it's done. Breakfast usually follows within another half hour or so. The idea is to do half of your packing before breakfast and half after. We each have two black rubber bags which carry all our gear; each is about the size of a large grocery sack. They get packed in the bow of one of the boats; one cannot get at them during the day. And so anything you need during the day—camera, books, maps, suntan lotion, or anything else—is carried in your medium-sized ammo can.

I've been back up to the Anasazi ruins to see the petroglyphs again this morning. The Anasazi certainly had a superb view, but one has to wonder if they really appreciated it the way we do. Not that I think there was some biological difference, only that it was an everyday view for them, associated with the toil of making a living in this stony place. Whenever they saw the Marble Platform (one can hike out through South Canyon), they probably thought that it was a great sight. And so it is.

No stargazing last night, at least none I've heard about. Perfect weather, nice exposure of sky, but a collection of sleep-deprived river-runners. It was nice and cool sleeping near the river. And besides, we'll be up late again the night after next—there will be an eclipse of the moon.

This second early morning in the canyon is different. The

Canyon has a hypnotic effect. People just sit and listen to the waters flowing.

And it sometimes happened that while listening to the river, they both thought the same thoughts, perhaps of a conversation of the previous day, or about one of the travellers whose fate and circumstances occupied their minds, or death, or their childhood; and when the river told them something good at the same moment, they looked at each other, both thinking the same thought, both happy at the same answer to the same question.

HERMANN HESSE, *Siddhartha*, 1951

□   □   □

ALAN PULLS US OUT of the eddy into the tail of the rapid. We pick up the current and gain speed. We now have thirty stories of Redwall on each side of the river. The water table seems to be in the Redwall as water seeps out here and there, marked by a little patch of greenery nestled into the steep walls. There are some caves higher up—solution caverns created by such seepage over the millennia—although most are dry now. It was in the biggest of those caves that the river surveyor Robert B. Stanton in 1889 hid his instruments when he decided to hike out via South Canyon rather than continue downriver. He was employed by a railroad that was considering a plan to run trains through the bottom of the Grand Canyon; happily, they abandoned the scheme before, rather than after, construction was begun.

In Stanton's Cave, archaeologists have found quite a few other things. In the Pleistocene (the last 2 million years, with all of the ice age oscillations in climate), condors evidently liked this cave, as some of them died there; one skeleton has a 4-meter wingspan. And some figurines made of willow branches were left there as offerings of some sort by Indians more than 3,000 years ago.

Vasey's Paradise seems even more remarkable than it did earlier this morning, once we get around enough of the river bend to see all of it. Major Powell described it well during his second expedition down the Colorado:

The river turns sharply east and seems enclosed by a wall set with a million brilliant gems. On coming nearer we find fountains bursting from the rock high overhead, and the spray in the sunshine forms the gems which bedeck the wall. The rocks are covered with mosses and ferns and many beautiful flowering plants. We name it Vasey's Paradise, in honor of the botanist who traveled with us last year.

JOHN WESLEY POWELL, 1871 river diary

□   □   □

ON THE LEFT SHORE, a mile downstream from Vasey's Paradise, there looms a giant cavern inset into the Redwall cliff just above the river level. It looks for all the world like a symphony-sized bandshell, but as we come closer we see that it is even bigger than that—it could accommodate a large audience as well. And they do hold concerts here, during the music trip. Its floor is a gentle bed of sand and, at this hour, it is entirely in shadow. The other boats have all paused back at Vasey's Paradise, but we passed up that stop, choosing to admire it from the river while drifting slowly along, because Alan dislikes the poison ivy hidden among the other greenery there. So in consequence, five of us have Redwall Cavern all to ourselves for a while. It's nice.

After poking around along the beach for awhile, Alan calls Marsha over to the shoreline and points down at the sand. Marsha, the teen-aged sister of one of the boatmen, picks up a basket-like figurine of a deer—actually more of a llama, with a tall body but short legs. What with the stories of archaeological treasures found in Stanton's Cave, Marsha immediately jumps to the conclusion that it is a valuable ancient Indian artifact. It doesn't look ancient to me; I suspect Alan of having planted it.

Marsha too became suspicious after a few minutes, and forced Alan to confess. Indeed, Alan had some unmodified willow branches on his boat and happily agreed to show Marsha how to make split-willow figurines in the manner of the Anasazi. First, you split a long branch, all except for one end. This unsplit end serves as the head, with a fold of one of the split halves sticking through the end of the crack to form the nose. Further folds of the two half-branches create a body and legs. The split willow is only folded, never severed, in the construction process. The final step is to use one end of the split willow to penetrate the wrapped layers of willow forming the body, so that the end sticks out like a spear. A hunting totem?

I wonder if the Anasazi knew about the medicinal properties of willow bark? That's where aspirin came from (acetylsalicylic acid, from the Latin for willow, *salix*).

The other boats float into shore, everyone having filled canteens and the lemonade coolers at Vasey's. The ravens have also arrived. Three of the large black birds strut along the beach and then fly up to perch on some low rocks. They look at us with a certain nonchalance.

The Redwall Cavern ravens are sleek and black, big and well-fed. They mostly keep their distance and impatiently await our departure, so that they can come in and inspect for leavings. I

MILE 33
Redwall Cavern

doubt they found anything to eat at South Canyon after we left, but they're ever hopeful.

THE MARBLE PLATFORM really isn't marble, but Kaibab Limestone. This Redwall surrounding us in Redwall Cavern is also limestone. Rock isn't living matter, yet this rock has been made by life itself. Slowly.

The calcium shells of all the little microscopic organisms in the sea that die over the millennia, slowly fall to the bottom. In 25,000 years or so, the ocean bottom accumulates a layer of limestone that, when compacted, is one story high.

Limestone. Polish it, as the river sometimes does, and it might fool someone into thinking it was marble. That's how the Marble Canyon got its name, back before the geological professionals got here to look. Real marble is limestone that has been metamorphosed, made plastic under extreme heat and pressure deep under the earth's surface, and then cooled, looking thereafter somewhat like the chocolate bar I had the other day, which first melted and then solidified as I drove through the cool desert during the night. It acquired a somewhat novel shape in the process, the lines between the squares getting a little wavy, as in marbling.

The limestone of Marble Canyon has thus far escaped melting and marbling. I hear that the Grand Canyon itself, far downriver near the volcanos, has a bit of real marble.

The high walls we see upriver used to be ocean bottoms, ancient seashores, sand dunes, or river deltas. Actually all those things. The land sinks beneath the seas, is resurrected, eroded and rearranged, and then sinks again. There have been many ups and downs over the ages, literally. Only in the last 200 years have we learned to read this rock-layer history. That's how we know that the summit of the highest mountain on earth used to be at the bottom of the Indian Ocean: Mount Everest is also marine limestone. Continental drift caused the Indian subcontinent to creep across the Indian Ocean, ram into Asia, and push up the Himalayas about 40 million years ago. Besides the Rocky Mountains, pushed up perhaps 60 million years ago when the West Coast got tacked onto the North American protocontinent, nothing so dramatic happened here. This canyon we're inside at the moment was probably in business by 30 million years ago, carrying the rainfall from the Rockies down to the sea.

PETER HARTLINE, Dan's brother, a neurobiologist specializing in unusual sense organs such as the infrared heat detectors of snakes, has decided to climb the rocks which lead up the canyon wall at the downriver end of Redwall Cavern. Dan and several others join him, and soon our group talking on the beach sees four figures in profile against the sky. The rock climbers love this hard limestone. One of the ravens flies up to inspect them, and we jokingly shout at our friends to look out for bombs being dropped. But the raven flies away, looking bored, and comes back down to watch us instead.

The shadows have been shortening, and the people left out in the sun are picking themselves up and moving up the beach into the shade. That's how long we've been here. We have been joined by another river group, taking what is called a private trip. In addition to river companies running commercial trips—of which several trips depart each day—the Park Service allows one private trip to leave Lee's Ferry every day during the summer season. There is a waiting list for private trips, and it takes years to work one's way to the top of the list. This group consists of only five people: two couples paddling kayaks plus an experienced Canyon boatman who is running their supply boat. The supply boat, a rubber raft much like ours, has a waterproof guitar case strapped atop it. One thing leads to another and soon one of our boatmen has borrowed the guitar and starts playing a classical piece. Probably Bach. It has that feeling of depth, the music retracing and elaborating a pattern, cresting and falling. He plays another piece and then passes the guitar back to its owner, who also plays some classic piece of more modern date, possibly Granados. Here we are, stretched out on the sand of Redwall Cavern, half in and half out of the sun, listening to real music in this incredible bandshell.

The ravens watch the crazy people. The requests start and we begin to sing—not exactly Bach chorales but rather Pete Seeger songs and the like. We're starting to get the idea that we're not on a schedule anymore, though finally the boatmen ask "Who wants to see the fossils?" and that gets us started back to the boats.

THE MUAV LAYER HAS EMERGED along the riverbank in places; it's another limestone, though somewhat greenish in color, and it is much older than the Redwall Limestone atop it. Quite a few intervening layers are now missing, at least in this part of the Canyon, so there is no evidence of the rock laid down between about 360 million years and nearly 535 million years ago at this level. Omitted as a result of ancient erosion are those Devonian layers whose fossils would have recorded the evolution of the vertebrates from the echinoderms (the phylum that includes the sand dollars and starfish), the early part of the Age of Fishes, the first land plants, and the first amphibians to crawl ashore. If we keep our eyes peeled, we'll see some of those miss-

MILE 35
Nautiloid Canyon

ing layers further downriver where erosion wasn't so efficient. Alas, fossils are rarely found in the Muav around here.

The left riverbank was getting closer, Alan rowing us over to where several other boats had tied up on the shore. I jumped off with the mooring line and found a suitable rock. Alan asked Ben to pass forward a big bailing bucket. At this, Ben was somewhat puzzled, since we hadn't been through any rapids and the boat was dry.

Alan scooped up some river water in a bucket and bounded off across the boulder pile, heading up the narrow side canyon. "Maybe he has a fixation with carrying heavy containers of liquids above his head," I observed to Dan, as everyone followed. "Coffee, I can understand. But water comes out of side canyons. Carrying a bucket of water up one is like carrying coals to Newcastle."

At the base of the Redwall, the side canyon dead-ended, with no stream to be seen. Just the memory of one, in the form of sculptured red and gray rock. And various people bent over, admiring it.

"See! Here's a good one," said Subie, and pointed at the weathered, gray rock underfoot. We could barely make out the outline of an invertebrate animal. It was almost like a weathered footprint from some strange corrugated-sole boot. "I'll get Alan's bucket."

She returned and splashed a little river on the ancient Redwall limestone. Suddenly the animal's outline was much clearer, as the color of the rock deepened and the dust washed away. Developing the image with river water.

"But what is it?" asked Ben, after puzzling over it for several minutes.

"Ah, you molecular biologists, you don't know your fossil animals!" Subie joked. "It's a nautiloid, a relative of the modern Nautilus. You know, it's a cephalopod like the squid and the octopus. Except it grows a series of chambers for flotation."

"The Nautilus is coiled into a spiral, like a snail," added J.B., who had come over to admire it. "This is the early uncoiled version, from about 350 million years ago."

"It's called going straight," observed Marsha, who was greeted by a chorus of groans. There's been an epidemic of puns today.

There were a whole series of fossil nautiloids in the thin layers of rock which the ancient creek had worn away. One was the better part of a meter long, looking like a giant's footprint. The fossils became easier to spot, thanks to wet patches left by other recent discoverers.

"Obviously a very successful animal," commented one of the biologists. "And their relative, the modern octopus, is probably the most intelligent of the invertebrates. It's a shame that they taste so good. An octopus is certainly as smart as a rodent."

"But their brain is built in an entirely different way from the general plan of vertebrate brains," noted Dan Hartline. "Just goes to show that there is more than one way to build a smart brain."

A curiously bell-like sound filled the air. Music again. Subie was demonstrating her favorite singing rock, a watermelon-sized chunk of loose rock in a pile at the head of the canyon. By striking it with another rock, it would ring for several seconds. It was, however, the only such rock to be found. Alas, it would have been great fun to construct a rocky xylophone.

THE SCARS on both sides of the river are man-made, a jarring note in this wilderness of running water. They are test holes drilled back into the limestone, extending several city blocks deep inside the Muav and the Redwall cliffs.

Surveyors' splashy marks dot the cliffs like graffiti. A tall, unnaturally steep pile of rubble can be seen below each hole, deposited so recently that the weather and river have not had time to spread out the pile. An abandoned barge lies half-sunk near the base of one pile. There used to be scaffolding and a tramline down the cliff to these sites, since removed by the Park Service.

This is not an old mine; the limestone here is rather too common for that. These test holes were the first stage in the construction of a large dam. Right here. The dam-builders planned to back up the Colorado 54 miles, back past Lee's Ferry to the base of the Glen Canyon Dam, burying all the places we've seen so far under a huge lake. That's why all the new government buildings back at Lee's Ferry are incongruously located high above river level—they thought the low-lying sites near the boat launch would soon be flooded. Thus the car campground is perched in a windswept location, and has had to be provided with sheet metal windbreaks to supplement the wilderness experience. Not only would Lee's Ferry have been flooded but also the nautiloids, Redwall Cavern, South Canyon, the Anasazi ruins and petroglyphs, Silver Grotto, North Canyon, and all the rest. As if burying Glen Canyon weren't enough.

The Glen Canyon Dam, just upstream from Lee's Ferry, actually did back up the Colorado to drown a 186-mile region every bit as spectacular as this section of Marble Canyon. There was no organized opposition to the flooding of Glen Canyon, perhaps because few realized how beautiful the area was. Lake Powell, a drag strip for speedboats, now covers those canyons and gradually fills them with red mud.

Marble Canyon Dam was defeated in the sixties by the en-

MILE 39
Marble Canyon Damsite

. . . most men, it seems to me, do not care for Nature and would sell their share in all her beauty. . . . It is for the reason that some do not care . . . that we need to continue to protect all from the vandalism of a few.

HENRY DAVID THOREAU
The Journals

We fear the cold and the things we do not understand. But most of all we fear the doings of the heedless ones among ourselves.

AN INUIT SHAMAN, quoted by an early Arctic explorer

ergetic efforts of Martin Litton, owner of one of the river companies, and the Sierra Club, then led by David Brower. Plus thousands of other people. The government dam-builders tried to promote the advantages of another new lake, saying that "people will like to sightsee by speedboat." I can still remember the Sierra Club's full-page newspaper ads headlined: "SHOULD WE FLOOD THE SISTINE CHAPEL SO TOURISTS CAN GET NEARER THE CEILING?" While the government cancelled the Sierra Club's tax-deductible status over that fight, the conservationists finally won the battle.

The Arizona and Utah politicians are endlessly fond of building dams with the federal taxpayer's money. The official Arizona state road maps still show a dam site inside Grand Canyon National Park at Mile 238 on the Colorado, variously named Bridge Canyon Dam or Hualapai Dam, showing that the fight to prevent the Grand Canyon itself from being flooded isn't over yet. Bridge Canyon Dam was officially cancelled by the U.S. government only in 1984. The "flooding easement" on the park and Indian lands was finally allowed to expire—but not without the dam-builders making a final effort to promote the flooding of the lower part of the Grand Canyon, scarring up the Canyon with access roads, and stringing it with high-voltage powerlines. But the Arizona politicians are still spending money on studies to promote it.

Unfortunately, the plans and the test-hole data for such projects get filed away, perhaps to be used in the future. And the local politicians are always trying to get Congress to give them money to build yet another dam. It's a tradition in this part of the world, one which has been repeatedly successful, this waiting game of exploiters. All it takes is a recession, and long-term preservation goals can be overridden by a short-term drive for profits and jobs. Those who would preserve the wilderness have to fight repeated battles with each new generation of politicians to keep the exploiters out. To lose once is unthinkable.

Even national park status seems no obstacle to the dam-builders and their powerful supporters. The badly overcrowded Yosemite National Park in California's Sierra Nevada Mountains used to include a second similarly spectacular valley just to the north, named Hetch Hetchy. Since 1920 it has been drowned, a Yosemite we'll never see. That generation probably rationalized flooding Hetch Hetchy by saying that one valley remained and that was enough. Today, the map handed out to the Yosemite visitors ought to remind people about why the valley is now so badly overcrowded, but it doesn't. You'd think that one such mistake would have been a sufficient lesson.

The outstanding example of exploitation and despoliation of a national park feature for private gain was the damming of Hetch Hetchy valley in Yosemite National Park. . . .

Isabelle Florence Story, in the *Encyclopaedia Britannica,*
1953

A GIANT COOKIE-CUTTER has been at work on the land-scape. That's what Marsha reported seeing on her flight out to Phoenix. Great circular spots of green amidst the brown.

"Those are irrigated fields," Ben explained. "From giant lawn-sprinklers that march over the fields, swiveling around a central pumphouse."

"But those cookies were giants!" exclaimed Marsha. "Some-one on the plane told me that they could be seen from the moon more easily than the Great Wall of China!"

"The lawn-sprinklers are giants too. They put out a stream like a fire hose. It'd knock you flat on your back if you wan-dered into it," explained Ben. "Those sprinklers are several sto-ries high."

"Is there a white ring of salt around the cookies yet?" asked one of the boatmen whose name I haven't learned yet. "There soon will be, you know."

THE SALT OF THE EARTH can be the downfall of civiliza-tions. The boatmen are ardent ecologists. They speak of the shortsightedness of our irrigation practices as well as the lost beauty of the landscape. Just fly over the world's largest irriga-tion system in the Indus Valley of Pakistan, they say, and you'll think there is snow down there. It is salt, encrusted atop the soil—ruined soil in which crops will no longer grow. Short-term gain yielded long-term disaster. And one can see that same white salt buildup along stream beds in the United States, from Col-orado to California.

The reason for this problem is familiar to anyone who knows a little about drilling wells for water. There is a water table, even beneath a desert, below which water sinks no further, thanks to a resistant rock layer such as shale. Above the porous layer that contains the water supply is likely to be another layer of rather salty rock, perhaps a sandstone or siltstone that was com-pacted beneath an ancient ocean.

As water drains through soil it picks up a bit of salt on the way. Where rain usually falls, the salt gets washed out over the millennia, carried underground along the water table. But if an unnatural amount of water comes down through the soil in an area that doesn't normally get much rain—as in the irrigated Southwest—there is lots of salt left to pick up. The well-water in the area of Phoenix, Arizona, is already starting to go salty from all the irrigation. By the time the Colorado River water reaches the Mexican border, it has been through the soil re-peatedly, and has become so salty that the United States was obligated to build a desalination plant for what's left of the Col-orado River (the Mexicans aren't left much) in order to live up to a treaty with Mexico which guaranteed the quality of the water delivered to that nation.

Such technological "quick-fixes" draw our attention away from the real danger: that poorly managed irrigation will raise salt to the soil's surface. After all, irrigation converts local land with less than 20 centimeters (8 inches) of rainfall a year into well-watered farmland. And all that rock and soil between the water table and the surface becomes wet but then, when the irrigation stops and the surface starts drying, water is wicked back upward, carrying salt with it. The salt emerges slowly but irresistibly, not unlike the way manganese is drawn out of the limestone around here to create desert varnish. Eventually the topsoil becomes salty and infertile. A white "irrigation varnish," just like the white ring that builds up around the tops of the pots used for houseplants, becomes the harbinger of stunted growth and crop failure.

Or the salt washes out downhill somewhere and contaminates the streams there. If a valley that lacks natural drainage— such as California's great central agricultural valley, the San Joaquin—is irrigated with even slightly salty water, the salt continues to build up over the years as the water evaporates. The water that does run off is so salty that evaporation ponds containing it may be a health hazard because of heavy metals leached out of the earth: in the San Joaquin, waterfowl signaled the problem with a high rate of birth defects and fetal mortality.

The politicians and farmers down here in Arizona and Utah know most of these things, but short-term money talks louder. They assume that by the time the long-term arrives, science and technology will have discovered a way to bail them out, again with the taxpayer's money.

History, too, speaks of the dangers of soil salinity, as revealed by irrigation canals over 6,000 years old that have been found in the Fertile Crescent of the Middle East. The great civilization of Sumer, which invented writing 5,000 years ago for us all, owes its downfall partly to soil salinity. That region of the Mesopotamian floodplain of the Tigris and Euphrates rivers once supported 17 to 25 million people; today this once-fertile river delta has been transformed into a desert. To most experts, salt heads the list of probable reasons for this disaster. There are some archaeologists who suspect that the same thing happened to the Anasazi over at Chaco Canyon in New Mexico, which for several centuries a thousand years ago was the focus of Anasazi culture in this area.

Farmers in the American West don't use modern irrigation technology now, so long as the taxpayers are willing to build more dams. In fact, American irrigation practices are not all that different from Pakistan's. But irrigation has been vastly improved by the drip irrigation systems developed primarily in Israel, where farming the desert is a matter of national pride. And, because the Israelis make do with far less water, I wonder how many of the Southwest's demands for more agricultural water—the American taxpayers are currently footing the $1,300 million bill for the Central Arizona Project and it's got $2,300 million to go—are simply a consequence of a wasteful technology.

Consider those giant garden-sprinklers and the large percentage of the water they emit that simply evaporates before landing on those round plots. Even the evaporation from the less wasteful flood-the-fields techniques is significant. In Israel, they cover all irrigation canals to limit evaporation. They run pipes down each row, dripping the water out of little holes directly into the soil where it is needed, wetting the soil only to root depth and no more. Moisture meters buried in the ground measure how dry the soil actually is. Microcomputers, hooked up to those moisture sensors, control the water valves so that they deliver only the amount of water actually needed to maintain the proper amount of moisture in the soil. This avoids waste through overwatering. The water is also delivered in the middle of the night, to further minimize evaporative loss. And the Israelis erect clear plastic tents over some fields to trap the humid air, slowing further evaporation. If one flies over Israel's northern valley, the Hula, there seem to be giant ponds dotting the landscape—but they're actually fields covered by giant plastic canopies.

And since the Israelis don't soak the depths of the soil with water, they run less long-term risk of ruining their soil via salt wicking up through it. It would be tragic if the rest of the world finally switched to drip irrigation only after its soil was ruined, its civilizations already scarred by starving mobs.

In the Southwest, building more dams is simply another way of subsidizing the farmer. To allow the farmer to get along without installing efficient technology, we raise taxes rather than food prices. This approach, in the minds of many thoughtful people, is appallingly wasteful and, most importantly, a luxury we cannot afford because of what it does to the land. It not only drowns beautiful canyons beneath new lakes, but risks crippling the soil that the lake water irrigates—by allowing the salt of the earth to rise to the surface.

BUSY AS BEAVERS have been our dam-builders. A few years ago, Dave Brower came along on this float trip. He stood atop one of the tailing piles below a test hole here at Mile 39 to recount how the battle over this particular dam was fought by the

Salt problems are particularly insidious. They do not come charging at you with trumpets blowing and battle flags flying, a sight to set stirring the hearts of activists in any century. Rather, they slip in almost unnoticed . . . They have quietly destroyed, without fuss or fanfare, more civilizations than all of the mighty armies of the world.
WARREN A. HALL, 1973
Office of Water
Resources Research,
U.S. Department of the Interior

At least 50 percent, and presumably now close to 65 percent, of all irrigated land will be destroyed by salt before the end of the century.
GEORG BORGSTROM, 1984
Michigan State University
food expert

boatmen and the Sierra Club. And temporarily won—but reminded everyone that fighting the dam-builders was a continuing battle, that we only have to fail once to lose permanently.

In a lighter vein, Brower compared dam-builders to beavers: they simply can't stand the sight of running water. Actually, that is quite a good characterization of beaver behavior if you substitute "sound" for "sight." It was once thought that beavers were terribly intelligent agricultural engineers, executing a preconceived plan to flood lowlands so as to raise more trees to eat. Instead, it seems that beavers have a strong instinct to shove mud and sticks toward the sound of running water. In fact, someone who wanted to investigate this took a loudspeaker, placed it up on a dry riverbank, and played a tape of a burbling brook. The beavers plastered the hi-fi speaker, not the river, with mud and sticks. When the tape was turned off, they stopped, presumably feeling some sense of accomplishment.

So beaver dams are built (and repeatedly repaired) thanks to this primitive instinct, stopping noise. Who would have ever predicted that dams and irrigation would emerge as a result of an animal's liking peace and quiet? One wonders if human dam-builders are operating on a similarly unreasoning principle, a blind expediency that we can no longer afford; our irrigation practices hardly seem to be the product of the insightful, reflective intelligence on which we humans pride ourselves.

Earplugs might slow down the beavers, but it will take more to stop the dam builders. Eternal vigilance is also the price of wilderness.

IN ANOTHER TWO MILES we see the Royal Arches, great natural caverns in the Redwall limestone where wet rock has fallen out of the cliff. Since the water table along here is in the Redwall, it results in outflows such as we saw back at Vasey's Paradise. These often weaken the rock, which eventually falls out, leaving an overhanging arch. Within these three large caverns, well above river level now, greenery clings to the Redwall where the water emerges and drips down to the river. We are getting hot now, and the caverns look refreshingly cool.

We pull over to a sandy beach on the right shore. There's shade, and we'll have lunch here. But first more lemonade. It's very easy to get dehydrated in a desert if we don't change our drinking habits. Yes, I know this place is wall-to-wall water, but we sweat a lot on a day like today. Because it evaporates immediately in the dry air, one usually isn't aware of the sweating. The boatmen's rule of thumb: if you aren't putting out more urine than you usually do back home, you aren't drinking enough. One wants extra body water in a desert, not less. So drink before meals, during meals, after meals, from the canteen on the boat and on hikes. The boatmen remind me of the noncoms in the Israeli army, one of whose duties is to make sure that every soldier drinks three canteens of water daily while in the desert.

And drinking beer doesn't count toward one's quota; because of its diuretic effect, one can lose more fluid than consumed, one reason why tavern restrooms are so busy. The conversation takes a small detour into medical physiology: normally, the brain senses how salty the blood is getting and regulates it by sending "antidiuretic hormone" (ADH) through the bloodstream down to the kidney, telling it how much water to extract from the urine that the kidney is creating. If there were no ADH, you would produce enormous quantities of urine. But too much beer on the brain, and it stops sending ADH to the kidneys. And so one starts dumping water. The dehydration that results is one of the causes of hangovers. If, in a desert, you start feeling a hangover coming on, you are probably dehydrated from sweating instead of imbibing. A sweat hangover, no less. Except that you may have been unaware of sweating in this dry air.

With both hands, we are hanging onto giant sandwiches which we have created from all the makings that the boatmen set out. It turns out that the prime use of the boatmens' belt knives is to slice up things for lunch, such as tomatoes, avocados, cheese, sausage, and onions. There are so many good things to try that one never winds up making an ordinary-sized sandwich. The lemonade cooler, propped up atop an overturned bailer bucket, is sitting next to Marsha, and she cheerfully refills cups that are passed over to her.

THE RIVER MAKES A LONG LOOP around Point Hansbrough—a real hairpin turn—and we get a little wet in our second small rapid of the day. It wasn't wet enough, we complain, getting hotter. Looking behind us, we see that the eastern rock-wall of the Canyon appears shattered. It is not like an erosional valley; no stream has run through it leaving a tell-tale silver color in the red rocks. Instead it looks as if a giant meat cleaver had descended from the sky, landing on the Supai and Redwall layers and creating a long valley of broken rock.

Enlightenment soon follows. A north-south fault line, the Eminence Break, comes through here, and the periodic slips and uplifts along it have created this long, high valley of fractured rock. Like the other major fault lines near the Canyon, it can be seen from out in space, appearing as a long straight line on Landsat pictures of the area taken from 900 kilometers up.

Alan tells us that we'll see an even more dramatic fault line in several days, the Bright Angel Fault, running north-south through Phantom Ranch and then up through the hotels perched atop the South Rim. Looking over there from the North Rim with binoculars, one can compare the east and west walls of the side canyon. The layers are offset about fifteen stories, just under the hotels. The trail out of the canyon leads up that fault line, but happily we will not experience that mile-high climb.

MILE 47
Saddle Canyon

THE WHOLE IS MORE THAN THE SUM OF ITS PARTS. Things in combination have properties that, separately, they may each lack. The additional properties "emerge" from the merger. They're called emergent properties. As we have seen, beaver dams, and the consequent irrigation of upstream areas, may be due to the beaver's propensity to push mud and sticks at the sound of running water. Dams and swamps emerge from that simple trait. Bird flight probably emerged from the simple invention of feathers for insulation.

We can't always predict what will happen. Most of the novelties in evolution are probably due to such emergent properties. Natural selection may shape feathers into good thermal insulators in a series of logical steps, but then there's this sidestep to flying—a result completely unrelated to heat conservation. Of course, natural selection thereafter starts shaping the feather arrangements into better airfoils, as flying is exposed to natural selection. But the surprising thing is the sidestep, in which natural selection changes tracks from insulating to flying. We resolve, while sitting beneath the shade along the riverbank, to collect some more examples of emergent properties during this trip.

Is cleverness one of those emergent properties? One thing that many of the clever animals have in common is that they're omnivores. They'll seemingly eat anything; at least they are broader in their tastes than their less clever relatives. It takes a lot of changes in an animal's body to be so versatile. It must be able to digest various kinds of foods, have the right digestive enzymes, and have defenses against the toxins that many plants use to discourage browsers. The animal also has to have the behavioral strategies that allow it to find the food, maybe even ambush it.

Now an animal that's got a dozen choices in diet, switching back and forth among them depending on their availability, has a lot of behavioral strategies in its repertoire. But they're not necessarily like the dozen fixed habits a bee uses to forage for nectar. They can be used in combination, sometimes with surprising results. The whole is greater than the mere sum of a number of such strategies. Is that the beginnings of cleverness?

Dogs and cats, indeed many of the carnivores, are clever. They have to outwit the escape strategy of each animal they prey on and, since they usually prey upon more than a dozen species, they may have a whole series of ways of making their living.

Chimps are clever, and they're the most omnivorous of the apes, nearly as omnivorous as humans except that chimps dislike dead meat (they have to catch the meat alive in order to treat it as food; offer a wild chimp a nice raw steak and he'll probably reject it). The octopus loves to catch crabs, quite unlike his squid relatives, who just strain seawater for the little plankton in it. The ravens and crows are adapted to a varied diet—and some of that diet requires tool use to get at the encased food. Pigs are smart: their diet is varied and includes things like roots and tubers that most animals pass up.

We thought of some other smart animals that didn't quite fit the hypothesis—the mountain gorilla, which eats great quantities of plants each day, the porpoise, which sticks to fish, and a few others. But maybe they've just retreated—maybe their ancestors got smart by accumulating food-gathering skills, but then later specialized in just one food. Or maybe there are more ways of becoming clever than versatility alone. Maybe some special skills have more potential for increasing intelligence than others. Perhaps the playful porpoise's echo-location specializations also aid its brain in doing other things. I can see that we are not finished talking about this subject.

We, in this case, are the people who didn't go on the hike back up Saddle Canyon, staying instead in the shade. Tamarisk grows thick along the riverbanks. It's just too hot to hike. Though the returning hikers, once they have cooled off in the river, say that we really missed something. Alas.

Remote from universal nature, and living by complicated artifice, man in civilization surveys the creatures through the looking glass of his knowledge and sees thereby a feather magnified and the whole image in distortion. We patronize [the animals] for their incompleteness, for their tragic fate of having taken form so far below ourselves. And therein we err, and greatly err. For the animal shall not be measured by man. In a world older and more complete than ours they move finished and complete, gifted with extensions of the senses we have lost or never attained, living by voices we shall never hear. They are not brethren; they are not underlings; they are other nations, caught with ourselves in the net of life and time, fellow prisoners of the splendor and travail of the earth.

HENRY BESTON, *The Outermost House*, 1949

☐   ☐   ☐

THIS IS THE MOST PHOTOGENIC STRETCH of Marble Canyon so far, to my eye. Between Saddle Canyon and Nankoweap, one starts seeing classic Canyon profiles, scenes that seem to have been laid out with composition in mind. And today the cliffs frame just the right assortment of clouds, the right blue sky, the right shadows.

The Canyon is opening out on the right because the Eminence Break fault line comes through here again about Mile 50— and East Kaibab Monocline's uplift of the North Rim makes for long side canyons on the right bank. Soon we'll see Nankoweap and some more Anasazi ruins. Major Powell got the name in 1872 from a Paiute Indian who said that the big canyon was remembered as the place ("weap") of an Indian battle ("nun ko").

We've become real Redwall fans. Its sheer vertical face is an enormous expanse, being nearly fifty stories tall all by itself. Its color is jewel-like. Life makes some hard rock, and that's a classy rust coloring it too.

MILE 52

Nankoweap Ruins

Third Campsite

This is a day when life and the world seem to be standing still— only time and the river flowing past the mesas.

EDITH WARNER

IT IS LATE in the afternoon by the time we make camp, given our leisurely songfest back at Redwall Cavern. Nankoweap is a long valley on the right bank which the Anasazi farmed. Now we are stretched out under the willows and tammies along the shore, having again raided the supply of cans kept cool by the river in the bow of each boat. A number of people have decided to bathe in the shallows of the river, and it lends a pastoral appearance to the scene. The colors, however, are not those of Monet or Turner; Europe really doesn't have colors like these great expanses of red-orange. Nor are the bathers dressed in Victorian bathing costumes; indeed, several have even gone to the opposite extreme, covering up only with shampoo.

To those who are shocked, a word about the inverted wilderness practices here on the Colorado. The desert which surrounds the riparian corridor is relatively fragile; one doesn't want to pollute it (or the sidestreams) with soap—or anything else. This river corridor, however, is unusually robust because of the high volume of water flowing through it. The dilution factor is enormous; by the standards of cities that draw their drinking water out of quiet rivers into which other cities upstream have dumped their wastes, the Colorado stays very clean even though riverrunners bathe in the river, urinate in it, and wash their dirty dishes in it—all things one shouldn't do in a creek or slow river. "The solution to pollution is dilution" in this special case. The toilet wastes are simply sprinkled with lime, triple bagged, and hauled out in large ammo cans on the baggage boat. As a result of this practice, the river corridor is quite clean in comparison to civilized rivers and to many well-traveled wilderness areas.

Though one can often drink the river water, there can be

pollution when a side canyon like the Little Colorado River is in flood. After an Independence Day weekend in the late seventies, a lot of people got sick on the river, and the suspicion is that the sewage treatment plant up at the dam overflowed from all of the holiday crowds. The river tour groups make a policy of providing chlorinated (one drop of bleach per liter) or finely filtered drinking water, encouraging passengers to drink from a canteen even when they're on the river surrounded by cold water.

The more energetic have set out to hike a little ways up Nankoweap Canyon. I am saving my energies. When we got down to Mile 52, we saw many caves high in the Redwall, as much as fifty stories above the river. And our birdwatchers' binoculars revealed that some of them showed distinctive signs of modification by humans: square openings, framed by timbers. They can even be seen with the unaided eye; it's surprising that Major Powell's expedition missed seeing them in 1869 (they didn't spot any ruins from Lee's Ferry to Mile 61, the entire length of Marble Canyon). Those square openings, we hear, are entrances into rooms in which the Anasazi stored their grain and took refuge from marauders. I cannot understand how they ever reached the caves unless they used ladders, but a moonlight hike is proposed for after sunset. Tonight's moon should be almost full and will brightly illuminate our path.

Dan and I resolved to again camp at the water's edge, and have found a nice spot just above the high-water line. Alan told us that the river would start rising about midnight, when the water that was released this morning—when all the air-conditioners were turned on down in Phoenix—reaches this point on the river. The water travels about 90 miles a day, so we're now seeing water released before dawn today.

Tides are nothing new for those of us used to camping on the ocean beaches. Yet these are freshwater tides, not saltwater. The usual animals that one sees inhabiting the ocean intertidal zone, such as the starfish uncovered at low tide, have no counterpart in freshwater fauna. Lakes are seldom big enough to have tides; even the Mediterranean has minuscule tides, but Glen Canyon Dam has repaired this omission in nature and, if intertidal specialists are to develop anywhere in fresh water, the Grand Canyon now seems a good place.

The predators are certainly ready for them. Already, whiptail lizards with their jerky movements, lashing their long bluish tails, come to forage on the riverbanks. Normally they stick to the desert and avoid the riparian, but they've discovered that the little shrimp-like amphipods (introduced into the Colorado in

1932 to provide food for the rapacious trout, which are also not native) are stranded when the river level falls, and the lizards venture out to eat them. A new niche, invented and filled.

The people who once lived here could have used the extra source of food too; we learned a lot about the Anasazi by listening to the boatmen talk over their beer. The native Americans who inhabited this area a thousand years ago were scattered, and their numbers greatly reduced, by a grim drought lasting from A.D. 1215 to 1300. By A.D. 1300, most villages were empty except the pueblos now known as Hopi, Zuni, and the Rio Grande group. The Navajo, who hunted and gathered their way into this area all of the way from western Canada from A.D. 1300 to 1500, called the remaining Indians the *Anasazi*, which translates as "old enemies" (the often-quoted translation "The Ancient Ones" seems to be a polite euphemism). These surviving Anasazi, however, probably served as the role models for the Navajo as they abandoned their primitive wandering existence to settle down to agriculture supplemented by hunting (and, as usual, raiding). The Navajo even borrowed substantial features of the Anasazi religion (which is not surprising, since it included instructions for agriculture). Even today one sees additional "borrowings." The national monument just east of here features two giant Anasazi cliff dwellings—Betatakin and Keet Seel. Paradoxically it is called "Navajo National Monument" and Navajo guides show the way to Keet Seel. Perhaps it was the same with Greek ruins in Roman days.

Many native American tribes call themselves "The People" in their own language (locally, the word is *Diné* and not "Navajo," which is what the early Spanish explorers mistakenly called the "Apaches with cultivated fields"). They certainly didn't call themselves "Indians," the name which commemorates one of the most important errors in the history of mapmaking. The Europeans underestimated the size of the earth (the ancient Greeks had estimated it quite accurately, long before) and mistook America for India. Of course, if Columbus had known that the earth is as large as it really is, his sailors (and sponsors) might not have had the courage to try the westward route to India.

But what did the Anasazi call themselves? Since they left no written records, all we can do is ask their relatives. The Anasazi's living descendants are thought to include the Hopi, Zuni, and Rio Grande Pueblo Indians. The present-day Hopi, who live on the mesas just southeast of here, refer to the Anasazi as the *Hisatsinom*, or "our ancestors," so that was hardly the Anasazi's word for themselves. The Hopi call themselves *Hopituh*, which

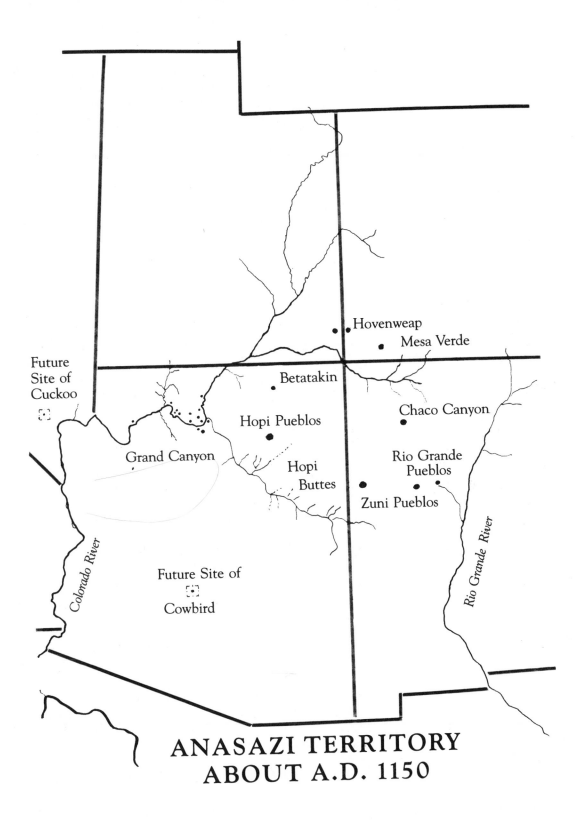

Future
Site of
Cuckoo

Hovenweap

Mesa Verde

Betatakin

Chaco Canyon

Hopi Pueblos

Grand Canyon

Hopi
Buttes

Rio Grande
Pueblos

Zuni Pueblos

Colorado River

Future Site of

Cowbird

Rio Grande River

ANASAZI TERRITORY
ABOUT A.D. 1150

When asked by an anthropologist what the Indians called America before the white man came, an Indian said simply, "Ours."

VINE DELORIA, JR.

means "the peaceful ones." With hindsight, perhaps the most genuine name we could give the ancients would be something like "ancestral Hopituh," but the pejorative Navajo word "Anasazi" has come to signify the natives of 2,300 to 700 years ago in this Four Corners region where the present-day states of Utah, Arizona, New Mexico, and Colorado meet.

THE MOON IS UP, at least far enough to illuminate the canyon walls and the Anasazi ruins, though the moonlight is still creeping toward our camp. Watching the moonlight has become a favorite after-dinner pastime along the river. The pale moonlight descends like a curtain, inching down the western wall of the Marble Canyon as the moon rises in the southeast.

We set out through the brush north of the campsite, cursing the local darkness as we get hit in the face by unexpected branches. Then we start uphill and soon look down on an area where the Anasazi grew their crops, alongside which they built their dwellings. We head up through the fallen talus slopes, emerge into the moonlight, and change gears again when we get into the Muav limestone. The view down the river is already spectacular. Looking down the river for four miles, one sees a long, straight stretch of red-walled box canyon, even though the course of the river is serpentine, formed by an alternating series of sandbars and back-eddies with greenery on their edges. A textbook lesson in meanders.

Though we cannot see colors in the moonlight, I am able to visualize this scene in color because—I now realize—this is a famous landscape found in nearly every picture book of the Grand Canyon. Many big cameras have been hauled up this steep path. I have enough trouble hauling myself up.

When the trail hits the Redwall, it gets quite steep. The ledges formed by the Redwall layers are quite shallow, and one is thankful for shoes that grip. Alan is, of course, wearing sandals. When we reach the last ledge before the ruin, we sit down and look around; Alan doesn't want us to sit right next to the ruin itself. One tends to be a little tired after the climb, and also tends to lean back to avoid the view looking forward—and down. Whatever the reason, a tourist leaned back against the ruin in 1982 and collapsed a section of wall. The Park Service archaeologists have since rebuilt it. Despite such problems, the Park Service has not yielded to the usual temptation to plaster signs everywhere forbidding this and that. We haven't seen a single sign since Lee's Ferry, except for petroglyphs we couldn't read.

Looking straight down forty stories and suppressing acrophobia, one sees in the monochromatic moonlight the farmlands of the Anasazi, now dotted with desert shrubs but once cultivated for corn. Alan pointed out where building foundations had been found and where lots of broken pottery had accumulated. Since there is often nothing left at these sites that can be dated from its radiocarbon content, broken pottery is the lifeblood of the Southwestern archaeologist, as its decoration changed with nearly every generation. Just as many people can accurately date a dress style from earlier in the twentieth century, so an expert like Robert Euler can look at a collection of potsherds and name the half-century in which they were made a millennium ago.

Why did the Anasazi store their grain high on a cliff? The usual explanation is the same as that offered for the development of such cliff-side urban ventures as Betatakin and Mesa Verde in the 1200s: protection from hungry have-nots. Here, a guard could deal with unauthorized visitors by just rolling a few rocks down the hill. That may, however, overdramatize the situation: perhaps they were trying to protect their stored grain from the rodents that frequent the delta itself. Maybe they also liked the view.

With a natural cave in the Redwall Limestone providing a floor, ceiling, and rear wall, all the Anasazi had to construct with mud and stone were the front walls and room dividers of their storehouses—though, as Alan pointed out, they did have to haul the water up here to make the mud. No small chore. The small rooms were probably not primarily dwellings but storage rooms: this modified cave was probably a granary, a place to store the corn which the Anasazi farmed on the narrow plains below, on the river's right bank. This is not a large place, several hundred baskets would strain its capacity. Outside, perched on a slightly lower ledge, was a small, topless enclosure—perhaps a guardpost, with enough of a wall to keep the guard from falling down the cliff if he dozed off, or perhaps it is just the remains of a granary annex built in the year of a bumper crop.

In the moonlight there was a surreal quality to it all, definitely dreamlike. And I began to wonder just how it felt to be an Anasazi, to scratch out a meager existence in the desert, to sit long nights up here as a guard with the whole Marble Canyon spread out below, all the sky above, perched on the edge of an abyss, a ringside seat on the universe. There were no textbooks of agriculture, or astronomy, or first-aid. Most of what he knew, he probably had learned from a hundred people, inhabitants of Nankoweap Canyon and neighbors. Knowledge trickled in from the outside by word of mouth, by legend. This place was not the center of the Anasazi culture, but perhaps he had heard of the fabulous medicine men of Chaco Canyon who studied the sun and the moon, who perhaps warned when the moon or the sun might be eaten by a sky monster.

Like the present-day Hopi, the Anasazi watched sunrise and sunset every day, noting the point on the horizon where the sun first peeked over the canyon rim or a distant mountain ridge. One sees present-day Pueblo peoples sitting on their rooftops and meditating over sunset or sunrise. Pueblo tribal leaders often have special viewing places in the surrounding hills, to which a responsible elder treks to be in position for the viewing. The position of sunrise and sunset on the horizon changes a little from day to day, coming to a halt at the summer and winter solstices and turning around. This, rather than a desk calendar, told the Anasazi when to plant or hold celebrations.

The Hopi have a system of cardinal directions quite different from our north-east-south-west. They reckon direction from the northeasterly location of the summer solstice sunrise, the southeasterly winter solstice sunrise, the southwesterly winter solstice sunset, and the northwesterly summer solstice sunset. Thus, watching for the position of the sun on the horizon was important for directions, a calendar, and religion.

It was easy to imagine an Anasazi perched up here, watching the place of the sunrise move along the craggy eastern horizon from week to week as the seasons changed. I wish that we were going to be here tomorrow night, when the lunar eclipse occurs, so that I could try to see it through his eyes. Surely, to a people who studied the sun and moon so assiduously every day, an eclipse must have been a major event. Disappearance, renewal. Being eaten, being recreated? Were there monsters in the sky who engulfed the moon, who sometimes blotted out the sun? What did they do to placate them?

An eclipse of the sun is a rare event in any one locality; few Anasazi would have seen one in their lifetime, but they probably knew from legend that it could occur. But there is an eclipse of the moon about every 170 days, visible from somewhere on earth. Many Anasazi would see several in a lifetime. In a world without scientific explanations describing the intersection of orbits and shadow cones, eclipses would have been especially impressive.

What would an Anasazi have thought of a comet? Or a supernova? During that A.D. 1054 supernova in the Crab Nebula, there were Anasazi living in the Canyon; perhaps my imaginary Anasazi perched up here would have seen it. By running the clockwork of the heavens backward (in a computer) into the position they were in on the morning of the fifth day of July, 1054, we can know what he saw.

Three hours before sunrise, the moon would have risen over

the Canyon wall in the northeast, a quarter-moon of white against a still-black sky. Then, shortly after the moon cleared the horizon, something strange and bright would have appeared on the horizon several degrees (four moon diameters) south of the crescent moon hanging there in the sky. The Stranger didn't sit on the horizon like a distant forest fire, but rather rose into the sky, following the crescent moon. It would have appeared as a very bright star, extraordinarily bright, a spotlight hard to ignore. Three hours later, the sun would have risen at about the same spot on the horizon. The sun on the horizon, the Stranger, and the slightly more elevated crescent moon would have formed a triangle in the morning sky. The Stranger would have stayed there, some distance from the moon, all day.

I hope that my Anasazi didn't fall off his perch in surprise when the supernova rose, or break a leg on that steep trail we came up, running down to alert the sleeping families below. It wouldn't have been unreasonable for him to have thought it a harbinger of the end of the world, this Stranger coming between the revered sun and moon, presumably another monster about to gobble up one or both of them. Of course, when he got down to the dwellings near the river, the Stranger would not have been visible yet because of the high canyon wall across the river, so perhaps no one believed him at first. Then, as the disbelievers watched, the moon rose with that spectacular giant star right behind, just as advertised.

Even after sunrise, the Stranger remained visible—even at midday, it beamed in the blue sky. They might have felt some relief 23 days later when the Stranger could no longer be seen during the day—but it remained very bright at night for many months thereafter, before settling down to being some semblance of an ordinary star in the sky. The moon, of course, moved away from the Stranger's position in the stars, perhaps to the relief of many watchers of the sky on the Colorado Plateau.

There is indeed some evidence that the Anasazi, both at White Mesa 30 km east of here and in Chaco Canyon 300 km further east, recorded this event of 1054 in pictographs and petroglyphs. Crescent moons are rather infrequently depicted in rock art of the United States; yet a number of those found in Arizona, New Mexico, and California are dated to this period and have a "star" associated with them. The White Mesa pictograph actually shows a star half the diameter of the moon itself, taking a bite out of the lower corner of the crescent moon. Some of the pictographs show a "sun" as well, forming a triangle. Until the calculations were done and the sun and moon positions were worked backward in time to see where they were early on the morning of July 5, 1054, the assemblage on the pictographs was without significance. Now it suggests that the big star was the Crab Nebula supernova, which appeared so suddenly that morning. Its close-to-the-moon configuration is one that would have been seen only on that first morning, as the moon would rise nearly an hour later than the Stranger the following morning. So, if the pictographs are indeed of the supernova, they depict that first appearance, the big surprise. Though there have been six bright novae in the twentieth century (1901, 1918, 1925, 1934, 1942, and 1975), there haven't been any of the longer-lasting bright supernovae since the one Kepler observed in 1604. The astronomers eagerly await one, though they've been happily studying the more modest supernova in the Virgo Cluster that appeared in 1979. Supernovae are surely one of the universe's great spectacles.

On the way back down the trail, the moon was poised just over the river, still somewhat low in the sky. From each of the meanders, the moonlight reflected up into our eyes, a long silver snake stretching out for several miles.

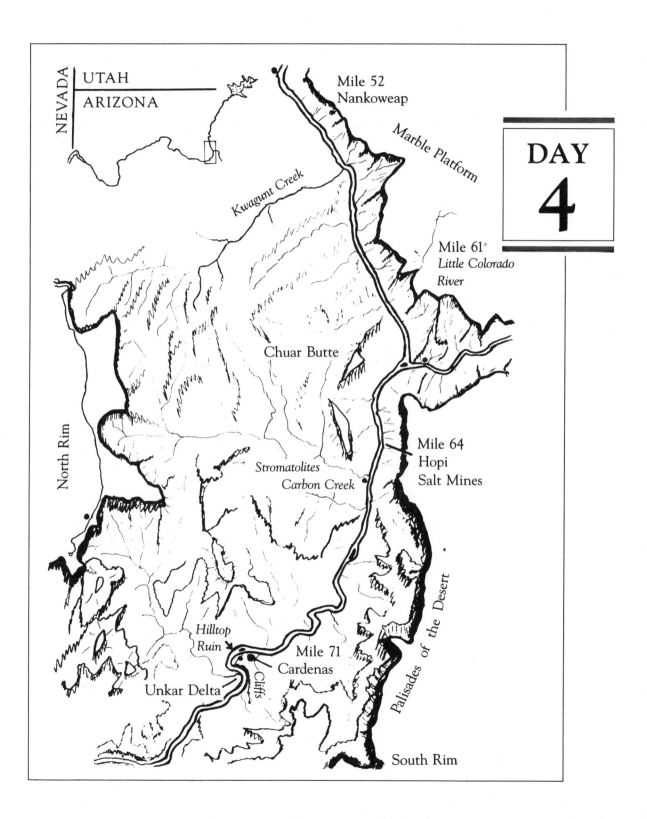

NEVADA

UTAH

ARIZONA

Kwagunt Creek

Mile 52
Nankoweap

Marble Platform

DAY
4

Mile 61
Little Colorado
River

Chuar Butte

Mile 64
Hopi
Salt Mines

Stromatolites
Carbon Creek

North Rim

Hilltop
Ruin

Cliffs

Mile 71
Cardenas

Unkar Delta

Palisades of the Desert

South Rim

MILE 52
Nankoweap Canyon

AFTER BREAKFAST, Marsha came back from a hike up the beach and reported that there were lots of tadpoles in one of the pools of the creek, amidst the willows and tammies. They were cute, and she offered to show them to anyone who was interested.

"Ah, yes," Alan replied. "We put out a package of freeze-dried tadpoles last night to rehydrate. Nice to hear they're doing so well."

A half-dozen people raised their eyebrows but said nothing (these days, the idea of freeze-dried tadpoles isn't totally impossible). Marsha examined Alan's face carefully for signs of a smile, she hadn't forgotten the split-willow figurine which Alan "found" on the beach. Alan kept a straight face and said that the boatmen also had several packages of freeze-dried cicadas in one of the freezer chests, just in case the bats got too hungry. Alan went on to say that these were special C-minor cicadas, rather than the common cicadas which, he claimed, sing in D-major—that the bats had been getting fussy lately about their food.

Without a word, Marsha turned and walked down to the boats, grabbed a bailer bucket, scooped up some cold river water, and chased Alan down the beach. The rest of us cheered her on, sounding like a softball team exhorting a baserunner from the sidelines.

THE NORTH RIM can be seen from several places along this stretch of river, but only when we pass the mouth of a side canyon. It's hard to believe how high it is. We've been encased by Redwall, and haven't been able to see what's atop it, set back out of sight.

The East Kaibab Monocline has pushed the North Rim up as high as 2,700 meters in places, while the South Rim is more like 2,100 meters high. If we look carefully back up Kwagunt Creek's canyon, we can see one of the highest points on the North Rim towering in the distance. It is more than a mile high from where we are, about the height of a 500-story building. And I thought the Canyon was deep at Navajo Bridge, where a 30-story building would have just fit inside it. That means we've cut 500 stories deep into the earth in just three days on the river. The view doesn't last long, but it is sobering.

Floating the rivers takes you through the land, not merely over its surface. Entering a canyon is akin to entering the living body of the earth, floating with its lifeblood through arteries and veins of rock, tuning your perceptions to the slow pulse of the land, single beats of river current marking the steady rhythmic changes in geologic time. This particular form of intimacy . . . can only be had on the rivers.

It flows through your memory and leaves behind a ripple of emotion: reverence.

The writer-photographer
STEPHEN TRIMBLE, 1979

□   □   □

SIXTY MILE RAPID has come and gone. No creek there, just a dry wash. A mere 4, meaning that we held on tight but didn't have to bail much afterwards. We are now seeing patches of the Tapeats Sandstone at river level, which is a sandy brown with lighter patches here and there where slabs have fallen away in recent years.

Alan says that there are several varieties of fossils to be found in the Tapeats, but that he hasn't seen any along the river. We're about to run out of fossils. We are currently in the Cambrian period, laid down nearly 570 million years ago, the age when there was the first big explosion of life forms in the sea, when evolution really took off. Rocks from earlier than that, which we'll see a little further downriver, have little in the way of fossils because the life-forms themselves often weren't sturdy enough to fossilize.

Presently, as we round a bluff on the left bank, we see a stream of light blue water—the Little Colorado River—running down the left side of the river in much the same way as the Paria appeared at Lee's Ferry long ago. We can now see up into the canyon of the Little Colorado River. No rapids. Just two peaceful rivers, gracefully merging.

Alan pushes us over into the bluish waters and then turns the boat around so that he can use a backstroke, rowing upstream into the Little Colorado's canyon. Behind us, another boat rounds the corner and follows us. The side canyon is so wide that we see a good expanse of sky. Back in the Marble Canyon the walls were never far away. And the water—it is now a pure stretch of the most amazing azure blue. From the morning shadow of Marble Canyon, we have seemingly arrived at a sunny tropical resort.

THE AZURE BLUE WATERS are warm and swimmable, not at all like the cold Colorado. We are just a mile upstream in the Little Colorado River, where the waters from Blue Spring flow. When Dan Richard stopped on the bridge over the Little Colorado near Cameron on the drive up to Lee's Ferry, he saw a dry river bottom. When the river runs wet there, these waters run red. Otherwise the Little Colorado's waters flow from some big springs a few miles upriver from here. And we love the blue spring waters.

After tiring of swimming, we sat around in the shallow waters

MILE 61
Little Colorado Confluence

talking. Topics such as water color. We have already seen a brief example of the old red Colorado, after the distant rainstorm of the first day. Usually the Colorado is mint green. When the azure blue of the Little Colorado empties into the Colorado proper, it quickly mixes and makes no dent in the colors of Lake Dominy (we have decided that Major Powell surely would not have approved of a reservoir that buried the beautiful Glen Canyon he so admired, and so—following Edward Abbey—we call Lake Powell after Floyd Dominy, the chief of the Bureau of Reclamation which created the abomination).

This talk of names led us to discuss what might be an appropriate name for the new, improved Colorado River. "There is already a Green River upstream, and a Rio Verde down south," Dan Richard pointed out.

I reminded them of the other great misnaming by color. "Do you realize that the brain's gray matter isn't gray at all?" I inquired.

"The gray matter isn't gray?" repeated Abby, incredulously.

"No, not in the slightest."

"Well, is the white matter white?" she asked.

"Oh, yes. The color of a pale porcelain. The white matter's just a bundle of cables, and the white color is from the fatty insulation on the wires. Except the wires are really axons, the long stringy portion of nerve cells."

"So why isn't the gray matter gray?" persisted Abby.

"Because it's red. Sort of reddish-brown. About the color of the river that night after the sandstorm," I ventured.

"Then why was it called the gray matter?"

"Well, it is gray sometimes. In a dead brain. The gray matter's where most of the action is, and that takes a lot of oxygen and sugar. Which means a big blood supply." I sipped my lemonade. "So the region looks reddish-brown when it's alive. Of course, the only people who see it that way are neurosurgeons and neurophysiologists."

"Maybe we ought to rename the gray matter too. But the reddish-brown matter just doesn't have the right ring to it," Ben said.

"How about the Colorado Matter?" asked Abby. "You said it was the color of the old Colorado River, back before damnation."

We roll that one around a little, taste it, and decide we like it—the Colorado Matter it is. If anyone asks our opinion on the gray matter.

In our enthusiasm, we even got around to renaming some cities—for birds that deceive other birds. An aside for those not of the cuckoo cognoscenti: the cuckoo practices parenthood piracy. Cuckoos leave their babies on someone else's doorstep: their eggs in the nest of some other bird species, such as Bell's vireo. Their eggs are speckled, just like those of the vireo; and when the cuckoo hatches, it has a scarlet throat just like the real vireo babies. But thereafter—ouch! First, the newly hatched cuckoo chick has a built-in instinct to shove the other eggs out of the nest, thus reserving all the baby food for itself. And does it ever grow! Yet even when it is twice the size of its foster parents, they feed it faithfully. Apparently that scarlet throat is the main way they recognize their young; like the beavers shoving sticks and mud toward the sound of running water, adult vireos have a powerful instinct to shove food at scarlet throats. The cuckoo has successfully imitated that trait, thereby enslaving the poor vireo parents. Hence parenthood piracy. (Who says the scientific literature is dull?)

Now to cities: the Phoenix was a mythical bird whose birth was not your usual event—it arose fully fledged from ashes. The city of Phoenix also arose unnaturally from the middle of a desert. Not from ashes but from Indian ruins, that being the comparison made by the drunken Englishman who did the naming. It is, however, more like a cuckoo rising from a nest from which Indians and farmers have been pushed out. A city that has fooled its foster parents, the American taxpayers, into feeding it with water and electricity for air conditioning so that it can grow, unplanned, sprawling, over the countryside—like a cancer, metastasizing here and there by following county roads and turning them into sad cluttered strips, turning cotton fields into tacky subdivisions. Some "developments" look like they will fall into tatters before the mortgage is paid off.

The same might be said of Las Vegas, each of whose gaudy hotels consumes the electricity of a city of 60,000 inhabitants, again subsidized by you-know-who. I suppose that it's probably named for a vega, the Mexican word for a moist meadowland, but we prefer to think that it is named after Vega, the brightest star in the constellation Lyra, whose brilliance is perhaps due to its being a mere 26 light years away—a near neighbor on the celestial scale of things. Why do we prefer the bright star interpretation? Because silliness has struck again: Vega comes from the Arabic word for the constellation in which the Arabs envisaged a falling vulture.

The brightest star among fallen vultures. . . . That sounds like Las Vegas, all right. Are you sure that's lemonade in the cooler jug?

Cuckoos are not the only species to enslave those birds with insufficient ways of recognizing their own young: cowbirds do it too, right here in the Canyon, enslaving the Bell's vireo.

As long as we're renaming things, Cowbird would make a nice new name to replace Phoenix. They can call the airport "Cowbird International" instead of Sky Harbor.

We're saving Cuckoo for Las Vegas.

We're not usually this silly. We must be starting to relax.

And this our life
  exempt from public haunt
Finds tongues in trees,
  books in the running brooks,
Sermons in stones,
  and good in everything.
I would not change it.
                    WILLIAM SHAKESPEARE
                    As You Like It, 1599

THE ROCK LEDGES NEARBY are the Tapeats Sandstone laid down in Cambrian times just after the time when life forms first diversified massively. The surrounding corrugated ledges and overhangs make perfect shelters along the shore if we want to get out of the sun, as we do for lunch. The Little Colorado may lack the underwater life around the coral reefs of the azure Caribbean, but it's rapidly becoming home to us. Some people are still floating in the translucent waters, not even tempted by food. The lemonade tastes excellent, and the supply is endless.

That says something about how much we've gotten into the mood of the river trip. I think we've finally left many of the cares of civilization behind. That may sound incongruous, what with our discussions of science, but technology and science are two separate things to us, as separate as farming and biology. Except for our boats and propane stoves and air mattresses, we've largely escaped obvious reminders of technology. I haven't heard anyone ask what time it is for a day now. We are starting to object when civilization's noisier artifacts intrude, such as the airplanes that fly below the rim of the Canyon. And the motorized boats with their whine and oil haze. I could even do without the Los Angeles-bound airplanes that crisscross the Canyon at night, winking and roaring across the Milky Way. They can't fly over the White House—why not ban them over the Grand Canyon too?

Across the river, beneath the overhang of a large Tapeats slab, stands an old prospector's cabin from 1890. Today, it's no more than three walls propped up against the cliff overhang, filled with the usual junk of the last century. Major Powell mentioned seeing some Indian ruins near here back in 1869, but the archaeologists weren't able to find any ruins until they finally tried excavating the prospector's cabin—he'd evidently improved on the old Anasazi cabin and moved in. There were arrowheads but also split-twig figurines, suggesting that the archaic Indians were here 3,000 to 4,000 years ago.

One of the springs which feeds the Little Colorado is a present-day Hopi shrine, or *sipapu*. The *sipapu* is about 7 kilometers upstream from the Colorado confluence. It is a huge travertine dome, built up from the minerals in the flowing water. The Hopi believe that man emerged into this world through this spring.

There are other shrines in the area, along a sacred trail leading down to the Colorado River not far below the confluence. The Hopi, who live about 100 kilometers east of here, make cere-monial journeys to collect salt from near the river.

WE'VE HIT BOTTOM WITH THE TAPEATS, at least as far as fossils go, here where the rock is 570 million years old. This is the oldest of the Cambrian layers; everything below it is Pre-cambrian. Cambria is merely the Latin name for a town in Wales which kindly lent its name to the layer. The reason scientists make such a fuss over Cambrian and Precambrian is that the dividing line marks the occasion of a great success story: while some forms of life had existed for over 3,000 million years be-fore then, a great diversity of life forms seems to have been cre-ated by the end of Precambrian times. And these forms had shells sufficient to fossilize. In Precambrian times, the microfossils are as rare as they are hard to see.

We subdivide the animal kingdom into 28 phyla, each of which employ a very different way of structuring a body. Most of them seem to have been present 570 million years ago, when fossilizing started in a big way; that suggests that they may have diversified earlier, but often weren't hard enough to fossilize. Several more phyla seem to have originated during the Cam-brian, during the time represented by the Tapeats and Muav layers around here. One of those phyla, the chordates, seems to have arisen from the echinoderms (sand dollars and brittle stars are among its better-known members). The chordates further diversified into vertebrates, into fishes, into amphibians, and into reptiles—all during the period represented by the layers above us—and then later into the mammals, primates, apes, and us.

New species were invented all along the way. Most of them died out. There has been a continuous creation of new life forms as specialized versions of older species have split off. The typical "lifespan" of an invertebrate species within the marine mollusks is about 3 to 10 million years (though in deep-water species of foraminifera it is three times longer than among the shallow-water mollusks). Then, usually rather suddenly, the species dis-appears from the fossil record.

Sometimes, superimposed upon this background of individual species coming and going, whole families of creatures became extinct simultaneously. Family? A family is the third of the classification groups; *Homo sapiens* is in the family of hominids, the genus *Homo*, and the species *sapiens*. But a family with only one living representative isn't a good example. How about cats? It would be as if all of the 37 feline species among the carnivora, from lion to domestic cat, had gone extinct together. There are occasions when more than 20 percent of all families of sea-going animals disappear, all within a few million years or so. That is indeed a major pruning of the tree of life; it makes one wonder what happened.

Such an event is called a mass extinction. About nine of them have occurred in the last 250 million years, and probably another dozen during the period covered by the Grand Canyon fossils, between 248 and 570 million years ago. Indeed, they tend to occur at regular intervals, seemingly every 26 to 30 million years or so (the last one was 11 million years ago, so relax for a while).

Two of these mass extinctions have been particularly dramatic. At the end of the Permian period about 248 million years ago, half of the families of marine invertebrates (90 percent of all species) died out within a few million years. At the end of the Cretaceous, about 65 million years ago, a quarter of the families died out, not to mention the dinosaurs. However, the animals lowest in the food chain fared even worse: some 90 percent of the zooplankton (the little microscopic creatures that float beneath the ocean's surface) were wiped out. Of course, that suggests that there wasn't much around for the zooplankton to eat, and since they virtually eat sunlight—consuming the little plants that do the photosynthesis in the ocean, the phytoplankton—it may be inferred that the sunlight was blocked for a while. Did a giant cloud cover the earth?

There are various ways of producing such devastating cloud cover. The impact of a large meteor could send a lot of dust into the air. If a dust cloud gets no higher than the tops of the rainclouds—about 10,000 meters up (33,000 feet)—rainfall will wash it out of the atmosphere. If the dust (and soot from burning vegetation) gets into the upper atmosphere, it could take several months for such a cloud to clear. Volcanic eruptions, the more frequent generators of such atmospheric disturbances, occasionally turn the sunsets red for a year because of all the tiny particles injected into the upper atmosphere. Temperatures drop around the world, as one can see in the growth rings of long-lived trees such as the bristlecone pine, a tree that grows high in the mountains around here and records faraway volcanic eruptions in the Mediterranean and Southeast Asia. The final scenario resulting in massive cloud cover is called nuclear winter, where cities and forests, consumed in monster firestorms, send smoke particles into the upper atmosphere.

In the search for explanations of extinctions, terrestrial causes such as volcanos and plagues have been suggested, but the betting is on the meteors because the dates of the impact craters seem to cluster around the periods when extinctions occurred. Both craters and extinctions show a recurrence cycle of about 28 to 32 million years. The impact dates for the post-Permian craters cluster right around the dates of the extinctions so tightly that the chance of their accidentally coinciding is said to be less than 0.1 percent. The DuBois family visited the big meteor crater east of Flagstaff before coming on this trip. Jim says that it is over 1,300 meters (nearly a mile) wide and 40 stories deep. This "splash" was made by the impact of an iron asteroid about 25 meters in diameter that punched through the atmosphere about 50,000 years ago, during the most recent ice age. So that's not one of the big ones. But it's very impressive; I can do without anything larger.

While some meteors come from outside the solar system, most are from clouds of ice balls that orbit the sun at great distances, the so-called Oort cloud out beyond Pluto's orbit. A passing attraction kicks them out of their usual orbit and they fall toward the sun; as the sunlight melts the ice and releases gases, sunlight and the solar wind sweep the gas and dust back into a tail— a comet. Most comets don't come close to us because of Saturn and Jupiter, whose gravity is sufficient to deflect them. A small percentage still make it through to the "inner" solar system. The question is, what could send comets into the inner ring of planets with such *regularity* that a big impact from one might stir up things on earth?

One possibility is that the sun is part of a binary pair of stars, the unseen companion appearing to orbit the sun at a great distance in an elliptical path, coming close enough every 28 million years to perturb the Oort cloud and send comets into the inner ring of planets. About 15 percent of all stars surveyed turn out to be binaries, though most are rather closer together.

The sun's hypothetical companion would probably go out into space a distance of 3 light years (our closest known neighbor, Barnard's star, is 4 to 6 light years away) and come in as close as half a light year. This could perturb the inner Oort cloud enough to send a billion comets into the inner solar system during the following 1 to 2 million years, a few hitting the Earth. The long duration of the meteor shower might explain why the dinosaurs took several million years to die out.

Extinctions seem rather important in the biological scheme of things, as when the mammals got their big chance after the Cretaceous Extinction, thanks to all the niches vacated by the dinosaurs (someone in the next boat remembered the doggerel: "In Cretaceous times the earth was flat; the fools fell off, and that was that"). The birds and dinosaurs took off just after the Permian extinction. The apes got started after the puzzling end of the Eocene. The rhythm of the extinctions suggests that such major pruning and subsequent blossoming has been a regular feature of evolution for a long time, almost a drive *toward* more complex creatures. Even if biology were to reach some "balance of nature" (and it probably wouldn't anyway), the comets would stir the pot occasionally, giving newcomers their big chance.

Let's see now. A billion comets in a million years. That would be 1,000 new comets every year coming in from the Oort cloud, so they'd really streak up the night sky like graffiti, possibly preventing a good view of the close approach of the companion star even if it were bright enough. A viewer would see three apparitions per night (creators of ghost stories notwithstanding, an apparition is the technical name in astronomy for the first appearance of a new comet) except, of course, in the year after a meteor hit the earth, when the dust cloud might spoil the view as well as ruin one's food supply. Those will be exciting times, 17 million years from now. It is likely that the current version of *Homo sapiens sapiens* will have been replaced by then, but we can hope that we will have an improved descendant species around to see the show. Although, John DuBois suggests, our descendant may be part Homo, part silicon.

If and when the companion star is found, we suggest that it be named Nemesis, after the Greek goddess who relentlessly persecutes the excessively rich, proud, and powerful. We worry that if the companion is not found, this paper will be our nemesis.

> MARC DAVIS, PIET HUT, and RICHARD A. MULLER, 1984
> Proposers, together with DANIEL WHITMIRE and
> ALBERT A. JACKSON IV independently,
> of the companion star explanation for mass extinctions

May we not name the sun's potential companion for a figure who embodies [the] central features of creativity in destruction and "neutrality" towards the evolutionary struggles of creatures in preceding normal times? Siva, the Hindu god of destruction, forms an indissoluble triad with Brahma, the creator, and Vishnu, the preserver. All are enmeshed in one—a trinity of a different order—because all activity reflects their interaction. . . . Unlike Nemesis, Siva does not attack specific targets for cause or for punishment. Instead, his placid face records the absolute tranquility and serenity of a neutral process, directed toward no one but responsible for the maintenance and order of our world.

> STEPHEN JAY GOULD, 1984

Evolution loves death more than it loves you or me. This is easy to write, easy to read, and hard to believe. The words are simple, the concept clear—but you don't believe it, do you? Nor do I. How could I, when we're both so lovable? Are my values then so diametrically opposed to those that nature preserves? . . . we are moral creatures in an amoral world. The universe that suckled us is a monster that does not care if we live or die—does not care if it itself grinds to a halt. It is fixed and blind, a robot programmed to kill. We are free and seeing; we can only try to outwit it at every turn to save our skins.

ANNIE DILLARD, 1974

□   □   □

SALT CRUSTS ON THE TAPEATS near the shoreline catch everyone's eye as our boats splash along below the confluence of the two Colorado rivers. These salt deposits come out of the bottom of the Tapeats and, looking like painted waterfalls here and there on both sides of the river, they drip down several stories. They are dramatic evidence of how salt washes out of the earth.

Fritz is telling her passengers about the salt deposits on the left bank, and Alan rows us over so we too can listen. They are sacred to the Hopis, and probably were to the Anasazi as well. A modern-day scientist rediscovered the ancient Indian salt trail leading overland from the Little Colorado's canyon to this site. The salt, which the Hopi call *sieunga*, is used in ceremonies as well as for dietary purposes. The salt is also found on the stalactites and stalagmites in caves, where it has leached out of the rocks as groundwater percolated through them. Perhaps a solo trip to these sacred salt mines, stopping at each of the shrines along the way, was a feature of the Hopi's "rites of passage" ceremonies.

The trail runs down a platform atop the Tapeats; getting down to the sandy beach is a problem. But once down, a block downriver are the mines, a series of small rectangular holes in the side of the cliff, little larger than picnic baskets, about knee-high above the sandy beach. The *sieunga* was taken from the stalactites and stalagmites within these shallow caves. The mark of the young man's clan was apparently left above the mine after each journey, and even from the boat floating past, we can see the weathered red and black symbols lining the wall.

As the salt mines recede behind us, the Tapeats ends and a loose red rock emerges along the shores, the beginning of the Dox Formation. Right here, something is missing: more than 250 million years of rock! That's more rock than we have already cut through in order to get to this point. At the bottom of the Tapeats, which dates only to 570 million years ago (the

MILE 64
The Great Unconformity

Cambrian-Precambrian boundary), the next rock layer ended 820 million years ago. The Dox Formation, whatever that is. It isn't that nothing happened for all that time, but the rock it produced was eroded away before the Tapeats Sea started up nearby and swept sand dunes across this region.

Yet another unconformity. The last big one was the gap between the Redwall and the Muav, which we saw yesterday. And while today's 250-million-year gap is usually called the Great Unconformity, there is an even wider 450-million-year gap downstream called the Early Unconformity, representing the period between 1,700 and 1,250 million years ago.

Now, suddenly, the Canyon begins opening up. We are no longer enclosed by two often symmetric walls, as in the Marble Canyon. On our right the cliffs of Redwall are far back from the shoreline and getting even further away as we look ahead. The Dox is soft stuff, easily eroded by the former spring floods. This undercuts the harder Tapeats, and it collapses into the river, bringing with it the Muav, and the Redwall, etc. And so the Canyon widens massively, becoming the Grand Canyon of the Colorado River, the successor to Cataract Canyon, Glen Canyon, and Marble Canyon. The Grand Canyon emerged, thanks to soft rock in the basement.

We can now see long distances. A great wall of cliffs stretches to our left once we pass the salt mines. The Palisades of the Desert, they are called, as one promontory after another juts out from the very long expanse of distant cliffs, looking somewhat like the folds in a drapery hanging before a window.

RIVER CORRIDOR CROSS SECTION

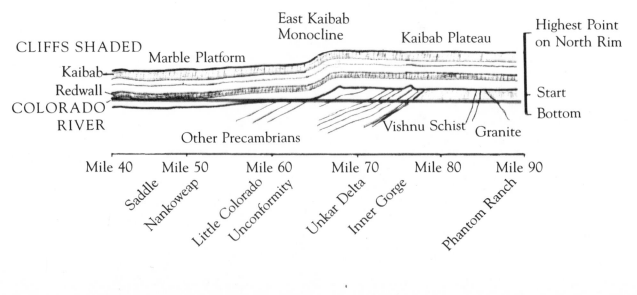

WE MAKE A QUICK STOP on the right bank at Carbon Creek to investigate its main attraction, a giant mushroom of a rock. Most Precambrian fossils are microscopic, but this one is several meters across. It is a fossilized clump of algae known as a stromatolite. One can still see stromatolites forming in some hypersaline shallows on the sun-baked Australian coast. I don't know how old this one is—probably it's Dox age, about 820 million years old—but stromatolites are among the earliest of known fossils, dating back over 3,500 million years. The individual cells are small, but great mats of them can form, something like coral reefs but without the specialization one can see in corals (which are animals, not plants or single cells). In some cases, one can see annual growth rings with little layers corresponding to each day—and that tells us that there were about 440 days in a year, back 820 million years ago. Probably due to tidal friction, the earth's spin has been slowing down.

Things have warmed up back on the river. For some reason—which I think we're discovering—this stretch of river is known to the boatmen as "Furnace Flats." The breeze is gone. The sun is high. The river has widened and slowed. The boatmen row and row and row. This is a completely different sort of canyon than we've been traveling through until now.

THE MARBLE CANYON, though lacking marble, is slender and elegant. This Canyon is grand. Despite the heat haze, we can see 30 kilometers, not 5. There are all sorts of seemingly free-standing buttes and pinnacles everywhere. They have names like Vishnu Temple and Cheops Pyramid. Their expanse is mammoth, dominated by the 10 km length of the Palisades. In the Marble Canyon it was like having mountains building up around us. Here we see that we are inside the mile-deep canyon that tourists see from the rim. Indeed, civilization intruding again, we note a little man-made tower atop the southern extreme of the Palisades; Brian tells us it is the Desert View Tower, where admission is charged so that tourists can climb several stories higher, as if the mile depth of the Canyon weren't enough, and had to be augmented with observation towers like those built above the "cannonball" national parks back east. Fritz insists that it is nonetheless a nice piece of architecture.

My fellow river-runners can be subdivided into those that want suntans and those who keep covered up. Covering up is becoming more popular as we gain experience with the river; it isn't that likely to make one even hotter, as desert peoples like the Bedouin of the Sinai Desert demonstrate with their long robes. The suggested packing list for the trip emphasizes "long-sleeved shirts" and "long pants, such as surgical scrub pants or

MILE 65
Furnace Flats

pajama bottoms." Short of necessity (and convincing the folks back home that you really went on a trip doesn't qualify), tans aren't worth the trouble and risk (sunburn, dry skin, skin cancer) they carry with them. Back when people only lived four decades, the sun damage didn't catch up with one so often. And here on the Colorado, your suntan oil or sunscreen gets washed off by every rapid, causing an endless cycle of reapplication. It's much easier to wear loose cotton and stay covered up.

Another rapid—Lava Canyon comes in from the right and Tanner Canyon from the left, all the way down from Desert View. We see hikers who are following a long, 25-kilometer waterless trail leading down here from the South Rim. Tanner Rapid is a good ride, and we get happily soaked, cooling down. Liz, one of the boatmen for another river company with whom I talked back at the Little Colorado, told me she'd hiked down the Hopi Salt Trail in the wintertime, stopping at the great travertine *sipapu* a few kilometers up the Little Colorado, then continuing over past the salt mines, taking the equally unofficial Beamer Trail on to Tanner, and then up and out by way of the semi-official (but unmaintained) Tanner Trail to Lipan Point, several kilometers west of Desert View Tower. Now that would be the way to spend Christmas vacation.

Row, row, row your boat. . . .

Ahead on the left bank is a hill of perhaps forty stories. There is an unoccupied campsite below it. Ours for the night, happily. Atop the hill we can now see a rectangular ruin, right at the apex of two cusps of the hill's drainages. The red silt hill is capped by a layer of gravel, typical riverbed stuff from the looks of it. Fritz explains that this is an Elston Gravel, the boatmen's name for a geological phenomenon explained by geologist Don Elston, whose theory for the formation of the Grand Canyon explains why there are rounded river gravels 35 stories above the river. The big problem with the straightforward explanation of the Colorado River cutting the Grand Canyon as the dome uplifted—the theory that Major Powell himself originally put forward—is that there are some sediments downriver, across Lake Mead, where the river flows over some rock formations only 6 million years old. Over? When Marble Canyon itself is 30 million years old? That's right. First puzzle: the river is cutting into rock a mere 6 million years old. Where did it drain before then? That gets the geologists' attention.

Second puzzle: the Gulf of California didn't open up to the Pacific Ocean until about 4 to 5 million years ago, so where would the river have emptied anyway? Sure, the San Andreas Fault has since provided a convenient opening to the sea for the Colorado River (tectonic plates moving Los Angeles north and all that) but that's very recent. Where did all that water go, back before that? Just dumping it into a pond to evaporate doesn't seem reasonable. Sure, the Jordan River empties into the Dead Sea and the water just evaporates—but the Jordan River's a creek by Colorado River standards. This is a lot of water we're riding. You'd think that it'd find a way out to sea.

This has led to all sorts of conjecture about how the river might have once come down Marble Canyon and then hooked a left turn into the Little Colorado canyon just like we did for lunch, but continued east into a lake. What lake? The geologists simply postulated one and named it "Lake Bidahochi." It supposedly emptied into the Gulf of Mexico. But there are no Marble Canyon sediments to be found in New Mexico, as there ought to be for that theory to work. Another proposal has the Colorado turning north at the end of the Grand Canyon, draining up into Utah (and then what? Evaporating in the Great Salt Lake?).

Elston, according to Fritz, explains the puzzling 6-million-year-old Muddy Creek Formation to the west by saying that the Grand Canyon and the Marble Canyon were both dry somewhat before 4 million years ago (indeed, the Pliocene climate was quite arid then), with no river to carry away sediments. Nevertheless, erosion continued while the river was dry. The summer sun loosened the cement holding the surface sandstone layers together, so that they continued to erode. Ice and wind in the winter loosened rock, so there was still some spring rockfall. All the loosened rock slid downhill and piled up in sloping terraces crisscrossing the bottom of the dry canyon, covering up the original riverbed. There were few flash floods to rearrange the rocks.

Then the climate changed and the Rocky Mountains again sent rainwaters down the Canyon, complete with a dose of river gravel. But over time, the Colorado washed away some of the crisscrossing talus slopes and cut a new channel, leaving lots of new river gravels atop the recent talus. The Elston Gravels. Then the river cut deeper and deeper, finally arriving at the present riverbed, carrying the sediments off to the new Gulf of California and leaving the post-drought river gravel stranded high and dry atop the talus slopes. This scenario would explain the square cut at the bottom of the talus slopes in the Marble Canyon near Nankoweap, and explain why there is river gravel at the 35-story level atop these hills we see on Furnace Flats. And maybe also explain how the 6-million-year-old Muddy Creek Formation got beneath the present riverbed. Correct or not, you can see why river gravels atop that hill behind our campsite are so interesting, the possibilities they raise.

Geologists love such problems, and we too are beginning to appreciate the stories of how this giant four-dimensional puzzle (three plus time) called the Grand Canyon is being unraveled—though, as Subie observes from the adjacent boat, every theory for the formation of the Canyon seems to be missing a crucial piece of evidence. Such as where the river flowed to, 30 million years ago when the Marble Canyon was surely in business? Or what carved the western part of Grand Canyon? Details, details—the lifeblood of better theories.

MILE 71

Cardenas Creek

Fourth Campsite

AFTER THE BOATS HAD BEEN UNPACKED and we had all found campsites in the brush surrounding the sandy beach on the left bank, Jimmy Hendrick asked who wanted to join him for a quick trip across the river to see the Anasazi ruins at Unkar Delta. I think that Jimmy hasn't had enough exercise today. He got a half-dozen takers despite the domesticity engendered by setting up camp, and he rowed us across the river. We were carried a bit downstream, of course, and we'll have an upriver stint to do when we return. After Jimmy tied the mooring line to a rock, we clipped our life jackets to the boat rigging and set off to hike the rest of the way down the right shoreline.

This 10-mile stretch of river, with its frequent sandy shores and open low hills, has more Anasazi ruins than any other. While the Anasazi may have lived here because it was easy to reach, old Indian trails have been found all over the Canyon, some leading to cliffs that no modern-day hiker will tackle. I think their skills exceeded ours. Furnace Flats probably was popular because the Anasazi could grow crops such as maize (corn), beans, and squash close to the river. Only a few more miles downriver the rock walls close in again, at the Granite Gorge.

There is a new dig just across from our Cardenas campsite, but most of the Anasazi ruins are two miles downriver, next to Unkar Rapid. There is a big "delta" where Unkar Creek opens out, a broad plain around which the river hooks. The delta is now several stories above the river, with a channel cut through it for the present course of the creek (actually it is not a true delta formed by the creek, but instead river gravel and the like which the Colorado has piled up here, perhaps because a bottleneck once choked off the river a few miles downstream from here). The pseudo-delta has pushed the river to the left against a high cliff of some 30 stories, cut into that hill up behind our campsite at Cardenas, the one with the ruin atop it.

While some Anasazi lived here briefly about A.D. 900, it wasn't until 1050 that Unkar Delta was inhabited again. They would have seen the 1054 supernova rising right over those cliffs across the river above the rapid. And then, between 1064 and 1067, they would have seen the eruptions of the Sunset Crater volcano about 50 kilometers south of here, which would have darkened their southern sky. In 1066, Halley's comet would have lit up the night sky, just as it did for the Normans invading England. An exciting time for the people here at Unkar.

The rainfall always varies from year to year in the Grand Canyon, some years getting ten times as much as others. The longer-term rainfall trends seem to have been important in determining whether the land could support the people. Judging from the tree rings, the years between A.D. 1050 and 1070 were exceptionally wet years all over this area. An Anasazi population explosion ensued, with new settlements springing up all over southern Utah and northern Arizona during this period; a few families settled at Unkar Delta. Then a drought hit between 1070 and 1080; what happened to Anasazi population numbers is unknown, but many of the baby-boom generation or their children must have starved. Unkar was deserted. Unkar Delta was resettled in 1080 by a larger population, perhaps ten families since ten hearths have been found. Drought again caused the abandonment of the Delta between 1090 and 1100. The final period of Unkar habitation occurred between 1100 and perhaps 1130, the beginning of a long dry period.

From this, one might get the impression that opportunity created by rainfall attracted Anasazi to live in the Canyon year-round. However, the rainfall at Unkar Delta during the corn growing season probably produced no more than half of the water necessary for that crop; irrigation of some sort seems likely. Of course, the Anasazi were still hunting. Nearly half of the bones found here are from rabbits and hares, and most of the others are from bighorn sheep. That there are hardly any deer bones to be found suggests that the inhabitants weren't hunting much up on the rims and hauling the carcasses home. The bighorns live in the canyon, but have to come down to seeps and waterholes in the side canyons for water; there are many places along Unkar Creek where they could have been easily ambushed by Anasazi hunters. And the Anasazi were surely still gathering beans, fruit, and seeds from inside the Canyon. The edible prickly-pear cactus grows everywhere on Unkar Delta and the surrounding deserts; mesquite trees with their beans are also here. But mainly, the Anasazi were growing corn, squash, and beans wherever there was water nearby.

Jimmy showed us the pueblo-like apartment buildings, row houses of two to seven rooms facing a subterranean ceremonial room called a kiva that was probably in use on such occasions

Unkar Delta is breathtakingly beautiful, with a spectacular setting deep within the Grand Canyon. But the beauty seen by the contemporary visitor may not have been appreciated in the same way by the prehistoric farmers who occupied the delta, for the canyon would have been a demanding environment for early Indian agriculturalists, allowing little time for aesthetic contemplation.

The archaeologist
Douglas W. Schwartz, 1980

as the full moon we'll see tonight. In the 1080-to-1090 group of buildings there were two kivas, one dug into the earth almost two meters deep, the other barely a meter deep and of quite different construction; this makes one wonder if the ten families included several different subcultures that required different religious housing. Or if there were a lot more families, but some built where the floods have erased their traces.

The group that came after A.D. 1100 was less addicted to linear row-house construction, and tended to construct complexes of living and storage spaces—but again, probably no more than ten families lived here. They had only one kiva; none of the kivas were circular as was the fashion over in Chaco Canyon; all were square or oblong.

The North Rim towers 500 stories above us in the western sky, Cape Royal being the most obvious landmark. There is a triangular gap in the topmost cliff, where blue sky can be seen through a giant hole in the rock. This is Angel's Window, and we could probably see tourists standing atop it if we had brought the binoculars along. From up there I once saw Unkar Delta spread out below; I could even follow the course of Unkar Creek as it descended the side canyon. The Anasazi had a string of settlements along that creek. Starting several miles up from the delta, there are seeps where willows and even cottonwood trees grow. A series of twelve granaries and twenty rooms have been found so far, many in the upper reaches of the creek just below the Redwall cliffs. From Angel's Window I could look down 300 stories and see the cottonwood grove around which the Anasazi farmed in upper Unkar Creek.

Some Hopi-style pottery was found here on the delta, dating from about A.D. 1300, but in quantities and locations which suggest that the Hopis were just passing through on a trading expedition. That, together with the Hopi's creation myth which says that they arose from the *sipapu* up the Little Colorado's canyon from whence the azure waters flow, is part of the circumstantial evidence that says the Grand Canyon Anasazi are indeed among the Hopi's ancestors.

WE NAPPED AFTER DINNER for a few hours and then arose for a quick cup of coffee. Some people turned over and went back to sleep. "Seen one eclipse, seen them all," someone said. The full moon was up, judging from the way the canyon walls to the west were illuminated, but it was out of sight behind the hill that had the ruin atop it. After a second cup of coffee we set off on a trail that led out of the back of the campsite and continued right around the hill we'd seen from the river.

Flashlights, as usual, were discouraged by the boatmen, who

believe in the virtues of dark-adaptation, and so the group of us went in serpentine fashion along the switchbacking trail that led around and up the hill. It looked exactly like that moonlit hillside scene from the classic Ingmar Bergman movie of the nineteen-fifties, *The Seventh Seal*, where Death is leading off a long line of his victims along the skyline. And soon the leader of our line, a boatman named Howie Usher (who can best be described as the living incarnation of the character Zonker Harris in the Doonesbury comic strip), was furnished with an appropriate scythe-like stick to carry. He already, for reasons known only to himself, had a white bedsheet draped over his head and flowing as a cape.

Around and around, up and down we went. Lots of moonlight, though there's already a nick taken out of the side of the moon. After about half an hour, we arrived at the top of a cliff overlooking the Colorado River at Unkar Rapids, Mile 72. Laying down to peer over the edge, we not only saw but heard the great rapids pounding away about thirty stories directly below. Moonlight. In the bottom of the Grand Canyon. Looking down at a great, long rapid and feeling its roar.

Howie disappeared somewhere. Soon, from a promontory somewhat above us and a short way downstream, there issued an Independence Day sparkler, thrown in a great bright arc out over the cliff and eventually winking out in the rapids below. Subsequently, holding a second sparkler out in front of himself, Howie came running down the slope toward us, white cape flying behind him and illuminated by the sparkler. A strange apparition, in both senses of the term. But even without the embellishments, the Unkar cliffs provided a majestic spectacle with the light of the full moon and the sound of the rapids.

The Anasazi living on the delta would have had a spectacular view of burning objects thrown off these cliffs. As we saw this afternoon, these cliffs towered above them like a row of skyscrapers above an inner-city park. Where we were lying had probably been the site of ceremonial bonfires in which burning coals were pushed over the cliff. This is, of course, all conjecture; but if one were an Anasazi shaman, it would surely be too good a spectacle not to utilize. Ancient fireworks. They probably made the same "ooh-ah" sounds that we made in response to Howie's sparkler.

The obscure moon lighting an obscure world
Of things that would never be quite expressed,
Where you yourself were never quite yourself
And did not want nor have to be. . . .

WALLACE STEVENS
The Motive for Metaphor, 1943.

BESIDES THE SPECTACULAR CEREMONIAL SITES all around them, one has to ask why the Anasazi bothered to farm in the bottom of the Grand Canyon. They were undoubtedly attracted to the Canyon's bighorn sheep and rabbits, edible cactus and the beans of the mesquite. Long before the Anasazi settled here, their hunter-gatherer ancestors surely visited the Canyon regularly for such things. The Canyon bottom would have attracted them with its long, almost frost-free growing season. It can be snowing on both rims without any snow falling near the river itself, a mile below—just as one February morning I once drove from Jerusalem down to Jericho, and in 30 minutes went from snow at the ridge of the Judean Hills to orange blossoms near the Jordan River and Dead Sea. We're used to thinking that it's colder up in the hills, but we're often surprised when it's warmer down in a valley.

I wandered off to look at other views in the fading light, and I got to thinking. Back before farming, when hunter-gatherer bands were wandering around the southern Colorado Plateau, they probably had to migrate south—down toward Phoenix— for the winters. It's just too cold above 2,000 meters elevation. Once agriculture started down in the southern valleys (it spread north from Mexico), there would have been population pressures: too many people living down there year-around who also wanted to hunt in the winter, competing with the seasonal visitors. I'll bet that as a result, the pre-farming Anasazi started congregating right here: instead of going south for the winter, they descended into the warmer bottom of the Grand Canyon. The bands probably were small—less than twenty-five people. And so eligible marriage partners were likely to come from another band. Winter was probably the marriage season. So farming here at Unkar Delta might have been just the outgrowth of an old tradition of meeting here in the winter.

From up atop the Cardenas cliffs, we could better see the obvious places to farm on the delta and explained the Unkar Anasazi story to those who hadn't taken up Jimmy's offer to row across in the afternoon. The Unkar Anasazi spread up the creek as far as possible, we mentioned, using every spring or seep to grow food. But, as Barbara noted, there isn't as much sunlight back up the creek year-round, given the long winter shadows. And it got colder as the Anasazi went higher up the creek.

The problem is even worse when farming the North Rim itself, which towers a mile above Unkar Delta. No problem finding lots of land up there on the Walhalla Plateau and elsewhere, but snow would have been a limiting factor. Warm as it remains on the Canyon floor during the winter months, the North Rim is usually buried under several stories of snow from October to May. There are only about 102 days free of frost up there, which poses a severe problem. Judging from present-day Hopi corns, it takes about 120 to 130 days for a crop to mature. Plant a week too late and the autumn frost would come when the corn was still immature, lacking all that substantial late growth.

Since the winters are pretty severe up top, those people likely went south for the winter—about 8 kilometers south, back down to Unkar Delta. After the snowmelt the Anasazi went back up there to plant crops and repair their summer homes, maybe clearing some more forest to create more planting space, to let in some more light. I suggested that they could have carried starter plants up from their open-air hothouse on the Canyon floor. That forest floor is good soil, far better than anything in the bottom of the Canyon, where the ground is often too alkaline and nitrogen-poor. And it rains regularly in the summer up there, as the monsoon clouds form at lower altitudes and are then pushed higher as they are swept toward the North Rim, cooling and losing their moisture over the forests.

And as Dan Hartline then pointed out, they could also have carried soil downhill, improving their sandy plots near the river with some good soil from the forest floor atop the North Rim.

The tight growing season suggests that the Unkar Anasazi badly needed an accurate calendar. While they could have planted a staggered series of crops in the bottom of the Canyon, they'd have needed something more than the improving weather to tell them when to plant higher up the trail, and on those terraces atop the North Rim.

The moon's cycle is, of course, one of the most tempting calendars—"we'll meet there when the moon is full," etc. But errors accumulate; year-round, counting the number of full moons is no better than sniffing the air on the first nice day of Spring—because 12 lunar months is about 11 days short of one solar year, so that a moon calendar quickly falls out of synchronization with the seasons. This didn't keep the Egyptians, Romans, and many others from attempting lunar-based calendars. Moreover, correcting the calendars after they drifted away from the seasons surely aided the development of mathematics (as one can see down in Mexico, where the Mayan 260-day ceremonial calendar meshed even more poorly with the 365.24-day length of the solar year and the seasonal cycle). And 11 days is a serious error when, as at the North Rim, one's growing season is less than 102 days long.

It makes you wonder how they did it. Marginal agriculture gets humans into solving some interesting problems. It's not like hunting and gathering.

AND MEANWHILE, BACK ON THE LEFT BANK, we watched the moon being eaten up to the accompaniment of the

It is a mark of modern ignorance to think that we have become progressively smarter. . . . Who is to say whether the task of tackling a problem without the benefit of a well-developed body of methods and information may not have required far greater intellectual vigor and originality than is needed [today] for proceeding from problem to problem within the safely established disciplines? Prehistoric, early historic, as well as medieval science have faced such a task.

The historian
THOMAS GOLDSTEIN, 1980

roar of the rapids. This cliff is one of those special places, a natural spectacle that suggests human ceremonies. I was reminded of when I first saw Delphi, near the top of a steep-walled Greek valley which opens out to the sea. One stands there looking out, the wet cliffs behind one—a real feeling of being perched on the edge of the universe. Especially when the springs which made the cliffs wet were emitting steam. A perfect setting for an Oracle. And temples.

Besides the ruins on the right bank which we saw earlier, there are ruins over on this side of the river too. A particularly enigmatic ruin is on the hilltop up behind our campsite, the rectangular one we saw from the river as we arrived. By the time that the moon had lost a big nick out of its lower left rim, Alan asked who wanted to go up to the ruin and watch the eclipse for a while longer. About six of us decided to go and started out. There was plenty of light for picking our way cross-country up the hill, then walking along a high ridge which led to the hilltop.

The rough walls of the ruin, which we could see in the fading moonlight, stand less than chest-high, and are made of piled-up rocks. No mortar. No sign of a roof. It seemed like a single room of house-trailer dimensions, almost 4 meters wide and 9 meters long. The second Powell expedition discovered this hilltop ruin in 1872. People were around here about the year A.D. 1100, to judge from the pottery styles found nearby, but otherwise the ruin is undated. It is not a sensible place to live, far from the water and exposed to the winds, but it has a spectacular view up and down the Canyon, a panoramic skyline. Was it perhaps a lookout? A guardpost? A temple, perhaps an above-ground kiva?

We explored the hilltop and caught the expansive view back upriver toward the Hopi salt mines. The Palisades were all spread out to the east, but the view was fading, the moon now down to a crescent. So I settled down on the southern slope of the hilltop ridge, facing the disappearing moon, hands behind my head, and looked up at the canyon walls and the sky. You'd think we would be sleepy, but no—everyone's wide awake with the excitement of this place. There's a gentle breeze blowing through the darkening night, freshening our faces.

As I took in the view and wondered why they had built here, another possible use for the ruin occurred to me. This would have been the perfect place for the Unkar Delta people to keep a calendar for their agriculture. The position of sunrise on the horizon provides a simple calendar, requiring none of the fancier knowledge of astronomy ascribed to the builders of Stonehenge (and a simple seasonal observatory is surely how they, too, got started). Each morning in winter and spring, the sun rises further north. Then, at the summer solstice, the sunrise turns around and heads south again.

One can use that horizon calendar scheme almost anywhere on earth, as long as the horizon is subdivided—mountain peaks work nicely as markers—and one has a customary point of observation, such as a favorite hilltop. I examined the eastern skyline in the moonlight. The most prominent landmark is the Palisades of the Desert, that expanse of canyon rim where the Kaibab, Toroweap, and Coconino layers form a vertically scalloped cliff, extending from northeast down to about due east. A regular series of promontories stick out, like columns on a Greek temple. That's where the sun would rise all through the spring and summer. No trouble with giving those promontories names, just as we name the months. I counted the number of notches in the skyline as best I could in the fading light, and decided that between the approximately due-east sunrise of the spring equinox and the northeasterly sunrise at the summer solstice, the sunrise position would traverse at least a dozen easily identifiable markers over that three month period. One every week, on the average.

Then I looked to the southeast. I couldn't see the South Rim because of a large butte inside the canyon, obscuring the view. It seemed no more than a few kilometers away and rose up rather high in the sky, meaning that sunrise in the winter must have been pretty late [9:14 A.M., *I discovered the following winter, but that little expedition is another story*]. The winter solstice sunrise, I mused, must come up over that butte somewhere—maybe in that nice V-shaped notch? [*Not quite: if we stood in exactly the right place, it first peeked through a hole in the cliff, looking like a brightly illuminated eye in the profile of an Indian chief*].

So that's where the sun turns around—if one prays hard enough. The winter solstice occurs during the Hopi's high religious festivals, I remembered from a display at the Museum of Northern Arizona just outside Flagstaff. For at least a week or so, the position of sunrise would change so imperceptibly that it would seem to stand still on the horizon. Then it would slowly begin rising somewhat farther north each day, reaching the Palisades by spring and then continuing through that series of notches during the springtime. Each one of those notches on the Palisades could mark a time to plant, the earliest ones for the lower elevations, the later ones in May—such as that big promontory with the finger projecting from it, Comanche Point [*the sun rises there on 30 April, it turns out. . .*].

I was feeling very pleased with myself. It felt distinctly extraordinary, as if I were rediscovering how the Anasazi thought a thousand years ago. Not merely as if I were slipping into their frame of mind, but as if I were glimpsing one of the ways in which our even-more-distant predecessors got started doing science.

The last sliver of white disappeared from the upper right edge of the moon, and suddenly the Canyon seemed much darker, the moon dusky (the reddish glow from all the sunlight bent and scattered by the Earth's atmosphere into the shadow cone). And the stars much brighter, Milky Way and all. But I could barely see the Canyon rim, my calendar. I settled down again, hands behind head, and looked up at the skies.

WE WERE GETTING IMPATIENT, awaiting the end of totality, trying to guess when the first signs of sunlight would again appear on the shadowed moon. And always guessing wrong. I was reminded of when I was a child, being impatient when the family car was stopped at an endless traffic signal, wanting the red light to change to green. And then my father would command the traffic signal to change—all he had to do was wiggle his ears.

Once I knew of his magical ability, I would always demand that he make the signals turn green. He would usually demur, but would finally yield to my pleadings to wiggle his ears. And sure enough, the signal would promptly turn green. I was amazed. Not being able to wiggle my ears myself, I was frustrated that I could not command the signals. It took some time before I discovered for myself his trick of watching for the green to change to yellow on the cross-street's traffic signal—my very first scientific triumph. But I never did learn how to wiggle my ears.

Eclipses weren't merely mysterious in the good old prescience days—eclipses were magic. High drama. To some peoples an eclipse was probably the harbinger of the end of the world. Anyone who could manipulate an eclipse, or seem to do so, surely reaped whatever rewards a society had to offer. It would, of course, have been an impressive performance if an Anasazi shaman could have ordered the end of the eclipse, successfully commanding the reappearance of the lost moon by performing a brief ceremony before anyone else could detect that totality was almost over. But, hard as we tried to guess when our eclipse was ending, we kept guessing wrong. Still, the shaman's tradition probably told him that eclipses didn't last forever, just an hour or so. The shaman could start up his "ear wiggling" ceremony after a while—one can always stretch out a prayer—and sure enough, pretty soon the eclipse would start to end. It would probably convince most of his naive audience—not being so well advised by tradition that eclipses always end after a little while—that his magic was powerful.

Still no sign of sunlight on the moon. It remained a dusky red orb, an unnatural disk in the starry vault of the heavens.

Of course, predicting the start of an eclipse would be an even neater trick. To do that, you've either got to have detailed records in the manner of the Mayan astronomers down in Mexico, or you've got to watch both sun and moon carefully and apply some simple rules. The Anasazi certainly became sophisticated about sun and moon cycles over in Chaco Canyon. A pair of spiral pictographs, much like the petroglyphs we saw pecked into the rock slab back up at South Canyon, serve to track the annual sun cycle as well as the 18.6 year moon cycle. It's not very accurate—you'd do better watching sunrise on the horizon to determine the solstices—but it demonstrates that the Anasazi knew about the moon movements on the horizon. Not bad. If the Anasazi attained such sophistication (probably in the years between A.D. 920 and 1130, when the finest architecture and road-building took place at Chaco), what simpler methods were in use out on the agricultural fringes of their civilization, such as here on Furnace Flats?

[*Well, to my surprise, they were pretty sophisticated here in the "wilds," predicting both solar and lunar eclipses by a method simpler than Stonehenge's. No counting, no records needed—just the Palisades of the Desert: they measured the moon's movements with the sun's ruler but restarted their calendar names every half-year ("January" and "July" were called by the same name in the historic Pueblos). You wouldn't think that you could predict eclipses with just those two practices and no records, but you can—and the Anasazi did. The simple rule: whenever the sun's date is almost the same (or at least has the same ambiguous name) as the moon's "date" (read off the sawtooth horizon calendar as if the rising moon were the sun), watch out for an eclipse! Tune in next time for another exciting episode in Anasazi astronomy—and find out why such often-inaccurate eclipse warnings and the frequent partial eclipses probably persuaded the ancient peoples that prayer was powerful, that it could deflect the moon from its normal path, preventing it from being consumed by sky monsters.*]

Still no sign of the end of totality. I had half a dozen false alarms, thinking I'd seen a sliver of sunlight on the left side. And I was getting sleepy, even though we had been vigorously discussing how the earth and moon were formed out of the primordial dust cloud. Alan said that maybe we should head back down anyway. So I got up onto stiff legs. Walking in total star-light? But I just followed the leader, my feet telling me when I strayed from the path—the loose stones all seemed to have been kicked off the trail by previous hikers, so the true path felt more comfortable for walking. No sooner did we get down to the cliff overlooking Unkar than the first sliver of light appeared on the moon, considerably brightening our path. We couldn't find any moonwatchers at the cliff; they'd evidently all gone back to camp long ago. So off we went, on a real trail and with the light getting better and better. At one point I looked up at the Palisades and remembered that the Unkar Anasazi would have seen the Crab Nebula supernova rise up there. And I wondered if they marked the spot where it rose in some way—whereupon I promptly wandered off the trail and stumbled into a small prickly-pear cactus. So much for that train of thought.

By the time we arrived back at the silent camp along the riverbanks, we had almost half a moon. We virtually ran the last downhill section of trail, it was so easy. I think that the Anasazi must have gotten around pretty well without flashlights.

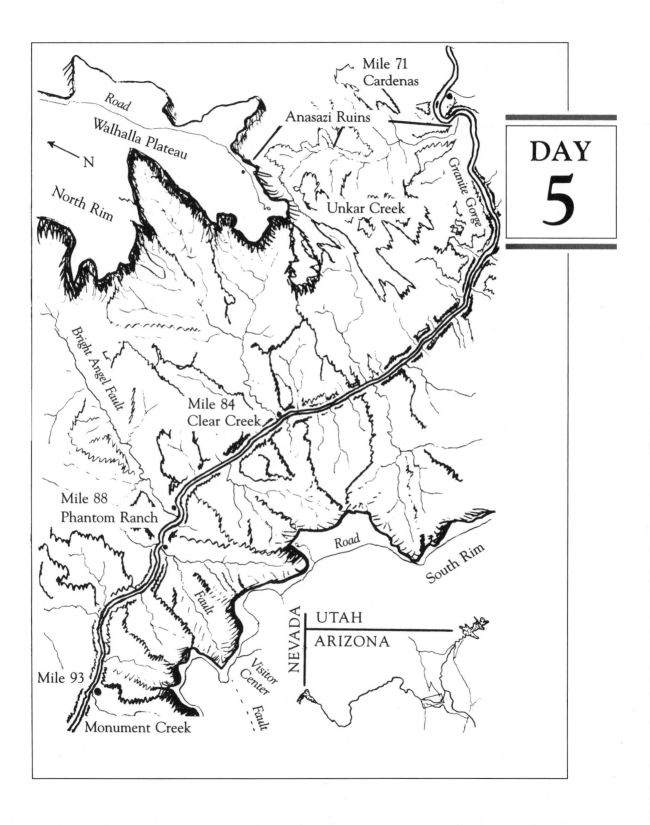

MILE 71
Cardenas Creek

THE ENIGMATIC ANASAZI HILLTOP was all the talk at breakfast. Those who stayed the course had to tell the people who slept through it what they'd missed—the view of Unkar Delta and the rapids seemed to take precedence over the moon. The half-dozen of us who'd gone on to see the hilltop ruin extolled its commanding view and enigmatic nature.

"If you're quick, you can run right up to the ruin and back down again," added Alan, not looking a bit sleepy. "We took the long way last night to see the cliffs. It's only about 40 stories up, and there's a trail in back of camp that starts straight up that ridge line," he said, pointing. Five people actually packed up their black bags in a hurry, left them down by the boats, and set off up the path, promising to return soon. "You can always stop at the 35th floor to admire the river gravels," Alan shouted after them.

While my calendar idea was discussed briefly, what really held the attention of the people eating breakfast in the alcove of tamarisk was the Unkar Delta story. Particularly the boom-and-bust nature of the Anasazi population, controlled by the intermittent droughts.

"That's almost as bad as the deer," Ben said. "A good summer means a lot of starvation the next winter."

"I thought that humans in primitive tribes held their population pretty constant," Abby ventured. "You know, the Kalahari San and the Australian aborigines. Even without modern birth control they average about four years between babies."

"But how?" someone asked.

"Prolonged breastfeeding suppresses ovulation, for one thing," Ben volunteered.

"That doesn't work so well if you're well-nourished, I hear," said Rosalie. "Maybe a poor diet holds population growth constant."

"And maybe it's a constant climate," Ben said. "The big population booms occur when a new niche is opened up, as when more food becomes available. Maybe the stability of the native tribes they've studied is just because they haven't experienced big improvements in living conditions."

"Sounds like inflation to me," Rosalie said. "The population explosion as the archetype of monetary inflation! Maybe both are due to a rapid improvement in living conditions."

Abby looked dubious. "You mean that the tribes with stable populations perceive the world as unchanging? While people in an obviously changing world have more children?"

"Could be true," said Ben. "Certainly people have fewer children when times are bad."

"That's partly because the infants don't grow up—infants

haven't acquired much immunity to diseases. They're being stressed all the time, and so die more readily if they're malnourished," explained Rosalie.

"But it's also planning," Ben said. "Humans plan. And there are social pressures—when another baby comes along too soon in an Aboriginal family, the man loses social status, he's blamed for it."

"So if people plan, why do we have such a big population problem?" asked Abby.

Rosalie pointed out that we've strained things badly, leaving very little insurance against fluctuations in climate or natural disasters. It's inhuman. A humane world ought to have no more people than it can support in its worst years; the way it stands, ten good years of weather in a poor country is almost a sure prescription for starvation, because the weather never stays that good during the next decade. As the statisticians say, it regresses toward the mean. Not that we're any smarter: even in our modern civilization we see college-educated people ignoring the obvious—such as when they build a house in the flood plain of a river, when it's perfectly obvious that it will be flooded out sometime in the next few decades (they expect, I suppose, that the equally gullible taxpayers will either pay to protect them with dams or reimburse them with disaster assistance when the inevitable happens).

Yet boom-and-bust cycles may have been common on the frontiers, where living conditions were marginal and fluctuating. The ice ages probably produced a lot of such conditions, running the ratchets of natural selection quite regularly. And, while I'd grown somewhat accustomed to thinking in terms of such stresses every 100,000 years, the Anasazi experience is sobering: it suggests that significant selection cycles could also occur every decade or two for those living on the margins.

THE STANDARD SWINDLE about the population explosion is that it will cure itself once the standard of living is raised even higher in the developing countries. Of course, the rising standard of living is also blamed for these countries' population boom in the first place. Confused? Someone is. Wishful thinking? Probably.

Medicine, or at least public-health measures such as sanitation, is supposedly the cause of the population boom. All of those babies who would have died, the story goes, have been saved from childhood diseases by improved sanitation and modern medicines. You'd think that population growth had been held in check all those millennia by disease. True, there has been a correlation between better medicine and increases in tropical populations during the last three decades, but to look no further back in history than this one recent example is indeed short-sighted. The world's population started booming long before modern medicine, back when there were still open sewers in the city streets. Europe's population boom started about 1600, not 1900. And 1600 was not the start of either modern medicine or improved sanitation.

Puncturing that fallacy only requires a little history, but to understand why the population explosion will remain a serious, continuing disaster requires a few lessons from population ecology. Back to the birds, while we wait for the boats to be packed for our little trip down what Major Powell called "The Great Unknown."

Some animals, such as mosquitos, lay lots of small eggs and merely hope for the best. Nearly all their young will perish. Other animals—and birds are good examples of this—put their reproductive efforts into the well-aimed shot rather than the scattergun. Postnatal care is the most obvious way in which such animals "invest" in their offspring. To insure the quality of the offspring raised, some birds also adjust the number of eggs they lay according to what the food supply will bear that season. The snowy owl may raise only one or two eggs some years, ten eggs in others. It depends on the supply of baby food, namely the little arctic mice called lemmings whose availability tends to fluctuate in cycles of about two to seven years. The snowy owl accurately estimates the food supply, and doesn't create a lot of mouths that cannot be fed without making them all weaklings. By spending their reproductive efforts wisely, more snowy owls' offspring reach maturity.

To estimate in advance the resources available during the coming season is rather clever of the owls. People are even more clever than birds at reading the environment, guessing the future, making plans, and implementing them. We have been in the family-planning business for a long time, using primitive versions of contraception and abortion, social rules and sexual taboos, and so forth. Zero population growth may have often been implemented during human history. Look at today's remaining primitive societies and you will often find a stable population rather than exponential growth. They know how many mouths they can feed, and they adjust their reproduction accordingly. Prolonged breastfeeding suppresses ovulation, we now know, but that's been utilized for millennia; it's one reason why the average birth spacing is four years in hunter-gatherer tribes.

But then there are the social devices for birth control; to take but one example, almost any form of sexual taboo helps reduce babies. Social rules also limit the total number of babies per mother by effectively decreasing the reproductive span, that period between puberty and menopause. They delay the first pregnancy: marriage is put off through a variety of devices, such as initiation ceremonies, bride prices, getting together a dowry, building a house for the new couple, and so forth. Social rules may have other functions too, but one of their results is to limit total reproduction.

Primitive people also practiced abortion as best they could, usually in the form of infanticide. In many recent societies and probably most ancient ones, families would carefully evaluate the family resources before letting a newborn baby join the family. Even aspects of our physiology facilitate this: lactation is not triggered by giving birth but by suckling, making it possible to delay mother-infant bonding. If there wasn't going to be enough food to go around, child-rearing was often postponed until a later pregnancy. Today we have the technology to make that decision much earlier, long before the brain develops any uniquely human functional abilities (a far better test than the simpleminded and unanswerable "when life begins"). And in most cases, we now have the ability to prevent conception in the first place. But while our technology may be more sophisticated, family planning has been done by both humans and birds for a very long time.

AND SO IF FAMILY SIZE is normally regulated, one cannot intelligently address the population explosion without asking: Just what factors determine the size of the family one can afford? If it is a control system like a thermostat and furnace, just what determines the setting, the family size around which it hovers? Remember, we're not necessarily talking about rational choices here, but also about the intuitive cues that even birds could use as their target family size. What are the target cues which, in particular, the human species follows?

Until modern societies such as India and China, it seems unlikely that family size was ever regulated primarily for the good of the larger community. Social rules, which initially suggest that population growth was controlled for the sake of the community, may be only a way of decreasing the competition, of holding down other people's family size. Instead, each family was probably trying to rear as many offspring as it could. After all, during prehuman evolution, those who maximized their offspring did wind up with more genes in the next generation than those who limited them.

Such "looking after number one," however, results in some appalling suffering and waste by our humane standards. As a result of such maximizing, most species try to raise far more off-

To assume that the recent invention of mass medicine has made any fundamental difference to the number of children raised in any contemporary society is to assign to people the small-egg gambit of a mosquito; it is to assume that women are mere baby factories and their output is a function of what the doctors can keep alive. It is unscientific as well as literally inhuman.

The ecologist
Paul Colinvaux, 1982

spring than can survive as adults. To take an omnivore not un-like humans, bears rear many more cubs than can ever grow up. There is only so much adult bear food around, so only a frac-tion of those cute cubs can ever raise a family themselves; in-deed, like most lion cubs, most bear cubs starve after their par-ents stop caring for them. Stupid? Just natural. The overall effort expended on raising bear cubs (the "reproductive effort") is ab-surdly in excess of the number of job slots for adult bears. Yet it was a matter of keeping up with the Joneses—for an individ-ual bear to do less would mean getting fewer copies of her genes into later generations than the bears who raise many cubs to reproductive age. Regulating current clutch size (the number cared for at any one time) is one thing, as it makes for healthier babies, but to limit lifetime numbers (clutch size times the number of seasons as an adult) makes less Darwinian sense. The excess means that natural selection and chance determine which cubs actually survive to reproduce.

Limiting clutch size by the projected availability of baby food is not the same thing as limiting total reproduction over a life-time according to the availability of adult food. The standard rule in population ecology is that the resources devoted to re-production have no relationship at all to the population size which results. The numbers of offspring reared are often ab-surdly in excess of the carrying capacity of the environment and there is a lot of starvation. It is the niche size—the number of bear job slots available—that determines the population size.

A niche used to be just a recess in the wall of a room, used for housing statues and such. But the ecologist's use of the word connotes something more like a job slot. For example, there are only so many dentist jobs in Flagstaff. To be a dentist requires a combination of skills and opportunities: one has to have in-born ability (nimble fingers) and the acquired training (eight years of college) to be a dentist, but one cannot function as a dentist unless there is also sufficient dental work for one to do. The number of dentist slots depends on the population of Flagstaff and the prevalence of dental disease there (all that good moun-tain water can be rather low in fluoride, unfortunately). Thus, the concept of niche implies both a set of skills conferred by inheritance and culture, and a set of environmental constraints such as food availability, climate, predators, disease, and the right setting for successful reproduction. Lack any of them, and one doesn't fit the niche, one can't make a living. Few animals can switch niches successfully; surplus dentists can usually find a dif-ferent job, thus modifying their niche (making silver jewelry for the tourists would be a good bet if a dentist wanted to remain in Flag).

The niche of human hunter-gatherers is determined by skills and resources too; being even smarter than birds, they too limit their clutch size in accordance with family resources. Birds raise a different clutch every year, but humans mostly raise one big "clutch" of various ages due to the long rearing period for each, replacing the ones that die and repeatedly estimating how many extra can be afforded. In contrast to the birds' situation, this means that human clutch size also represents the number of children produced in a lifetime. This may allow the number of adolescents coming into the human breeding pool to approximate the number of job slots opening up, thus allowing most adult humans to reproduce. We have improved on the birds who, like the bears, usually produce more offspring than can ever survive or reproduce.

Whenever a niche broadens, there is room for a bigger population: when the bears learned to fish, there was a bear population boom until the limits of that new niche were reached. And whenever either human skills or environmental resources improve, there has usually been room—in the past—for more humans. For a while.

Before Columbus, says the ecologist Paul Colinvaux, the native Americans were likely packed into the Americas just as tightly as their technology allowed. The European settlers had agricultural technology that supported more people on an acre of land; they also had the weapons that allowed successful aggression against the original inhabitants. And so, back home, the European populations boomed starting in the 1600s. The family planning in the old countries undoubtedly took into account the possibility of emigration to the new world; the new Americans had big families, as there always seemed to be resources for lots more. The European niche had expanded at the expense of the Indians; the world population had a net increase because the Europeans could live at higher density than the Indians. The Anasazi niche also expanded about A.D. 1050 because the rainfall allowed crops to be grown in new places; but their population boom was, alas, in trouble after just a single generation.

ONE CONVENIENT RATIONALIZATION for not worrying about the population explosion is that family size drops as middle- and upper-class economic status is attained; it even happened in ancient Rome (though people who cite that usually fail to note that the *total* Roman census continued to expand). Perhaps better-off parents don't need all those children to make sure someone will support them in their old age, and so forth.

Thus, the soothing story goes, when those developing coun-

> Evolution is what it is. The upper classes have always died out; it's one of the most charming things about them.
>
> GERMAINE GREER

tries are further along, the problem will take care of itself. This was the prevailing thinking up until the nineteen-fifties (although U.S. President Ronald Reagan found it convenient to revive it, like an old movie, in 1984). As early as 1944 demographer Kingsley Davis called this view into question, warning that if India's population followed the pattern of the West's demographic/economic transition, it would reach 750 million by the year 2025. Davis was considered an alarmist at the time. But his prophecy came true in only half the time: by 1985 India's population had exceeded 750 million, despite decades of birth control programs.

In *The Fates of Nations*, Paul Colinvaux points out that both rich and poor probably have as many children as they can afford; the reason there may be only two or three children in rich families is that each child requires such major resources. Rich parents' expectations for their children are at least as high as their own attainments. While a physician may earn a lot in comparison to a laborer, the physician may still be able to afford to send only two children to medical school or its equivalent; the laborer without upward mobility, on the other hand, has no such expectations and may be able to afford seven or eight children who get by on mediocre diets and who all sleep in one room rather than in separate rooms. For the poor, children are cheap. They may even contribute by going to work at an early age, providing another wage-earner to help the family.

Both the rich and the poor family may regulate clutch size just as the snowy owl does, but their standards of what is sufficient differ greatly; thus the number of children from each social class that reach reproductive age may be contrary to what income suggests. We might say that the quality of the product is different, but that's our cultural bias speaking, not biology: rich or poor, all of our offspring are competitive for mates unless they're grossly malnourished, and in evolution that's what counted for getting one's genes into further generations in greater numbers than the competition. I might note that, for humans, such competition is not a consideration anymore, as human biological evolution by standard means has probably ended, what with our mobility stirring our very large gene pool.

Once beyond malnourishment, poverty is relative. And as long as the poor don't have great expectations for their children that require the parent to set aside resources, the poor will be able to afford big families. And they'll have them, too. That, says Colinvaux, is why the population explosion won't go away.

Humans are animals that, rather than being born to their niche, learn their niche: we can learn a hunter-gatherer niche or a dentist niche. And at various times in our history, we have greatly expanded the possible niches. Occasionally this occurred when new land opened up for habitation, as when *Homo erectus* used fire and clothing to survive Peking's climate, as in the European takeover of the Americas, as in the irrigation of the Negev desert by both the ancient Nubians and the modern Israelis. As in when the land around us here on Furnace Flats was opened up to agriculture by the rainfall improving about A.D. 1050.

Usually niche expansion has been aided by technology, creating new jobs as it were, so that more people can be supported. In the developed countries, we have created so many new niches that 10 percent of the people can now feed both themselves and the other 90 percent as well; and while some of the other 90 percent must occupy niches that supply clothing, housing, fertilizer and fuel to farmers, society has a great deal of choice in what else it will emphasize. It could, I suppose, spend the rest of its efforts at bookkeeping and auditing the bookkeepers, keeping track of every transaction with a passion (this seems to be the goal of our tax laws). Assuming that doesn't happen, what fraction of those new "nonessential niches" will go to lipstick or books, to adult education or spectator sports? You are what you pay attention to.

Peoples' perception of a changing niche is, of course, part of what family size is based on. If they see more-of-the-same in the manner of the traditional hunter-gatherer, they will plan their family size differently than poor Mexican peasants exposed to movies and television who therefore hope to slip their children into the United States someday. Or at least Mexico City's teeming tenements. They're just doing what the Europeans did during these last few hundred years.

We were in Guaymas, Mexico, with a guy from Chicago. He was busy denigrating the area, "who could stand to live here, you wouldn't know anything about the world, it is so squalid, etc." I was busy taking pictures of houses perhaps 25 feet square with a 1954 Chevy pickup truck in the driveway and a satellite dish on the roof. An area of perhaps 1,000 people, with about 50 satellite dishes! He said, "What do those dishes do anyway?" I said, "Well, these people can get 130 TV channels in five languages, and subcarrier FM stereo. They have Quebec, Venezuela, Mexico City, all of America, BBC, and they get the Chicago Symphony as clearly as you do." He was stunned. And silent for a while. And then he said, "What do they think when they see all that, and they look at this, where they live?" And I was silent, and Nan was silent, and he was silent. And I can't get rid of the notion that Scarcity and Abundance will have to be dealt with by the materialistic nations (today's equivalent of the monarchies that went down to democracy's force with the advent of the cheap printed word).

CHARLES HOUSE

□   □   □

WE NOW SEE UNKAR RAPID from a new vantage point, and the waves sure look larger from down here. Unkar's a long rapid, sweeping in a U-shape, cliffs on the left bank and the Anasazi's ancient cornfields on the right. Those fields were used for not much more than one century, mostly during the Anasazi population boom.

We're holding just downstream of the rapid, waiting for the other boats to come through. Once the boats are bailed out, Jimmy repeats a bit of the Unkar Delta story to those who hadn't ferried across yesterday afternoon.

There is an old Anasazi granary on the right bank, just downstream of us. It's not up as high as the cave at Nanko-weap, so maybe the rodents got more of the stored grain here.

We're soaking up the morning sun, having heard stories about the big rapids up ahead. This is reputed to be the hardest day on the river, with lots of really big rapids coming up. Besides which the canyon narrows down, and that means lots of shadow, too.

The human population explosion represents hubris. . . . If we make use of birth control, we can affect the amount of time it takes for the human population to double. At present, this doubling time is shrinking constantly, and the world's population is burgeoning in accordance with a hyperbolic law. The potential for catastrophe is great. The self-regulating mechanism that will, because of the inherent limits of our environment, inevitably go into effect is inhuman.

MANFRED EIGEN and
RUTHILD WINKLER
Laws of the Game, 1976

THE POPULATION EXPLOSION might level out, of course, if people's perception of the future was as unchanging as the hunter-gatherer's—for example, if the society became very rigid, with no chance to rise as in a caste system, with no opportunities for emigration, with barriers everywhere created by a bureaucracy that has to ration strained resources. There are, and have been, some stagnant societies like that.

Rigidity does stop growth. Rigid societies are, of course, police states in addition to everything else. They may eventually become ripe targets for an aggressive neighbor. If we want anything like a free society, with lots of choices and the constant opportunity to better ourselves, we will also have the natural tendency for the population to grow—in the absence, that is, of some unnatural intervention. Couples, left to themselves, will continue to have as many children as they think they (without regard for their neighbors) can afford; for the poor, that will likely be many more than is needed to replace the dying in both rich and poor segments of the society, for they're unlikely to be influenced by ecologists' warnings printed occasionally in the big city newspapers.

Human societies have choices, however, that other animal

societies don't. The choices are the benefits of our ability to discover and accumulate new knowledge, and apply it to simulating scenarios for the future, choosing the better-appearing alternatives. We can choose to apply our medical technology, for example, not so much to increasing fertility (by treating infertile individuals and saving problem pregnancies), but more to decreasing fertility—by improved contraception, by making spontaneous abortions somewhat more likely rather than less likely (they've always been many times more likely than induced abortions: 48 to 72 percent of all conceptions spontaneously abort, most in the first month where they are never noticed because the woman does not miss a menstrual period), by removing barriers to a woman's right to terminate a pregnancy.

Other effective measures include training every woman for a niche other than full-time mothering, so that she always has a choice. However, one should not deprecate the important niche of full-time mother to achieve such ends; a diverse society should include the possibility of some families having no children and others having four. If one's goal is to decrease overall numbers rather than to uniformly decrease the size of everyone's family, and one doesn't let planning get contaminated by eugenics-type considerations (some of us have great faith that the gene pool of the poor is little different from that of the rich), one can avoid many of the most difficult problems posed by a society trying to implement zero population growth.

Our addiction to "growth" is really an addiction to an expanding niche. We often call it "freedom": to be free to choose, to be free of the bureaucratic constraints associated with the rationing of scarce resources, to be free of the repression employed in stagnating police states as those in power protect their own niche. Niche expansion is, in the natural course of things, conducive to a growth in population as well—individuals will naturally plan to have larger families, just as the Europeans and Anasazi did when things improved.

And, conversely, some people think that more babies mean more jobs. But that's illusory. For some occupations, of course, a baby boom does mean more jobs—but we must not allow shortsighted "more is better" thinking to dictate our policy. The postwar baby boom has propagated through our society; the decline after the peak reduced the number of jobs for baby-carriage manufacturers, police officers (fewer erratic teenagers), and teachers—but during the same period, we nevertheless expanded our niches all the same, the industrialized nations' economies having somehow created an enormous number of additional jobs (which is how the percentage of employed women has soared). We must disassociate niche growth from population growth, or the population growth will eventually overwhelm niche growth and its freedoms, just as has happened before in crowded parts of the world.

The alternative to doing something? Default. Zero population growth will instead be attained by perfectly natural but very undesirable methods—lots of aggression from overcrowding, rigid caste systems, stagnation, police states, and all the rest. To maintain and expand freedom in the world is going to require vigorous action to decrease average family size. To allow the issue to be swept under the rug by shortsighted politicians and special interests is to abrogate our freedoms, to sentence our children to a world for which they will not thank us.

Just remember those young Anasazi of the years 1070 and 1130, whose parents started their population boom before the agricultural economy was really secure enough to guarantee themselves—much less their children—a living. They probably starved to death. Taking those kinds of gambles—with lives—has been important in the past, but a humane society doesn't have to continue the practice when it can do better. We aren't deer.

[Spinoza's truth] that outside civilization (privilege) we are nothing, mere battered brutes without choices, whereas inside, however unfair that may be, we have hope, including the hope that our good fortune may spread to others.
The writer JOHN GARDNER, 1978

THE CANYON, which had been so broad along Furnace Flats, begins to narrow below Unkar Delta. For us it was a sudden transition, as we weren't paying attention to the scenery, arguing as we were about population problems. Our sense of the world closing in on us was mirrored in the canyon walls closing in on the riverbanks.

The tilted Precambrian layers flanking the riverbanks give an abrupt illusion of heading downhill. Steeply. The river is indeed going downhill—the Colorado's gradient averages about one story every 1.5 river miles—but when layers ascend from the riverbank level to many stories high within your several-block view downriver, it gives you the distinct impression of being funneled down into an abyss.

The first view of such V-shaped expanding sightlines, just below Unkar, is reinforced after the river takes a turn or two and the walls have really begun to close in. What is going on? The view of the Palisades is lost and we only catch glimpses of the South Rim; the North Rim is completely obscured. This is Shinumo Gorge, and the prominent white bands in the walls are of quartzite, which is much more resistant to erosion than the usual Dox stuff—hence the narrower canyon.

But we have other concerns: namely, Hance Rapid, the second of the biggies, rated a 9. It drops nearly three stories and it looks BIG. We see hikers camped here; there is a steep trail down from the South Rim. The ride through Unkar was long and wet as we swept in a broad curve to the right around the foot of Unkar Delta. Hance is a straighter shot and another wet ride as we flush through.

We are now ready to start on our way down the Great Unknown. Our boats, tied to a common stake, chafe each other as they are tossed by the fretful river. . . . We have an unknown distance yet to run, an unknown river to explore. What falls there are, we know not; what rocks beset the channel, we know not; what walls rise over the river, we know not. Ah, well! We may conjecture many things. . . . Heretofore hard rocks have given us bad river; soft rocks, smooth water; and a series of rocks harder than any we have experienced sets in. The river enters the gneiss! We can see but a little way into the granite gorge, but it looks threatening.

POWELL EXPEDITION DIARY, 13–14 August 1869

Just below Hance at mile 77 comes another V-shaped illusion as the Bass Limestone emerges steeply from the river. The Canyon profile narrows further and then we are abruptly into the Vishnu Schist. Nothing gradual about this emergence—just "wham," like entering a black tunnel whose roof has been left off.

THE INNER GORGE is like nothing we have seen before. Its Vishnu Schist is finely layered, almost foliated like the Tapeats sandstone on which we rested at the Little Colorado. But at river level it has a polish like marble, that varies from a buff red (where granite has intruded) to an ebony black. The vertical slabs never extend very far before they are distorted, overlain, intruded—the impression is of a marbled cake, chocolate with swirls of strawberry red. All this runs a few stories high before terminating abruptly. We often see sky beyond the top of this narrow canyon, though at other times there are a few layers of corrugated Tapeats Sandstone capping the marbled walls. This makes it even more like a cake: horizontal layers of Tapeats frosting atop the vertically-swirled marble layer-cake. The river-polishing of the schist extends more than one story above the current river level.

Then, near Mile 79, we come to the first of the inner-canyon rapids, Sockdolager, whose name is not very reassuring once you learn that it supposedly means "knockout punch" in Swedish. The Canyon is so narrow that sandy beaches are infrequent; even if we wanted to stop and look at this rapid, it would be hard to find a place to park. And we are traveling ever so much faster now that the Canyon has squeezed the river into a

MILE 77
Inner Gorge

narrower channel. We are swept in. Through we go, up and down, getting soaked from one side and then the other, splashed from the rear when we don't expect it.

We pass the last of the good campsites for 11 miles, and what a difference—Vishnu camp at Mile 81 is a little sandy beach on the left, hardly big enough to hold us. Then "wham!" Grapevine Rapid, another biggie.

Once more we bailed, and then looked around, somewhat breathless by now. The canyon walls continue to display one variation after another on marbling. The river too is marbled with swirls of water, the currents milling about, diving under one another. This occasionally sucks one side of the boat down.

And the boatman yells "Highside!" We quickly move to the high side of the boat to counterbalance it, to keep the other side from subsiding into the swirling waters. And I thought that highsiding was going to happen only in rapids—but there's no rapid in sight! This river is full of surprises.

The schists here form a medium-gray background for a series of red, black, and white bands. Early geologists gave names to all the variations on granite and schist: Brahma Schist, Vishnu Schist, and so on. Now the fashion is to just talk about schist, granite, and gneiss, without further subdivision. We neurobiologists understand this immediately—in the perpetual war between the splitters and the lumpers in science, the lumpers are currently predominating in this descriptive geology. The same thing happens in any branch of science, where different names are initially assigned to every variant in the hope that they will prove useful (as not infrequently happens). But a later assessment may suggest that one name, lumping them all together, is more advantageous and less tiring.

There are many granite intrusions into the schist, streaking the canyon walls like a crisscrossed lace. The schist is metamorphic rock, made from old sedimentary layers of the same general kind we saw during our descent through Marble Gorge and Furnace Flats. These sandstone and shale sediments were pressed and cooked deeper within the earth at some point, producing the metamorphosis, a transformation of sandstones and shales and limestones into a harder schist that will take a polish. Hotter, more fluid rock from the earth's mantle—granite—managed to push its way up through weak cracks in the schist, while it was still buried deeply, and we now see the result in the form of these crazy laces running every which way. Sometimes they become so extensive that it is hard to find the original schist—the wall instead looks as if the red-white granite had somehow acquired patches of black schist.

The narrower river channel is due to the harder rock. But the same amount of water has to pass each second if it is not to back up. So the river is deeper and faster here, and the swirls abound in this torrent. Often we must pick our way between two back-eddies, each of which would carry us back upriver. The boatman needs a sharp eye to thread a path that keeps us going forward.

It is, in theory, possible for there to be no path downriver whatever, even though that's where the river is flowing. If the deep water flowed faster than the surface water, eddies could make the surface water all flow back upstream. The river, from surface appearances, would actually seem to run uphill! And the surface waters are what we have to ride—we can't just ride the "average" current. Fortunately, we're able to find a little surface current heading downriver.

It's literally The River That Flows Uphill, not just my metaphor for evolution. As metaphor, the phrase is handy to remind us that the downhill flow of energy also has consequences for jacking systems up to new heights of complexity. And us.

WE ALSO LIVE in a part of the universe that isn't average, that is going two ways at once. What's true for the whole "average" universe isn't necessarily true for local sections of it, such as the solar system. Instead of things getting more and more disorderly as time goes on, which is the usual conclusion drawn from the second law of thermodynamics (entropy and all that), things locally often get more and more orderly, just as a consequence of a flow of energy.

This river, by flowing downhill, creates whirlpools below the rapids, nice orderly spirals. And the river sorts rocks by sizes, the small ones getting carried along further than the big boulders; the sand settling out of the river earlier than the silt. Many crystals arise when heat dissipates, as in the formation of a snowflake or the quartz crystals we see here and there in the riverbanks. Or the cooling of lava (Gary says we'll see big hexagonal columns of lava down near Lava Falls in another eight days). That's creating order locally as the universe as a whole supposedly runs downhill to chaos.

Inferences about the long run give one a totally erroneous impression of the short run—and inferences about the whole universe give an erroneous impression about particular localities. The downhill flow of energy can build up order, quite without any help from intelligent beings. Indeed, this tendency towards order may well be what created life and then intelligent life. "Order through fluctuation" is the phrase that characterizes

Classical Laws of Thermodynamics, Simplified:
1. You cannot win.
2. You cannot break even.
3. You cannot get out of the game.
ANONYMOUS

Consequently: he who wants to have right without wrong,
Order without disorder,
Does not understand the principles
Of heaven and earth.
He does not know how
Things hang together.
CHUANG TZU, about 300 B.C.

a new school of thermodynamics; this ordering principle was clearly recognized only as recently as 1967, a century after the advent of classical thermodynamics.

There are other ordering principles too. In 1944 the physicist Erwin Schrödinger claimed, for the Law of Large Numbers, the distinction of being the "order from disorder principle," and we're still discovering the implications this "law" has for brain size. For certain things, bigger is really better. But which things?

MILE 84
Clear Creek

The canyon is narrower than we have ever seen before; the water is swifter; there are but few broken rocks in the channel; but the walls are set, on either side, with pinnacles and crags; and sharp, angular buttresses, bristling with wind- and wave-polished spires, extend far out into the river.

POWELL EXPEDITION REPORT,
1869

I AM HIGH UP the Inner Canyon walls, looking down on the river from an overlook sparsely decorated by a few hardy plants that have gained a foothold in cracks in the rock. All the rock around here is foliated—sharp, spiky schist and Zoroaster granite, leaf upon leaf of it sticking up almost vertically, and so hard that little erosion is evident. Certainly nothing has blunted the sharp edges. Having found one small place where I can sit without a knife-edge beneath me, I have let the other hikers continue up this unusual side canyon without me. The rain clouds have drifted away and the sun has already dried my clothes. I yawn and rub my eyes, wishing for coffee.

Some leftover notes to take from last night's marathon discussion, which lasted until the middle of the night up at the hilltop ruin, while the lights were out. The Great Totality Discussion: just how did life get started? From a mere dust cloud? As Abby said, surely that is highly improbable.

True. Looking backwards, any particular outcome is always highly improbable. Nonetheless, the percentages are sobering. For example, the earth happens to be in just the right orbit around the sun. If we were always 6 percent closer, our atmosphere would have become dense clouds of carbon dioxide. And we would have had a runaway Greenhouse Effect like the one on Venus—which traps heat, raising the temperature to 900°C. at the surface. The same effect plagues cars here in the Southwest: the visible light gets in and heats things up to produce infrared radiation instead. The infrared photons, having a longer wavelength than light, can't get out through the glass as well as those shorter wavelengths got in. And so things inside get hotter and hotter if the air cannot mix with that outside.

However, if we were always 1 percent farther away from the sun, the oceans would have frozen solid about when this spiky schist was formed, nearly 1,700 million years ago, two-thirds of the time between the dust cloud that gave rise to the earth and now. That 1 percent is calling it uncomfortably close, especially when there is already a 3 percent annual variation in our distance from the sun as we travel around our elliptical orbit.

And by happy coincidence, the earth is also the right size. What determined the size? Part of the dust cloud formed an eddy and coalesced at just the right distance from the sun, becoming a "planet" with a lightweight crust floating atop a dense core. Had the earth been smaller like the moon, any atmosphere would have escaped from its lighter gravity. And the heat trapped in the core would have dissipated into space rather than generating volcanos. And so the gases trapped inside the earth would not have vented as they happily did, escaping just far enough to help build up a trapped atmosphere, for the expelled water vapor to have condensed into rainfall. And oceans. Life would have had a rough time of it without water and methane.

For hundreds of millions of years the earth was a hot, inhospitable place as volcanism poured out noxious fumes and vapors at an enormous rate. There were no oceans, a scant atmosphere, and a surface barren, pitted, and scarred by fissures and fiery eruptions from within. . . . But vast amounts of water bound in the rocks as hydrates were being liberated into the atmosphere and remained there as the surface was hot. After a very long time, with the air saturated and the surface of the earth cooling, a new phenomenon took place.

It rained.

It rained, and the rain evaporated, and it rained some more. It poured down on the bare rocky surface and ate the rock and collected in great flat basins. . . . The acid rain dissolved the rock . . . and where the water evaporated the salts formed broad, flat salt plains.

WILLIAM DAY, *Genesis on Planet Earth*, 1984

Methane? Don't you mean oxygen? No, methane. This simple but smelly molecule, just a carbon atom surrounded by four hydrogens, was essential to the formation of the carbon compounds that all life utilizes to build structures and store energy trapped from the sunlight. And methane, ammonia, and other simple molecules are even found in interstellar space. Molecules of oxygen came much later, mostly given off as a byproduct of light-induced photosynthesis—which is getting ahead of the story.

Not only were there lots of volcanos on the early earth, but there was also lots of lightning. The early earth had severe weather. So the oceans were stirred by storms, tickled by lightning, and had hot lava dripping into them. This is not unlike what one can see fairly often these days on the south coast of the island of Hawaii, as Kilauea spouts a 160-story-high fountain of bright orange lava. The lava spreads in underground tubes to reappear at the coastline, dripping orange into the ocean waves as they crash into the lava cliffs of the shoreline. Except for the present-day oxygen atmosphere and the tourists, it is all rather like a scene 3,700 million years ago.

It was a stark, barren earth over which the sun rose quickly each morning, searing in a black sky in a blaze of intense ultraviolet radiation. The accretion of the unmelted mass of dust, aggregates, and stones which formed the planet had left it looking much like the dry, barren face of the moon. And as the sun followed its diurnal course, it rushed across the sky in a few hours to descend below the horizon just as quickly. For on this airless, waterless, hadean world, the day was only five hours long. Nightfall brought the rise of the moon, an awesome globe so close as to appear to touch the earth's surface as it loomed over the horizon, brightening the austere landscape with its huge glowing face.

WILLIAM DAY, *Genesis on Planet Earth*, 1984

Back in the fifties, California graduate student Stanley L. Miller tried a simple chemistry lab experiment, stimulated by the 1936 ideas of the Russian biochemist A. I. Oparin. Miller took some methane, ammonia, hydrogen, and water. He boiled them, hopefully to simulate conditions on the early earth. Nothing much happened. Then Miller added lightning, in the form of a 60,000-Volt spark between two wires. And in the residue which formed at the bottom of the chamber after a few days, he discovered that an amazing variety of more complex molecules had been formed or, as they say in the biochemistry business, synthesized. Actually, as later investigators found, ultraviolet light will do as well as lightning—and the early earth had even more of that, since there was then little atmosphere to screen out the ultraviolet in the sunshine. Lots of heat—which volcanic lava could have easily provided—will also cause the synthesis.

Among the most important building blocks of life are the amino acids, twenty simple organic molecules which are essential for present-day life. And the ones most easily created in these early earth experiments were exactly those most abundant in life forms today.

If one gently heats a mixture of those individual amino acids, proteins are formed—long chains whose links are the little amino acid building blocks. These chains fold here and there, like the tire chains in my car trunk. Cross-links also form, tying together adjacent loops of amino-acid chain to make a pretzel out of it (I have often suspected that my tire chains form new cross-links too, as I try to unravel them with cold fingers). Proteins, all folded up pretzel-fashion, have some amazing tendencies to speed up chemical assembly lines. They act as catalysts, providing lots of little nooks and crannies in which simple molecules can be temporarily trapped. And, if such neighboring "prisoners" can stick to each other with a chemical bond, they'll go into solution stuck together when they are eventually freed from the confines of the protein. Imagine a figure-of-eight pretzel, a small one, laying on a table. You could seat two jelly beans inside the pretzel. And if you wanted to cement two jelly beans together, you'd want a jig—something like that pretzel, to hold them for awhile until the cement dried. After popping out the linked jelly beans, the pretzel could then serve as a jig again (catalysts aren't used up). Catalysts like proteins not only make chance meetings far more likely than if the constituent molecules were just wandering around in solution, ricocheting off one another, but they also hold those molecules close together long enough for a chemical bond to form between them.

So a protein can be a matchmaker, helping the "loving couple" to get together in a "loveseat" when chance meetings would be rare. As a result, unlikely couplings become the norm, and formerly rare combinations become commonplace. Different proteins catalyze different chemical reactions because they have different nooks and crannies (some metals, such as platinum, are also good catalysts because of their surface structure).

And the rate at which a reaction happens, the speed of the production line, is controlled by these protein catalysts (usually just called enzymes; those chemical names ending in the suffix "-ase" are usually enzymes). When two production lines run at different rates because of different amounts of enzyme, amazing things can happen. Timing is everything. A plant curves toward the sunlight because the cells grow faster on one side of the branch than the other. Embryos form arms and legs in the same way—just let two connected groups of cells grow at different rates and they'll form a curved surface. That's how gastrulation occurs: because neighboring cells grow at different rates, a spherical sheet of cells invaginates to form a pouch—used as a stomach—that is evolutionarily an important step towards our particular phylum of animals. Faster and slower growth rates are also how the convolutions of the human brain form.

Protein-type enzymes control growth rates, and relative growth rates control form, and form controls function (except on those occasions, also important, when form follows function). It's hard to overemphasize the importance of relative rates, when it comes to living systems.

But that gets ahead of the story again. Stability is the other key concept in this nooks-and-crannies tale. It's the stable which survives fluctuations. It's the stable configurations in the right place that go on to do more interesting things, such as progressing from chance proteins to faithfully replicating proteins, and progressing from that to life itself.

□   □   □

At the time when Yahweh God made heaven and earth there was as yet no wild bush on the earth nor had any wild plant yet sprung up, for Yahweh God had not sent rain on the earth, nor was there any man to till the soil. However a flood was rising from the earth and watering all the surface of the soil. Yahweh God fashioned man of dust from the soil.

Genesis 2:5

Very old are the rocks.
The pattern of life is not in their veins.
When the earth cooled the great rains
came and the seas were filled.
Slowly the molecules enmeshed in
ordered asymmetry.
A billion years passed, aeons of
trial and error.
The life message took form, a spiral,
a helix, repeating itself endlessly,
Swathed in protein, nurtured by
enzymes, sheltered in membranes,
laved by salt water, armored with
lime.
Shells glisten by the ocean marge,
Surf boils, sea mews cry, and the great wind
soughs in the cypress.

Thomas H. Jukes, *Molecules and Evolution*, 1966

□   □   □

WE ARE HAVING lunch here at the riverside, in a space so small that many people have perched up on the rocks with their sandwich, almost overhanging those of us with a spot on the sand. Gargoyles with sandwiches, yet. The returning hikers are exhilarated; they found a waterfall that shoots horizontally out of the rocks and arches out over the bathers in the creek below. Much farther up the canyon is said to be Cheyava ("intermittent") Falls, which comes out of a cave in the top of the Redwall and cascades down into Clear Creek Canyon, the tallest waterfall in the Grand Canyon. You'd never think that a side canyon began just downriver of us, as this sand beach is only big enough to precariously house a few sleeping bags—at "low tide." Such is the change made by hard rock. From having breakfast amidst the softest rock in the Canyon, we are having lunch amidst the hardest.

We are in the part of the Canyon that reveals the oldest layers of all. Some are as much as 2,000 million years old, the earth itself being about 4,600 million years old. There were bacteria 2,000 million years ago, but not much more (yes, there were blue-green "algae," but they're now classed with the bacteria, the lumpers being triumphant).

The steep slabs of schist and Zoroaster granite that flank our little beach wouldn't show any fossils anyway, having been laid down more than 1,000 million years before things started leaving fossils. Furthermore, the schist has been melted and re-formed too many times in the depths of the earth, which is why it is called a metamorphic rock. But there are original rocks 3,500 million years old remaining in Australia which show small fossils, looking very much like the fossil stromatolites that we saw yesterday at Carbon Creek. And so it is suspected that life itself got started sometime in the first 1,000 million years of the earth's history.

Even simple cells like blue-green "algae" have much more complex properties than those proteins. They have a way of trapping sunlight and using its energy to create ever more complex chemical compounds that store the energy; they use the energy to build another alga, to reproduce their kind.

But how does one trap sunlight, put it to work? One of the other theories that Albert Einstein published in 1905—the same year that he tossed off $E = mc^2$, the special theory of relativity, and his statistical explanation of the Brownian Motion—was a model for the photoelectric effect. When metal surfaces were illuminated, electrons were kicked loose from the metal and went zooming off, generating an electric current (as in solar arrays for electrical power generation these days). Blue light was better at causing this than red light; often red wouldn't work at all, no matter how intense, but a dim blue light would generate an electrical current.

Einstein was able to explain or predict all of the puzzling aspects of this photoelectric effect by postulating that light was packaged into photons, little bundles of energy whose content was inversely proportional to the light's wavelength. This (and Planck's use of quantized energy five years earlier in explaining "black body" heat distribution) was the foundation for what became known as quantum mechanics. Einstein received the Nobel Prize for his explanation of the photoelectric effect, as relativity was still in dispute in 1922. Essentially, the photon of light collided with an electron in the metal and gave it a good kick. This kick, however, caused the kicker to disappear; the vanished photon's energy was simply added to the kinetic energy of the electron.

Fortunately, that doesn't happen to the kicker in football—but the same thing happens in molecules, especially the ones

In each of the 1905 papers, Einstein has totally transcended the Machian view that scientific theory is simply the "economical description of the observed facts." None of these theories, strictly speaking, begins with "observed facts." Rather, the theory tells us what we should expect to observe.

JEREMY BERNSTEIN, 1982

called pigments (the best-known pigment is chlorophyll). The electron kicked by the photon rattles around for awhile, permitting other chemical reactions to occur. This energy, deriving from the sun 8.5 minutes earlier, when two heavy hydrogens fused together to form a nucleus of helium and packaged their spare binding energy into a photon, is used to build up a storehouse of energy inside the cell. This stored biological energy is available for doing various jobs, rather as our dams store rainwater that can later be dropped into generator turbines to spin them around and generate electricity (cells generate electricity too, in a somewhat more subtle manner).

So simple cells like bacteria take in sunlight and use it to rearrange the atoms inside six molecules of carbon dioxide (CO_2) and twelve molecules of water (H_2O). They split the oxygen off the water molecules and it becomes six molecules of good old O_2, better known as molecular oxygen. However, oxygen is a waste product of photosynthesis. The cell really wants the other product of the reaction, which is a simple sugar, stored energy that will be later used to construct things. Glucose, $C_6H_{12}O_6$, is what I eventually get from the many cups of lemonade I've been consuming; it is "quick energy," and just about the only fuel on which the brain will run (glucose, not lemonade!). I drink two cups more.

Brains get rather ahead of the story. What's so important about this simple reaction is the oxygen that is discarded. It eventually gets trapped as a gas in the atmosphere. There wasn't much of an atmosphere in the beginning; life had to build it up. Even today, this simple photosynthesis process in the microscopic plants that float in the oceans (collectively called phytoplankton) contributes 90 percent of the oxygen we breathe. That's one reason why we worry about the health of the oceans.

But other chemical reactions gobble up oxygen. Iron rusts into Redwall-colored iron oxide. Silicon liked oxygen too, producing our sand beach. And back near the beginning, there was a lot of exposed iron on the earth's surface and dissolved in the oceans. For perhaps 2,000 million years, not much oxygen remained in the air, so ravenous was the appetite of the iron and silicon. But eventually, rusting was satiated so that oxygen began to build up in the atmosphere, reaching the 20 percent level that it has today. This helped shelter the earth's surface from the ultraviolet radiation in the sunlight (a molecule containing three atoms of oxygen, called ozone, O_3, is especially effective at absorbing UV). This shielding made it possible for life to eventually leave the sea and take up residence on land. Some UV still gets through, of course, which is why everyone has been rubbing on sunscreen lotions today.

The oxygen leveled off at 20 percent because photosynthetic production was then in balance with continuing rusting—and with oxygen consumption by animals. It is estimated that if photosynthesis stopped making oxygen, we'd run through the 20 percent reservoir in the earth's atmosphere in only 2,000 years. That is not the best imaginable safety margin.

It reminds me of those botany bumper-stickers which read, "Have You Thanked a Green Plant Today?" Especially the phytoplankton drifting the oceans, which produce most of what we breathe.

MARSHA, the blossoming teenager who was one of the moonwatchers last night, just teased a boatman about when we were going to have prebiotic soup for dinner. A truly organic soup that would be—hopefully not stirred by lightning, not while I'm around. With a straight face, he replied: "At dinner, with the clams linguine."

However, the boatmens' stock answer to all questions about dinner menus is always "Clams Linguine," spoken with a flash of the eyebrows. People took it seriously on the first day of our trip, until the steaks were served. On the second day, inquiries also elicited "Clams Linguine"—but no clams, no linguine. Clams linguine has been picked up like a buzzword. Asked the name of a strange bird, a passenger who doesn't know the name is now likely to reply knowingly: "Must be Clams Linguine."

"The prebiotic soup is sure a catch-all, isn't it?" remarked Rosalie. "Surely our genetic code—and that fancy chain of manufacturing processes that goes from DNA to RNA to protein chains—wasn't the start of life."

"Our clams linguine is a catch-all too," Alan volunteered. "Just wait until you see what we throw into the pot."

"Yes, but in our case the prebiotic soup is a catch-all for ignorance," I said. "It's everything that happened before our present-day genetic code evolved. Surely there were simpler versions of replication that competed with one another, some sort of progression in complexity, back before about 3,500 million years ago."

"The real problem," said Dan Hartline, "is how does self-replication start? Molecules that'll make more of their own kind?"

"Remember what happened to Ben's breakfast dish that first morning on the river," said Rosalie, laughing. "He forgot to wash it, left it setting out in the sun, and the pancake syrup dried up hard. When he went to wash it, he popped the hard syrup out, all in one piece. A perfect copy of the inside of the plastic dish!"

"I suppose that it's possible for a protein to serve as its own mold," I answered, "but I'll bet that the key to their evolution lay in RNA or DNA chains evolving alongside, and forming a series of molds for amino acid chains."

"That's what a protein is, just a chain of amino acid molecules?" asked Abby.

"Right. And genes are just chains of DNA base molecules. Except DNA chains don't fold up and form cross-links in quite the fancy ways that amino-acid chains do," I answered. "They like to spiral instead, like a corkscrew. The DNA chains are the master memory for the cell—they don't *do* anything except let themselves be copied, making a complementary RNA chain. Which then goes forth from the nucleus of the cell and serves as the instruction tape for the assembly of an amino-acid chain."

"There's a translation scheme—what's called the genetic code," Rosalie explained. "The first three molecules on the RNA chain determine which of the twenty types of amino acid will form the first link of the protein chain. And the next three RNAs determine the second amino acid type to be tacked onto the first one. As so the protein chain grows. That's fancy, which is why I don't think it was the first scheme tried out."

"Some simpler self-replication scheme probably got started using clay as a catalyst," I said. "Once the rains cause rivers, the particles get sorted by size. And you get clay. Clay is really nice as a matchmaker, its nooks and crannies will catalyze various simple carbon reactions."

"Somebody told me that every cell in my skin contains the information necessary to make my brain," Abby said. "Is that really true?"

"Probably," I answered. "The skin cells that I scraped off today on the knife-edged rocks around here had the complete instructions for how to make a copy of me. Or at least how I was at conception. The ants have probably already carried home those cells I left behind. I sure hope they don't have the requisite technology to translate the code and clone me."

"We'd have to award them the next Nobel Prize if they did," Rosalie joked.

MILE 87

THE WHAAP-WHAP-WHAP SOUND of a helicopter is heard, an unwelcome reminder of civilization's casual pollution of the environment. When seen, it is not the usual chopper from the touristy strip of scenic-flight establishments just outside the South Rim entrance to the park, but a builder's beast of burden: dangling from a cable is a truckload of construction materials. J.B. says that Phantom Ranch at Mile 88—literally just around the corner from us—has been "improved" by the Park Service to include flush toilets, hot and cold running water, and blow dryers as a service to the wilderness hiker. And a heliport as a service to the pilots. At least the bulldozer that used to sit beside the river has disappeared, perhaps helicoptered out, perhaps hidden nearby in case more improvements are desired. Mule power sufficed for earlier construction of the bridges, grumble, grumble.

We can hardly wait to see these millions of dollars in wilderness improvements. We have to stop there—in the old days, you sped by as fast as you could, some passengers keeping their eyes shut so as not to have such sights disrupt their wilderness experience—because of a new park service regulation that the float trips check in at the Phantom Ranch ranger station.

Since the 1983 overflow of Lake Powell, when the Park Service received hundreds of long-distance phone calls from worried relatives of river-runners, a new layer of bureaucracy has been added—you have to stop and give them a trip roster, get cleared for the next stage of your journey. You wouldn't, after all, want a park ranger to have to walk down and post a sign on the bridge to flag the boats down, would you? Next, hikers will likely be required to carry beepers so that they too can be summoned.

WE ARE IN LIMBO, pulled up on the sandy shore here where the Bright Angel fault line crosses the Colorado River. We are as close to civilization as we'll get on this trip, what with all the blatant construction and the two fancy footbridges spanning the river. They connect the trail descending from the North Rim with the two trails that ascend to the South Rim. But the outside world has intruded in a bigger way.

Signs of civilization first appeared on the right bank, an old brick tower with boarded-up openings—the old river-gauge station that estimated water flow in the Colorado. Then, after a left turn, came the first footbridge. And the uncamouflaged shiny new building complex. It used to be that buildings were hidden, five minutes up the trail, near the guest ranch built before Grand Canyon National Park was created.

A sand bar gave us some trouble as we approached the beach, and we finally walked the boat along it until finding a path to the beach proper. The other boats followed our example. One of the boatmen disappeared to check us in. And then returned, shouting to Howard that there was a message for him to phone the Park Service emergency operator.

Someone started to kid Howard about his patients tracking him down even here. He quietly said that he didn't have pa-

I want you to do one thing in connection with [the Grand Canyon] in your own interest and in the interest of the country . . . Leave it as it is. You cannot improve on it. The ages have been at work on it, and man can only mar it.
THEODORE ROOSEVELT, 1903

A man is rich in proportion to the number of things he can afford to let alone.
HENRY DAVID THOREAU

MILE 88
Phantom Ranch

tients, that he was a Ph.D. researcher. And everyone then realized that it could only be bad news—personal bad news.

One of the boatmen has gone up the trail with Howard to show him where the emergency phone is located. Most people are out on the shore, but with their lifejackets still on, waiting. We generally have our backs turned to the signs of the outside world, such as the footbridge. I think we're in shock, having gradually let down the workaday mask we all wear, gradually starting to relax and enjoy this unparalleled experience of being away from civilization, in increasing contact with the world of our ancestors, increasingly coming to grips with the great age of the earth and what a recent arrival humans are.

The boatman comes running back alone and holds a quick conference with the other boatmen. Then leaves again. Gradually word trickles along the beach that Howard's father has had a stroke. And that Howard plans to hike out of the Canyon, up the South Rim trail, this afternoon. Several other boatmen have taken off to try to find the mule skinner. Mule trains carry freight, and the idea is to get Howard's black bags hauled up on a mule. Someone else starts putting together some trail food. Dan digs into the bottom of one of his black bags and retrieves his car keys, so that Howard will have a car to drive down to Phoenix as soon as he makes it to Flag, where Dan's car is stored.

Howard arrives back, looking somewhat shaken. He goes with the boatmen to identify his black bags, and they take them off the boat. The boatmen appraise him of the arrangements they've made. And so he sits down to open his black bags, looking for heavier hiking shoes than the tennis shoes he is wearing. Then, river wear exchanged for hiking gear, the boatmen run off with the black bags, down the trail to where the mule train is waiting impatiently.

Howard tells us the Park Service emergency operator had somehow lost the exact message. But that he was able to dial out and get hold of his mother, who said that his father had a stroke four days earlier, just after we set out on the trip. Things seem somewhat stable now, Howard's father is in the hospital being treated for the pain, and will undergo diagnostic tests when he is feeling better. And Howard was able to get a good description of what happened. His father had gone to bed the previous night with a bad headache. But got up at dawn and walked downstairs and started to fix breakfast. He went out to pick up the newspaper, brought it back indoors, and spread it out on the table. Then he found that he couldn't read it.

He obviously wasn't blind. Indeed, he could see and name

individual letters, even some two-letter words like "is" and "do"—but he couldn't make any sense out of longer words, he could read a sentence only with many, many errors. He could speak correctly and had no problem with understanding the doctors. So it wasn't a paralytic stroke or one causing language difficulties in general (known as "aphasia")—it seemed only to affect his reading. He could even write, taking down dictation when the doctors would read a short paragraph to him. But, asked to read back what he had just correctly written down, he couldn't. Except letter-by-letter.

This relieved Howard considerably, since he knew that it meant his father had had a small stroke. And people with small strokes almost always get better. Rosalie, a neurologist, confirmed his judgment on this, saying that alexia (reading disturbance) alone was quite rare: that usually writing was affected too and that there was some aphasia. That, given his father's pain, it must have been a bleed—a ruptured blood vessel, releasing blood cells into the brain and irritating its dural covering, the dura being capable of signaling pain (brain tissue itself is not). But no one could agree on exactly what part of the brain was most responsible for reading. Apparently a number of places on the periphery of the known visual cortex can, if damaged, produce a reading disturbance.

Howard added one additional piece of information, that his father seemed to ignore objects on the right side of his visual world. It was odd, because he could see objects there—if that's all there was to see. But if there were some other object on the left side, competing for his attention, then he'd pay attention to the left-sided object and ignore the waving fingers on the right side. Aha, left hemisphere stroke, said Rosalie and several others simultaneously. That makes sense, alexia usually comes from left-sided strokes. The neglect of objects on the right side will disappear, Rosalie predicted—it was probably due to the brain swelling that occurs near the damaged area. In a week or so, that would probably decline and the selective-attention problem would fade away. But she wasn't equally confident about whether the reading problem would disappear.

So I expect Howard felt somewhat better, what with all the expert consultations in the bottom of the Grand Canyon. It's quite amazing, how much you can predict just from knowing the details of a stroke patient's symptoms. Every part of the brain generates different symptoms, and they serve as excellent clues. Except for the frontal lobe which, when damaged, may cause little detectable malfunction. Until the damage becomes extensive.

THE HEAT HAS BECOME OPPRESSIVE. Only mad dogs, mules and Englishmen go out in the midday sun (to amend Noel Coward). As soon as we're under way on the river, we'll cool down again. No one seems to know whether to commiserate with Howard over his long, hot, hike or just say nothing. The boatmen explain that they'll save Howard walking the first two miles of the trail by floating him downriver until the trail emerges from the ups and downs in the inner canyon rock and turns to start up the Bright Angel fault line toward the south rim. So we all pile back into the boats and set off into the Colorado again. And have our previous trouble getting across the sand bar.

Once out into the channel, we observed that the waters were very unpredictable around there, many rocks having been washed into the stream by flash floods of recent years along the northern side of the Bright Angel fault line. And so we had a splashy mile until the boats pulled over to the left bank, getting soaked several times despite the lack of real rapids. High up a talus slope, we could see the trail emerging from the schist. All of the broken rock here is because the Bright Angel Fault leaves the river at this point to create Garden Creek, which the trail will follow up to the South Rim.

Howard climbed out, handed Subie his lifejacket, tightened his climbing boots, and thanked the boatmen for arranging things so nicely. At Subie's suggestion, he soaked his clothes with cold river water, for a little evaporative cooling. He also dipped his big canvas hat into the river, filled it up, and lowered his head into it, then stood upright. The water began trickling around the hatband and dripping down onto his face. Subie was delighted, and noted that there was water along the way for refills—just not to drink out of the creek, since it was contaminated by all the people up above (the Park Service has permitted the South Rim to become a small city). Howard shouldered his day pack, loaded with canteens and trail food, and began hiking out of the Canyon, waving good-bye to us.

After we cast off, Subie commented that it was indeed going to be a hot hike. It was nearly 47°C. (117°F) in the shade at Phantom; with the river moving along at a runner's pace, we are reasonably comfortable. The trail is nine miles long, in the sunlight and still desert air of mid-afternoon. And the trail ascends one vertical mile (a good 1,500 meters), from about 1,900 feet to 6,900 feet. About like climbing a 425-story building. The air would, at least, cool down to room temperature by the time Howard reached the South Rim in mid-evening.

I'D SAY WE WERE still in shock, about how our splendid isolation had been brought up short, about how the real world out there can intrude and pluck someone out of our midst. But we got little opportunity to think about it. Despite the steady diet of big rapids before lunch and the continuous knocking about along several miles of the Bright Angel fault, we next got hit by Horn Creek Rapid (rated a 9) at Mile 90.

Now we are pulled over just upstream of Granite Rapid, having endured today all of seven rapids rated higher than 5. It's a good thing we didn't do this on a cold day. Or in more difficult river conditions—I think I've been battered around enough for one day. And Granite Rapid, from the roar of it just downstream, may tomorrow live up to its rating of 9.

Instead of getting domestic, as we're wont to do after making camp in the afternoon, many people just sit around with their lifejackets still on, soaking up sun and gradually shedding the river. People who would normally drink one beer consume two or three in silence. And then finally set out to look for a campsite. That's usually the first thing anyone does, competing for the best sleeping spots. Today is different. The silence is palpable, broken occasionally by someone talking too rapidly. It has been a tiring, upsetting day for some people.

BARBARA SPREAD OUT the tarp on the sandy shore. Then she picked up two potato-sized rocks from the collection deposited by the last flood. "Want to see how easy it is to make stone tools?" she asked. Her audience was hunching together under some willow trees, escaping the afternoon sun. "Sure," we said, expecting the anthropologist to sit down on the tarp and tap away delicately. Instead she put on her sunglasses—in the shade. What?

The two rocks were each the size of big, elongated potatoes. Her grip on each rock was simple: she held it by one half, so that the other half protruded unobscured by her fingers. But she didn't sit down. She stood facing the tarp, away from her audience. And began pounding furiously, hitting the two stones together at waist height, really hammering hard. Chips began flying away from her, a few dropping at her feet. After a minute of this furious performance and its shower of rock fragments, a big piece of rock fell and, lacking enough protruding rock to continue, she stopped.

The size of the audience had miraculously tripled. Nothing like a little action to attract attention. Trust the women to invent a distraction from the gloom.

Barbara took off the sunglasses—eye protection, evidently—and picked up some flakes, and passed them around. "See these sharp flakes? You hold onto them just like a razor blade. Not only can you butcher a rabbit with these, but you can get through the tough skin of an elephant or a rhino. Now even hyenas and vultures have a hard time doing that, at least until the big animal has been dead long enough for the skin to rot. You can cut open knee joints with these little flakes—that makes it easier to carry the meat away, a section at a time, off to a safer place to eat it. Gets you away from the other scavengers. And you can cut muscles loose from bone." She paused. "Anyone lost their knife? Steak knives, anyone?" she said to some stragglers just arriving.

Barbara retrieved the two original stones, or what was left of them. "And these big fragments, which are still large enough to fit comfortably in the palm of your hand—they're sharp too. You can use them for all the same purposes, but they're safer. You can cut your own skin while holding one of these little flakes with your fingertips. And ancient people didn't have band-aids, either. But the original rocks, minus the fragments, still have a nice smooth surface over the back half. A nice handle." She demonstrated the grip.

"And you can bring a lot more pressure to bear, more safely than with a flake. If you spent ten minutes pounding a number of rocks, you'd have dozens of big fragments to choose from. You'd probably find one that had a comfortable grip. Maybe with an indentation in just the right place for your thumb, so you could pull really hard. Maybe cut through roots when you're out gathering. But I'll bet that they used sticks to dig out the goodies—and that they carried along a sharp piece of rock flake to resharpen the stick with. That's what the women of primitive tribes do today when they're out gathering."

So when did prehumans start making tools this way, we asked.

"Well, hominids were walking upright more than 4 million years ago—and looking fairly human too. I mean, if you saw Lucy and family over on the opposite riverbank waving at you, you'd immediately classify them as human—even though they went out of style nearly 3 million years ago. What else stands upright and waves? It's only if you looked carefully, especially if you saw one from the rear and noticed that small skull behind the face, that you'd start to wonder." Barbara paused. "But they do *not* find simple rock tools with the early Australopithecines. Only starting at about 2.4 million years ago do you find flaked stones like these."

Scientists are prone to probe for holes in an explanation, even in the afternoon heat. Dan Hartline started in: "I'll bet that I could find flaked stones just like those if I looked carefully around any of the waterfalls. All it should take to make fragments and little flakes is for one stone to be dropped from a great height. It's the kinetic energy of the rocks when you strike them together that breaks open fracture planes." Dan, like many other neurobiologists, started out in physics (well, to be more precise, he and his brothers started out collecting horseshoe crabs from Chesapeake Bay for their father's biology research lab).

Barbara smiled. "Right you are. There's even a geologist up in Utah who found a batch of rocks looking like stone tools. Except the sediments in which they were buried dated back to when the biggest primate around was a tree shrew. Turns out that nodules of chert were eroding out of a high cliff, falling and fracturing. You're also right that it's mostly brute force that makes these fragments—it doesn't take much skill to pound hard like that, just enough to avoid smashing your own fingers." She examined the side of her thumb. "The main problem with the method is blisters, if you're not in practice."

"So what makes you so sure that rock fragments were made by hominids?"

Barbara nodded, then turned and pointed to the tarp, littered with stone flakes. "See that pattern? A big fan of flakes, plus a little pile where I was standing? Like a fat exclamation mark? When his group excavated a big area, that's the pattern Glynn Isaac found in Kenya, time and again. And there were no cliffs around, not for a long, long ways. They were even able to reconstruct some of the original stones from the fragments. Just think—with random banging around, you too can create an archaeological site in only one minute!"

"But," interjected Ben, "just how often do they find flakes?"

"Some places like Olduvai Gorge in Tanzania," reflected Barbara, "are just littered with stone flakes. I mean, you literally cannot take a step in some places at Olduvai without stepping on a hominid stone tool. That's why Louis Leakey started digging there—with all those stone tools, he just knew there would be hominid bones if he looked long enough. But it took from 1935 until 1959—that's when Mary Leakey found the Zinjanthropus skull and teeth. Olduvai goes back to 2 million years ago before the sedimentary layers run out and you hit rock bottom, but Koobi Fora and Laetoli go back earlier—and have stone tools as early as 2.4 million years."

I smiled, recalling when I'd met Louis Leakey not too long after that first East African hominid find. He wasn't famous yet, having just come to North America to tour anthropology departments. A physics undergraduate, I'd talked myself earlier that year into a graduate anthropology seminar, never having had an introductory anthro course. Late in the term, my professor, Melville Herskovits, smiled his dapper smile and, with that characteristic twinkle in his eyes, announced that he had a treat for us: Louis Leakey and the casts of the Zinj skull and teeth.

Louis Leakey was a real presence—comparable, in my experience at the time, only to Harry Truman (around whom I had worked for a week a few years earlier, when I was a fetch-and-carry photographer's assistant at *Life* magazine and he had just finished his Presidential memoirs). I don't know which was the more impressive, the large and muscular Louis Leakey or the massive Zinj skull with the peaked sagittal crest like a gorilla's. Louis was pleased as punch, cradling that skull in his large hands, replying to the excited questions which indicated that everyone in the room realized that a new era had just begun in paleoanthropology. What I didn't realize then was the 24 years he'd spent, on and off, in Olduvai Gorge paying his dues. And 1959 was the same year he persuaded Jane Goodall to study chimpanzees at Gombe. A good year.

"I wonder if pounding rocks got started from hammering open hard nuts?" asked Jackie. "That's what chimps do. They take a rock, place the nut on a hard surface, and pound away quite skillfully. And the female chimps are the experts—they tackle nuts so hard that they sometimes break open the rocks instead. Sure looks to me like a perfect setup for accidentally producing rock flakes and then discovering what they're good for. But that's precision hammering, not the brute-force hammering you just used."

Marsha perked up. "You mean that women might have invented tools, rather than the men?"

"At least the female chimps," Barbara replied. "They're certainly the most frequent tool-users, and the most skillful. All of the chimps—male and female—try their hand at making sticks for termite-fishing. They strip the leaves off the stick, thus violating Ben Franklin's definition of man as the toolmaking animal. Then the chimps push the prepared stick into a termite nest. The termite defenders attack the stick, grabbing on. And the chimp slowly withdraws the stick and licks off the termites, rather like the Darwin's finch. The female chimps spend many more hours at this task than the males. However, it is in hammering that the big differences between females and males show up: more than 92 percent of difficult nut-cracking is done by females, even though males engage in the simpler tasks. And she doesn't hit her own fingers, either."

"And so, once you take up eating nuts, you develop the skills to make lots of tools too," Ben ventured. "That could have been what started the technology roller-coaster."

Barbara began gathering up the flakes from the tarp, throwing them far out into the river to avoid having anyone step on them. "You know," she said, "once this crude rock-hammering was invented, a basic tool kit was developed by about 1.5 million years ago. But there weren't many improvements in it for the next million years—maybe the tool-users' behavior altered, but the tools that have been recovered didn't undergo any fundamental change until about 300,000 years ago. More than a million years with little change. Progress was very slow. Think about that." She shook the sand off the tarp.

Silence. "Okay, so why?"

"So whatever did they need fancier tools for? Glynn Isaac used to say that the question isn't why nothing changed for so long, but rather why it changed when it did. Maybe they tried to live in colder climates and needed sewing needles to fasten up animal hides. No one knows yet."

AFTER DINNER, Rosalie sat down on the rock ledge next to Marsha, who was busy rubbing something against a flat stone. I was sitting nearby and eavesdropped. "Indian arts and crafts?" asked Rosalie.

Marsha looked up with an engaging grin. "This is the way the Anasazi women made necklaces for themselves." She brushed her blond curls back and then held up a small bead for Rosalie to see. "These are juniper nuts."

"So how are you going to make a hole through them for stringing?"

"That's what's so nice about these nuts. If you grind off both ends, the middle core drops out. You just blow out the dust. See? Perfect hole." Marsha fished a handful of finished beads from her jacket pocket and displayed them on the rock's flat surface. "Then you roll them around to make them round."

Rosalie admired them. "Where did you find juniper nuts around here?"

"Brought them with me," laughed Marsha. "That is to say, I forgot that they were in my jacket pocket. I picked them up last week, on the ground outside the archaeological museum at Mesa Verde. After seeing that exhibit there on the Anasazi and their life styles. They had real necklaces on display, beautiful things."

"Did the Anasazi women color the beads?" asked Rosalie.

"Well, I remember that they got some of them to turn black. All they had to do was wear them awhile and their sweat would stain the nuts black. I thought that I'd wear a necklace for a few days and see how it works."

"So were there any other colors in the Anasazi necklaces?"

"I don't remember. I suppose not, for everyday necklaces, because the sweat would just turn them black sooner or later. But maybe I could get some of the Redwall color, that stuff that

The most powerful drive in the ascent of man is his pleasure in his own skill. He loves to do what he does well and, having done it well, he loves to do it better.

The polymath
JACOB BRONOWSKI, 1973

washes down from the Supai layer, to stick awhile. Maybe I'll try that."

"Did the museum exhibit say anything about the Anasazi using the beads on strings for counting things?" asked Rosalie.

"You mean like an abacus?" answered Marsha. "Sliding the beads back and forth to count? I don't remember that."

"No, not in that manner. What I'm thinking of is the Aztec scheme of keeping tax records and the like on knotted strings. You know, where the number of knots and their spacing records how many bushels you've paid. They could have done the same thing with beads on a necklace. I was just curious whether the Anasazi had any such schemes." Rosalie tossed a stone into the river.

"Gee, I don't think there was anything in the museum about that," said Marsha. "That's a neat idea. You know, they could wear a necklace whose beads spelled out 'This necklace cost a thousand dollars' rather than wearing diamonds!"

Rosalie laughed. "That might take a lot of beads, a sentence that long."

"It's just a couple of dozen letters."

"But how many different colors of beads would you need?" Rosalie asked.

Marsha thought for a few seconds. "I suppose that twenty-six different colors of bead, one for each letter of the alphabet, is a bit much. How about Morse Code? I could use long and short beads."

"I'll bet a necklace that long would reach your waist," Rosalie estimated. "How about a code with maybe four letters in its alphabet? Four different colors of beads."

"You mean like DNA, the genetic code? It spells everything out with just four different types of letter—you know, the RNA bases G, C, A, and U." Marsha held the nut that she was rubbing up to the sky, then blew the dust out of the center hole and looked again. "There aren't too many words that I can spell with just those letters."

"You just have to use a two- or three-letter sequence from that four-letter alphabet to stand for each English letter," replied Rosalie. "Like GCA stands for B, GCG for E, and so on. Remember how the genetic code works?"

"I remember. It uses groups of letters too."

"How many letters in the amino-acid alphabet?"

"Oh, you mean like twenty-six letters in English?" Marsha stared at the beginning of sunset downriver. "Isn't it twenty? The DNA is telling the cell what proteins to make, and there are twenty different amino acids that serve as the building blocks of the protein, strung out in a chain. Isn't that right?"

"You've got a good memory. So how many letters of DNA does it take—you know, to tell the cell which one of those twenty amino acids to tack onto the end of the protein chain under construction?" asked Rosalie, with a raised eyebrow and a grin.

"I think it's three," said Marsha. "Three consecutive bases tell the protein assembly line which one of the twenty amino-acid possibilities comes next."

"Could you get by with only two DNA bases?"

Marsha looked puzzled.

"Well," continued Rosalie, "how many possible ways are there, of arranging two beads on the string there, if each one can be of four different colors?"

"I see. Well, the first bead can be one of any four colors. If the first one is black, the second one can be any of four colors. So that's four possible pairs. If the first one is white, the second one can be. . . . I guess that's four plus four plus four plus four. Sixteen. Sixteen different pairs."

"Right you are," Rosalie answered. "So with a pair of DNA bases, you could specify only sixteen different types of amino acids."

"But that's not enough, so you have to use triplets so that you can count to at least twenty! Oops!" Marsha exclaimed, having spilled the beads from her lap onto the sand. Both she and Rosalie bent down to gather them up. I tossed over several that had landed on my foot.

"I wish that these nuts came in four different colors, instead of just dirty and clean," Marsha mused. "Then I could make a necklace that told how to construct a real protein."

"Well, this one could be U, for unfinished," Rosalie laughed, holding up a nut with only the ends ground off but without its nut shape rounded into a bead yet. Marsha had smoothed most of the other nuts by rolling them around between two flat rock faces.

"And this polished bead is sort of auburn," observed Marsha. "We've got an A!"

"G for green? Oops, no green nuts here. What else is there?"

"Well, as soon as the sweat goes to work on these, they ought to get pretty dark," Marsha noted, then fished around in her pockets again. "Here's the color that I got by rolling it around in my hot, sweaty hand. On the bus up from Flag."

Rosalie looked at the bead in the soft evening light. "Not really black, Good thing, too. We don't need a B. What colors start with G, or with C?"

"How about chocolate?" Marsha exclaimed.

"Okay. The sweaty ones are C, chocolate stands for cytosine."

Marsha counted. "Now we've got U for unfinished, A for auburn, C for chocolate. Back to G. Of course, the other problem is that I only see three different kinds of beads in this collection here." She brightened. "We could always paint some. Got any green nail-polish?"

"Sounds ghastly."

"I suppose that no one else has any, either. Maybe gray? I could rub them against the gray stones! I remember now, that's what happened at Mesa Verde when I was rubbing the nuts against the rocks there!"

Rosalie clapped her hands with delight. "G is for gray. Good old guanine." They looked around for a gray rock. "You know, I think that it's getting a little dark out here. And everyone seems to have finished brushing their teeth by the river."

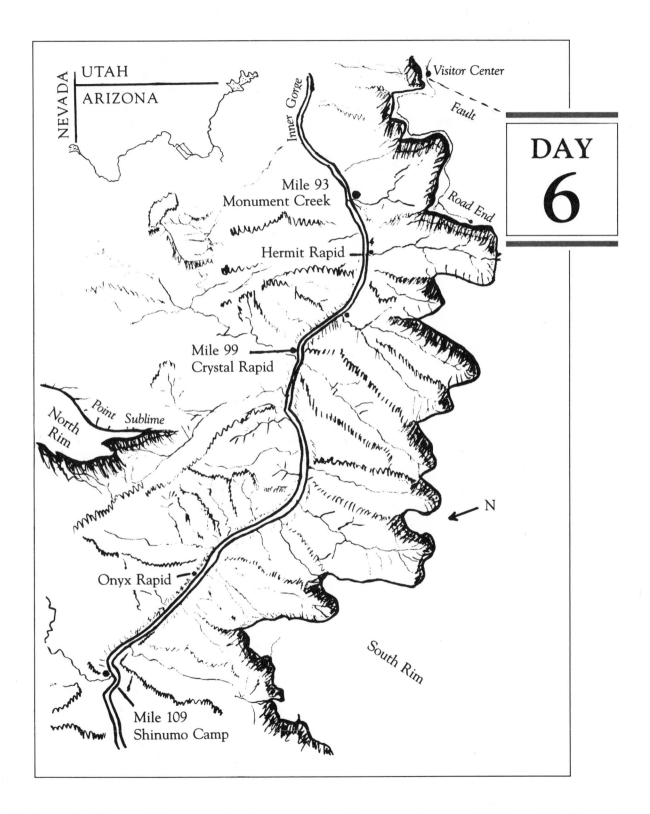

NEVADA

UTAH

ARIZONA

Inner Gorge

Visitor Center

Fault

DAY
6

Road End

Mile 93
Monument Creek

Hermit Rapid

Mile 99
Crystal Rapid

North
Rim

Point Sublime

N

Onyx Rapid

South Rim

Mile 109
Shinumo Camp

MILE 93

Monument Creek

[The late Arthur Koestler] radiated a rare passion for life, a deep merriment in the face of the unknown. He seemed to exemplify Nietzsche's insight that there is in men and women a motivation stronger even than love or hatred or fear. It is that of *being interested*—in a body of knowledge, in a problem, in a hobby, in tomorrow's newspaper. Koestler was supremely interested.
                The literary critic
                GEORGE STEINER

Happiness goes like the wind, but what is interesting stays.
        The artist GEORGIA O'KEEFFE

MONUMENT CAMP LOOKS DIFFERENT by morning light. We're still deep in the inner canyon, surrounded by schists veined with granite. Marsha came over as Rosalie and I were standing by the water's edge, sipping coffee. She held out her hand to Rosalie.

"See? All four colors. The gray worked, I used some wet stones that I found by the river this morning. And the chocolate ones are getting darker and darker."

"Been sleeping on them all night?" Rosalie smiled, then finished off the last of her coffee. She clipped the Sierra cup back onto her belt loop and picked up the beads to examine them.

"Do you have a sewing kit?" asked Marsha. "I need some heavy thread to string them on."

"No sewing kit, but I'll bet there is some heavy suture thread in my medicine bag," Rosalie said. "Let's go look."

"Are you a real doctor?" asked Marsha as Rosalie rummaged through a compact metal box holding an assortment of medical supplies. "I mean, not a professor like the others?"

"Both, I teach neurology. And I have even been known to sew up a wound—ah, here's that heavy thread."

"Gee. That's thick," Marsha replied. "Just right for the necklace. You really sew up wounds with thread this thick?"

"Not usually. The last time I used any of that thread was when my suitcase was slashed open at the airport, by one of their mechanical baggage-handlers. So I sewed up the hole in the leather with the proper interrupted stitches that I learned during my training in the emergency room. I kept hoping that the leather would heal so that I could take out the stitches!"

Rosalie draped the thread around Marsha's neck. "Is this long enough for you?" Marsha opted for a longer length, and then they sat down to string the beads.

"Well, what protein can I create with these beads?" asked Marsha, laying them out on a flat rock.

"How about a nice short chain, maybe a string of five amino acids making a little peptide hormone?" answered Rosalie. "Do you know about enkephalin?"

"No. What does it do?"

"Reduces pain. It's one of those drugs that the brain manufactures for itself. Acts rather like morphine."

Rosalie thought for a few seconds, glancing out across the river at the sunlit wall of the Canyon. She turned and asked me, "How does that sequence of amino acids go? I seem to remember it as tyrosine, glycine, another glycine, phenylalanine, and finally leucine." I nodded and said that sounded familiar.

"That makes morphine?" Marsha asked me.

"No, but enkephalin is sometimes called the brain's own

morphine," I replied. "Morphine might look just enough like enkephalin to impersonate it under some circumstances."

"That's neat. A real pain-killing necklace. So what beads do we use?"

"Well, first we have to specify tyrosine," said Rosalie. "The genetic code for that is—well, there are two that mean tyrosine. Let's use UAU. So we need an unfinished one, an amber, and then another unfinished."

Marsha tied a knot in one end of the thread and started stringing the beads in the proper order. "There's the instruction for tyrosine."

"Next comes glycine. You can specify that with GGG, so three gray beads are needed in the RNA string to fasten a glycine molecule onto the chain." Rosalie sorted through the juniper nuts.

"Three gray beads, coming up," Rosalie said, passing them to Marsha.

"Great," Marsha said, "Just like what goes on in the cell nucleus."

"Not quite," Rosalie corrected. "The amino acid chain that is going to become the protein actually gets constructed outside the nucleus. The messenger RNA is a copy of the master set of instructions kept in the DNA within the nucleus. This RNA copy goes out into the cytoplasm. There, just like a tape being fed into a mechanical loom, it starts up the assembly of the amino-acid chain."

"Oh, I remember!" exclaimed Marsha. "We saw that funny film in class of the dancers acting out protein synthesis. The RNA triplets—wearing balloons—selecting the proper amino acid and then adding it to the growing protein string. Snake dancers!"

"I remember that film," laughed Rosalie. "With all the narration in the style of Lewis Carroll's 'Jabberwocky'. What was it that the Bandersnatch did in the dance?"

I said that I thought the Bandersnatch danced the part of the enzyme that cut loose the new protein from the ribosome, when the stop code came along. It's something like the worker in the automobile plant who unhooks the car from the assembly line after it is finished.

"That's right! I remember!" Marsha was inspired to get up and imitate the Bandersnatch's dance, and eventually came swooping down on the necklace held by Rosalie, going "Snicker-snack, snicker-snack." We all collapsed laughing at the memory of the outrageously costumed dancers, gyring and gimballing in the wabe of RNA.

"So what's next?" Rosalie asked herself, rubbing her eyes.

"Next is another glycine. Three more G's, so three more gray beads."

Marsha slid three more gray beads onto the string. Which was indeed beginning to look like a proper necklace. "Then phenylalanine, which is UUU. So here are three unfinished beads. And the last amino acid is leucine. Let's see, there are several different triplets that specify leucine. Let's use CUU. A chocolate, an unfinished, then another unfinished. There you have it. The instructions for making the brain's own morphine!"

Marsha held it up around her neck. "Do you suppose anyone'll guess what it is? I mean, they won't know that the unfinished ones mean U, the auburn ones mean A, and so on."

Rosalie pondered this, contemplating the necklace with a raised eyebrow. "I suppose that we could drop some hints. But that would be cheating." Rosalie kicked the rock at her foot, shaking the sand off her shoe. "I know! We can add the start and stop codons."

"You mean, those special three letter groups that mark the beginning and end of the code string for a protein?"

"That's right," Rosalie said. "But beware the frumious Bandersnatch, my child! So we'll start the necklace with AUG, the start code. Then we'll have the fifteen beads coding for the five amino acids, then three more beads for the stop code. UAA is the stop triplet that I remember. That'll be a good hint. They'll see two auburn beads on the right end and another auburn one starting the string on the left side. Then maybe the unfinished ones will suggest U to them." Rosalie was looking pleased with herself. For Marsha, this was taking on the aspects of adventure, a secret mystery in the making.

Marsha was delighted as she strung an unfinished bead and two auburn ones onto the end. Then she undid the knot at the other end of the string and slid on an auburn-unfinished-gray sequence. "There are only twenty-one beads, total. That's really all it takes to tell the brain how to make morphine?"

"Well, if they were really the RNA bases, that's all it would take to tell a brain cell how to construct leucine enkephalin," answered Rosalie. "Simple, isn't it? There are even laboratory machines that can mimic the cell in constructing the chain. I mean, if you were to show that necklace to the people in the lab down the corridor from my office, they might be able to construct synthetic enkephalin from it. That's the code for it. And it was probably invented in evolution before these rocks were made," Rosalie gestured at the Redwall across the way.

I was sworn to secrecy. Piltdown revisited? One always wonders about the great Piltdown hoax, in which a whole generation of anthropologists was misled because someone placed an artificially aged human skull, together with part of an ape jaw, right where it could be found in an English gravel pit in 1915. Was it an elaborate practical joke that got out of hand, or was it a fraud, done with malice aforethought? But this is a river trip, I remembered, and surely they'll think of practical jokes before anything else.

WHILE WE WERE STANDING AROUND waiting for the final packing to be done, several people noticed Marsha's necklace and promptly nicknamed her the "Indian Princess." Were the nuts substitutes for a string of pearls, she was asked? No, she teased, who would want to wear a collection of oyster kidney-stones? Some of the laughter was, I thought, a little strained. When asked how she drilled the holes, she explained all about what she called the "holy" virtues of juniper nuts.

And, having everyone's attention, she also explained that she'd copied the pattern for the necklace directly from a real Anasazi necklace at the Mesa Verde museum. And threw in a few facts about Aztec record-keeping. Did anyone know what this pattern meant?

GRANITE RAPID turned out to be a real washing machine. If any one rapid had to be selected as the "Boat Wash," this would be it. Granite works just like the agitator in a washing machine —first we were met by a big lateral wave from the left, then another from the right overlapping it, then another from the left to slap down atop the previous one. Something like shuffling a deck of cards. When we emerged from Granite, we felt as though we'd been to the laundry. J.B., thirsty as usual after a rapid, discovered that his big coffee cup had been left full of water. He sipped it with gusto and said, "Thank you, Granite."

HERMIT is certainly one of the longest rapids we've ever seen, stretching out over several city blocks. We are viewing it from upstream, at our scouting spot on the left shore. When an ordinary amount of water is flowing down the river, Hermit is a long roller-coaster of swells, a series of giant standing waves, sometimes one-and-a-half stories from peak to trough. It is relatively predictable as rapids go. There is even a quiet route through it—just stick to the left side of the river. But no one wants to miss riding the roller-coaster on the right. The boats are to go through in two groups, the first group getting to photograph the second group and vice versa. Most rapids aren't suitable for such "photo runs"; the only other such rapid, we hear, will be Lava Falls, a week down the river from here. Lava is a 10; after yesterday's string of heavies, I don't want to

MILE 95
Hermit Rapid

even think about it. But Hermit looks like sheer fun, even if rated a 9.

I am riding with Jimmy Hendrick today, trading stories with him about other parts of the world. He too spent some time in Jerusalem, working as a security guard at United Nations headquarters there after a stint in the Marines, before knocking around Africa, before training as a paramedic, and then as a boatman. Jimmy is an amazing young man, one of the most natural athletes I have ever seen, though I have no idea what his favorite sport might be—but sports are only artificial outlets for the kinesthetic skills. Being a Grand Canyon boatman is a more natural outlet, more akin to the activities of our ancestors, whose successes shaped our skills.

All of the boatmen are perfectly at home in the outdoors—all natural guides, well-suited to their rowing and hiking lifestyles. Many have been teachers or graduate students, and they are all learned as well as passionate ecologists. But Jimmy, who is redheaded and modest in stature compared to handsome giants like Alan and Sandy, does everything with not only energy and confidence but often with grace as well. It reminds me of watching a ballet star making effortless leaps and spins, convincing one that gravity encumbers only ordinary mortals. It is hard to imagine Jimmy in an office job or cooped up in a library or laboratory, rather than in graceful motion. In addition to his fund of knowledge about the world, he is passionate about the Grand Canyon, knowledgeable about the ancient Anasazi, acute in his judgments of western politicians and water politics. I hate to imagine a world without varied outlets for people like Jimmy; he's a reminder to us that exceptionally talented people are found everywhere, not merely among those who choose to pursue advanced degrees or high salaries in the city canyons or suburban strips.

We row back upriver a little, just to get positioned on the far side of the river channel, since the entrance to the roller-coaster is to the right. Jimmy likes to stand up on the seat as the boat approaches the lip of the pond, just before being washed into the waves. Planning his moves, he sits down after his last-minute fix and then strokes us into the fastest moving water. We are carried up to the top of the first swell.

In a roller-coaster, the passengers tend to rise up out of their seats as the top is crested. We don't travel that fast. Yet just before we reach the top, while the boat is still nose-up by 30 degrees, Jimmy rises up out of his seat, hops atop it, and catches a quick look ahead over the bow, at the previously hidden downslope. And manages a quick stroke on the left oar as he sits back down again. We again are carried along the fastest of the currents, speeding downhill at a steep angle. It looks as if it would be easy to miss the path, to be carried around the side of the next swell. But we climb up it, dead in the center of the ridge of current, Jimmy rising up again as we start to crest, ascending to his full height atop the seat, then stroking us downhill. Again and again we rise and fall. These are steep hills, and out of the corner of my eye I see the photographers on the left bank catching us at dramatic angles. Each crest sees Jimmy, perfectly coordinated and full of grace, carrying the boat through the very top of the wave. It is like seeing someone make love to a rapid.

Eventually we swing toward the right bank. Well trained by now, I automatically reach for a bailing bucket. Then I realize that there is no water in the bilges. Indeed, we scarcely got splashed. All of the water is below the tops of the waves, and we rode the tops.

THE RIGHT BANK is getting the morning sun, and we warm up quickly while waiting for the second group of boats to get their act together. Passengers from the first two boats have scattered along the rocky shore, hiking back upstream from where we put ashore below the rapid, trying to find the best vantage points from which to photograph the various standing waves. I join the laziest group, the one which figures that the penultimate wave is as good as the first for dramatic pictures.

Seeing that my camera has only a few shots left on its roll of film, and not wanting to have to change film in the midst of the run, I snap a few portraits of my distinguished companions. Gone are the attempts at sartorial elegance of our first day on the river. We are now all windblown and achieving a well-worn look. Like a pair of jeans which has been through the wash numerous times, we too have gained character. We fit better.

As I change the film, I hear the first mention of Howard's father since yesterday. "If," Barbara asks, "there is a place in the brain for reading, is there also one for writing?" And, Ben jokes, for spelling? Several people agree that they must have lost that part somewhere along the way.

Strangely enough, while there are several sites for reading surrounding the visual part of the brain in the rear of the head, there is no one place for writing. Writing may be disrupted, of course, but only as part of numerous other symptoms. When you do see a writing-but-not-reading disturbance, it is usually from poisoning of some sort—carbon monoxide, for example—causing widespread damage to the left brain, out in the periphery (the "watershed") of the middle cerebral arterial tree.

No spelling area has yet been found—spelling is probably one of those skills which requires wide areas of the brain working together as a committee, not just one group of neighboring nerve cells. It's likely that the committee can limp along without a few of its usual members, so that less-than-massive strokes seldom eliminate the function.

Indeed, I asked, why should the brain have a reading area at all? Writing has only been around for 5,000 years, since the Sumerians, and surely a reading area hasn't evolved in that short a time. Now a special area for recognizing faces, that would make some evolutionary sense. Our prehuman ancestors may not have needed to read, but they certainly needed to recognize one another from rock-throwing distance to tell friend from foe.

This prompted Rosalie to tell a tale about a stroke patient who couldn't recognize his own wife. At least, not by sight; once she said something, though, he could tell who it was that had entered the room. Indeed, he could recognize her by her footsteps. He wasn't blind; he could look at yearbook portraits and match up twins. It was just remembering particular faces that gave him trouble. So is there really a special area for facial recognition or memory in the brain? The strokes that damage this ability are mostly in the rear of the brain, along its undersurface, but they aren't very discrete—they're usually associated with a lot of damage to the visual association areas and the underlying white matter. You'd expect a lot of other problems too from such widespread damage, and indeed, many of these patients have blind regions and color-vision problems.

Perhaps faces are just one application for the specialized neural machinery for recognition, and the specialization is more general than that. Indeed, that seems to be the case with the patient who cannot recognize his wife. They tested him on cars. While he can pick out different makes and models, try to get the face patient to pick out a picture of his automobile from a collection of pictures of very similar automobiles, and he'll have trouble doing that too. Recognizing one particular face, from among the memories of many faces, or recognizing one particular automobile using its distinctive dents or embellishments, suggests that the visual area destroyed by the stroke has something to do with recognizing unique individuals among populations of similar items. These stroke victims seem to have trouble recognizing and resolving the near-identical in their memories. Some would say that these strokes destroy the area where the detailed long-term memories of faces (and cars) are stored.

A FEW READING-DISTURBANCE-ONLY PATIENTS cannot even tell the different letters from one another. Not even a "T" from an "I." But it is now possible to say how normal people probably do it. There are some nerve cells in the rear of the human brain that become specialists in recognizing vertical lines, and others in horizontal lines. There is probably a committee of cells, including representatives from both the horizontal and vertical specialist groups, that works together to identify a "T." And another committee, some of whose members probably also belong to the "T" committee, likely specializes in "L." We may not yet understand how the brain distinguishes words such as "now" from "how," but we're starting to get the letters down.

We have gotten that far rather recently in the history of science, in about one generation of neurophysiologists. Indeed, it was Keffer Hartline, the father of Dan and Peter (and Fred, a biophysicist who is not along on this trip), who first realized in 1938 that individual nerve cells in the visual pathways were specialists in contrasting light and dark. They're most involved when something changes, either a light patch becoming dark or vice versa. For a cell to show sustained interest in what's going on, there may have to be a dark area adjacent to a light area (this spatial contrast aspect was later discovered by Stephen Kuffler). Contrast in time, or contrast in space: without one or the other, a cell may pay little attention to the visual world.

The eye is not like a television camera, faithfully registering the light intensity in each cell of the retinal mosaic of rods and cones (the nerve cells that act as "photo cells"). There are a hundred times more photosensitive cells in each eye than there are lines leading back to the brain in the optic nerve: the information has to get funneled down. Keffer Hartline and his followers showed that cells did this by playing off one group of photosensitive cells against a neighboring group, so that messages were sent only when the neighbors were seeing something different from what the first group was seeing. For example, a small white spot of light caused a report to be sent back to the brain, but a bigger spot, which also illuminated the neighbors, would cause a different message to be sent. Indeed, sometimes, no message was sent at all.

This work led to the realization that a cell could be attuned to some particular configuration of light. Frogs weren't interested in the difference between "T" and "I," but they were sure interested in moving black spots on light backgrounds—such as an insect to eat. The lines back to the brain weren't carrying a television-like report for some viewer back in the brain—they were carrying reports which, in effect, said "delicious fly at three o'clock."

"You mean that my eyes don't tell my brain about everything they see?" asked Abby.

. . . To study Metaphysics, as they have always been studied, appears to me like puzzling at astronomy without mechanics [physics]—Experience shows that the problem of the mind cannot be solved by attacking the citadel itself.

CHARLES DARWIN
the N notebook, 1838

"That's right," I answered. "They censor things. And re-arrange things."

"But how do I know what's really happening out there?"

"Isn't your eye part of you?"

Abby was impatient. "Oh, you know what I mean. That's just a piece of machinery like a camera. How come it censors things? Why don't I know about everything that comes into it?"

Brian is also puzzled. "And how do you keep from seeing everything upside-down? I mean, the lens projects the image of the sky onto the bottom of the eye, the ground onto the top. Where are things turned back right-side up?"

The little person inside the head. A philosophical problem that bedevils our thinking about the brain, and about ourselves. It's a point of view. Literally. No matter how much of the optic and neural apparatus is explained, we keep thinking that the "real me" is somewhere deeper inside, viewing the sensory inputs just like a person watching television.

"But there is no one place in the brain where an executive sits, receiving reports and issuing orders," I attempt to answer. "The real me is a little bit of everywhere in there. It's a committee of nerve cells."

Rosalie attempts to rescue me. "It's like asking exactly where this rapid is located. Sure there is the approach, when you pass the lip of the pond upstream and enter, just like there is a boundary between the outside world and the surface of the eye. But the rapid goes on for a long time—although damned if I can tell you, looking down that river, where the rapid stops. It's spread out along the river. And the little person inside the head is spread out too, all through the brain. From the sense organs leading into the brain, to the muscles on the pathway leading out."

Abby was not convinced. "But I have a single sense of myself—a unity of consciousness, if you will. I can focus my attention from listening to you to watching the rapid, from fantasizing Lava Falls to recalling the eclipse. It doesn't all happen at once, out of control. Your committee description of the brain sounds like a Tower of Babel."

I concede the inadequacy of the metaphor. "But in the brain business, we try to stand before we walk, walk before we run. Or dance. To understand the neural machinery that operates the legs, we don't start out by trying to explain dancers or gymnasts or Jimmy—we start with what keeps you standing up straight when your knees start to buckle. For reading, we don't start with a sentence, or even a word or letter. We start with simple patterns of light and dark like the little dots that make up an Impressionist painting or a newspaper illustration's halftone, and build our way upward. So far, we're about to the level of understanding where we can make an educated guess about how the brain handles one letter."

The first boat of the second group now appears at the top of Hermit and claims our attention. It slips over the edge of the pond and into the swirl that leads to the first standing wave. The boatman has it just right, with the boat in the center of the wave, and they crest the wave riding high. Now they head downhill at a steep angle. Up again, with the boatman trying to see over the crest, picking his way down the center of the channel so as to soar over the very tops. Down again, up again. It is a kind of music.

WHILE WAITING for the boats to get underway again, Abby admired Marsha's necklace and asked how to make one for herself. Marsha gave her 21 juniper nuts, some of which were the leftover beads from the first necklace. The pattern of beads began to replicate itself.

We soon passed through Boucher Rapid, a 6. It is named for Louis Boucher, a turn-of-the-century prospector who did a little mining down here. He also had a grove of 75 fruit trees just up the side canyon. And a garden where he grew tomatoes year-around. He even built some little cabins for tourists hardy enough to hike down and back. It wouldn't be surprising if the Anasazi had farmed that side canyon too, though they probably stuck to beans, corn, and squash. We pulled in to stop briefly on the beach below, to deliver some supplies to a team of researchers working there, studying the bighorn sheep.

BALONEY BOATS are giant rafts the length of a truck, with two outrigger tubes looking rather like big sticks of baloney. The tubes are lashed together, forming a center platform on which up to twenty passengers ride among the freezer chests. They are propelled by a whining outboard motor, and we usually hear one coming up behind us long before we see it. We now hear that distinctive announcement, back up the canyon. Purists, we have come to resent motors. I irrationally consider the baloney boats roughly on a par with the F–15 fighter jet that illegally buzzed us yesterday in the inner gorge. I have since heard that it was probably one of the jet jockeys from the Air Force base outside Phoenix, which trains foreign pilots as part of our massive arms sales abroad.

It is not only incongruous to be suddenly buzzed by a high-performance jet when you're floating quietly down the river, it is doubly incongruous when buzzed by a joyriding Middle Eastern fighter pilot in the bottom of Arizona's deepest canyon. And now we're about to be buzzed instead by a floating All-American beer-drinking party. Grrr. I think that I'm a little irritable today, maybe worried about Crystal Rapid up ahead (which some boatmen say is more of a real worry than Lava Falls).

Soon two of the baloney boats approach us. It is only mid-morning, but nearly every passenger on board has a beer in hand. Which they raise in greeting to us. We wave politely, empty-handed. Little is said. Their party looks to have been in progress for days. I cannot imagine them hiking up side canyons. The baloney boats grind past, the Doppler shift of the motor's whine dropping its pitch to announce they've taken the lead. The gasoline exhaust forms a leaden haze atop their wake, and the headwind blows it back toward us. Smog seems the final insult.

We naturally feel superior. The us-and-them psychology of groups being what it is, they probably think themselves superior to us too. I think that our boatmen are used to seeing some "oar jingoism" develop, for they assure us that the motor boatmen are really nice guys who run good trips, even if they're not privileged to row such fine small boats. Into this headwind.

We are not convinced, already nationalistic to the core without even being a nation. If we can become so us-and-them in just six days, one can imagine how hard real tribalism and nationalism will be to eliminate. Finally, perhaps fifteen minutes after the baloney boats first whined into sight, they disappear around a downriver bend. Quiet again, thanks to entrenched meanders. We begin to notice the bird songs once more. But the mood of Hermit is gone.

The baloney boats seldom stop to scout rapids. They just plow right on through, their length and weight serving to span holes and flatten out waves. While we take two weeks to cover 225 miles, they may spend only three to six days on the river. In the late 1970s, the Park Service proposed to phase them out, restoring the Colorado to oar-powered boats only. But the plan got shelved by a new government in power, whose Secretary of the Interior boated down the river for several days and then had himself helicoptered out. The river trip was, pronounced James Watt, "boring." Conservationists, kept busy trying to keep Reagan and Watt from selling off the remaining wilderness, had no time to speculate about what might happen if Watt had tried to improve the river tour, to make it a little snappier and keep it moving right along. His tastes in water transport probably ran to hovercraft, but he never got around to doing more than reprieving the baloney boats. And letting the river tour companies markedly expand the number of boats in the Canyon at any one time (that's obviously "good for business").

We resolve to change the topic of discussion. Back to brains.

THERE ARE TWO DIFFERENT CAMPS of brain researchers, too, though not quite as different as our group and that particular motor-trip party. There are the top-down types and the bottom-up types and we all get along fairly well together.

In a top-down approach, one starts with something general, like reading. Or recognizing faces. A neurologist studies a stroke patient and discovers that his problem is a failure to match up the face he sees with a face stored in his long-term memory, rather than merely an inability to spot yearbook portraits of twins, which only involves short-term memory mechanisms. Dissecting this further with clever tests, the neurologist discovers that the patient has a problem distinguishing between long-term memories within the same broad classification, not merely familiar faces but familiar cars or other high-order forms of ambiguity. This is an example of top-down in science, working from the general to the particular.

Bottom-up is another way to approach the visual part of the brain. Here we first attempt to understand the building blocks, then the architecture created by them. Cells, then circuits of cells such as reflexes, then brains. The followers of Keffer Hartline (he got the Nobel Prize in Physiology in 1967 for his discoveries) have, in the last quarter century, discovered many varieties of the building blocks. And they have followed the architecture up through more than a half-dozen stages in the brain's analysis of the images focused on the back of the eyes.

The two approaches should meet in the middle someday, when enough stages have been uncovered at each end. Then we will get a picture from start to finish of how the brain recognizes a face as an old friend, of the many stages through which the upside-down image from the eye must pass before "eureka" or "familiar friend" is triggered. Then we should be able to give a more adequate description of the "committees" of nerve cells that carry out each task along the chain, of how the shape of a friend's face is stored in memory, of what "eureka" consists of, in neural terms.

The key concept in the bottom-up approach to vision consists of describing the world from the viewpoint of a single nerve cell, as if you were inside the nerve cell and seeing only what its inputs provided it with. In fact, you're only seeing the net sum of its inputs, not the individual entries. Whenever you get confused, remember that essential viewpoint.

If it's a photosensitive cell like the rods and cones of the eyes, then you've got to shine a light on the cell via the optics of the eye. Shining light on other photoreceptor cells doesn't (usually) matter. But for the other nerve cells in the long chain leading back into the brain, the view is via other nerve cells: all a neuron back in the brain "sees" is what some other neurons tell it. Dan Hartline points out that a brain cell is like a general getting telephone reports of a battle that he does not personally observe.

Some of the inputs counteract others, just as withdrawals counteract deposits in determining the balance of your savings account. It's all a matter of balance between push and pull. As you gaze upon a newspaper halftone (which, like those Impressionist paintings known as Pointillist, is comprised of lots of little dots), some of those dots are providing positive inputs to the cell, while other dots are producing negative inputs via inhibitory synapses. The balance in the cell is not measured in dollars but in volts: the nerve cell is a little computer, keeping a tally of what hundreds (sometimes thousands) of inputs tell it, using voltages about a hundred times smaller than those in our flashlights.

For any one nerve cell, you can make a map of the halftone dots which cause positive inputs to this one cell, marking down a little "+" at each such dot, and marking down a "−" for a dot from which the cell evidently gets a negative input. Most dots in the picture don't affect the cell at all. But there will be a little cluster of "+" and "−" symbols. In some cases, it will be a circular cluster of "+" signs but with the very center of the cluster all having "−" signs instead. Something like a donut.

Now take away the newspaper halftone, so that the eye is staring up into the cloudless sky instead. Light falls evenly on the cluster of photoreceptors, some of which were connected to this cell to yield pluses, some minuses. The cell may give no response to the even illumination of this cluster: the "−" area in the center may contribute a negative input that cancels out the positive input from the periphery of the cluster. Despite all the inputs, the cell does nothing, sending no message to other cells further back in the brain. But let a fly come along, a black spot on the light background. The photoreceptor mosaic is no longer uniformly illuminated anymore. If that fly is imaged onto the center of the cluster that leads back to this cell, all the negative inputs to the cell disappear. Only the positive ones are left, and the cell goes wild, crying the neural equivalent of "Fly! FLY!"

The cluster of "+" and "−" inputs predicted how this one cell would respond to a natural input: it said that this cell ought to be pretty good at detecting a fly if its image were centered on the cluster. It is as if the cell constituted the neural template for a fly, always silently sitting there observing the world and getting excited only if a fly happened by. Neurophysiologists tend to call these templates "receptive fields": they are really just descriptions of what a particular cell likes, of what turns it on. And different cells like different things, simply because they are wired up to the retinal mosaic of rods and cones in some other way. To call a cell a "fly-detector" because it responds well to the fly can, however, be misleading as the cell doesn't correspond to an Aristotelian category; it's more analogous to what the mathematicians call a "fuzzy set". Such a cell also responds to other objects that almost look like flies, even to part of the letter "T" if it were imaged to include the cell's cluster.

And a map isn't a complete description of what the cell likes, because the cell is sensitive to time sequences as well as spatial contrast. Moving a light spot from the "−" area to the "+" area, for example, is usually the most effective stimulus for a cell, producing a much greater response than merely turning on the stimulus to the "+" area *de novo*. This means that moving stimuli, such as a fly flying along, get preference over stationary stimuli: they're literally "seen" more intensely. Most cells have some version of this movement preference property and there are analogous phenomena at many levels of the nervous system. So the functioning of the cell depends on both a map and a motion—in a sense, it serves as a search template for them. I'd hate to attempt Aristotelian logic with such fuzzy elements, but that's the brain's way.

Shapes more complex than flies are analyzed by the brain using combinations of the donuts. The donut shape of the search templates favored by retinal cells is rearranged by the time the cerebral cortex goes to work at analyzing the image. A cortical cell looks at what a series of cells are doing "upstream" from it. And the ones it chooses to examine give rise to a new type of favorite input. Rather than favoring small dots with dissimilar neighbors, the cortical cell favors lines and edges. Just as one can construct a black line with a series of black dots, so the cortical cell seems to have inputs whose template centers just happen to lie along an imaginary line in space. And so instead of a "black fly detector," the cortical cell becomes a "black line detector."

Unlike dots, lines have orientations. Some cortical cells specialize in vertical lines, others in horizontal lines. And for every angle in between, there will be some cortical cell that likes it better than other degrees of tilt.

Granted, the black line may have to be in just the right place—if it is moved sideways a little, the cell may not like it any more. But another cell will. And so among the millions of cells in the visual cortex, there are specialists in all sorts of lines in all sorts of places. The image of the world, projected camera-like onto the back of the eye, has been taken apart during its transmission through about six cells in the chain that leads from the eye's photoreceptor mosaic back to the visual cortex. It has been taken apart into lines and into edges between regions of different brightness or color.

And what happens next? Does the next cell in the chain look at several such line-loving templates and specialize in the letter "X" or "T"? Well, that may happen somewhere down the line but the next stage is not that specialized. At the next stage, a so-called "complex cell" will like lines or edges of a certain tilt—but they can be anywhere within a somewhat bigger region of space. Move the line sideways a little, and the complex cell will still respond to it (whereas the just-described "simple cells" won't). And so the restriction on exact location has been relaxed somewhat. Yet change the tilt just a little and the cell will become uninterested in the line. Thus, the principle of this next stage of image analysis seems to be position generalization.

Next? Probably line length—there are "hypercomplex" cells interested in lines only if they are of a certain length and tilt, though they are not particularly fussy about the line's exact location. But it gets hard to talk about stages, because this network of nerve cells isn't a chain. It's really a web, where a cell may look at what many inputs—not all from the same earlier "stage" of analysis—are doing. Still, one can see how a nerve cell might come to specialize in a "T" but not an "I." Whether there is, in fact, a "T" detector cell isn't yet known. Personally, I'd bet that T's are detected by a committee of cells—that the committee has abilities that no one committee member alone has. Color sensation, for example, is probably coded by no one cell but by a committee of cells that compares the signals from three different types of receptors in the retina; it is the relative size of those three signals which tells us the hue, but color sensation may not correspond to the actions of any one specialist cell or cell group. (Taste works the same way in all likelihood, for all but the most basic sensations such as salt and sweet). Emergent properties again—hue emerges from the merger, and doesn't have a separate existence.

Perhaps three "stages" of analysis occur within the so-called primary visual cortex, a region at the rear of the brain that is easily defined by its twice-the-usual packing density of cells (one layer of tightly packed cells forms a stripe easily seen without a microscope, hence the name "striate cortex"). If there is a "T" detector cell type, or one specializing in the image of your grandmother's face, it certainly isn't in that primary visual cortex.

But there are a series of secondary visual centers, some surrounding this primary one, others further forward in the brain, near the centers for hearing and language. At last count, there were over a dozen such secondary centers. Some specialize in depth perception, in telling us how far away something is located. Some do rather fancy jobs. There is the one that I mentioned earlier, just above the right ear of most people, which specializes in looking at a person's face and analyzing whether it looks happy, sad, mad, surprised, disgusted, and so on.

The wonder of it all is that we can see so much, things for which evolution did not prepare us. Such as the words in a book. Neurobiologists didn't really appreciate this until about 1959, when four MIT neurophysiologists published a paper entitled "What the Frog's Eye Tells the Frog's Brain." It turned out that the nerve cells going back to the brain carried few signals at all when the frog was merely looking at a stationary scene. No TV-like picture was being transmitted back to its brain, from which it could have reconstructed a scene such as we see. Even the frog's favorite food, a fly, caused no signal—unless it was moving. But if a moving fly did happen by, then all sorts of nerve cells got interested. In fact, the frog evidently couldn't even see the fly unless it was moving. A high school teacher later noted that she knew that all along, since frogs in captivity won't eat dead flies placed on the floor of their cage. She invented a merry-go-round, with dead flies (or little meat balls) dangling from the ends of black threads and twirling around—that the frogs then snapped up.

Curious, I took a pencil from my pocket and touched a strand of the [spider] web. Immediately there was a response. The web, plucked by its menacing occupant, begin to vibrate until it was a blur. Anything that had brushed claw or wing against that amazing snare would be thoroughly entrapped. As the vibrations slowed, I could see the owner fingering her guidelines for signs of struggle. A pencil point was an intrusion into this universe for which no precedent existed. Spider was circumscribed by spider ideas; its universe was spider universe. All outside was irrational, extraneous, at best raw material for spider. As I proceeded on my way along the gully, like a vast impossible shadow, I realized that in the world of spider I did not exist.

LOREN EISELEY

□   □   □

THE BRAIN'S CELLS not only individually have map-like sensory templates of the outside world, but there is another map which arises because of the way the cells are located in the brain itself. Cells that individually seem to specialize in the same patch of the visual world also tend to cluster together within the cerebral cortex. And the same mapping principle holds for other sensory surfaces as well, such as the surface of the skin.

"This is the little-man-in-the-brain map?" asked Barbara. "Where the arm region is next to the hand region, which is next to the face, and so on?"

"That's it, all right. Except that the amount of brain devoted to each body part tends to be proportional to the number of nerve cells coming from that region—there's as much space devoted to your thumb as to your whole arm," I replied, "but that's because the thumb is so richly endowed with sensory nerve cells."

"The face is next to the thumb?" asked Ben. "Is that what Barbara said?"

"It sure is—if you listen in on the electrical activity of a nerve cell in the thumb region of the brain, you'll find that it takes notice when a small region of the thumb is touched. And no other place will stir it up. But then move toward the ear just a fraction of a millimeter, and listen in to a nerve cell there. You'll find the cell will only respond to a region of the face," I added. "Move a little further to the side, and you'll listen in on cells that will only respond to the tongue, or the larynx. It's called the sensory strip."

"It comes this way in a newborn baby, or does the baby's experience cause it to arrange itself that way?" asked Barbara. "Nature, or nurture?"

"Both. It comes that way at birth in monkeys, but the standard map can also be later rearranged by experience. Suppose the monkey loses one finger as an adult? The patch of brain representing that finger doesn't just sit there inactive for the rest of the monkey's life. Within a day that inactive patch of brain will start specializing in the adjacent fingers."

Rosalie remarked, "We're always telling stroke patients that the brain recovers after damage—that they usually get better, recover some of the functions that they are initially missing—but what happens to one of those big maps of the body surface if it's damaged?"

"At least in monkeys, it rearranges itself within days. Kill the nerve cells specializing in the thumb, and pretty soon the rest of the finger map will have rearranged itself to devote less space to each finger, while still representing all five fingers. The brain map seems to be constantly changing, though just a little. In some brain areas it may be quite rigid after infancy—such as the primary visual map, for example—but in others it may be in a constant state of remapping. Dynamic mapping, even when you're an adult. That may be why some areas recover better than others after a stroke, for example."

"Whoa," requested Ben. "What do you mean, the map's always changing?"

"Well, one day the neurophysiologists tested hundreds of cells and found out where the boundary between the thumb and the face was located—the region of the brain where 'thumb' cells had neighbors on one side which weren't interested in the hand at all—these neighbors were more interested in some region of the face. They photographed the little surface blood vessels in the area so they could locate this patch of brain again with great accuracy. Then, a week or two later, they went back in and recorded from another few hundred cells and once again located the thumb-face boundary. It had moved. Not much—less than a millimeter, but it sure looked as if there were cells that had been thumb cells several weeks before and had changed in the meantime to become face cells."

"But what had they done to cause that to happen?" asked Barbara.

"Nothing, so far as they knew. The animal had just been playing in its cage. It sure makes me think that the face and hand are always competing for space in the brain, and that the truce line moves around from week to week."

"Suppose the whole hand region is killed off by the stroke?"

"Well, there's always one of the secondary maps. Last time I counted, there were six complete body maps of the skin surface in the monkey cerebral cortex."

"Are they backups, like the various backup systems for lowering the landing gear in an airplane if the main hydraulics fail?" asked Ben.

"I doubt it. I suspect they're all working, all the time. In tandem."

"Are there extra visual maps too?" asked Barbara.

"Yes, those were the first duplicate maps discovered, in fact, back about 1942. But now there are more than a dozen complete maps of the visual world, and that's in monkeys again—who knows how many we have?"

A second map of the body musculature was discovered long ago—it's forward of the motor strip; since it was smaller, it became the "supplementary motor area." Additional motor maps have now been found. For hearing, there is a brain map of the tonal scale; indeed, four such maps. I haven't heard of any orderly maps for smell or taste but, if one is found, I confidently predict a few duplicates will also be located.

Duplicating a sensory map must surely be one of the easier

tasks of brain construction, something like making a second casting of a bronze statue once you've got the first one done. The first time, though, is harder: it takes a lot of self-organization to wire up the cortex in such a way that neighboring areas on the retina remain neighbors in the cortex. Imagine you had to move the flashcard section from one side of the football stadium to the other, each person having to pass single-file through a narrow corridor. Getting them reseated so that neighbors are still neighbors might be a little tricky, especially if there weren't seats with numbers on them. The brain's "developmental manager" has solved that problem, not by an efficient clipboard-holding traffic cop but by self-organization principles that make natural neighbors congregate.

Furthermore, the wiring patterns leading up to the cerebral cortex produce the ability to detect line orientation and to compare the left eye's image with the right eye's. There is a standard way of doing all of this wiring, called a hypercolumn; it's like one square in a patchwork quilt. Within this small patch of the visual world, both eyes and all possible orientation angles are represented. In the brain, one hypercolumn occupies the space beneath a 1x2 mm patch of brain surface. In monkey brains, the whole primary map (the "quilt") is created by simply repeating the genetic instructions for wiring up a hypercolumn over and over, up to about 400 times, until the whole visual map is constructed.

Making an extra whole map is only a little extra work. Just let branches of the nerve cells go to another area and organize themselves according to the same set of genetic instructions. So the second map is just a repeat, like making a second casting of a work of art. What, however, is the advantage of an extra complete map? Let alone a dozen? Sheer numbers is one possibility, particularly in the case of the primary visual cortex where the cells are already packed in twice as tightly as is usual for cortex. To get more cells to operate on the same region of visual space, it may have been easier to simply duplicate the map elsewhere and then coordinate things. There are circumstances in which having two cells do the same job and pooling their results can be useful for improving precision and reducing uncertainty.

But I expect that the big advantage of duplicated maps lies in the ability to have the new one eventually specialize in something slightly different from the original. So-called "Visual 4," the fourth map of the visual world discovered in monkeys, has cells duplicating most of the properties of those in "Visual 1", the primary map—but many of the "Visual 4" cells exhibit slight changes which make it easier to detect how far away an

object is located from you. In "Visual 4," the further specializations are for depth perception or for color discrimination. It
looks as if "Visual 1" was duplicated, but that "Visual 4" then
proceeded to diversify a little.

Is the principle here duplication, then followed by diversification? Repeated 12 to 20 times? And that's only in monkeys—
no one knows how many maps a human has.

DUPLICATION, THEN DIVERSIFICATION may also be a
principle at the level of genes. Duplication of DNA itself is, of
course, something that DNA does very well, very reliably. That
is, after all, how cells divide—by first duplicating the chromosomes which contain the stored DNA strands, then pinching in
the cell membrane between the two sets, and then separating
into two cells—the original photocopy machine. Both halves of
the chromosome pair are duplicated. That's mitosis, the process
used in almost every organ of the body to make new cells.

In the sex cells of testis and ovary, another step follows, which
pares down a cell to a half-set of chromosomes, 46 chromosomes down to 23 in the case of humans. Thus when a sperm
and ovum unite, the offspring winds up with the standard set,
but roughly half from each parent. The production of that half-
standard sex cell is called meiosis; it has an interesting twist in
that your two matching chromosomes (one from each parent)
are first shuffled before separating, a process called "crossing over,"
which insures that the offspring winds up with some combination of its grandparents' genes, not just either its grandfather's
or its grandmother's.

Some strange things can happen during crossing over; some
DNA strands may, for example, be broken at inopportune places.
A strand may be replaced upside-down so that it reads like nonsense when the cell goes to use it as an instruction for assem-
bling a protein. Sometimes the two half-standard sex cells produced by meiosis do not wind up with an equal split of the DNA
(analogous to the deck of cards not being split evenly), one getting more than the other. Indeed, some DNA sequences may
wind up being kept in duplicate so that, once fertilization occurs, the paired chromosome now has three copies of a particular gene rather than two.

Missing information may well prove fatal to the zygote, and
many zygotes are probably spontaneously aborted at an early stage
of development and never seen. But an extra set of some genes
may prove useful (though an extra whole chromosome is often
unfortunate; in Down's syndrome, for example, there are three
rather than two copies of chromosome 21). Whatever
the mechanism for the duplication, the chromosomes seem to

have a lot of DNA sequences which are virtual duplicates of others.

"But what are the duplicate genes used for?" asked Abby. "Backup copies, in case there's a mutation in the original?"

"Maybe, but genes have proofreading mechanisms that correct simple errors. Another case of nature inventing it before the computer designers," I explained.

Ben brightened. "Perhaps they're just for playing around with? When a computer programmer wants to make some improvements in a program that's already operating, the first step is to make a duplicate. Then you make your modifications in the copy, and save the original."

"And, of course, the modified program usually doesn't work at first. So it's a good thing you kept an unmodified copy," smiled Cam. "It's only after I've fiddled around with it for awhile that the new version works at all. Much less working better than the original."

"So duplicated genes, however they might arise, would be handy for evolving a new improved version of a living thing," Rosalie said. "And there are sure a lot of near-duplicates of genes in the cell nucleus, strings of DNA which are almost like the ones that make the proteins, but not exactly the same."

"Of course, if the changes are made randomly, with no intelligent programmer masterminding the modifications, you'd expect that a lot of the DNA sequences would be nonsense, simply nonfunctional," I added. "Nothing but junk."

"So that's what is called junk DNA?" asked Abby. "Or is it garbage DNA, I forget?"

"Someone once called it garbage DNA, but the more appropriate name is junk. After all, garbage can be thrown away. Junk is the stuff that you never manage to get rid of," Rosalie said, laughing.

"So why can't the cell get rid of the DNA that isn't useful? Wouldn't natural selection eliminate it?" asked Abby.

"No, not if it wasn't actively harmful," I said. "It's a lot easier to photocopy a whole notebook, for example, than it is to sort through all the pages and make individual decisions about what's worth saving. And the cell probably doesn't have the intelligence to make such decisions anyway. And just duplicating is so easy—at least for a cell."

So evolution at the gene level may well involve extra copies of genes, kept off-line in the genome, where they don't do any harm if they're a little crazy, with diversification arising when accumulated modifications of some genes happen to provide a better-than-original version. Duplication, then diversification. The expression of such a modified duplicate gene (when, for example, the regular gene was damaged beyond repair) might even have caused a cortical map to duplicate.

It is now suspiciously quiet on the river. Ever since Boucher, we have been in "Crystal Reservoir." We are approaching Crystal Rapid, considered the most unpredictable and dangerous rapid on the river by many boatmen. An angry young rapid that thrashes around.

BEFORE 1966, CRYSTAL WAS A MINOR RAPID. Then there was a storm which dumped 350 millimeters (14 inches) of rain on the North Rim within a 36-hour period. Three-story-tall walls of water came roaring down both Crystal and Bright Angel creeks. The sound alone must have shaken loose rock fragments from the nearby cliffs. That massive a flash flood is capable of moving house-sized boulders. Many lesser boulders were carried all the way into the river channel, creating a new Crystal Rapid overnight. Big Ponderosa pines, which grow only on the North Rim, are seen in the debris, testifying to the origins of the flood waters as well as to their force.

I'm reminded of the river below Phantom Ranch, in the mile from Bright Angel Creek to the talus slope where we deposited Howard, where it's very rough and splashy, unpredictable from one minute to the next. That too is from the 1966 flood. Crystal is similarly unpredictable, but on a much larger, more threatening scale. In the space of a city block, the river drops nearly two stories—that's how much water is dammed up by the new boulders. Its rating of 9 or 10 depends on how "big" the water is, boatmanese for how much water is being released from Lake Powell every second. The holes of white water where the river pours over a big boulder—which can trap and over-turn boats—keep changing around as I watch them, waves cresting and crashing, then building again. Every so often, one will grow larger as the river current shifts a little. I watched a hole in mid-channel briefly expand to include the right channel as well, as the wave feeding in to it built up and then crashed down.

The boatmen huddled and appraised Crystal from our up-stream vantage point. One catches the mood of a rapid, and this is no Hermit.

Flash floods do something this spectacular every few centuries, somewhere along the Colorado, thanks to the steep gradient of many side canyons. Some twelfth-century Anasazi ruins were destroyed by the 1966 flood, showing how long it had been since this area experienced a flood of that magnitude. But most rapids aren't such bad actors as Crystal is—they've had time to be smoothed out a little. Over the centuries, the pre-

MILE 99
Crystal Rapid

damnation river's Spring floods pushed around the new loads of boulders, rearranging them into stable positions in the river, sorting them by size as the small ones were carried farther downriver than the big ones. Now, without the flushing action of the natural floods, the managed river will eventually turn into a series of waterfalls as the rapids fill up—provided, of course, that Lake Powell doesn't fill up with silt first, which dam critics say will happen within several centuries.

So spring floods are a thing of the past: that's what many said prior to 1983. They assumed that the people who run the Colorado River dams knew what they were doing, were competent to manage the lake levels and release rates during the spring snowmelt. But the dam managers' promises and their performances are two different matters. Early in 1983 they promised to limit peak releases to about 900 cubic meters (31,500 cubic feet) per second; that's double a typical release. In June 1983 they admit to having released 2,600 cubic meters every second (92,000 cubic feet); at one time, the Bureau of Reclamation (known hereabouts as "BuRec") reported 3,000 (108,000 cubic feet) to the Park Service, so the boatmen suspect revisionism.

This flooding was not done intentionally for old-times' sake, to mimic a predamnation spring runoff. It happened because BuRec mismanaged the dams so badly that Lake Powell overflowed in a big way. And the dam managers nearly destroyed Glen Canyon Dam itself, quite without any help from the Monkey Wrench Gang (see Edward Abbey's 1976 novel of the same name).

There had, of course, been a lot of snow in the Rockies that winter; the National Weather Service predicted that two winters' worth of water would be coming down the river that spring, and they were quite accurate. But to watch the performance of the dam people, you'd never have known it wasn't an average year. Beginning in May, the river people were getting worried because Lake Powell was pretty full; the dam managers were still hoarding every drop of water, turning down the river flow at night when they couldn't sell the electrical power. Surely, the boatmen thought, if they intend to open up those big spillways and flood the river, they wouldn't keep hoarding water at night, which only makes their situation worse.

But the damn dam's controllers practice a form of logic that few can recognize. So there was little warning when they finally flip-flopped and the flood came roaring down the river, all that extra water that should have been released gradually over the nights and days of the preceding months. Here at Crystal, three of the giant baloney boats capsized (those inflatable tour buses weigh four tons each and are normally regarded as unflippable). One person died; dozens were hurt. Some passengers bobbed along in their life jackets for eight miles, being carried through seven other major rapids before reaching shore. Helicopters evacuated 140 people in the aftermath.

The problem, of course, was that a rapid melt of an oversized snowpack filled up Lake Powell behind Glen Canyon Dam. That should have presented no problem: the managers are supposed to release a lot of water during the winter to make room for any flooding in the spring. Anyone knows that—one learns it as a child, to let water out of the bathtub before rinsing off with the shower.

But it had taken seventeen years to finally fill Lake Powell to its designed maximum (a matter of some embarrassment to the dam-builders, as they'd predicted it would fill up much more quickly), and the water managers were reluctant to draw down the lake during the early spring as a precaution, even when presented with the measurements of the giant snowpack waiting to melt up there in the Rockies. The room they left was only one-fourth of what they needed—not just a slight underestimate, but a major screwup. I can remember Subie saying, in 1980, that something like this was sure to happen, given BuRec's attitudes about keeping Lake Powell close to full. This suspicion was widely shared among professional boatmen. They were right.

And so the dam managers caused a disaster: for the boaters, who got surprised in midtrip by water much higher than "allowable" and by helicopters dropping messages of worse to come. And it was a disaster for the river ecology, as the river forever lost sandy beaches with their wildlife habitats (unlike the pre-damnation spring floods, the upriver sand will not be replaced, since the dam traps any new upstream sand and keeps it from entering the Grand Canyon). It was also a major disaster for the people downstream in Arizona, California, and Mexico, whose supposedly safe farms and towns were flooded out.

The managers even caused $50 million in damage to the dams they were supposed to be managing. Indeed, they almost lost Glen Canyon Dam, things were so serious at one point. When they finally opened up the two giant spillways to cause the "Fool's Flood of 1983," the four-story-high tunnels, poorly designed in the first place, were damaged by all the water that came thundering through. The thick concrete walls broke apart in places, and the torrent of water tore into the sandstone cliff between the spillway and the adjacent dam. A three-story-deep hole was dug in the cliff under one section of the west spillway. The huge stream of water arching out into the river turned red, the color of the Navajo Sandstone comprising the canyon wall. To some, it looked as if the dam was bleeding to death.

The bleeding cliffs. The dam managers got even more worried when house-sized boulders of sandstone started flushing out into the river. I should think that they'd have been "sweating blood" themselves. Does civil service protect the job of a bureaucrat who destroys a dam?

For a while it looked as if they were going to have to shut down the spillways to prevent the cliff from being torn apart. The cliff, of course, forms the edge of the dam, that concrete plug which keeps all of Lake Powell from washing down the river. The cliff could also have collapsed from all the vibration, dropping sandstone into the spillway and plugging up the river's new path.

The managers were not very happy about this prospect. They now had a new, urgent reason to reduce the water released. But there was no room left in the reservoir because they had foolishly left themselves no safety margin: the gates on the spillways were as high as they would go. So they added 2.4-meter (8-foot) panels of plywood atop them, raising the lake to new record heights, all the way up to within a meter of spilling over the top of the dam itself. And creating a magnificent 50-story-high waterfall.

A little more sunshine up on the Rockies and they'd have had the second disaster scenario: the waterfall washing away the powerhouse at the bottom of the dam. It wasn't built to withstand the force of the Colorado River falling on it from a height of 50 stories. And so in two different ways, they almost lost a dam—what would have been the biggest, if not the most spectacular, dam failure of all times.

WHAT CAUSES THE DAM MANAGERS to disregard elementary precautions such as safety margins? First, there is the western states' fear of drought—"saving" water behind the dam (where a goodly percentage evaporates anyway) is easier than conserving water by modern irrigation practices. Then there is the petty bickering between the states over the water that caused the Glen Canyon Dam to be needlessly built in the first place. Phillip Fradkin's book *A River No More* tells the sad story.

Even the resort uses of Lake Powell create pressure, since commercial interests like Del Webb Corporation (the major concessionaire at Lake Powell, who runs the hotels and marinas) have advertised the lake as a resort lake rather than a working reservoir. The promoters cringe when paying guests have to traipse over mud flats littered with tattered styrofoam and shredded plastic bags (from their previous paying guests) in order to get to the boat dock or a "beach." And so Del Webb et al. want the dam managers to keep the lake full, with no unsightly bathtub ring. The resort operators aren't local residents who remember the predamnation Glen Canyon; hotel and transportation conglomerates run the Park Service concessions in this region (small businesses are not "in" these days); the hotel manager is likely to be an imported management trainee with his eyes set on the big time. Del Webb makes Lake Powell an exception to the rule, but don't cheer yet: besides its expertise in casino gambling, Del Webb is a giant land developer in the Southwest; having any developer run Lake Powell always reminds me of the tradition of putting the fox in charge of the hen house.

Finally, there is peaking power, the cause of the daily tides on the river downstream from the dam. Dams are better suited to handling the peak loads of midday, because they can be turned on and off more rapidly than coal-fired power plants such as the nearby Navajo Power Plant which pollutes the clean air of the Grand Canyon; furthermore, the government can sell that peak-hour electricity for four times as much as the electricity produced in the middle of the night. And so the dam people are moving, without first researching the legally mandated environmental impact statement (EIS), to using the dam so as to create daily floods on the river, closing it down at night (they can't dry up the river entirely since the dam leaks too much; there are even small waterfalls down its western seam with the canyon wall). They are spending many millions of the taxpayers' dollars to rewind the eight big generators at Glen Canyon Dam's powerhouse, so as to better operate under peak power conditions; this is the equivalent of a developer saying "we'll get around to doing an EIS—after it's built."

When one visits the dam's visitor center, not only are there no exhibits showing the beauty of the drowned Glen Canyon (see Eliot Porter's book *The Place No One Knew*) but the BuRec is a little selective about recent history as well—one gets no sense of the bungling and near catastrophe of 1983, which a few newspaper clippings of the time would have nicely illustrated. There are engineering pictures of the spillway damage and the contractor's efforts to repair them—but to read their accompanying messages, one would think that the heavy snowfall the winter before was the sole cause of the problem. The commissioner of BuRec, a Las Vegas politician, also tried to blame the computers. There was nothing mentioned about insufficient safety margins, a matter very much under BuRec's control.

Now how would you react to a child practicing brinkmanship in the bathtub, who explained that the bathtub overflowed because someone else turned on the shower too hard? Plug? What plug? Who, me? People of that mentality are running the dams on this river, controlling the plug in the drain. It is not reassuring to us river-runners, nor to the people living downriver. So much for the wisdom of the Bureau of Reclamation. A Congressional subcommittee held oversight hearings a few months afterward but, since the western water politicians were as much to blame as the dam managers, they were very low-key and dwindled off into praise of BuRec for preventing a worse disaster. For something that was the Three Mile Island of the water power industry, the Fool's Flood has been strangely hushed up.

And if you think the BuRec learned anything from 1983, you'll be interested to know that in 1984 they again allowed the lake level to creep up above "full" while both spillways were inoperable, as workmen in them repaired the previous year's damage—and then proceeded to shut down half of the "river outlets" in use (the junior-sized versions of the spillways) to keep the overfull lake level from dropping. Safety margins seem not to be part of their vocabulary, suggesting that legislation is needed to establish simple rules for these gamblers to follow, so that the dollars from power generation will not become their sole monomaniacal focus.

Did this bungling imitation of a predamnation spring flood tame Crystal Rapid a bit by rearranging the boulders? They're rearranged some, but there's still that nasty rock bar at top right which pushes you left, and still that series of constantly changing holes all down the left channel that you can be swept into. The boatmen haven't downrated Crystal one bit. Alas, there was no silver lining to the Fool's Flood of 1983.

We made it through Crystal. Jimmy insisted that I crouch down much lower in my corner than I usually do, and it was a good thing, too. You could get whiplash from that rapid. We'd barely bailed the boat before we hit Tuna Creek Rapid (a 6) half a mile later, and felt somewhat frazzled by the time we staggered ashore at Mile 104 to make lunch. But the sun warmed us.

Comparing notes once ashore, it sounds as if Howie's boat had a more exciting trip through Crystal than we did—Dan Richard says he'll never forget skirting past a gaping hole in the river. And looking down one story deep into churning waters. I shuddered. It does give one a new perspective on why they're named "holes."

Looking up the Colorado, the tongue of Crystal Rapid appears broad and silky, but the smoothness is deceptive. The water actually powers down Crystal's initial drop at speeds approaching 20 miles per

hour. . . . Along the tongue small rocks and their ensuing holes
pock the right side of the river. Increasing in frequency and size,
they funnel the Colorado inexorably toward a truly unbelievable
hole. . . . It exists because of several enormous rocks directly at the
end of Crystal's long, racing tongue. Most of the Colorado River
plunges over the rocks and down twelve feet into this hole.
Rebounding, the water shoots twenty feet into the air. It is this
mountain of water that fills boatmen's nightmares . . . The hole is
only a quarter of the way through the white water. Below it and
slightly to the right is a rock that many Grand Canyon veterans
think of as the worst on the river. Actually it is rather pretty: orange
in color and nicely smoothed, a block of Supai sandstone. The problem with this rock is its location. Boats slamming off the right side
of the big hole will, if the boatman loses control, wash directly into
the orange rock and then careen onto a barely submerged island of
large boulders.

ROBERT O. COLLINS and RODERICK NASH, *The Big Drops*, 1978

HAWKS AND FALCONS can often be sighted in the Canyon, soaring along on the updrafts near the cliffs, and they become our after-lunch preoccupation as we lie on the sandy beach.
Several days ago we spotted a red-tailed hawk circling high over
a side canyon. The local falcons are kestrels. We haven't seen
a kestrel catch anything yet; besides cicadas, they prey on small
birds. And while the small birds are plentiful, they are also cautious when it comes to hawks and falcons: they recognize the
profile of the predator seen from beneath and take evasive action promptly. Does this mean that birds have special "hawk
templates" in their brains? Is it inborn, or do they have to learn
it?

When they spot a hawk, young birds crouch down, remaining immobile against the ground. Shadows and movement help
a soaring bird to spot prey against the background camouflage,
so this stationary posture reduces the nestling's chances of being
detected and getting eaten. But how do they know to hide when
the hawk flies over? Presumably they haven't learned by getting
half-eaten once—experience would seem grossly inadequate as
a means of protecting young birds. Thus we might conclude that
the young bird comes with a built-in template for the shape of
a hawk (short neck, wings set forward unlike geese, that distinctive fan tail—the "trigger features" for the protective reflex). A little more observation of animals would have saved the
philosophers from mistakenly thinking that the young brain was
a tabula rasa, a blank slate on which experience wrote.

When the ethologist looks more closely at the behavior of
young birds, however, it turns out that nestlings react defen-
sively to all birds flying past. It's just that they will stop doing

MILE 104
Onyx Rapid

[When a redtail hawk] spots
something live and edible, down
she goes at an angle of forty-five
degrees, feet first, talons
extended, feathers all aflutter,
looking like a Victorian lady in
skirts and ruffled pantaloons
jumping off a bridge.

EDWARD ABBEY
Down the River, 1982

it for the familiar birds. They may react to robins, but they eventually tire of it. The shape of a robin no longer triggers the reflex. But the shape of a crow still does—until the nestling gets enough exposure to crows too. Just as we eventually become habituated to strange noises in the night, so the birds get used to the repeated, harmless profiles. Once they habituate to the shapes of the common birds in the region, the only birds that then trigger the reflex are the uncommon ones.

So is it only strange, exotic birds that now trigger the reflex? Not solely. Birds may be infrequently seen in a particular place for two reasons. They may be exotic (literally, from another place), just a few travelers passing through. Or they may be from a local species whose numbers are naturally few, a species that the food supply cannot support in large numbers. And there are very few hawks in comparison to other bird species because hawks prey on small animals rather than more abundant insects or seeds.

That's a simple and well-known consequence of a food chain: there is not much room at the top. To put on a gram of body weight, a predator may have to eat ten times as much. Not only is digestion inefficient, but warm-blooded animals waste a lot of what they eat, just in keeping their body warm around the clock. Furthermore, predators are usually larger than their prey (a big fish, for example, has to eat a lot of small fish to survive). So there cannot be as many predators as prey—indeed, many fewer. And thus any bird that preys on other birds must be pretty rare, compared to robins and ravens. That may be the reason why nestlings freeze when a hawk flies overhead. Hawks are relatively rare and nestlings just never have the chance to get used to them.

And so nature provides this general way for young birds to avoid predators, taking advantage of this order-of-magnitude difference in population densities between bird-eating birds and other birds. Instead of wiring up the young bird with a built-in template for the hawk profile, it wires it up so that a rough template fitting many different bird profiles will trigger the reflex. And then, with experience, a series of more specific templates are formed for each common bird species. If none of these fit the passing bird, the alarm sounds.

If the nestling were born into a different habitat with different predators such as falcons, the end result would still be the same: the rare predator would still trigger the reflex. That's a rather different design principle than providing the baby bird with a genetic template for specific predator species. It's a more general principle, suitable for many different times and places. So long as the young birds can initially afford all the false alarms, the population statistics of the food chain will shape the triggers

Perception is not determined simply by the stimulus patterns; rather it is a dynamic searching for the best interpretation of the available data.

RICHARD GREGORY
Eye and Brain, 1966

. . . each person's knowledge base is made up not of isolated facts but of established mental codifications of behavior patterns and of generalized theories about the world. We are able to handle information rapidly only because the regularities of the world, as well as our routine dealings with it, are internally represented as schema. When available information (derived either from the senses or from memory) is sketchy, we draw on certain schemata—old ideas and generalizations—to fill in the missing data.

JAMES REASON, 1984

for the protective reflex against the youngster's true predators. This shaping process may, of course, have other side effects—a general suspicion of strangers, for example, which could have been avoided with the inborn exact template method. The rough-template defense mechanism is yet another example of a young animal being "tuned up" by early experiences so that its brain is better wired for the particular environmental circumstances in which it finds itself.

SERPENTINE CANYON RAPID is only rated a 7, but it has one of the biggest "holes" of any rapid on the Colorado River. But the hole is easy to avoid. We just ferried sideways across the river channel long before reaching it, and swept past, getting a good view from a safe distance. It was indeed a giant, frothy pit, quite capable of trapping a big boat. Because the frothy water has so much air in it, its buoyancy is reduced (uplift, saith Archimedes after issuing his "Eureka!", depends on the weight of the water you displace). And so a boat can literally sink if the water it displaces weighs only half as much as normal. Like a black hole in space, these "white holes" may not give back what they take in.

LEARNING is, of course, often a more complicated matter than mere habituation. We learn associations, just as Pavlov's dogs came to salivate at the sound of the bell. Sometimes we gradually learn something, as when we practice a new skill. Other times, once is enough for a strong memory to be formed.

As compared to other primates, we humans aren't fussy about what we eat. Indeed, we'll seemingly try anything, once. We're always putting something new in our mouths to taste, maybe chewing on it a little. There are a lot of advantages to being an omnivore, as compared to sticking to salads and bamboo like a gorilla. For one thing, there is more to choose from, and that gives you more choices of places in which to live. The gorilla is stuck in a rut: by eating only its favorite plants, it must stick to where those grow in quantity.

But there is an obvious hazard to eating a new food—it might be disagreeable. Skunks may defend themselves with smell, but plants often defend themselves from browsing animals by incorporating toxic chemicals. Which is what taste is all about, small samples being taken and analyzed before subjecting the gastrointestinal tract to large quantities of the potential food. And so, if you are going to eat a new food, you need to remember what it tastes like (yes, it also helps to remember how it looks, but taste is a more sensitive, definitive test). One needs to remember the item's taste for as long as it takes to get sick from it, so that it can be avoided next time by taste alone.

Prehumans didn't exactly invent that strategy for avoiding toxins. Even lowly animals like snails and slugs have this one-trial learning ability. Feed a slug some fancy exotic lettuce which it has never eaten before. Then, an hour later, inject it with something that makes it retch. The next time the slug encounters the lettuce, it will taste but not ingest—presumably on the theory that it was the exotic lettuce which made it sick before. But the one-try taste mechanism isn't foolproof. We too indiscriminately avoid foods that we mistakenly associate with getting sick; one should never eat favorite foods while coming down with the flu, as it may ruin one's taste for these foods forever (this is probably why some people can no longer stand the taste of chicken soup!). It's not too surprising that the slug commits the logical error of *post hoc, ergo propter hoc* (after this, therefore because of this); it seems that we're not much more logical most of the time ourselves.

And so there seems to be a lingering memory of the taste of the lettuce, lasting long enough for the gastrointestinal tract to discover any toxins in it. Furthermore, the reaction to the toxin somehow "develops" the lingering memory of the taste, just as a photoprocessor develops a latent image on a film. The developed memory is then made into a permanent sensory template for detecting the taste of the toxic food, and is apparently then provided with strong connections to the "Ugh" circuits of the brain. Wildlife ecologists have been trying to explain this to farmers, so that they won't poison coyotes and eagles. It may be sufficient to put out some bait loaded with a drug that makes the predator briefly sick, so that he will think that chickens taste bad. Just as in spraying for pests once a year, farmers can train a new generation of predators every year.

So much for explaining bad tastes. But why, Abby asks, do we take such pleasure in good tastes? Where did that come from? Why is dinner likely to taste so good tonight? We are stumped.

THE RIGHT TIME TO LEARN, for the slug's taste avoidance system, is only after the slug has gotten sick. Learning is similarly programmed in other types of animals.

Back on the river, Alan reminded us of the beekeeper's wisdom about moving beehives. If a hive is moved in the middle of the day, the bees become disoriented and confused. But get up in the middle of the night, to move the hive before their first flight of the day, and they'll come and go from the new location with no trouble: a bee memorizes the landmarks that it will need for its return flights during the rest of the day as it flies away from the hive on its *first* flight of the morning.

A coherent natural philosophy will only be possible once we have understood how the brain, itself an object of physics, generates the description of the physical world.

VALENTINO BRAITENBERG
Gehirngespinste, 1977

And a bee does not learn the smell of a flower by hovering around it. The odor of the flower is learned only if the bee is actually standing on the flower. Furthermore, if any aspect of its food source changes, such as its location or color, the bee must relearn the whole thing: it's stored all together, not as separate fragments. Thus bees are carefully tuned learning machines: just as their eyes see only certain aspects of their environment, so a new memory is recorded only when the conditions are just right.

This kind of memory is not the gradual tuning up which the hawk template suggests; rather, the bee seems to take a sensory "snapshot" when the right conditions trigger the shutter. But we humans seem to be open for learning much of the time. It seems to be stored in two different forms. In episodic memory, we seem to record a series of events almost like a motion picture camera, storing a whole sequence of memories of a particular episode: say, of getting into a car and driving it to the grocery store. And we can, if we try, distinguish this episode from other episodes, such as going to the store the previous day.

But the more common kind of memory, seen more widely among the animals, is the schema. This would be the generalized concept of "car," not any particular car but all cars; what we use to distinguish it from a truck. There can be a subschema for a particular car, what we use to tell our car from others of similar appearance. Our vocabulary is composed of schemata, which examine sequences of sounds to see if they approximately fit a word template already stored in our memory.

SYMMETRY IS ONE ELABORATION OF A SCHEMA, a handy way of generalizing on an observation. The human body seems to be two halves, each the mirror image of the other. Surface appearances are deceptive, however. Inside any mammal, you can see that the huge liver has no counterpart on the left side. Indeed, it has enlarged so much as to make the right lung smaller, pushing the heart over to the left side of center.

As for the paired organs like the kidneys, we still assume they're identical twins, just mirror images of one another (surgeons know better). But aren't the two sides of the brain just mirror-images of one another? Not at all, they do different things, and they aren't even anatomically symmetric. Not even in rats.

How the presumption of symmetry crept into our teaching—that's how I learned it myself when I took neuroanatomy at Harvard Med back when I first met Subie—probably has something to do with our notions of symmetry in the universe. Or with esthetic considerations, which play a bigger role than non-

Symmetry, as wide or as narrow as you may define its meaning, is one idea by which man through the ages has tried to comprehend and create order, beauty, and perfection.

The physicist
HERMANN WEYL, 1952

scientists might guess in our formulations of how nature seems to work.

But its origins are not the issue, so much as how it has persisted for so many years. Even freshman biology students in my human brain lab can spot the differences in the two halves of a human brain if you ask them to look for differences, rather than prejudicing the issue by saying "Of course, they're just mirror-images." You only have to look inside a typical skull (a real one, not a plastic replica that an artist has tidied up) to see that the hollows made by the front of the brain are different on the two sides (the right frontal tip is usually larger than the left), and that the back of the left brain produces a bigger hollow than the right side.

One way in which the notion of anatomical symmetry has persisted in textbooks is that the author's rough sketches for illustrations are forwarded to a medical artist for a professional redrawing. They always come back looking much nicer than you can manage yourself. They are sometimes even beautiful. But esthetics once again enters the picture—the artist, too, thinks

THE TYPICAL ASYMMETRIC, SKEWED HUMAN BRAIN

Right frontal pole protrudes beyond left

Right hemisphere wider than left

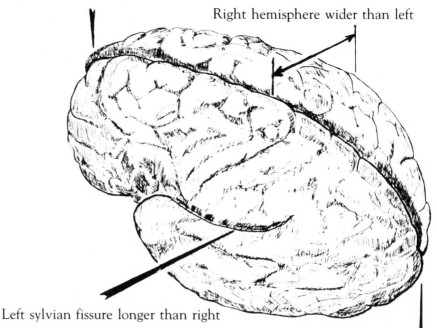

Left sylvian fissure longer than right

Left occipital pole protrudes beyond right

that brains are symmetric. A few years ago, when George Ojemann and I were making up the 88 illustrations that went into
our paperback book, *Inside the Brain*, we carefully sketched the
right front and left rear of the brain as protruding beyond their
neighbors. But the finished illustrations came back looking like
mirror-images. As far as the artist was concerned, we had obviously been sloppy in our preliminary sketches (not, I admit,
an unreasonable assumption in most cases!). I think that I dis-
turbed a cherished notion about the universe when I explained
to the artist that brains really aren't symmetric.

Of course the primary blame must be laid at the feet of the
people like me who teach the subject, for not noticing the natural asymmetry themselves and then educating others. I am reminded of how the biology textbooks and reference books, back
when I was in school, all proclaimed that human cells had their
genes arranged on 24 pairs of chromosomes. Ahem. We really
have 23 pairs. The textbook karyotypes indeed show 23 pairs.
Someone couldn't count. And then no one blew the whistle for
some time.

How can careful scientists make such glaring mistakes? And
how can other scientists take so long to correct them? Scientists
belong to the same general culture as everyone else. Unless a
matter is important for some specific reason (and brain asymmetries and absolute chromosome numbers haven't been really
important in anyone's analysis until recent years), they may not
take careful note of it. Or if they do notice, they may not think
it worth the trouble to proclaim that the emperor has no clothes
unless they're sure that it makes some important difference.

When one of these fictions is unmasked, you usually find that
the people in the field will say with some impatience: "Yes, of
course. Everyone in the field knows that, has for a long time."
Some of that is covering one's tracks, but it does represent a
truth of sorts. There is always a lot of knowledge about a subject which isn't published: things that aren't sure yet, things that
are out of fashion, things that "everyone knows" so that claim-
ing credit for the discovery by writing it up yourself seems pre-
sumptuous. The only way to find out about such unpublished
things is to listen carefully in seminars to the questions afterward, or to the gossip at tea time among the professors and
graduate students.

One of the things that makes science different from other
enterprises is that everything is fair game, always up for possible
revision (if you can find the time and money to tackle it). There
is a real sense of correct and incorrect, it's just that explanations are assumed to be imperfect. A plurality of competing
viewpoints is assumed to be the normal, desirable state of affairs

This elaborate cartoon on plate
tectonics was assembled, and it
was beautiful, except for one
detail: The earth was rotating
the wrong way. When I pointed
that out, nobody. . . could
really see it being that important. What was the big deal? I
came to realize that "wrong"
means something different to an
artist than to a physicist. The
artists thought we were just
being argumentative, quarrel-
some, picky, when we said
things were wrong. To us, a fact
is either right or wrong. To
them, "wrong" is more of an
aesthetic question.
SCIENCE ADVISOR TO A
TELEVISION PROGRAM, 1980

once one gets beyond simple facts such as chromosome number and brain symmetry. We like—even though we do not always immediately practice—the principle that juniors can correct their seniors and the textbooks.

AND WHAT ABOUT brain functioning: How symmetrical is that? When we think of right-handedness and language—which are most strongly developed in humans—it's obvious that human brain functioning isn't symmetric. But we still tend to think that the other animals are largely symmetrical in their brain organization, that humans are the exception to the rule. That's not the case: animals have a great deal of asymmetry when one observes them closely. Rats usually circle to the left, and their tails also curl left. In pressing a bar to avoid a shock, a large percentage of lab rats prefer to use their left paw. And when one looks inside the brain, there are various asymmetries in chemistry as well as anatomy. Some of them are more pronounced in male rats than in females.

When one looks at "emotional" behaviors, one finds that the brain anatomy can predict emotionality. There is, of course, lots of variation in a population, even in an inbred strain of laboratory rat. If you find a rat with a much larger right hemisphere than its left hemisphere, it will probably be cautious when exploring a new environment, taking a long time to visit all the corners and sniff them. And it will likely be an unhesitating mouse-killer, unlikely to live-and-let-live if a mouse is placed in the same cage. Rats with a less pronounced size difference between the hemispheres exhibit more exploratory behavior, and have more of a tendency to coexist with a passing mouse. The rats that explore the most, and mouse-kill the least, are those uncommon rats whose left hemisphere is bigger than the right.

It is thought that the right hemisphere is more emotional, and that the left hemisphere holds it in check, since splitting the brain or removing the left hemisphere causes more mouse-killing and more cautious exploration. There has been some suggestion of this in humans, which was once symbolically illustrated by a drawing in the *New York Times* showing a split-brain patient swinging an axe with his left hand (controlled by the right hemisphere) but with the right hand swinging over to grab the axe on its way down.

So the things we notice most easily—human right-handedness and left-hemisphere language—may have developed from a foundation that was already skewed in early mammals by this "emotional" specialization. Are humans like the rats, being less likely to explore, or coexist with a passing mouse, if they have an oversized right hemisphere? I don't think anyone has looked.

□   □   □

The flame of conception seems to flare and go out, leaving a man shaken, and at once happy and afraid. There's plenty of precedent of course. Everyone knows about Newton's apple. Charles Darwin said his *Origin of Species* flashed complete in one second, and he spent the rest of his life backing it up; and the theory of relativity occurred to Einstein in the time it takes to clap your hands. This is the greatest mystery of the human mind—the inductive leap. Everything falls into place, irrelevancies relate, dissonance becomes harmony, and nonsense wears a crown of meaning.

The novelist JOHN STEINBECK, 1954

It is a wondrous thing to have the random facts in one's head suddenly fall into the slots of an orderly framework. It is like an explosion inside. . . . I think that I spend half my time just talking and listening to people from many fields, searching together for how [plate tectonics] might all fit together. And when something does fall into place, there is that mental explosion and the wondrous excitement. I think the human brain must love order.

The marine geologist TANYA ATWATER, 1981

What's beautiful in science is that same thing that's beautiful in Beethoven. There's a fog of events and suddenly you see a connection. It . . . connects things that were always in you that were never put together before.

The physicist VICTOR WEISSKOPF

There are not many joys in human life equal to the joy of sudden birth of a generalization. . . . He who has once in his life experienced this joy of scientific creation will never forget it.

The geographer PETER ALEKSEYEVICH KROPOTKIN, 1842–1921

Intelligence . . . is the capacity to guess right by discovering new order.

The neurobiologist HORACE B. BARLOW, 1983

GETTING WET in the bottom of the Grand Canyon is usually something that happens in the daytime, incidental to running a rapid, taking a bath in the river, or getting involved (sometimes with malice aforethought on a hot afternoon) in a waterfight between adjacent boats. The nights are usually comfortably dry. Though river-runners carry along tents, they don't expect to have to use them in June or early July in the Canyon. And it's a good thing too, because the nighttime temperatures often stay high enough so that you don't want a tent between you and the breeze.

This year the monsoon season started early, the cumulonimbus clouds building in the late afternoon as the heat rose from

MILE 109
Bass Camp
Sixth Campsite

the Canyon to push the moist upper air from the oceans to higher altitudes, producing a lightning show for dessert. Peach flambé— canned peaches, but with the fire in the sky reflecting off the juice. Tents that had been carried for years but never unrolled were reluctantly erected, that being the surest known way of making the rain fall elsewhere.

My own tent stayed home; instead I had brought a tube-tent, the closest thing to a single-use throwaway item included on my packing list, never unfurled in over ten years (and for good reason, given their soggy reputation for interior rainfall via condensation). Forsaking seconds on the peaches, I too joined the brigade of pole-and-string architects in the fading twilight. To my surprise, the "instant tent" was intact and didn't shred into a million pieces from age.

We are still in the inner gorge and the metamorphic rock sticks up here and there within the sandy camp, providing me with two places to tie up the tent.

As the freshening winds were added to the lightning, it became evident that our superstitious ploy for avoiding the rains was going to fail. So I decided that I might as well stay up to watch the show. Though there were surely better places than from inside that tube tent. Grumble, grumble. Nevermore. I'll bring a real tent next time.

Fortunately there was a cave nearby. Not in the Redwall, where we found caves upriver, but inside a very large, room-sized boulder. The boulder was really a chunk of old riverbed conglomerate, a lot of medium-sized rocks that had been cemented together and later dumped near our campsite. At some point it had lost some of its constituent rocks, leaving a considerable cavity in one side. The resulting "cave" was full of nooks and crannies, just the place for a scorpion or a rattlesnake to live. Luckily, I was able to inspect the smooth sand in front of the cave for footprints and snake tracks. It seemed uninhabited—except, perhaps, for bats. If they lived there in the daytime, they were surely out gathering insects at night. So I crawled in and hoped that they wouldn't return just because of the storm.

In short order a magnificent desert thunderstorm began, heralded by ruffles and flourishes. Lightning, thunder, driving rain, blowing brush tumbling past, wind waves on the river. Added to the colors of the sunset on the high walls of the Grand Canyon, it had its virtues. It became one of those scenes that you could lose yourself in. Its wonders were hypnotizing. Rumbling bass notes, cracks of thunder. Sheets of lightning, then jagged extravaganzas. Thor outdid himself. Fresh cool breezes on the face, new smells brought in by the storm. And a little rain on one leg and foot, which didn't quite fit inside the one-person instant cave.

DURING A LULL when the rains stopped and the hypnotic spell wore off, I stood up and stretched, shook the dry foot which was tingling from lack of blood. The bats were still out working hard at making their living. For humans of even modest size, the cave was hardly suitable for sleep, only for long nights contemplating the elements.

Surely, it occurred to me while awaiting the second act, I was not the first person to take shelter from a storm in this little cave. This boulder has been lying here for many thousands of years while Indians had been hunting in the Canyon. Nearby, up on the hill behind our campsite, are numerous Anasazi ruins. Where I had reclined, with most of me inside the enclosure, had probably been where a lone hunter took refuge during a similar thunderstorm in ages past. In this very place, he probably looked out and saw much the same sights, felt the same damp breeze, was shaken by the same thunder claps. And worried about similar rattlesnakes. Unless he was a lot smaller than I am, he got one foot wet too.

He was undoubtedly in better shape than I am physically—certainly his feet were less tender and he could run farther. But he was probably hungry, and his teeth were surely worn down from eating too many gritty roots or too much corn (sand gets mixed into it when grinding with the Anasazi *mano*, which is made of sandstone). He was probably half my age, since a man past forty was ancient and perhaps toothless back then, unless extraordinarily lucky. Those conditions made it rather hard to accumulate knowledge, especially if you were also on the move all the time, just trying to get your children to a self-sufficient age before you passed from the scene yourself.

It was really his level of culture that made the difference between us, not just his lack of agriculture or technology. A properly organized culture means that the dead can speak to you.

Archimedes speaks to me from thousands of years ago, his "Eureka" echoing whenever I wonder why I float better in my lifejacket. But not as well in white water.

Ptolemy too speaks to me about the stars from back then, just as Galileo speaks from four centuries ago about the planets.

Isaac Newton speaks to me from three centuries ago, telling me the laws that apples and planets both obey.

James Hutton speaks to me from 200 years ago whenever I contemplate the layer-cake geology of the Grand Canyon, even though he never set foot near this greatest geological spectacle on earth.

Ben Franklin speaks to me from that same era when I look up at the lightning, telling me of nature's electricity. And I still use Clerk Maxwell's equations relating magnetism to electricity, the first of the "field" theories in physics, one of the magnificent intellectual achievements of the nineteenth century.

As also was Charles Darwin's achievement; he still speaks to me, each time that I contemplate the simplest problem in evolution, just as Paul Broca and Hughlings Jackson speak to me about brain organization from the nineteenth century when I struggle to understand maps in the brain.

Albert Einstein's words of 1905 still speak to me about space, time, and the packaging of energy.

The venerable Hans Bethe speaks to me from only decades ago, telling me how distant supernovae created the very carbon atoms which are now found in every cell of my body, indispensable to the simplest motion or metabolism. And he continues to speak to me in this decade, about how it is absolutely essential to control nuclear weapons.

And my scientific contemporaries speak to me constantly—across the dinner table, when I visit their labs, in the hallways and conference rooms, in print and on television. It is an exciting time to live, as most of the scientists who ever lived are alive today. Our river-running group is just a microcosm, biased toward those who concern themselves with how brains work. Neurobiology has developed so recently that even young researchers are likely to meet and talk with the pioneers—real two-way talk, in which you can still ask questions of the pioneers and get answers.

THE SECOND ACT has started, and I am back in the Anasazi's mini-cave. I see brief snapshots of the Canyon during each lightning flash. Certainly the difference between that Anasazi and myself is not biological. The human gene pool has changed significantly over 100,000 generations (for example, the brain has tripled in size), but hasn't changed much over the last forty generations, the last 0.04 percent of hominid evolution. At birth we were probably very similar, as similar as any two babies born yesterday in the same hospital in Los Angeles. But all that neural hardware in the brain is versatile—it can tune itself up to detect a bighorn sheep hiding amidst a thicket of mesquite trees on a slope of jumbled rocks. Or to recognize an arbitrary symbol like the letter "T." Or to piece together a faint buzzing sound, when walking down a hot, dusty trail, with a mental representation of the combination that results in "Stop. Rattlesnake. Look before leaping."

That Anasazi could have spotted many more bighorn sheep

than I've seen so far this trip. He probably had a dozen names for that spectrum of canyon colors that I merely call red, reddish-orange, and orange. He surely knew the stars better than I do, having long, clear winter nights in which to contemplate them without the distractions of books and television. The names of many of the constellations come down to us from well before the invention of writing 5,000 years ago. And recognizing a constellation by fitting seven stars to your mental image of a ladle—well, that's schemata for you, par excellence.

We see if things fit the mold. These are all schemata, mental templates for situations, which come to mean something. A schema (as in schematic outline) is pieced together from those simpler neural templates that Keffer Hartline began studying, using those higher-order cells of visual cortex that specialize in lines and edges, those cells in the dozen even-higher cortical regions that carry out even more complex analyses of the visual images we see, those committees with emergent properties.

Some schemata are probably inborn, perhaps the common primate fears of snakes and deep water. Babies are certainly born with a firm idea of what a human face ought to look like, as newborns will cry if shown drawings of faces with a missing eye or misplaced nose. But we acquire most schemata during life. Some, perhaps, are acquired much as the baby bird is tuned up to the overhead profile of the hawk, by editing some connections between schemata. Surely, however, some of our new schemata are created by building up, more like a carpenter does with building blocks, than by selectively removing material as a carver does.

We are always trying out new sensory information against our resident schemata, seeing what mold they fit among the multitudes in our cephalic library. And the human brain seems to have acquired an almost unlimited capacity to create new schemata. Indeed, given our compulsions to distinguish this from that and thus create dichotomies, we might be said to have a passion for new schemata, creating a new mold when the old ones don't quite fit.

We also have a passion for creating new molds for concepts as well as facts, for lumping various elements together under a new heading. For discovering new order. We love to distinguish one thing from another—and that's an evolutionary clue. To some extent, that which gives us particular pleasure is likely to have once been important in evolution—and the singular sense of pleasure we get when things fall into place testifies to the importance of forming new schemata.

Watching the stars and galaxies that first night on the river, we contemplated the evolution of matter such as the elementary particles. That night waiting for the eclipse, we contemplated the evolution of the organization of matter, not just into stars and planets but into life itself. But here—this is a new kind of evolution, one that involves mental structures, webs of relationships. In a sense, they have become emancipated from the material world, living a life of their own on a new plane of existence. And as these webs, these schemata, become established and stable, they serve as building blocks themselves, as when the "journey" schema helps build new schemata such as "run-around" or "grid-lock." Supporting further evolution into more complex, higher forms.

And since behavior usually is the first thing to change, with anatomical variants only later being edited to streamline the body shape to optimize the new behavior, so a new schema is often the first step in evolving a flying squirrel—or snake!

Schema evolution—and its behavioral counterpart, cultural change—happens on a time scale far faster than biological evolution. It is transmitted to others without biological reproduction as the medium—rather through gestures, drawings, words, images, books, inventions. As the sociobiologist Richard Dawkins has proposed, we can call this cultural unit the "meme"—as in mime. They are contributions to the culture pool to be mimicked, rather than contributions to the gene pool. Mimicking genes, memes propagate themselves by metastasizing minds—sometimes even against your will, as when an advertising jingle keeps running through your head despite your best efforts to shut it off.

And onto this new evolution, we can attempt to impose humane values, those considerations largely missing from earlier evolution. When the foundation of these values rested only on an appeal to a higher authority (by analogy to the parental "You'll do it that way because I told you so"), the responsibility wasn't firmly in our laps. If the emerging facts of primate societies say what I think they say, we humans have made some important choices along the way of evolving our societies—we call them ethics, values, sometimes morality—that make our high civilization a far better place to live than some other human and primate societies. They may not be inevitable and, if we value them, we'll have to work hard to retain them in the face of the vicissitudes of time. What is natural isn't always good.

THE LADDER OF LIFE is an old metaphor, standing for the gradual progression to more intricate forms of life. But since a branching tree better describes the world of our ancestors, ladders are somewhat out of fashion; yet they do seem applicable to the hierarchy of schemata in the brain, to more complex ways of representing information. But a ladder is not quite the right metaphor. A staircase is better, simply because one can imagine resting on each step. Without slipping backwards. As a matter of esthetics, I like to imagine a spiral staircase. DNA makes a lovely spiral staircase, those C, G, A, and T bases being the steps.

Darwin marshalled a mighty weight of evidence for the existence of evolution, an idea that had been around for many decades. But Darwin also put his finger on a crucial piece of the mechanism of evolution, natural selection. The survival of the fittest, as his contemporary Herbert Spencer later phrased it, leads to plants and animals that are even more cleverly suited than their ancestors to the environments in which they live. Since the climate keeps changing, the life forms gradually change too, becoming even more complex in order to beat out their less versatile competitors.

As Darwin presented it, this process is gradual. Rather than a spiral staircase, one imagines a spiral ramp, like one of those spiralling driveways that connect different levels of a giant parking garage. With life gradually creeping up the ramp to higher and higher levels, driven by natural selection.

THE PARKING GARAGE is an attractive metaphor, now that I think about it, since the floors attached to the spiral ramp suggest the ability of life-forms to spread out on a stable level. While a minority continue to creep up the spiral ramp and change, others may have a population explosion to populate a new empty level—the empty niche of the ecologist's lingo. In this parking garage, the Model T's would be on the bottom level, the finned cars of the 1950s on several middle levels, and our latest creations on the top level.

If you were an archaeologist digging up a parking garage, nearly all the cars you'd uncover would be parked on one level or another; few would actually be on a ramp between levels. And so it is with the evolutionary history uncovered by paleontologists. As they dig deeper, they find relatively sudden changes in animal species, not the gradual changes they might have seen had they been lucky enough to locate the spiral ramp off on the edge of the garage. One of the things which has happened in the century since Darwin is the realization that new species arise off in isolated corners, not out in the middle of a floor. This "allopatric speciation" was first argued convincingly by the evolutionary theorist Ernst Mayr some decades ago.

The point has been made even more forcefully of late—by people like Niles Eldredge, Stephen Jay Gould, and Steven Stanley—that there really are floors, that species as a whole do not change gradually. Indeed, large populations are surprisingly resistant to change, contrary to what one might expect from the Darwinian idea of gradual natural selection. The floor of the garage is the equilibrium of punctuated equilibria. When the creep up the spiral ramp—Darwinian gradualism occurring to an isolated population off in a corner—reaches a new stable level, there will be a population explosion to fill the new floor (a new niche, in ecological terms). So that to the historian digging down through the layers, the fossil record will appear to be one of punctuated stability.

And our cultural evolution looks much the same. Writing wasn't gradually invented everywhere, but rather by what was probably a small group of tax accountants in Sumer, and then the idea spread around. Mathematics and geometry owe much to what happened on the Greek island of Samos in the sixth century B.C. among the followers of Pythagoras. Because ideas reproduce themselves in virgin minds, thanks to our passion for new schemata, our thoughts have come to have lives of their own, and thus an evolutionary history of their own.

THE SPIRAL RAMP is not just for life forms and ideas—genes and memes—but is perhaps a metaphor for the entire physical and prebiological history of the universe. There is, of course, a romantic tendency to think big when looking out at the stars in the clearings between the passing thunderclouds. But it is an exciting idea, one I cannot avoid pursuing. If we are ever to contemplate the grand sweep of evolution, from the Big Bang through all the intermediate stages to the Big Brain, it will have to be with the aid of some such metaphor. Is this the forest, whose trees we have been individually describing?

Of course there are many gaps in our knowledge—it is a spiral ramp seen through the clouds, still obscured in places, still fuzzy in others. Many a floor is missing because it disappeared long ago, having served only as scaffolding for another floor. But the metaphor of the spiral ramp with attached floors expands on Jacob Bronowski's notion of stratified stability, encompasses evolutionary species and ecological niches, and handles the hierarchy envisaged by the old one-dimensional ladder of life. It provides a chance to rise above the details and contemplate the grand sweep of all of evolution.

I feel like shouting "Eureka!", awakening the camp. But caution reasserting itself, I satisfy myself with a broad smile instead, and look overhead at the drifting clouds. I must try this out, see just how much of the universe's known mechanisms can be appreciated from this new viewpoint.

Suppose, even if it were true, that I woke someone up and

announced the spiral-ramp parking garage as the grand metaphor for the mechanisms of the universe? Hmmm. I'll have to see what I can do to improve that image. It just doesn't have the elegance of Michelangelo's God reaching down from the ceiling of the Sistine Chapel to create life on Earth. Or even Einstein's Watchmaker God, who supposedly made the universe and then started it running, leaving it alone thereafter (presumably having better things to do than rescue individuals from their follies), watching it go on to eventually invent its own customer complaint departments, and provide its own limited warranties.

THE SHOW'S OVER, I think. The luminous clouds have drifted farther west and darkened, the air seems warm again, and the lightning hasn't been seen for quite a while now. I contemplate extracting myself from the boulder to wend my way in the quiet darkness through the trees and tents, back to my imitation of a tent.

Then a great sheet of lightning brightens the camp. And I dimly and distantly see a nude female figure coming up the path from the river, her right hand stabilizing a towel wrapped around her head obscuring her face, her left hand holding a tube of shampoo. The light flickers out, and the apparition silently disappears into the dark camp. I await another flash of lightning, but see only faint shimmers deep inside the retreating clouds.

What is there in life except one's ideas,
Good air, good friend, what is there in life?
                    WALLACE STEVENS, *The Man with the Blue Guitar*

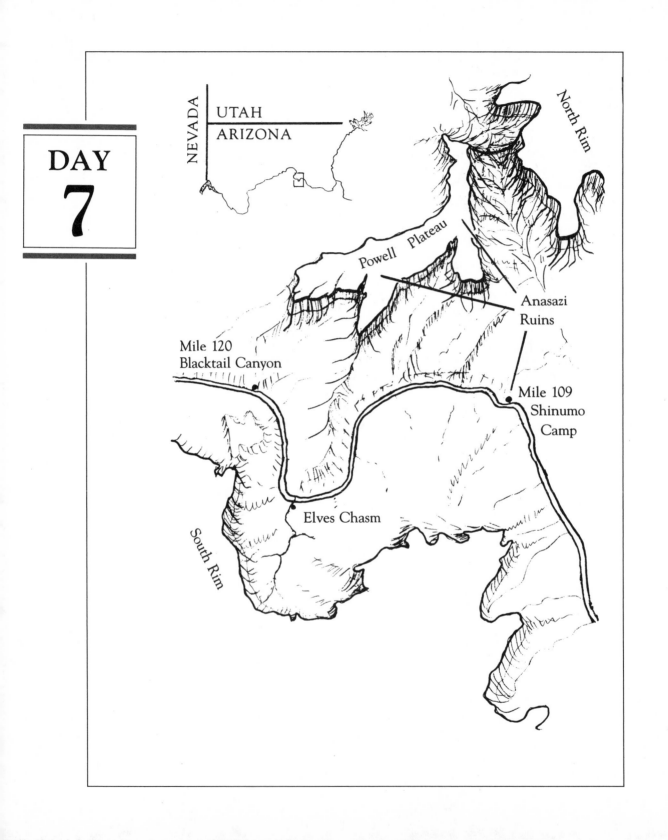

THE GREAT SANDAL BOAT RACE is run at Shinumo Creek, just downriver from our camp. The boatmen compete to see whose sandals can get through the rapids the fastest. The race is run in the creek, where there is a cascade of water through the side canyon. Just as in the Colorado River where the water cascades too steeply and becomes a local waterfall, there are white holes in the creek too. And if you think that white holes are bad, the boatmen joke, just wait until you see that black hole in Lava Falls.

The idea is to start your sandal on the far side of the creek's channel at the top, so that the current will carry it away from the minihole below the little cascades. But sandal after sandal, cheered on by the spectators, falls prey to the hole, sailing around and around the eddy, getting pushed beneath the surface again when swept under the little waterfall. What those sandals need are miniature boatmen to steer them. Elves Chasm is just down the way. . . .

In a steady relay, boatmen run tirelessly from the bottom of the cascade, carrying their sandals back up to the top. Bets are placed, the racing sandals are urged on. The boatman with the biggest feet won. Like the baloney boats, his sandals were so long that they spanned the hole, continuing on through.

THE POWELL PLATEAU is in our way, and the river swings south to take a 10-mile U-shaped detour around it. Unlike other mesa tops inside the Canyon, this one has trees growing atop it in profusion, though we cannot see them from the river. The Powell Plateau is isolated from the North Rim, however, by a deep valley. And so it sits there, a little island in the sky.

The Anasazi lived on top of Powell Plateau. Indeed, your chances of stumbling upon a ruin there are considerably higher than anywhere else around northern Arizona. Hundreds of people at a time must have lived there. Considering the resources (water was scarce, for example, once the snowbanks were exhausted) and the archaeologists' analysis of what the Anasazi left behind, they were probably seasonal visitors. Perhaps they came down to the river for the winter, as there was a whole collection of south-facing Anasazi ruins up behind Bass Camp last night. The situation certainly reminds me of Unkar Delta, right below those Anasazi ruins on the eastern side of the North Rim. "Going South for the Winter" may have been popular even a millennium ago.

There are quite a number of animal species living in the forest on Powell Plateau today—deer, squirrels, chipmunks, rats, mice. To visit others of their species living on the North Rim proper, they would have to leave the woods and descend to the naked saddle, climbing back up 75 stories again on the other side. Because of this trek, the animals of Powell Plateau are largely isolated, inbreeding rather than mixing their genes with their neighbors across the way. Biologists love situations such as this. It seems to speed up the slow grind of evolutionary processes, producing new species from old.

This near-isolation happens in island chains all the time. An animal species will arrive on an island—perhaps only a single pregnant female carried along by the winds or currents. Her progeny then populate the island and slowly spread to the other islands in the chain. Initially the animals on different islands can interbreed, though they will tend to breed among themselves. Pretty soon the collection of genes on one island may become sufficiently idiosyncratic that individuals from that island won't breed too successfully with individuals from other islands, even when given the chance. When the odds of successful interbreeding become low enough, a new species has effectively been formed.

Fruit flies (the same *Drosophila* that geneticists raise in milk bottles) arrived in the Hawaiian Islands long ago; indeed, the original island they inhabited has since sunk. Every remaining island has its own species of fruit fly—indeed, because of all the ridges of lava that isolate the major drainages from one another, every major valley on each island is likely to have an endemic species of its very own. Now it is true that each valley has somewhat different vegetation, and the various species are to some extent specialists. That's the traditional Darwinian view of how new species spring up, that natural selection means only the variants that are best equipped to the valley's particular environment will survive, so that eventually each valley will have somewhat different-looking fruit flies from every other. But that isn't the whole story—indeed, heresy triumphant, perhaps the least important aspect.

APPEARANCES USED TO BE ALL-IMPORTANT. When a paleontologist looks at shells or bones, appearances may be all there is to go on. And so the dividing line between one species and another is largely in the eye of the beholder, although there are some standards about such things. Biologists have a more functional definition of a species: a population of individuals that can interbreed successfully.

"Know the story about the squirrels on the North Rim?" Alan asked as he rowed us downriver. We were in one of those lazy spells on the river. "Those Kaibab squirrels look pretty much like the Abert squirrels over on the South Rim. They've got pointy ears, just like the cartoon characters. Both kinds build their nests pretty much alike. Sure seems likely that they used to all belong to one species. But then the river got in the way. Isolated them."

The river cut its path through the middle of the squirrel population? Ben asked. "Maybe," said Alan. "But then too, perhaps the squirrels moved up to the South Rim after the Canyon started forming. And some of the squirrels crossed the river. Had themselves a little population explosion, with no competition for all the squirrel food on the right bank. Probably happened a long time ago, maybe back when the river was dry, 4 million years ago. In any event, after all that time of being unable to

Kaibab Squirrel (North Rim)
Sciurus kaibabensis

Abert Squirrel (South Rim)
Sciurus aberti

mix their genes with the ones across the river, they probably couldn't interbreed now if they tried."

"We could always try and find out," volunteered Marsha. "I'll bet that Alan could catch a squirrel and take it across the river." Alan's raised eyebrows suggested that Marsha could catch her own squirrels. Marsha, however, is becoming irrepressible. The necklace has emboldened her.

Two populations may look identical, but be unable to interbreed because their gene pools have become too idiosyncratic. They are called sibling species. In other cases, two populations may look very different but still be able to interbreed. Such as German shepherds and miniature poodles—both part of the single species, *Canis familiaris*. So appearances can be deceiving.

And experimental geneticists can create new species of fruit flies in the laboratory, with ease—all without any selection. They just mimic what would happen in the island-hopping example. Select eight individuals from a cage (actually a little milk bottle), and put them in an empty bottle with plenty to eat. This is essentially what happens when a new island is invaded by a few individuals from the adjacent island—a founder population. They will, as the phrase goes, breed like flies. Soon the empty bottle will be full of flies, all bearing some combination of the genes found in the eight founders. Now take eight of their offspring from that bottle and give them a new bottle, again mimicking another one-island hop further along the archipelago. Another population explosion occurs, all descendants of those the latter-day pioneers, who were in turn descendants of the original eight founders.

Keep up this bottleneck-and-boom sequence, mimicking the island-hopping that probably occurred as the Hawaiian-island chain was populated. Now, from the fourth such "island" bottle in the chain, take some individuals and see if they can interbreed with ones from the original bottle's population. You will find that the "inter-island" matings are nowhere as successful as "intra-island" matings. Some barriers to successful reproduction have appeared, not because of natural selection and adaptations (the bottles are such perfect environments that everyone lives), but just because of inbreeding followed by a population explosion, repeated a few times. With enough islands to hop, one is almost guaranteed a new species of fruit fly—even without natural selection.

But why doesn't this speciation happen on the original island; why doesn't the original population fragment? Because they keep the gene pool stirred up, having far more choice in mates. On a secondary or tertiary island, one has to mate with someone who is a close relative, everyone sharing the same grandparents, etc. A sufficiently inbred population seems to lose its compatibility with the ancestor population, and that idiosyncrasy is speciation: reproductive isolation.

Of course, in real life, separate populations also become specialized, because natural selection is also involved in the process. The natural variability in offspring, caused by having sexual reproduction shuffling the chromosomes constantly, means that some will survive better than others in less-than-perfect environments. The islands with bananas will come to have fly populations which thrive better on bananas than do the islands without them. The invasion of the island chain by the immigrant species will thus give rise to a diversity of new species—the new species may not have to look and act differently to achieve reproductive isolation, but in fact the less-than-perfect environments will select for physical characteristics such as wingspan, behavioral characteristics such as fear of predators.

"So you only find one species of fly on each island?" Marsha asked.

"At one time, but by now some of those new species on the out-islands have been blown back to the original island. If enough of them blow back, they'll interbreed with each other, even though they can no longer breed with the original parent population. So you'll end up having multiple species on each island." Alan paused, and decided to start rowing again. "The physical isolation isn't needed anymore to maintain the two different populations, once reproductive isolation also develops. Whenever you see two similar species living together, you know that they probably got started living apart."

And the squirrels on the two sides of our river provide a simple example of how another permanent barrier is erected between populations. There are inheritable variations, for example, in the month when the compulsion to mate strikes different squirrels. Some squirrels mate only during one day of the entire year. Alan noted that the Kaibab squirrels breed three months after the Abert squirrel's mating day, which is in early March. The later spring thaws on the North Rim eliminated those variant squirrels whose breeding seasons were normal by South Rim standards but which gave birth during the fatal North Rim snows. The North Rim survivors were those whose gene combinations happened to produce an extremely late breeding season—usually a day in early June.

Selection and speciation—there can be one without the other. Domestic dogs are a good example of selection without speciation (though achieved by artificial rather than natural selection). The ancestor of all dogs was a relative of the jackal. But by breeding the smaller offspring with each other, subpopulations were obtained. Both German shepherds and miniature poodles resulted as the body-size genes were segregated into subgroups. But they can still interbreed, since dogs don't speciate as easily as some animals (beetles will speciate if you look at them and frown). If the reproductive affairs of dogs were no longer controlled by humans, dogs would mix up those genes. Then most dogs would be mongrels, probably not unlike the original jackal-like dog.

So selection by the environment, whether natural or artificial, need not produce a permanent effect. Even if squirrels with heavier fur coats survived better on the North Rim, those heavier fur genes could easily be lost by subsequent mixing of the gene pool. Indeed, most natural selection is a fleeting thing, of no permanent significance. How, then, can the results of natural selection become permanently established?

The answer? Prevent remixing. Speciation is the cog on the ratchet. It prevents backsliding. A little change in the mating season, thanks to a difference in the month of the spring thaw, and presto—you've got a new species, because the males and females of the different populations will never be interested in one another at the same time. And that will prevent adaptations such as better fur coats from being lost in a mixup of genes. A fur-coat ratchet, the delayed mating season serving as the cog that prevents backsliding to less hair.

"And here Marsha was all set to have me ferry a poor Kaibab squirrel across the river," Alan kidded. "Just think how unhappy a Kaibab would've been when mating season came and no one was interested. Such heartbreak!"

Marsha looks like she's plotting revenge on Alan, though. And Alan doesn't know about the necklace hoax.

The finches evolved in isolation. So did everything else on earth. With the finches, you can see how it happened. The Galapagos islands are near enough to the mainland that some strays could hazard there; they were far enough away that those strays could evolve in isolation from parent species. And the separate islands were near enough to each other for further dispersal, further isolation, and the eventual reassembling of distinct species. (In other words, finches blew to the Galapagos, blew to various islands, evolved into differing species, and blew back together again.). . . It is as though an archipelago were an arpeggio, a rapid series of distinct but related notes. If the Galapagos had been one unified island, there would be one dull note, one super-dull finch.

Annie Dillard, *Teaching a Stone to Talk*, 1982

□   □   □

EVOLUTION HAS MANY CAUSES. First of all, you need variations on a theme. Indeed, nature is so fond of having lots of variations on a basic plan that it doesn't leave the matter to mutations. While cosmic rays sometimes change one DNA base to another, thus coding for a somewhat different protein, and while mutagenic chemicals occasionally change the instructions too, the number of variants can be further increased by shuffling the deck, literally snipping the long DNA chains on a chromosome into shorter segments and recombining them in different ways. That shuffle is what biological sex is all about.

I'll bet that isn't what you thought sex was all about. Sex, however, isn't just a means of reproduction—budding off, cloning, whatever, will take care of that. There are even virgin births in some otherwise sexual species where females do their own thing occasionally. Sex involves making a new individual that isn't quite like either parent.

That's what sex is all about? Added randomness producing more grist for the mills of natural selection and speciation? How disillusioning.

THE GREAT UNCONFORMITY confronts us again, this time with the Tapeats Sandstone sitting atop the far older Precambrian schists. The schists have dikes of pink granite injected into them (that's geologist talk for the cracks in the schist being filled up by molten granite). There are flexures and a fault, where the Unconformity has been locally thrust a few stories upward by some ancient uplifting event. Hiking along the shore, we see travertine—calcium carbonate deposits formed by mineral water flowing along the rocks. The travertine along the shoreline is sharp stuff, and you learn to walk carefully enough so that a handhold isn't necessary to keep your balance. But then the trail leads up the canyon and the handholds are worn smooth and are safe to use, thanks to hardy predecessors on the trail.

And the trail comes to another idyllic waterfall, tucked back into a narrow crack into which large boulders have become wedged. Greenery drapes down the waterfall, and the spray keeps finer greenery growing on adjacent walls. Elves Chasm, it was called by someone who overrode the local fascination with Spanish and oriental names. You can swim to the grotto and then climb back up behind the waterfall, ascending up a level or two inside the rocks while getting a cold shower, and then jump off an elevated perch into the pool below.

There is a trail of sorts up the right side, with plenty of ledges for sunning available in the Tapeats, looking out over the view below. The trail leads higher up the valley to three more waterfalls. But before it leaves the chasm of the lower falls, there is a great overhanging ledge at one point on the trail, blocking the path like a giant flatiron. If you are elf-sized (and this is the

MILE 116
Elves Chasm

only reason that I can see for the name), you can walk under this slab (ordinary mortals crawl). If you have the sticky fingers of a gecko, you can hug the rock and inch, spread-eagled, around the outside, exposed to the chasm. But somehow Gecko Chasm doesn't have the right ring to it.

Marsha is holding court down by the edge of the pool. Even sitting up above on the trail, I can hear the conversation perfectly. The bait has been taken—just the suggestion of a code, from her question yesterday about Aztec bookkeeping, has gotten three scientists talking about what sort of message could be hidden in the necklace. And, the genetic code being the one they are most familiar with, it is not long until someone asks the obvious question: how many letters in the alphabet? Four different kinds of beads, it seems. And how many letters in the message? Twenty-one beads in all.

"Were there more beads—is that a segment of a longer necklace?" asks Ben. Marsha reassures them that this was a complete necklace, according to the label on the museum display.

"So it could be a message 21 units long. Or maybe pairs of beads mean something?"

"No, that can't be right or there'd be an even number of beads. But triplets would work, seven of them giving 21. Triplets, just like the genetic code for proteins," explains Brian.

"See," Alan kids Marsha, "maybe you're carrying around the chemical formula for a deadly Indian arrowhead poison!"

Everyone laughed and began drifting away, several swimming to the base of the waterfall and climbing up inside it. Marsha waves at me, discreetly but triumphantly. She's really changed in the last few days on this trip; it's not so much that she feels safe flirting with the boatmen, but that she has a newfound confidence in judging other people correctly, in giving as good as she gets in repartee.

BRIAN AND BEN are back looking at Marsha's necklace again. It could just be that the puzzle is such a good excuse to stare at the anatomical territory over which the necklace is draped. But they are, in any event, pretending that it is a serious scientific matter. They are discussing which Indian poison is a peptide formed of seven amino acids. Certainly not curare, but. . . .

And then, remembering start codes and stop codes, Ben suggests that it might be a peptide of five amino acids instead.

Cam, who has come over and listened skeptically, points out that one could eliminate that possibility easily. If those first three beads were the standard start code AUG, then the last three would have to be a stop code. And, since all stop codes begin with U, the third bead from the end would have to be the same color as the second from the beginning.

How about that, it is! And the last two on the end are the same color as the first bead. . . hmmmm, the last three beads could be the stop code UAA. The four types of beads do match up in the right way at the far ends of the necklace. But that's ridiculous.

Brian is not to be deterred, pointing out that the remaining bead type must therefore be a C. They don't have our names for them—Auburn, Unfinished, Gray, and Chocolate—but they've named them with the letters from assuming that the first three beads, Auburn-Unfinished-Gray, must be AUG if they represent a start code. And that leaves the fourth type, what we called Chocolate.

Of course the last three beads could correspond with the starting beads just by chance. So it's a chance in a hundred that they match up. So what?

Everyone laughs again. What a funny coincidence! But the boatmen are starting to move people back down the canyon towards the boats.

Shortly after we get underway, the river takes a sharp right turn and heads due north, the third leg of our detour around the Powell Plateau. This long lovely stretch of river is known as Stephen Aisle. The Tapeats Sandstone is at river level in a number of places, with Precambrian rocks sticking through here and there. Some of these are thrust faults, four stories worth of uplift. At one point the shoreline Tapeats layers are thrust up several stories, then bent over and dropped vertically into the river, looking like a giant question mark laid on its side.

THERE IS AN ISLAND in the middle of the river, Precambrian metamorphic rock. But this is not another thrust fault; instead, we see the Great Unconformity protruding like an ancient thumb. This island, like some other protrusions of metamorphic rock sticking up into the Tapeats Sandstone in the canyon walls nearby, used to be an island in the Tapeats Sea, because it was hard enough to resist the erosion that earlier flattened the rest of the neighboring Precambrian rock. Then they were all covered with the sandstone. Now the sandstone has been worn away by the Colorado and the hard Precambrian rock stands exposed, an island once more. Even surrounded by water again.

Heaven knows where on earth this spot was originally located back during the Precambrian, while it was being eroded, or during the Cambrian, when the sandstone was being laid atop it. The continents have moved around quite a lot since then.

RIVER CORRIDOR CROSS SECTION

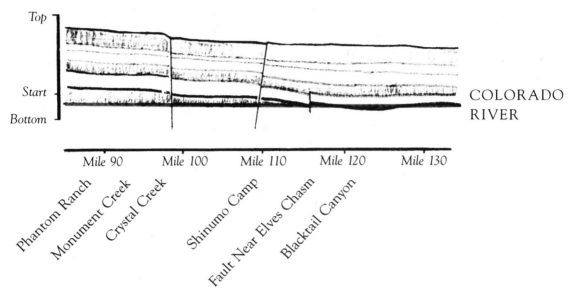

The story of continental drift and seafloor spreading is one of the key scientific discoveries of all time, ranking up there with Darwinian natural selection as an all-important pervading influence on how life has developed.

Back to Hawaii. Granted that islands are handy for diversifying a migrant species, that the isolation is handy to speciating so that the effects of all the natural selection that takes place are maintained even when remixing occurs. But seafloor spreading is what caused the Hawaiian islands to become a long string of volcanic islands in the first place. The volcanos that are currently active are all in the southeast corner of the southeast-to-northwest-tending chain. And now we know that the other islands used to be located where the active volcanos are now—that they have moved northwest since then. The oldest remaining islands are the ones at the northwest end of the chain at Midway atoll, at 17.9 million years. The youngest island, dating only to the last half million years, is the big island of Hawaii. Where Kilauea and Mauna Loa still spew out enough lava to add many miles to the coastline every century.

It seems that there is a weak spot in the earth's crust underlying the drifting plate, so that magma can be pushed up to the surface. The active volcanos are currently sitting atop this weak spot. Thanks to seafloor spreading to the southeast, the Pacific plate is slowly drifting northwest, no more than a hand's width per year. Periods of volcanic activity punch holes into the drift-ing plate overhead and push lava upwards to sit atop the sur-face—a volcanic eruption. It is at first an undersea volcano, forming a seamount; then it breaks the surface and goes into business as an island—and land plants, birds, and insects all manage to find it in short order, thanks to the wind and cur-rent. The island chain is like a giant paper-roll record of the volcanic activity of the last 18 million years.

In another million years there will be another Hawaiian is-land growing atop the hot spot. There are already growing sea-mounts beneath the Pacific Ocean southeast of the big island, submerged volcanos, islands in gestation. The local joke has it that real estate promoters are already selling retirement lots on them. Of course the islands are sinking too, as the plate appar-ently cannot support all that weight from the lava; this down-ward bowing of the plate has created a deep trench around the islands, like a moat around a castle.

Thus the Hawaiian islands form a microcosm showcase for the processes of evolution everywhere. Even in the tropics, where making a living is relatively easy, the physical environment is constantly changing. Animals and plants have to adjust to is-lands sinking, with their mountains therefore catching less rain-fall from the passing clouds. Volcanos periodically flood the landscape with new lava, so that a new round of natural selec-tion operates during the ensuing centuries. New land will form on the margins of volcanos, opening up new opportunities for colonization. And the fact that the land is parceled out into a series of small islands rather than one long strip means that geo-graphic isolation can work the ratchet in the gear wheels of evolution, conserving the creatures that variation and selection happen to produce.

Such forces have been operating on a worldwide scale for most of time, certainly since the land was first colonized nearly 400 million years ago but also earlier, since bays and troughs in the seafloor provide much of the same kinds of isolation as islands and are also disrupted by seafloor spreading. Life forms never had the chance to rest, perfectly adapted to their environ-ments, because the environment kept changing. The ocean currents, and therefore the continental weather patterns, were always slowly shifting. The fact that the plates are not firmly anchored has an overwhelming implication for evolution: it provides a constant drive to the evolutionary machinery, pre-venting a status quo from ever developing. Think for a moment of the unchanging moon if you want a contrast, what might have happened instead. It isn't just physical environment that is so important for evolution—it is a *constantly changing*, yet not chaotic, physical environment. Most of the universe wouldn't qualify.

SELECTION IS THE OTHER SIDE of the randomness coin. One doesn't do much good without the other. It is hard to appreciate just how powerful this combination is when the random variation is inheritable. People are always saying that our marvelous brains, or our precision eyes, are too complicated to have been designed by mere chance—that surely their sophistication of design speaks to a guiding hand from above. It seems like common sense. But what we don't see are all the failures that chance also produced—they're no longer around, those brains that got their owners into trouble before reproductive age, those eyes that didn't see the predator approaching. Selection usually brings with it a narrow, selective view of history.

This can be illustrated with a simple, presumably legal, get-rich-quick scheme (not my own invention; I seem to remember B. F. Skinner telling the story) which works because everyone's view of reality is partial, edited by circumstances. Suppose you send out a thousand postcards to people who gamble on the horse races, predicting that Pretty Boy will win the April race. Of course, you do exactly the same thing for Sunny Girl and the other eight horses in the race, except that you send each prediction to a different thousand bettors. After the race, no matter which horse wins, there are 1,000 bettors out of the original 10,000 who believe—indeed know—you predicted the race correctly. Forget the other 9,000 bettors who know you called it wrong. To those 1,000 who got the postcards correctly predicting that Sunny Girl would win in April, you try predicting the May race—to 100 of them, you send postcards reminding them of your previous success and predicting that Naughty Nag will win in May. And do this for all the other nine horses on the May schedule as well. After the May race, there will be 100 people who'll know you've called two races in a row correctly.

To those 100, you now send a telegram offering them a chance to subscribe to your racing newsletter for a mere $100 per month. Don't make any claims about your methods or successes, just let them draw their own conclusions. They'll think you've got an inside track, because your record is so much better than mere chance (even those who calculate your one-in-a-hundred odds of being right by chance won't know about the other 9,900 postcards). And so (even after the expenses for all those postcards and telegrams) you'll have thousands of dollars in profit.

And so it is with judging evolution in hindsight—we see the animals that survived, the organs that worked. The healthy ba-

Arrogance comes in a variety of forms. The arrogance of great wealth, the arrogance of great power, the arrogance of great beauty, and the arrogance of a great master are bearable because they rest on an acknowledged and measurable base. The arrogance of ignorance, however, is unbearable because it is rooted in smug satisfaction with being isolated from the facts of the case. The anti-evolution plank in the platform of Christian fundamentalism is a classic example of the arrogance of know-nothings.

The biologist
WILLIAM V. MAYER, 1984

bies we see born are those that survived the pressures for spontaneous abortion every day, from conception onward for nine
long months. We seldom realize the editing that has gone on
for thousands of generations. If one merely repeats the horse-
race scheme for 10 races (generations), the probability of any
one outcome is one in a billion; for 101 generations, it's one in
a googol. A *googol* is a mathematician's term for a ridiculously
large number, 10^{100}; there are, for example, only about 10^{81} elementary particles in the universe. We've had not just 101 but
100,000 opportunities for this selective view to compound
itself.

Which goes to show why probabilities based on looking
backwards are nonsense when many cycles of natural selection
are involved; selection biases the results of evolution generation
by generation, recycling the failures as food for another organism lower in the food chain, ratcheting the successes up from
one stable state to the next. All it takes is sunlight to pump
those probabilities—and enough generations to discover the
emergent stable states created by our environment. Natural selection is a mechanism, as R.A. Fisher used to say, for making
common that which is highly unlikely. Evolution too buries its
mistakes. Unlikely as we are, we're the survivors.

The next time someone laughs about monkeys typing Shakespeare, tell them that horse-race story—and the trouble with
thinking backwards.

Among all the events possible in the Universe the *a priori* probability of any particular one of them occurring is next to zero. Yet the
Universe exists; particular events must occur in it, the probability of
which (before the event) was infinitesimal . . . Destiny is written as
and while, not before, it happens.

                    JACQUES MONOD, *Chance and Necessity*, 1970

A depressingly large number of . . . scientists with metaphysical
proclivities [John Eccles, Karl Popper, Fred Hoyle, Francis Crick]
have posed this problem [marveling over the thousands of coinci-
dences necessary for life to exist]. . . . To infer that super-intelli-
gent beings are doing this on purpose [the so-called anthropic
principle] is a strange reversion to the supernatural and proves not so
much imagination as bankruptcy of imagination. The concept of life
emerging as a natural, perhaps inevitable function of existence is too
miraculous. We must have gods. What a shame we have such a lack
of imagination.

                    The science teacher RALPH ESTLING, 1983

☐   ☐   ☐

SELECTION is the reason why randomness can be so spectacularly successful. Both Charles Darwin and Alfred Russel Wallace read what the economist Thomas Malthus had written a

half-century earlier on population, about how quickly we would have a standing-room-only earth if all offspring survived to reproduce themselves. But animal populations haven't grown that rapidly—because not all offspring survive, and not all reproduce even if they have an ordinary life span. Their numbers are held in check by various factors, some more important than others. For some animals (say, polar bears) that have few predators, the availability of food becomes the limiting factor. For others (say, tropical species) which have almost unlimited food supplies, it is a predator population that regulates their numbers. And all suffer from disease, from pathogens which are themselves constantly mutating to defeat the immunological defenses erected by the host organism to protect itself.

Some variations in construction plan, produced by all that mutation and shuffling, are better than others for coping with the particular set of these factors we call the environment. They will be less likely to be weakened by pathogens or eaten by predators, more likely to be successful at locating food. And so they will produce more offspring. The particular genes that code for their version of body and brain will live on. The natural environment has, in essence, selected those genes that survive best—hence the term "natural selection." This was the key discovery. Natural selection.

By itself this need not lead to more complex bodies and brains—a new gene arrangement that simplified something might also be advantageous (greater energy efficiency, for example). But selection is never over. The next time the climate changes—it might, for example, revert to the original weather pattern—the altered environment will once again put each organism to the test. A more complex organism is more likely to be able to cope with several different environments. So while there is probably no upwards-to-complexity drive to variation and initial selection, there is a tendency for more complex multi-environment organisms to ride out the ensuing waves of selection better than the variations which were simply better suited for the first environmental change. In the long run, fancier lasts longer since versatility is a virtue. Lasting longer means more chances to mutate to a new species, more variants in the species competition. Ultimately, it is the fancier organisms that evolve—a mere consequence of the simple interaction of variation, selection, and the constantly drifting environment.

SO EACH SPECIES IS QUITE VARIABLE—obviously in body form, probably as a result of variations in relative growth rates, but also in inborn behavioral traits. I suppose that if the Irish elk entangled his giant antlers while running through the forest

The initial survival value of a favorable innovation is conservative, in that it renders possible the maintenance of a traditional way of life in the face of altered circumstances.

Romer's Rule, as phrased by C. F. HOCKETT and R. ASCHER, 1964

General progress occurs in changes that are not only adaptive to single environments but also are prospectively more widely useful in other environments.

The evolutionary theorist GEORGE GAYLORD SIMPSON, 1974

away from a wolf, one could say that a certain body form was being directly selected against. Certainly a fetus with too large a head (in the days before cesarean sections) would not only have killed itself but its mother too—which would make for very rapid selection against oversized heads (one reason why there sure must have been a strong counter-influence, why bigger brains must have been far better).

Selection, however, usually operates on how well something works (function), not on how it looks (morphology). Selection for function rewards one aspect of a morphological variant, while also hauling along any related anatomy at no extra charge, "for free." For example, variations in the time of sexual maturity result in some adults being more childlike than others, their development truncated. If juvenile playfulness were rewarded by selection (because, say, juveniles were more likely to try out new foods than traditional adults), and the successful adults were those who remained more juvenile, other anatomical changes would occur without themselves being exposed to selection (for example, the flatter face of juvenile primates, their smaller teeth, their larger brains compared to body size). Cause and effect are often so indirect in biological evolution as to completely obscure the reason why a useful variant arises.

Thus, natural selection may produce adaptation to an environment in terms of one function but, in passing, change another subtly-linked anatomical feature. And so the path of evolution meanders, like this river (though, now that I look, this is one of the straightest stretches of river I've ever seen—we must be following an old fault line).

And sometimes we see a sidestep in evolution, where a structure under selection because of one function becomes secondarily useful for a novel function, as in the thermoregulation-to-flight story of feathers. As Darwin emphasized, "In considering transitions of organs, it is so important to bear in mind the probability of conversion from one function to another."

Are there trends to evolution, principles that would predict us as an inevitable product of the evolutionary machinations? Nineteenth-century naturalists were fond of the notion of orthogenesis, saying there was a straight-line tendency to evolutionary paths that was independent of natural selection (for example, a predetermined "upwards to perfection" tendency). While that isn't believed anymore, there are several tendencies that are thought to operate. One is the aforementioned tendency towards multienvironment organs ("complexity"). A second is a tendency to speciate, the reproductive isolation thus preserving the editing done by natural selection from subsequent dilution. A third is some tendency toward increased size; the punctuated-equilibrium theorists note that shell size may creep upward during the otherwise static period of 3 to 10 million years that a single marine molluscan species exists (the bigger you are, the more choice you have in food and the fewer that can eat you). These three mundane trends lack the appeal of "perfection" as a principle, but they do explain a lot. I wouldn't be surprised if there were additional, yet to be discovered, mundane principles to add to this list but to postulate cosmic goals is to simply short-circuit the discussion.

The otherwise wandering and opportunistic path of evolutionary success leads to all sorts of Rube Goldberg arrangements in nature, the roundabout contraptions loved by cartoonists that any reasonable Creator would have thrown in the wastebasket. There is, for example, the mixed up wiring of the brain, where the nerves from the right side of the body cross to the left side somewhere in the spinal cord or brainstem, and go to the left cerebral cortex. Our right-hand movement commands start from the left cortex and then cross over to the right side in the brainstem, finally exiting to go to muscles on the right side of the body. How did this mixup get started?

Dan Hartline points out that to escape a threatening stimulus to one side of the body, a fish has to contract the muscles on the opposite side of its body in order to flip out of the way of harm. Thus, sensory nerves conveying "threatening nibble" have to connect to the muscles on the opposite side of the body. And we're a late-model fish—our fancier wiring is superimposed on the more elementary wiring that is crisscrossed, for the purpose of escaping from predators.

My favorite example of meandering design, however, is the sequence of preliminary forms that a mammal goes through before attaining the familiar adult form—what gets called prenatal and postnatal development, or ontogeny. Just imagine constructing a digital computer by first setting out to build fingers to count on, then switching to an abacus, then changing your mind again, backing up a few steps and scraping the abacus beads, taking off in a new direction to build a mechanical calculator that whirls little wheels and clanks a carriage, scrapping it for a programmable player piano, then superimposing an electrical design based on vacuum tubes, pulling the tubes and replacing them with transistors, scrapping them for integrated-circuit chips even before all the tubes have been replaced, and so on. And going through this nonsense each and every time you wanted to build an additional computer.

Yet to construct a human brain and its attached body (which, someone quipped, is still the only general-purpose computer that can be made by the unskilled labor of two workers), one cell divides into a collection of cells that looks something like an invertebrate called an ascidian. It then changes course to head in the direction of a shark's elongated body form, but shifts toward a proper fish's specializations such as gills, then scraps the gills after a few weeks and remakes the body into the image of a reptile, then into that of a primitive mammal, then realigns things into the primate ape format, and finally, with some fine tuning of the relative growth rates, grows the big brain of the human form.

The possibility has to cross your mind: *Maybe the cell's DNA doesn't know any other way to make a brain.* It's like a treasure hunt, with new instructions opened at each stage of the game, telling the developing organism where to go next in words that can only be interpreted in the context of its present position. Instructions, overlain by modification after modification. An architect would scathingly dismiss it as "design by change-order." But I think it is rather nice to evoke your ancestors, to bring them to life ever so slightly, each time you make a baby.

> The large brain, like large government, may not be able to do simple things in a simple way.
>
> DONALD O. HEBB, 1958

NATURE ISN'T EFFICIENT, and often roundabout even in the simplest, most important matters. Abby didn't quite believe my Rube Goldberg analogy, so I told her about how her brain regulated her breathing rate.

The idea is to keep enough oxygen circulating in your bloodstream so that all your cells are happy; half as much oxygen, and brain cells in particular don't work very well. When you run, the muscles use a lot of oxygen and so something needs to tell you to breathe faster. When you are in a confined space, like a cave where the oxygen concentration in the air may be lower than the usual 20 percent, you need to breathe faster to deliver the usual flow of oxygen to the blood circulating through the lungs. So what controls breathing rate? Any reasonable engineer would say the oxygen levels in the bloodstream. If you wanted to regulate the temperature in your house, you'd sense the room temperature with a thermostat and use low readings to turn on the furnace. So you expect breathing rate to be controlled by blood levels of oxygen, right?

Guess again. What the body reliably does is to sense the carbon dioxide concentration in the bloodstream to regulate the breathing rate and thus the oxygen delivery. Usually the O_2 and the CO_2 levels are reciprocally related: when you need more oxygen, it's usually when the muscles are letting loose all sorts of additional CO_2 into the blood. And when you're using up the oxygen in a cave, you're usually building up the CO_2 levels in the air there at the same time. So sensing increased CO_2 instead of decreased O_2 isn't ridiculous—a little roundabout (something like regulating your room temperature by sensing relative humidity instead of temperature), but maybe it was easier to sense CO_2 than the blood's O_2 back in the days when the scheme was invented by evolution.

Yet it can get you into all sorts of trouble if you go into situations that evolution didn't prepare you for. Such as flying at high altitudes where taking a standard breath only yields you about half as much oxygen as it would on the ground. Pilots get silly and do stupid things if they forget to breathe extra oxygen—and all because their bodies have failed to sense the low oxygen levels and increase respiratory rate. Unfortunately, CO_2 doesn't increase with altitude as O_2 thins out—and so the usual stimulus to increased respiration is missing. (Actually there are O_2 sensors and they do affect breathing, but it's impressive how often the system fails if CO_2 doesn't increase at the same time as O_2 falls.)

So even something as important as regulating breathing was a roundabout scheme, never improved because it worked most of the time. It ruined my faith in the efficiency of natural selection when I found out about that.

MILE 118
Stephen Aisle

WE'RE STOPPED at a broad sandy beach on the left shore of Stephen Aisle. We hoped to see Powell Plateau from here, but we're down deep in the inner gorge, and so our view of the North Rim is blocked. Some hardy souls are trying to find a hiking route that will allow them to climb up atop the Tapeats. If they succeed, I hope they'll take some extra pictures of the famous Powell Plateau for me, but I'm enjoying the shade here near the river.

This would make an excellent camp for the night, but we're going down to an even better one, Blacktail Canyon, just another two miles. It's not known so much for blacktail deer as for a spectacular canyon of corrugated Tapeats Sandstone leading back up to Powell Plateau.

Our Rube Goldberg story has been spreading to the people on the other boats, and so our little shade-loving group has been talking about making babies.

"You mean that the baby looks like a shark at one stage? And then an ape?" exclaimed Abby.

"Well, it has gill slits at one stage, a few weeks into gestation. They disappear in a few more weeks," explained Rosalie. "But you don't see what look like familiar adult animals. They're really more like fetal versions of those animals. And even that isn't quite true, because the evolutionary changes have been made merely by varying the growth rates of different parts of the body."

"Maybe the head grows a little faster than the body," I interjected, "and therefore winds up bigger when it is finished. Different rates, just like thermostats."

"Thermostats?"

"Sure, just take a look at that little sandwich of two metals inside any wall thermostat, sealed together. Both expand when heated, but one expands faster than the other. Since they're glued firmly together, this means that the straight strip of metal begins curving sideways. And trips the furnace switch at some temperature."

"But babies aren't metal."

"No, but the baby has lots of curved surfaces, and they form in exactly the same way," Rosalie resumed. "Two sheets of cells, one of which grows faster than the other, and the surface curves into all sorts of shapes. And there are master clocks too, which set the overall time schedule of development. They cause monkeys to become adult in three or four years. In apes, they're slowed down so it takes eight years. In us, they're slowed down even more."

"It takes longer to make us because we're fancier?" asked Ben.

"No, there's no real reason why it takes nine months rather than the monkey's four months, except this evolutionary history, everything getting slowed down by half at each transition. It only takes a month to make one of the local squirrels—that's the time between the mating day and birth," added Rosalie.

"It isn't just time to grow, you know," I said. "It's also the time it takes for some cells to die and be removed. Not all of development is growth, where cells are added and the fetus gets bigger. Quite a lot of development is carving, removing parts selectively via the death of cells. Just as in the computer story, where the abacus is scrapped, the body is sculpted by development."

"I read somewhere that adults lose 10,000 brain cells every day," said Abby. "Is that true? Am I degenerating?"

"Not that we've noticed," said Rosalie, smiling. "All that cell death seemed ominous back when we didn't understand that development was accomplished by both growth and sculpturing. That daily loss of brain cells started way back before birth. And development's never over—it doesn't just stop when you become adult. That's why you're losing cells today."

"Mind you," I explained, "we don't understand what the adult cell death is in aid of, but I suspect that it's refinement of structures. Brain cells start out by making lots and lots of ties to other cells, but then some of the connections are broken. When a rat is born, many regions of its brain make connections to its spinal cord. But months later, only a few regions have remaining connections to the spinal cord. The different parts of the brain aren't anywhere as well defined early on as they later become—and a lot of that finer detailing comes from connections being withdrawn, from cells simply dying."

"So what determines if a cell dies?" asked Ben.

"Some of it seems to be good old Darwinian selection," answered Rosalie, "on a small scale. Overproduction, then editing. Take, for example, the spinal cord cells that command the muscles to twitch. At first, there are more of them than there are muscle fibers for them to operate. They send out little threadlike axons to make contact with the muscle fibers. But once a muscle fiber has a connection, it'll reject other axons that approach it. Some spinal cord cells wind up without a muscle fiber to operate. They're likely to die. Mini-Darwinism?"

"And one of the Rube Goldberg aspects," I picked up, "is that whole muscles are created, then killed off. And many of the spinal cord cells that run the temporary muscle also die."

"I just can't get over the cells dying right and left," said Abby, shaking her head. "Just as I can't get used to the idea that half—or is it three-fourths?—of all fetuses spontaneously abort."

"Welcome to the club," said Rosalie. "It was a shock to me too, but I think the problem is that we try to trace ourselves back to our individual beginnings. And think that it's a miniature of ourselves, fully determined. That it really has an identity."

"Remember the Doonesbury comic strip that a lot of newspapers censored? That series on the emotional appeals of the anti-abortion publicists?" interjected Ben. "Trudeau did this parody by starring a twelve-minute-old zygote named Timmy!"

"Thinking backwards gets us into trouble," replied Rosalie. "That zygote or fetus was no more me than a cell of my skin, scraped off by the boat this afternoon, whose nucleus contained the same genetic information. That skin cell could, in theory, have been cloned to produce a duplicate of how I was at conception. But inevitably it'd grow up very differently than I did, make different decisions than I did, and its whole personality would wind up somewhat different, even if it did have red hair and look like my twin. Worrying about fetuses that could potentially grow up is like worrying about the lost opportunities to make a baby with each menstrual period, each of those unique, never-to-be-repeated ova down the tube. A fetus that grows up into a baby, and from a baby into a real person, has had a lot more invested in it by the parents and society—it's far more than just the genes it started with."

"That beginning fetus is just the foundation onto which all the rest has been added," I said. "If nature makes more foundations than the ecological market can ever bear, that's because nature's method of building is different than when we build a house. We don't start three foundations but then finish only one of them. Nature does."

Rosalie turned to Abby. "Just imagine clearing a lot for a house every month—but usually nothing else happens and the weeds grow back. But some months, the lumber and blueprints are actually delivered just after clearing has taken place, and construction starts. Still, most starts are scrapped—maybe the carpenters and the plumbers got their schedules tangled-up. And so it's all cleared away and the weeds come back—that seems to be easier than untangling the snafu. Only some of the starts are actually carried through to be finished houses, completely furnished. Now at what stage are you going to call that building-in-progress a 'home'? Sure, each cozy home was once only a foundation, but we wouldn't call that collection of lumber and nails a home, would we? I wouldn't even call it home on the day that the builder finished it and delivered the house to its new owners. It's a home only after it's furnished and lived in."

"And all that elective abortions have done," I added, "those abortions that all the fuss is about, is to make it 25 foundations that are finished for every 100 started, rather than maybe 33. In the good old days, malnutrition probably changed the odds even more than that, maybe only 15 finishing for every 100 starting. All we ever see are the ones that finish. It's a very selective view of reality. Beware of thinking backwards."

A LOT OF FETUSES never see the light of day. Many gene combinations from the parents, with all the shuffling that results from genes crossing over from one chromosome to another, probably cause malformed embryos in one way or another. After all, development is a great orchestration of many separate growth patterns happening all at once on different schedules, and it is easy to see how something might occur too late to make a needed connection, throwing things out of whack.

There is probably a constant pressure to spontaneously abort, which only a particularly successful fetus can overcome by sending enough of some sort of "I'm okay, mom" signals. Mothers that didn't have such an abortion mechanism would repeatedly waste nine months on nonviable fetuses, rather than being able to try anew after several months and so be able to squeeze many more tries into her reproductive years. As in the horse race prediction scheme, we only see the winners. The unsuccessful exist briefly, but we are simply unaware of them.

Thus abortion seems to be quite natural, editing out the more pernicious combinations of genes; indeed, much natural selection may take place in the womb, unobserved. These natural abortions are not, however, the first stage at which selection acts. There is the great sperm race, an obstacle course of mammoth proportions. And at the end of it, one may see an ovum sitting there, sometimes surrounded by hundreds of sperm trying to gain admittance through its outer membrane, the meditating ovum somehow deciding which one to admit.

BECAUSE OF THE GREAT DISPROPORTIONALITY in numbers of potential offspring, between the human male's 40 million sperm a day and the female's 1 to 2 dozen pregnancies in a lifetime, it follows that the female is in a buyer's market. She becomes more selective with whom she enters into joint ventures than do males. Quite a number of interesting phenomena follow from that disproportionality, including many of the phenomena that a human thinks of under the rubric of sex.

One is a line of selection wholly different from the usual one. Sexual selection is the name that Darwin gave to an effect which seemed to differ from the "natural selection" exerted by such elements of the environment as the availability of food, predators, disease, and so forth. Sexual selection usually evokes a vision of competition between males for access to females, though there are examples of females selecting for males in those species in which the males perform a lot of the infant care that greatly increase the chances of offspring survival. Certainly females tend to select males that look healthier, which shows how two supposedly separate things, sexual selection and natural selection, can get all mixed up (sexual selection involves the appearance of fitness, not its actuality—advertising versus performance). While the usual examples of sexual selection involve the development of bright colors and strange courtship displays among the birds, one can see it right down at the level of the sperm surrounding the unfertilized ovum, banging at the gates.

The sperm does, of course, have a long way to go before getting there, what with the obstacle course created by courtship, the long passage through a hostile chemical environment from vagina to uterus to the Fallopian tubes where the fertilization actually takes place. But many make it. So which sperm are admitted? Sometimes it is simply a matter of sheer numbers. Relative numbers, that is (in absolute numbers, sperm production is absolutely profligate; in three weeks, one human male produces enough sperm, given the perfect delivery system and indiscriminate ova, to impregnate every woman on earth).

In many types of animals that do not compete for mates, where all males get a chance to mate with a female in heat (male chimpanzees will actually stand in line behind a receptive female, waiting their turn—the queue itself could be a product of sexual selection!), relative numbers can be important. A male producing only 4 million sperm a day rather than his neighbor's 40 million will stand, everything else being equal, only one-tenth the chance of having one of his sperm be the lucky one. That mating system is literally a lottery, where one's chances of winning depend on how many tickets one can afford to buy. Monkey and ape species with such multi-male mating systems may gradually develop an arms race in testis size, as variants with copious sperm production will tend to be more successful. The woolly spider monkeys of Brazil have baseball-sized testicles as a result, and chimpanzees are not far behind, with testes three times the size of a gorilla's even though their bodies are only one-fourth as heavy. That's sexual selection.

Another common result of sexual selection is that males may be larger than females. This may have come about because, at some time in the history of the species or its ancestors, the mating system involved competition between males for access to females. The bigger males likely won the competition, on the average, and thus propagated their genes on the Y chromosome for making extra testosterone, that male hormone having quite an influence on muscle growth. Gorillas have a harem type of mating system, and the males may be twice as large as the females, reflecting generation after generation of male competition for the proprietorship of a harem.

Besides all this competition for getting sperm up to the courtyard of the ovum, selection may also occur in the final act of fertilization itself. As indicated by the microscope picture of a meditating ovum surrounded by hundreds of anxious sperm, fertilization is not like shooting an arrow into a ripe melon. Some sperm may be more "acceptable" to the ovum than others, once their surfaces have been tasted for recognition signals. Should the sperm and the ovum both possess the same genes for controlling the immune system (the genome's major histocompatibility complex, or MHC), the sperm will probably be rejected. This promotes variety, since successful fertilizations yield an offspring that has two different versions of the MHC, and thus more strategies from which to choose later in defending against invading organisms ("heterozygous for the MHC" is what it's called in biology, "homozygous" meaning identical copies of the gene on each of the chromosome pair).

Thus the ovum is something like a suspicious shopper sniffing all the produce offered her by anxious merchants who have just finished running a marathon—then she decides, with a great thunderclap that seals the deal. That's the way it can sound if you've hooked up a wire from the ovum to a hi-fi system—the electrical signal announces the acceptance of one sperm and seals the ovum's membrane against further penetration by additional sperm. It's the first use of electrical signals by the new individual—they're subsequently used to contract muscle, warn of predators, secrete saliva, and even think great thoughts.

Both testicle size and sexual dimorphism are, in these examples, mere side-effects of the disproportionality in the numbers of male sperm and female pregnancies, shaped in turn by the particular mating system in use. These size excesses are not produced by the environment, in the manner of natural selection. Sexual selection could become maladaptive. Adult male mountain gorillas can no longer take to the trees—they are simply too heavy, though the females and juveniles can still use trees as a refuge. Just another interaction between sexual selection and natural selection that blurs the boundary.

It's one more example of the lack of planning, of many different random plans being tried out and let run for as long as they can. It's no way to run a railroad—no foresight, no planning ahead. But it works, given enough time and the right conditions. And it just may be the only way in which the universe has been run, up until now.

WE NOW HAVE ARTIFICIAL SELECTION in addition to natural selection and sexual selection. Humans have used it to shape our domestic dogs and cows into varieties never seen in nature. All it requires is an ability to control an animal's reproductive life, usually with fences, and make its sexual choices for it. We have been helping select the offspring's sex for decades: spinning sperm down in a centrifuge, for example, so the slightly heavier ones carrying an X chromosome rather than a small Y chromosome will sink to the bottom. Artificial inseminations of such sorted sperm can shift the sex ratio of the offspring from 50/50 to more than 70/30, which makes the farmers happy (dairy farmers have always known that females are more valuable than males; among beef cattle, heftier males are preferred).

In recent years, genes have even been snipped out of a chromosome with restriction enzymes, then spliced into the DNA of a bacterium. In this manner, one can fool the bacterium's cellular machinery into producing a new product that is coded for by the excised DNA strand. Thanks to the fact that we shared a common ancestor with the bacteria billions of years ago, we both still speak the same internal language of protein manufacture, the same genetic code. Human insulin and human growth hormone are two things that have been produced by bacteria in this manner, to the great relief of those people who do not produce enough of their own.

Some people say that genetic engineering "isn't natural," that it is fiddling around with nature. In one sense it is only doing what nature itself is always doing each time that crossing-over occurs, every time selection shapes up a new population, each time that geographic isolation runs the speciation ratchet that conserves new traits. We help that along every time we swat a fly, thus helping to breed smarter and faster flies for tomorrow. Genetic engineering is just faster, much faster.

Of course, some changes in speed can become important changes in kind; rockets were a big step over slingshots, especially when we managed to sling a spacecraft called *Pioneer* all the way out of the solar system, never to return. To create something that will probably outlive the death of our sun a few billion more years down the line—that's a human accomplishment of immemorial proportions, not just a little improvement in speed.

Our whole civilization is one of those changes in kind, not just the genetic-engineering aspect of it. The dangers of genetic engineering are very much those of our whole farming and pharmaceutical industries: namely, that we don't know what will happen down the road as the new pesticides and drugs perturb the system, because our culture is still so ignorant of ecology, of how the elements of the environment hang together and buffer one another. We do know that the natural ecosystems cannot absorb some insults forever. Unless we somehow limit our pollution and our population growth, the earth may fall apart on us as we ruin one carefully-wrought ecosystem after another.

THE TAPEATS SANDSTONE stands like a cliff of corrugated cardboard back of our camp, an expanse of little rounded ridges. We've come up out of the schists and other Precambrians. We are reversing our direction in time, as it were; we must be coming out of the far side of the dome. Blacktail Canyon is a deep, narrow cut through the ropy layers of the Tapeats. Layer after curved layer is stacked vertically, and the path taken by the canyon meanders back toward Powell Plateau.

The floor of the canyon rises in a little series of steps, forming what can only be called bathtubs—modest-sized depressions in the floor filled with water from the slow-flowing creek. But sculpted when the water was thundering down: standing waves cut these little bathtubs for us.

Soaking tubs! But no soap is allowed, not in any side creek, as they are fragile ecosystems. And the water, while not as cold as the river, is not exactly warm. The sun penetrates this narrow canyon only at midday. The bathing, however, is going on in a big way back at the river, as we discover upon our return to camp. It has become a tradition of the late afternoon.

Evolution, of course, is the vehicle of intricacy. The stability of simple forms is the sturdy base from which more complex stable forms might arise, forming in turn more complex forms, and so on. The stratified nature of the stability, like a house built upon rock on rock on rock, performs, in Jacob Bronowski's terms, as the "ratchet" that prevents the whole shebang from "slipping back."

ANNIE DILLARD
Pilgrim at Tinker Creek, 1974

MILE 120
Blacktail Canyon
Seventh Campsite

BEN HAS BEEN PERSISTENT. Once in camp, he located a pencil and paper and got Marsha to pose for a sketch. Next he created a list of the beads on her necklace, using the AUCG letters to represent the beads' colors. And then he divided them into groups of three: AUG-UAU-GGG-GGG-UUU-CUU-UAA. Next he set off in search of information.

Ben first asked Cam if he remembered the amino acid that was encoded by the GGG nucleotide triplet. "Ah, must be glycine," said Cam.

What about UUU? Cam was uncertain, and called Brian over. He remembered that UUU was phenylalanine. And what about CUU? Neither Cam nor Brian could remember the genetic-code table that well, so together they all went in search of an expert.

After drawing two blanks, they asked Jackie about CUU. "Leucine," she said, "definitely leucine. Why do you want to know?"

"Just a little test," said Cam hurriedly before the others could open their mouths. "We're just playing a little game. Do you remember UAU as well?"

"Sure," said Jackie, "that's tyrosine. What do I win?"

Ben was scribbling it all down, and the others were looking over his shoulder. Taking the sequence AUG-UAU-GGG-GGG-UUU-CUU-UAA, he now had written "(start)-tyrosine-glycine-glycine-phenylalanine-leucine-(stop)."

He shook his head, then showed the list to Jackie. "Does this amino acid sequence make any sense? I mean, is it nonsense or a real peptide?"

THE GENETIC NECKLACE

AUG—UAU—GGG—GGG—UUU—CUU—UAA

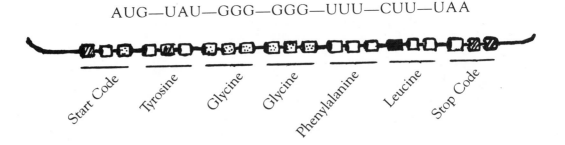

Start Code · Tyrosine · Glycine · Glycine · Phenylalanine · Leucine · Stop Code

ENKEPHALIN

"Let me see. Sure, it's enkephalin," replied Jackie cheerfully, "it's leucine enkephalin. What ever is this game you're playing, anyway?"

"You mean it's a real hormone?" exclaimed Ben, doubt setting in.

"Of course it's a real peptide hormone, you idiot. It's also a part of the longer chain of beta-endorphin. That's a classy sequence of amino acids you've got there," explained Jackie, warming to her subject. "Stops pain, supposedly makes you feel good. You've probably got a lot of it on the brain right now, after romping around in all that cold water at the beach. Good old enkephalin, good for what ails you. What does ail you, anyway? You look a little green around the gills. What's this all about?"

Ben sat down. "I think maybe I've been out in the sun too long."

Cam and Brian looked sheepish as Jackie turned toward them with raised eyebrows, waiting for an explanation.

"So where did you get that paper with the letters on it?" she demanded of the mute trio. "Manna from heaven? Old homework papers stuffed in your jacket pockets? Something from a fortune cookie?"

"Okay, Cam," said Ben, ignoring the question, "so you calculate the odds of this happening by chance. Now it isn't just the three beads at each end being consistent with the start and stop codes. It's twenty-one beads of four types, all in the right order for an important natural substance. What's the chances of that being random?"

Cam looked up to heaven. "I can't count that high."

"Beads?" interjected Jackie. "Whatever are you talking about?"

"Marsha's necklace," replied Brian at last.

"Well, what about it?"

"Marsha's necklace spells out leucine enkephalin. That's all." Brian was looking at the ground as he spoke.

"An alphabet necklace? How clever. Just like an anatomy T-shirt."

"You don't understand," said Cam miserably. "This is Marsha's Indian necklace."

"Are the Indian reservations making anatomy T-shirts too? They've branched out from pottery and silver jewelry? Getting the university bookstores to sell molecular biology necklaces? So what's the problem?"

Cam stood up and looked around for Marsha.

The trio hauled Jackie along with them as they went in search of Marsha. She was down at the water's edge, flirting with the boatmen, giving Alan a hard time as he fished beverage cans out of the bilges.

"Marsha," began Ben, "could you show Jackie your necklace?"

"Sure. Did you figure out how many bushels of corn the poor people had to pay in taxes?"

Ben held up one finger, asking her to wait a minute, and turned to Jackie. "Marsha copied the necklace from the museum at Mesa Verde. And thought that it might be like those Aztec knotted strings that were used for keeping tax records."

Jackie took off her sunglasses and looked closely at the necklace. "I see. There really are four different types of beads."

"Now look over here at the beginning," Cam pointed. "If you assume that those first three beads are the start code, AUG, then this other dark type of bead must be C. What got us interested is that assigning AUG to the first three types suggests that these last three beads are UAA, which is a stop code. And there are exactly 21 beads, seven triplets worth. Just as if this were a string of messenger RNA, all that's needed to tell the ribosomes how to make a five-part peptide."

"And if you work through the rest of the beads, you get this list I wrote down on the paper," exclaimed Ben. "Here, you check to see if I copied them down right."

Jackie took the paper and began working through the necklace. "Well, I suppose this bead could either be a C or an A— it's sort of dirty and ambiguous. But you're essentially correct. These three would be the start code, then tyrosine, glycine, glycine, phenylalanine, leucine, and a stop code." She shook her head, disbelief finally setting in. "That is truly amazing."

The boatmen came over to inspect the necklace, demanded an explanation of what everyone was so excited about. So Ben explained the genetic code to them. And what the necklace seemed to be spelling out—the genetic code for how to make enkephalin, the powerful pain-killing hormone which the brain itself produces. Supposedly, in some people, producing euphoria just like morphine.

Jackie and the trio are feeling very pleased with themselves for solving the puzzle, even though they still didn't know what to make of it.

"Boy, dip your arrowhead in that stuff, and your prey would sure die happy," Alan observed. "You really think they did that?"

"But it's absurd!" exclaimed Cam. "How old did you say that necklace is, the one you copied the pattern from?"

Marsha, looking as astounded as the rest, replied that it was at least a thousand years old, according to the museum's sign.

She held out the necklace so that she could look down and see it, her eyes wide. Not only does that girl have stage presence, but she can improvise too. She denied any knowledge of the genetic code herself, deflecting suspicion. But she hyped the discussion a little, suggesting that it would have made a great necklace for an Anasazi medicine man to wave over his patient as a symbolic pain-killer.

Thanks to all the loud exclamations, a crowd had gathered around Marsha and her necklace, Rosalie among them. They too wanted the mystery explained to them. Soon everyone was saying how amazing it is—or how absurd it is, that nothing that old could be that scientifically advanced. After all, enkephalin wasn't even sequenced until the 1970s. How could the Anasazi have known about it?

The reaction went in waves. First came the astonishment that the trio, with Jackie's help, had figured out that the necklace was a code. And then broke the code. With the secret message being no less than enkephalin. Then came the rejection of the notion that the Anasazi could have known about it a thousand years ago. Impossible!

"Now I'll bet that's just what some astronomer said," teased Rosalie, "when they showed that Fajada Butte over in Chaco Canyon was a fancy device for tracking the nineteen-year cycles of the moon. If the Anasazi were that sophisticated in astronomy so long before we discovered such cycles, maybe they were sophisticated in other areas too. Just think how the Indians domesticated corn. Maybe they knew more than just practical genetics?"

The bait caused some discussion between neighbors. And much head-shaking. Someone started to explain how big the 20 corn chromosomes were, how different types of corn hybridized. More beer cans popped open. After all, the enkephalin molecule is about the same in the octopus as in us. That probably means that enkephalin has been around since the Cambrian, is half a billion years old. It isn't as if it has been around only since the 1970s, when its sequence was determined and some of its functions discovered. Still. . . . Impossible.

Entering into the spirit of things, I reminded them of Peter Medawar's dictum, that scientists treat a new idea the same way that the body treats a foreign substance: it is rejected.

They tried to stretch their credulity. And they were most intrigued—after all, usually when you hear "Impossible!" uttered with delight, it's a sign of a scientific problem posed critically, possibly about ready to crack. And it attracts scientists like flies. But no one took enough of the bait to emerge as a champion of ancient Anasazi molecular biology. Several people did, however, sound determined to stop by Mesa Verde on the way home, to check out this necklace for themselves.

"But that Chaco Canyon observatory is a feat of naked-eye astronomy," replied Jackie finally, addressing herself to Rosalie, "and this is more as if those Fajada slabs had all pointed, not to the sun and moon, but to the black holes known only from radio astronomy." The more excited Jackie gets, the faster she talks. "Have the archaeologists dug up any Anasazi microscopes lately? Or chromatographs? Or written records of chemical formulas? This isn't just kitchen chemistry that's required, you know. There's simply got to be some other explanation for this necklace."

Silence. Then more head-shaking. Finally, Ben stood up and bounced onto the bow of the boat in a perfect imitation of the boatmens' loose style, causing a low booming sound as he balanced himself, arms outstretched. Having gotten everyone's attention, he solemnly raised his beer can in a toast to Marsha, cocked an inquiring eye at Rosalie, and mused aloud: "Piltdown, Piltdown, wherefore art thou, Piltdown?"

Marsha and Rosalie could keep straight faces no longer, and collapsed in each other's arms. Soon everyone was laughing as the truth dawned.

DINNER WAS A LITTLE LATE. This time, the clams linguine turned out to be a collection of Mexican dishes. Everyone seemed to have a story to tell about a hoax, though some of them required elaborate explanations for the nonscientists. I suppose one reason that people think that scientists are white-coat serious types is that science jokes don't travel well. For a joke to work, the setup has to arouse expectations in the listener that are exploded by the clincher, often with some sort of screwy twist. The punch line is usually a mismatch to the expectation. No predictions about what's coming, no joke. You've got to know enough to guess ahead (and have enough time to think about it—which is one reason why timing is so important in telling a joke). Schemata again—they're not just templates for special configurations of sensory inputs, but some are also mental images of the future, waiting for something to come along and tickle them. Maybe, for humor to work, one has to have our peculiarly human consciousness, with its overblown ability to project sequences into the future.

There are nautiloids just downstream from the campsite, and we've been over to see the fossils in the fading light. I took a canteen of water and, with the aid of the light from a flashlight nearly parallel to the surface, we were able to see the chambered forms. There is no way to estimate how intelligent they were, there being no bony braincase as for hominids. If they were particularly omnivorous, perhaps they were as smart as their living cousin, the octopus. As clever as dogs and ravens. We last shared a common ancestor with the dog back in the Mesozoic, with the raven back in the Paleozoic, and with the octopus back just before when this Tapeats Sandstone was being laid down atop the eroded Precambrian unconformity. So there were a lot of routes to intelligent life, unless one defines intelligence so narrowly as to make elaborate language a requirement.

And it doesn't even take a big brain to pull off great feats of engineering—the ants can manage quite well as a collective army with many specialized roles, being quite capable of building elaborate cities and air-conditioning them too. Or farming fungi. Or enslaving other ant species. The local ants haven't carried off our camp yet, but I have no trouble imagining a well-organized horde of specialists, complete with military policemen to direct traffic.

It is dark as we pick our way through the rocks to return to the campsite. There is, however, a group down by the boats, staying up to await the moonrise several hours from now. Another emerging tradition.

THE MOON HAS ARISEN, judging from the milky sky, though it hasn't peeked over the canyon walls yet. We have been talking about ants again, how they almost upset Darwin's notion that selection could explain how species evolved. Some of the advanced insects like bees, ants, and wasps have sterile castes—animals that leave no offspring of their own. How, one might ask, can evolution explain such a dead end, if inheritance and selection based upon an individual's success cannot operate? One would think that, once the tendency toward decreased fertility began, the line would wipe itself out. Did a benevolent Creator provide special sterile slaves for the other ants?

Darwin, who was his own most severe critic, asked that question himself, since he was familiar with sterile castes from his youthful days of insect collecting. He recognized it as the "one special difficulty, which at first appeared insuperable, and actually fatal to my whole theory." The answer that Darwin came up with not only saved his theory but started a whole new branch of evolutionary theory, though it began to flourish only a century later: selection, it seems, is sometimes based not on individual success but on the joint success of relatives and other group members.

In cultural terms, we have no problem understanding this

theory. Whoever invented sewing helped her imitating neighbors, who were probably relatives sharing many of her genes, to survive better in a cooling climate. Even if she left no offspring herself, she increased the number of copies of her genes by her relatives' success. But what happens if biological genes are the only means for passing the information, and successes must be expressed in terms of leaving progeny? How does this get started in simpler animals without culture?

It's simple. The sterile individuals perform similarly useful work for their relatives who do reproduce, work that enhances the relatives' reproductive success markedly beyond the average. The sterile worker thus propagates copies of its genes through anothers' reproductive success. This altruism would obviously work better when helping a twin sister than when helping a second cousin.

I sometimes dream of spinning off a clone of myself to serve as my alter ago, personal assistant, errand runner, computer programmer, and library researcher—someone who thought much as I do because of identical genes. I might even let him go through Lava Falls in my place and report about it afterward. Some insects have, in their own way, managed to get others to live for them, as when the queen bee lays all the eggs and the others do the rest of the work. This does, however, smell of slavery—in which some ants engage, quite in addition to putting sterile relatives to work for them. Darwin doubted the existence "of so extraordinary and odious an instinct as that of making slaves" until he witnessed a slave raid himself on an ant nest near his country home at Down.

ALL THIS ACTION FOR A COMMON GOAL is not so extraordinary if one thinks of the beehive or ant nest as a single individual, with specialized cells for digestion, waste disposal, communication, and reproduction. In an individual human body, most cells are, in a sense, merely supporting the germ-line cells that make sperm and ova—they are after all the only ones to make cells that carry on after the death of the individual. A cell in my brain does not reproduce itself at all, just like a worker ant. The anthill's "cells" just have legs in this interpretation, the anthill being the individual and the ants its cells.

Are most of my cells therefore slaves, in need of emancipation? Is slavery a "natural" thing, somehow excusing the human slavery that persisted until this century? Questions relating biological principles to society arise whenever we start looking backwards, trying to see from whence we came, attempting to figure out rationales for our actions. And they're not easy to answer, even with great caution and care.

When this topic came up, we wound up discussing Social Darwinism. This, of course, has little or nothing to do with Charles Darwin; it was a pet idea of Herbert Spencer's, about which Darwin showed little enthusiasm. Science, thanks in part to its extraordinary usefulness and occasional ability to predict the future, has long enjoyed a prestige that politics does not. People arguing one or another partisan political viewpoint will sometimes try to bolster their case by borrowing from the authority of science. They usually borrow one fact or principle, out of context.

This happened earlier in the century when it was argued that laissez-faire capitalism was "natural" and "scientific"—that nature's principle of the "survival of the fittest" meant that attempts to modify monopolies were therefore unnatural and unscientific (and, undoubtedly, against God's will too, that being the traditional rationale for keeping things as they are). Railroad barons and timber magnates, captains of industry—they all tried to argue that they were only sterling examples of self-made men, the natural ascendancy of the fittest, and that anyone could do it if they only had what it takes, that attempts to modify this "natural order" would only weaken society.

It was a great puffery and helped disguise the fact that monopolies had effectively created a lid on the ladder to keep anyone else from rising—short, perhaps, of Hercules. (Someone noted that this was in the days before advertising agencies were brought in for such campaigns—just imagine a catchy jingle singing, "The survival of the fittest is *good, good, GOOD* for you!")

One still hears this argument, usually from reactionary politicians, though there is also a tendency for it to be trumpeted by "self-made men" and women, both those who have indeed, against all odds, pulled themselves up by their own bootstraps—and by their many imitators (often, alas, hard-working professional people) who merely lack the imagination to see the role that accidents of birth and opportunity have played in putting them on the right track to success. It is often a self-serving argument, though one can sometimes hear the same argument even from the poor.

Another survival of the early social ideas stemming from the theory of evolution is the eugenics movement, that attempt to apply animal-breeding practices to humans by sterilizing the "feebleminded," the deviant, and the mentally ill. While there is indeed some tendency for the bright and the dull to run in families, the extremes—the geniuses and the idiots—seem to wink on and off in the population regardless of parentage. Many parents of ordinary IQ have been surprised to have a genius on their hands, and many bright parents have had to help a dull child learn to cope. A historical relative of the eugenics movement was the raising of "IQ" to a single-number quantitative index of human capacity (numbers are, of course, thought to be *very* scientific) and it was early applied to help decide matters of public policy: immigrants were tested en masse at Ellis Island, and there was an attempt to limit Italian and Jewish immigration because of their low scores on the tests (an early example of the cultural bias of such tests). That the eugenics movement had a limited scientific basis is now clear, in retrospect, as are some of the underlying motivations for the particular items that were selected from science to be waved about in the arguments. And given the gene shuffling that goes on, the eugenicists' schemes would probably have produced little change. Greater effects have likely been inadvertently achieved merely by sending offspring to college at an age when mate selection is at its most intense (thus promoting breeding between those able to meet college entrance requirements!).

But effects from any form of selection are likely to be small when one is talking about the present-day human population. Short of artificial selection with its complete control over an animal's reproductive life, it now seems that the evolution of large populations is very limited, contrary to what was once thought. Natural selection can most effectively act on small populations, and its sorting of the gene pool is essentially lost when they again interbreed with a larger population with its well-stirred gene pool. Permanent "improvements" perhaps occur only when complete reproductive isolation is achieved in a small geographically isolated population of animals.

Lifting natural selection out of this tangle, simplifying it into a stand-alone slogan such as "the survival of the fittest," and enthroning it in isolation as the guiding principle for success is certainly not scientific now, and never was.

THESE BORROWINGS from early evolutionary thinking show that single findings, even something as important as natural selection, often do not transpose readily into the making of social policy. Taken out of context, they seldom deserve the prestigious aura that science may lend them. Yet because they seem "harder" than many of the competing "softer" arguments, they may overwhelm the many other sides of an issue. While this is occasionally the fault of a scientist overselling his or her subject in the competition for insufficient research funds, it is more typically the product of decision-makers seizing on a simplistic solution and running with it. It gives science a bad reputation in the process. Denigrating *science* itself—the search for relationships, as opposed to the often reckless *technological* applications that follow fundamental discoveries—will reverse this unfortunate situation only at the price of weakening our ability to bail ourselves out of the problems we have already created with pollution and overpopulation.

Try though we must to create a better future for ourselves through social policy, we must be cautious when seeking guidelines in the animal kingdom; it may be better to use our considerable abilities to foresee the future, to imagine alternative scenarios and judge them, and create new principles to guide human society. If the animal kingdom indeed arose without planning, fortuitously finding ways that worked and exploiting them, then we should—eventually—be able to do better with our enhanced abilities to reflect and plan, to simulate the future in our heads (and computers) before acting to see where a course of action might lead, and thus increase our chances of success by picking the better-appearing alternative. In some areas, the principles we can create might well be superior to the shopworn principles seen in nature. But in any case, we must know our biological selves—and that means knowing animal behavior as well—if we are to plan and decide intelligently.

THIS HISTORY OF POLITICAL EXPLOITATION is, of course, one reason why human sociobiology is not always greeted with open arms: many people can envisage how theories about the evolutionary basis of "human nature" could be misused. But one must not confuse the scientific knowledge with its conceivable technological applications (even if the newspapers are forever conflating the two, perhaps because they like shorter words for headlines). And because of our deep curiosity about our origins, the probing will continue. It may have much to teach us about our funny quirks, about how we gamble when we make decisions, about our sometimes difficult relationships, and about the mental illness to which so many of us are prone. In a world in which tribalism and gambler's instincts still rule the actions of world leaders, we need to understand as much as we can—even if applying that new knowledge is fraught with difficulty.

But I suppose that the main reason why people become upset with sociobiology, which one can see in any letters-to-the-editor column, is that they think that "to explain is to excuse." Yet this indignant attitude about excuses is not only uncritical but fails to understand the motivation of the scientists involved.

Take, for example, infanticide. There has been important ethological research on monkey males who kill the infants sired by another male. Some letter-writers assume that this must have been done to provide excuses for those stepfathers who batter children.

In societies in which the young are especially cherished (and this includes many primate societies), infanticide is puzzling as well as repugnant. But there is indeed a devil's payoff for infanticide under some conditions in the animal world, such as harem mating systems in which the male-in-charge is regularly replaced every few years, the new one proceeding to kill off infants. The ex-mothers, no longer breastfeeding and thereby producing hormones that suppress ovulation, will come into heat—and can thus be impregnated by the male taking over the troop a year sooner than otherwise. Since his reproductive years are limited by the mating system to those several years when he can manage to hold onto the top slot, this practice may double the offspring he leaves behind. If the tendency to kill infants upon taking over is inheritable, then a new generation of males may come to carry that trait. Indeed, our close relatives, the gorillas, are apt to suffer a wave of infanticide when a new silverback male takes over the harem. To reveal the chain of mechanisms involved in infanticide is to understand how genes for such murderous behavior arising by chance could have been preserved in evolution.

This odd sexual-selection mechanism, in these harem-less days of bottle feeding and birth control, probably wouldn't operate anyway in our society, even if battering infants to death were socially acceptable. But if such genes were left over from some harem-ruling ancestors, it might give some insight—without in the least condoning or excusing their behavior—into potential subconscious motivations of battering stepfathers.

Though a whole book would be needed to adequately explore the subject, this possible evolutionary scenario does demonstrate the physiological and evolutionary mechanisms by which genes for murder could be promoted by a harem-type mating system. As a reflective society we can elect to promote the opposite, such as outlawing harems. We have long known that society must combat murder and child abuse; knowing that there can be a genetic underpinning for infanticide doesn't excuse it, even though it may help us devise better ways of educating battering stepfathers. Rather than looking to behavioral research for excuses, we should value it for the new directions it can suggest in solving our problems as a society. What's natural isn't always a good policy anymore, nor a good excuse.

□   □   □

When we die there are two things we can leave behind us: genes and memes [*contributions to culture to be mimicked*]. We were built as gene machines, created to pass on our genes. But that aspect of us will be forgotten in three generations. Your child, even your grand-child, may bear some resemblance to you, perhaps in facial features, in a talent for music, in the colour of her hair. But as each genera-tion passes, the contribution of your genes is halved. It does not take long to reach negligible proportions. Our genes may be immor-tal but the *collection* of genes which is any one of us is bound to crumble away. Elizabeth II is a direct descendant of William the Conqueror. Yet it is quite probable that she bears not a single one of the old king's genes. We should not seek immortality in reproduc-tion.

But if you contribute to the world's culture, if you have a good idea, compose a tune, invent a sparking plug, write a poem, it may live on, intact, long after your genes have dissolved in the common pool. Socrates may or may not have a gene or two alive in the world today . . . but who cares? The [cultural contributions] of Socrates, Leonardo, Copernicus, and Marconi are still going strong.

The sociobiologist RICHARD DAWKINS, *The Selfish Gene*, 1976

I don't think writers are sacred, but words are. They deserve respect. If you get the right ones in the right order, you can nudge the world a little or make a poem which children will speak for you when you're dead.

The playwright TOM STOPPARD, *The Real Thing*, 1984

Any suggestion that the child's mathematical ineptitude might have a genetic origin is likely to be greeted with something approaching despair: if it is in the genes "it is written", it is "determined" and nothing can be done about it; you might as well give up attempting to teach the child mathematics. This is pernicious rubbish on an almost astrological scale. Genetic causes and environmental causes are in principle no different from each other. Some influences of both types may be hard to reverse, others may be easy.

The sociobiologist RICHARD DAWKINS, *The Extended Phenotype*, 1982

The behavior of animals is determined mostly by evolution, while humans have options for self-improvement in line with their civi-lized ideals.

The primate ethologist SARAH BLAFFER HRDY, 1983

Socrates was put to death in 399 B.C. on the charge of corrupting the youth of Athens. He subjected traditions and custom to the fire of pure reason and in so doing threatened the traditions of the soci-ety. As one of the first and greatest philosophers and as one who unhesitatingly espoused reason, he showed us once and for all that it is possible to break with tribal lore, traditions, and the cultural luggage that we have brought into the world and look at ourselves anew, in the light of reason. Socrates, more than any other teacher, has shown us that we need not be slaves to the promptings within, the whispers from the limbic lobes. That is where our genes speak, where they hold our hearts: reason alone can free us from their ancient leash.

The anthropologist BERNARD CAMPBELL, *Human Evolution*, 1985

It used to be thought, in the bad old days of social Darwinism when evolution was poorly understood, that life is an uninterrupted struggle—"nature red in tooth and claw." But this is only one side of natural selection. . . . The same process also leads to altruism and reciprocity in highly social groups. Thus the human species has evolved genuine sentiments of obligation, of the duty to be loving and kind. . . . In this sense, evolution is consistent with conventional views of morality.

The philosopher MICHAEL RUSE
and the sociobiologist EDWARD O. WILSON, 1985

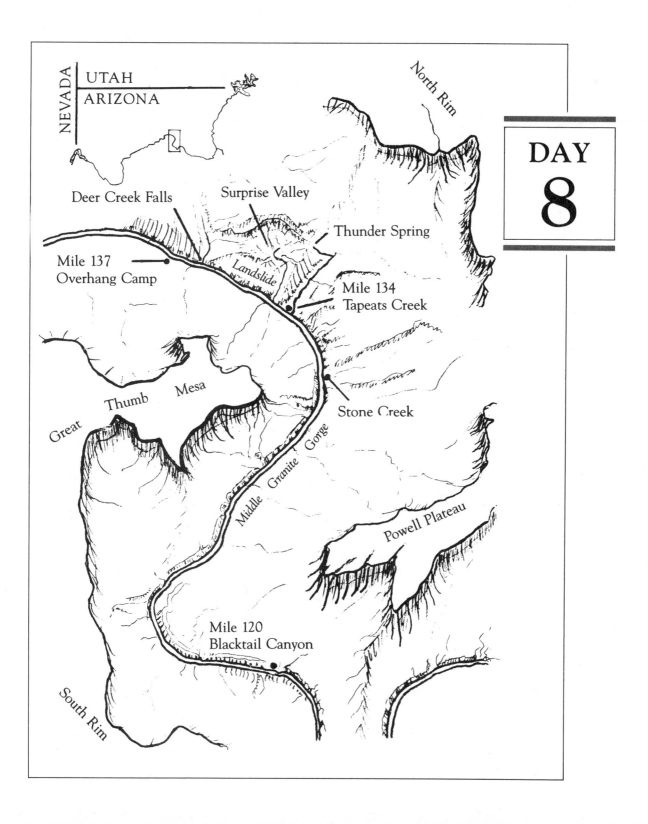

NEVADA
UTAH
ARIZONA

North Rim

DAY
8

Deer Creek Falls   Surprise Valley

Thunder Spring

Mile 137
Overhang Camp

Landslide

Mile 134
Tapeats Creek

Thumb   Mesa

Great

Stone Creek

Middle Granite Gorge

Powell Plateau

Mile 120
Blacktail Canyon

South Rim

MILE 120
Blacktail Canyon

It is unwise . . . to assert that evolution could not have done this or must have done that, except in the broadest possible terms. It is a good working rule for the biologist that evolution is a lot cleverer than he is.

> The molecular biologist
> F. H. C. CRICK, 1979

CLONING DOES ALLOW FOR VIRGIN BIRTHS which, as Cam pointed out at breakfast, ought to make some people happy.

"You know how virgin births came about, don't you?" asked Ben. "I mean, in religion?"

"It's an Old Testament prophecy, from way back, many centuries before Christ," Rosalie replied.

"Well, in the original Hebrew, it said something about a young woman giving birth to a prophet," Ben said, sipping his tea. "But by the second century B.C. in Alexandria, Hebrew was getting to be like Church Latin—not too many people could read it. The educated people all knew Greek, so to promote their religion, the religious scholars translated the Old Testament from Hebrew to Greek. The only trouble was that in the process, they translated the Hebrew phrase for 'young woman' using the Greek word for 'virgin.' "

We laughed. "That's one little translation error that really started something," Cam replied, chuckling.

"I heard of another Hebrew translation error," Jackie volunteered. "Well, maybe not an error but a little problem of double meanings. You know about how women are supposed to give birth 'in pain'? The original Hebrew word in that passage of the Bible is *b'etzev*. Now, one meaning of that is pain. But the other common meaning one would translate as 'in sadness.' So maybe that Biblical passage isn't about the pain of childbirth—maybe it's an early description of postpartum depression?"

CONQUISTADOR AISLE is a long straight stretch of river just down from Blacktail, with the Muav on the right bank creating sculptures much like Gray Castle back in the Photogenic Fifties. These scallops look like an oblique view of a row of chessmen, lined up before the match starts, extending into the distance.

One of the first rapids here is another of those "No Name Rapids"—at least in the eyes of the boatmen and the authors of river guides. Imagine the surprise our boatmen got when they looked at the American Automobile Association's otherwise excellent road map "Indian Country" and found that this rapid had been given a name that no one on the river had ever heard of—Enyeart Rapid. I suspect that the AAA threw in a fake name, in the abominable manner of mapmakers generally, to serve as a tipoff if someone copied their copyrighted map—while, of course, confusing everyone else. Intentional lies in a reference work are most offensive. One never knows where they'll lead.

Naming an unnamed rapid, however, is less hazardous than adding a road or bridge that doesn't exist, which is what paranoid mapmakers often do. I once discovered, on an official government map for pilots, where a road had been added around the northwest side of Mount Rainier in Washington State, connecting the dead-end West Side Road with the dead-end Mowich Road. Such a grand loop road, I am happy to report, does not and never has existed; I wrote the Federal Aviation Administration and asked them to remove it from that map as a hazard to lost pilots trying to follow a road back to civilization. And then I got to thinking: maybe it's another copyright ringer? But why would the government bother to do this, since anyone is free to copy their maps? Or did the government mapmakers get lazy and copy an oil company's maliciously mangled map when they made the pilot's map, transcribing the nonexistent road? Of course, perhaps (the wilderness hiker's paranoia) they're just planning to build yet another road through the remaining wilderness.

About two-thirds of the way down Conquistador Aisle, there is a side canyon on the right which has an excellent natural amphitheater. The music trip sometimes stops here, and the boatmen haul the cello several miles into a charmed place called the Delphic Amphitheater.

COWARDS ARE THE BASIS OF CIVILIZATION, it says somewhere. That's because cooperation—you go first, but reciprocate next time, please—needed some way to get rolling, some way in which an animal could gain long-term advantages while enduring short-term disadvantages.

Many species have rules for helping to minimize conflicts, allowing something else to decide who gets the reward (simple conflict-avoidance rules—such as deferring to whomever arrived first—are seen even in butterflies). And there are individuals—call them "doves" if you like—who avoid conflicts with others of their species. When challenged for possession of a choice resource, doves prefer to avoid the costs of losing a fight and wait for another chance at the rewards. The opposite type lets no one get in the way of immediate rewards; this "hawk" naturally spends a lot of time and energy fighting other individuals, risking injury but also wasting time that could otherwise be used in searching for other food.

I suppose that if every individual were a hawk and the food were concentrated in one place, most would be injured fighting over food. One might expect there to be some optimal ratio of hawks and doves for a species, just enough hawks so that they encounter doves more often than other hawks, enough doves so that they usually get to eat before a hawk arrives to contest their meal. In fact, one can even predict the ratio of hawks to doves by knowing the relative costs of each alternative. Costs here might be measured in calories: how many calories in the food, how many calories spent searching for food, how many calories wasted fighting, how many calories burned while waiting for another chance, and the costs of injury and disability. For a given set of reasonable numbers, one might wind up with a 30:70 hawk/dove ratio. Note that being born a dove into an all-hawk society can be an advantage—you may lose every encounter and get to eat only when uncontested, but you won't suffer the costs of fighting and can potentially be better off than everyone else.

This hawk/dove strategy can yield a stable ratio: if one starts with a 50:50 ratio, enough hawks will die so that the ratio becomes 30:70; if one starts with too many doves, the hawks will out-reproduce them until a 30:70 ratio is achieved. This situation is an element of the evolutionary stable strategy or, as it is known in evolutionary biology, an ESS. The only way that the 30:70 ratio can be changed is to modify the relative payoffs, and even that may exhibit a stability that confounds permanent change. However, suppose you play dove most of the time and hawk some of the time? What would happen if you played hawk in dealing with an individual who usurped your rightful due the last time, but played "after-you" otherwise, taking your turn when it came. Might such qualified cooperation work better than the hawk/dove strategy's payoffs?

Yes, but there are many variants on cooperation, and some work better than others. Some are not evolutionary stable strategies—should some hawks invade, they could wipe out the cooperators. Still other strategies are just not stable, with the population fluctuating in a boom-or-bust manner.

Take the simple matter of paying back cheaters, playing hawk with cheaters who don't take their turn when they should. If one plays hawk forever with such a defaulter, the population will soon become locked into a rigid collection of hawks. So that perpetual suspicion strategy is unstable, degenerating into the stable hawk/dove extremes with its poorer payoffs, the niche supporting fewer individuals. There is a virtue to forgiveness, to again cooperating once you've paid them back for cheating.

That is one conclusion of a big contest between computer simulations that tested various strategies for cooperation. A simple strategy called "tit for tat" was the winner: you initially cooperate when encountering a new individual, then expect him to reciprocate (or whatever the cooperation strategy is). If he cheats, you play hawk next time and pay him back. Then you forget about it, returning to cooperation. The animals in tit-for-tat need the ability to recognize one another as individuals, a memory that lasts until the next possible encounter, enough hawk in them to play the role on occasion, but that's about all—no altruistic nature, no higher thoughts about how it would be much better for everyone if we all just took turns. Tit-for-tat is one of the viable variants on the hawk/dove theme; an evolutionarily stable strategy which—provided those calorie ratios don't sink below certain critical values—will survive even if the cooperators are invaded by pure hawks. Tit-for-tat is a robust strategy, in that many different calorie payoff alternatives will work with it.

Most importantly, it will survive once established—as the economist Robert Alexrod and the theoretical biologist William D. Hamilton said, "the gear wheels of social evolution have a ratchet." It would be easiest for the "genes for cooperation" to develop in small groups—perhaps on a tropical island, where everyone is a close relative anyway, and where making a living is easy enough that one doesn't starve if they allow someone else to go first. Once an individual bearing the "cooperation genes" migrates elsewhere (I like the proverbial farm boy moving to the big city), he will encounter many cheaters. He'll lose to them only once, because tit-for-taters have good memories. Whenever he interacts with someone with the cooperativity genes who will indeed alternate with him, then the advantages of cooperation will manifest themselves in the increased payoffs. Thus, even though the payoff is reduced in the new environment, the cooperation genes won't necessarily be wiped out. Their population will grow, relative to all the pure hawks and doves, because of the more efficient food gathering and conflict avoidance they produce.

Via such a scenario, tit-for-tat (or something like it) could have engendered cooperation on a large scale: cooperation was a variant that found a niche and was preserved by evolutionary processes of selection and speciation. It was another emergent principle, a surprise consequence of some simple properties of memory and behavior, but one with far-ranging implications for the evolution of social species like ours (and the insects, and the dogs, etc.). We may now use strategies far more complex than the childish tit-for-tat, but cooperation got started somehow.

And now game theory—that mathematical subject that has been applied to both chess and war games—has shown evolutionary biologists one of the possible ways cooperation evolved by focusing our attention on the minimal set of rules necessary to move beyond hawks and doves. The cooperation genes may, of course, be little more than the genes for a brain that can recognize a large number of separate individuals, genes that produce enough body shapes and colors to create discernible individuals, genes that provide a memory good enough to pay back a cheater (but not too good, so as to get stuck playing the hawk

To be wronged is nothing unless you continue to remember it.

CONFUCIUS

Without forgiveness life is governed by . . . an endless cycle of resentment and retaliation.

ROBERTO ASSAGIOLI

forever!), and something to soften unconditional hawkishness (a bit, indeed, of the coward).

If cooperation is a variant along some hawk/dove continuum, we might expect a cooperating species to still contain a certain number of individuals who fall into the hawk or dove extremes. If this scenario for the evolution of cooperation is even half true, then the unusually timid and the sociopath are living reminders of our evolutionary past—and a reminder that variation still prevails, is still being industriously created by those busy permutations during crossing-over.

While we may have started with such a simple set of rules, happily emerging into an evolutionarily stable strategy encoded in our genes, we will probably have to create a far more complicated strategy to stay alive. Playing tit-for-tat in a nuclear age is far worse than merely childish, yet our national leaders mouth platitudes which suggest such simple-minded thinking.

MILE 127
Middle Granite Gorge

EARLIER WE NOTICED that the Tapeats ledges were going downhill, as if they were planning on disappearing into the river, reversing their appearing act back in the Fifties. But they stopped, and now we see the Tapeats emerging again, more and higher sandstone ledges surrounding the river channel.

Soon schist appears again, and we once more cross the Great Unconformity, though without the salt mines this time. Unlike the tunnel-like abrupt appearance of schists back at Mile 77, this emergence is gradual in the manner of the other layers. We are entering the Middle Gorge, back in the schists again; Major Powell's expedition was none too pleased to see the schists reappear, given the big rapids that followed their original introduction to them. At least here there are no big rapids, no V-shaped illusions of plunging into an abyss.

But the black marble effect is much greater here: really black and highly polished. And an anomaly: here we see a polished black layer atop a dull schist layer. Now the bottom layer really should get more river polishing than the higher layer. Oops.

After some discussion we decided that the higher one must be a different type of schist, one that takes a shine better. Indeed, the guide book says it is called hacatite and that it is a metamorphosed basalt of volcanic origin; the dull stuff is sandstone and siltstone that has been metamorphosed instead.

There is a virtual row of trees on the right bank, one story above the river; they seem to form a green line along the bottom of the talus slopes. This is another little illustration of evolution in action: the trees that grow below the high water line get washed away in the floods. Those variants with long roots, which also happened to take root up away from the river, are what remain after natural selection. If you want a variety of riparian tree with extra-long roots, come and borrow a few seeds from these trees: evolution has been at work on them.

Strangely, the river is heading northeast, back in the direction from which we came a week ago. This is no mere meander. We can't continue west because Great Thumb Plateau looms ahead of us to the north and west. It's part of the South Rim—to the north of us! And the North Rim—in the form of Powell Plateau—is now south of us. In its early editions, the blue bible's river map for this section of the Canyon had the North arrow pointing the wrong direction—the artist must have decided that the South Rim was to the south. But only on the average, just as rivers flow downhill on the average but can appear to run uphill when one is watching a big back-eddy. All those variations from the average certainly do make things interesting.

LIFE IS CHANCY, to be sure, but it is still a surprise to find that nature has also gone out of its way to shuffle the deck. The average, even the nominal variations, appear not to be what nature emphasizes. With each generation, crossing-over introduces new noise even if point mutations don't.

Taken by itself, all this randomness seems like noise intentionally introduced into a well-tuned radio—like static, pops and crackles superimposed upon music, like stray notes being struck while playing the harmonic inventions of Bach. The Goldberg Variations would be ruined. We recoil from the notion, just as did Darwin's critics—and they didn't know even the tip of the iceberg about how randomness seems to be the name of the game. After all, we try to engineer quiet hi-fi amplifiers, reliable cars, predictable spare parts. What Creator would intentionally make her creation creaky?

And now it turns out that sex is all about increasing the noise, by intentionally shuffling the carefully preserved genetic instructions for how to construct a new body and brain. As if mutations weren't enough, and more randomness was needed. So scramble the blueprints a little. Mutations evolved a system for permutations—and that was a big step in evolution. It institutionalized randomness.

"THINK RANDOM" would, I suppose, be an appropriate sign to hang over the desk of the evolutionary biologist, though I doubt that this slogan will ever catch on because of the bad press that "random" has had. It would seem like an exhortation to woolly-headed thinking, to promoting disorder, incomprehensibility, chaos.

This nomenclature problem has been faced before, by mathematical theorists. They, of course, are quite used to the regularities that may occur in the superstructure of a noisy process; though the motion of an individual oxygen molecule in the air may seem quite random, winds do exist. There is even a whole branch of mathematics called the Theory of Random Variables. And so a near-synonym for "random" has developed which, because it is thoroughly Greek to everyone, lacks the unfortunate connotations of randomness. Thus, one reads up on the Theory of Stochastic Processes only to find good old random variables being slung around again. If a T-shirt exhortation to evolutionary thinkers is ever produced, I predict that it too will read, "THINK STOCHASTIC!"

This puzzling randomness cannot be understood by itself, in isolation from the other mechanisms involved in evolution: selection pressures such as disease and late winter snows, temporary barriers such as rivers, and permanent barriers such as speciation from shifts in mating seasons. Only in context does the randomness begin to make sense—if one looks at it long enough and hard enough.

The challenge of Darwinism is to find out what our genes have been up to and to make that knowledge widely available as a part of the environment in which each of us develops and lives so that we can decide for ourselves, quite deliberately, to what extent we wish to go along.

RICHARD D. ALEXANDER, 1979

. . . the more we discover about the mechanisms of genetic control, the better equipped we will be to escape those controls through an enhanced awareness, to transcend them so that we may, for the first time in our history, work for ourselves instead of our genes, exercise truly free will and free choice, give free reign to our minds and spirits, attain something close to our full humanhood.

A. ROSENFELD, 1977

I CALLED THE CREATOR "SHE" for some good biological reasons, not just equal time. You even inherit more than half your genes from your mother—you may get half of the DNA in your cell's nuclei from your father but all your mitochondria (the powerhouse of the cell with its own DNA and separate genetic code) come from your mother. You see, the sperm's mitochondria seldom make it into the ovum at fertilization.

Males are the oddballs, not being able to directly reproduce themselves (the females of some species can clone themselves if males are scarce or unsuitable). And we mammals all start off as female *in utero*; it's only later in prenatal development, when the Y chromosome causes extra testosterone to be produced, that female genitalia are modified into male ones.

There is some evidence that this male afterthought wasn't as well engineered as the female original. Males are more liable to birth defects. Boys die in childhood more readily than girls. Adult males are likely to start falling apart at an earlier age than females. Rather than Eve being metaphorically made from Adam, biology suggests that it should be stated the other way around—if at all.

SEX HAD TO EVOLVE TOO; this institutionalized randomness wasn't present at the Creation. Somehow, the crossing-over shuffle of the genome was superimposed upon ordinary cell division—but only in some specialized cells, those of the so-called "germ cell line," a fancy name ("germ" as in germination, not pathogens) for the cells that produce sperm and eggs. What, one might ask, would be the immediate advantages to the organism of such an additional complication? Sure, it's better in the long run for the evolution of more complex organisms (like us), but what on earth was the immediate short-run advantage? How was the ratchet run by selection and speciation to create a sexually reproducing organism in the first place?

Indeed, there is a serious disadvantage to sex that must be overcome in the short-run. Namely, males. Sex tends to produce numerous individuals (often half of the total) who cannot themselves give birth. It reminds one of the insects which almost ruined Darwin's theory for him. Those sterile castes of social insects (ants, wasps, bees) seem to have evolved only because selection sometimes acts on groups of individuals, rather than on each individual in isolation, and the sterile ones enhance the success of their sisters who do reproduce. That suggests that males can exist because they make the actual reproducers, the females, much more than twice as successful in getting offspring to reproductive age themselves. Now in advanced organisms such as frogs and birds, the male's efforts at brooding the young may improve the survival rate. But I suspect we may have to look to something more elementary, something that will work in simple organisms. Something that directly involves the increased randomness generated by sex. STOCHASTIC SEX—I can see it now, emblazoned on the students' T-shirts. And misinterpreted by most of the people who see it.

While sex in eukaryotic cells got started about 1,000 million years ago, there is an even more ancient form of sex in bacteria, in which cells exchange some genetic material without fusing. And the virus, that little packet of DNA that lacks the usual cell machinery for protein synthesis, is perhaps another one of the original ways of mixing up genes a bit. Often looking like a moon lander with a hypodermic needle protruding, the virus goes and, kamikaze-like, injects its RNA or DNA into a proper cell, even committing suicide as a means of producing more viruses. So crossing-over as we practice it is only a more recent version of what may be a variability scheme over 2,000 million years old. So we should not look solely at multicellular levels of evolution for the explanations of sex, but seek clues from more elementary cases of mixing things up.

Various schemes for the evolution of sex have been proposed, and have been given such catchy names as the "Red Queen Hypothesis" and "Pathogen Escape." The first takes its title from *Alice in Wonderland* in which the Red Queen tells Alice that she has to run as fast as she can just to stay in the same place. The arms race of this century has brought the Red Queen's quip into focus, a sobering reality. But the arms race is also a succinct way of summarizing the tendency of ecosystems to keep getting fancier rather than attaining a truly static "balance of nature": a plant that is eaten by an insect develops better defenses such as becoming toxic, the insect develops better ways of inactivating the toxin, so the plant raises the ante and the arms race continues. To keep up with the plant's ability to vary its defenses, the insect has to produce a variety of offspring, some of which will be able to cope with the changed conditions. The Red Queen Hypothesis says that the increased variability in offspring produced by sex had an immediate advantage, because some of the offspring could become much more successful than the run-of-the-mill nonsexual offspring who could only hope for a lucky mutation to strike.

While the Red Queen Hypothesis focuses on exploiting resources better, the Pathogen Escape hypothesis looks at one of the main sources of illness and mortality (which do tend to limit one's reproductive abilities): being inhabited by a parasite, or having your genetic machinery borrowed by a virus, or having your internal environment utilized by too many bacteria for their own ends.

Cells have ways of defending themselves against exploitation by pathogens, and multicellular organisms like ourselves have specialized cells assigned the job of cleaning out invaders that lack the right passwords—recognition signals in the form of proteins embedded in their cell surfaces. These defender cells are specialized to recognize different foreign proteins; when they find a protein "lock" that matches up with their "key," they kill the offending cell. The defender cell not only destroys but perhaps reproduces itself in the process, making more defender cells of that type. This is how the body fights infection; after the infection is over, it has a lot of defenders for that particular foreign cell and so makes a subsequent infection much less likely to succeed. This is how we acquire immunity to, say, the Asian flu virus. Immunization usually consists of stimulating the antibody-production mechanism without precipitating a major infection. Minor infections are sometimes good for you.

The defender cells in an individual's bloodstream are thus a history book of his exposure to infections, if one knows how to read it. There are six major variants on the Asian flu Type A virus; many old people have, circulating in their bloodstream, defenders against all of six types. Each is left over from an exposure to one of the flu subtypes (some of which may not have caused obvious illness but instead a subclinical "silent" infection that stimulated the immune system to produce more defenders). Children's blood will have defenders only against the strain of flu virus that has most recently been around.

By piecing together the pattern of defender cell types present in people of various ages, it can be seen that Asian flu subtype A5 was the one responsible for the epidemic of 1918, that subtype A0 occurred in 1933, subtype A1 in 1946. The 1957 epidemic was caused by subtype A2, which was last seen in 1889; the "Hong Kong" epidemic of 1968 was subtype A3, same as in 1900, and subtype A4 in 1978 was the same as in 1910. This suggests that we'll be back to subtype A5 before 1990. This hypercycle, as it is called, takes 68 years—about the average human life span for those who survive childhood. Since most of the people alive about 1990 won't have had the flu in 1918 and thus have acquired cells to fight A5, subtype A5 should have more success about 1990 than it would have had in 1970. Just like the "seventeen-year cicadas" whose reproductive cycle is a prime number of years so that they can escape predators with shorter life cycles (yes, I'm afraid that evolution invented prime numbers too), the Asian flu virus outsmarts the human immune system with a longer cycle; with the recent increase in average human lifespan, it will be interesting to see if the Asian flu will falter.

Pathogen Escape concerns how you develop defenders against, for example, subtype A4 after being infected. Your genes cannot possibly carry the code for every conceivable foreign protein that might work its way into your body, and then produce defender cells for each type; there just isn't room for so much information in the cell nucleus. I don't know if the following story will turn out to be true or not, but it illustrates how the immune system could work, using only simple rules.

Suppose that (at some developmental stage, not necessarily

always) a defender cell had, on its surface, the same protein that the cell attacked, sort of a lock and a key on opposite sides of the cell surface. This means that identical cells would tend to attack one another. Soon one would have a population of defender cells that were all different, a very simple self-organizing system emphasizing diversity. Suppose further that defender cells divided when they successfully attacked (just as when building up immunity)—but that they sometimes mutated in the process, making a slightly different password protein. Maybe they shuffle the genes as happens in crossing over? If the mutation happened to produce a protein on the cell surface identical to the one coded for by an existing defender—well, too bad. But if it produced a unique password protein, such a new defender cell would enjoy a long life. There would wind up being a massively diverse population of defenders, coding for far more invader types than the original genes could have done.

As I said, whether true or not, this example shows how a very capable system can arise from two simple rules: competition between identical cells, and an occasional random mutation. As I thought about it a little more, floating down the river, I realized that this shuffling and elimination need only happen in a setup period during prenatal development. Once the diverse password population was produced, the immune system could settle into a postnatal mode without further mutations or permutations.

And that has some advantages when one considers how to prevent my immune system from attacking my own proteins—what is called the self-recognition problem. Such attacks during the setup period—when so many of my own proteins are being produced that losing a few to defender cells won't matter much—wouldn't be a problem. Sure, I'd lose some structural proteins but the defender type might not reproduce as well without two defender cells involved (this is similar to the sterile male strategy for controlling insect pests). This means that when the mutation mechanism was later turned off by development, I'd have hardly any defender cell types corresponding to my own proteins. So I'd wind up with a broad spectrum of defender cells, far wider than any coded by my genes, yet the ones corresponding to my particular body's proteins would have been eliminated during the setup period. If something goes wrong with this sequence, of course, my immune system might start attacking me successfully in adult life, when I don't have so many structural proteins to spare (the production rate for many types of proteins drops dramatically between the ages of 20 and 70). This provides a model for "autoimmune" diseases such as lupus, myasthenia gravis, rheumatoid arthritis, and juvenile-onset diabetes, in all of which the body's self-recognition mechanism seems to fail.

So a gene-shuffling mechanism might have been handy in the immune system, enabling the organism to better survive infections by producing a broad range of defenders. Maybe escaping pathogens is what selected the gene shuffler, but the shuffler in turn may also have affected those cell divisions producing sperm and ova—and created recombination and crossing-over. If true, it was a sidestep in evolution—sex succeeded because its shuffling mechanism was a gift from the immune system.

While life on the individual level is indeed chancy, evolutionary processes have enthroned randomness as a virtue, and all because it turned out to be so handy in the short-run for gaining a temporary advantage in the "propagate-your-genes" sweepstakes. Its long-term advantage, of progressively more intricate organisms such as ourselves, may be another one of those emergent principles—a free bonus for more elementary efficiencies.

The effect of a cause is inevitable, invariable and predictable. But the initiative that is taken by one or other of the live parties to an encounter, is not a cause; it is a challenge. Its consequence is not an effect; it is a response. Challenge-and-response resembles cause-and-effect only in standing for a sequence of events. The character of the sequence is not the same. Unlike the effect of a cause, the response to a challenge is not predetermined, is not necessarily uniform in all cases, and is therefore intrinsically unpredictable.
ARNOLD J. TOYNBEE, *A Study of History*

If our kind of mind had been confronted with designing a [DNA-type] replicating molecule, starting from scratch, we'd never have succeeded. We would have made one fatal mistake: our molecule would have been perfect. . . . The capacity to blunder slightly is the real marvel of DNA. Without this special attribute, we would still be anaerobic bacteria and there would be no music.
LEWIS THOMAS, *The Medusa and the Snail*, 1979

HARD ROCK THAT COMES UNRAVELED? There is some fascinating rock around here which shows asbestos formed from contact metamorphism. When some crystalline basaltic rocks are overheated, simply by being in contact with a very hot substance, the subsequent cooling can produce fine crystalline fibers between the hotter and cooler regions. And so you can pick up a rock and see a white band very different from all the rest. Using a fingernail, you can pull off little white filaments. As-

MILE 132
Stone Creek Beach

bestos is handy for insulation against heat (if you can avoid breathing and drinking it); it used to be the best thing around. Several miles downstream from the sandal race this morning, there is an old asbestos mine that provided some of the long asbestos fibers used to make fire curtains for theatres in Europe, back at the turn of the century.

The long stretch of sandy beach here at Stone Creek is washed clean by the artificial tides every 24 hours. We are stopped here because Alan wants to take us for a beach walk. Sea shells? Here? No, Alan is preparing the beach, implanting sticks and drawing lines as he paces off distances.

Well, we are also stopped here for lunch, having just gotten soaked in Deubendorff Rapid, an 8. Alan is munching on an oversize sandwich as he paces along the beach, counting his steps, then stopping and drawing yet another line in the sand. Or planting a stick. Even making a little sand castle. Marsha is following along, asking questions. But Alan manages to keep his mouth too full to talk, and so she stews in suspense as he keeps muttering "Just a minute, just another minute. Gotta count." And he keeps pacing off the distance. What distance? The rest of us wonder, as we head back for seconds on lunch. Hard work, running rapids.

Finally—for dessert, as he puts it—Alan invites us all over for a little "walk through time." We first hike all the way down

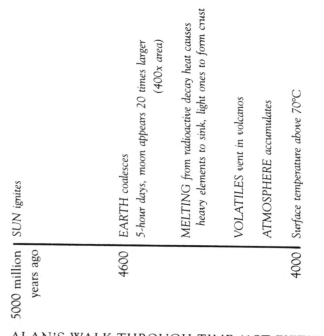

ALAN'S WALK THROUGH TIME (1ST FIFTH)

to the far end of the beach, more than a city block, where Alan has constructed his first sand castle. As we stroll down to the starting place, I am reminded of Alan's other famous walk: one winter, he and two friends started off 60 kilometers north of the North Rim, using cross-country skis through the forest up to the snowbound visitor center perched on the rim, then carried their skis as they hiked down to the bottom of the Canyon (the skis were certainly a novelty down at Phantom Ranch) and up the trail to the South Rim. Then another time, they hiked from Phantom up, and walked 50 kilometers south to climb Mt. Humphreys, the tallest of the volcanic peaks behind Flagstaff. From 2,700 meters elevation, down to 600, then up to 3,800. Alan's walks are ambitious.

"Now this here," began Alan, "is when the solar system went into business about 5 billion years ago, when the collapsing dust cloud finally got hot enough to ignite a thermonuclear reaction and, lo, the sun began to shine. And up there at the lunch table is the present time, today to be exact. And we're going to walk all the way through the earth's history. Now if you want to go all the way back to the Big Bang and work your way through the formation of elements and the local supernova that seeded the dust cloud that started this here sun," he said, pointing to the round sand castle at his feet, "you'll have to swim another 10 billion years upstream before you reach the Big Bang."

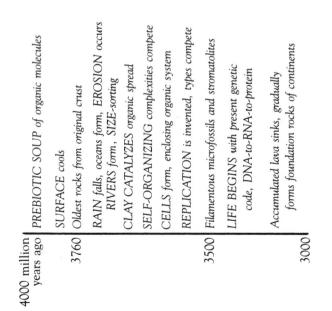

ALAN'S WALK THROUGH TIME (2ND FIFTH)

"How do we pace off the distance if we can't walk on the bottom of the river?" Marsha asked.

"Details, details. Now on the scale I've picked, one standard pace—my kind, anyway—is equal to 50 million years. All the way back up to the picnic table is 100 paces. Five billion years—call it 5,000 million for simplicity, since we'll deal in million-year units, just like the Anasazi probably thought in units of lunar months. Just to give you some idea of speed, it'd take about one pace for all that fifty stories of Redwall cliff to be laid down." He pointed up at the Redwall across the river. That's one percent of the total?

"Well, now, we walk eight paces, up to 4,600 million years ago, and the earth has finally condensed out of all that dust swirling around the sun, probably focusing around an eddy that formed in the disk of dust."

"Now just remember that," interjected J.B. "Back-eddies are useful."

"Another 22 paces," Alan resumed, "and we reach 3,500 million years ago, when the earliest known traces of life forms have been found." He gestured backward. "You just walked through the transition between physics and biology. Now those 22 little steps cover a mighty important period, when all those volcanos, and lightning, and ultraviolet light were making carbon compounds. Methane was in the air. Probably stank too,

ALAN'S WALK THROUGH TIME (3RD FIFTH)

though there wasn't anything around to smell it—now that, in my humble opinion, is the right way to do real organic chemistry. It rained, and rivers flowed, and the rocks got sorted into piles of big rocks and little rocks, even clay to catalyze the organic reactions. So here we are, almost a third of the distance covered, and finally organic chemistry has gotten to be a real self-organizing system that could presumably replicate itself. That is to say," and Alan drew the letters in the sand next to his sand castle with a leaf for a flag, " 'Life began'."

"So were DNA and the genetic code invented before then?" asked Cam.

"Until someone discovers otherwise," mused Alan, "that's the assumption. So the seas swelled with cells that had no predators—and the main food they ate was sunlight. Not too different from what all those phytoplankton do in the oceans today, making most of the oxygen we breathe—excepting, of course, that they now get eaten by everything from zooplankton to whales.

Alan started walking again. "The important thing happening now—with of course, our parochial hindsight, is that photosynthesis was churning away, throwing away oxygen in the same way that we discard carbon dioxide. Since the oceans couldn't hold any more after about our first step, or 50 million years, the atmosphere became the big dumping ground for all that useless

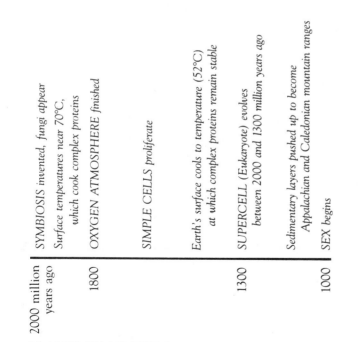

ALAN'S WALK THROUGH TIME (4TH FIFTH)

oxygen. Twenty-nine, thirty. By about here, at 2,000 million years ago" and Alan stopped at his second stick, "our present 20 percent oxygen atmosphere was complete. It took 1,500 million years to develop, and the reason it took so long is that all the exposed iron and silicon and whatnot on the earth's surface happily gobbled up any oxygen they could snatch out of the air. That's why the Redwall's red—good old rust. So until everything was rusted, the oxygen percentage stayed pretty low. So there you see," and Alan pointed up to the Redwall once again, "what used the oxygen before we did."

He kicked the sand underfoot. "So here we are, already more than halfway from the start of the earth to the present, and we're just getting the oxygen atmosphere that our kind of life requires. And now a whole new ballgame starts. What's next, baseball fans?"

"How about bacteria finally coming up with a nucleated cell?" volunteered Ben. "You know, a nice storehouse for all that genetic code, instead of scattering it around the cell like those simple-minded bacteria do? Supercell?"

"Sold," said Alan, and started marching 14 more steps, up to 1,300 million years ago. "Now that's moving. We're finally up to the age of some of that Vishnu Schist you've been seeing again on the river this morning. And there were now fancy cells on the scene, with all sorts of specialized little internal factories

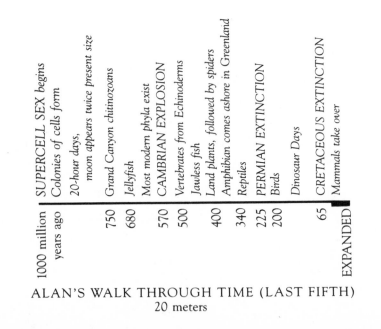

ALAN'S WALK THROUGH TIME (LAST FIFTH)
20 meters

like mitochondria and chloroplasts for energy, regular little powerhouses. All those good things. Supercell has arrived," he said, planting a third stick in the sand. "And nearly three-quarters of the time is already gone."

"You're going to have to speed up if you're going to get this all finished in seven days," Cam needled.

"That's all right—evolution's about to go into high gear." Alan gazed back upon his work. "Now just look at that. It took a whole 1,100 million years—22 paces—just to get cells going. Then it takes twice that time again before you finally get Supercell." Then he swiveled around to look ahead. "But it'll only take a few-hundred-million more years to get colonies of cells living together, making multicellular organisms. Sex probably started here about 1,000 million years ago. And those cells started becoming specialized. Some handled only digestion, while others took care of sensation but got fed by some specialized truckers, transporting cells that carry the goodies in between a gut cell and a sensory cell. Now that's real progress." Alan paced up to 600 million years, completing seven-eighths of the total span of time on earth.

"And finally here you get an explosion of life, particularly life with specialized cells that build strong shells by oozing out some calcium compounds. Which leave nice fossils for us to find. Thus marks the end of the Precambrian era."

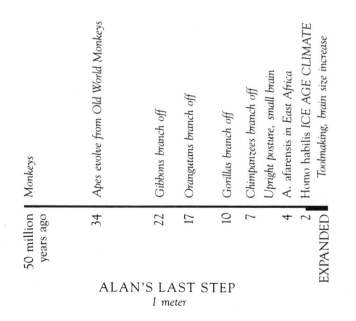

ALAN'S LAST STEP

1 meter

"We also just walked through the Great Unconformity," noted Marsha.

"Give that girl a gold star," announced Alan. "There is indeed a lot of rock missing from that period, leastwise around here. Our Tapeats Sandstone over there is from the Cambrian, this period starting maybe 570 million years ago when the fossils become abundant. And they're not just of one kind of organism, but all sorts of plants and animals, as if a lot had been going on back in that last section that we never saw—not because there's a Great Unconformity everywhere, but because it just plain didn't leave many fossils. Some microfossils, to be sure, and paleontologists are finding more and more. But here in the Cambrian, in the period when the Tapeats Sea covered this part of the world and then built up this sandstone, that period was when diversity got going in a big way."

"Can anyone tell me how many different branches of the evolutionary tree got started then, out of those Supercells?" asked Alan munching an Oreo cookie offered him by Marsha.

"Aren't there something like 28 phyla of animals? Hundreds of orders, millions of species? Plus the protozoa and the plants?" volunteered Jackie.

"Now the invertebrates that led to us were the tunicates. You know, sea squirts and such. Before they grow up, they're elongated with a primitive sort of backbone. And by not growing

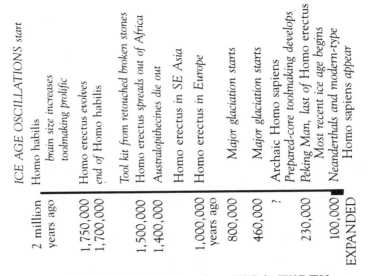

ALAN'S LAST TWO FINGERS' WIDTH
40 millimeters

up, they remain elongated. Some of those juvenilized tunicates turned into things like mudpuppies and sharks."

We all looked ahead at the ten paces remaining of the hundred. "Well," said Alan, taking a step forward, "here's where the tides bootstrapped us up to new highs. Out on the seashores, plants were getting uncovered by the tides. Every day too, not just once a century—that really speeds up evolution. Only the fancier ones survived that daily drying. By about 450 million years ago, there were land plants that managed all day without the seawater. Sure might have taken forever without tides to speed things up. Remember to thank the moon tonight."

And once there were land plants to eat, the intertidal animals followed." Alan took one more step. "About 400 million years ago, we get the first land animals, cousins of the spiders. The fish near shore got caught in the intertidal every day too, and that sure started something big—because some fish grew bony fins that turned out to be good for walking along beaches to food. So the fancier vertebrates were off and running. Evolution goes into high gear."

"And then come reptiles," he said, taking another few steps, "and here we are at the end of the Permian, 248 million years ago. What happened then?"

"The Permian extinction," said Jackie, "when 90 percent of

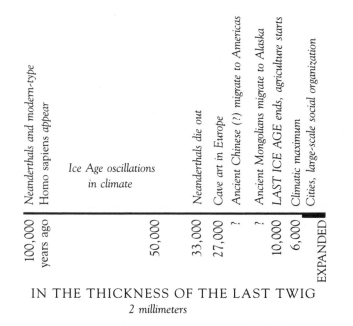

IN THE THICKNESS OF THE LAST TWIG
2 millimeters

the sea-going invertebrate species got wiped out. That's also not long before the super-continent of Pangaea broke up. But maybe a meteor helped things along too."

"Poor old Pangaea," said Alan, holding his baseball cap over his heart. "Shattered. But," he said as he fitted his cap back on, "you all know that ten continents are better than one for evolution to go its separate ways in isolation, so I suppose the breakup was a good thing. Too bad about those 90 percent of marine invertebrate species that died off during the breakup. I mean, there were some fancy animals that went down the tube then, like those trilobites you like so much. But, up with the dinosaurs. And, another step later, here at 200 million years, the birds split off from the dinosaurs. What somebody called a free bonus for excellence in thermal insulation."

Four steps remained. "You realize, of course, that the top of the Grand Canyon stops at about 245 million years ago. That fiend Erosion destroyed the evidence. Back about that time, the mammals and the placental animals went their own ways as they improved on matters reptilian. And then the mammals split up into all those orders, like rodents and carnivores and primates in these next few steps. But let's just step over all that and land up here at 65 million years ago." Alan plunged a stick into the sand and swirled it around. "Disaster strikes."

"The Cretaceous extinction. Goodbye dinosaurs," offered

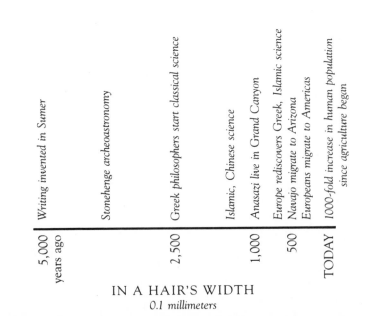

IN A HAIR'S WIDTH
0.1 millimeters

Brian, "as well as 50 percent of all the marine invertebrate species around at the time."

"Not to mention nearly all the zooplankton," Jackie observed. "That must have been some black cloud hanging over the earth, to stop photosynthesis to the point that nearly all the little ocean animals starved. I mean, since those phytoplankton produce 90 percent of the oxygen consumed by us animals, isn't that calling it a little close?"

"There are lots of plant and animal species that didn't make it through those terrible times," observed Barbara. "But that created some empty niches, and afterwards the primates expanded to fill some of them. What were mostly little tree-shrew sorts of animals, not unlike rodents in many ways, suddenly evolved into monkeys. And somewhere about this next-to-last step, they split up into New World monkeys and Old World monkeys, getting separate continents on which to go their own ways. South America and Africa."

"Thank you. And now, for my final step," announced Alan in a voice suggesting a roll of the drums, "we shall leap from monkeys to ape to man!"

"I've got to see this," said Rosalie. "For 99 steps you've fiddled around, and now for the last step you're finally getting down to serious business. The monkey business."

"You didn't like the nautiloids?" asked Alan in a hurt voice, "or my birds? I mean, I thought that the birds were a great invention, even if they were kind of accidental."

"You've got to look at the big picture, Rosalie," volunteered Cam. "Haldane once observed that the Lord must have been inordinately fond of beetles because He made so many different types. Something like 90 percent of all animal species are beetles."

"Oh, never mind," said Marsha. "I want to see this flying leap across the monkey gap."

Alan braced to leap, but then fell abruptly down on his hands and knees and started walking his fingers across the sand while everyone laughed. "I think we'll have to reduce the step size a little, so we go 1 million years at a time rather than 50. Now about a third of the way along," Alan walked his fingers along to 34 million years, "the apes split off from the Old World Monkeys. That deserves a small stick." Alan planted the twig he'd kept behind his ear. "So it took half the time since the Cretaceous extinction just for the apes to get started. Maybe we'll just keep dividing the remaining distance by half, just like in Zeno's Paradox."

"Now the apes lived in the trees and, unlike the monks, they developed some real anatomical specializations for genuine hanging-by-your-hands brachiation. We've got their brachiator's shoulder joints, and monkeys don't. Now Marsha," Alan said, "just take your right hand, reach around behind your head, and scratch your left ear."

She did it with a flourish. "Some women put on earrings this way."

"Did you know that a monkey couldn't do that? Their shoulders just don't have that many degrees of freedom. This business of apes being more clever—that might not have been the main thing when they initially diverged. Probably more like making a more efficient cherry-picker. You know, those trucks with little platforms that get positioned by hydraulics. Well, monkeys have to walk along branches like a squirrel, most of them. Now an ape can swing along under a branch, hanging on with one hand while picking fruit with the other hand. Sure, they can swing from tree to tree too, but that's nothing special. Just think of those flying squirrels that glide between trees with the greatest of ease."

Alan took another 17 finger steps, arriving at 17 million years ago. "Now in half the remaining time, the apes make it all the way to an extinct ape called Ramapithecus, or Sivapithecus—whatever, you can remember him easily by thinking of your favorite orangutan in the zoo. Now the orang is a pretty smart animal—somebody demonstrated to one how to flake a rock, took the sharp flake, and sawed through the rope that tied shut a box of goodies, and then went away to watch what the orang would do with a new set of materials and a new sealed box of bananas. Sure enough, the orang made the tool and then used it to get into the tied-up box of bananas."

"It's a pity they're not more social animals," observed Barbara. "The adults are loners, getting together only occasionally for mating purposes because their food is spread out so thinly that each requires a large territory. They're certainly clever enough that, with the boost provided by social life and observing the inventions of others, they might be more like chimps. At least as juveniles, they're certainly clever and social enough. Their adult life style is what limits them, I think. Evolution is full of dead-ends. That could have been us."

Alan was not to be deterred from his timetable. "Half again, and down here—let the fingers do the walking—we indeed get to chimps and gorillas. That is to say, we last shared a common ancestor with gorillas about 10 or 11 million years ago, with chimps maybe 7 or 8 million years ago. They keep changing those numbers on me every year, so I might be a little out of date. Since chimps and gorillas might also have changed some since then, you have to make allowances. But here at maybe 7 million years ago, you've got the last split in the hominid lineage for which there are several descendants still living today—though the apes may not be long for this world if the human population keeps growing and cutting down their forests. There were various splits since then, in this here hominid line, but all the side branches have died out—excepting us, of course. And we're working at that too."

"Now," observed Alan, "we've only got another eight little finger steps to go. And 8 million years ago, East Africa was getting pushed higher and higher by lava welling up, making a big blister in Kenya and Ethiopia—just like this here Colorado Plateau was rising up about the same time, creating this canyon we're in. Not only does elevation change the local climate, but the whole world was getting a whole lot drier back in the late Miocene—forests were changing into grasslands and all that. And those fancy apes had to either retreat with the forests into refuges like where the gorillas live now, or they had to get used to finding food out in the open country. Where there were lots of competitors. Even predators who liked succulent leg of ape. Dangerous place, there, out in the open.

"Well, somehow they managed, though there aren't many fossils from this period to show the gradual changes. All we know is that by 4 million years ago—halve the remaining time again— we've got old *Australopithecus afarensis*. Walking upright, almost as good as Jimmy. 'Course, they've still got ape-sized brains. Pint-sized brains, to be exact. Half a liter for you metric types."

Jimmy was hefting a softball-sized rock, an eyebrow cocked as he awaited Alan's next sentence.

"I didn't say it, honest," said Alan innocently. "Now some people I know may have pint-sized brains, but not Jimmy, no sir. You've all heard of ten-gallon hats? They were invented for our Jimmy."

Alan quickly resumed his march before Jimmy could reply. "So, halve it again, and we're at 2 million years. Something funny has started to go wrong with the earth's climate in the middle of that last little step, sort of hot and cold alternating ten times every million years. And surprise, the brain size has started to increase. Furthermore, stone tools start to be found all over the place, as Barbara showed you. And there are soon three hominid lines going at once in East Africa. One was a massively built fellow who died out. Old Zinj baby, who increased his tooth size rather than his brain.

"And in another step, at 1 million years, there is only one species left going, our ancestor *Homo erectus*, with a quart— pardon me, a liter-sized brain. Erectus has got the wanderlust, and by now he's spread out of Africa and is all over Southeast

Asia, maybe even into Europe. But, just a tiny little bit further—we've only got one finger step left before we arrive at today if Zeno's Paradox doesn't rise up to smite us—the Ice Ages start in a big way. And the brain gets even bigger—all the way up to three pints in Neanderthal, here in the thickness of the twig that marks today. But he died out too. Now in the thickness of the bark on that twig—actually no more than a hair's breadth—we arrive at the civilizations of the last 5,000 years, and science.

"Now in the last few years, less than a layer of dust on my fingernail, science has discovered much of what happened during all that time"—and here Alan swept his arm to indicate the length of the beach—"plus these estimates of when it happened. There's even knowledge of how it occurred—all that evolutionary bootstrapping."

Silence. "How about the 'Why'?" someone asked. "You've covered 'What', and 'When', and a little bit of 'How'. But why did it all occur?"

I volunteered an answer. "The usual scientific prejudice is that if one figures out the 'How', the 'Why' will take care of itself. But making some guesses about how it all fits together—which is perhaps our closest approach to giving an answer about 'Why'— that's a part of science too. The only trouble is that it's always a temporary summary, soon out of date. But we keep on making models for how and why it fits together, even though they'll be superceded shortly."

"So why do *you* think it occurred?" I was not to get off lightly.

"Well, one way of looking at it comes from the new thermodynamics. That says there is a self-organizing tendency whenever energy is running downhill in a system, just like spiral eddies form downhill of rapids. There are a lot of levels of self-organization, evidently, and we just keep encountering one emergent principle after another, getting surprised by bird flight as an offshoot of keeping warm with feathers, getting surprised by consciousness as a free gift of enough complexity in a brain specialized for handling symbols and sequences. Evolution is almost like a river that flows uphill, the increased complexity powered by the usual downhill river of energy flow."

If there is anything else, we'll never know except by wading through the long, hard process of eliminating the trivial explanations. If, indeed, one can use the word "trivial" for such a piece of magnificent creation. It's only the individual pieces that are workaday machines and processes. Yet the whole is much more than the sum of its parts, and this whole has still escaped the comprehension of our limited brains. Our brains are much better at comprehending the pieces, and so we are much better at dissecting things than at visualizing the whole—even when we know the individual pieces. It's only through clever metaphors, such as Alan's walk through time, that we can even attempt to comprehend the whole thing.

AFTERWARDS, Dan Hartline and I walked down the beach again talking about brains some more. We stood at about 700 million years, just back of Alan's Cambrian stick.

The way I figure it, nerve cells must have gotten started sometime back about that time. Before that, individual cells did a little bit of everything—they sensed the environment, they contracted to move away from trouble or toward food, they digested food. Paramecia are probably a good present-day stand-in for those Precambrian cells. They have specialized channels through their membranes—little gates that admit calcium ions, or maybe potassium or sodium ions on other occasions. It's the calcium entry that starts them swimming, beating their little hairs like so many Volga boatmen, to go zooming off in a new direction.

Dan suggested that sodium channels for sending electrical signals long distances must have been around before the time of the Cambrian, because even primitive nervous systems like the nerve net of a jellyfish use sodium to produce the nerve impulse, which is how an elongated nerve cell (some can be over two meters long—they are, of course, very thin) tells its far end what's happening elsewhere. The signaling codes are very similar. Dan and I once did some experiments together on lobsters, and their multiplexing scheme (how nerves, and the long-distance telephone companies, send two different conversations down the same line) was the same as I'd earlier studied in cats, monkeys, and humans. One has to go back more than 600 million years ago to find a common ancestor.

Standing at 500 million years ago, when all the major phyla were underway, we compared notes and decided that the major types of circuits of nerve cells had probably already been invented by then. It does make one wonder, when the sensitivity-adjusting mechanisms for sensing muscle length turn out to be the same in lobster neurons as in humans. These involve two different chains of cells, interdigitating in just the right way, so that the sensory nerve ending is kept under the right tension to sense any new changes in muscle length. So perhaps lobsters and humans inherited them from a common ancestor.

Either that or a lot of groups later invented the same thing on their own. That does, of course, occasionally happen: the

Numbers do not seem to work well with regard to deep time. Any number above a couple of thousand years—fifty thousand, fifty million—will with nearly equal effect awe the imagination to the point of paralysis.

JOHN McPHEE, 1981

Part of the resistance to Darwin and Wallace derives from our difficulty in imagining the passage of millennia, much less the aeons. What does seventy million years mean to beings who live only one-millionth as long? We are like butterflies who flutter for a day and think it is forever.

CARL SAGAN, 1980

camera-type eye was invented by the mollusks in time for the octopus to use it, although it was invented independently in the chordate line for the mudpuppies and the fish. And, of course, us. That it was independent invention is known due to differences in the embryology of the eye between chordates and mollusks. In the octopus, the photoreceptors sensibly point toward the incoming light; in our eyes, they point away. Indeed, the light must pass through three or four layers of nerve cells in our retina before reaching the photoreceptors. This is terribly inefficient, since those nerve cells are not entirely transparent—their DNA in particular is very good at scattering photons every which way, diffusing the image somewhat.

Now if the Creator had planned ahead properly, she would have done us the same way as the octopus. Instead, it seems likely that the pointing-the-wrong-way arrangement was an evolutionary patchwork job, which was sufficient for primitive chordates like mudpuppies, who live in murky river bottoms without much need for precision vision. And so the primates inherited the same arrangement. When monkeys needed better resolution for spotting fruit in trees, evolution just improved other parts of the visual system rather than starting over from scratch. As in other bureaucracies, one has to live with the shortcuts that predecessors took, procedures that have become so embedded in the system that redesigning them now is out of the question. The treasure hunt of chordate development just doesn't know how to build an eye any other way.

More recently than 500 million years ago, we're hard-pressed to put a date on an invention. We just don't know enough yet about the super-circuits (like those ones in the brain that tune up to detect hawks) to know if the birds invented them, or the vertebrates, or if they too were invented clear back here before things diverged into the many phyla.

Still, the major circuits for repeated movements—the ones we use to walk and chew and swim and tap out a rhythm—are all similar to one another. And they differ little between lobsters and humans. Again, that may be repeated invention; just like the eye's optics, there may be only so many really good ways of making a circuit oscillate. But it does make one wonder if the evolution of nerve circuits also hadn't been going on for hundreds of millions of years before things started fossilizing in a big way during the Cambrian. So a lot more may have been happening in that span between 1,300 and 600 million years ago than just the beginnings of multicellular animals. The foundations of our brains may be back in that Precambrian ocean.

Back to the boats.

The Powell expeditions through Grand Canyon [showed] that man had inhabited that seemingly inhospitable region centuries earlier. It should have been clear to the emaciated and battered explorers that those prehistoric aborigines were in many ways much better adapted to the environment than the explorers with their rancid bacon, soggy coffee, and mildewed flour. Indeed, the more intensive recent archeological studies [of Grand Canyon] have demonstrated not only that its depths provided adequate subsistence for a people technologically attuned to their habitat, but that movement on foot through its vast recesses was entirely feasible.

The anthropologist
ROBERT C. EULER, 1969

MILE 134
Tapeats Creek
Eighth Campsite

WE'RE MAKING CAMP EARLY this afternoon so that we can hike up to Thunder River. Thunder River is surely one of the few rivers that empties into a creek, which then empties into a river. So much for orderly names. We're anxious to see Thunder Spring, which gives rise to this short "river." The spring is one of the largest in the Grand Canyon. Certainly Tapeats Creek as it flows into the Colorado is the biggest stream we've seen since the Little Colorado, though it gathers its waters from a dozen springs up the drainage.

Tapeats has a large campsite spread out along the right bank, and it even extends along Tapeats Creek, going back in a ways. Tamarisk grow all along the shoreline of the creek, providing havens from the afternoon sun. Tapeats Canyon starts off easy, but then quickly narrows into a "box" canyon filled with a jumble of really big boulders through which the stream cascades. In some places, the stream fills the canyon from wall to wall, and one has to wade back and forth to pick through the shallow spots. Early in the summer, the water can be so high (and cold) that it is impassable. The walls are Tapeats Sandstone. Though we first encountered this corrugated-appearing khaki sandstone at the Little Colorado River, and explored it again at Elves Chasm and Blacktail Canyon, this canyon is the "type locality" for which the Tapeats Sandstone was named. And handsome it is.

It requires some agile climbing to get up over a steep talus slope. But once up, the slope becomes gentle, the ledges and terraces extending back for many miles. The Tapeats of the box canyon is replaced with the overlying Bright Angel Shale, which is easily eroded down to a gentle gradient (this is the same stuff that forms the Tonto Platform, that almost flat region one sees looking down from the Canyon rims just before the V of the granite gorge finally goes down to the river—it's such crumbly rock layers that give the Canyon its breadth).

On the tops of some of these terraces are Anasazi ruins, originally noted by the second Powell expedition in 1872. We explore one Pueblo-style ruin on the right side of the creek, which has four rooms flanking a series of storerooms. These ruins, alas, have been pot-hunted. But Subie says that the potsherds recovered have all been identified by Bob Euler as being from the period of A.D. 1100 to 1150, the same time as the final period of occupation at Unkar Delta. There are more than 2,000 sites like this in the Canyon, and most of them are from the one century between 1050 and 1150.

There is another one-room pueblo ruin on the other side of the creek, a good fifteen stories above the streambed, hidden behind a boulder that forms one of the walls of the room. Someone observes that one of the families must have sure liked their privacy. But of course it could be where the survivors of the lower pueblo moved after some disaster. Tapeats Canyon can be reached from the North Rim (even horses can make it down these days), and they might have had hungry visitors coming in along the same route after the drought set in about A.D. 1130. Thanks to Thunder Spring, this place probably had water long after others had dried up.

Somewhat farther upstream, Thunder River comes down from the left; it is obviously contributing most of the water we see arriving down at our campsite on the Colorado. Hiking up Thunder River's short V-shaped valley via a series of switchbacks, we soon see where all the water comes from: it bursts out of the cliff through two openings, falls eight stories, and then foams and cascades another half mile down to join the rest of Tapeats Creek. This is surely the shortest river in the world. Up there to the right of the falls is a cave which leads back into the underground river, shortly before its emergence.

Continuing up to the left of the falls, we reach a crest, and a valley opens out below us. Surprise Valley. Abruptly, the sound of Thunder River is lost. Intrigued, some people hike back to the point where the sound starts and the falls come into view, a most dramatic entrance for anyone hiking the trail in the opposite direction. Out of Surprise Valley and into Thunder River.

Surprise Valley has a most unusual shape, rather like a bowl. Though a creek has been cut down from the Redwall in several places, it is hard to see where the water leaves the bowl. A topographic map proves illuminating: Bonita Creek takes a few sharp turns, again most uncharacteristic of the valleys around here.

Subie tells us that Surprise Valley was formed by a great landslide. All of the left wall of the bowl has slipped toward the Colorado River. About four square miles of rock slid sideways and temporarily plugged up the river; geologically speaking, it wasn't even that long ago that it happened.

"And what caused this great prehistoric landslide?" Rosalie asked.

"Probably water," answered Subie, "lubricating the slippery shale of the Bright Angel Formation. Thunder River indicates that there is a lot of river draining down off the high Kaibab Plateau of the North Rim. Maybe there was enough in the past to grease the skids.

"Or maybe the Colorado River was backed up," she added, "by the lava flow which once dammed up the river farther downstream near Lava Falls at Mile 179. If this area was soaked by the backup, that might have lubricated things so that when the dam broke and the lake drained, the loosened block went sliding—and created Surprise Valley."

One of the great landslides of prehistory. I cannot resist telling the others about the greatest landslide of historic times. It happened in 1980, when the top of Mount St. Helens slid off and uncapped the volcano. The volcano had been getting restless, and a spotter plane happened to be flying overhead when it happened. A series of earthquakes occurred right underneath the mountain, and the observers reported seeing the seemingly solid mountain begin to quiver like a bowl full of jelly. The top of the mountain then slid sideways and created the great landslide. It crashed down one vertical mile before reaching Spirit Lake. When it hit the lake, it caused a great wave of water to splash out of the opposite side of the lake. The wave washed up the mountain ridge behind the lake.

One can still see where the wave washed away the soil, because for a few years nothing grew on that whole end of the mountain ridge. It isn't just that the trees are missing—they're blown down and stripped clean of branches and bark everywhere in that direction because of the great volcanic blast that followed the uncapping of the pressure cooker. The soil itself is missing, and so no new bushes or seedlings grow back. One whole mountainside, washed clean of soil down to the underlying rock by one gigantic wave splashed out of Spirit Lake. The ecologists have been studying how soils get started again in such denuded areas, as well as in the lifeless lava beds near the volcano.

SOIL ISN'T JUST THE SURFACE OF THE EARTH, as I thought when I grew up in the farm states of the midwestern United States. Rocks, which are mostly what one walks on in this desert, aren't soil. Soil is a living ecosystem; it can be killed, for example, by heat from lava flows. Soil is partly formed of things which are living or were once living and are now decaying; these organic (carbon) materials are mixed in with inorganic "minerals" such as potassium and nitrates. The organic and inorganic molecules that are useful to living cells are called nutrients. Soil also contains water and air spaces; the mix of particle sizes is very important, since sand alone won't hold water, and clay alone won't let in water. Bacteria in the soil do all sorts of useful jobs, such as fix nitrogen in the soil so that plant roots have nitrate fertilizers; the plant that extends a stalk up above the soil is only the tip of a mountain of subterranean goings-on.

In Tapeats Canyon as we hike back, Alan points out how soil gets started. Here and there among the sand and rocks are some dark patches of crusty stuff; often some plants grow adjacent to them. The dark material sometimes covers the ground like a lumpy black crust, looking almost like a skin disease. The dirty stuff is cryptogamic soil, the simplest of the soil ecosystems. Cryptogam means "hidden marriage," and tells of the cooperative relationship between bacteria and the simplest plants. Soil starts simple and co-evolves with the plant life. Knowledgeable desert hikers avoid stepping on the cryptogams; these primitive living systems have a hard enough time without disruptions, and a careless footprint can set them back decades.

The buildup of a soil can be aided by things blowing in from the outside; the new lava beds near Mount St. Helens are starting to build up new soil in nooks and crannies, just because that's where blowing things are trapped. Dead insects, for example, blown up from lower altitudes may lodge there and contribute their decaying organic compounds to the new soil. But cryptogams show how soil can get started without so much outside help from decaying higher life forms; their blue-green algae (now classed with the bacteria rather than the other algae) use sunlight to convert atmospheric nitrogen into a waste product containing nitrates, which serve as food for fungi (which cannot do their own photosynthesis). This symbiotic combination, called a lichen, also helps retain water and thus provides a home for mosses, another component of cryptogams.

Plant life has to build up through a slow succession of ever more complex types; each decade or century sees a new type of bush or tree dominate. The speed of the succession depends on the weather and the soil. For example, the Anasazi's corn needs the right amounts of potassium and nitrogen in the soil. Their beans could get along in soil that was low in nitrogen, so long as they had enough water. And once soil has had beans (or other legumes such as clover or alfalfa) grown in it for a while, the soil accumulates enough nitrogen to grow corn, thanks to the bacteria in the legume roots which fix nitrogen; while plants use most of the atmospheric nitrogen they convert to ammonium compounds, the bacteria convert so much that the excess is excreted as nitrates into the soil. Natural fertilizer.

I don't know if the Anasazi knew about this crop-succession principle; perhaps they just found the better soils for corn by trial and error. But the Indians didn't domesticate corn without many generations of selecting the right plants and soil (and corn is one of their major contributions to our civilization). So it wouldn't surprise us if they knew about crop rotation too.

THE RED SOILS OF THE TROPICS remind one of all the red rock and sand around here, but they're poor soils for a different reason. In the temperate zones, the good land has a very different soil than in the tropics. With proper crop rotation (such as planting legumes every few years to build the soil's nitrogen back up), good soils—if they're not ruined by salt from irrigation—will grow all sorts of things for a long time. But in the tropics, the soil has been so regularly washed by the rains that many of the soil minerals have been washed out to sea. The nutrients in the forest floor would wash out to sea too if it weren't for the fine network of plant roots that trap them as they wash down. All of the dead animals, the insect excrement, the decaying plant materials—they're all neatly trapped by the super-efficient network of living tree roots, with the help of special types of fungi that live on the roots. Cut down the trees and the roots die. What isn't burnt washes out to sea. And the remaining soil has little to give a new crop.

And so you can't simply plant a tropical rain forest, even if you had all the right seeds to sow. Even if a rain forest grew in the same region some years earlier, starter plants can't take hold, because of the lack of the right conditions (such as shade!); it might take millennia of slowly evolving soils and successions of plant life before a rain forest complex could ever exist again. Once a rain forest is cut down, the building materials are lost and the necessary shade is lost. It's not like a European or North American forest that might return in a century or two.

The web of roots in the rain forest reminds me of the mammalian kidney, that super organ that dumps the liquid part of the bloodstream into the plumbing that leads down to the bladder, but then—before the fluid actually reaches the ureter and is declared waste—neatly grabs back those molecules that it wants to save, thus keeping the right proportions of salts in the body.

The lush tropical forest, then, is a great accomplishment of slow evolution, but one that cannot be repeated on order, simply by reseeding a clear-cut. Once they're gone—and they're

Many European farmers have found out the hard way that the methods of their ancestors do not work in parts of the wet tropics. If you clear a typical piece of red tropical land, plough it up, and sow seed, your efforts are poorly rewarded. There may be a few years of struggle against falling yields, but then comes the bitterness of defeat, and a patch of red mud is left for the wild weeds. . . . How have the forest trees [of the great tropical rain forests] managed to thrive in a soil washed clean of nutrients?

PAUL COLINVAUX
Why Big Fierce Animals Are Rare,
1978

being cleared at a ferocious rate due to the Third World population explosion—the rain forests won't be back for a very long time. And the animals that live there will all be dead. The species that lived only in those forests won't ever be back: extinction is a very permanent fate. A large fraction—more than half—of the world's animal and plant species will become extinct *within decades* if the clear-cutting of the tropical forests continues.

Except in cases like that of Brazil, where the Amazon is often cleared simply to grow grass for cattle which will be exported to the rest of the world as cheap beef for the fast-food industry, it's hard to blame the people who do the clearing—they're us, just a little less educated and a little more hungry. The problem is the inflationary times in which we've lived since agriculture got started about 10,000 years ago: just as prices tend to rise in times of prosperity, so population numbers tend to rise as couples raise as many children as the local resources can bear in the short run. In the long run, a lot of people and animals are going to starve unless the renewable resources (which a tropical forest isn't, except at low human population densities) are brought into balance with the population.

Scientists aren't very popular when they come bearing such bad news, and one doesn't find newspaper headlines in Third World countries concerning what they've got in store for themselves only decades ahead if they keep expanding the population and clearing the forests. It's not quite like eating the seed corn, but it comes close.

Tropical forests are being besieged by armies of subsistence farmers who cannot survive in cities. . . . Each year humans destroy enough tropical forest to blanket all of England. Among the several dire implications of this devastation is that a mass extinction of tropical species appears imminent. And, since tropical forests are the homes of between two and four million of the estimated five to ten million species on the face of the earth, it could well rank with history's several great mass extinctions.

The biologist DANIEL SIMBERLOFF, 1985

. . . if no country pulls the [nuclear] trigger the worst thing that will *probably* happen—in fact is already well underway—is not energy depletion, economic collapse, conventional war, or even the expansion of totalitarian governments. As tragic as these catastrophes would be for us, they can be repaired within a few generations. The one process now going on that will take millions of years to correct is the loss of genetic and species diversity by the destruction of natural habitats. This is the folly our descendants are least likely to forgive us.

The biologist E. O. WILSON, 1984

THE SUNSET WAS UNUSUALLY RED TONIGHT, long before dinner was finished. Many thought it pretty, but some of us who live in timber country had mixed feelings. It was the kind of red that one sees when a forest fire has settled a pall of smoke over the western sky. Pretty, but discomforting at the same time.

Smoke sometimes spreads for long distances. In 1950, forest fires in Canada made the sunsets similarly red in Europe; they created a haze that cut the daytime sunlight in half in Washington, D.C. During a heavy overcast, only about 10 percent of the usual amount of sunlight reaches the surface of the earth. And volcanic eruptions have been known to reduce it even further: the towns downwind from the Mount St. Helens eruption in 1980 had their automatic streetlights lit at noon.

"That sounds like what happened to Moses," commented Jackie. "The people in Egypt couldn't see one another or move around for three full days."

"Another one of those pesky Mediterranean volcanos," Ben replied. "Suppose it was Santorini, popping off?"

Just as an overcast sky means a cooler day, so smoke or ash clouds also cool the earth's surface. Benjamin Franklin, as usual, had something to say on the subject: he suggested that the 1783 Laki eruption in Iceland was the cause of Europe's cool weather and poor crops. There is now evidence from the tree rings of very old trees, such as the bristlecone pines in the mountains of the western United States, that early frosts occurred in the years of major volcanic eruptions elsewhere in the world. Thanks to the accuracy of tree-ring counts, 1626 B.C. is now estimated to be the year of one of the greatest volcanic eruptions of historic times, the Santorini (Thera) eruption in the Aegean Sea. The climatic effects of such an eruption can be major: following Tambora's eruption in Indonesia, 1815 was called the "year without a summer" in faraway Europe.

Scientists had been studying the effects of dust injected into the atmosphere by volcanos ("a stratospheric veil of fine silicate ash and sulphur aerosols, with resultant surface cooling"), stimulated not only by the marked climate changes that have followed some eruptions but also by the results of one of the unmanned spacecraft which flew past Mars in 1971. There it found a giant dust storm which enveloped much of the planet and took 10 months to clear. Could that happen here? Why does dust take so long to settle out of the atmosphere? One answer is that, if it gets up high enough, rain won't wash it out anymore.

And how does dust get up that high? When the geologist Walter Alvarez discovered unusually high concentrations of the rare element iridium in 65-million-year-old layers of rock in both

Italy and Denmark, he considered whether the breakup of a meteor might have caused it. He, his father the physicist Luis Alvarez, and others postulated in 1980 that such a meteor could have kicked up enough dust to cause the Cretaceous extinction, that wiped out the dinosaurs and so many other species about that time. The giant dust cloud they postulated got everyone to thinking about extinctions and atmospheric disruptions.

But what about smoke? It was a new consideration to many scientists, despite the smoky sunsets of 1950 and other years. In 1977, George Woodwell of the Woods Hole Research Center suggested that all of the clearing of tropical forests that was going on might, because of the burning, be injecting more carbon compounds into the atmosphere than all the coal and oil burned in the Northern Hemisphere.

Smoke can also get high enough in the troposphere to avoid being washed out immediately; when it does wash out, it causes acid rain, as the people and wildlife downwind of industrial centers well know by now. Smoke at any altitude is far worse than dust—one big difference is that, while dust tends to reflect light back into space that would have otherwise reached the earth's surface, the black carbon particles tend to absorb light and heat up, thus heating the air molecules around them much more than dust does. Heating up the middle atmosphere, while simultaneously reducing the heating of the lower layers near the earth's surface, is just the sort of thing to give nightmares to atmospheric scientists: the circulation patterns that carry weather around are quite dependent on the temperature gradient between the lower and upper atmosphere.

El Niño, the Pacific Ocean climate change which seems to occur every half-dozen years or so, causes a lot of fishermen's families to go hungry (air temperatures affect ocean surface temperatures and thus ocean currents, such as the upwelling off Ecuador and Peru which carries nutrients to the surface and feeds lots of fish). El Niño's mysterious rearrangement of Pacific weather patterns seems to be associated with a change in the temperature gradient between the lower and upper atmosphere. It is clear that volcanos can make El Niño advance its schedule, causing it to arrive much earlier than normal—probably by modifying the atmospheric temperature gradient by injecting ash into the middle and upper atmosphere.

Injecting a lot of smoke into the atmosphere might be even more serious because black soot particles in the smoke upset the usual vertical temperature gradient even more than light-colored dust. Volcanos and other natural causes are bad enough when humans are living close to the edge of their food resources: burning a lot of vegetation in the tropics is a serious matter for people living anywhere there's weather. But that may not be the worst of it.

The nuclear winter story actually started with supersonic jets and ozone, the three-atom oxygen molecule that tends to accumulate in the stratosphere and screen out much of the sun's ultraviolet light that would otherwise seriously damage plants, not to mention human skin and eyes. In Germany, Paul Crutzen's studies of the ozone layer called into question the building of supersonic passenger jets in 1971. He then contributed to the subsequent studies which had led to the concern over refrigerator coolants and the propellant gas used in spray cans, because of fluorocarbon's potential for destroying the ozone layer. In 1975, a U.S. National Academy of Science report concluded that all-out nuclear war might destroy enough of the ozone layer to expose the earth's surface to lethal doses of ultraviolet light—lethal to plants as well as people. The president of the Academy, in releasing the report, offered his personal opinion. He chose to look on the report as "encouraging," characterizing it as suggesting that much of the planet could recover from a nuclear war. In the furor that followed, ecologists Paul Ehrlich, Anne Ehrlich and John Holdren challenged the report because it virtually ignored the "huge firestorms" that would follow a nuclear attack. Woodwell made his calculations about Amazon burning. By the late seventies, Crutzen was studying burning trees in Brazil and trying to figure out what happened to the constituents of the smoke and vapors, worried that they too might affect the earth's ozone.

All of this formed the background to one of those startling serendipities that sometimes occurs in basic science, when one problem suddenly illuminates another. Smoke had some effects on ozone, but what might they do to temperature? Smoke hadn't been taken seriously before, and atmospheric scientists began to reevaluate the old studies about the aftermath of a nuclear war. Never mind for a moment all those people killed by the blasts and firestorms and fallout—what sort of world would the survivors face? If volcanos can cause so much trouble, what would happen after all those bombs kicked up a lot of dust? And all those firestorms burned up all those cities with their fuel dumps and asphalt pavements and flammable buildings, sending smoke up high?

Crutzen didn't have data on burning cities, but he did have data on forest fires and he assumed that the city firestorms might spread to the forests. So Crutzen and an American colleague, John Birks, wrote a paper in 1982 for the Swedish environmental journal *Ambio* on the smoke from forest fires that a war might cause—and calculated that a typical nuclear war might cause enough atmospheric disruption from forest fires alone to prevent 99 percent of the sunlight from reaching the surface of the earth, and that the effect might last for weeks.

As is obvious from the fact that temperatures drop during the night anywhere from 5°–20°C. (9°–36°F.), lack of rewarming during the next several days could cause the earth's surface to freeze in short order. As Paul Crutzen said when contemplating the consequences, "I don't think they know what winter is in India." Plants in the tropics have not evolved any protection against frosts; even high-latitude trees which will survive prolonged winter freezes can be killed by a quick frost during their summer season. Even a few days of dense overcast can have crippling effects on forests and agriculture.

Is a simple calculation reliable? One can't just experiment by burning cities down, but there is the smoke-haze data from forest fires. The volcanos and the weather records have provided a lot of data with which to calibrate computer models of dust in the atmosphere. But the next part of the story came when people working on very different problems applied their expertise to Crutzen and Birk's scenario. Carl Sagan and two of his former students, Owen Toon and James Pollack, had developed computerized models to study how the giant dust storm on Mars might have operated; Richard Turco and James Ackerman had been using a more sophisticated version of this computerized model to test the notion that dust clouds kicked up by a meteor striking the earth might have been the cause of the mass extinctions postulated by Alvarez et al. Turco saw an advance copy of Crutzen and Birk's work, and realized that smoke was much more important than dust because of what it did to atmospheric temperatures.

The five had gotten together to study the biologists' mass extinction problem, but now they shifted and extended Crutzen and Birks' calculations using the sophisticated computer "working model" of the atmosphere; they included estimates for burning cities as well as burning forests. Turco, Toon, Ackerman, Pollack, and Sagan wrote a paper (soon known by the acronym TTAPS) published in *Science* in late 1983 detailing the consequences of nuclear exchanges of various sizes and types; the TTAPS report was delayed one year, Sagan said, because their U.S. government sponsors were nervous about the political reaction and wanted more studies done before letting it become public knowledge. But news circulated quickly in the scientific community anyway.

Turco coined the term "nuclear winter" to summarize the consequences of the cold and the dark that would come from the smoke clouds of a nuclear war. It would get very cold—Arctic winter temperatures—and stay that way for months, much longer than Crutzen and Birks' first estimate. Indeed, between four and nine months of subfreezing temperatures, depending on assumptions about the size and season of the war. In the interim year before the TTAPS publication, while the results were circulating privately, a group of physical scientists met to assess the Crutzen-Birks and TTAPS reports; every time they found a neglected factor that might lessen the effects, they also found several that would make things even worse. A group of biologists met to assess the longer-term consequences to the biology of the world. Sagan, the Ehrlichs, Woodwell, and fifteen other prominent scientists wrote a report that was published with the TTAPS paper; they evaluated the radiation doses, the ultraviolet effects, the bitterly acid rain, and the effects of the violent and frequent storms that would be generated by cooling land masses, and the disruptions to the ecosystems which the cold and dark would cause.

Because much damage could be done in the tropics by only a few days of slightly subfreezing weather, even the small-war scenarios looked dreadful. The biologists' report was understated, and had the language of compromise that nineteen different authors engenders, but it spelled catastrophe: "the possibility of the extinction of *Homo sapiens* cannot be excluded." A nuclear attack of any substantial size is, in effect, a Doomsday machine that would destroy the aggressors themselves within a month—and, unfortunately, much of the rest of the earth as well.

It would wipe out the agricultural and industrial system that supports a world population far larger than in preagricultural or preindustrial times; the grain harvests that provide 70 percent of the world's dietary calories are surprisingly fragile, even threatened by drops of 2°–5°C. in the average daily temperature. A full-fledged nuclear winter wouldn't merely reduce us to 0.1 percent of the world's present human population, the level that hunting and gathering supported before agriculture—there might also be too little to hunt and gather for that remaining one person in a thousand. Even if it didn't wipe out humanity, the war would likely reduce the population to a tiny fraction of its present size, and destroy civilization as we know it through the actions of starving mobs.

It would undo the world painfully built up by our ancestors, whose suffering and failures shaped the survivors into the species we are today. The apes, who today live in precarious habitats unlikely to survive even the cutting of the tropical forests, would surely succumb. Some monkeys might survive in the Southern Hemisphere, but no scientist can be sure. It might be more than 50 to 100 million years before the gearwheels of evolution again created anything as fancy as our civilization—or perhaps 500 million years, or never.

And we have ignored the possible effects of radiation. Someone once said that nuclear war could reduce life on earth to a radiation-resistant grasshopper eating a radiation-resistant grass.

The mechanism most likely to lead to the greatest consequences to humans from a nuclear war is not the blast wave, not the thermal pulse, not direct radiation, not even fallout; rather, it is mass starvation.
MARK HARWELL and THOMAS HUTCHINSON, Scientific Committee on Problems of the Environment, 1985 report

John Holdren . . . commented that what amazed him was that [any national leader] who had seriously contemplated the acceptability of losses implied by direct blast and radiation effects (which could be as high as a billion people) could be considered rational, and would probably be unmotivated by the further recognition that perhaps four billion people could be threatened by the longer-term climatic effects. . . . We would be appalled to learn that any governmental official who continues to believe in a winnable large-scale nuclear war could remain in a position of responsibility in any sane nation on earth. Perhaps most disquieting of all is the fact that people with such warped values are both responsible for strategic planning and are at the same time protected from public censure by the legal cloak of secrecy.
STEPHEN H. SCHNEIDER and RANDI LONDER, *The Coevolution of Climate and Life*, 1984

□   □   □

BAD AS THIS IS FOR HUMANS nearly everywhere on earth, it might also rate with the mass extinctions as a killer of whole major groups of plants and animals.

Despite the "winter" aspect, nuclear winter is not to be confused with just another ice age; the great extinctions said to be caused by meteors are the more appropriate comparison, if indeed anything in the earth's history is similar. When the climate changes slowly over thousands of years, there is time for humans and other animals to move around, find new ways of making a living, time for ecosystems to adapt and most species to survive. When the change happens in a matter of days, the results are far different. It's the difference between the melting ice caps causing sea level to slowly rise over the millennia and an earthquake causing a giant tidal wave to violently denude a whole coastline in minutes. Except that with a nuclear winter, it isn't just coastlines.

We have called into question the Old Testament reassurance about the continuation of life:

One generation passeth away, and another generation cometh: but the earth abideth for ever.

Ecclesiastes 1:4

Many more species have become extinct than are now alive. . . . We are unimportant in the history of our planet, which got along very well without us for several thousand million years. If we lose the flexibility to adapt, we too will become extinct. Other species will take our place, fill our niche, and carry on the evolutionary process—unless we, in passing, so alter the conditions for life that no existing organic forms can survive.

Betty Meggers

You know, there's no reason to believe progress is inevitable. I'm a medieval historian and believe me, people are quite capable of mucking things up.

Charles E. Odegaard

The Earth is just too small and fragile a basket for the human race to keep all its eggs in.

Robert A. Heinlein

The systematic mass murder of European Jewry made it clear that entire civilizations of the highest cultural and scientific attainments could in the course of a few years go rabidly mad; and the invention of nuclear weapons insured that insane nations of the near future would command the means to destroy life on Earth.

MATT CARTMILL, 1983

We have become, by the power of a glorious evolutionary accident called intelligence, the stewards of life's continuity on earth. We did not ask for this role, but we cannot abjure it. We may not be suited to it, but here we are.

STEPHEN JAY GOULD, 1984

We no longer have the choices to make, or the options of a few months ago to argue over. We simply must pull up short, and soon, and rid the earth once and for all of those weapons that are not really weapons at all but instruments of pure malevolence.

LEWIS THOMAS, 1984

If it should turn out that we have mishandled our own lives as several civilizations before us have done, it seems a pity that we should involve the violet and the tree frog in our departure. To perpetrate this final act of malice seems somehow disproportionate, beyond endurance. It is like tampering with the secret purposes of the universe itself and involving not only man but life in the final holocaust—an act of petulant, deliberate blasphemy.

LOREN EISELEY, 1963

Do not go gentle into that good night.
Rage, rage against the dying of the light.

DYLAN THOMAS

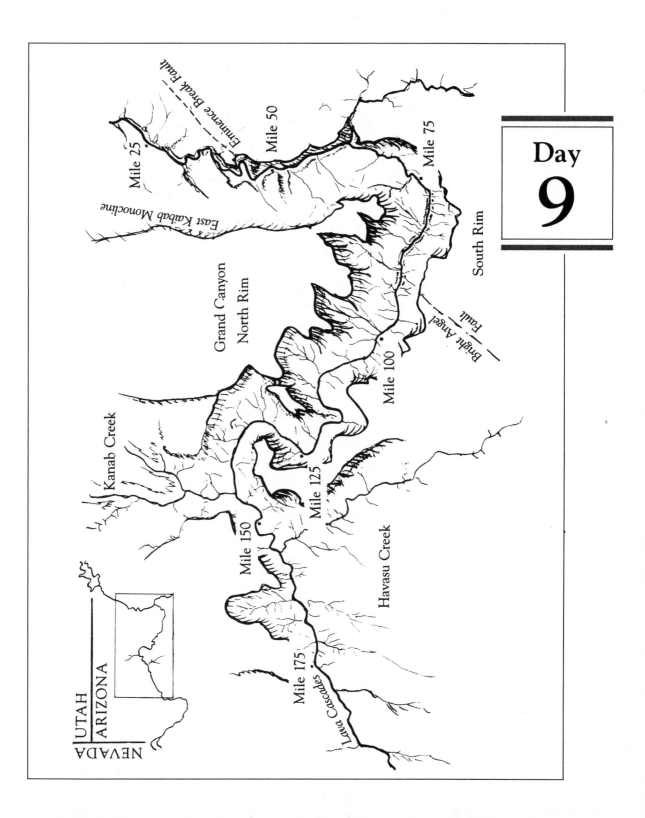

Day
9

Mile 25
Mile 50
Mile 75
Mile 100
Mile 125
Mile 150
Mile 175

Eminence Break Fault
East Kaibab Monocline
Grand Canyon North Rim
South Rim
Bright Angel Fault
Kanab Creek
Havasu Creek
Lava Cascades

NEVADA
UTAH
ARIZONA

Mile 134
Tapeats Creek

ALREADY IT'S A BIG DAY FOR BIGHORNS. Jeremy DuBois woke up this morning and was looking sleepy-eyed out of his tent, studying the boulder-strewn hillside across the river with approximately the attention one gives the back of a box of breakfast cereal. Then he thought that he saw a boulder move. Soon the binoculars were out and everyone was standing down at the edge of the river trying to count bighorn sheep. Three was about all that I spotted. But Fritz says that she once had some passengers who were experienced hunters, and that those guys could point out ten bighorns on a hillside where everyone else had only seen three. The Anasazi also probably had well-developed bighorn schemata. One of the tricks, of course, is to watch for slight movement. But the bighorns really do look like boulders otherwise.

There were tracks around the kitchen this morning when Fritz went to start breakfast, though no one saw the ringtail. They're not really cats but a relative of the racoon, with a cat-like body and fox-like face. The boatmen say that sometimes they see ringtail tracks around the kitchen almost every morning of an entire trip, demonstrating that there are plenty of them throughout the river corridor (or that they had a stowaway!). They're seldom seen because they're thoroughly nocturnal, spending their days up on a ledge or in a rock pile. They're quite agile and also bold animals; scientists studying rodents in the bottom of the Grand Canyon have had ringtails march into their tents during the night and make off with their specimen collections. Fritz says they spotted a ringtail one night who, having extracted the squeeze container for honey from a kitchen box which wasn't properly fastened, was having a feast. The ringtail ignored all the people that had gathered with flashlights, and calmly continued eating the honey. It remained long enough for them to count the rings in its long, bushy tail: ringtails sometimes have as many as sixteen black bands. Though the local ringtails probably eat mostly rodents and lizards, they also like rabbits, insects, snakes and fruit. And honey.

We're only going about three miles today, at least by river; we'll probably hike more than that. We shall go down to Mile 136 and explore Deer Creek all day, then take ourselves down to Overhang Camp at Mile 137. At breakfast, there were a group of people who hadn't seen Thunder River yesterday afternoon and who suggested a loop hike through Surprise Valley to Deer Creek, meeting up with the rest of us there in the afternoon. They'll have to do without a boatman for a guide, however; though several passengers have volunteered to row the short distance, there are three rapids between here and there,

Bighorn Sheep
Ovis canadensis

Ringtail
Bassariscus astutus

one with a big back-eddy known as "Helicopter Eddy." The river is at its narrowest and deepest here, making the currents tricky.

Alan gives the hikers some advice: don't drink the water, as the surface water may come down from some campgrounds up above us on the North Rim. And he advises all of us to watch out for the poison ivy on the trail somewhat above the river, going up around the lower falls at Deer Creek. Poison ivy is a problem in only two places, back at Vasey's Paradise and in that one small patch near Deer Creek Falls. The Canyon is amazingly free of stinging and itching hazards at most places and at most times of the year, just so long as one avoids the red ants in the daytime and shakes one's boots out in the morning in case a scorpion took up residence during the night. Even the Canyon rattlesnake is a sluggish coward.

DARWINIAN GRADUALISM is one way to get a new kind of animal, such as a Ringtail. As Darwin thought through the consequences of natural selection editing the variations within a species, he saw that there should be a drift toward those variants that were more successful in coping with their environment. Thus, he said, there would be a gradual shift in the characteristics of a species. It was perfectly good reasoning based on the data of 1858, before the days of the gene concept or the data from population studies. Darwin thought that nature was pretty well filled up with species, and that the evolving species would likely have to drive a wedge between existing species, taking over some of their niche (as we would now say). Darwin's metaphor of the wedge has dominated our thinking about evolving species.

But now it seems as if whole populations may not gradually shift their characteristics in such a conveniently gradual manner. The fossil record of marine invertebrates tends to show a species not changing at all (except, perhaps, for a slight increase in size) for a very long time. Then, without warning, it is likely to disappear, replaced by another similar species—which itself lasts for a long time without change. This is like the "model year" of American automobiles, where change occurs only once a year (it's just that the snail's model year lasts 10 million years). Variations may still occur within the model year (particularly, it is reported, in the cars that go down the assembly line on a Monday!), but they cause little steady drift in the overall character of the species.

Gradual change can, of course, be seen—Darwin was quite familiar with what animal breeders accomplished. The difference may well be in the size of a population: small subpopulations may be able to evolve gradually and rapidly; large populations with well-stirred gene pools may buffer much change and slow down the pace of gradualism so much that it becomes insignificant.

And so the events observed in the fossil record may simply be those of the large central population. Small subpopulations, off in a corner isolated from the rest, may evolve gradually and rapidly, as if—in my thunderstorm-spawned metaphor—on a spiral ramp off in one corner of the parking garage. Their adaptations might suit them to a new niche, eating a food that no other animal had been able to exploit. Or the adaptations might merely make them more efficient at earning its living in the same way exploited by their parent species.

If the subpopulation returned to mix with the parent species after attaining reproductive isolation, it would take a long time to displace the parent species by outcompeting it on equal terms. Mass extinctions would, however, offer a special opportunity to an improved species, when every bit of efficiency would count in the crunch of hard times. And hard times occur at least every 28 million years or so. It may be that several of the branches on the line to humans were affected by the mass extinctions. The apes split off from the Old World monkeys about 34 million years ago, not long after the "terminal event" of the Eocene, an unusual climate change that affected winter temperatures but not summer temperatures in the temperate zone's forests. The winters, judging from the botany, were about 20°C. colder than usual. In the seas, the protozoans called Radiolaria were almost decimated. And at the very same layers in sea-core samples of the radiolarian ooze in which the numbers of protozoans drop, geologists find tektites. These are little rounded pieces of glass, most of them smaller than the tip of a finger. This glass is particularly homogeneous, nonporous, water-free—all quite unlike volcanic glasses, and so it is suspected that tektites were made in space. Their distribution supports the idea of a meteor breaking up in the atmosphere: though the area in which they are found is called the "North American" strewn field, it extends from the Caribbean west through the central Pacific to the Indian Ocean.

Now how might such a meteor impact have caused a climatic change? Microtektites, or the dust kicked up on impact, in the lower atmosphere would be washed out by rainfall in a matter of weeks. In the stratosphere, it might take a few years. But the evidence for climatic change lasts 1 to 2 million years. That suggests that if something remained to shadow the earth, it remained out in space, orbiting the earth, unaffected by the atmosphere. But how could that produce this funny business of normal summers but extra-frigid winters in the temperate zones? In 1980, John O'Keefe suggested a clever model for a Saturn-like ring around the earth, composed of the tektites and microtektites that were pulled into orbit by the earth's gravity.

Rings tend to form around the equator because of collisions which dampen the north-south component of the velocity; the gravitational pull on an orbiting particle is not uniform because of the flattened-at-the-poles shape of the earth, that equatorial bulge associated with a none-too-rigid spinning body. And so, after a year or two, what started out as a widely distributed orbiting cloud would become concentrated in a narrow ring around the equator. Now when the sun is overhead at the equator on March 21 and September 23, the shadow cast by such a doughnut will simply be a narrow ring around the equator. But when the Northern Hemisphere is tilted 23° away from the orbital plane of the earth at the winter solstice, the ring will cast a broad shadow on the northern temperate and arctic zones. At the equinoxes, it would not matter how far the ring extended out into space, since the sun's light would be arriving edge-on; at other times, however, the depth of the ring would determine how broad a shadow was cast. O'Keefe simply assumed that the inner radius started 3200 kilometers above the surface and that the ring extended for another 6400 kilometers (an earth radius) out into space. This would block about 75 percent of the sunlight at the solstice, about enough to cause the 20°C. temperature drop. In the summer, the sunlight would come in above the ring, so there would be no shadow in the northern hemisphere (though, of course, the southern hemisphere would be shadowed then). Thus, there would be cold winters but normal summers.

And the extinction associated with this event might have given the apes their big chance by vacating niches. Their split from the Old World monkeys has been dated to about 34 million years ago using DNA differences and the characteristic rate at which they occur. An early fossil ape called *Aegyptopithecus* is at least 30 million years old. The DNA date for gibbons splitting off is about 22 million years ago. There were a number of subsequent splits, since we have fossil apes like *Proconsul* between 22 and 16 million years ago in the early Miocene, *Sivapithecus* at 17 million years ago, and the related *Ramapithecus* at various younger dates. The ancestor of the modern orangutan *Pongo* seems to have split off at about 16 million years ago, judging from the accumulated DNA differences, and indeed a *Sivapithecus* skull looks surprisingly like an adult orang, with its huge round eye sockets and long shelf-like snout sticking out in front.

But there were two hominoid splits about 10 to 11 million years ago: the common gibbon split off from what became the siamang, and gorillas split off from the line that went on to become chimps and humans. This date is about when the mid-Miocene extinction occurred, the most recent of the 28-million-year series of clustered extinctions and meteor craters. So, someone joked, maybe the last visitation of the comets gave us an opening, and kept us from remaining gorillas.

THUNDER IS HEARD from the Lower Deer Creek Falls as we approach it, walking up the beach. It is a tremendous volume of water, falling about ten stories without a break, in one narrow column. The spray rising from the pool has force too, as several people discover when they attempt to wade toward the falls: the spray blows them back, Jackie sitting down in the pool as a result—literally blown off her feet. Standing under that force of falling water would be like walking into the stream of a fire hose. But it is a beautiful sight, this waterfall and its pool, tucked into an alcove of rock and greenery.

But we do not stay long, as we are starting off on a hike up above the falls into the valley beyond. We have been hearing all sorts of things about the valley and the fossils to be found there at the entrance to the labyrinth that leads to the lower falls. The trail starts downriver of the falls, and we have a lot of climbing to do, not just the ten stories of the lower falls, but that of the upper falls and the cataracts as well.

As we gain elevation on the steep trail, views up and down the Canyon open up. We see the narrows produced by the Surprise Valley landslide, and marvel at the size of it. This doesn't look at all like a landslide because the whole block slid sideways. Then the trail turns in and the view narrows as we approach Deer Creek Canyon itself. The Tapeats forms interdigitating vertical scallops for several blocks in from the river. At the bottom of this corridor, three stories below our trail, thunder the waters of Deer Creek on the way to its plunge toward the river. Our trail is not wide, not for the severely acrophobic. But those who do look down are rewarded by the sight of a redbud tree in its own little alcove. The creek formed a pothole at one time, as stones were swirled around, too heavy to be carried high enough by the rushing waters to escape, gradually wearing themselves down. And gradually forming a deeper pothole via another emergent property. Eventually enough sandy soil gathered in this pot to support a tree. It is miniature, thanks to being root-bound in a pot of fixed size, but it looks as if oriental gardeners tended it every week.

The narrow canyon starts to open up and we see greenery ahead—and then the spray from the waterfall that moistens them. It is a beautiful waterfall of two stories, falling down one side of a U-shaped ledge at the same level on which we are walking. In several stages, it cascades down to the bottom of the narrow cataract.

The canyon opens out because we have reached the top layer of the Tapeats Sandstone; the Bright Angel Shale that overlies the Tapeats here is more easily eroded, leading to a wider canyon by undercutting in the same manner as the Grand Canyon itself widened from Marble Gorge in Furnace Flats. The falls here are surreal, an impression aided by our seeming inability to get a better view of them by moving around—just as in a dream where you cannot do what you command. You discover that there is really only one place from which to photograph the falls because of the horseshoe ledge connecting to the serpentine canyon. Move from the right viewpoint and the view disappears.

As one approaches the slippery top of these falls, a whole valley opens up, as if you'd just passed through a tunnel entrance to a secret interior valley. Here we encounter others looking at fossils. So they say. I look carefully for small details. Then someone tells me to step back and look—and then I see it. The entire slab of rock is completely covered with an intricate pattern of finger-diameter rope work, suitable for a wallpaper design. Except that these are the casts left by big worms burrowing through the mud. Something of the Cambrian equivalent of a dinosaur footprint. And they're all over. I now remember seeing small sections of rock bearing such worm works in a museum on the South Rim—but the size of this rock slab is not to be believed. It is just lying there next to Deer Creek, not covered by glass or Park Service warnings, probably getting washed off every time that Deer Creek floods. It also exhibits no damage, no graffiti from a hundred years of river-runners.

The creek flows knee-deep through an opening valley, and we wade in the water looking for rocks bearing fossils. I pick up hundreds of small rocks and find several possible fossils, though of what I cannot tell. The creekbed leads to a small rapid, suitable for bathing and frolic.

As I search for shade later, back at the upper canyon entrance, I try lying under an overhanging cliff of Bright Angel Shale. And to my surprise its ceiling is covered with fossil tracks—the paths of Cambrian worms and, it is said, trilobite tracks. This superb ceiling is larger than many dining tables, an exquisite collection of worm works.

There is, Alan tells us, more to see further along the trail: the source of Deer Creek cascades out of the canyon wall several miles back up the valley. And there is time. We'll probably meet up with the Surprise Valley hikers back there. Alan, his brother Ken, and his father Gordon, are all going. Temptation. But I decide to stay and explore the lower canyon instead. There are steep paths down into the cataract on the far side and, on the way, nice cool places to sit and admire the beauty. When I emerge from the cataract with the aid of a helping hand from above, I find a group collecting under one of the Tapeats ledges with a view out over the narrow canyon, talking about another kind of ascent.

FROM APE TO LUCY was the topic—all the problems in getting from a typical mid-Miocene ape, perhaps like the chimp, to an early hominid like Lucy, who walked around upright 3 to 4 million years ago in the Afar triangle of Ethiopia. She had the nice rounded pelvis and the indented knees that go along with walking around upright. But she was clearly only partway from chimp to human in such changes. And her skull was strikingly chimplike in size and shape—this, near the end of the *Australopithecus afarensis* line at 3.0 million years ago, at the end of the model year. After that, *A. africanus* came into style. The artist's reconstructions always show them modestly covered with hair, not naked in the manner of modern humans before the clothing mania. The great cover-up. No one knows if Lucy had ape-like hair, but it certainly was lost somewhere along the line—and it probably wasn't just when clothing came into style. What on earth could select for hairlessness?

The traditional explanation is that hairlessness is an adaptation for running on the plains. If, so the story goes, our ancestors needed to run down animals or run away from them, they'd overheat without the peculiarly human sweat glands that cool our blood. And sweating works better without hair in the way. If that were true, one would expect other animals to have discovered this alleged physiological principle too—but the people visiting a zoo are likely to be the only animals sweating. Indeed, no other primate has done anything quite as physiologically stupid as prolific sweating. Baboons are adapted to savannah life, and run around faster than humans just fine with more traditional temperature regulation mechanisms, though humans are better adapted to a really sustained long chase.

And sweating is profligate of both body salts and water; apes conserve water so well that they seldom have to visit waterholes where predators lurk in ambush, seldom have to seek out salt sources. In a hot climate, humans have to drink repeatedly throughout the day (as we are repeatedly reminded by the boatmen); in the hot savannah in pre-waterbag days, this must have caused hominids to stick close to creeks and lakes in a manner atypical of other savannah animals.

Furthermore, hairlessness has a truly serious disadvantage, since primate babies cling to the mother's fur for transport. As hair became scarce, one supposes the number of babies injured by falling would have increased considerably (even in hairy chimps, infant falls are the major cause of mortality). It makes you think that hairlessness must have been important for some other, much

Parts of [the world] are neither land nor sea and so everything is moving from one element to another, wearing uneasily the queer transitional bodies that life adopts in such places. Fish, some of them, come out and breathe air and sit about watching you. Plants take to eating insects, mammals go back to the water and grow elongate like fish, crabs climb trees. Nothing stays put where it began because everything is constantly climbing in, or climbing out, of its unstable environment.

Loren Eiseley
The Night Country, 1971

more important, reason—preferably in a situation in which infants falling wasn't an immediate problem. But where wouldn't that be a problem?

There really is such a place: while wading around offshore, catching crabs.

DID OUR APE ANCESTORS SPECIALIZE IN SHELLFISH?
Back in the forties and fifties, Alister Hardy was studying marine mammals, which of course are land animals that have somehow been forced to take up life in the sea and develop aquatic adaptations. He began to realize that humans had a group of peculiar features which, in any other species, would immediately lead one to surmise that they had once been land animals, were forced to become aquatic, and then returned to the savannah, keeping their swimming skills and other aquatic adaptations. Virtually all the hairless mammals today are either aquatics, or wallowers like pigs, or probably descended from such (the exceptions are the naked mole rat and an artificially bred Mexican hairless dog). The longer the animal has been in the water, the more complete the hair loss (seals and beavers are recent converts). As anyone who has tried to swim with clothes on can testify, they're a drag. Competitive swimmers have been known to shave off all body hair before a race.

Hairlessness is only one of those peculiarities of many marine mammals such as dolphins and whales. Another is the subcutaneous fat layer that they use to make up for the lost insulation of hair (which works only on land, via all the air it traps). We, and the naked marine mammals, have a subcutaneous fat layer all over our bodies, quite unlike the apes. It also helps the streamlining for swimming; an angular ape isn't the most likely candidate for an efficient waterfoil.

Human babies are born very plump, an addition of the last months of pregnancy (when they also lose the body hair they had earlier, called lanugo). They look quite unlike the cadaverous chimp infants, whose appearance is comparable only to either very old or very malnourished humans. Is the fat there to adapt human babies for life in the water, to make them buoyant enough (in salt water) and insulated enough so that they can bob around, hanging onto mother's remaining hair, that on her head? Similar scenes can still be seen in the waters of Tierra del Fuego, floating Indian infants hanging onto their mother's long hair as she swims offshore, collecting shellfish.

Then there is the little matter of upright posture: what preceded Lucy's pelvis? Two-legged locomotion is much slower than the four-legged version it must have replaced; baboons can zoom along at remarkable speeds. But mammals in the water often

Oftener than not, mammals who return to the water and stay there long enough, especially in warm climates, lose their hair as a perfectly natural consequence. Wet fur on land is no use to anyone, and fur in the water tends to slow down your swimming. She began to turn into a naked ape for the same reason as the porpoise turned into a naked cetacean, the hippopotamus into a naked ungulate, the walrus into a naked pinniped, and the manatee into a naked sirenian. As her fur began to disappear she felt more and more comfortable in the water, and that is where she spent the Pliocene.
ELAINE MORGAN
The Descent of Woman, 1972

adopt a vertical posture, peering about and observing, communicating with companions, eating the food they have just retrieved from the depths—all preferably while vertical. When treading water, when diving, and when swimming horizontally, their legs are positioned parallel to their spines, not perpendicularly as in four-legged land animals. And so the marine mammals lose the elongated pelvis characteristic of the four-legged land animals such as chimps and gorillas. And any land animal that wades into the shallows and maintains a horizontal posture gets its nose in the water a lot sooner than one that stands up on its hind legs. Thus, the horizontal wader would be restricted to about one-third of the shallow water foraging area otherwise available. Shoreline foraging in a drying climate would be a likely transition from four-legged walking to full swimming and diving.

Another human peculiarity among the primates is face-to-face copulation: whatever the reason for this reversal of the usual approach, most of the other aquatic mammals have done it too, probably as a result of the pelvic rearrangements associated with upright posture. There is even the little matter of tears: primates don't cry, but some aquatic mammals do. Tearing and sweating reminds one of salt glands, those adaptations of marine animals for getting rid of excess salt from their fishy diets.

To say that humans were once all professional swimmers and divers is, of course, heresy. In 1960, Professor Hardy let himself be persuaded to gave a talk to the British Sub-Aqua Club at Brighton, surely a friendly audience. Outside the conservative groves of academe, which at the time was quite happy with the savannah theory for the ape-to-prehuman transition (they still are), he put forward his aquatic ape hypothesis that had been gestating in his brain for 30 years. That might have been the end of it, but a reporter was present that Friday evening; the Sunday papers were full of the story Hardy put forward, some with distortions as wild as reporting that "Professor Hardy's startling new theory shows man to be descended from a dolphin." A little 100-million-year error, that being about when cetaceans branched off the mammalian tree.

Sir Alister later said, "I hardly dared to go back to Oxford on the Monday." And so he phoned up the *New Scientist* magazine and asked if it would publish a proper account of his talk, to counteract the embarrassing distortions. And it did. But, alas, he never wrote up a longer academic account for the professors to evaluate, having retired to concentrate on research concerning religious experiences.

The aquatic ape theory has, nonetheless, survived. Elaine

Morgan, a former Oxford scholar, has written two books popularizing Hardy's theory, the best-selling *The Descent of Woman* in 1972 and *The Aquatic Ape* in 1982; her updates appear in the *New Scientist* periodically as she locates new evidence in scattered places.

Anthropologists have been hesitant to discuss the aquatic theory, almost as if they were Victorians standing on ceremony, not having been properly introduced. The physiologists keep adding weight to Hardy's theory, however, as they discover more and more about aquatic mammals. There is something called the diving reflex which all successful divers have (even diving frogs), in which the heart rate slows and the blood supply to the skin is reduced at the beginning of the dive. It is evidently an adaptation to prolong the time that can be spent underwater, by reducing the oxygen consumption rate and thus make it possible to dive deeper and collect food longer. Humans have a well-developed diving reflex that halves the heart rate; water splashing on the face helps to trigger this reflex slowing, and so a face mask may prevent it.

Fueling the debate, the physiologists have been finding strange things about how we differ from other land animals in our regulation of salts, sodium chloride in particular. Most land mammals exhibit a salt hunger when their diet doesn't contain enough salt. And they'll stop eating salty foods when they don't need more salt. We humans, however, don't seek out salt even when we are seriously depleted, as before we start getting muscle spasms. This failing is, in fact, a leading cause of death in the world, given the mortality from childhood diarrhea in underdeveloped countries (it's the salt loss that kills), so that our poor regulation of salt intake was probably counteradaptive during much of hominid evolution too.

But marine animals have a hard time regulating their salt intake because everything they eat is salty; instead, they develop improved mechanisms to get rid of the excess. Kidney mechanisms, of course, but also tears (yes, that's one way to get rid of salt) and sweating. So why do humans exhibit salt regulation more typical of aquatics than land animals? To get rid of excess salt from a diet of fish and shellfish?

Many hominid-like anatomical changes are seen in one primate which did go aquatic, the swamp ape (some would say swamp monkey) *Oreopithecus*, whose bones were preserved in large numbers because they sank into the mud; one Italian coal seam yielded a virtually complete *Oreopithecus* skeleton. It has the short broad pelvis like the upright walker, the hominoid elbow modifications, the flattened face, the short canine teeth, the curved finger bones typical of Lucy and the other early hominids (physical anthropologists love nothing better than to talk about whether bones are straight or curved as a clue to function)—all the things needed to make *Oreopithecus* a potential hominid ancestor, were it not for its northerly location and disputed membership in the ape club. But it shows what life in the swamp can do to a primate as the sea rises and the islands become smaller and smaller. It also shows the likely fate of such experiments: *Oreopithecus* went extinct. One wonders how many other times this process has begun, only for the physical conditions to eventually change faster than the biological capacity to adapt.

One of the first proposals that humans arose from simpler animals also had an aquatic theme. The Greek philosopher Anaximander of Miletus pointed out 2,500 years ago that human infants are far more helpless than the young of other animals and require much more prolonged suckling: if they were originally as helpless as they are now, he maintained, humankind could have never survived. Therefore, Anaximander reasoned, humans must have originated as animals better able to take care of themselves when young. Anaximander thought this human predecessor was some sort of aquatic animal; his proposal, of a slow transformation from these "fish-men" into "land-men," represents a landmark in the history of evolutionary thought.

The objections to the aquatic hypothesis have varied. True, primates typically have a fear of falling into the water—but various water-loving primates have evolved nonetheless. Besides the extinct *Oreopithecus*, there are such present-day examples as the talapoin in the rivers of Gabon, the proboscis monkey of the mangrove swamps of Borneo, which sometimes swims well out to sea for unknown reasons, and the crab-eating macaque of the Philippines. Gorillas in zoos are reported to love swimming, especially the breaststroke. An ethologist studying wild chimps at several different African sites now reports that they have no fear of water. Wild pygmy chimps have been seen wading in streams and snatching at fish. So much for that objection.

Anthropologists are forever noting that we have just as many hair follicles as chimps, that our nakedness is merely an illusion. So what? As Elaine Morgan points out, Queen Victoria's face had no fewer hair follicles than Charles Darwin's, but Darwin would have been surprised to learn that his beard was an illusion. It's how thick and fast that hair grows that's the relevant factor, not the anatomical presence or absence of the factory. Such is their addiction to "hard" evidence that anthropologists are forever suggesting that the discussion should be postponed until such a day as there is incontrovertible fossil

I imagine him wading, at first perhaps still crouching, almost on all fours, groping around in the water, digging for shell fish, but gradually becoming more adept at swimming. Then, in time, I see him becoming more and more of an aquatic animal going further out from shore; I see him diving for shell fish, prising out worms, burrowing crabs and bivalves from the sands at the bottom of shallow seas, and breaking open sea-urchins, and then, with increasing skill, catching fish with his hands.

The physiologist
ALISTER HARDY, 1960

evidence for the aquatic ape. While seeming to strike a sober note of scientific caution, this tacitly assumes that fossil evidence is somehow the only evidence worth anything, that comparative physiological and behavioral clues to our origins are not worthy of consideration.

SINCE EVOLUTION WORKS FASTEST when animals are isolated in small populations under demanding climatic conditions, evolutionary biology must also become part of the debate. Whether proponent of savannah or shoreline or whatever, one must consider the suitability of the setting in which the ape-to-prehuman evolution is proposed to have taken place: how rapidly can change occur there? An ideal spot would be an African area which, in the late Miocene, perhaps 7 to 8 million years ago, was forested; had apes; and was then isolated from the rest of Africa, with the advantages of islands for speciation and selection. It would help if said island was later reconnected to Africa in such a way that the East African rift valley became populated with *Australopithecus afarensis* by 4 million years ago. For this, one must consult the evidence about ancient sea levels, geological events, and climate.

Such an ideal spot on the Red Sea coastline has been identified by Leon LaLumiere, Jr., and it fits very well with the aquatic-ape hypothesis, not with the savannah theory. It is just north of the Hadar region where Lucy and family were found, in the tip of the Afar triangle. Just north of Djibouti, just south of the present Dahlak Archipelago, this coastline is part of the Eritrea province of Ethiopia, a region of chronic political unrest often unsafe for, and forbidden to, travelers. Alas. The geologists call it the Danakil Alps; about 75 kilometers wide, it forms 540 kilometers of the African coast approaching the Straits of Bab al Mandab, just before the Red Sea opens out into the Gulf of Aden and the Indian Ocean.

Back about the beginning of the Miocene, say 20 million years ago, Africa and Arabia were one tectonic plate. This tectonic plate collided with the Eurasian plate, buckling up the area around the present Red Sea, which then downfaulted. Together with a little seafloor spreading that got started, this formed the proto-Red Sea, and it connected with the proto-Mediterranean, not the Indian Ocean (which had earlier witnessed the Indian "continent" crash into Asia, raise up the Himalayas, and become a "subcontinent").

A rift started to form the Gulf of Aden (what separates the Somali Republic on the horn of Africa from South Yemen on the Arabian peninsula, that feature which seen from space looks like a giant can opener had been used on the real estate), but

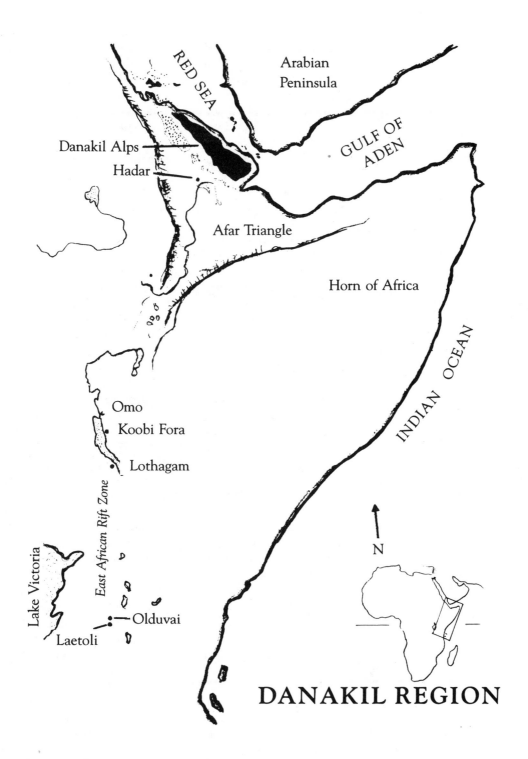

RED SEA

Arabian
Peninsula

Danakil Alps

GULF OF
ADEN

Hadar

Afar Triangle

Horn of Africa

INDIAN OCEAN

Omo

Koobi Fora

Lothagam

East African Rift Zone

Lake Victoria

Olduvai

Laetoli

N

DANAKIL REGION

it didn't connect with the Red Sea for a long time. Instead there remained a forested land bridge between forested Africa and forested Arabia (in those Miocene days, the moist tropics extended into southern Eurasia), and starting about 17 million years ago it was used as a migration route by numerous species of African land animals who expanded into Asia during the Miocene. This probably includes *Ramapithecus*, whose remains have been found from Hungary to China, as well as in Kenya. No one has yet explored the Arabian peninsula for hominoid fossils on the Asian side of the land bridge, though the anthropologists are working their way north along the African rift valley toward the ex-land bridge, in between civil wars in Ethiopia.

The collision, rebound, and further collisions between Africa and Arabia were accompanied by changes in Africa itself which were far-reaching in their implications. Before all this started, there were a few volcanos and no highlands of Ethiopia and Kenya. Africa, however, began to be torn apart, a process that continues today. By 15 million years ago, two large blisters had formed in Kenya and Ethiopia where lava upwelled and domed up the land surface by a thousand meters or more to form the highlands (a process perhaps not unlike the uplift of the Colorado Plateau, which has volcanos all around its edges). The crust cracked in numerous places, fault lines opening up all over the place, but especially in a north-south direction: a long valley began to be formed. The Great Rift Valley of East Africa today runs from the east coast of South Africa north through the Afar triangle, but the spreading continues up the Red Sea though the Dead Sea and Sea of Galilee to Syria. The associated earthquakes shook down the walls of Jericho numerous times (still, Joshua must have had a superb sense of timing). The Great Syrian-East African Rift is still splitting apart, currently at the rate of 1 millimeter each year (this is, however, ten times slower than Europe and North America are being pushed apart by seafloor spreading).

With all this, of course, came African volcanos even larger than the present-day Mount Kilimanjaro. As the Ethiopian and Kenyan highlands got tall enough to precipitate rainfall, they caused a rain shadow to the east, the tropical rain forests there began to dry up, and the land was transformed into the patchwork of woodland and open terrain called savannah. The primates that lived there either adapted to the foods and predators of the savannah, in the manner of the baboons, or retreated into enclaves in the manner of the mountain gorilla in locations where their old rain forest habits were still sufficient to make a living. (There's a price for this: only 240 mountain gorillas remain, pushed up into an "island" formed of wet mountaintops—a fate not unlike what happened to *Oreopithecus* surrounded by water.) Just as they had done many times over the ages, plate tectonics and sea floor spreading were again causing major evolutionary changes to accumulate.

In the late Miocene, the Red Sea was still a gulf of the Mediterranean. But the Med was undergoing a dramatic event itself: it dried up into a series of salty lakes. And then refilled. And repeated this cycle 11 to 14 times, probably causing all sorts of havoc at the southern end of what was then its southern gulf. Things were already lively down there, as increased tectonic and volcanic activity had been going on from 11 to 9 million years ago in the Red Sea and Afar triangle, all the way down the East African rift (this is about when we last shared a common ancestor with the gorilla).

While the sea level fluctuations were still going on about 7 million years ago, the African plate moved away from the Arabian plate and the Danakil Alps microplate was no longer squeezed between the giants. Like the crustal blocks in Nevada that one can see driving north from Las Vegas in the Basin and Range country, where spreading is also occurring, the Danakil Alps have tilted vertiginously so that their sediment layers are now at a dramatic angle; they also swiveled counterclockwise into their present position. Just one of nature's little rearrangements of things that pointedly reminds you that blocks of earth can bob around like icebergs before getting frozen into place again.

When the Danakil microplate finally detached from both the African and Arabian plates, the sea flowed in and that was the end of the great Miocene land bridge between Africa and Eurasia. Not only did the Red Sea come down into the northern part of the Afar triangle about 6.7 million years ago, but the Gulf of Aden came up from the south and joined it, opening up the Red Sea (which had now lost its connection to the Med as the Isthmus of Suez arose). The Red Sea opened into the Indian Ocean via both the present Strait of Bab al Mandab and the "Danakil Straits" to the west. The Danakil Alps became an island.

DANAKIL WAS A LARGE ISLAND, potentially twice the size of such familiar islands as Sardinia, Corsica, Jamaica, and Puerto Rico. It perhaps became a series of islands as volcanos popped up here and there, as coral reefs formed, as tilting land subsided to near sea level; if so, they covered an area like that of the major part of the Hawaiian island chain. The Hawaiian islands are also a good comparison because they are tropical—

and they have volcanos that push their way up to altitudes that catch rain clouds, and so provide streams of fresh water for drinking.

The apes trapped on the islands would have had problems, and not just from all of the exciting volcanos and earthquakes. The late Miocene was a worldwide time of drying up, when the forests changed to grassy plains, even desert. While there was likely a savannah period on Danakil, the major food resources might not have been in the center of the islands but along their shores. For those who have not stuck a face-mask underwater in the Red Sea, it may be hard to appreciate just how luxurious sea life can become. While there are nice examples of coral reef life to be seen in Hawaii and the Caribbean, the protected Red Sea is an order of magnitude more dense in its underwater life, comparable only to Australia's Great Barrier Reef. And one doesn't have to take a boat ride to an offshore reef to see Red Sea coral reef life—it is everywhere.

Just wading in the shallows of the Red Sea can be like walking through a supermarket for fish and shellfish. There is seemingly limitless food for the taking. It's not just clams and scallops and mussels and oysters, with the sorts of hard shells that might accumulate for the archaeologists to find as middens (but, unless carried back to a central site before consumption, were more likely to be thrown back into the water, and swept away by the tides). Apes there might also have dined royally on fresh lobsters and crabs, could cooperatively have herded whole schools of reef fish into the shallows where they could be grabbed. Some fish, such as the grouper, would have been particularly favored, for both their taste and their large size. True, by wading the apes wouldn't encounter too many of the big fish, but surface diving would allow them to spear some inside the reef caves. Just as chimpanzees fish today for termites with a stick, so Danakil apes might have learned to probe for fish with selected spearlike sticks.

And one must not forget the tides. Near the mouth of the Red Sea, the tides might have been large, just as they are near the mouth of Puget Sound. Every day up around Seattle and Vancouver, the beaches are uncovered to a depth of one story. With tides like these, many stranded animals are exposed to even the most hydrophobic land-dweller—which might be how the apes got started on a seafood career. While the tidal range tends to diminish with distance from the outlet to the sea (tides are minor up at Suez and Eilat), Danakil was in an optimal place for the exposed intertidal beaches to serve as an inducement to apes. Just as the little shrimp-like amphipods of the Colorado attract the whiptail lizards at low tide.

This is, of course, a description of what Danakil might have been like in the good times. All of the geological rearrangements of the Miocene-Pliocene boundary probably produced disruptions; furthermore, shellfish populations seem to be periodically decimated by diseases. Life on Danakil might have gotten harsh, periodically selecting for apes able to swim offshore, and dive deeper and deeper to find increasingly scarce food.

About 5.4 million years ago, lava flows along the southwest coast probably closed the Danakil Strait and reconnected Danakil Island to the African mainland. The extensive basalts would have made this base of the Danakil peninsula a biological desert for some time, still providing something of a barrier to the migration of land animals who had to eat their way along the surface. But, of course, the aquatic apes could have eaten their way along the shoreline—provided there was drinking water in creeks.

So from 6.7 to 5.4 million years ago, the Danakil region would have been particularly isolated. Did some ape evolution occur there, which split the hominid line off from the apes? The chimps' DNA differences from humans suggest that the split occurred 7.7 to 6.3 million years ago, nicely overlapping the Danakil isolation period.

ONE EARLY HOMINID SCENARIO thus looks remarkably like the Hardy hypothesis, if Danakil is accepted as an ideal spot for ape evolution to take place. On the grounds of evolutionary biology, it is ideal for a number of reasons. The Danakil apes would have been isolated from the African ape gene pool, allowing natural selection to quickly bias the genome in the direction of the traits under selection. The population would have been small enough for speciation to occur; a series of islands might even allow for multiple species of hominids to form, with subsequent mixing as in the Galapagos birds and Hawaiian flies, with occasional replacement of the less "fit" species. There too, waves of selection might have taken place if the Red Sea dried up with the Med, then refilled, as the Danakil Strait opened and then closed periodically as lava flows crossed Danakil's southwestern coast. The drying-up and the volcanos and changing tidal patterns would have made the plentiful sea life occasionally scarce, reducing the Danakil ape population to only the most fit. Evolution could have operated rapidly there, much more so than in the savannah of East Africa itself.

And what would have been the traits enhanced by natural selection? Wading ability, certainly, but eventually swimming and diving skills, an ability to remain in the water for a long time, perhaps even to babysit infants there. Angular hairy apes would not have fared as well as naked, curvaceous apes insulated with subcutaneous fat. Those with a pelvis that allowed their legs to be operated parallel to the spine would have been better waders and swimmers than the typical apes, and thus better providers for their offspring. Those with an improved sense of balance would have been better at exploring the underwater environment with its subtle gravity. And those able to control their breathing would have eventually been able to dive; a diving reflex would have let them stay down even longer. Hard times could have selected for such abilities.

Toolmaking doesn't really appear in this scenario, as the chimp's hammering abilities with nuts would seem adequate for pounding shells open, just as the chimp's probing of termite nests with a stick serves as a model for spearfishing in reef caves (even birds poke sticks into holes, as Dan Hartline mentioned on the first day of our trip). These kinds of tool use really don't demand much toolmaking, though of course it might have incidentally occurred, as when the chimp flakes a rock that it was using to hammer open a particularly hard nut.

Nor do the needed adaptations particularly demand bigger brains—though it has been noted that mammals that became aquatic often wound up with bigger brains in the bargain, as if the acquisition of an entirely new locomotor repertoire were facilitated by some extra brain in which to house the new neural-command machinery. The river-swimming monkey of the Gabon, the talapoin, has a significantly larger brain than an average Old World monkey of the same body size. With few fossil ape braincases from the period of 4 to 16 million years ago, we have no idea of when the hominid brain size started increasing, whether the 500 cubic centimeter ballpark was attained early, or whether it occurred shortly before 4 million years ago. But some brain growth is consistent with the aquatic ape hypothesis.

So the Danakil version of the aquatic hypothesis suggests that natural selection acted on a number of ape features independently in a mosaic fashion, but particularly on hair and fat, locomotion abilities, and diving physiology. It suggests that quite a number of rounds of speciation and selection could have taken place within several million years, thanks to the island setting, its unsettled geology, the end-of-the-Miocene climate, and the poor Med's periodic problems with the erratic Straits of Gibraltar. We need only look at how fast artificial selection can reshape domestic animals to realize that a million years was probably enough time in which to make all those changes, given the opportunities for repeated selection and speciation. Even if rapid natural selection is a thousand times slower than artificial selection, there's still time.

The result would have been an ape-hominid with a number of omnivorous adaptations; we need not talk of intelligence to recognize that this might have been a cleverer animal, retaining the earlier ape fruit- and plant-eating versatility but with an overlay of new skills related to living along waterways and regularly eating the flesh of a number of species, acquired in a number of different ways. It would have been an animal capable of filling various African niches, more capable of improvising in hard times.

If they were going to venture forth from Danakil, these aquatic apes might well have brought along some disadvantages from their aquatic interlude, such as the naked skin and the salt- and water-wasting sweat glands, such as the need to keep an arm occupied by holding an infant who could no longer hang on, such as an inability to run as fast as its quadrupedal ancestors. The logical emigration routes would have been along the Red Sea shoreline. But, particularly if it were a bad year for shellfish, the apes could also have gone inland, up the Afar triangle following the Awash River valley upstream past such places as Lucy's home of Hadar. Then perhaps south down the Omo valley to Lake Turkana, farther along the rift to Olduvai and Laetolil, even all the way down the Great Rift Valley to South Africa and the Transvaal caves. Actually, one cannot conclude anything about the rift being a favored path of migration for hominids, as the rest of Africa is largely unexplored and negative evidence from it means nothing. The rift is the favorite site in which to dig because it is pulling apart, tilting strata in the earth's crust, and exposing the 1–4 million-year-old sediments so that you need not dig down twenty stories to find them. So one has to take the Great Rift Valley as something of a special case—but maybe *the* case, where it all happened.

BACK 34 MILLION YEARS AGO, apes evolved from the Old World monkeys, losing their tails, gaining a shoulder joint of increased flexibility. But there is more to the monkey-to-ape transition than just cherry-picking and some increase in brain size. More impressive to behavioral scientists is the doubling of the length of childhood. Monkeys may reach sexual maturity in three to four years, chimps need nearly ten years.

Now if one wants to teach by example, to pass on memes as well as genes, that's very important. Not only do more things happen in twice as many years of childhood, but there is also the fact that juveniles are primed to play, to mimic. The Japanese macaques—the same ones that washed the potatoes and

The salt of those ancient seas is in our blood, its lime is in our bones. Every time we walk along a beach some ancient urge disturbs us so that we find ourselves shedding shoes and garments, or scavenging among seaweed and whitened timbers like the homesick refugees of a long war.

LOREN EISELEY
The Unexpected Universe, 1969

sifted the sand out of the wheat—demonstrate that the young are more likely to experiment with a new technique, eat a new food. The older animals then copy them, except for the old males who seem particularly inflexible.

Playing around is not universally a good thing—one often has to take action without thinking, instinctively do the right thing on the basis of inborn or acquired propensities. When one is old enough to have offspring, one had best be able to forage efficiently rather than fiddling around half the time. Because the young are protected by more serious-minded adults, they can afford to play around. And twice as long a play period, before becoming a more reliable adult, was great as long as the species could afford it.

Ah, but that's the rub, it seems. Barbara pointed out that the remaining apes have seemingly overdone the extended childhood. A chimp female may have to wait six years before bearing another offspring because ovulation is suppressed by suckling—which is a good thing, since she simply can't look after more than one at a time. Because of the infant and juvenile mortality, a mother may have trouble getting two offspring to reproductive age before she passes from the scene herself. Given that the mother chimp has to do all the work of child-rearing, it would be hard for chimps to ever expand their population, even in good years. Even without the situation created by the expanding human populations near their tropical habitats, the apes are marginal. They are excellent candidates for extinction, given some bad years. That's not only a serious matter for them but for us as well; because behavior does not fossilize, the apes are our best clues to what we once were, to what we could alternatively have become. We need to see how they cope in the wild as part of their native ecosystems, not just in the artificial setting of the zoo or circus.

Humans have gone even further than apes and doubled childhood again. However, child spacing has been reduced to every four years in primitive hunter-gatherer tribes, with further reductions possible in agricultural societies.

"But we've doubled the length of childhood, compared to the apes," Rosalie said. "How did we do that without having 10 or 12 years between babies?"

"That's right," added Abby. "Even in primitive hunter-gatherer tribes, the birth spacing is about four years. So it isn't agriculture that did it, though that may be why the birth spacing can drop down to two years in modern times."

"In a word," Barbara said with a big smile, "Lovejoy. That's the reason."

"Is that a person or a process?" asked Ben, suspiciously.

"Both," Barbara chuckled. "It's C. Owen Lovejoy, who's a physical anthropologist. But it's also a key feature of his—and some other peoples'—theory that accounts for how we've overcome the bind that the apes got themselves into." We all listened more carefully, I thought, wanting to know what either love or joy had to do with population ecology.

"Back to the birds," Barbara began. "As you all know, one of the traditional strategies for promoting one's genes is to spread them around as widely as possible, even indiscriminately. But there is also another strategy, to care for those genes after the birth of one's offspring and help assure their survival. Females often practice it. Males sometimes do, typically in situations where they can be sure the young are carrying their genes and not some other male's."

"I've seen male frogs that brood tadpoles in a special throat sac," added Ben. "And male birds may sit on nests, too. The males may bring home food to the young, sometimes to a stay-at-home mother too."

"Aha, but that's birds for you. Monogamy—because the male is investing in babies which indeed carry his own genes—is one way of making it worth the male's while to babysit and provide. Something like 92 percent of bird species are monogamous, while a mere 5 percent of mammals are. One ape is monogamous, the gibbon, but we parted company with gibbons about 22 million years ago, and none of our closer cousins seem to believe in monogamy."

Our closest relatives, the African apes, do not excel in one-on-one relationships; male gorillas have contests for temporary possession of a harem, leading to sexual selection for big males. They are now twice as large as the females, when adult. The chimps have their multimale mating system in which the sperm instead compete in a lottery outside the ovum. Only the pygmy chimps are reported to have longer-term male-female relationships.

Even without monogamy, ape males are somewhat useful in caring for their young. In particular, they protect the troop. But a male may not have a way of promoting his particular genes: he most likely does not know which young he fathered, unless he is the longtime proprietor of a harem. And he seldom helps out with the food—a chimp or gorilla mother finds her own food and that for the infants and juveniles. So his post-conception efforts do not promote the survival of his particular gene combinations over those of the other males in the troop. A mother's efforts, on the other hand, go preferentially to infants carrying her genes; her pre- and post-conception success promotes her gene combinations. His pre-conception efforts promote his genes, but he needs to stick alongside those genes as the mother does if his post-conception success is to help them along up to reproductive age. The birds seem to have discovered this principle in a big way.

"What got monogamy started, given that's it's so useful?" asked Abby. "I can see why it has advantages, such as supporting the longer childhood, or the offspring of a particularly fit male surviving better through his post-conception efforts. But what converted hominids to monogamy?"

"Well, you can see a minor form of one-on-one in the chimps, which might have developed into real monogamy in other extinct apes," answered Barbara. "When a female chimpanzee is in estrus she is often followed around for days by one or two males. Occasionally a pair will even disappear into the bushes for a few days. That's called a 'consort relationship.' If the female climbs a nut tree, the consorting male will likely find something important to do up the same tree. While the female doesn't spurn the advances of other males, the consorting male probably gets quite a few more sperm into the lottery, besides being more likely to be there at ovulation time.

"Now suppose," she continued, "that a female happened not to advertise her time of ovulation—human females don't, which is a big puzzle, since it is unusual among the primates. Ovulation occurs halfway between menstruations. . . ."

"Is that the same as estrus?" Abby asked.

"Yes, the behaviors you see at about ovulation time are simply called estrus," Barbara replied. "Instead, the prehuman female seems to have become sexually receptive all the time, with the time of ovulation neither marked for all to see by sexual swellings on her rump—which is what most monkeys and apes do—nor advertised by changes in her behavior. No more estrus.

"Now what would have been the consequence of such a genetic variant?" Barbara asked her attentive audience. "The male most likely to impregnate her would be the one who followed her around and tried regularly. The concealed ovulation—that's what this lack of estrus at ovulation time gets called—in females would then select for a certain variant type of male, one who consorted and tried regularly."

"Hah! So that's where 'lovejoy' comes in!" exclaimed Ben, laughing.

"That's the idea. Presumably the sex drive became strong enough to sustain all this time-consuming, out-of-season mating activity," Barbara said, smiling. "After all, the oviducts are empty, conception can't occur. Few other species waste a lot of time and energy mating when it serves no purpose."

"It sure would select for males that stuck close to a favorite female," Rosalie said, "because they'd be more likely to impregnate the female with concealed ovulation. We seem to have lost salt hunger, but we have certainly enhanced sex hunger."

SURELY THE KEY ASPECT of concealed ovulation exposed to natural selection—as Richard Alexander and Katherine Noonan noted in 1979—would be the provisioning and infant care into which it led the male. For monogamy to evolve in the hominids, consorting would have to have become a real habit, a substantial one-on-one attachment, something like mothers develop for their infants, that would bond a prospective father to the mother gestating his genes in the manner of bird monogamy. Did the females set this up by rewarding food gifts with sexual receptivity, much as the mating rituals of many birds involve displays of masculine skill at nest-building, with sexual receptivity the reward for satisfactory building skills?

The ape females whose genes led them to reward food gifts and companionship would certainly have been more likely to have a well-fed infant if the consort relationship continued. Nor need this have been the direct type of short-term deal suggested by modern prostitution; the usefulness of a consort relationship would instead only seem to require a correlation, such as the female being more likely to consort with a male who had meat to share than one who didn't. Just being around her more, he'd get more tickets to the pregnancy lottery.

One must focus on plausible lines of evolution, the things that lead to explaining some of the major differences between us and the African apes. Those differences include concealed ovulation, virtually nonstop sexual receptivity, pair-bonding, and male provisioning. Somehow those developments occurred by the usual genetic mutations and permutations. Somehow they became more prevalent via the usual natural or sexual selection processes. And they were probably conserved now and then by speciation.

But when did they occur? Early, middle, or late in hominid evolution? Before the chimp split, with the chimp perversely retrogressing later? During a Danakil-like pre-Australopithecine interlude? After *Australopithecus afarensis* went walking upright back to the savannah, but before the brain started to enlarge? Or during the spectacular period of brain enlargement of the last 2 million years? The fossil evidence is thin but not entirely silent: rather like gorillas, *A. afarensis* had a much greater degree of sexual dimorphism than modern humans (some experts say; others interpret the size range as not male-female but two different species). If *A. afarensis* did have sexual dimorphism of a considerable extent, that would suggest an earlier period of

If we could interview a chimpanzee about the behavioural differences separating us, [food sharing] might well be the item it found most impressive— "These humans get food and instead of eating it promptly like any sensible ape, they haul it off and share it with others."

The archaeologist
GLYNN LLYWELYN ISAAC
(1937–1985)

harem-type mating systems, not a prolonged period in which monogamy had stopped sexual selection for overblown males.

An argument can be made that our tendencies toward monogamy developed initially in the period between 5 and 3 million years ago, during the aquatic ape's readaptation to the highlands and river valleys of East Africa proper. The Tierra del Fuego practices suggest that floating childcare is not incompatible with the mother gathering food by wading and diving, so the Danakil ape females might well have managed to provide for themselves and their offspring in the usual ape manner, without a home base or male provisioning or delayed consumption. But in subsequently coping with the savannah, an arm (and an upright posture) would often be continuously required to carry an infant that couldn't cling to the now-missing maternal fur. It would be harder to park the infant while gathering, what with the carnivorous predators of the savannah. The mother could, as some human mothers still do, take the children out gathering with her, but they would wind up with a meat-poor diet—just those small animals and birds that she could grab in the underbrush in the manner used by baboons (when the infant didn't cry at the wrong time). The ape's taste buds might have been attuned to the regular taste of calorie-rich flesh by then. The males, able to range more widely and engage in longer chases because they lacked immediate responsibility for the children, would be more likely to possess meat in the chimpanzee manner.

Consort relationships might very well hinge on who happened to have tasty meat, an extension of the chimpanzee's tolerated scrounging for meat; the female and juvenile have-nots beg the typically male possessors for a handout; it's the most prominent food-sharing seen in apes outside of mothers and their infants. Add concealed ovulation to this food-sharing ape, and one has a scenario for the development of male provisioning of the mother and her offspring. And thus for developing the full benefits of two-parent investment: the offspring survival based on the father's (as well as the mother's) post-conception performance a la birds but also the doubling of childhood.

THAT'S MY PRE-ENCEPHALIZATION hominid scenario, borrowing heavily from Alexander and Noonan, Lovejoy and other biologists and anthropologists who have thought about the matter. No doubt others can fit the pieces together in other ways, perhaps for the other possible time frames just as well. You'll note that I've divided up the post-common-ancestor period into an early (aquatic, upright?) phase and a middle (savannah, monogamy?) phase; there is also a late bigger-brain phase (temperate zones, hunting?). Each phase was about 2 million years long, underway by perhaps 6.5, 4.5, and 2.5 million years ago, respectively.

We decided that one important feature would make a good slogan for our T-shirt philosophy sweepstakes: *CONCEALED OVULATION WAS RESPONSIBLE.* Though people would probably misinterpret it too, thinking it merely appropriate for wearing by an expectant mother who had been using the rhythm method of contraception.

All this pervasive sexual activity is, of course, what humans usually think that sex is all about. But this is largely nonreproductive sexual activity, when the oviducts are empty, the female unable to conceive on more than 80 percent of such occasions. *It really has to do with pair-bonding for raising children and lengthening childhood, not with making another baby.*

And it's ironic: in such elaborations of the concealed ovulation hypothesis, the *nonreproductive* aspects of sexual activity emerge as the distinctly non-ape human feature that made two-parent families possible. But biology having been only partially understood by some religious groups, they insist that sexual activity be firmly linked to reproduction—as in the barnyard. One would think that if they wanted to promote family life rather than just more babies, they'd be in favor of nature's own nonreproductive sexual activity, in favor of birth-control devices that would let pair-bonding continue when reproduction had run its desired course but there were not-yet-grown children to rear. To say that nonreproductive sex is unnatural is to misunderstand one of the things that made us human—indeed, an aspect that the church most cherishes, family life.

SURPRISE VALLEY was as far as Alan and his companions went, they report upon returning. They ran into the hikers making the loop up in the bowl-shaped valley who had spent some time exploring the Anasazi ruins. And playing around Thunder Spring.

In the boat during the half mile from Deer Creek down to camp, we ran wild making up more T-shirt slogans after explaining *CONCEALED OVULATION WAS RESPONSIBLE* to the hikers. *DIG AT DANAKIL!* was what got us started. *USE YOUR COLORADO MATTER* to promote the gray matter's new name? Here we go again. I can just imagine what they'll think at the T-shirt store when we get back to Flag. *THINK STOCHASTIC! BEWARE OF THINKING BACKWARDS?* Silliness has struck again.

MILE 137

Overhang Camp

Ninth Campsite

Everything that happens now in churches, schools, town halls, and theaters happened concentrated and intense and all at once in the caves. It was the only way in those days to create a human unity, a body of conforming and obeying people. People who were individuals in the modern sense could never have survived.

JOHN E. PFEIFFER
The Creative Explosion, 1982

ROSALIE CAST A CRITIC'S EYE on the sandy beach, which was shadowed from the afternoon sun by a great overhanging slab of rock where the river had undercut the cliff. It formed a giant cave, with space enough for everyone to spread their sleeping bags, even for the kitchen as well. No tent to pitch tonight. It seemed unlikely that river-runners were its first inhabitants, nor the first to name it Overhang Camp.

"I don't know about those Anasazi," Rosalie said, hand on hip, looking up at the overhang. "First, little caves in steep cliff faces, only forty stories down to the water. Straight down. Now this—lots of room for all the relatives, but with the river so close that it probably cleaned house for them every spring. Thus depriving archaeologists of their due, the trash pile." She turned away and looked back at us as we leaned against the boats, laughing and sipping refreshments. "I'm afraid that Anasazi dwellings remind me of that classic architectural description in the *New Yorker* that called somebody's homely masterpiece—let's see if I can remember the quote—'an anomalous piece of domestic architecture, combining the small, familiar pleasures of the hearth with the headier excitements of Doomsday'."

After the laughter had died down, J.B. tossed her a cold beer from the bilges of his boat. "Actually," he said, "Overhang Camp has a reputation to maintain. We don't call it Hangover Camp the next day for nothing."

"Ah," Ben exclaimed, "now we see the true origins of the word Hangover. A twisted tongue, contorted by the evil brew. Did the Indians brew beer?"

"They probably discovered it by accident, storing grain in jars that somehow got filled up with rainwater and fermented away in the hot sun," Cam ventured.

"Maybe they got their antibiotics by accident that way too," Rosalie smiled. "Grain storage bins like those Nankoweap granaries are great places for mold-like bacteria such as *Streptomycetes* to grow. They're present in soil and they like a very dry, warm, alkaline environment. And they produce tetracycline to use in their war for survival competing with other bacteria. Fouls up water regulation in other bacterial cells, so they swell up and go pop. If you use grain from such contaminated granaries, you can get an incidental dose of antibiotic with your beer and your bread. Every day. Makes your resident bacteria go pop too."

But did the Indians really get antibiotics that way, we asked?

"Well, the Nubians of the Sudan apparently did about 1,600 years ago. One of the peculiarities of tetracycline is that it likes bone, binding to the calcium and forming compounds which, it just happens, fluoresce. And bones from an old cemetery near the Nile River show the characteristic tetracycline fluorescence. Debra Martin discovered that quite by accident when she went to look at some thin slices of bone to make a routine measurement of wall thickness. Now normally you wouldn't use a fluorescence microscope for a routine job like that because their light bulbs are so expensive and burn out so fast. But the only microscope that wasn't busy was a fluorescence microscope, so she used it. And when she turned on the microscope's ultraviolet light source, the bone lit up like a fluorescent Christmas tree, just like it would from bone biopsies in patients treated with modern tetracycline."

"Were these mummies?"

"They were naturally mummified by the dry desert air, but there was none of the fancy Egyptian embalming. No, contamination isn't likely the cause. And it wasn't just a few of the bones that showed the fluorescence, as would happen if you studied a modern autopsy series—so far, all the bones from that cemetery have the tetracycline. Suggesting that they all got it as food contamination or as some other sort of environmental pollution."

"I always said," volunteered J.B., "that beer was good for you. Sounds like old-fashioned beer was even better."

"So did the Nubians grow bigger faster, just like the cattle and pigs that farmers now dose routinely with tetracycline?" Sue Gilmore interjected. "You know, half of the antibiotics produced these days go to fattening up healthy animals for market. It probably works because it suppresses the subclinical infections that otherwise slow down growth."

"Well, ancient cemeteries have been studied pretty extensively by the anthropologists who are interested in ancient disease patterns. And they say that the Nubians had extremely low rates of infectious disease," Rosalie replied. "Of course, they might have suffered from some of the typical side effects of tetracycline too—such as when your intestinal bacteria get killed off and you think you have dysentery. Tetracycline also slows down sperm, and extended exposure reduces the number of sperm produced. Bone growth in infants can be slowed. Vitamin B can be depleted. You don't want to take it unless you have to.

"Yet the widespread use of antibiotics nowadays—both from adding it to the feed of healthy farm animals and from the underdeveloped countries selling it over-the-counter, so that it gets taken routinely as a cure-all—is causing a really serious problem," Rosalie continued. "It results, because of good old Darwinian natural selection, in bacteria that no longer burst open and die when the antibiotic gets to them. These resistant strains of bacteria aren't created by our antibiotics. But the antibiotics kill off the competition, so that the otherwise-rare resistant ones prosper. The indiscriminate use of antibiotics is capable of putting us right back where we were before such wonder drugs were developed. And that affects you, not just the people who abuse the antibiotics—you won't be cured by the antibiotics anymore either. So you've got an interest in what the users do with them—you can't take the live-and-let-live attitude you might otherwise adopt toward recreational drug users."

Rosalie sipped her can of beer. "Now when this problem started popping up, such as in that cholera epidemic in Mexico where they were frantic because a lot of patients didn't respond to the usual drugs, people thought that resistance was new, dating from the widespread use of antibiotics after World War II. But then they found that 'virgin' populations, supposedly never before exposed to antibiotics, also had some resistance factors in the cytoplasm of their cells. So maybe indiscriminate use of antibiotics has been around for a long time, at least in desert peoples who irrigated fields to raise grain and then stored it for long periods in hot, dry, dirty storage bins."

"Did the Anasazi get dosed with tetracycline too?" asked Marsha.

"So far as I know, no one has checked Anasazi bones yet— maybe you should investigate that yourself. This is a perfect setup for it," Rosalie gestured at the surrounding canyon, "with the same desert climate that should make *Streptomycetes* commonplace, with the Anasazi irrigating the fields much like the Nubians, using mud-lined granaries and such. Maybe. It's a real possibility."

"Can you just eat Sudanese desert dirt and get a good dose of tetracycline?" Sue ventured. "They probably didn't always wash off their food, so they might have gotten a dose that way too."

"Well, if you place a bit of the soil in a culture dish, it sometimes shows obvious antibiotic activity, inhibiting the growth of bacteria in a zone around it. I don't know how much soil you'd have to eat to get a decent dose, or what the side effects of eating that much dirt might be," she laughed. "The advantage of a storage bin full of grain is probably that it provides excellent culture conditions, a protected place with lots of nutrients. See, Marsha, there are all sorts of things left for you to discover."

> He prayeth best who loveth best
> All creatures great and small.
> The Streptococcus is the test
> I love him least of all.
>   WALLACE WILSON

LIVING IN CAVES has probably been around as long as there have been both caves and humans. Cats and bears, sloths and birds—everyone likes a good cave. And from the standpoint of humans, a cave sometimes came with an additional advantage: a floor that helped keep the campfire burning. Bird and bat guano accumulates on cave floors, which are sometimes mined for making gunpowder. The problem could have been in keeping the fire under control. The *New Yorker*'s critic would have had a field day: the caveman's humble abode with its homely hearth might indeed have produced the headier excitements of Doomsday. Booms-day?

So the earliest cavemen might have been *Australopithecus afarensis*, if they could have found a cave. Certainly Neanderthals liked caves. And we're the latest cavemen, spread out here under Hangover. I mean Overhang. Oops.

Not too much happened for several million years or so after upright posture developed—so far as we know, that is. Hominids were upright by 4 million years ago, maybe even earlier. But the next bit of hard evidence of progression isn't until about 2 million years ago. And that, to our eyes, is impressive—tools and brains blossom.

Starting about then, stone tools became plentiful, the kinds of flakes and remaining half-stone fragments that Barbara made back at Monument Creek after that eventful day. They haven't been found earlier, though the hominids might well have been using tools without making them in Barbara's manner, which results in lots of leftovers for archaeologists to find. They probably enjoyed nuts, and worked to crack them with the same techniques employed by the chimpanzees today, using a handy stick or stone as a hammer. But a hammerstone, unless the same one is employed regularly, doesn't acquire the pockmarkings that would label it as an artifact; indeed, were such a stone found in a 4-million-year-old context, one would have to consider whether a chimpanzee might have used it rather than a hominid.

Besides this stone-flake evidence of hominid toolmaking at 2 million years, the size of the brain is also seen to undergo some enlargement. Nothing dramatic, mind you. Indeed, it is only in retrospect that one would affix a date for the enlargement as having started between 2 and 3 million years ago. If you plot brain size from 2 million years ago to the present, you can fit a straight line that suggests a regular increase in brain size from 500 cubic centimeters (473 cc is a truly pint-sized brain) up through the recent 1500 cc of the Neanderthals. Extrapolate the curve backwards in time, and it will suggest that 4 million years ago, we had no brains at all.

But brain size stays at 500 cc from 4 to about 2.4 million years ago, then curves upwards and meets the straight line fitted through the points from later hominids. As it happens, 300 to 500 cc is also the adult brain size of the modern chimps and gorillas, so it is often said that hominids had ape-sized brains

BRAIN SIZE THEN AND NOW

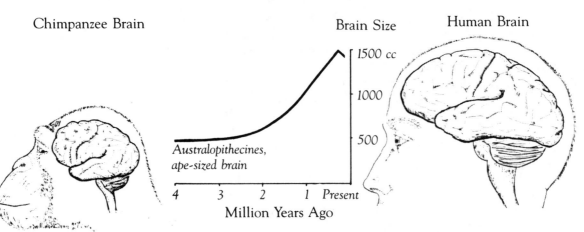

Chimpanzee Brain

Brain Size

Human Brain

1500 cc

1000

500

Australopithecines,
ape-sized brain

4   3   2   1   *Present*

Million Years Ago

until then. One wonders what was selecting for bigger brains back around 2.4 to 2.0 million years ago.

Tools? That's the other thing we know was happening then. And the seafloor oxygen samples suggest that the mini-ice-ages were getting started back then, as early as 3 million years ago. But we must not let the hard evidence bias our view too much. Just think of all the things that don't fossilize, the artifacts that reliably crumble into dust. There were probably wooden spears long before rock spear tips appear in the archaeological record. And hunters were probably throwing handy stones, knocking down rabbits and birds, long before they accurately threw specially shaped rocks or spears.

Gathering was probably once even more important than hunting, but split-cobble-sharpened digging sticks aren't preserved either. Waterbags from animal bladders aren't preserved. One of the key inventions, the anthropologist Richard Lee notes, may have been the carrying bag. If you've got to carry food back to a home base to feed your family, you can only carry so many separate items in your hands and arms. A sack or a basket is very handy, once you pick up more than four items at the grocery store. And the carrying bag is handy for hunting too—

it allows the hunter to carry along a supply of familiar, favorite throwing rocks. Without it, a hunter would only get several tries before having to resort to whatever rocks were lying around nearby. But carrying bags aren't preserved for very long. We can go look at the deteriorating, thousand-year-old Anasazi carrying bags at the local museums, but not those of the African hominids. Did the post-aquatic women invent them for baby slings, then adapt them for shopping bags? It seems likely, but we'll probably never know for sure.

Now the big thing that happens after this blossoming of brains and toolmaking in Australopithecines is the first multi-track hominid experiment. Just as there are currently two major types of apes in East Africa (chimp and gorilla), there were once three quite different species of hominid living there at the same time, in about the same places. Starting at about 2.0 million years ago, there was *Homo habilis* who lasted until about 1.7 million years ago. Then there was *Homo erectus*, the even larger-brained successor to *Homo habilis*, seen as early as 1.75 million years ago. And continuing until 1.4 million years was a more robust form of the earlier Australopithecine, what Louis Leakey initially called Zinjanthropus.

In Zinj and his robust relatives, the molar teeth's grinding area was doubled rather than the brain size. Zinj was generally heavily built, as in the gorilla-like sagittal crest running along the top of his head, needed to anchor his massive jaw-closing muscles. The newspapers called Zinj "Nutcracker Man" because of that formidable chewing apparatus, though surely Zinj had better ways of cracking nuts than by trying to chew them whole. Big grinding surfaces like that suggest high-bulk, fibrous diets, such as those leafy plants that modern gorillas consume daily in large numbers (each must eat about 27 kilograms—60 pounds—each day). Zinj and relatives died out by 1.4 million years ago, leaving *Homo erectus* with its 800 cubic centimeter brain as the only hominid on the scene. The triumph of brain over brawn? A change in climate wiping out Zinj's major plant food, with Zinj too inflexible to try other foods? Who knows? Also, no one knows where the new species came from; LaLumiere suggests that *Homo habilis* might have been the latest arrival from Danakil, if it was still in business producing new species from its lava-isolated section of Red Sea coastline.

INDIRECT TOOLMAKING, as opposed to our usual notions of careful craftsmanship, may have been the way rock toolmaking got started. Not only chimps but hominids might have pounded nuts open with rocks that fractured—and might have found a use for the sharp edges of the fractured rock. Glynn

One of the specific characteristics of the human evolutionary lineage has been the propensity to make tools—and to discard them. This has created a trail of litter that can be traced back some 2 to 2.5 million years.
                    The archaeologist
                    GLYNN LLYWELYN ISAAC
                    (1937–1985)

Isaac's model of pounding two stones together for a while, then sorting through the fragments for particularly useful ones, would be a more advanced type of "stochastic toolmaking." The profusion of stone fragments seen starting about 2 million years ago may simply represent the advance from incidental to intentional fracturing.

The basic choppers, scrapers, and flakes seen at the earliest toolmaking sites, Olduvai Gorge and Lake Turkana, were augmented gradually over the next half-million years. Then, at 1.5 million years ago, an interesting development occurred at Olduvai: just as we have no problem distinguishing the different styles of kitchen knives and silverware manufactured today, so archaeologists can distinguish a new style of toolmaking, which they call Acheulean. And like modern silverware styles, the Developed Oldowan and the Acheulean stone tool styles began a long coexistence. Eventually, more than a million years later, the Acheulean took over the market. And then was itself replaced by 0.3 and 0.1 million years ago, when a new style of toolmaking developed that involved more than just touching up selected broken rock fragments.

A GIANT ARROWHEAD pretty well describes the shape of an "Acheulean hand ax," a teardrop-shaped rock artifact that goes back 1.5 million years to the days of *Homo erectus* in Africa. While named after the find at Saint Acheul, France, the Acheulean hand ax has been found from Europe to South Africa, from the Mediterranean east through the Indian subcontinent to southeast Asia. It was evidently a popular item of the times, and its times lasted for well over a million years.

I can spread my fingers just about enough to reach from one end to the other of an average hand ax; sideways, it fits in the palm of my hand. Unlike the arrowhead, hand axes have no handle or attachment area; the back end is rounded like a discus. They are flat stones to start with, shaped by chipping away their edges into a taper. And therein lies the problem in believing that it was really used as an ax: because the sharpened edge extends all around, hammering something with one seems as likely to damage the hand as the target, not quite as bad as hammering on a double-edged razor blade, but the same general problem. Whoever named this artifact the "hand axe" must not have tried using it as one.

It is much easier to convince yourself that they were used for throwing. This was first proposed over a hundred years ago, and H. G. Wells even popularized the idea in his 1899 book, *Tales of Time and Space*. Flat stones have some nice aerodynamic properties, seen in the frisbee and the discus: because spin can stabilize such a projectile into an edge-on attitude to cut through the air, it can often be thrown farther than a round or irregular stone of the same weight, which will encounter more air resistance.

Small "hand axes" can be thrown overhand in a vertical orientation, and are said to be appropriate for hunting birds. A small hand ax is set spinning by holding it near its pointed end between the thumb and bent forefinger, and then flicking the wrist while uncocking the elbow. It may have been this method of setting the spin that required the teardrop shape. The largest hand axes are too awkward to throw overhand, but a discus thrower can do quite well with them. For her undergraduate honors thesis, the anthropologist Eileen O'Brien tried some experiments with a fiberglass replica of a 30 centimeter (1 foot) hand ax from East Africa, enlisting the aid of several varsity athletes. The typical distances achieved were more than 30 meters (about half a dozen parallel-parking spaces). Though starting off in a horizontal spin, the large hand ax would shift to vertical as it descended (what often happens when I throw a frisbee). And on nearly every throw, the hand ax would land on edge, sticking into the ground—often, point first.

This tendency for the thrown replicas to land vertically may explain some puzzling aspects of the archaeology of hand axes: they are often found standing on edge. The most common place to find them is in what was once shallow water; yet the surrounding countryside may be barren of them. This would make sense if they were used to ambush game animals as they came to the water to drink. While one would expect a hunter to retrieve a favorite throwing stone, the ones that landed in the lake might not be found, accumulating there in the mud like so many lost golf balls (Indian arrowheads in North America similarly accumulated in shallow water). Only if they were projectiles would one expect such a shallow water distribution; if used as axes, there is no reason to expect to find them preferentially in the water. Especially standing on edge.

So I wonder if they weren't a stage in our development of throwing. I doubt that they were the earliest stage; perhaps they were an improvement on throwing peach-sized rocks. At East African sites dated to 2 million years ago, Mary Leakey finds groups of rocks that she calls manuports—hand-carried—that are suitable for throwing; they are not indigenous to the local geology, as if carried in from some distance. The primary advantage of a hand ax over a round rock is its narrow edge, important for aerodynamics. It is also true that such a shape would be the best way to get a heavy rock to travel any distance (a large hand ax may weigh 2 kilograms); though speed is theoretically a better way to achieve great stopping power than is weight—because of the square-law relation of kinetic energy to velocity—they might not have been able to achieve both speed and accuracy at an earlier stage in brain development.

It is unlikely that a large hand ax could be thrown sidearm with the same accuracy achieved using a dart-like overhand throw of a small round rock or small hand ax. Yet because of their weight, the large hand axes might have been efficient for knocking down a medium-sized game animal; striking anywhere on the body might delay the animal's escape long enough for the hunter to run up and grab it. A good aim might not initially be important if throwing into a whole herd of animals coming to drink at a waterhole; it wouldn't matter which one was hit. Clustering is one way that animals minimize their exposure to predators (only animals on the outside of the group are exposed, a small percentage of the total), but it would have worked against them, once throwing was invented and a hunter could lob a large stone onto their midst.

DESSERT AFTER DINNER featured a choice of cake and cookies. The cookies were the sandwich type known as Oreo. And so we toasted *Oreopithecus* with Oreo cookies, saluting all the sophisticated species that didn't make it.

Then Marsha suggested that perhaps *Oreopithecus* was the original cookie-monster.

HUNTER-GATHERERS OR GATHERER-HUNTERS? What was the major source of the hominid diet, meat or vegetables? The living apes are mainly gatherers; some are specialists in plant food, as are the gorilla and the orangutan, but chimpanzees are omnivores—they'll eat much of what's seasonally available, except that wild chimps seem to pass up dead meat. Nice fresh meat is quite another matter—chimps will skillfully stalk and kill antelope, small monkeys, and bush pigs, tear them apart and consume them with relish. But chimps too are primarily gatherers of seeds, leaves, blossoms, and fruit. Are chimps therefore gatherer-hunters (if we are to adopt the revisionist anthropological nomenclature which seeks to stress the vegetarian side of things over the carnivorous side)? Well no; gathering, to the anthropologists, suggests carrying the food back to share it with a family, and chimps forage and consume their food on the spot. To delay consumption is very unchimplike. Chimps carry unconsumed food, all right, but only to keep it away from other chimps, so they can eat it in peace while hiding back in the jungle.

One can eat meat without hunting—it's called scavenging,

Modern humans are notoriously expert at killing from a distance. The hand ax may be proof that this behavioral strategy was refined long ago. . . . Is it possible that the ancient Greeks preserved as a sport [the discus throw] a tradition handed down from that distant yesterday?

The anthropologist
EILEEN M. O'BRIEN, 1984

and some anthropologists stress its probable role, since defleshing tool marks overlie carnivore tooth marks on some animal bones. It is clear, however, that some early peoples were primarily hunters—perhaps not in Africa, where there are alternatives to hunting, but in colder climates where there just isn't any plant food available during some of the year, and the dead animals available for scavenging wouldn't support very many people. Inuits were an extreme example of this hunting life style around the Arctic Circle. Gathering is a problem up there—even the berries are quite small. Only the grasses and shrubs grow well in such cold climates, but one cannot digest them without the enzymes and extra stomachs found in the digestive systems of grazing specialists. The easiest way to get those calories in grass is by eating the muscles they produce in a grazing animal. Or the muscles of a predator who got to the grazers beforehand.

There are presumably all the possible intermediate mixes of hunting and gathering; the question is which mix played the predominant role in hominid evolution? Which diet required advanced toolmaking and tool use, which diet demanded a bigger brain, a longer childhood, whatever?

And which diet is associated with the best opportunities to "make progress," to *rapidly* turn the ratchets of evolutionary change? (Hominid brain enlargement, once it starts, progresses with extraordinary rapidity). Island seafood diets? Danakil provides one example, but there are other ways of getting the evolutionary advantages of islands as well.

A good case can be made for hunting as the most important hominid dietary source, simply because of the reliance in marginal climates upon meat. That's because margins are more important than population centers. Selection pressures are harsher in marginal climates, so change is more likely to be made by natural selection biasing the population towards those with important traits such as the ability to stalk and aim and throw. As the Inuit suggest, hunting skills may become terribly important in such climates, for keeping the family alive through the winter; they cannot fall back on gathering after missing the target, the way Africans could. And those essential-on-the-margins traits are also more likely to be made permanent by subsequent speciation, since they occur in isolated places where the gene pool isn't buffered by a large interbreeding population. On the margins, tribes are few and far between because the land won't support a higher population density.

While the gathering skills may be used more of the time in the tropics—as many anthropologists are quick to point out whenever hunting is stressed—the bias exerted there by natural selection is not likely to be as rapid or as harsh as in marginal regions. For one thing, there is no hunting-only winter once a year to nudge things along. Nor, when a bias towards more successful reproduction is finally achieved by natural selection in the tropics, is it likely to be made permanent, because speciation cannot readily occur with all the interbreeding opportunities, short of an island situation, such as in the Danakil aquatic ape hypothesis. The African savannah and forests, as well as other hominid sites such as in tropical Asia, will support higher population densities than the margins, preventing large deviations from the average that might make the genome idiosyncratic enough to speciate and preserve adaptations.

All this suggests looking for the real action in hominid evolution on the margins, places such as our Colorado Plateau— say Unkar Delta—where success was sporadic, life was chancy, where populations underwent boom and bust, where every bit of cleverness counted. Not that early hominids were ever around here (even their ancestors, the apes and the Old World monkeys, never made it across to the New World—though some early primate teeth are to be found in Wyoming). But along with the life style of the Inuit on the Ice Age frontiers, the life style of the Anasazi on the mountainous desert frontiers serves better as a model for the cutting edge of hominid evolution than that of the tropical populations that have contributed most of the bones and stones to the anthropological record.

The hominids of equatorial Africa were probably the products of evolution that happened earlier on the African margins, beneficiaries of—rather than participants in—the important selection and speciation events. But because Africa doesn't extend very far south into the temperate latitudes (no further south than Mexico or Israel extends north), winters aren't very spectacular even in South Africa, making islands like Danakil especially important in African evolutionary considerations before the ice ages began. When ice ages altered climates worldwide, South Africa and some of the mountains around the Mediterranean Sea might have had more significant winters, nudging selection along each year in those subpopulations which couldn't retreat to the tropics.

It didn't always seem that way. Darwinian gradualism suggested that the center of the whole population was a representative place to look, as the low numbers on the margins meant that they didn't count very heavily in the average. But the progress in evolutionary theory over the last few decades has shown that Darwinian gradualism, while it may operate in small populations, does not realistically depict the detailed mechanism of the ratcheting up of a whole species, which involves a sequence in both space (the allopatric speciation of Mayr) and time (the punctuated equilibrium of Stanley, Eldredge, and Gould). That has implications for where to dig.

The people who dig in the tropical sun for years to find a few hominid bones will protest that this is unfair, that it asks them to instead dig where the population density was ten times lower and the geology or climate for preservation unfavorable, so that finds will be even rarer.

True, but it reminds one of the story about the person who was crawling around on the sidewalk under a streetlight, sorting through bits of broken glass while looking for a lost contact lens: That wasn't where he lost the contact lens, but the light was better there. . . .

At the present stage of hominid investigations, the questions to answer about hominid origins are What and When—and so it makes some sense to look where there's a chance of finding something, anything. But if we want to see hominid evolution in action—to answer Where, Why, and How questions—we'll eventually have to look in the right places. Even if the light is poor there.

Just as in contemporary industry, where the cutting edges of innovation (as well as high failure rates) often lie in small companies outside the big industrial cities, we may have to look where small groups struggle if we are to understand how lasting change comes about. The industrial centers may wind up doing the mass production which results in the most common artifacts which some future archaeologist of the computer age on earth will dig up, but their antecedents will be hard to discern. IBM's best-selling computer, the PC, wasn't really designed or built by traditional IBM; it only stepped into a well-developed small computer field that was leaving it behind in the late 1970s, and packaged together a computer whose parts were designed and already being manufactured by small innovators. Hundreds of different small companies were taking those same disks, memories, displays, keyboards, and software, then integrating them into systems for small business use.

IBM did the same thing in 1981 but the familiarity of the IBM name captured the market in a classic bandwagon effect; only later did IBM begin manufacturing more of the parts themselves (many jokingly classified the IBM PC as an import, since many of its parts were made abroad—but that's better than AT&T, which literally stuck their familiar name on a well-designed Italian computer). The buyers mostly thought that the computer was designed and built by those reliable, experienced engineers at IBM who made all those big computers. Actually, it was a small, temporary offshoot group that IBM set up in

Florida which did the shopping and packaged the product (it wasn't even state-of-the-art for 1981). IBM cashed in on its name, not any special talent that the hundreds of smaller competitors lacked. That computer archaeologist will not, I hope, dig only near IBM headquarters in New York. As in hominid evolution, one has to distinguish between where the experiments and failures advance the technological evolution, and where the standardized mass production subsequently takes place.

THE BOATMEN ARE AT IT AGAIN. We are having a boat-jumping contest. The seven boats are, as usual, all pulled up, stern on the beach and bow in the water, parked side by side. One can, although barely, jump from the bow of one boat to the next bow. The target bow, of course, compresses into the water when you land—and then stiffly rebounds. If you lose your balance, you fall into the shallow water, or perhaps the front compartment of the boat. Ordinary mortals wobble upon landing, and fall—if they haven't already fallen while launching themselves.

Fueled by beer (presumably without tetracycline), the boatmen are getting a running start, hopping onto the first boat's left bow, then over to the right side, and then bouncing from one boat to the next, trying to get through all seven before crashing. To get an idea of the dimensions, imagine seven soft waterbeds strung out end-to-end, each with two standard-sized beer kegs tied down across them to serve as the stepping stones. This is what the physicists call a gedanken ("thought") experiment; if someone, heaven forbid, should actually have seven waterbeds, fourteen beer kegs, and the space to string them out and get a running start, I disclaim all responsibility for the flood that will result.

Eventually all the boatmen try their luck, and a half-dozen passengers as well. Howie wears his white sheet as a cape. After a few practice runs, Alan and Jimmy get through all seven, to cheers. Everyone keeps trying, and eventually even the better-coordinated passengers like Dan Richard manage to get through seven bounces without falling.

Then Jimmy—superbly coordinated Jimmy—tries to do it on one foot. Well, he gets his running start with both feet, but then hops on his right foot from boat to boat, his leg pumping like a piston. On the third run, he makes it through all seven bouncy bows. What a finale. The Overhang cave resonates nicely to our shouts.

I wonder what the Anasazi improvised for athletic contests here? And when did such spontaneous contests begin in hominid evolution? One never sees apes performing in turn, cheering one another on, trying to better their performance on the next round. This is more than the usual monkey or ape playfulness. Maybe it happened during the hominid's redoubled childhood, during all that extra time to play.

From Apes to Homo Sapiens

A Tentative Timeline

7.0 Myr	Chimp-Hominid Common Ancestor
	Like chimp, perhaps already omnivorous and clever?
	Assume mother-infant family as African apes?
	Aquatic ape phase for hairlessness, upright posture?
	Frequent selection cycles as volcanos, tides change and when shellfish supply ruined by pathogens
4.0 Myr	Early savannah phase of Australopithecines
	More helpless mothers due to carrying infants?
	Concealed ovulation develops?
	Pair-bonding develops, male supports family too?
	Gathering, small game hunting as in chimps, baboons
	Waterbag, carrying basket invented?
	Throwing for threatening carnivores (defense, scavenging); minor selection for throwing accuracy?
	Selection cycles due to African drought, volcanic eruptions; every-winter cycle only in South Africa during some climatic periods or in "mountain islands" on slopes of high volcanos
2.4 to 2.0 Myr	Brain size increase starts with *Homo habilis*
	Hit-or-miss rock flaking for cutting tools
	Major climate change every 0.1 Myr as ice ages come and go
1.5 Myr	Discus-like "hand ax" throwing into herds at waterholes; selection for length of throw, good aim not essential
	Aimed throwing for hunting small, then larger animals?
	Continuing selection for accuracy, length of throw
	Retouched toolmaking from broken stones; standard toolkit
	Fire-starting from sparks during toolmaking?
	Every-winter selection cycles for *Homo erectus* in temperate Europe, Asia; ice age oscillations continue
	Continued selection for hunting abilities
	Secondary uses of throwing and hammering neural machinery?
0.1 Myr	Brain size increase ends with *Homo sapiens*
	Shift from biological-plus-cultural evolution to cultural evolution alone.

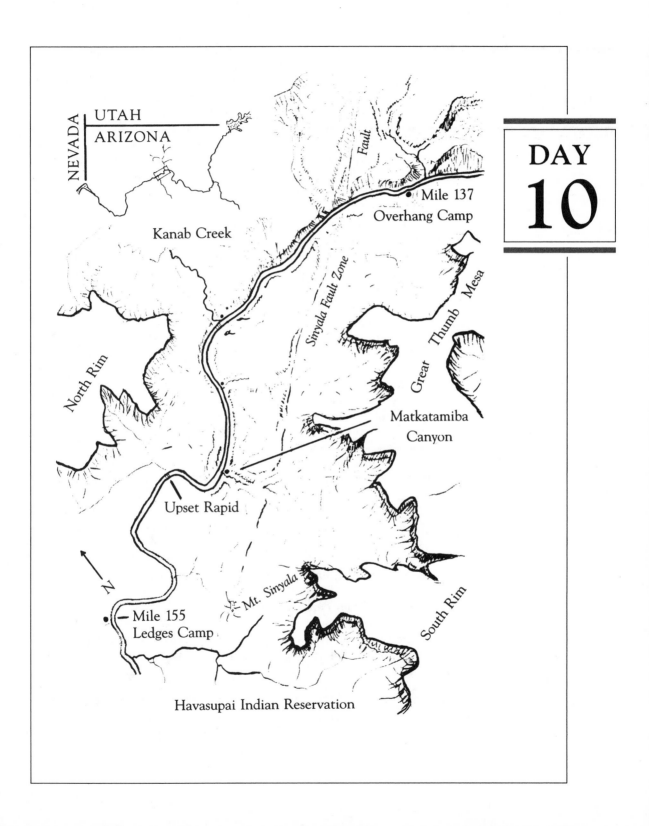

NEVADA

UTAH

ARIZONA

DAY
10

Kanab Creek

Sinyala Fault Zone

Fault

● Mile 137
Overhang Camp

Great Thumb Mesa

North Rim

Matkatamiba
Canyon

Upset Rapid

N

Mt. Sinyala

South Rim

● Mile 155
Ledges Camp

Havasupai Indian Reservation

MILE 137

Overhang Camp

NO HANGOVERS THIS MORNING as Overhang Camp awakens. As I stand at the shore brushing my teeth, I notice that the river seems exceptionally swift. It's probably because the Canyon is so narrow here. I smell bacon cooking on our homely hearth. It's what woke me up—the overhang "cave" tends to fill up with the cooking smells.

I suppose the Anasazi cooked bighorn sheep instead. And I've heard that there are some Anasazi granaries just downriver. They're in the Tapeats, just above the underlying schist.

I've been trying to see up above the overhang, at the canyon above. We still haven't figured out the geology, but I suspect that an old fault comes through here—there is a lot of broken rock above the Tapeats cliff, but no creek along its path. It's something like the Eminence Break back at Mile 43, where it looked as if a meat cleaver had fallen out of the sky and shattered the rocks. The broken rock here extends up through the Muav and a bit into the Redwall. We're now on the same side of the river as where Jeremy spotted those bighorns yesterday morning, and we're only three miles downstream. But I cannot spot them.

We're all in the shade, though the sun almost peeked in when it first rose. But Overhang Camp faces north, and probably stays shaded most of the day. It fills with the sounds of a sociable river camp. And we're a group comfortable with one another by now. There's always a lively round-table discussion going. Without a table.

"So Australopithecus and Homo habilis never made it out of Africa, never got to see an ice age?" asked Jackie as she sipped her second cup of tea.

Barbara nodded. "Of course, the ice ages probably changed the climate in the tropics too, simply because the ocean currents and weather patterns altered. So they'd have had to move around some in Africa, to follow the game or find enough rainfall to keep them supplied in plant food. But that doesn't mean it was a more severe climate."

"But Homo erectus saw the ice ages?" asked Ben.

"Surely. Homo erectus made it out of Africa not long after the time that the two tool-kit styles developed—about 1.5 million years ago—taking his handy spinning projectiles along. Even if you stick to the classically described four ice ages that left rockpiles rearranged by the glaciers, you've got dates of 0.8, 0.46, 0.2, and 0.1 million years ago. That's when those ice ages started, anyway. Homo erectus surely saw the first two or three, at least—plus a lot of the others that didn't leave such a nice record."

"And Homo erectus was far enough north to see them?" Jackie inquired.

"Well, Peking Man was late Homo erectus, living up in that northern latitude by 0.5, dying out by 0.2 million years ago. There are sharp, cold winters in Beijing these days—much colder than in other cities like Naples or St. Louis that are the same latitude—and I doubt Beijing was any warmer in an ice-age winter. So Homo erectus sure must have been wearing fur coats and living in cozy shelters by then," explained Barbara.

"Didn't Peking Man live in caves, though?" Dan Richard asked. "Isn't that where they found them?"

"That's right. That cave system got used repeatedly for a quarter of a million years. And they presumably had fire. It's not just that the climate would seem to require a source of heat. They've found charcoal in the caves. And the cave floor has been repeatedly burned," Barbara said. "So they were probably cooking food, and huddling around campfires for warmth at night."

"Is that when fire-making was invented?" asked Jackie.

"No one is very sure about controlled fire. There are some reports from East Africa of fire-damaged stones arranged in what looks like a hearth, but it's still hard to eliminate grass fires and other accidental causes. That's several million years back. I expect that sometime between then and Peking Man at a quarter-million years ago, fire was invented. And lost. And then re-invented."

Ben brought over the coffeepot and refilled cups for most of us. "But you say that the tools didn't change much over that period?" he asked.

"Well, the Mousterian style came in late in that period, but that's mostly an improvement in manufacturing, handy in places where the raw material is scarce. True, you can get some nice long blades that are hard to produce simply by touching up a handy random rock fragment. I'd say that the improvement was one of economy rather than an advance in what they could do with the tools they made. It isn't like the jump from wearing skins to sewing clothing that keeps the drafts out, or the jump from eating raw food to preparing cooked food, which greatly expands the possible diet by inactivating plant toxins. But I could be wrong," Barbara added.

"And brain size increased all through that Homo erectus period?" asked Jackie again.

"At first glance, that's what you'd think. They start at about 800 cubic centimeters in Africa 1.7 million years ago, and Homo erectus finishes up with Peking Man at 0.23 million years ago.

And some of those Peking skulls are as big as 1140 cubic centimeters, though they average about 1088. But there's a lot of scatter. Some experts, like Philip Rightmire, argue that there isn't much steady improvement."

"So what replaced Homo erectus?" asked Ben, returning from putting the coffeepot back on the breakfast table. "Was it Homo sap?"

"Well, I wish that I knew," said Barbara, brushing her hair back with annoyance. "There are some skulls 0.4 million years old in Europe which we class as 'archaic Homo sapiens' because they are more like Homo sapiens than Homo erectus. But modern-type Homo sapiens doesn't appear until about 100,000 years ago in South Africa. So there's 300,000 years of transitional types, and they're really not very well defined yet. And 100,000 years ago is also about when the Neanderthal type appears. How Homo erectus changed into the archaic form, and then into the two Homo sapiens types is a big question."

"Neanderthal is Homo sapiens too?" asked Ben.

"Well, it sure wasn't an ancestor—they were heavily-built contemporaries, with bigger brains than ours. So we just call them Homo sapiens neanderthalensis. And so we got a subspecies name, too. Homo sapiens sapiens."

"Man the wise, but doubly wise? I don't think so, not the way we're heading," commented Jackie.

"Now let me get this straight," said Ben after thinking a few moments, turning to me. "You don't think that the big brain era is just a continuation of the savannah phase in Africa, right?"

"Maybe the beginning—Homo habilis and early Homo erectus—was in the African savannah or hills or the Danakil tidelands. But no, I doubt that the Rift Valley was a good place to repeatedly run the ratchet for a bigger brain," I replied. "I think that the interesting events were probably happening elsewhere after, say, 1.4 million years ago. That's when Homo erectus started spreading all over. And I think we were hunting in a big way by then. Loren Eiseley used to say that meat supplied the energy that carried man around the world."

"But couldn't brain enlargement have been due to toolmaking?" queried Jackie.

"But," interjected Ben, "tools just don't change all that much during the period of enlargement. That was just my point."

I shrugged. "When you get down to it, we're just not an order-of-magnitude better than chimps are when it comes to hammering skills. I think it's hunting and, while hunting is handy anywhere there is game, it is essential on the frontiers. In Africa, it's just too easy to fall back on gathering if the hunting skills fail. It's where groups are over-extended, living beyond their normal niche, that selection is most do-or-die."

"But why is a bigger brain so great for throwing things? Wouldn't a big brain be better for outsmarting animals, or remembering your territory, things like that?" persisted Jackie.

"Carnivores," I explained, "are the real experts at outsmarting other species, and they haven't been experiencing a bigger brain boom. Nor have squirrels and packrats, who remember where they hide things, or orangutans who find their way around big territories. I think we're dealing with something fundamentally new in this third phase of post-chimp evolution—that big brains involve something that other apes just don't do very much."

"Like language?" suggested Rosalie, looking up from threading film in her camera. "That's sure fundamentally new, and it's what our cultural boom is built on."

"That, and general intelligence itself, are surely most people's favorite candidates for why big brains became so popular," I agreed. "But I think they're too slow to do the job—I prefer to put my money on something like hunting. And particularly on the kinds of hunting that the apes don't do—such as throwing rocks. That's really a new invention, not just an improvement in hammering or social communication. And throwing also has this great growth curve—bigger and bigger brains continue to be better and better performers."

"But why is a big brain so much better at throwing stones?" asked Jackie. "That's not exactly obvious to me. I can understand why a bigger brain could store more information, or why it might have to enlarge if it were to add on a new language center. But throwing is an arm motion—it's not unlike hammering. And those chimps seem to already have that. Why does it take a bigger brain to throw? Isn't it just a little improvement in hammering-type motions?"

"And why all the emphasis on natural selection?" asked Ben. "I thought that variations were the flip side of the selection coin. Why aren't we talking about the anatomical variations that lead to bigger brains?"

I started to reply, but Gary called everyone over to the shore to discuss what we were doing today. So we picked ourselves up and walked down to the boats. Head boatman's announcement time. The answer wouldn't have been brief, anyway.

"We're going down today to a real pretty place called Matkatamiba. It's down at Mile 148, and we'll hang out there all afternoon," Gary began. "We'll probably stop for lunch just before Matkat at a neat waterfall in Olo Canyon. But it'll be a quiet morning. We'll go through a couple of fault lines, Sinyala and Fishtail. And Fishtail Rapid's a good ride. Then we'll get to Kanab Creek, probably stop there and let you hike up to see the meanders."

Gary held up a cautionary hand. "Just don't drink the water from that creek, or just downriver of it—Kanab Creek comes all the way down from Utah. The town of Kanab's up there at the head of the canyon. We'll be filling our water jugs before getting to Kanab Creek. Why don't you fill up your canteens this morning, top them off before we break camp?

"Keep your eyes open for bighorn today," concluded Gary. "Oh, yes. There's a big rapid this afternoon, after we leave Matkat. It's called Upset Rapid. A real good ride. But that's the last big one until we get to Lava Falls, day after tomorrow. We'll camp tonight down around Mile 155 or 156, so we can do Havasu tomorrow, bright and early. Anybody got any questions?"

"This Oreo Canyon where we're having lunch," asked Marsha, "is that where the cookie-monster lives?"

Groan. It's going to be one of those days. First we rename Overhang Camp as Hangover Camp, and now poor Olo Canyon is about to be renamed too.

MILE 143
Kanab Creek

THIS SIDE CANYON IS LONG, with the characteristic treelike branching of a river that isn't in a hurry. Just up the creek from the confluence, it twists and turns with the typical meanders that one sees when flying over the Mississippi River. Such long rivers in flat country can change their meanders every century or so, but Kanab Creek cannot. Its meanders have become "entrenched"—that is to say, they've dug such a deep canyon into harder rock that they can no longer actively meander about the way they did in the softer rock layers above; they are locked into an old wiggle from ages ago.

One wonders what old patterns have become entrenched in human evolution. Abundant toolmaking and brain enlargement may have started up together more than 2 million years ago but to judge from the merely minor progression of the Acheulean tool kit from 1.5 until 0.3 million years ago, it wasn't the demands made by toolmaking that caused our ancestors' brain size to keep increasing. Yet, if not toolmaking, then what? What used natural selection to make bigger brain variants survive better, reproduce better?

The usual answer to this question would surely be "general intelligence": smarter is better when trying to catch food that can run away from you, better in coping with changing environments. If bigger brains are also smarter, then bigger brains are better. It fits in perfectly with our preconceptions: that intelligence is what humans are all about.

The first problem with this appealing explanation is that one doesn't see other examples of it. Why didn't some other primate double and triple its brain size too? Even if no one made it as far as we have, surely there would be some robust examples in evolution of bigger-is-smarter-is-better, demonstrating its efficacy for us to see. It doesn't take other examples of 200 percent. Even a 50 percent increase would help make the point. But none obliged. The monkey-to-ape enlargement is about all we've got with which to compare. It may be that every time the brain enlargement was tried out, the mother died in childbirth because the baby's head was too large to get out. That's about the strongest form of natural selection that I can imagine: It's the equivalent of, every time a teen-aged hunter was gored, his mother also died, along with all her younger children. Bigger hominid heads had to be pretty spectacularly better at something, for their advantages to exceed such a negative selection pressure. An incremental improvement in IQ doesn't seem likely to overcome that barrier.

The second problem is that within the present population of the presumptuously named *Homo sapiens sapiens*, bigger isn't particularly smarter or wiser—though some correlation between brain size and some aspect of "intelligence" isn't ruled out, the geniuses certainly come with all sizes of brain, persons of low intelligence don't have a smaller than average brain size, and generally all bets are off. Knowing someone's hat size won't do you a bit of good.

And to look at dolphins and gorillas and orangs and quite a few other animals, there are certainly species that are more clever than they need to be. These animals could perhaps get along fine with much less learning ability, manipulative ability, and mimicry ability than they have—in their present niches. Maybe they were once faced with a series of environmental challenges that selected for those qualities, but they've settled into lives which no longer demand them for survival—they found a reliable way of making a living and stuck with it, like the taxi drivers with Ph.D.s. One may not get to see the world that way, but by sticking to fruit and leaves, one doesn't have to worry if the game animals or the grain harvest will be sufficient to see one's family through the winter. Smarter may be better, but only if one's environment continues to make demands, only if speciation opportunities continue to save those biased genomes from subsequent dilution.

BIGGER DOESN'T EVEN MEAN MORE CELLS, much less a smarter brain. A bigger adult body usually means a bigger brain as well, but it may not have any more nerve cells than before! Typically, when a mammalian species gets bigger like the horses did, the brain enlarges along with the rest of the body. And the nerve cells simply spread out—the same number, just more space between them. But sometimes there are also more cells as a result, and the reason may lie in one of those Darwinian aspects of development: many more nerve cells are produced early in development than can ever survive in subsequent stages. As gardeners know, the sprouts come up too close together in flats of young seedlings, so not all survive—but if the gardener spreads them out, more will make it. Our threefold larger human brain doesn't have a proportional increase in the number of nerve cells it contains; the current estimates suggest that there are perhaps 25 percent more nerve cells in the human cerebral cortex than in a chimpanzee's cerebral cortex. The other 175 percent growth is just because they aren't as close together.

How does one relate this to fossils, when all there is to go on is their cranial capacity and some estimates of their body weight, derived from the thicknesses of their bones and the size of their muscle-attachment zones? One can compensate somewhat for the differences in body size by reducing things to the brain/body ratio. There are formulas for brain/body weight ratios, but the safest thing is to compare mammals of the same body weight, such as a 40 kilogram bear, a 40 kilogram chimp, and a 40 kilogram human. On that basis, we still have a brain that is 3.6 times as large as most apes would need to run a body our size, and 8.6 times that of an average mammal of our body size.

One way of judging brain growth over successive species is to fall back on the analogies between ontogeny and phylogeny. Brain size certainly grows as the fetus-infant-child enlarges, but at very different rates during the various stages. In the first trimester of gestation, a human fetus may be half head, making the brain/body ratio quite high. The head continues growing quite rapidly, but eventually it slows and the body grows faster, the brain/body ratio dropping steadily through childhood until reaching its adult value. To get a bigger adult brain in a new species means modifying those rates somewhere along the line, and that means varying the brain/body ratios. Comparative anatomy shows that there is a very simple way to increase relative brain size. Just grow young. It is called juvenilization, and it results in a bigger adult brain/body ratio. It also enables evolution to work around entrenched meanders in matters developmental.

LUNCH IS NEXT TO AN OVERHANGING WATERFALL which is quite a beautiful sight. And not a cookie monster in sight, just a rope dangling from atop the waterfall, left by someone trying to get up-canyon. It's rotted by now, and Gary cautions us against trying that route.

We were just saying that sometimes in evolution, one gets something for free, in apparent contradiction to the adage "There is no such thing as a free lunch." Most random change is, of course, bad—and natural selection may eliminate it. Natural selection may seemingly operate on individual features of the human body, selecting for hairlessness separately from the diving reflex, so that our body is a mosaic of the ancient and the recent. This adaptationist view of the body tends to suggest that every feature has been shaped for a purpose, that nothing came *gratis*. Mosaic evolution.

But it's misleading. That's because natural selection isn't perfect; the physiologist Lloyd Partridge emphasizes that the result is more like "good enough engineering" in which a sufficient solution to an environmental problem removes the feature from exposure to the natural selection that might lead to further improvements in it. A neurophysiologist can imagine ways to improve our sense of taste; important as it is in the evolution of omnivores, our present system hasn't been streamlined. Natural selection also has yet to eliminate nearsightedness, the inflammation-prone appendix, muscle cramps, flat feet, headaches, premenstrual tension, and other such evidence of imperfection in human evolution. And natural selection may exercise little influence on some change, neither rewarding nor penalizing it. Mosaic evolution can happen, but selection on a one-feature-at-a-time basis has been greatly oversold as the architect of change.

Thus, there are "free" ways to get change: because many traits are anatomically linked, functional selection for one will carry other anatomical features along for free. Hitchhikers, no less. One family of linked traits, of crucial importance for human evolution, is commonly known as juvenilization.

You may remember a fad in architecture in which new buildings looked unfinished, even though the occupants had moved in and the building was open for business. The structural beams were still exposed, the heating ducts and plumbing visible as if the builders hadn't yet gotten around to installing the usual false ceiling. In short, the building looked unfinished by the

MILE 145
Olo Canyon

Whenever you happen to take your children to the Zoo you may observe in the eyes of the apes, when they are not performing gymnastic feats or cracking nuts, a strange strained sadness. One can almost imagine that they feel they ought to become men, but cannot discover the secret of how to do it.

BERTRAND RUSSELL

usual standards of its ancestors, the buildings of earlier decades. I remember wondering how far they'd carry this trend, whether they'd leave off the windows as the next phase.

I don't know if the architectural critics knew enough biology to see the analogy, but a good name for the unfinished-look fad would have been "architectural juvenilization." Juvenilization (also known as neoteny and paedomorphism, by those who can figure out how to pronounce them) is a biological fad, one important way in which new animal species evolve from old ones— and there's nothing trivial about this fad: It's the fad that helped produce the apes from the monkeys, and the humans from the apes. And probably the vertebrates from the invertebrates, back much earlier in the Cambrian, during Tapeats time. That's not a bad track record.

Juvenilization doesn't really refer to juveniles—it's a fad affecting adults. And indeed among the best-known and longest-living of fads, one we see every day: Adults trying to appear younger than they really are. It's appearance and behavior, changed in the direction of juveniles, though not necessarily attaining it.

Jackie explained it by analogy to fashions in women's clothing. It's as if this year's style for "Women's" dresses were to look suspiciously like last year's fad in dresses for "Junior Misses." Well, we're talking about the analogous biological trend that produces adults who look and act younger than an adult of the previous model year. There are several mechanisms for inducing this fad, though we try not to confuse them with the fad itself.

In its simplest manifestations, juvenilization appears as a way of escaping overspecialization, of backing up in evolution. Sometimes the latest model of the body finds itself unsuited to the environment, as when an amphibian discovers that a prolonged heat wave has dried out its swamp. An adult cannot return to the safety of the water by regressing on the spot to its fetal form, retrieving its gills. But a youngster coming along can put the brakes on its development, so that it keeps its gills. This is best seen in the Mexican salamander, much valued in the restaurants of Mexico City, as it was by Julian Huxley for his developmental studies. This newt-like amphibian, *Ambystoma*, usually goes through a larval stage corresponding to the tadpole stage of the frog, then loses its gills and emerges from the water as an air-breathing, land-dwelling animal getting around on all fours. But when the weather has been bad for salamanders, this metamorphosis from tadpole to salamander doesn't happen. The immature salamander is better off staying in the water; by putting the brakes on its development, it retains its gills and swims happily ever after.

Now the usual trouble with remaining a child forever is that you don't reproduce your kind. Happily, however, the tadpole form of *Ambystoma* becomes sexually mature; in fact, this early sexual maturity is the main reason that the tadpole's body development comes to a halt before it makes the water-to-land modifications in its body. A minor form of this phenomenon can be seen in humans: the main reason that men are taller than women is that girls mature earlier than boys, slowing growth. And earlier-than-average sexual maturity in girls is likely to lead to their being shorter adults than girls whose menstruation begins at age 16. Accelerated puberty is, however, just one mechanism for inducing the juvenilization fad.

A delay in puberty, but with even more delay in the general body-development timetable, is another mechanism used. And it seems to have been used repeatedly by the primates: the whole primate lineage has been postponing the later phases of its development in favor of retaining the more juvenile forms.

Reflecting this is a tendency for the primate lineage to become more and more juvenile in appearance—not only do the faces of successive species often become flatter but the teeth become smaller and the brain becomes larger (relative to body size). That is, chimp adults are more like juvenile monkeys; adult humans are more like juvenile chimps. This trend toward a more juvenile adult was even mentioned by Darwin, and was termed neoteny in 1884 by Julius Kollmann, a zoologist at Basel. Havelock Ellis in 1894 applied the idea to human evolution. Louis Bolk, an anatomist in Amsterdam, coined "fetalization" in comparing primate fetal stages with human stages back in 1926. Stephen Jay Gould calls it paedomorphism ("child-shaped"). Julian Huxley in 1952 liked "juvenilization," and that's my favorite too, since my tongue trips on the others. But take your pick.

Ben asked if names lasted only a quarter of a century, or whether each new generation of biologists had to rediscover juvenilization for itself? It is, alas, a topic rarely found in the textbooks, and many anthropologists and neurobiologists have never heard of it under any name.

THE LINKAGE BETWEEN ALL THOSE JUVENILE TRAITS comes about because they share a common mechanism: altered clocks. Rather than simply speeding up the sexual maturity clock, as in *Ambystoma*, the road to *Homo sapiens* is marked by a simple slowing of two rates of maturation. Sexual maturity comes later and later: a monkey may become sexually mature in three to four years, a chimp in eight to nine years, and humans much later. The puberty alarm clock is slowed down; its mechanism

Since the perimeter of the [scallop's] shell grows at a faster rate than the center, the perimeter curls and wrinkles. No genes carry an image of how to place the wrinkles; no genes remember the shape of the shell; they only permit or encourage faster growth at the perimeter than at the center.

PETER S. STEVENS
Patterns in Nature, 1974

is thought to be related to the secretion of melatonin by the pineal gland and some other midline areas of the brain.

The second slowing is in somatic growth. A juvenile chimp and a juvenile monkey may become playmates one year, but the next year the monkey will have grown much more than the chimp—and the "retarded" chimp usually has to find a younger playmate. The regulation of the somatic growth rate is traditionally attributed to the growth hormone secreted by the pituitary gland (though the issue is known to be more complicated than that). A hypopituitary dwarf can, as a child, be treated with a two-year regimen of human growth hormone that will accelerate its body growth (originally, the hormone was gathered from 100–200 human pituitaries at autopsy, but it can now be produced by bacteria fooled with recombinant DNA technology).

The slowing is seen in all stages of life, with longer lifespans for the more "advanced" species (one reason why ageing isn't just a matter of wearing out). If both sexual and somatic clocks were slowed down equally, the eventual adult body form would probably remain the same—it would just take much longer to reach it. But at each stage of primate juvenilization, body growth is slowed down more than the puberty alarm clock—this achieves much the same end as speeding up sexual maturity à la *Ambystoma* but additionally provides the extended childhood for cultural learning. Thus, puberty arrives when the body form is still juvenile by the standards of the ancestral adults. This is inferred from the numerous "neotenous" traits, things which adults now have but which are merely retained from their juvenile selves, things which were no longer altered in adulthood.

Take the little matter of flat faces. Monkey, chimp, and human infants all share a flat face, with the nose and lips lined up vertically beneath the eyes—and the brain coming far enough forward to sit atop the eyes. But as these three primates grow up, the lower face starts to grow forward until—in the monkey and chimp—the adult brain sits largely to the rear of the eyes, the eyes to the rear of the nostrils, with the lips protruding even further forward. The same thing happens to many animals, such as our pet cats and dogs. We find the young ones particularly appealing because, like human infants, they have flat faces with large eyes (relative to their face size). Child face shape is a trigger feature that attracts adults, a matter important if the child is to receive adult care and protection. Much like the cuckoo's scarlet throat attracts the vireo stepparents, the attractiveness of a baby face may also serve other ends besides the one for which evolution first imperfectly designed it, such as identifying the appropriate target for parental affection and care-giving.

Then there's playfulness. Behavior is one of the big differences between juveniles and adults. The young are more inclined to play, amusing themselves by exercising their newfound abilities. And they are far more flexible than adults: the classic story of the Japanese monkeys tells of how novel foods were gradually adopted by a troop of macaques on a small island. The young would learn to unwrap caramel candies and eat them. They would learn how to wash sand off of potatoes. They would throw grains intermixed with the sand on the beach into the shallow water nearby, scooping up the floating grain after the sand sank. Not only didn't the adults ever invent these adaptations to new food, but they were slow to adopt them even after observing the success of the juveniles. Maybe chimps and prehumans adapted themselves to new niches by learning to eat a wider variety of foods than their fruit-loving ancestors. It is easy to imagine that juvenile curiosity and experimentation, retained into the adult stage of life, would have made possible the exploitation of many new foods.

And then there are the teeth. Our ancestors had big molars for grinding down food. Indeed, for an animal that tries to eat everything, it is hard to cite advantages of small teeth. Yet the grinding surfaces of the cheek teeth shrink during prehuman evolution, decreasing by half in the time that the brain triples. Were the smaller teeth somehow better, to use a traditional adaptationist approach, or was the tooth-size reduction another case of a hitchhiker: retaining the half-size juvenile molars into adulthood because some other aspect of juvenilization was rewarded by natural selection?

A bigger brain is also part of juvenilization. But isn't the adult's brain larger than the juvenile's? True, but it is the ratio of brain size and body size, rather than the absolute size itself, that seems all-important. Early on, the embryo is half head. By birth, the head is only a quarter of the crown-to-rump distance. In adults, maybe 10 percent. So one simple way to get a bigger brain/body ratio in an adult is to retain the relatively larger juvenile head size.

Human adults exhibit many other juvenile traits: for example, the big toes face forward in juvenile monkeys and chimps, but come to point outward (are "rotated") in adults. The human forward-pointing big toe might again be most simply explained as "juvenilization strikes again," though adaptationists strive mightily to link upright walking to modifying that big toe.

Some primate offspring have more juvenilization, others less. Selection operates on this genetic variation, biasing the gene pool one way or the other. The adult of the pygmy chimpanzee, *Pan paniscus*, looks like a juvenile of the common chimp, *Pan troglodytes*. And so the adult chimps look even "more human" than the adult common chimp, thanks to juvenilization. They split off from the common chimps about 3 million years ago. Pygmy chimpanzees are rare, and given how important they could be for understanding prehuman behaviors, we really ought to be building breeding colonies to assure their survival.

Dog breeders have artificially selected for juvenilization in the various steps starting with a jackal-like dog and ending up with a pug, simply by breeding together the flatter-faced offspring. Most of our domestic animals are juvenilized versions of their wild ancestors: pigs, cows, sheep, dogs and, to a lesser extent, cats. It seems likely that the artificial selection that humans exercised on these animals operated on some aspect of the juvenilization collection of traits, such as behavioral plasticity. But since young animals also solicit care, the ones that continued this trait into adulthood were also more likely to be fed and sheltered by humans. Perhaps humans too were "domesticated" by a selection for juvenilization.

Juvenilization was important at another juncture in our evolution: in the passage between the invertebrates to the vertebrates. The embryonic form of the sea squirt looks surprisingly like a primitive chordate, and it is thought that a truncation of adult development in the sea squirt led to the first of the chordates. There's a French phrase which summarizes all this: *reculer pour mieux sauter* ("step back to leap better").

> The problem which remains is in fact not "how have vertebrates been formed by sea squirts," but how have vertebrates eliminated the [adult] sea squirt stage from their life history? It is wholly reasonable to consider that this has been accomplished by paedomorphism [juvenilization].
>
> The pioneer neurobiologist
> J. Z. Young, 1950

ADAPTATION OR "FOR FREE"? Because the traits that exhibit juvenilization all share one common mechanism—the puberty alarm clock is slowed down less than the body-growth clock—natural selection affecting any one of the these traits can haul the others along for free. For example, if our ancestors became more successful via expanding the acceptable items in their diet, the selection for behavioral plasticity would have favored those individuals who were more juvenilized over those who were less. But a bigger brain/body ratio, a flatter face, smaller teeth, and a nonrotated big toe might have been incidental changes. In short, not all of these traits need have been directly shaped by selection—it is sufficient for only one to have been a big success to have indirectly carried along the others. However, while one gene controlling many seemingly unrelated features is a well-recognized fact in genetics (it's called pleiotropy), neoteny-paedomorphism-juvenilization is not the traditional teaching in human biology, though first recognized over a century ago.

The variations tend to be families of anatomical features; the natural selection tends to act on the *function* of one of the family. Anatomy varies but physiology succeeds.

Do we owe our big brains, then, to the success of the juvenile's playfulness, or perhaps only to the tendency of individuals to select mates whose flat-faced, big-eyed appearance mimics the child's? Sexual selection could, after all, do the job rather than natural selection. I once asked students on a final exam a comic relief question: construct a hypothesis that could connect bigger brains to the common practice of changing the appearance of a woman's face via eye-shadow and -liner. What happens with eye makeup, of course, is that it is used to enhance the apparent size of the eyes, making the face look more juvenile. I wanted the students to recognize that such makeup was used to mimic juvenile appearance, and that adults were "tuned up" to like children's faces and to protect and provide for them. And that relatively larger eye appearance in an adult woman might stimulate a man to provide her with the care he might otherwise reserve for a child. But since women are even more tuned up to respond to young faces, this ought to also work the other way: as one of the best students pointed out to my surprise, this means that eye shadow for men might attract women. And that maybe I should shave off my beard if. . . .

Ah, but back to juvenilization. If all these traits are linked, thanks to their sharing the sluggish clock genes, cause and effect become harder to distinguish. The selection for juvenile facial appearance in mates might occur at the same time as selection for juvenile experimentation with novel foods, at the same time as direct selection for neuron numbers via general intelligence. There is no single "cause" for any evolutionary happening, but for linked traits like those of the juvenilization family, cause is particularly fuzzy.

While juvenilization has been recognized for a hundred years under various names, it has not been widely adopted as an explanation for human phylogeny; you'll seldom hear an anthropologist mention it when spinning a scenario for hominid evolution. And Dan Hartline voiced what has probably been a widespread reaction to the juvenilization hypothesis even among biologists: How can you advance by retreating? We're not juvenile chimps, after all.

Juvenilization goes against the widespread notion of "progress" in evolution. After all, it suggests that an adult ape-hominid was overspecialized, that it had to back up to produce us. It suggests that the child may be better than the adult, contrary to our personal experience of becoming more competent as we grow older. Yet once you begin studying the subject and get beyond these surface reactions, you see that juvenilization has to be at least part of the answer to hominid evolutionary mechanisms—there are just too many facts staring one in the face, like the doubled and redoubled childhood, the flatter faces and smaller teeth, those greater brain/body ratios.

The issue isn't juvenilization, but whether there is some other important mechanism involved in addition to juvenilization. For example, there might be a developmental tendency for the head end of the body to enlarge faster than the tail end. This may happen in the squirrel monkey, whose 1/31 adult brain/body ratio is even bigger than our 1/49. One can see the opposite in the cheetah, whose body is much larger relative to its head size than an average cat. If there is an additional mechanism for relatively larger head ends or tail ends, we don't know much about it yet: it's undoubtedly a matter of relative clock rates in development, but what are the linked traits? What selects for those traits? Which get hauled along for free? What are its disadvantages?

Tune in next year. But in the meantime, the advice we'd offer ambitious chimps is: *Grow young.*

□ □ □

I do not know what I may appear to the world; but to myself I seem to have been only like a boy playing on the seashore, and diverting myself now and then finding a smoother pebble or a prettier shell than ordinary, while the great ocean of truth lay all undiscovered before me.

The natural philosopher ISAAC NEWTON (1642–1727)

In our innermost soul we are children and remain so for the rest of our lives.

The early neuroscientist SIGMUND FREUD (1856–1939)

Man's maturity: to have regained the seriousness that he had as a child at play.

The philosopher FRIEDRICH NIETZSCHE (1844–1900)

[Children] are fantastically interested in making things and in asking "Why? Why? Why?" Then, at a certain age, the children just become adults and are no longer very deeply interested in anything, except in the process of making a living and in sex and power. . . . Profound curiosity happens when they are young. I think physicists are the Peter Pans of the human race. They never grow up, and they keep their curiosity. Once you are sophisticated, you know too much—far too much.

The nuclear physicist ISIDOR ISAAC RABI, 1975

In a sense, all science, all human thought, is a form of play. Abstract thought is the neoteny of the intellect, by which man is able to continue to carry out activities which have no immediate goal (other animals play while young) in order to prepare himself for long-term strategies and plans.

        The mathematician JACOB BRONOWSKI (1908–1974)

MATKATAMIBA CANYON is special. We pull into a narrow side canyon just before hitting the rapid; unless you knew about this secret place, you'd zip right past, spotting the canyon entrance too late to pull in. It's hidden around a corner. The boatmen come down hugging the left shore. Then, as we round the corner, a lot of hard rowing and we enter the quieter waters.

    The entrance to Matkat is very narrow, with only enough room for a few boats to moor. The others tie up behind them and the passengers pick their way across the other boats. Carefully.

    Matkat stays narrow: usually I can keep one hand on each wall. As at Silver Grotto, I have to wedge myself up in some places where there are waterfalls and some greenery. I can manage to walk along one side of the creek while pushing with both hands on the opposite wall, edging along at an angle. The creek looks easier to descend than ascend—there are narrow spaces where one could slide downhill, as in a children's playground. Getting up them is the problem, as the stone is worn smooth and the microgreenery makes it slick near the flowing water. But the canyon layers of Muav limestone have handholds, and so I can wedge up in chimney fashion, always keeping at a 45° angle.

    No sooner is this first obstacle surmounted than I reach a pleasant flat section that wets my ankles again as I slosh along happily. Then comes another chute which I must wedge myself up. But if you arrive at a rock-plugged crevasse that requires both a boost from below and maybe a hand extended down from above, you've gone too far—go back and climb the Muav cliff to the right, up away from the creek.

    And then the canyon opens out, soon reaching an amphitheater in the Redwall, right where it sits atop the Muav. The Unconformity is very obvious here, those missing layers from between 535 and 360 million years ago. You may not be able to see them, but here the Muav looks to have been sanded flat and then another layer-cake glued down atop it.

    The gray-green limestone-sandstone forms the floor of this natural theater, and the red walls are streaked with black desert

MILE 148
Matkatamiba Canyon

varnish, punctuated by patches of greenery. The creekbed in the Muav has a series of bathtub-sized pools with slowly flowing water, probably carved by a series of standing waves during flash floods. The water is warm, and we tried them all, one after another. I kept returning to the middle one, and decided—as I lay there with the warm waters flowing around me—that if I ever made a fortune, I'd have a landscape architect copy this magical place, right down to the desert plants that surround it, and have it installed somehow in my back yard. Unfortunately, it would require a crew of gardeners to maintain. But Matkat manages nicely without help, because each of the ingredients has been selected by the environment over the centuries to work together with the others. It is a small ecosystem that cannot be readily transported elsewhere.

The rock slab where I am resting, I now notice, is another masterpiece of Cambrian wormworks, just as at Deer Creek. The fossil casts are in just one layer of the Muav; the lower layers lack any sign of the finger-sized grooves running every which way.

BUT BIGGER BRAINS MIGHT ALSO BE BETTER, not just freeloaders, to come back to the usual hypothesis. Bigger-is-smarter-is-better is representative of a large number of explanations for the Great Encephalization that come readily to mind. Some "explanations" are mere romantic nonsense, articles of faith such as Robert Ardrey's resounding dictum: "We do not think because our brain is big; our brain has grown big because we think." (This dramatic statement is at least from a dramatist; alas, it echoes the statements of many anthropologists and neurobiologists who should be more suspicious of such comfortable notions).

Other "explanations" are based on mechanistic analogies to systems that work very differently from the biological brain: users of digital computers, for example, immediately comment that a larger memory capacity might have been useful (but such computers use pigeonhole memory storage of the kind that fills up, not the overlapping committees of the brain's distributed memory storage system, which may not saturate but merely require progressively longer times to find something). My objections do not, of course, rule out the possibility that there is more than a grain of truth in such proposals. Indeed, almost everyone's favorite proposal might well be right, in that the proposed mechanism could have played some role in hominid evolution. Fortunately, it is possible to focus the discussion a little.

Of the many things which might have benefited from a larger and more versatile brain, which was in the best position to work the evolutionary ratchet? And to do it most often? Was there a fast-track for brain enlargement, some one factor operating over and over again to increment brain size? The problem any candidate faces is not only to have evolved a bigger brain, but to have done it very rapidly, in the last two million years or so. From the lessons of evolutionary biology, one can create a recipe for rapid evolution:

FIRST, take a variable population, some with smaller, some with bigger brains. Expose it to severe natural selection. That means severe limitations on food, severe culling by predators, severe selection by disease, severe actions of climate—with which some variants in the population can cope better than others. Overextended subpopulations, barely making a go of it in a somewhat foreign habitat that strains their existing skills, is the sort of setup that comes to mind. Small batches are best for this recipe. Many small isolated bowls are better than one big bowl.

SECOND, do not stir after selection. Not only can natural selection bias a small genome faster than a large one, but boiling the population down to a residue, and then having a subsequent population explosion based on those few survivors, is a fast way to make the genome idiosyncratic enough so that speciation occurs. Just repeat this bust-and-boom cycle (in the business, this is known as the Founder or Bottleneck Effect followed by a Population Flush) a few times and (at least in insects) reproductive isolation will start becoming noticeable. Speciation means that when the severely selected folk do eventually find their way back into the parent central population, they won't interbreed very well. Since their successful copulations are only with each other, it saves their own new-fangled genome from being badly diluted. After all, that central population has a lot more individuals than any isolated subpopulation. Though the biased genome of the selected subpopulation will shift the gene frequencies of the whole species a little upon remixing with the central population, it will be nothing compared to the shift achieved in the subpopulation itself before mixing. It may work eventually, but here we're talking about speed. The way to make rapid changes is to build atop the subpopulation, rather than by the tiny biases to the whole population that Darwin first envisaged. Thus the recipe calls for the speciation ratchet now and then, to prevent dilution of the progress achieved so far by selection, just as the ratchet on an automobile jack prevents the car from slipping back to the ground, just as the ratchet in the clockworks prevents time from seeming to run backwards.

THIRD, repeat the cycle as often as possible. The unsettled geology and tides of Danakil? But even more frequent cycles can be achieved by a locale in temperate climates, where there are real winters unlike the tropics, so that the selection process can be nudged along by yearly episodes of hard times. And there is that 100,000-year cycle in climate, starting 2.5 million years ago, with the mini-ice ages taking rainfall out of circulation. In our classic examples of adaptive radiation, such as those arising after a mass extinction, there are many niches available and few rivals, and so there is a rapid diversification. But here we are concerned with repeated adaptation in a particular direction. That's a very different problem. Repeating the cycle only produces results as long as natural selection continues to have an effect. Suppose, for example, that bigger brains were a mere side effect of selecting for hairlessness via juvenilization. Infants do have finer fur than adults, and maybe an aquatic environment's selection for less hair would therefore sometimes use the juvenilization family of features, when selecting for the clock rates that give less hair in adults, dragging along a bigger brain for free. But continuing selection pressure won't have any effect after a while: one can, after all, become only so naked. That less-hair growth curve flattens out at a limit. But some things can grow over a wide range. So it would be best to base natural selection for bigger brains on some feature other than hair—a feature that could forever encourage brain growth, preferably one with a steep growth curve.

Now my reliable recipe for rapid ratcheting is not obligatory; for example, the speciation step might be eliminated if one doesn't mind the risks of losing everything to a premature remixing with the central population. Cultural aspects of behavior can substitute for speciation in many cases: when remixing, the two groups might tend to maintain their own cultures, just as the Developed Oldowan toolmakers and those preferring the Acheulean tool kits (the hand ax throwers) managed to coexist for so long. And that same separation by culture might tend to minimize interbreeding. There are many other such "barriers" (as they are called in evolutionary biology) to interbreeding.

But because there is always the chance of tumultuous remixing, as in raids and rape, episodes of regular speciation are good insurance against the loss of a specially selected genome. Who knows what creatures developed, omitting the insurance of a ratchet, and then got diluted out of existence? And it is certainly not obligatory to start in temperate climates with the selective nudge provided by every winter; one doesn't have to speed up evolution in every possible way all at once to ensure rapid growth of the brain. In reality, the mix of rapidity-encouraging elements probably changed, with episodes of two steps forward, then one backward.

THE FAST-TRACK ARGUMENTS for human brain enlargement thus center around ape-human differences that are climate-dependent, more important on the periphery or islands than in the central tropical population, directly related to survival skills rather than contemplative intelligence, and likely to involve some aspect of the juvenilization collection of traits open to natural selection.

Could diet have done it, since the smartest animals are often omnivores? Learning to eat more types of food is useful in expanding one's niche, enabling one to live in different kinds of environments. But however good a general principle that may be, I doubt that diet will explain the special case of the Great Encephalization: that's because chimps are already pretty accomplished omnivores; we may, or may not, have picked up a taste for dead meat along the way, enabling us to take advantage of dead animals, steaks that chimps would pass up. I don't want to minimize scavenging; it might have aided the development of throwing (driving away hyenas with thrown rocks, etc.) and hammering (well-protected brains and bone marrow are among the leftovers), and gotten hominids into the hunting-by-throwing business gradually. But while applicable to the savannah of equatorial Africa where there are lots of game animals, scavenging is intrinsically a way of life that spells a low prehuman population even there: we'd have been dependent on the top predators for our living—even though not eating them—and it takes a lot of game animals to support a single lion (and even more if we were stealing part of the lion's food). For standard food-chain reasons often forgotten by enthusiasts of the scavenging hypothesis, that means far fewer prehumans than lions. And scavenging would give a very low yield outside the densely-populated savannas. Scavenging would thus surely have been only one minor part of a more complex food economy but, because of its influence on hammering and throwing, perhaps of major importance via its cultural stimulus to a biological change.

Gathering? Human gathering isn't all that different from what chimpanzees or baboons do. True, we may make use of digging sticks; true, we tend to carry things back to others, postponing consumption and sharing our food. But what is the connection of gathering to juvenilization or bigger brains? What kind of growth curve might it have?

How about predation of the usual snatch-or-chase type? One

. . . the increase in brain size in such a short period from an average of 460 g to more than three times as much is almost unbelievably fast.

The evolutionary theorist
ERNST MAYR, 1973

starts with the baboon and chimpanzee picture—again already at a near-human level. Their predation involves group cooperation in stalking—of a kind we used to think was uniquely human. One can say that improved spatial skills would be useful for hunting, but one comes up against the considerable baseline of chimp and orangutan skills—they unerringly and repeatedly locate fruit trees in distant corners of their range during just that week of the year when the fruit will become ripe. So navigation doesn't look like such a dramatic improvement.

What about throwing-type hunting? It fits a number of the aspects of the recipe. It's more important in temperate and arctic climates, if only because gathering is so restricted at certain times of the year. Though they throw in order to threaten, apes don't seem to use aimed missiles for hunting to any extent. However, their skillful hammering and threat throwing are obvious stepping-stones toward displacing predators and other scavengers from a kill, toward developing crudely aimed predatory throws at groups of animals visiting a waterhole (the hand ax story), and then to aimed throws of the familiar type. There is a long growth curve in hominid throwing, just judging from improvements in missile type along the way: selected rocks, hand-ax-type discuses, wooden spears, rock-tipped spears, throwing sticks, slings and slingshots, bow-and-arrow—not to mention all the advanced projectiles.

There is another substantial growth-curve: in throwing technique. You can see it by watching children of various ages. At first a child tosses things without much aim or control, reminiscent of how chimps and gorillas throw in their threat displays. Then smaller rocks are selected, with more of an emphasis on distance achieved, and on hitting a target. The child learns to "get set," concentrating on the task, throwing in a stereotyped way over and over, making minor modifications in speed or release point in order to change the impact point of the projectile.

Applied to hunting, you immediately see a third kind of growth-curve: accuracy, or, as it manifests itself, "approach distance." It's easier to hit a nearby target than one farther away, and so the hunter tries to get as close to the prey as possible. While prey animals will often ignore a two-legged human when they would run from a four-legged carnivore, there is still a point at which they will move away from you (their "approach distance"), sometimes just moving back to maintain a certain distance, at other times simply picking up and running. The farther back you keep, the less likely they are to be spooked by the beginning of your throwing motion. So an ability to throw farther with the same accuracy means more successes.

But there is a big bonus for learning to hit a target from twice your former distance. To throw twice as far typically means launching the missile with double the former speed, as distance achieved with a nearly-flat trajectory is proportional to initial velocity. Ignoring air resistance for the moment, this means that the missile arrives at its target with twice the velocity, so that its kinetic energy—being proportional to the square of the velocity—may be four times greater than formerly. Thus the "stopping power" of the missile quadruples when one doubles the distance. This means that one can tackle bigger prey, graduating from birds to rabbits, rabbits to bushpigs, bushpigs to gazelle, and so on. Farther is also better for this second reason. This has a nice kind of growth-curve too, following a square law rather than merely being linear.

So there are four kinds of growth-curves for throwing, all seemingly unlimited. The only trouble is that *throwing twice as far means making decisions more than twice as fast. Indeed, nearly eight times as fast.*

TIME IS OF THE ESSENCE, once one starts looking carefully at throwing with a neurophysiologist's eye for detail. Traditionally, the first thing about which a neurophysiologist would remark is the impossibility of feedback corrections late in the throw. Muscles have sensors embedded in them, as do the tendons and joints; they tell the brain where the arm is located, via messages coded in nerve impulses.

But they don't tell the neighboring muscles, except via that long round trip into the spinal cord and back out again. The brain only knows where the arm was about 1/25 of a second earlier. It can take a message 1/50 of a second to travel from the arm into the spinal cord; it can take another 1/50 of a second (and usually longer) for the spinal cord to tell the brain about it too. Unlike wires through which electrical signals travel at almost the speed of light, nerves use a relay system not unlike a burning fuse or a row of falling dominos. It's not as slow as the mail service, but it isn't as instantaneous as the telephone. It takes even longer for a command message to travel back out, from the spinal cord to a muscle in the arm (the motor nerves aren't designed for speed in the same way as sensory nerves). And it also takes time to make decisions in the brain—the reaction time is anywhere from 1/10 to 1/4 second, or even longer if you're indecisive.

One can make little corrections early during the throwing motion. Though not, of course, after you've let loose—that's one of the disadvantages to unguided missiles. But one also can't make corrections in the last 1/10 second or so before letting go—there just isn't time to gather new data, make the decision, and send the new commands out to a muscle. So there's a point of no more feedback. Once past it, one can't make corrections any more. Your brain is on its own.

The faster the throw, the shorter the throwing time. But the "period of no more feedback" doesn't change; it stays at about 1/10 second. Thus, a larger and larger percentage of the throwing time is impossible to modify as one throws faster—one has to predict what to do on the basis of early data fed back from the arm, telling how rapidly it is actually accelerating, then do the calculations of the trajectory of your rock based on that, and set the release time accordingly.

For some particularly rapid movements (eye flicks, for example), you just have to forget about muscle and visual feedback altogether and send out exactly the right command sequence to the muscle in the first place. You plan carefully for ballistic movements, so that you don't have to correct the command sequence in midcourse. Throwing farther may be better, and faster may be its critical mechanism, but it sure does make life hard for the poor brain.

Take a simple overhand throw, with the body considered rigid just to simplify things down to the arm's motion. You cock your elbow, hand atop your shoulder grasping a rock, and then contract both sets of muscles: the extensor muscle groups that uncock the elbow, and the flexor muscle groups that cock it. Contracting both opposing sets (known as co-contraction) serves to stretch the muscle tendons, storing energy in them just as if you'd stretched a spring. You keep the two tensions large, but exactly equal so that the arm doesn't move in either direction. Then the brain gives the command to stop contracting the flexor muscles. And the elbow starts uncocking, both the stored elastic energy and the active forces from the ever more active extensor muscles serving to accelerate your forearm so that it moves faster and faster in its upward arc. At some point, the rock you're grasping flies loose. The time at which this happens is under the control of your hand muscles. Essentially, you want to open your fingers at just the right moment and so let the rock slip free. Imagine a robot hand, flapping open upon command. Human hands are more complicated than that, but whatever the thumb and finger muscles do together has to be timed with a precision equal to when that command would be given to a robot hand.

And what is the "right time," the right moment for releasing the rock? That depends on how far away your target is. And how big it is. Release too soon, and the rock will lob too high, going too far and impacting behind the target. Release too late, and the rock will hit the ground in front of the target. The right time is whenever the resulting trajectory will cause the rock to come down somewhere on the target.

Suppose that the target is a rabbit—the rabbit is facing you calmly eating a bit of greenery. Little does it know, evolution not having informed it yet, that you're a new-fangled action-at-a-distance predator. The standard rabbit, let us say, is 10 centimeters high and 20 centimeters from front to rear (never mind its width, since that turns out not to be as crucial). The range of correct times for release (in analogy with a moon rocket, we can call it the "launch window") are those between an early release where the rock travels a bit too far and hits the top rear of the rabbit, and a late release that would land the rock on the rabbit's front paws.

Now it is a simple matter for any freshman physics student to calculate the rock's trajectory. So just plug in the numbers for various different release times and see which ones hit the target. This is equivalent to what artillery gunners do in "walking" the impact point of a shell onto the target, except that they just adjust the angle of the barrel. But that's essentially what adjusting release time is doing: release early and your rock will head upwards at an initial angle; release late and it'll head out horizontally instead. Intermediate release times are just the intermediate angles.

To hit a standard rabbit from 4 meters away is pretty easy; most of us could do it with a minor amount of practice, since the distance is the length of a subcompact automobile. Just imagine standing alongside the front bumper and throwing at a stuffed rabbit sitting on the ground near the rear bumper. For 4-meter throws, the average launch window is 11 milliseconds. This is about as long as a camera shutter stays open when set at 1/100 second. Release anywhere within that 11-millisecond window, and the rock will hit the standard rabbit somewhere on its front or top.

Now move the rabbit so that it is twice as far away: two small cars, parked bumper-to-bumper. Throwing will become much harder, though most of us nonexperts would succeed with some practice. You're throwing twice as fast, so you expect the launch window to halve just from that. But the rabbit also presents a smaller-looking target to you; at twice the distance, the target angle between the top rear and bottom front of the rabbit will more than halve. Alas, this target angle drops down to a quarter of its original value. So it comes as no surprise that the launch window at 8 meters has dropped to 1.4 millisecond, 1/8 of its value for the 4-meter throw. You have to get eight times better in your timing to throw twice as far with equal success rates. That's why it's so much harder.

Now real machines are not infinitely accurate. Neither are we. When we practice and manage to hit the target at double the distance, we've done something to improve the precision of our brain-and-muscle combination. We've improved our timing.

Accustomed as some of us are to clocks that can split a second into a billion equal parts, it may come as some surprise that nerve cells aren't capable of doing this too. In fact, as clocks, they're pretty poor, jittery as can be. But brains still pull off some great feats of timing, as an expert thrower demonstrates. How? They use lots of jittery cells, all trying to do the same job.

Hearts use the same trick. Take a single embryonic heart cell, resting on the bottom of a glass dish. If one uses a microscope, it can be seen twitching a few times every second. It isn't a very regular beat, with some intervals between beats being twice as long as others. Played through a loudspeaker, a lone cell sounds like rain on the roof: highly irregular. Now take another such cell and push it over until it touches the first cell. Heart cells are not only sticky, but they exchange electrical currents with one another. Both cells were beating independently of one another when separate, but once stuck together, their beats synchronize—they beat together. And a funny thing happens: the beat starts sounding more regular. There aren't as many long pauses or short, quick double beats.

Just keep sticking cells together (how to build a heart!) and one will soon have a mass of synchronously contracting cells. And the beat will get more and more rhythmic, ticking along with great regularity, each interval pretty much the same as the one before. It sounds like a rapidly-dripping faucet, not at all like the irregular beat of the single, isolated cell. The jitter—the range of fluctuation—narrows by half when you quadruple the number of cells in the cluster. When there are a hundred cells in the cluster, the fluctuation range is ten times narrower than for one cell by itself. More and more is better and better. To make a really rhythmic beat, use lots of cells. Our regular heartbeats come from thousands of heart cells (in a region called the sino-atrial node) all beating together like this, setting the pace for the rest of the heart to follow. If only a few dozen pacemaker cells were on the job in the sino-atrial node, our heartbeats might be rather erratic, bouncing around between too fast and too slow.

Nerve cells can use the same trick, solving the precision

problem with large numbers of cells, even though they don't visibly twitch like muscle cells (to a neurophysiologist, a muscle cell is just a nerve cell that can also contract). A nerve cell can beat in an electrical rhythm (you can hear it by hooking the cell up to a hi-fi system; it sounds like a dripping water faucet going tap-tap-tap), and that's how cells count time. To make a large number of nerve cells "beat" together in synchrony, you don't have to literally stick them together; nerve cells are much more sophisticated than heart cells, and their wiring diagrams can accomplish the same end. And it doesn't even take special, fancy wiring patterns—the simplest kind of parallel summing circuit will suffice to create really precise beats, timing with any degree of accuracy you need.

All it takes is lots of cells. To make a fluctuation range 8 times narrower, as you need to do to double your throwing distance to a standard target, you just use 64 times as many nerve cells as you used before. To triple the throwing distance, all you need is 729 times as many cells. This isn't just square law for a growth curve: the number of nerve cells needed rises as the sixth power of throwing distance. Accurate throwing has an insatiable appetite for more and more synchronized nerve cells.

MORE NEURONS, BUT FROM WHERE does one get so many additional timing neurons? This isn't just a tripling that we're talking about. In the short run, I suspect you borrow them from elsewhere in the brain, the primary region getting the neighbors to come and lend a hand.

Where are we talking about? Rapid movement sequences like hammering and throwing are likely orchestrated from a region of the left brain in the frontal lobe, just in front of the motor strip for the hand and arm; besides this premotor region of cerebral cortex, the cerebellum (which also enlarges nearly three times from ape to human) probably plays a major role in coordinating things too. When the cells in those areas have done their collective best to reduce the jitter, you perhaps create an even bigger circuit by using other regions of the frontal lobe, or perhaps by borrowing from the language areas of the temporal and parietal lobes. These regions have lots of connections with one another; you just turn off the business-as-usual connections and turn on the connections that create the massive parallel circuit that synchronizes them all. That means that you might not be able to talk and throw accurately at the same time. Or listen carefully to speech while launching. This suggests that as you concentrate and get set to throw, you're creating a really big parallel brain circuit just for the throwing command sequence. After the big push, the circuits relax and go back to their separate business as usual—it says here, with more than a little guessing and wishful thinking.

And so evolution might be a matter of selecting for brains that are wired in a manner that allows such temporary synchronizations to occur. Do any developmental trends hold out the promise of facilitating that? Yes, indeed. Early in development, it sometimes appears as if everything is connected to everything else, with many connections eliminated later. As I mentioned the other day when we got to discussing cell death, neurons from nearly all brain areas send connections down to the spinal cord; later in development, most of these connections have been broken, with only those from the motor strip remaining. The other connections have been somehow pruned or withdrawn. Thus, juvenilization might also select for wider connections, if this ontogeny observation can be so extrapolated. This fits nicely with a new theory for mammalian brain development; the neuroanatomist Sven Ebbesson says that things are indeed wired up widely at first, then selectively "pruned" (my word) to more clearly define the subsystems of the adult brain. Freezing the brain development at an immature stage might thus maintain a more widespread system of connections useful for those occasions when large numbers of neurons are needed in parallel, to gang up on a throwing problem.

But evolution could also just select those variants with brains that have extra neurons in the particularly important places, such as premotor cortex. And the easy way to do this is also through juvenilization: rather than selectively increasing the size of the premotor area, it may be easier to simply make the entire brain bigger. The other regions of the brain would thus get increases in their cell population "for free," even though they hadn't contributed to the cause. This might improve hearing, or memory for faces, or any number of functions unrelated to the throwing skills.

Thus, those prehuman adults who had greater juvenilization might have made better hunters than those with less-than-average juvenilization. A bigger brain might, in its own right, have been useful for the throwing skills so exposed to natural selection via hunting success and failure.

The growth-curve for throwing-style hunting being what it is, there is no danger that this selection effect would saturate in the manner of hairlessness. Faster and faster is always better and better for throwing. Bigger and bigger brains can be faster and faster with the required timing precision. Thus bigger is faster is better. At last, a suitable mechanistic scenario for bigger-is-better.

This mechanism is, of course, only one possible way in which a bigger brain might also be a better brain, or in which a bigger brain might have arisen incidentally as a consequence of the success of some other juvenilized traits. But it fits the recipe for rapid evolution especially well: it provides an immediate reward in hunting success for any bigger-brained variants that come along from genetic permutations, and the hunting success is particularly important during winters and ice ages, capable of repeatedly driving the selection cycle. Bigger brains for better throwing looks like a fast-track for evolution. Whether other tracks are even faster remains to be seen.

> The hand is the cutting edge of the mind.
>
> The polymath
> JACOB BRONOWSKI

MATKATAMIBA'S AMPHITHEATER has a Muav floor with a series of cracks running along parallel to one another. Indeed, they almost subdivide the floor into a great checkerboard. Aha, the map says that the Matkatamiba Syncline is near here, so the Muav was probably flexed and cracked during some ancient upheaval.

A throwing contest has developed, using my poor hat for a target. We are standing on one crack and trying to hit the target at the next crack, then moving the target back another crack to make things more difficult as the contestants get better and better with practice. Now if only chimps had learned to hold such throwing contests, they might have indeed bootstrapped themselves up.

PARENTAL PRIDE BEING WHAT IT IS, you need to discount some of my enthusiasm for the throwing theory. I stumbled on it while throwing rocks at the beach one day. Back in the dark ages, when I was doing my Ph.D. dissertation, I happened to study the sources of jittery beats in the nerve cells of the spinal cord that run the limb muscles (the primary source turned out to be "bumps" from the small, but quantized, inputs to the cells—not unlike the random walk of the Brownian Motion). I was, though I didn't realize it at the time, taking a lesson from Charles Darwin: he recognized that the motive force in evolution was not the species type but the individual variations about that average type. If you like, the "jitter." I had investigated whether there was something important about the variations in cell timing, rather than the average time. I didn't strike gold at the time, but learned a lot and filed it away in my head.

Sitting on that beach fifteen years later, I knew that individual cells just couldn't time things very accurately, no closer than about 5 parts per hundred. And my instincts told me that throwing surely needed better timing than that—but how good?

You don't have to take slow-motion movies of baseball pitchers to answer that question—just work backwards from the physics of trajectories. So when I got home from the beach, I finally cranked up the computer and did the physics calculations, though it turned out that the needed equations weren't quite the ones in the physics textbooks (they assumed initial conditions that were too simple). There was a little delay while I derived the equations from scratch, starting from Newton's Laws and using integral calculus. And then wrote a computer program in BASIC.

Sure enough, throwing sometimes required an accuracy more like 1 part per thousand. And so how did circuits of many nerve cells become more accurate than an individual cell? Then I remembered reading about those heart cells in the *Biophysical Journal*, recalled reading in *Science* about some computer simulations of common nerve-cell circuits involved with circadian rhythms in sand fleas. Lots and lots of cells could do the job, and thus there might be a way in which bigger brains were better. Later, I remembered what the mathematicians call the Law of Large Numbers, and discovered that the physiological examples were just manifestations of this fundamental law. It seems that nature discovered the Law of Large Numbers even before Bernoulli did in 1713, using it to make heartbeats regular and throwing more accurate.

IF BIG BRAINS DEPEND ON HUNTING SKILLS and the hunters were male, then does that mean we owe our human brain development to our male ancestors? That's too simplistic. A little knowledge is a dangerous thing, and all that.

Even if men did 95 percent of the hunting, the occasions when women hunted could have been of crucial importance. Hunting is a hazardous business, what with the dangers of being gored by an animal or freezing in a storm when caught out in the open. It was surely not uncommon for the man to fail to return from the hunt. Then it would have fallen to the mother to provide all of the food, and in wintertime her hunting skills would have been the only way to stave off starvation. Even if infrequently exercised, female throwing skills would have been used in life-or-death situations rather than everyday ones.

But of more fundamental importance is that the evolutionary base for the throwing skills is probably the same rapid muscle-sequencing abilities that chimpanzees use for hammering on nuts. They involve the same arm motion, the same precise control of a ballistic movement, only without the release and with the elbow held lower. Since female chimps do more than 92 percent of the most skillful hammering tasks, we may owe much of our throwing skills to female ancestors; the subsequent brain enlargement may only have duplicated these basic ballistic sequencing circuits many times over. The neurological foundation for throwing may be female, even if males make more regular use of the extra copies in tandem. Which is more important, the foundation or its overelaboration? That seems a useless question.

TODAY'S ONLY BIG RAPID is rated an 8, and it is our last rapid of any size until we get to Lava Falls the day after tomorrow, another 30 miles downriver. The rapid's name brings to mind an incident that makes the boatmen very careful about how they rig their boats, and keeps them wearing a belt knife while going through big rapids. In 1967, a boatman was drowned here when his motor rig flipped and his lifejacket became entangled with the boat ropes. The passengers all survived.

MILE 150
Upset Rapid

The small oar-powered boats are rigged so their load remains intact if they flip; if there are no loose ropes to start with, there shouldn't be any after a flip, if the boat has been rigged correctly. When three of the big motor rigs flipped in Crystal in 1983 during the Fool's Flood, their ice chests, black bags, and ammo cans were found scattered downstream over a hundred-mile stretch; many probably wound up buried in the mud flats of Lake Mead.

We all got very wet in Upset, but stayed upright. Our last real warmup for Lava Falls. And its black hole. Well, its alleged black hole.

Sinyala Rapid down at Mile 153 is only rated a 4, and the boatmen consider it permissible to let passengers swim some such rapids if they have an overwhelming urge to do so. The river water has had three days since its release from Lake Dominy to warm up, and it's almost tolerable now. The air's downright hot.

Rosalie had for days been contemplating swimming a rapid. She had, I thought, a certain morbid fascination with the subject (I myself have never been the least bit interested in swimming a rapid). She decided that she was going to do it, having her adrenaline still up from our trip through Upset Rapid. So Jimmy told her how to do it: she should keep her feet out in front of her, so as to push away from rocks. And should keep her mouth shut.

Rosalie tightened up her lifejacket. With a great whoop she jumped overboard and went bobbing down the river, Jimmy keeping the boat just behind her and off to one side.

All was fine, with only minor complaints about the water temperature, until we went into the first big wave of the rapid.

Which, when one's face is so near the surface, must have looked a lot larger than we were used to seeing from up in the boat.

Quite audibly, we heard a quick, breathless "Hail Mary, full of. . ." and about that time, a large cold wave struck Rosalie full in the face. She came up sputtering, "Holy Shit!"

We were all still laughing when we picked her up below the rapid and hauled her back aboard. She didn't understand what was so funny, and asked what we were laughing about. So we told her about the interesting sentence that she had constructed. And Rosalie turned a deep shade of purple. Proving that with sufficient cause superimposed upon the right education, one can successfully blush despite a sunburn.

I then commented that her supplementary motor area must have really been disinhibited, something of an in-group joke among the more clinical neurobiologists among us, and which, being a stroke and paralysis expert, Rosalie understood just fine. But we had to explain it to everyone else. Most people know about the language center being located in the left side of the brain, out just above the left ear. But there is a second language area in the middle of the brain, just above the corpus callosum, known as the supplementary motor area. The two areas are far away from each other. People who have strokes that leave them unable to speak or understand what others say (aphasia) can usually still swear like sailors, much to the distress of their families. The only strokes that leave someone entirely mute are those of the supplementary motor area, not those of the main language cortex. And so the swearing center of the brain (it's also Sir John Eccles' most recent candidate for the seat of the soul, but not for that reason) tells you something rather interesting about the origins of language.

In monkeys, the brain areas that have something to do with monkey's vocalizations—cries and barks and chattering—are not the areas that you would guess from a knowledge of human language. In the monkeys it is that supplementary motor area that is the main piece of cortex involved in vocalization; all of the cortex homologous to the main human language area seems to have little to do with monkey vocalizations. So it looks as if swearing in humans is analogous to the monkey's vocalizations—and indeed they are both rather emotional kinds of utterances. People who say swearing is rather primitive and unsophisticated may be more correct than they know.

But this leaves you wondering from whence the main human language cortex arose in evolution, if human speech didn't build on top of the more common emotional vocalizations. If you don't know, one starting hypothesis would be to assume that an adjacent area expanded, and then later specialized in language. So

LEFT BRAIN LANGUAGE CENTERS

Medial language area in Supplementary Motor Cortex seems homologous to cortical region for species-specific cries and calls.

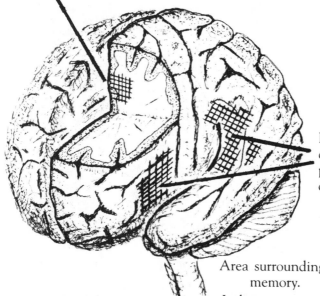

Lateral language area has central core devoted to detecting sound sequences, producing oral-facial movement sequences.

Area surrounding core is involved in short-term verbal memory.

In between core and surround are isolated cortical areas affecting grammar, reading, naming.

to what is the main human language cortex a neighbor? Most obviously, its neighbors are the auditory cortex, where sounds are deciphered. And the motor cortex for running the throat, mouth, lips and face, which is in turn right next door to the motor strip for the hand and arm. So those become the logical candidates for the origins of human language specializations. Did we get especially good at hearing? Or mouth movements? Or maybe hand and arm movements? Did language then build atop one such improvement to achieve our elaborate language abilities?

□   □   □

While chimpanzee calls do serve to convey basic information about some situations and individuals, they cannot for the most part be compared to a spoken language. Man by means of words can communicate abstract ideas; he can benefit from the experiences of others without having to be present at the time; he can make intelligent cooperative plans. All the same, when humans come to an exchange of emotional feelings, most people fall back on the old

MILE 155

The Ledges

Tenth Campsite

chimpanzee-type of gestural communication—the cheering pat, the embrace of exuberance, the clasp of hands. And on the occasions when we also use words, we often use them in rather the same way as a chimpanzee utters his calls—simply to convey the emotion we feel at that moment. . . . This usage of words on the emotional level is as different from oratory, from literature, from intelligent conversation, as are the grunts and hoots of chimpanzees.

JANE GOODALL, *In the Shadow of Man*, 1971

THIS PLACE LOOKS LIKE a Cambrian resort hotel, its ledges forming suites on three levels stacked up above the river. There is a seep dripping quietly in its middle, building up travertine. There is greenery around the wet rock. The Canyon is narrow here, the open sky almost looking like a skylight in a roof. There are a series of scalloped outcrops into the river itself, looking like a series of small piers in a waterfront development. It's all enough to make one look around for the registration desk. And for the little bronze plaque that tells who the architect was.

The suites are in natural caves formed by overhangs. That means they're hot, and Dan and I have learned by now. If instead we pick part of the flat Muav platform next to the river's edge, so as to get the breeze, we run the risk of losing things into the rushing river. I have already littered the river, a full can of soda got away from me and rolled in. Everyone is carefully weighting down anything that can blow away. And as usual, none of the rooms has a private bath. The toilet has been located a two-story climb up a rock-filled gully. It was hard enough to find at dusk; I hate to imagine someone looking for it by flashlight during the night. We also have to watch out for the wall-to-wall carpeting. This is travertine-coated Muav we're walking on; Gary warns us to keep our shoes on.

We were lucky to get this camp; we can't camp at Havasu (or any other of the places that get heavy day use, such as Redwall Cavern, the Little Colorado, Elves Chasm, and Deer Creek), and there is only one more campsite before we get there—a little spot downstream called Last Chance Camp, which has all the disadvantages of The Ledges plus being smaller and more precarious to navigate at night.

Neither place has any sand beach. The Muav ledge just drops off steeply into the river, which is therefore flowing past the shore much more rapidly than usual, without any sand to slow it down. Gary suggested that we wear lifejackets if making a nocturnal visit to the river's edge, just in case we were to slip.

PLAYING CHARADES reminds us that nonverbal communication is quite sufficient for many purposes. One can tell a lot just from a person's posture. Moving toward someone, or staring at them, carries a message, as does turning one's back. Gestures are an elaboration of this, where hand and arm movements convey additional information. Facial expression is particularly important in monkeys and apes; one reason why we find chimpanzees "so human" is that they hug and kiss, raise their eyebrows, pucker their lips, and sometimes look sad. And sometimes angry. Human brains have a region of the right brain that specializes in interpreting facial expressions; if the area is put temporarily out of commission, the patient will mistakenly label a happy face as sad, or a sad face as disgusted, enraged or neutral. The extensive communication between a human mother and her baby makes use of postures and facial expressions, plus some soothing words whose function may be prelinguistic, and since mothers tend to hold infants in their left visual field (which reports first to the right brain), we surmise that this emotional-facial-judgment region is being extensively used in this elementary form of human communication.

Verbal communication adds to all this, being particularly important when two animals are out of sight of one another, as when up in the trees—or have a particularly urgent message to deliver, concerning the arrival of a leopard. But when we start counting up the different types of vocalizations, we may wind up with a dozen different messages in a monkey, several dozen in a chimp. It is a long way from human language.

Human language doesn't utilize that many more basic sounds than in a chimpanzee vocabulary (though our phonemes are different, mostly shorter). Instead, we have evolved the trick of stringing those sounds together, with the order of the sounds being especially important for conveying information. We interpret a string of sounds terminated by a silent pause as a word, fitting that phoneme string to an auditory schema in our brains and coming up with a set of associations from memory—the connotations of the word.

Just as a string of phonemes can make a word, so can a string of words make a sentence. And the order of the words is very significant—the interesting sentence that Rosalie constructed (and she blushed again when we told the story after dinner, then threw a cookie at me with considerable accuracy) would not have been embarrassing had the order of the phrases been reversed. We interpret the word string using mental rules for word order, so that we interpret "Bill called Rosalie" differently from "Rosalie called Bill." The subject-verb-object order of a simple direct English sentence is not universal; Japanese, for example, assumes a subject-object-verb order and classical Arabic assumes a verb-subject-object construction. One of the things that comes with learning a language is a set of expectations about word order, which enables us to interpret the sentence in the same way as other speakers of our language do. Those expectations regarding word order are called grammar, or syntax.

So the brain needs a greatly improved sequencing ability for language, and a trainable memory for sequential order, but those capabilities need not be special to language per se. Just as the right brain has an emotional reputation, the left brain (more exactly, the language-dominant hemisphere) has a general reputation in humans for being obsessed with temporal sequences. Language is only part of it: rapid movement sequences of hand and arm, whether on the right or left side, are controlled from left brain. Ditto for oral-facial movement sequences: it is left brain that controls both sides of the face in sequential facial expressions. It is the left auditory cortex that specializes in detecting rapid sound sequences, whether they are language, musical phrases, or nonsense noise sequences. And it is the left brain that puts together the string of motor commands for such rapid ballistic movements as hammering and throwing (they are the most strongly right-handed of skills). Perhaps it is sequencing that is the key function, and language is just one of its latter-day applications.

As far as we can tell, human language results from a certain type of mental organization, not simply from a high level of intelligence.

Noam Chomsky
Language and Mind, 1965

LINGUISTICS HAS NOT HAD any traditional relationship to biology, and it perhaps took some audacity for Noam Chomsky to propose that there is a "language bioprogram" (as it is currently called) in the brains of all humans, and that this "innate bias" accounts for the many puzzling similarities in diverse languages and the ways in which they are learned and in the characteristic mistakes made while learning them. The bioprogram does not supply word order—as can be seen from the way languages differ around the world—but it does supply case relations (agent of, goal of) and grammatical functions (subject of, direct object of).

In many ways, Chomsky's proposal for a uniquely human "language organ" in the brain is merely using Descartes' "language is uniquely human" dictum to explain such regularities in the comparative study of languages. It has been criticized as being an *organum ex machina*, in analogy to the way in which ancient Greek playwrights solved thorny plot problems by bringing in the gods, who lectured the players and audience and resolved the difficulty. There was literally a "god machine" in classical tragedies, an elevated lecture platform on wheels that was rolled onto the stage and from which the gods spoke. Thus the phrase *deus ex machina* ("god in a machine") has come to signify any particularly contrived resolution of a storyteller's difficulty; *organum ex machina* is a commentary on Chomsky's language organ made by people who think the explanation contrived, that language may instead be an emergent principle, arising from the coordinated use of other mental facilities such as cognition, memory, perception—and, I would add to the head of the list, sequencing.

Someone asked about whether Neanderthals could talk, at what stage of hominid evolution the speech apparatus was sufficient? Barbara explained how the issue came up (on most campuses, if one has a question about some aspect of primate anatomy, the local expert may be in the anthropology department). The upper respiratory tract changes a lot in mammals and also in human infants during development: the larynx, or voice-box, moves down in the neck. When the larynx is up high in the neck, the animal can simultaneously breathe and swallow, thanks to an interesting criss-cross anatomical arrangement called the piriform sinus, which solves an earlier design blunder: the trachea being in front of the esophagus rather than behind it. Until about 18 to 24 months of age, a human infant has a high larynx, much as do most mammals. Newborns breathe, swallow, and vocalize much as do the chimps and monkeys, for example. Sometime during the baby's second year, however, the larynx starts to move down, and this dramatically alters the way in which the baby breathes, swallows, and vocalizes. In this lower position, the larynx does not allow for simultaneous swallowing and breathing; rather, the two must be carefully coordinated to avoid aspirating food and water. And suffocation.

It is not known why the larynx descends. It is surely not part of juvenilization, for example. It has all sorts of disadvantages, such as choking when the coordination fails. But there is one lovely advantage: the vibrations arising from the vocal cords can be modulated by the shape of the throat, tongue, and lips over a much wider range of sounds than is possible with a high larynx. Maybe this is why babies cannot talk sooner than they do (they certainly hammer and throw at an earlier age!). But that also suggests that perhaps our ancestors lacked the human range of sound production too.

How does one investigate prehuman sounds, given that the larynx does not fossilize? The comparative anatomists have discovered an interesting correlation between the larynx position and the shape of the bottom of the skull, which does fossilize. The base of the skull is rather flat in most mammals and in human infants before the larynx descends. In humans after the descent, the base of the skull becomes flexed. Thus the obvious question (in retrospect!) is: When in hominid evolution does the flexed base of the skull show up? Australopithecines have flat bases much like the chimps and monkeys. *Homo erectus* shows signs of incipient flexing, suggesting that its larynx was moving down and its vocal repertoire improving. Some people see this as meaning that human language had to wait for crucial anatomical developments.

But, as was pointed out rather forcefully in our discussion, chimps have dozens of different vocalizations, not too different from the number of phonemes that any one human language uses. They might not be our phonemes, but chimps can sure tell the difference between them all. What chimps lack is the practice of stringing them together in a meaningful special order. The *deus ex machina* of the people who try, and fail, to teach chimps and gorillas a spoken language is that the ape larynx is insufficient for producing our range of vocal expression. So what? They can produce—and distinguish—almost as many elementary vocalizations as we ordinarily use, and if they had the proper neural sequencing machinery, should therefore able to string them together in an orderly way to achieve the benefits that we accrue from this clever coding method for conveying information.

We might have to learn their "phonemes" just as we learn those of the dolphins and whales, and it might be a slower language in which to speak a long sentence than human languages, but they'd have a language if they could just master the sequencing problems: producing a sequence; listening to a sequence and holding it in their short-term memory long enough to match it up with sequence schemata (word-order rules) in long-term memory. And doing their planning in terms of such sequence schemata, just as we do while talking to ourselves, would convey to them more of what we call consciousness.

One can't tell whether apes have sequential language from the failures and half-successes of teaching sign language to apes, because such gestural languages do not usually rely on sequential ordering; in many sign languages, several different parts of the message may be expressed simultaneously, just as in our ordinary nonverbal communication methods.

It wasn't vocalizations that made the language revolution— it was sequential ordering and its rules. Maybe the chimps sequence their facial expressions and body postures instead. If there were rules about the order of elements, that greatly multiplied the number of possible messages that were sent, we'd have to concede that the chimps had a real language with syntax, even if it didn't involve sound.

But, of course, emotional speech doesn't utilize the rules of sequential speech: it's mainly one-word or stock phrases which aren't varied. Therefore, Rosalie pointed out, we were applying the wrong rules when stringing together her interesting construction in the rapid: each phrase stood independently, it isn't fair to string them together for an additional meaning since they were emotional speech.

Quite right, we agreed. We'd take back our laughs, we said, if we could watch her take back her blush. Like a movie run backwards.

SEQUENCE IS THE *SINE QUA NON* of language. So if you want to start looking at the neighbors of the lateral language cortex for cues as to how it developed, out there away from emotional language predecessors, you might want to ask about the extent to which sequence is important for each neighboring function.

Auditory cortex—well, the most prominent sound sequences (as opposed to single sounds) in the ape's environment are those emotional vocalizations of other apes and monkeys and leopards, at least until you get to language itself. Escalating sequences of vocalizations signal increasing social tension. There might be an intermediate sound sequence skill that's important between the apes and us, but we couldn't think of an example.

Then there's the motor cortex and premotor regions of the frontal lobe; the premotor cortex in particular has a "planning sequential movements" reputation. Down at the bottom of the motor strip is the control area for the larynx and pharynx, mouth and lips. Now at some point, we had to learn a lot of breathing regulation for diving (though to simply override the breathing rhythm, inhibiting it for a minute or so, doesn't take fancy circuitry). And it probably took some new coordination of breathing and swallowing whenever the larynx started moving down, along about the time of *Homo erectus*. But things like breathing and swallowing sequences usually aren't handled in the cerebral cortex—they're handled down in the brainstem, closer to the spinal cord. So again, short of language itself, our group had a hard time coming up with any suitable examples of sequential movements of those structures that would have been exposed to selection pressures during hominid evolution.

Next on the motor-strip map comes the face, then the thumb and other fingers, the hand, the wrist, the arm, and the shoulder. You can find language regions in the frontal lobe just in

Language, like other cognitive structures, is useful for some tasks and worthless for others. I cannot tell you, because I do not know, what my language prevents me from knowing. Language is itself like a work of art; it selects, abstracts, exaggerates, and orders.

ANNIE DILLARD
Living by Fiction, 1982

front of such regions of motor strip, so it isn't getting to be too far away. This premotor cortex, with its sequential reputation, has particularly extensive interconnections with the wrist area of motor cortex.

It is possible that language developed through serial improvements in hand and arm gestures, then in facial expression, and finally in spoken sequences. Or the sequencer abilities in the neural machinery might originally have had nothing to do with language or gestures, only being used later for sequencing sounds. And the most prominent rapid-movement sequences are for hand and arm motions such as clubbing, hammering, and throwing. They certainly are exposed to natural selection, though each has a different growth curve; some, such as hammering, may not have improved much over chimpanzee abilities. And one may have improved as a result of improvements in another; converting a throw into a hammering motion (or vice versa), for example, doesn't take much change in the motor sequencer. The fast-track hypothesis provides one way of dealing with many interrelated causes, and throwing seems to win that conceptual competition so far, though the results are only beginning to come in.

And so, as the evening talk wound down, we were left facing a hypothesis that assigns our rapid acquisition of language, as well as the rapid growth of our brain, to getting better and better at a non-language sensorimotor skill: throwing rocks and spears at prey animals. Starting from general philosophical principles about human qualities in Descartes' manner, you'd never have stumbled upon such a hypothesis. Nor, starting from the knowledge base of linguistics, would you ever arrive there.

The ancient question is still awaiting an answer: What features in our brain account for our humanity, our musical creativity, infinitely varied artifacts, subtlety of humor, sophisticated projection (in chess, politics, and business), our poetry, ecstasy, fervor, contorted morality, and elaborate rationalization?

The neurobiologist
THEODORE H. BULLOCK, 1984

Assigning a major role in language evolution to throwing will probably remain heresy for a long time, even if it turns out to be the least awkward solution to the difficulties. Given the usual fate of most scientific hypotheses, it may well turn out to be another *deus ex machina* when we are farther down the road. But maybe it is the fast track, maybe language is an emergent property of brain circuits facilitating fancy time sequences, itself selected by hunting success, out in the fringe subpopulations where selection was harder and speciation was easier.

I JUST WOKE UP from a wild dream, thanks to some noise nearby (so I'm now scribbling in my notebook by the light of a dim penlight). My wife, in my dream, was looking out the window and remarking upon a dead mouse or shrew that the cat had hauled home as a present. It was left just outside the cat's basement entrance to the house, as if the cat had second thoughts about its acceptability inside the house. Katherine went outside to pick it up, and I came over and leaned out the window to look. It was some strange animal we hadn't seen before. It had a tail (bushy and striped, however, most unratlike). But its head, as she described it, "has a high domed forehead, just what they need for eating cheese."

What? And then I recalled, in the dream, that some animals like pigs have special head adaptations for rooting around, butting their heads into the earth in search of roots and other such goodies. Those side-projecting teeth are also what make piglets so dangerous to other piglets competing for the same teat (farmers routinely clip them to prevent bloody sibling rivalry). Why did the rat-shrew-whatever have a high domed forehead? I had, in the dream, a good knowledge about the inside of the backward-sloping skull of such animals (it comes with being a neurophysiologist), and so knew that it was strange for any of them to have domed foreheads. Except humans. And the animal, whatever it was, certainly wasn't even vaguely human.

The domed forehead was, my zoologist-wife said in my dream, for butting into a block of cheese, pounding off a chunk so that it could be carried away to eat elsewhere. (I now recognize this take-the-money-and-run scenario as coming from the pictures I've recently seen of chimpanzees carrying off bananas into the forest to hide them from the other chimps, so they can be eaten in peace).

But pounding with the forehead on a block of cheese? Good grief! What animal does that? At that point I woke up.

And I lay there in the moonlight trying to puzzle out where I could have possibly gotten the notion of animals pounding on something cheese-like with their heads—in which the shape of the head was somehow important for pounding. Had I really invented something entirely out of whole cloth, or did I really have those concepts already in my brain from some source? The striped tail was easy—that was appropriated from the ringtail episode we discussed the other morning back at Tapeats Creek. But the head . . . ?

It has finally come to me. It wasn't cheese, but wax. The dome-shaped head was the hemispherical shape of the bee's head (well, I do mix up my phyla sometimes). They pound their heads against the wax walls of the tunnels through their honeycomb. What's so interesting is that hexagons miraculously appear when a lot of bees are all pounding on the same piece of wax with their round heads. Suppose some miners were tunneling through soft clay, and in order to shore up the walls in the network of tunnels, they butted into the soft walls with their round miner's helmets. And that miners in the neighboring tunnels were doing the same thing, all without coordination, just butting at random. The tunnels would begin to take on a hexagonal shape, quite without anyone intending it to happen. It's an emergent property.

LATER BACK HOME: I located the source of my dream schemata in a scientific journal I'd read just before the river trip:

"A casual observer noting the perfect hexagonal structure of honeycombs is tempted to conclude that the universality and perfection of the hive structure are ensured by 'instinct' or, more specifically, by some kind of innate hexagonal principle responsible for the bee's construction behavior." [I hope no anatomist ever went looking for a hexagon in the bee's brain].

"However, it is now well understood that the hexagonal structure is an inevitable outcome of the 'packing principle,' a mathematical law governing the behavior of spheres packed together at even or random pressure from all angles. The bees' 'innate knowledge of hexagons' need consist of nothing more than a tendency to pack wax with their hemispheric heads. . . ."

"By the same line of argument, grammars [this is from Elizabeth Bates' critique of Chomsky's innate bioprogram for language] may be taken to represent a set of possible solutions to a much more complex formal problem, with some solutions falling out more easily than others on purely formal grounds."

It's an *organum ex machina* criticism, suggesting that a lot of neurons pushing around their electrical signals might have produced some patterns just like the hexagons, and that language makes use of them. Emergent principles, in short, have struck again. And I had a dream about them (I doubt the Anasazi would have). I wonder if any of those Cambrian wormworks we saw had hexagonal cross-sections? Ah, well, back to sleep.

. . . The way we think in dreams is also the way we think when we are awake, all of these images occurring simultaneously, images opening up new images, charging and recharging, until we have a whole new field of image, an electric field pulsing and blazing and taking on the exact character of a migraine aura. . . . Usually we sedate ourselves to keep the clatter down. . . . I don't necessarily mean with drugs, not at all. Work is a sedative. The love of children can be a sedative. . . . Another way we keep the clatter down is by trying to make it coherent, trying to give it the same dramatic shape we give to our dreams; in other words by making up stories. All of us make up stories. Some of us, if we are writers, write these stories down, concentrate on them, worry them, revise them, throw them away and retrieve them and revise them again, focus on them all our attention, all of our emotion, render them into objects.

Joan Didion, 1979

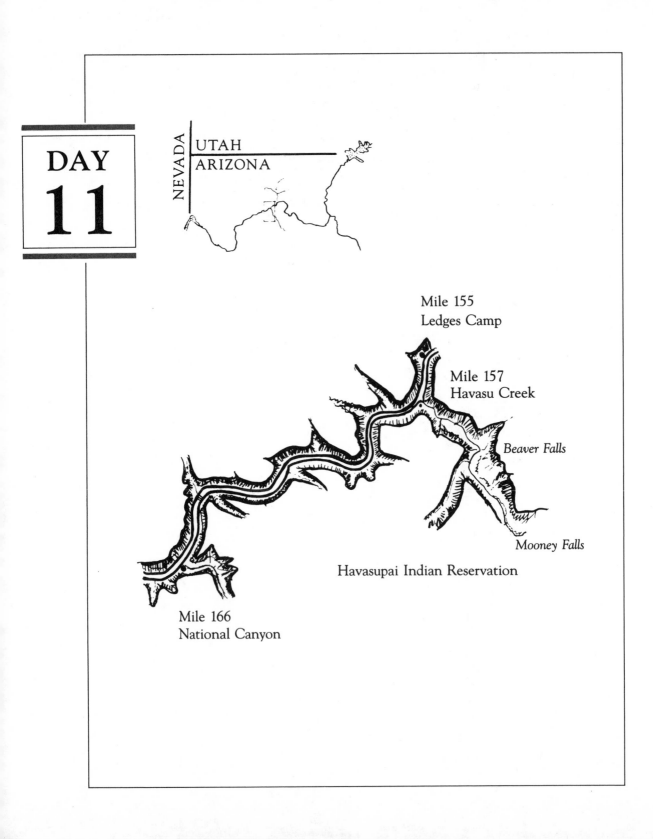

DAY

11

NEVADA

UTAH
ARIZONA

Mile 155
Ledges Camp

Mile 157
Havasu Creek

Beaver Falls

Mooney Falls

Havasupai Indian Reservation

Mile 166
National Canyon

ONE TROUBLE with sleeping at the river's edge is that other people arrive in the middle of the night and spread their air mattresses, having finally been driven out of their hot suites. But the place, by morning light, really does look like the dream of some resort-hotel architect.

At breakfast, Michelle DuBois told of her great discovery last night before I had a chance to tell them of mine. "You know, the other night, before I fell asleep, I looked at the stars for a long time. It was just incredibly clear out, except for one long, thin cloud. Then last night, when I looked at the stars again, there was that cloud again. The same funny, long transparent cloud. In the same place. Now, I thought, how can that be?"

"And then it dawned on me," Michelle said, knocking her head with her hand, "that's not a cloud, that is the goddamned Milky Way galaxy. I must not have seen it for, well, more than ten years, living in the Boston suburbs." And it seems as if half of our breakfast companions have had the same experience on this trip, seeing the Milky Way and not recognizing it at first. Now, no Anasazi would forget the Milky Way. One can lose touch with elementary things appallingly easily. We're getting closer to our roots, but it's hard—I still haven't felt tuned in to the ways that our ancestors thought. I'd still like to be able to see things through their eyes. I can, of course, imagine being a hunter, hauling home the bacon, but life then was surely much more than just that.

WHY COULDN'T LANGUAGE HAVE COME FIRST, with hunting skills then borrowing language's muscle-sequencing machinery to run the limb muscles for throwing? That's a "have your cake and eat it too" proposal that would retain the primacy of language and conscious reasoning as the engine of human uniqueness. I think that there was a general sigh of relief when Ben asked that question. The idea of a skill like throwing as being pivotal in human brain evolution is not usually congenial.

But the problem is speed. The brain enlarged mainly during the last 2 million years—unbelievably rapidly by the standards of natural selection, getting up into the speed range closer to artificial selection. No doubt bigger-is-smarter-is-better could have done the job, eventually. But is there a fast-track such as throwing that worked the gearwheels of evolution much faster than that, giving us a big head start on improving language and sequential reasoning skills?

Thinking our way to success just doesn't have any of the hallmarks of speed. It doesn't work dramatically better in small, isolated groups exposed to the selection cycles of winter every

MILE 155
The Ledges Camp

As an evolutionist I am familiar with that vast sprawling emergent, the universe, and its even more fantastic shadow, life.

LOREN EISELEY
The Night Country, 1971

year and to ice ages every 100,000 years. Thought, and the cultural improvements that go with it, seem to flourish best in situations involving agriculture, cities, educational systems. Those aren't as likely to be found out on the life-is-hard fringes of the population—they flourish in the parts of the world where making a living is somewhat easier, where the population density is higher, where the rumor mill can pass around ideas more easily. Big central populations may be good setups for rapid cultural evolution, but for biological evolution they spell slowdown— no isolation, no small numbers, no repeated do-or-die waves of selection as on the frontiers.

And however useful culture was, it was biological evolution that had to enlarge the brain very rapidly, had to overcome that terrible tendency for big heads to kill their mothers. Our intuitions about cultural evolution just don't carry over to biological evolution very often.

MUSIC EMERGES FROM SOMEWHERE. Someone, sitting up out of sight on one of the ledges above me, is playing a flute while we sit around waiting for the boats to be packed. The clear notes drift out over the water and faintly bounce back to us from the canyon wall across the river. While there is some competition from a canyon wren with its descending trill, the flute music is Bach, its recursive temporal patterns repeating and building, changing and retracing, elaborating its sequence in a soul-satisfying manner.

To what do we owe such an appreciation of music? Music certainly reminds me of language—the same time-sequence elements, with their order all important, with certain underlying patterns repeating and elaborating like the rhythms of poetry. Is music like the hexagonal beehives, one of the consequences of our time-sequencing machinery settling into patterns? Does our language cortex have even more temporal-patterning machinery than it needs for mere spoken language, with music plumbing those depths of our ability to perceive and remember elaborate patterns of time sequence?

When our memories are stirred by the first few bars of a piece of music, we start anticipating the next notes and predicting what's coming. You get a nice feeling from predicting the future like that (provided someone doesn't play the wrong note and sour things). Just as you get a nice feeling when you successfully predict the future in other ways, such as when you let go of a rock at the right time, knowing that it's going to hit the target this time.

And if there are universal rhythms, surely they are due to inborn properties of our brains. Just as deep grammar is, according to Chomsky's comparative study of languages around the world. Some music ought to resonate with the brain's natural rhythms. Resonant rhythms, I should trademark it now. I can hardly wait for composers to start mining the neurophysiological literature for leads to catchy tunes.

□   □   □

The morality of music is faithfulness to the immutable laws of musical gravity (the laws by which melody tends to fall and progressions sink to resolution and rest) and faithfulness to the particular work's emotional energy; that is, the power and thrust of an ascending scale, a blast of trumpets, a crash of drums, a flute note. Great music pushes upward, soars, sinks, fights, and at last gives in or fails or wins or accepts, in sorrow or triumph, with a comic burp, or in some other of its infinite ways. Its devices are inexhaustible, vastly beyond capture in any theory of composition. . . .

JOHN GARDNER, *On Moral Fiction*, 1978

Music is the effort we make to explain to ourselves how our brains work. We listen to Bach transfixed because this is listening to a human mind.

LEWIS THOMAS, *The Medusa and the Snail*, 1979

□   □   □

IS MUSIC ANOTHER EMERGENT PROPERTY of our highly developed time-sequencing abilities? Did it come directly from sequencing—could a child raised without learning any language still appreciate music nonetheless? Or is music dependent upon language, with its more elementary dependence on sequencing abilities?

I don't know. But I think we've become *Homo seriatim.*

There emerges from this view of our brain, with its relentless reorganization and enlargement for ever more precise pitchers, some glimpses of the neural foundations on which we construct our utterances and think our thoughts. The brain may have begun precisely uncocking the elbow while hammering nuts in the tropics. Overextended on the ice age frontiers, however, our ancestors staved off starvation according to their inborn throwing abilities. Those with bigger and better-organized brains survived with the aid of the Law of Large Numbers; eventually even their babies came to instinctively hammer and throw.

From such an evolutionary ratchet jacking up brain size, there arose unbidden our own brain of unbounded potential. From basketball to tennis, this mosaic brain expresses its ancient pleasure in precisely timing a sequence. Transcending its origins, our brain can now create novel sequences using grammar and music. Blind to our foundations, we nonetheless created poetry and reason; with a clearer footing, we can perhaps contemplate how our enlarged consciousness evolved and is evolving.

The animal, by and large, seeks to satisfy his immediate hunger and his reproductive instincts. Man, as his vocabulary and memory extend, becomes apperceptive rather than plain perceptive. He envisages what is out of sight, or an hour off, or a year away. . . . As Hallowell has so ably pointed out . . . the concept of self emerges. The "I" can think of "me." It is here, in intimate association with language, that the quantum jump is glimpsed.

The anthropologist LOREN EISELEY, 1967

Our great human adventure is the evolution of consciousness. We are in this life to enlarge the soul and light up the brain.

The novelist TOM ROBBINS, 1985

MILE 157
Havasu Canyon

THIS IS THE LARGEST of the side canyons. Havasu Creek pours down a gradient leading to a regular series of waterfalls and pools, a staircase that has emerged because of all the dissolved limestone falling out of the water over the years onto tree roots and the like. A quiet travertine staircase of little pools, each spilling over a broad lip, dropping only a meter or less into the next lower pool—it's a series of steps where only a slope existed before, order again developing out of disorder as stored potential energy is dissipated. Beaver Falls, several miles up the canyon, descends into a large travertine pool; it is an underwater wonder of hidden passages one can swim through, of cliffs from which those who like to splash can jump into the quiet waters from heights of one to four stories.

One can find a shady spot and settle down with a good book. Or join the five-mile "death march" to Mooney Falls high up in the canyon; as Fritz said, "It's just run up, look around, and run right back down again." That scared off all but two runners. We made lunch even before eating breakfast this morning, and have sandwiches and fruit in our day packs; we carry loaded water bottles of lemonade, as one can't drink the water.

The main problem is that everyone stops here. There are even hikers in this paradise, a whole troop of Boy Scouts who descended from the South Rim through the Havasupai Indian Reservation, camped above Mooney Falls, and then hiked down to see the river. In addition to our group, I have counted six other noisy river groups already, and it is still mid-morning.

The other big problem, not unrelated to the first, is that the canyon is full of false trails. One thus gets to relive how someone else got lost. Since some of the dead-end trails go up three stories of rock before turning around, it wears one down.

We have found an island retreat in the middle of the creek, cooled by the waters flowing by on both sides, shaded by the trees growing there. This little riparian resort is surrounded by the desert of the lower Canyon, sun-baked, lizard-explored, studded with cactus and ocotillo. Everyone seems to have brought a book with their lunch, but no one is reading. They're either arguing about consciousness or looking at the landscape while keeping an ear cocked.

Ah, a cloud drifts across the sun. Too small to hold much promise of a cool afternoon, but enough to instantly drop the temperature nicely. The sun is not quite overhead here in the weeks near the summer solstice, but it is only about 14° off. And that is hot. You can see why the serious hiking season down here is every season but summer.

There is something soothing about having water flow past me and tumble over a small waterfall not far away, with the breeze wafting back a suggestion of spray with its coolness. I just sit and watch the travertine build up, ever so slowly, in the midst of a few green leaves against a background of red and gray rock.

When I saw any external object, my consciousness that I was seeing it would remain between me and it, enclosing it in a slender, incorporeal outline which prevented me from ever coming directly in contact with the material form.

MARCEL PROUST, *Swann's Way*

Subjective conscious mind is an analog of what is called the real world. It is built up with a vocabulary or lexical field whose terms are all metaphors or analogs of behavior in the physical world. Its reality is of the same order as mathematics. It allows us to shortcut behavioral processes and arrive at more adequate decisions. Like mathematics, it is an operator rather than a thing or repository. And it is intimately bound up with volition and decision.

The psychologist JULIAN JAYNES, 1976

The most important problem which our conscious knowledge should enable us to solve is the anticipation of future events, so that we may arrange our present affairs in accordance with such anticipation.

The 19th-century physicist HEINRICH HERTZ

NEUROBIOLOGISTS CALMLY discussing consciousness? I can hardly believe my ears, but some of my fellow neurobiologists are actually having a civil conversation about consciousness. Another sign that the Canyon has had a mellowing effect on us. This subject ordinarily evokes turned backs, people making for the door. Or vehement verbal rejection, reminiscent of Schopenhauer describing Hegel as "scribbling nonsense and dispensing hollow verbiage that fundamentally and forever rots people's brains."

Ever notice how those commentaries on consciousness in *The New York Review of Books* tend to involve treatises written by eminent physicists, critiqued by Nobel Prize-winning molecular biologists, neither of whom seem to know anything more about consciousness than that gleaned from their own introspection? Brain researchers—as well as professors of chemistry and economics—usually keep quiet about consciousness, and for good reason. But physicists and DNA experts are somehow assumed to have a leg up on the subject—and the brain researchers have, admittedly, left the field open to them. Why?

Now neurobiologists are people who haven't always been neurobiologists. And most of them got into the field because they share the natural urge to understand our Minds. They come with questions such as: What is Consciousness? Is there a Higher Consciousness? What is Meaning? What does it mean to Think? How do I form Beliefs, a Will to do something? Is there a Soul? Is there anything more to it than Materialism? How do I really Know something? What about Intent and Motive, the Self, the Ego? Is there room for Dualism?

It seems obvious that our sensations such as touch and color must be different from our thoughts and feelings, our memories and dreams, our imaginings and insights. We form intentions to do something, our acts are usually voluntary—we think. And so, quite aside from any religious notions of a material body and an immaterial soul that somehow escapes the laws of physics, many people distinguish between mind and brain. But is Mind and Brain a distinction without a difference?

These are, of course, the bread-and-butter questions of philosophy, and while I suppose there are a few people who start out with computers and then move on to the biological "computers" without pondering some of them, such questions are typically how people get interested in the subject of brains. So what goes wrong? Why are hard-core neurobiologists so unlikely to ever mention such Words again, some of us even avoiding "the mind"?

It isn't that we have a superior substitute, and it certainly isn't the reductionism-holism business (think what a great coup it would be for a reductionist to reduce consciousness to a neural circuit!). It is mainly from despair, considering such virtually unanswerable questions to be a waste of time in comparison to a host of more approachable problems. Or coming to see them as meaningless distinctions, prescientific questions posed the wrong way, questions that aren't heuristic—they don't take you forward. Sometimes when one does get an answer out of a neuroscientist, it's a narrow answer. Ask neurologists about consciousness and you'll get a working definition of coma. Ask them about higher consciousness and they'll define it by an ability to paraphrase proverbs (patients with frontal-lobe damage often cannot explain what is meant by "people who live in glass houses shouldn't throw stones"). Pragmatic, important, sometimes life-saving distinctions—but not, I suspect, what most people hoped for.

It all reminds one of behavioral psychology's complete denial of consciousness. And of John Dewey's observation that philosophy progresses not by solving problems but by abandoning them.

The reasons for bypassing the philosophical questions do have something of the quality of the I-have-better-things-to-do excuses that one finds for not cleaning out the basement. We neuroscientists are periodically taken to task for our negligence by writers like Arthur Koestler and E. F. Schumacher, who think we're being unscientific by ignoring the obvious. Even Annie Dillard chides certain scientists for trying "to make a virtue of ignorance by denying that anything else exists." Touché.

THE LIZARDS ARE DOING PUSHUPS AGAIN. This happens mainly when they encounter another lizard. Then they chase one another around the rocks. One small lizard crawled down my arm and ran across my book. Was it curiosity, or just because I was in his accustomed path? He did seem to stop and ponder his decision before taking that path. Does that mean he's conscious?

Ah, well, basement-cleaning time. Can one say anything useful about the neurobiology of consciousness? Consciousness isn't all of mental life, as a lot of things go on of which we're unaware—not just autonomic things like regulating the body temperature and blood pressure, but also subconscious thinking and reasoning. As when we come up with an answer—such as "This is heavier than that"—but cannot give the reasons for our answer. Learning is a poor definition of consciousness, and there is also no use in lumping into consciousness the various template-like cognitive processes that we use in matching up a stimulus configuration with a memory schema. Our inner state not only involves mental representations of objects and concepts—those schemata of our memory—but the ability to play games with them: to mentally see an object, turn it around, mentally prod it. To string schemata together into stories.

The neurologist's definition of consciousness really isn't just non-unconsciousness, though awareness and alertness play a major role in it. Neurologists think of consciousness as the human ability to respond to one's environment in an organized manner. This isn't a bad definition, if we accept it as only the ground floor. However, neurologists, neurosurgeons, anesthesiologists,

To classify consciousness as the action of organic machinery is in no way to underestimate its power. In Sir Charles Sherrington's splendid metaphor, the brain is an "enchanted loom where millions of flashing shuttles weave a dissolving pattern." Since the mind recreates reality from the abstractions of sense impressions, it can equally well simulate reality by recall and fantasy. The brain invents stories and runs imagined and remembered events back and forth through time.

The sociobiologist
EDWARD O. WILSON
On Human Nature, 1978

and others who regularly deal with the disturbances of consciousness distinguish a continuum of levels of alertness and the ability to be aroused into a higher condition of alertness. Drowsiness is the state characterized by ready arousal, verbal responses, fending-off movements to painful stimuli such as a pinch or pinprick. In stupor, painful stimuli don't really arouse the patient fully; he doesn't moan and groan, but still has purposeful fending-off movements. Light coma means no arousal, and only primitive and disorganized movements to painful stimuli; even those movements are lost in a deep coma. In mammals there is even a seat for this type of consciousness—not the pineal gland, as Descartes imagined, but the reticular formation of the brainstem; the clusters of giant nerve cells found in the locus coeruleus are particularly important in waking us up. If someone is in a coma and we've ruled out such common causes as drug overdoses with standard blood tests, it is usually due to damage to the brainstem. And that's usually due to not wearing one's seat belt, an incredible stupidity.

Well, I suppose that a healthy plant could be said to be in a light coma if your time scale for a response encompassed days of growth, and an amoeba could similarly be said to have attained stupor—but that really doesn't get us anywhere. Levels of alertness are not really levels of consciousness, in the way we intuitively use the latter word.

Beyond irritability and alertness lies self-awareness, in the philosophers' scheme of things. We are aware of an intention to act before acting; electrophysiologists have shown, however, that the brain's electrical activity starts changing more than one-third of a second before we report being aware of our intention to act. This, of course, raises the question: if conscious control of one's body is not movement initiation, then what is it? The ability to veto an act before actually carrying it out?

SELF-AWARENESS ALSO INVOLVES imagination or foresight. I'm inclined to substitute "scenario" or "simulation" ability, as I think that such dry-run simulation inside the brain, choosing between alternative scenarios, is the important quality that goes beyond mere alterations in alertness to the immediate environment.

We have an ability to run through a motion with our muscles detached from the circuit, then run through it again for real, the muscles actually carrying out the commands. We can let our simulation run through the past and future, trying different scenarios and judging which is most advantageous—it allows us to respond in advance to probable future environments, to imagine an accidental rockfall loosened by a climber above us and to therefore stay out of his fall line.

But is that qualitatively any different than what the lizard did, in deciding to investigate my book rather than take a path around my feet? I don't know how much simulation ability lizards have, but animals do differ in their responses to situations that evolution hasn't prepared them for, such as a collar and leash: dogs often hang their leashes up on an obstruction. They just keep lunging forward instead of backtracking to free themselves; chimps would figure it out, so we are tempted to say that they have more "insight."

> Animals studied by Americans rush about frantically, with an incredible display of hustle and pep, and at last achieve the desired result by chance. Animals observed by Germans sit still and think, and at last evolve the solution out of their inner consciousness.
>
> BERTRAND RUSSELL, 1927

One might say that the lizard doesn't look very far into the future, that its behavior is just the result of a motor-pattern generator for foraging, not conscious choice. We, on the other hand, can look months ahead in our simulations—but, as Michelle pointed out, so can horses. She said that her family finally figured out why one of their horses always failed to grow a thick winter coat; every year, Bumper had to be provided with a blanket when it got cold. In the autumn, they always left the barn lights on until mid-evening because the boys had a lot of afterschool activities. The artificially long day evidently confused the horse by removing the cue—the shortening period of daylight—that she used to start growing her winter coat, evolution never having prepared horses for the difference between sunlight and artificial light. Michelle's other horse seems to have been able to use other cues as well, such as air temperature, since he grew a winter coat despite the artificially long days. Now a timer switch on the barn lights avoids the need for Bumper's winter blanket.

Good old melatonin, one built-in way of physiologically guessing the future by using the nocturnal secretions of the pineal gland. Apparently the increasing amounts of this hormone released each night (light inhibits its release from the pineal) as the nights lengthen serves as the internal calendar signal for "winter's coming" in many animals. Decreasing amounts each week similarly signal spring; that's probably what turns on the mating seasons of the Abert squirrel in March (a different sensitivity setting turns on the Kaibab squirrel in June instead). I suppose that consciousness tends to suggest simulating less predictable scenarios than the seasons, and using higher parts of the brain to do it, but who is to draw the line? If a scenario for the future is part of your definition of non-trivial consciousness, you can make a case that Descartes was right after all, that the pineal is one seat of consciousness. At least in Michelle's horse.

The first sign that a baby is going to be a human being and not a noisy pet comes when he begins naming the world and demanding the stories that connect its parts. Once he knows the first of these he will instruct his teddy bear, enforce his world view on victims in the sandlot, tell himself stories of what he is doing as he plays and forecast stories of what he will do when he grows up. He will keep track of the actions of others and relate deviations to the person in charge. He will want a story at bedtime. Nothing passes but the mind grabs it and looks for a way to fit it into a story, or into a variety of possible scripts . . .

The writer KATHRYN MORTON, 1984

Our lives are ceaselessly intertwined with narrative, with the stories that we tell and hear told, those we dream or imagine or would like to tell, all of which are reworked in that story of our own lives that we narrate to ourselves in an episodic, sometimes semiconscious, but virtually uninterrupted monologue. We live immersed in narrative, recounting and reassessing the meaning of our past actions, anticipating the outcome of our future projects, situating ourselves at the intersection of several stories not yet completed.

The writer PETER BROOKS, 1985

BUT WE MAKE UP STORIES, with ourselves as the central character, and I'm not sure that lizards and horses are likely to bother with that level of abstraction; they probably just "feel like doing" something and do it. Our ability to tell ourselves a silent narrative about the future is the key to the modern conception of consciousness.

There is often a leap of faith which accompanies this conception, concluding that our fancy human verbal language is therefore essential to consciousness. People too readily forget the silent movies. Or playing charades. Stories can be told without words or even word concepts; certainly getting up and going somewhere, bringing back something, and eating it—things like that were around long before language, long before humans. Words are often much more powerful concepts, however, and so elaborate scenarios can often be expressed succinctly, encapsulated by a pregnant word schema such as "the runaround." But language per se may not add much more to narrative consciousness than the sound track added to the silent movie, simply building atop a story-telling technique of more ancient design.

It's for such reasons that I cannot get very excited about theories which posit that humans were lacking in this self-narrative ability until just a few thousand years ago, less than a millennium before the Greek philosophers. Instead, so the theory goes, self-admonitions were heard as auditory hallucinations, and therefore people thought that the gods were speaking to them. The psychologist Julian Jaynes calls this the bicameral mind, and sees it as an intermediate stage before the development of modern consciousness with its narrator.

That is to say, I'm inclined not to believe it on neurophysiological grounds—yet he may be right for the wrong reasons. I think it likely that many people said they heard voices speaking to them, and that this indeed had an important influence on our culture. There is a certain percentage of people who hear voices. Some are temporal-lobe epileptics, some are schizophrenics, some have temporal-lobe tumors (which were common in tuberculosis, back in the good old days). Others are apparently normal people; for example, a substantial percentage of children are reported to hold conversations with imaginary playmates. Training may well bring out the phenomenon; the voice may not speak spontaneously but rather be brought on by certain mental states, such as meditating on a scene, perhaps an idol in a grotto.

Leaders of primitive societies had an especially good motive for saying that they had heard voices: it lent authority. An Anasazi shaman, for example, had the problem of instilling in his people a sense of direction, togetherness, and destiny. (Why? Because it works—groups with such cohesion survive better.) Yet a shaman is also a long-time everyday member of a small group of people, in which everyone knows each other quite well, complete with little foibles and pretenses. For such a person to episodically get unquestioning obedience from such a group can be quite a feat—and a shaman could pull it off, probably by creating a distance between his ordinary self and his role as a spokesman for something bigger than himself. And a distance between himself and the others, so that they wouldn't argue quite so readily.

The most natural way to create both kinds of distancing would be to report hearing voices commanding you (whether or not you actually do—as I say, the result's the thing). Given the percentage of people who hear voices anyway, this probably got started because some shamans actually did hear voices, were very persuasive, helped their people through hard times or a battle, and thus started a tradition. Other shamans probably imitated it or trained themselves to hear voices. And people tend to imitate their leaders, so I wouldn't be surprised if a lot of people besides shamans reported that they heard voices, social conformity being what it is. If that's true, then the course of our cultural development may well have been influenced by this tradition of reporting conversations with the gods. And given the way that fads come and go, there may well have been "historical stages" in the phenomenon that appear in the literature and myths.

But self-narratives emerging as some sort of biological stage all mixed up with the right brain talking to the left brain but interpreted as an external voice—no, I can't buy it; it's not impossible but it's not necessary on the basis of what we know about evolution and brains.

As masters of illusion, specialists in the evolving art of social control, [shamans] held exalted positions. It could not be otherwise. As equals, they could never have done what they had to do, indoctrinate people for survival in groups, devise and implant the shared memories that would make for widening allegiances, common causes, communities solid enough to endure generation after generation. . . . The ceremonial life promoted, not inquiry, but unbending belief and obedience. . . . To obtain obedience it helps if shamans . . . can create a distance between themselves and the rest of the group. . . . One must appear and remain extraordinary (by no means an easy task when one is a long-time member of a small group), look different with the aid of masks . . . and sound different, using antique words and phrases, reminders of ancestors and a remote past, and special intonations conveying authority, fervor, inspiration.

JOHN E. PFEIFFER, *The Creative Explosion*, 1982

But I think Jaynes is right about his main point, that at some cultural stage, metaphor flowered and people began seeing themselves as the narrators of their own personal story. The question is *when* this happened. Jaynes says 3,000 years ago, based on his analysis of the western literary tradition. "The characters in the *Iliad* do not sit down and think out what to do. They have no conscious minds such as we say we have, and certainly no introspections." That changes in the *Odyssey*, and even more by the time of the Greek philosophers about 2,300 years ago. It might be nothing more than a change in literary style (one can argue that Jaynes' historical stages are just that), but the result was nonetheless impressive and important: the change from "we" to "I", from admonitions made by an inferred authority to an ethical self who has to make one's own decisions, who is an actor in one's own life story.

"So the old style was—if we ignore hallucinations for a moment—like an authoritarian religion or social caste, where you have little autonomy," said Ben, trying to rephrase it all. "Maybe like today, when people try to lose themselves in a team sport, take on a group identity, let a religious commune or an army take charge of their lives. And then there was a transition to a new style of the self as the narrator of a personal history contemplating alternate futures, deciding between alternatives. Right?"

"That's the general idea," I agreed. "There was a Freudian psychoanalyst who once called the self 'a milling crowd of self-narratives,' and that pretty well captures the essence."

"You know," volunteered Rosalie, "I can see the development of that even in religion. Take the whole concept of confession. It didn't exist until many centuries after Christ. Then you get Saint Augustine confessing to sodomy and poetry in the same breath. Even in the Catholic Church, going to confession was once an annual thing, then tended toward a weekly event—at least if you lived in Boston! And the autonomous self is very important in confession—you've got to have a lot of self-awareness to do it properly, a real sense of personal history, a sense of wrong choices made."

"Jaynes thinks that consciousness, and our concept of self, is a rapidly evolving thing," I reported. "He even thinks that it has changed in the last few centuries since Machiavelli and Shakespeare, believes that great changes will occur in several more centuries. And I tend to agree. But even if I were to accept Jaynes' notion about an hallucinatory bicameral mind of 3,000 years ago developing into the more modern narrator—which I don't—I'm left with wondering how much of the prior state of affairs was a consequence of agricultural civilizations starting 6,000 years ago and their high population densities. Did their hunter-gatherer ancestors have modern consciousness in Jaynes' sense? Did the civilized peoples then lose it slaving away in the fields, getting their brains baked? Only to regain the narrator when empires loosened up enough, and travel became freer? Maybe the storytelling tradition flourished as a consequence, and re-established the suppressed indigenous narrator of the hunter-gatherers. As far as I can see, all of his evidence is consistent with such an alternative explanation."

"What I find absurd," commented Rosalie, "is how, in only 700 years, one could get from Jaynes' pre-conscious being to the Greek philosophers. How much has our thinking changed in the 700 years since the Renaissance? I find it improbable that the Greeks accomplished such a quantum leap in only 700 years."

EQUATING LANGUAGE CAPABILITIES with our active conscious mental lives may also be right for the wrong reason. Creating a scenario, holding it in memory while making another, and then comparing them for reasonableness may require neural sequencing machinery that was much improved during human evolution by something like throwing. And the comparisons with memory are surely the basis for metaphor. Our enhanced language and scenario-making consciousness may both be results of a common cause, rather than language causing consciousness.

Of course, that implies that the natural selection enhancing language and consciousness may be far different than is usually supposed. Rather than shaping them through selection for their usefulness, we may have gotten them as gifts. Gifts that we're still trying to figure out how to operate.

□   □   □

Man might be described fairly adequately, if simply, as a two-legged paradox. He has never become accustomed to the tragic miracle of consciousness. Perhaps, as has been suggested, his species is not set, has not jelled, but is still in a state of becoming, bound by his physical memories to a past of struggle and survival, limited in his futures by the uneasiness of thought and consciousness.

JOHN STEINBECK, *Log from the Sea of Cortez*, 1941

□   □   □

THE LIZARD IS BACK, contemplating a return trip across me but looking very hesitant. He finally detours around me. Rosalie suggests that I let her sit in the lizard's path next time, to see if he'll explore a new person. I accuse her of a devious plot to acquire what is now the best patch of shade on the island, now that the sun stands overhead. But it's time that I got up to stretch anyway. So I give her the seat on the condition that she practice lizard calls.

Somehow, the laws of thought must be the laws of things if we are going to attempt a science of reality. Thought and things are part of one evolving matrix, and cannot ultimately conflict.
JOHN E. BOODIN
A Realistic Universe, 1931

Our memories are continually being altered, transformed, and distorted.
The psychologist
ELIZABETH LOFTUS, 1980

THE SCHEMA IS THE STARTING POINT for a discussion of scenario-type consciousness. A schema is like the round hole that you're supposed to fit the round peg into, rather than the proverbial square one; you can imagine a family of cookie-cutters being tried out on a Christmas cookie, seeing which one fits. The schemata-templates in the brain, always on the lookout for a passing pattern in the sensory input that matches one or another of them, are each an average of past experience with that pattern, not a specific instance of a past experience. We see something not so much by making a permanent record but by a back-and-forth process of matching the input pattern with candidate schemata.

Perfect fits aren't always required—and that can produce some appalling consequences. One tends to fill in details that aren't there; they're in the stored schema so one perceives that they're present in reality (an imperfect star-shaped Christmas cookie may, for example, be seen as perfect unless one studies it closely). This poses a terrible problem when it comes to eyewitness testimony, since people really do tend to see what they expect to see. Thoreau said it well: "We hear and apprehend only what we already half know."

That's probably where the canals on Mars came from. The American astronomer Percival Lowell, who correctly predicted the existence of the theretofore unknown planet Pluto, sketched what he saw of Mars through the telescope he had built in 1888 on a hilltop down in Flagstaff (known locally as Mars Hill). Lowell drew a network of interlocking lines which suggested to him a network of canals of the kind that were very popular in the eighteenth and nineteenth centuries before the railroads took over. They were just too regular to be natural. Hence there was not only life on Mars, but civilization!

Others looked through their telescopes to see these wonders and saw only a patchwork of features which, to them, looked nothing at all like canals. Did some people see things that others didn't, in the manner of visual illusions? The British astronomer Walter Maunder at the Greenwich Observatory tried an experiment with a class of schoolboys at the beginning of the twentieth century, at the height of the canal craze. He made a series of drawings showing the main patterns of light and shade on Mars, but without the canals. He set them up at a distance from the class, so that they saw them about as large as the image of Mars appeared in the telescopes to the astronomers. Then he asked the schoolboys to draw them. Quite a few of them inserted canal-like features into their drawings. Arthur C. Clarke repeated the experiment with a group of schoolgirls in Sri Lanka seven decades later, and got the same result. In modern psychological terminology, we'd probably now say that Lowell and those schoolchildren were "filling in" according to a schema already in their heads. Different people do see different things.

We usually distinguish between schematic memories of overlearned things, such as familiar words, and the episodic memory of a unique happening. Granted, schemata are comprised of a number of episodes. But suppose you cannot keep the first episode separated in your memory from the developing schemata for the repeated occurrences? Recalling a memory, mulling it over, can constitute such a repeated occurrence. Alas.

A schema develops over time, from a series of experiences. It's the sensory equivalent of a motor skill. Episodic memory is the storage of a brief series of events, something like a strip of movie film. Naturally, schemata are built up of the average of a number of episodes. Unfortunately, the memory of the first episode can be blurred by somewhat similar repetitions (I can no longer remember the first time that I heard the word "runaround"). And there is now some evidence that even recalling

The mind itself is an art object. It is a Mondrian canvas onto whose homemade grids it fits its own preselected products. Our knowledge is contextual and only contextual. Ordering and invention coincide: we call their collaboration "knowledge." The mind is a blue guitar on which we improvise the song of the world.

ANNIE DILLARD
Living by Fiction, 1982

Theories that explain the mind in material terms will affect our concepts of praise, blame, and responsibility, profoundly changing the way we think of ourselves.

The philosopher
PATRICIA CHURCHLAND, 1984

Objectivity does not mean detachment, it means respect; that is, the ability not to distort and to falsify things, persons, and oneself.

The psychoanalyst ERICH FROMM

the memory of the first episode constitutes a repeated experience, that the recalled memory modifies the stored memory. That wouldn't be a problem if we never made mistakes, or never filled in things that weren't actually there. But we do, and so our memories are malleable.

Eyewitness testimony, as Elizabeth Loftus has shown, is often modified by previous retellings of the story: should a witness make a mistake in the third retelling, it may tend to be adopted as the true version in fourth and fifth retellings.

You can literally fool yourself. And of course skillful prompting during witness rehearsal before a courtroom appearance may tend to make you see things differently (and this need not be intentional—simply showing a witness mug shots may make that witness, during subsequent questioning, substitute the face in a photo for the actual face seen). Since you no longer have the correct memory stored to nag your conscience, you may make a very persuasive witness.

A SCHEMA CAN REPRESENT a triangle or a box; in hearing, it can be the sound of "Ah" or of a door closing; in skin sensation, the feel of a key or of a pencil. And then there are higher-level abstractions that are made from these more elementary ones.

Take a comb: there is a visual schema which represents a comb, all those teeth attached to a spine; indeed, because the comb may be seen from many different angles, the schemata must be able to recognize it as seen from on end and obliquely. There is the sensation of a comb running through your hair, and a quite separate sensation of a comb which you use to find it while rummaging through a pocket or purse. There is also an auditory schema that signals "comb"—that characteristic sound of plucking the teeth of the comb. Then there is the characteristic smell of a comb. A chimpanzee could have all those schemata, if it were experienced with a comb, and it would probably associate them all, too. With language comes another schema, the tone-time pattern that monitors the sound of "comb" being pronounced. Finally, there is a motor template (to stretch the traditional schema concept a little) for producing the breathing-oral-laryngeal muscle sequence that ends up producing the sound "comb."

Asking where the concept "comb" is stored in the brain can thus become a little complicated; if a stroke patient cannot name a comb when shown a picture of it, you have to find out where along the line the message got lost. Let us assume the patient can match up pictures of combs, and can say "comb" if you ask him what "C-O-M-B" spells. If a stroke has severed the connections between visual and language cortex, the patient may have difficulty naming a picture of a comb, but will immediately name it if allowed to handle one. This is one of what are called the "disconnection syndromes." But they're not so simple. Since there are intact connections between visual and somatosensory cortex, and between somatosensory cortex and language cortex, some patients might eventually succeed by using the visual schema to trigger the somatosensory schema (of how the comb feels), and thus the language schema in this roundabout way.

Rosalie pointed out that such ingenious loops are one way in which patients like Howard's father eventually overcome their reading problems: since they can still recognize individual letters, they spell a word out loud to themselves: "C-A-T, why that's cat!", thus constructing a loop that actually goes out the mouth and back in through the ears. Hearing "C-A-T" triggers the word schema in language cortex, even though the direct connections from the visual cortex to the language cortex will no longer match up the visual three-letter group "CAT" with the word, because the nerve fibers have been severed. Eventually, such patients may speak silently, the muscle feedback from mouthing the word seemingly sufficient for them to identify the word. Such examples also show that we don't normally piece together a common word letter by letter, but instead have schemata that recognize multi-letter groups all at once.

There are lots of paths interconnecting all the schemata representing a common object; some paths are faster and more secure than others. Indeed, there might merely be a "comb committee" of all the varied sensory schemata of a comb, any one of which would set off the motor apparatus for pronouncing "comb." You have to allow that some higher-level concepts, say your associations with this particular book, won't be represented that securely, only by a loose web of connections, none effective alone. If you read this book ten times and describe it to fifty friends, it may come to have its very own special schema in your language cortex. But I suspect that most things are represented by loose committees with members from all over the brain, not by a specialist established by overlearning.

Consciousness is ever ready to explain anything we happen to find ourselves doing. The thief narratizes his act as due to poverty, the poet his as due to beauty, and the scientist his as due to truth, purpose and cause inextricably woven into the spatialization of behavior in consciousness. . . . A stray fact is narratized to fit with

some other stray fact. . . . A cat is up a tree and we narratize the
event into a picture of a dog chasing it there.

JULIAN JAYNES, 1976

Having a companion fixes you in time and that the present, but
when the quality of aloneness settles down, past, present, and future
all flow together. A memory, a present event, and a forecast all
equally present.

JOHN STEINBECK, Travels with Charley, 1962

WE STRING THINGS TOGETHER into scenarios. Consciousness seems like memory, in the sense that it allows one
to call up a schema and "look at it." But consciousness usually
does much more than that: it creates a string of schemata. And
then a somewhat different string. It sees which is better, and
perhaps stops there, or maybe keeps inventing and comparing a
little longer. If we're talking about word schemata, that's how
you can construct a short sentence in your head before uttering
it. Sometimes we're aware of the picking and choosing process,
as when I look at the river and think it is blue, switch to green,
search my memory a little more, perhaps settle on blue-green
or muddy, and then say: "It reminds me of the snotgreen sea,
which was James Joyce's parody on Homer's wine-dark sea."

Consciousness is often very sequential: we literally create a
stream of consciousness, piecing together elements from memory and fantasy, manufacturing a narrative, rejecting it as too
fantastic (tasting a comb?), or playing around with it until it
"makes sense." In dreams, our criteria for making sense are relaxed and so the narrative skips around, creating fantastic juxtapositions of impossible times, places and people.

But when awake, one does a good job of matching schemata
to input patterns, and consciousness does a good job of weaving
together past and present into a reasonable narrative. One can
see this process fail in people who have lost their ability to create new memories, as in Korsakoff's syndrome. Ask them what
they had for breakfast, and they'll invent something reasonable,
not having successfully stored that information earlier in the day
while actually eating breakfast (making up stories for such reasons is known as "confabulation" in neurology). These patients
are probably unaware that they're doing this; they're simply filling holes in a sequence as best they can. Our stream of consciousness often fills in missing details, not unlike the way in
which a visual schema fills in the missing spatial details of an
imperfect cookie.

Our sequencing ability gives us the neural machinery to handle the words we hear, and those we choose to speak. The sequencer might also, independently, give us an enhanced ability

to rehearse sequences, an ability to search through more possible candidate sequences, a longer attention span for planning before acting. Even if a human infant were raised by chimpanzees without sequential language and grammar, in some reverse-Washoe experiment (Washoe was one of the first chimp infants reared in a family of psychologists), the human neural sequencing machinery might still provide an expanded consciousness that was more capable of imagining scenarios—perhaps even extended sequences of bluff and counterbluff (something which would be very handy in chimpanzee society!).

This notion of competing scenarios can, of course, take place on one level or several levels. An example of comparing scenarios on the same level would be comparing two different ways of catching a monkey, a frontal rush versus a flanking ambush. Between levels, you might compare an ambush scenario with an imagined scenario for how the monkey might react, which of two trees he might leap towards. If you've got the machinery to handle it, you could imagine a bluff, a counterbluff, a counter-counterbluff, and so on. We've got the ability to project many moves into the future, as you can see in planning chess strategy or labor negotiations.

Metaplanning would, I suppose, be the word for planning about planning. Is that, then, higher consciousness: your ability to watch yourself thinking about something else? Perhaps—but again, I suspect that isn't quite what you may have had in mind. It may be that the higher-order schemata formed when summarizing and abstracting the lower-order schemata are rather hard to put into words; as the Chinese philosopher Chuang Tzu said about the impossibility of communicating absolute knowledge, "If it could be talked about, everybody would have told their brother."

There the eye goes not,
Speech goes not, nor the mind.
We know not, we understand not
How one would teach it.
THE UPANISHADS

Consciousness will always be one degree above comprehensibility.
GOESTA CARL HENRIK
EHRENSVARD, 1965

OUR PASSION FOR FORECASTING THE FUTURE, though of obvious usefulness, can give rise to problems as well. Worry is perhaps the most common example, the kind of nonproductive fretting that no longer produces alternate scenarios but instead dwells upon several known scenarios.

Fortune tellers (sometimes said to belong to the world's second-oldest profession) still successfully exploit the human obsession with forecasts. Our appetite for hearing a weather forecast three times a day back home can hardly be accounted for by their accuracy and usefulness. And, as Abby pointed out, there is astrology—the notion that the configuration of the planets at the time of one's birth affects the course of one's life. Notwithstanding the fact that astrologers' predictions about personality, based on birth date and time, have been repeatedly shown to be no more correct than chance (picking a horoscope at random rather than yours), the newspapers still print more about astrology than science.

□   □   □

Schemata within the brain could serve as the physical basis of will. An organism can be guided in its actions by a feedback loop: a sequence of messages from the sense organs to the brain schemata back to the sense organs and so on around again until the schemata "satisfy" themselves that the correct action has been completed. The mind could be a republic of such schemata, programmed to compete among themselves for control of the decision centers, individually waxing or waning in power in response to the relative urgency of the physiological needs of the body. . . . Will might be the outcome of the competition, requiring the action of neither a "little man" nor any other external agent. . . . It is entirely possible that the will—the soul, if you wish—emerged through the evolution of physiological mechanisms. But, clearly, such mechanisms are far more complex than anything else on earth.

The biologist EDWARD O. WILSON, *On Human Nature*, 1978

A central aspect of consciousness is the ability to look ahead, the capability we call "foresight". It is the ability to plan, and in social terms to outline a scenario of what is likely going to happen, or what might happen, in social interactions that have not yet taken place. . . . It is a system whereby we improve our chances of doing those things that will represent our own best interests. . . . I suggest that "free will" is our apparent ability to choose and act upon whichever of those [scenarios] seem most useful or appropriate, and our insistence upon the idea that such choices are our own.

The biologist RICHARD D. ALEXANDER
Darwinism and Human Affairs, 1979

[Loren Eiseley] reveals himself as a man unusually well trained in the habit of prayer, by which I mean the habit of listening. . . . The serious aspect of prayer begins when we have got our begging over with and listen for the Voice of what I would call the Holy Spirit, though if others prefer to say the Voice of Oz or the Dreamer or Conscience, I shan't quarrel, so long as they don't call it the Voice of the Super-Ego, for that "entity" can only tell us what we know already, whereas the Voice I am talking about always says something new and unpredictable. . . .

W.H. AUDEN, 1970

The idea that psychological complexities can in principle be identified with the structure of a highly organized piece of matter, the human brain, is unappealing to many people. Something in their mental setup balks at the idea that the colorful, lovable experience of themselves and of other persons is translatable into the black and white drawing of a set of logical relations. They would rather leave the psyche unanalyzed and think of it as a separate substance that has a fleeting liaison with the body as long as it lives. This view is called animism when it is encountered by ethnologists in other societies. It is also the most widespread psychological theory in our own society. . . . It is important, however, to realize that the animistic heresy has been competing against the analytic tendency of science throughout the history of philosophy.

The biophysicist VALENTINO BRAITENBERG
Gehirngespinste (The Texture of Brains), 1977

Our capacity for deceiving ourselves about the operation of our brain is almost limitless, mainly because what we can report is only a minute fraction of what goes on in our head. This is why much of philosophy has been barren for more than 2,000 years and is likely to remain so until philosophers learn to understand the language of information processing.

The molecular biologist FRANCIS H.C. CRICK, 1979

We wish to be angels, not made out of meat.

The neurophysiologist RODOLFO LLINÁS, 1984

☐   ☐   ☐

THERE ARE A LOT OF REASONS WHY we attempt to separate mind from body. And scientists often try to adapt their ideas to popular notions. For example, the computer scientists are forever promoting the notion that the distinction between software and hardware is like that between mind and body. Neurophysiologists like Walter Freeman tend to reply that the computer as we know it is a hopelessly inadequate analogy in the first place: "Animals and children even more than adults . . . behave in ways expressed by the colloquial insight that 'they have minds of their own'. . . . They exhibit traits of independence and self-directedness, which are to be expected and admired in any being that has a brain, but which are intolerable in a computer and causes it to be overhauled or discarded. . . ."

Consciousness seems to imply free will, individuality—and with them, responsibility for one's actions. But one can have that without separating off "mind" as a separate entity from the brain. My conception of consciousness is that it is fundamentally the brain's ability to simulate the past and future, to make quality judgments about alternative scenarios, and thus pick and choose. Individuality arises not so much because we each (identical twins excepted) have a unique collection of genes, but because everyone's life experiences are different; thus, each of us has a different collection of schemata, quality judgments, and so forth. We have made a series of conscious choices in the past, each of us differently.

Those aren't necessarily absolute quality judgments, only relative ones. Thus, a lack of imagination, or the lack of the requisite schemata to play games with, could make for poor scenarios—and thus poor relative quality judgments, because one wouldn't wind up with very many candidate scenarios from which to choose. Or you might get stuck after imagining one scenario, unable to go on to imagining another because you were fixated on the first one, and so wind up doing the first thing that "came into your mind."

As Kenneth Craik once pointed out, a little initial confusion can even be helpful (so long as one eventually recognizes that the two things aren't identical) because it brings several schemata "to mind" (much as I try, it's sure hard not to use that word) and helps one to recognize analogies. That expands the number of schemata with which one can play scenario games.

But where (to recall the searching of Pirsig's Phaedrus) does quality arise? Although some quality judgments are probably inborn like the primate preference for the taste of fruit over the taste of zucchini—we instinctively favor certain flavors—they mainly come from our experience with the external world, the trial-and-error encounters of our lives so far. That experience may, however, be several times removed: we may reject a scenario for approaching the boss for a pay raise not because someone else tried it and was turned down, but because we've thought about a similar situation before and chose not to act it out then. That previous choice is still on file, and so thought becomes part of our experience, along with our actions and the direct evidence of our senses. Experience is not only what we have done, but what we have chosen not to do, having imagined a scenario and made a quality judgment about it.

The Quality which creates the world emerges as a *relationship* between man and his experience. He is a *participant* in the creation of all things. The *measure* of all things—it fits.
    ROBERT M. PIRSIG
    Zen and the Art of Motorcycle Maintenance, 1974

One definition of an expert is a person who knows all the possible mistakes and how to avoid them. But when we say that people are "wise" it's not usually because they've made every kind of mistake there is to make (and learned from them), but because they have stored up a lot of simulated scenarios, because their accumulated quality judgments (whether acted upon or not) have made them particularly effective in appraising a novel scenario and advising on a course of action.

HAVING SAID ALL THAT, we concluded that the most puzzling role of consciousness remains that of the selective attention mechanism. Just as the brainstem reticular activating system is what controls our levels of alertness and wakes up a sleeping brain, neurophysiologists tend to think that the thalamus is the brain structure most associated with switching our attention around. It's certainly at the center of things: anatomically, it's to the cerebral cortex what an avocado pit is to the avocado's skin.

A few aspects of selective attention are even understood at the level of single-cell function. My Jerusalem friend Shaul Hochstein has, for example, shown that some nerve cells in the monkey's brain are "switch-hitters" (my phrase), able to register color better than line tilts when the monkey is rewarded for correct color choices, but the same cell becoming better at registering tilts (and less sensitive to color) when the desired tilt is rewarded instead. Thus some templates aren't fixed—focussing one's attention on the color of an object rather than its orientation may actually assign more cells to the color task than usual. And assigning more cells is a way to make more precise discriminations, just as assigning more cells to a timing task is one way to improve pitching accuracy. This shows how selective attention, via controlling the assignment of sensory priorities to multipurpose cells, influences that to which we pay attention—and how that influences how skillful we are at sensory and movement tasks.

But what determines whether I pay attention to the external world or, instead, spin a scenario inside my frontal lobes? Whether I remain fixated on my first trial scenario or spin another one? How do I hop around the memories of the candidate scenarios, seeing "how good they taste"? What is it that shifts my attention around like that—now listening, now remembering, now spinning a scenario, now freeing me from it to spin another scenario, now deciding, then removing the inhibitions that disconnect my thoughts from my muscles and letting me act?

Alas, we imagine a conductor up on a podium, leading the orchestra. Or the switchboard operator, the executive presiding over the board meeting, the circusmaster running the three-ring circus. Like Descartes, we tend to see both an operator and something separate, operated upon—but is that really necessary? The orchestra conductor really isn't playing a single note, only keeping them all coordinated; were the conductor to fall asleep, the orchestra would finish up the piece without his help, though perhaps without some of the sharp transitions and balancing of effects that the conductor helped achieve. Conductor/coordinators don't have to be single spotlit entities. Just as the frog heart creates a sharply rhythmic beat from the interactions of a lot of jittery cells, so may the brain's coordinator be the emergent property of a widespread committee.

Selective attention might simply be many processes going on simultaneously, each competing for access to the language mechanism (since we cannot say two things at once, this produces something of a bottleneck). In short, one might simply be going from parallel to serial: when we say that we can only think, or pay attention to, one thing at a time, it may just mean that we cannot express more than one thing at a time. Lots of things can happen simultaneously, but if they "want out" through our language system, they may have to jostle for access to it.

Yes, but some thoughts may be channeled more narrowly, Rosalie replied. The serial nature might be the important thing, not merely a bottleneck. Our sequential language system is often—though not always—an important part of how we think, as silent speech helps us frame propositions by using the powerful schemata of language. Even if we don't formulate a sentence, we're making a scenario, and that may require the same neural-sequencing machinery as we use to speak. So, to the extent that sequences are part of the three-ring circus, there might be some limitations on how many can go on at once. This is probably a matter of individual variation; some people can probably manage two simple sequences at once in their heads, just as some individuals can indeed rub their stomach and pat their head at the same time.

Sometimes, those background sequences take over consciousness in a big way. Is an hallucination a runaway thought that gets into one's sensory channels, seeming to arrive from the eyes or ears instead of from memory? There's another lizard trying to get around me, and he's doing pushups. Suppose he's hallucinating another lizard, or just seeing me and hoping I'll give way and move out of his path if he tries his usual bluff?

Rosalie suggests that I respond to him by getting down and doing some pushups myself. I get out of that by replying that, like Eiseley's spider not seeing things outside of spider world, the lizard probably thinks that I'm just a rock anyway.

WE'RE NOW DROWNED by the waters backed up by Bridge Canyon Dam at Mile 238, the boatmen announce as we get ready to leave Havasu. Indeed, had this dam been built (and there are still Arizona politicians who want to build it), it would have backed up the waters all the way past Matkatamiba, drowning that special place. But that's all right, said the dam-builders, no one would be able to see the lake—from standing up on the Canyon rim. All they'd have been able to see from the rim would have been the high-voltage lines crisscrossing the bottom of the Canyon. And the access roads scarring it up. Signs of progress. There would surely have been a new visitor center at the dam, full of construction pictures for people to admire. But, had they run true to form (as at the Glen Canyon Dam visitor center), there would not have been displayed a single picture of Matkatamiba or Ledges or Havasu or Lava Falls or anything else buried. That, after all, might discourage future dambuilding.

The chief reason so many people are fleeing the cities at every opportunity to go tramping, canoeing, skiing into the wilds is that wilderness offers a taste of adventure, a chance for the rediscovery of our ancient, preagricultural, preindustrial freedom. Forest and desert, mountain and river, when ventured upon in primitive terms, allow us a sort of Proustian recapture, however superficial and brief, of the rich sensations of our former existence, our basic heritage of a million years of hunting, gathering, wandering.

EDWARD ABBEY, *Down the River*, 1982

When one is hunting, the air has another, more exquisite feel as it glides over the skin or enters the lungs, the rocks acquire a more expressive physiognomy, and the vegetation becomes loaded with meaning. [The hunter] will instinctively shrink from being seen; he will perceive all his surroundings from the point of view of the animal, with the animal's peculiar attention to detail. This is what I call being *within* the countryside. . . . Wind, light, temperature, ground contour, minerals, vegetation, all play a part; they are not simply there, as they are for the tourist or botanist, but rather they *function*, they act. And they do not function as they do in agriculture . . . but rather each intervenes in the drama of the hunt from within oneself.

JOSÉ ORTEGA Y GASSET, *Meditations on Hunting*, 1972

FLOATING DOWN THE RIVER below Havasu in mid-afternoon, we are quite laid back. There are no rapids for seven miles, and we only have nine miles to go until camp at National Canyon. Our boat, Mike's, is tied side-by-side to Fritz's boat, and they float down the river together, one or another boatman occasionally giving a tug on an oar to keep us from running ashore. It's that kind of afternoon.

Everyone is talking together, comparing experiences. Various people have swum, stood under the falls, explored farther up-canyon. It seems that one has to ford the creek four times before getting to Beaver Falls, and then another three times to get up to Mooney Falls, an 11-mile round trip from the river. Fritz and her two followers did indeed run up and then right back down again, then jumped into the river near where we moored the boats for a cooling-off swim. But most people sat around, stayed wet, and enjoyed the setting. It seems that everyone's lunch was a soggy mess by the time they got around to extracting it from their plastic bags, having been jostled around on the hike up. The apples and oranges pulverized the soft sandwiches.

□   □   □

Do the reflexive structures and intellectual patterns and purpose which we find in art—do these obtain elsewhere? Or do we merely make them up because our minds are uniquely adapted for making things up?

This is an appalling possibility. If our minds are selected for inventing bits of order, then art's highest function is to shed light on the mind. And, terribly, any human artifact is the mind's own simulacrum. A play or a government, a canal or a culture, is a physical replica by means of which the mind duplicates its own structures unwittingly, as a strand of DNA replicates itself inside a banana leaf. And if *this* is true, and the natural world which churned out the mind is a wreck and a chaos, like a rock slide, then the mind is a marvelous monster indeed. And the work of art (in addition to being the least of our worries) is always a tour de force in which the mind displays abilities absurdly in excess of, or at least incidental to, their survival function. For the ability to conceive and execute murals and epic poems and symphonies and novels is a grotesque trick of tissue which sprang from the pot of the possible, like the grossly overdeveloped antlers of the extinct Irish elk. . . .

By these lights, there is no order anywhere but in our brains, which are uniquely adapted for inventing it and for handling complex abstractions. These abilities have served us very well. The only significance and value which obtain anywhere are in the mind's discernment of these fictive qualities in its own manufactured models. We create value and locate it in our monstrously overdeveloped mental self-replication, our stuttering repetitions of our brains' own order, with which we have covered the gibbering earth.

This is the most dismal view—of art and of everything else—I can imagine. It must be admitted that one idea in this book is consistent with this view, and even points to it: the suggestion that . . . human significance is the only significance. . . .

Do art's complex and balanced relationships among all parts, its purpose, significance, and harmony, exist in nature? Is nature whole, like a completed thought? Is history purposeful? Is the universe of matter significant? I am sorry; I do not know.

ANNIE DILLARD, *Living by Fiction*, 1982

□   □   □

Rosalie was asked how much progress she had made with the thin volume of Annie Dillard's essays that she'd carried along today. "Three pages," she replied. "We," she said, sweeping her arm to indicate a few more of us, "kept talking about consciousness. At one point, they even exorcised the mind from the brain."

Now how was I supposed to answer the inevitable questions about consciousness after that introduction? I insisted that Rosalie summarize our discussion, since she had gotten us into this.

She replied that since I wouldn't do pushups to test her theory about the lizards' pushups, the least I could do was to explain consciousness. So I explained about Eiseley's spider—that in a spider's world, Eiseley probably didn't exist. That the lizard similarly probably thought that I was a big rock. If I'd done pushups, I'd have created a psychologically scarred group of lizards that thought big rocks were alive, since they did pushups, and would starve because every time they encountered another rock in their search for food, they'd waste time demonstrating to it. The mental health of lizards didn't distract the group from consciousness for very long.

Rosalie started by saying that no one would buy her neurologist's definition of levels of consciousness—that those were brainstem levels of consciousness, and that what most people meant by consciousness were, in effect, the diencephalic (thalamic and cortical) aspects of consciousness that regulated where we direct our attention. And she neatly summarized the arguments about scenarios for the future—then told the group about Michelle's horse Bumper who seemed to favor Descartes' pineal gland as the seat of looking-into-the-future consciousness.

Of course, where she got into trouble was when she started to tell them about how one might explain many of the things ascribed to the mind—individuality, free will, thinking, intentions, responsibility, motives—simply on the basis of the brain's overdeveloped capacities for stringing together schemata into scenarios, for making quality judgments when comparing various scenarios, and then turning the body's inhibited muscles loose to act out the best scenario. People who aren't used to thinking in terms of schemata in the brain aren't going to accept strings of them as explanations for the varied, colorful, and willful experience of human consciousness. To perceive that argument, one needs the right building blocks of perception: including a schema for schemata! Not unreasonably, they balked.

Now it's hard to give a short explanation of schemata when everyone wants to ask a question or volunteer an opinion on consciousness, and some had not heard the earlier discussions about the "hawk templates" of the baby birds. And so we had a somewhat frustrating discussion on a different level, working from the top down instead of bottom up.

"Descartes sure did get us into trouble when he tried to reason out the basis of will," commented Rosalie. "The rigid categories of Aristotelian logic led him to see the controlled and the controller. And since he didn't have any notion of self-organizing systems or machine intelligence, he assumed that anything physical—the body—was controlled. Leaving the controller, the mind, as some separate entity."

"Didn't Descartes say that only humans had consciousness?" asked Abby.

"Descartes never would have said that if he'd owned a pet dog or cat," added Ben. "I think it's pretty obvious that my dog is conscious. Damn near reads my mind. And he sure knows about the future—the day before I leave on a trip, he sulks around the house like a lost soul."

"Descartes and his followers," replied Rosalie, "were perfectly happy to grant consciousness to humans—self-evident and all that—but they wouldn't grant it to animals because animals couldn't tell us about it, nor could we measure it in some indirect way. But that created an artificial division between humans and the rest of the animals, one that probably doesn't exist in nature."

"I'll agree with you on that one," I said. "I'll concede a degree of consciousness to animals, especially for detecting and responding to the emotions of the people that feed them. I just don't want to assume that consciousness is separate in some way from the hardware of the brain, from things we can observe."

"Just why do you start off assuming that there is no separate mind—soul, consciousness, whatever you want to call it?" Abby asked me.

"It's part of being a neurophysiologist for some of us," I tried to answer. "You avoid assuming anything more than you need to. I mean, how will you ever know that mind is something more than brain unless you do your best to prove that the brain's hardware can manage just fine by itself?"

"But we've seen a whole generation of behavioral psychologists," responded Abby, "who were so addicted to sticking to the observable that, if they had been physicists, would have discarded all of quantum mechanics because they couldn't describe the atom without making unmechanical assumptions. And very unphysical, fuzzy assumptions they were too, those principles of quantum mechanics. But the physicists who followed that path were very successful in explaining the world." She added triumphantly, "So why don't you just assume the mind exists and get on with it?"

"Rosalie," I pleaded, "you got me into this. You get me out of it."

"I can't help that you didn't do your pushups," she teased. I threatened her with a bailer bucket of water, but she knew me too well to flinch. "Just explain that there is an alternative to the amorphous mind floating around inside the head, tickling the brain cells."

"Oh, what's that?" asked Abby. "How do you get free will out of electrical and chemical parts, pushing one another around like the insides of a clock? Why do I choose to talk, rather than throwing a bucket of water at you instead? Did I slip a cog somewhere?"

"Explain!" added Mike, taking a lazy stroke on his right oar. "If we don't like your explanation, we won't even wait until sunrise, just a quick firing squad with eight loaded bailer buckets."

"If we think you're all wet," Marsha added, "we'll make sure you look it too."

Trapped.

"I shall have to speak metaphorically," I began sadistically, "about metaphors. And make analogies about analogs. Remember Heinrich Heine's romantic poem that starts 'Du bist wie eine blume'? That's 'You are like a flower' except it sounds better in German. Technically a simile, but never mind." Oops, the natives are getting restless with those buckets. "It ties the concept of a flower to that of a particular person. It doesn't say they're equal, the same in all respects, that the person has green leaves, for example. And there's another comparison, when I translated 'Du bist' as 'you are'—they're not really equivalent, because the German 'du' carries the additional information that Heine is speaking to someone with whom he is on intimate terms. English doesn't have that familiar form of the verb.

"Now each of these words or concepts has a group of nerve cells in the brain that is on the lookout for it, that sort of springs into activity whenever it detects 'flower' or 'du bist' or whatever. That committee of neurons constitutes the schema, or template, or search image, or whatever you want to call it. And it can be put into activity in various ways—when you look at a flower, certainly, but also when you just remember a flower. Fantasize a flower. Wish for a flower. There are schemata for all the words in our vocabularies, with ties between them when metaphors exist, or translations. And there are schemata for actions, like walking and running and rowing and standing under waterfalls."

But where shall wisdom be found?
And where is the place of understanding?
                        BOOK OF JOB

Can all the sky
Can all the World
Within my Brain-pan lie?
THOMAS TRAHERNE (c. 1636–1674)

"So you can make a scenario out of schemata," volunteered Abby, "taking the schema for walking, combining it with the flower schema, and imagine walking over to pick a flower. Right?"

"Exactly. And you can make an alternative scenario out of sitting still and continuing to read your book. Then you can compare the two, and decide which you'll do. A lot of the combinations of schemata are nonsense, such as this boat flying over to that mesquite tree. We edit those out, having some means of testing them against reality. We've never seen a rubber raft fly."

"Oh no?" interrupted Mike. "Just wait until Lava Falls."

"Some people apply this sort of reality testing to their daydreams more reliably than others," I chided, "but at night, we all dream of scenarios that are silly, impossible juxtapositions of people and places. The schemata themselves aren't usually crazy, it's just the way they're strung together. One schema calls up a related one, and that leads somewhere else, and so on it goes. The stream of consciousness. And unconsciousness, I might add."

"So that's the unconscious? All those scenarios not currently connected to language consciousness?" asked Rosalie in a bit of friendly prompting. I agreed, happily.

"How many schemata can you string together?" Ben asked.

"Well, it depends. If you want to keep them in the correct order, maybe half a dozen at a time. It's been said that when we begin to speak a sentence of more than a half-dozen words, we don't know what words will conclude the sentence. If you want to remember a longer string, you need to subdivide the string: make a higher-order schema out of a group of schemata and substitute it, to make room for more schemata in the string."

"And how many strings can you keep going at the same time?" asked Dan Richard from the other boat. "The most fascinating aspect of consciousness to me is the subconscious problem-solving that goes on as I go about something else. I think about what to buy Sue for her birthday, and I'm stumped. And then the answer pops into my mind when I'm eating dinner and talking about something unrelated."

"I don't know how many can be juggled in parallel. But the throwing theory suggests that you might have a lot of independent sequencers available in the brain, at least when they're not being forced to work in tandem for precision timing. Maybe only one can be connected to the language circuits at a time, but that's no reason other sequencers would need to stop making new arrangements of schemata," I replied.

"You know," began Ben, "that does sound a lot like dreaming. Those elaborate sequences that shift gradually into something quite different, hinging on some minor detail that brings forward a scene from some other story line. As if a second story had been running unseen."

"Exactly," I agreed, "I suspect dreaming is just the scenario-making machinery free-running, without the usual quality judgments that we use when awake, labeling something as ridiculous or incorrect. And in dreaming, the memory mechanisms are also altered, so that long-term memories aren't formed so readily from short-term memories. You really have to recall a dream after awakening—go over it when finally awake—to store a long-lasting memory of it. But except for those differences in judgment and memory, our dreaming may just be the scenario machinery being exercised, switching occasionally to another story running in another sequencer. Animals without such fancy scenario-making machinery might not dream in the same way that we do."

Abby was still dubious. She finally asked, "So the brain can create scenarios. But who decides between them? Where do those quality judgments come from?"

Rosalie answered. "Quality judgments come from your experiences in life—which as a group are something unique, which only you have experienced in that combination. But thought is experience too—if you once created a mental scenario, judged it unrealistic or another scenario better, then that judgment might still be on file, as part of your experience. You don't have to actually make every mistake in the book to become an expert—you can just imagine them all! Quality's in your brain."

"How does this view differ from what the cognitive psychology types come up with?" asked Abby. "What do they call it? Cognitive science? I saw where someone called it an 'hallucinated subject,' introspection revisited. Isn't it just another version of the little person inside the head? Except that one little person recognizes symbols or situations, another runs the filing cabinet of memories, still another runs the muscles. And we're supposed to take it on faith that the mind emerges from this collection of dumb computers?"

"We neurobiologists want to know not only what the 'brain programs' are, but how the brain machinery operates them. The Artificial Intelligence folk figure that if they can postulate a program that seems to do the trick, then they can build a hardware computer that will mimic the actions of the mind, running the same program using silicon chips rather than wet and unreliable nerve cells," I replied, pausing for a drink from my canteen.

"We neurobiologists work up from the bottom much of the time, trying to fathom the computation processes of the building blocks. We're constantly coping with parallel processing, a notion which is still novel in AI. I happen to think that the AI types are missing the boat, by trying to ignore the unreliable nature of the individual cells, the real brain's computing elements. Instead of trying to work around jittery cells by using

Making variations on a theme is really the crux of creativity.
DOUGLAS R. HOFSTADTER, 1985

reliable pigeonhole computers, unreliable cells should be seen as the essence of the brain's way of doing things, just as sex's institutionalized randomness is the essence of how evolution has done more and more elaborate things. But philosophically, both neurobiologists and the AI folk start from the premise that the mind can be explained, that it isn't beyond understanding. And most of us would assume that mind is going to emerge from a lucky combination of more elementary 'dumb' processes."

"Look, something I can't understand," began Steve, who had only been listening up until now, "is how you can get something as fancy as thought out of something as simple as strings of templates being compared. That's like saying that the human eye—a damned fancy optical device, not to mention all the image processing that goes on in the retina—was constructed only from differences in growth rates. It's just too fancy for something simple to have caused it. And so is the mind."

"I have the same trouble too, sometimes," I replied. "It's like saying that the speed differences between the Tortoise and the Hare created a fancy racetrack, grandstands, and popcorn machines. But our problem is that we just don't have much everyday experience with such things, we don't have analogies that spring to mind, that help us over the hurdles. We can't fathom the improbabilities caused by thousands of generations of selection shaping up our world. Biologists, psychologists, and computer scientists have more useful examples stored in their heads than most people have handy for comparisons, but they have trouble too.

"The key issue here is that old phrase: the whole is more than the sum of its parts. Consciousness is one of those things that emerges when you sum up all those nerve cells. It doesn't exist independently of the nerve cells. You can't pin consciousness down to any one nerve cell, you can't spotlight some identifiable piece of the puzzle and say: 'Here it is, folks, that's where consciousness lives, right in there.' Consciousness is more closely related to some things than others: it doesn't have much to do with the brain regions regulating the heart rate or the body temperature, and it has a lot to do with the sequencing mechanisms that string together the schemata. But it's really an emergent property, one of those unexpected sidesteps in evolution in which a novel combination of preexisting things turns out to be handy for something completely new."

This went back and forth, interrupted only by the minor rapid at Mile 164. The boatmen didn't even bother to unhitch the boats—we just rode through it, lashed together, rippling over the waves. We had some diversions, such as discussions of ecology and holistic medicine, situations where you have to concern yourself with the good of the whole, preserve the in-terrelationships as well as the pieces. But we eventually came back to more cases in which the whole was greater than the sum of the pieces, creating some new unrelated property.

"I think that the problem is that most of us," Rosalie said, "myself included, just aren't used to thinking about problems where the whole is greater than the sum of the parts. Where something emerges from a merger. But surely they're all around us, if we'd just look and build up our vocabularies a little. Get the right schema!"

National Canyon was just ahead on the left bank. Mike and Fritz were uncoupling the two boats in preparation for maneuvering into the beach below the little rapid. So I proposed that we make a list of all the emergent properties we had seen on the river, starting with the birds. If people would just come and tell me when they thought of one, I'd write it down in the river diary.

□   □   □

You won't locate a traffic jam if you restrict your search to the insides of a single taxi. . . . A traffic jam is just not on the level of an individual car. . . . The nature of collective phenomena is that they are patterns composed of parts, and they in turn exert powerful influences on their parts, acting to keep them in line. Think of hurricanes, life, intelligence.

> The computer scientist DOUGLAS R. HOFSTADTER, *Metamagical Themas: Questing for the Essence of Mind and Pattern*, 1985

In matters of visual form we sense that nature plays favorites. Among her darlings are spirals, meanders, branching patterns, and 120-degree joints. Those patterns recur again and again. Nature acts like a theatrical producer who brings on the same players each night in different costumes for different roles. The players perform a limited repertoire; pentagons make most of the flowers but none of the crystals; hexagons handle most of the repetitive two-dimensional patterns but never by themselves enclose three-dimensional space. On the other hand, the spiral is the height of versatility, playing roles in the replication of the smallest virus and in the arrangement of matter in the largest galaxy.

> The architect PETER S. STEVENS, *Patterns in Nature*, 1974

THOSE OF US who sat out the hike up Havasu this morning, staying on the island instead, were still game for a hike after we made camp. And so we discovered the great chute that the creek has sculpted out of the rock. With the colors accentuated by the long shadows, it was indeed nice. And the sunset was especially beautiful, some clouds in just the right places. We got back after the dinner-line had already formed.

Various people came by after washing their dinner dishes by

MILE 166
National Canyon
Eleventh Campsite

the river, while I was still working on my second helping. They had examples of emergent properties seen along the river, and so I juggled my notebook and dinner plate for a while. Here is our catalog of emergents:

□   □   □

Waves are good examples of how a faster and a slower rate interact. Wind waves occur when the surface of the water is driven to move faster than the water currents beneath the surface, and so the surface water overruns the deeper water, creating a crest and a splash. Waves near shore are created in an inverse manner. When a wave comes ashore, deep water gets slowed down by scraping the bottom; again the surface water tumbles over the slower depths.

Where the flow meets a solid surface, it slows down; indeed, the closer to the surface, the slower it gets until—at the very interface—nothing flows at all. That's why wind doesn't blow the dust off leaves—or airplane wings—in between rains. Even when we stick an oar into the water, the water molecules at the very surface of the oar don't flow. The gradual slowing near the surface creates tumbling, and so we see spiral eddies coming off the back edge of the oar.

□   □   □

And that's how back-eddies arise, another emergent. The water slows down at the edge of the rapid, and so a "sideways wave" is created as the river widens out below the rapid. Spirals seem to emerge easily during downhill flows of energy, just because of those edge effects where the flow is slowed down near a boundary like a riverbank. But two currents moving in opposite directions also have a region between them where the water flow drops to zero. And so new eddies can form out in the middle of a stream, far from shore, peeling off from the region of zero flow.

The average eddy moves a distance about equal to its own diameter before it generates small eddies that move, more often than not, in the opposite direction. Those smaller eddies generate still smaller eddies and the process continues until all the energy dissipates as heat through molecular motion . . . thereby inspiring the beautifully apt verse of L.F. Richardson:

> *Big whirls have little whirls,*
> *That feed on their velocity;*
> *And little whirls have lesser whirls,*
> *And so on to viscosity.*

Quoted by Peter S. Stevens, 1974

Albert Einstein once turned his mind to the problem of river meanders, that tendency of rivers to keep changing course rather than going straight down a hill. He concluded that it was just a fancy three-dimensional version of the same principles seen in ocean waves and back-eddies.

This organization emerged out of the downhill flow of energy. Emergents, and particularly evolution itself, are pumped up by this energy flow. Evolution is the river that flows uphill.

□   □   □

Bighorns are emergent! The spiral twist of the sheeps' horns is just a consequence of the growth rate being higher at the front side of the horn than at the back side, leading to the horn arching backward. If, in addition, the central edge grows faster than the outside edge, the horn will tend to grow out to the side. But suppose both processes occur at once? The combination of the two differences in growth rates results in the corkscrew horn of the bighorns.

Snails get their shell shape from the same set of differences in growth rates. However, the helix of double-stranded DNA arises in another manner, not from growth rates; there is more than one way to make a spiral or a corkscrew. The astronomers are still trying to figure out spiral galaxies, those heavenly things that look like a galactic lawn sprinkler had spewed out stars as it twirled around.

□   □   □

The travertine pools at Havasu are an example of organization arising during the downhill flow of energy—in this case, water running downhill. Instead of just a creek flowing downhill, creating meanders all the way, you get a series of pools, little dams all along the path, just like a terraced hillside. The dams arise quite without beavers and their instincts to push sticks and mud toward the sound of running water (though that's another emergent property too). The calcium carbonate (the limestone dissolved in the water) precipitates out on the tree branches that fall into the creek, on the tree roots that are exposed by the running water, and anything else handy. Like a plaster cast on a broken arm, this enlarges the branch. A loose branch being swept downstream becomes entangled. Stuck in place, it too starts getting coated, becoming cemented into place. Even when the wood rots away, the travertine cast remains and continues to grow. And this goes on for centuries.

Eventually there is so much resistance to water flow that the water is pushed over the top of the tangle instead of flowing through the openings between branches. But then the top starts building up too, forming a smooth level lip. From this simple process of precipitation in flowing water, a series of little dams are formed, creating the staircase of quiet pools that we all enjoyed today. Order arising out of chaos.

□   □   □

There's driftwood trapped atop ledges along the river, several stories above the present water level, showing you just how high the waters used to get during the spring floods. That's an example of stratified stability, Jacob Bronowski's phrase to describe how tumult could occasionally trap something at a higher level of organization, preventing it from falling back. The ledge under the driftwood isn't exactly an emergent property, but it illustrates how the chaos of a spring flood can give rise to order if there is something to catch the driftwood and keep it from falling back.

The stability of protein chains is especially important; like pretzels tacked together in the middle, they have a certain shape. Their shape is important for their nooks-and-crannies function as an enzyme. It is specialized for controlling a biological rate—one rate in a whole family of rates—in an interacting chemical process.

□   □   □

Potholes are emergents! Well, at least the kind that we saw at Deer Creek with the tree growing in it. When a rock gets into a depression and the water current swirls it around, it can grind a deeper hole. In most cases, a flood will carry the rock downstream so that the process is interrupted until another rock is similarly situated. But when the hole gets deep enough, and the rock is heavy enough, not enough water can get down into the depression to ever carry the big rock away. It is then trapped, even more firmly than the driftwood on the ledges. The pothole principle—I wonder if there's a corollary that applies to city streets?

Stratified stability strikes again. And so, year after year, the rock is twirled around inside a hole that grows deeper and deeper. Eventually making a nice pothole. Smaller rocks or sand will collect in the hole between major floods, and thus trees and flowers may take root there for a while. They catch water during the rains, and so serve as a source of drinking water in times when the side streams dry up. In the Canyon, the potholes are sometimes marked on the hiking maps as a source of water for human travelers. The bighorn don't need maps.

□   □   □

Standing waves emerge. And creeks in flood dug the series of bathtubs that we enjoyed at Matkat, and at Blacktail.

Washboard roads are another manifestation of standing waves, the corrugations in the dirt road an outcome of a particular dirt consistency, the shock absorbers' and tires' resilience, and the typical speed of passing cars.

□   □   □

Another emergent: sorting by size. We can see it here at National Canyon, walking down the sand beach. Up near the creek, the rocks are big. They get smaller as one walks downstream because the river can carry smaller rocks along more easily during a flood. So given enough time, the river can sort rocks by size, again simply as a consequence of the downhill flow of energy. That was very important back before biology: clay makes a good catalyst.

And order arises when volcanos blow their tops: when trees are blasted down, they lay in nice parallel rows, like matchsticks. The hills around Mount St. Helens look like disintegrating fragments of some giant wicker basket.

□   □   □

Packing principles, like the hexagonal cross-sections of honeycombs from my dream last night. Similar rules decide the form of crystals, or how the grains on an ear of corn are packed together. Maybe even the structure of space itself.

Einstein . . . held a long-term vision: There is nothing in the world except curved empty space. Geometry bent one way here describes gravitation. Rippled another way somewhere else it manifests all the qualities of an electromagnetic wave. Excited at still another place, the magic material that is space shows itself as a particle. There is nothing that is foreign and "physical" immersed in space.

The physicist JOHN A. WHEELER

□   □   □

Cleverness in omnivores, simply because the combination of several different food-gathering strategies can result in behaviors that are more versatile than the sum of the component behaviors. For example, the seagull's ability to carry food home in its beak, in combination with its ability to eat clams already cracked by waves crashing ashore, could have been what resulted in its ability to crack open clamshells by dropping them onto rocks from a height. Once in the possession of those two abilities, all the seagulls had to do was discover the joys of dropping shells. As a child discovers the joys of dropping spoons from high chairs.

□   □   □

Sharp stone tools from falling rocks. Barbara's demonstration of stochastic toolmaking was just a way of speeding up what nature does more slowly, dropping rocks a long enough distance so that the impact fractures them. I guess the reason that you don't find a pile of sharp rocks at the bottom of every cliff around here is that the smaller rocks tend to get carried away by floods, and are worn smooth by all the tumbling they do as they're carried along downstream. Getting sorted by size.

□   □   □

There are the major sidesteps in the evolution of multicellular animals. Like feathers for insulation facilitating bird flight, they produced something quite unlike what the competition seemed to be all about.

A major portion of the world's story appears to be that of fumbling little creatures of seeming no great potential, falling, like the helpless little girl Alice, down a rabbit hole or an unexpected crevice into some new and topsy-turvy realm. . . . The first land-walking fish was, by modern standards, an ungainly and inefficient vertebrate. Figuratively, he was a water failure who had managed to climb ashore on a continent where no vertebrates existed. In a time of crisis he had escaped his enemies. . . . The wet fish gasping in the harsh air on the shore, the warm-blooded mammal roving unchecked through the torpor of the reptilian night, the lizard-bird launching into a moment of ill-aimed flight, shatter all purely competitive assumptions.

LOREN EISELEY

Just think of the advantage that the first warm-blooded mammal would have had at night, all the reptiles cooled down to somnolence and unable to defend themselves. And all because of an abnormally inefficient animal (by cold-blooded standards!) that wasted energy by metabolizing food when it wasn't needed for movement. But this kept body temperature up and so the animal was pleasantly surprised by all the sleepy prey he encountered, which more than made up for all the wasted energy. The next time that you hear an evolutionary argument based on efficiency, remember those profligate warm-blooded animals.

□   □   □

Surface-to-volume ratio. Take the little matter of bundling up small children against the winter weather. You know how babies can get heated or chilled much more readily than adults? That's because they have a higher surface-to-volume ratio. The number of calories we contain depends on how big we are, our weight, our volume. We typically gain or lose heat through our body surface. When a baby grows to be twice as heavy as it was (has twice the volume), its surface area doesn't double too. And the baby can't change temperature as rapidly anymore. The percentage rate of heat loss (the fraction of body heat that you can lose in a given amount of time) is proportional to your body's surface area divided by your volume: the surface-to-volume ratio, in short. If one doubles the diameter of a ball, the surface area goes up four times. Yet its volume goes as the cube of diameter, so it goes up eight times. Doubling diameter halves the surface-to-volume ratio (1/1 goes to 4/8). And so the big ball's temperature will drop at only half the rate of the smaller ball. It's the same with babies: the bigger they get, the slower they lose heat, and so the less parents have to worry about bundling them up for a brief trip down the street in wintertime. Polar bears are big for a reason.

The same simple size principle (which lies at the core of what biologists call allometry) is found operating in many other ways in nature. For example, consider two schools of fish, one containing twice as many fish as the other but with the same average spacing between fish. Big fish intent upon a meal naturally approach the school from the side, and the school veers away from them. Only the fish on the outside of the school are likely to be caught. Thus, while more fish will be exposed in the larger school, the percentage of the fish population exposed to predation is smaller, simply because volume (proportional to the number of fish in a school) grows faster than surface area (number exposed to predators). The fish need not "know" allometric principles—it's just that those fish that like lots of company will be more likely to live long enough to raise a family. Of course, the herds of animals that visit African waterholes had this schooling principle used against them by *Homo erectus*, who lobbed that pointed discus into their tightly-packed midst. Circumventing their circumference.

On the other hand, if you want to maximize transfer rates, keep the surface-to-volume ratio high by preferring small sizes. For example, to cook a steak quickly, cut it up into lots of small pieces which—having a much greater surface area available for heat transfer—can therefore heat up faster.

We are, you may have guessed, having steak tonight, everyone cooking his own. I just showed Marsha my mother's technique of first slicing her raw steak into thin strips, then cooking them separately (she has a passion for "well-done" meat). In a similar way, trees also increase their rate of photosynthesis by increasing their surface area via lots of thin flat structures called leaves rather than just doing their photosynthesis on the surfaces of their cylindrical branches (yes, that's why Mormon Tea doesn't have leaves—the "bark" does the photosynthesis instead). Just another little rule from geometry with all sorts of implications for the sizes of things.

□   □   □

Later it occurred to me that the rate of evolution may, in part, be another consequence of surface-to-volume ratio. Natural selection is most effective on the boundaries of a population where the survival conditions are already marginal (the school-of-fish problem again). But how fast can selection there gradually change the characteristics of the whole population, if the gene pool is kept well-stirred?

Think of the population as the area of a circle, of change occurring only around the perimeter of the circle: the circle's perimeter-to-area ratio behaves just like the sphere's surface-to-volume ratio, so that the percentage change you can make is inversely proportional to the diameter. Whenever the population grows four-fold, the perimeter where natural selection takes place only doubles, thus slowing the rate of evolution to half, everything else being equal. When a population grows to a hundred times its original size but change still takes place only at the boundary, its rate of evolution should drop to 10 percent of what it originally was. For example, the human population

SIZE AFFECTS RATE OF GRADUAL EVOLUTION

If selection occurs primarily on the periphery, but the gene pool mixes, then four times the population only doubles the number under selection, *so the rate of gradual change is slowed to half.*

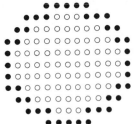

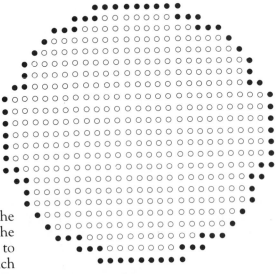

When a population grows 1000-fold, as has the human population in the last 10,000 years, the rate of gradual biological evolution is reduced to three percent of its original value under such circumstances. This is one reason why large populations change slowly, small ones alter rapidly.

has increased a thousand times over what it was before agriculture, thus any gradual human evolution should have slowed to 3 percent of its rate only 10,000 years ago, simply from that population increase and this simple size principle (in practice, bigger populations change nonuniformly because the gene pool is no longer well-stirred). When the uplift of East Africa broke up the big lakes there into many smaller lakes, it prevented the fish from getting around as much as earlier. The cichlid fish species promptly subdivided into many separate species and each started evolving at a faster rate.

Success, at least as measured by numbers, thus tends to slow evolution down to a crawl. Of course, there are other influences on evolutionary rates as well—such as the meteors that occasionally rock the boat.

□   □   □

Self-organizing systems are prime examples of emergent properties. Such as my example of how defender cells in the immune system could, with two simple rules, produce a widely varied array of defender types—none of which corresponded to one's own proteins. The widely known computer automata, known as the Conway Game or the Game of Life, neatly illustrates how two simple birth-and-death rules can generate fancy patterns in space and time; as it evolves on a checkerboard, some patterns emit "gliders" that move away; other patterns can absorb gliders without being altered.

The attainment of a new level of dimension is . . . a critical event in evolutionary history. I propose to call it evolutionary transcendence . . . to transcend is to go beyond the limits of, or to surpass the ordinary, accustomed, previously utilized well-trodden possibilities of a system.

The theoretical biologist THEODOSIUS DOBZHANSKY, 1969

□   □   □

I suppose that transcendence is another name for sidesteps—Charles Darwin's "functional change in structural continuity" is most evident when dealing with obvious structures such as feathers, but where it really comes into its own is in behavior, involving structures that are hidden in complex neuroanatomy. Our ability to ride a bicycle, for example, involves the secondary use of neural machinery that was shaped by selection pressures for things other than riding bicycles. The pedaling is probably just the circuit governing two-legged walking, temporarily modified within the range of possible strides. But the superb balancing act probably comes from something like our underwater skills, perhaps most extensively exposed to natural selection in an aquatic phase 6 million years ago. The combination of the two behavioral skills, walking and balancing, yields a novel skill far more readily than the combination of two digestive enzymes yields a new item available for the diet. Behavior easily combines unlike elements. That's why brains are such a powerful invention in evolution.

□   □   □

Natural selection could only have endowed savage man with a brain a few degrees superior to that of an ape, whereas he actually possesses one very little inferior to that of a philosopher.
ALFRED RUSSEL WALLACE (1823–1913)

And sidesteps are also emergent properties, new uses for old things. They're what so many people have missed when they say that human brains just couldn't have resulted from natural selection. Of course, in a sense they're correct—but evolutionary explanations encompass more than just adaptations. Natural selection shapes up the original skill, say throwing, but then jumps the track to something unexpected, say language. Natural selection again operates on this new track to shape up the emergent skill to something better than its crude beginnings, although natural selection itself really doesn't cause the sidestep-transcendence. It emerges, willy-nilly. Just as the lungfish invaded the land, as the feathered reptile invaded the air, our philosopher's brain has emerged by a self-organizing sidestep of evolutionary history, and invaded a new realm.

Sidesteps are something like "jumps into hyperspace," as in the computer games in which one can escape from approaching rockets by pressing a panic button, causing one's warship to disappear from the screen and reappear at some other, randomly chosen place on the screen (not necessarily a safe place either—sometimes the random jump is from the frying pan into the fire). There is natural selection before the jump and after the jump, but the jump itself is a discontinuity.

Are evolutionary sidesteps really steps to a random result, or are there principles governing sidesteps that we haven't discovered? Just as many mathematical principles break down at discontinuities, so our adaptationist reasoning cannot bridge a sidestep.

□   □   □

Are there classes of emergent properties? Packing rules and surface-to-volume ratios certainly seem to give rise to whole families of emergents. That's encouraging—it says that an emergent property needn't be completely unique, *sui generis*, but that some of them cluster into families, that principles may be understandable.

Indeed, there are emergents that make possible more emergents: the neurobiologist David G. King calls them metaptations (think "meta-adaptations" but, as Steve Gould and Elizabeth Vrba showed in their discussion of exaptation as a term to replace the misleading "preadaptation," the "ad-" is inappropriate because of the "toward" presumption).

What's a metaptation? It's an evolutionary change that opens up an entirely new set of evolutionary changes. Yes, it's a sidestep, an emergent, but a special kind, more fundamental in the long run than feathers leading to flight. Sex is a metaptation: by institutionalizing randomness rather than leaving it to chancy mutations, it opened up a whole series of other possible sidesteps. Gene duplication, then diversification, is a metaptation in my book.

And the invention of brains was another important metaptation: just as brains can add together "apples" and "oranges" to get the number of pieces of "fruit," so they can combine unlike behaviors to create novel behaviors. Brains add together behaviors, memories, and strategies far more readily than merely irritable cells can, and so brains have set into motion a whole series of evolutionary developments.

□   □   □

And the Law of Large Numbers itself gives rise to another whole family of varied emergent properties. It gives rise to the regular rhythm of the heartbeat and the precision of the hunter's throw. It's maybe even the underpinning of our appreciation of music? The physicist Erwin Schrödinger, in his influential 1944 book on biology, *What is Life?*, called the Law of Large Numbers the "order-from-disorder principle".

Applied to sequences, the Law of Large Numbers says that a lot of parallel sequencers, all trying to do the same job, ought to be able to produce more accurately timed sequences. That's handy for throwing. But maybe those separate sequencers are hitched up in tandem only on special occasions, and can each go their own ways in between the occasions that demand peak timing performance. What might emerge from lots of sequencers sitting around, amusing themselves by stringing together scenarios? Is this what we call consciousness? Did it emerge from just a lot of sequencers? Is human consciousness an order of magnitude more complex than that of animals, simply because we evolved so many sequencers on the way to becoming good throwers?

I got some requests from the after-dinner group to explain just what I meant by sequencers, and Rosalie provided the perfect example: the switching device that controls washing machine cycles. The schemata it sequences are all movements, called "Fill, Wash, Rinse, Empty, Spin, Pause." It can vary the duration of each cycle, can omit some if you like, perhaps repeat a rinse-empty sequence. The sequencers of the brain operate in fractions of a second rather than in minutes, but otherwise the principle is the same.

Suppose that we wanted, for some special occasions, a washing machine whose cycles lasted exactly ten minutes, right down to the split second. But that the available model of washing machine sometimes had an eight minute cycle, sometimes an eleven minute cycle—was, in short, jittery. There is a clever, though extravagant, way around this problem. We could take a hundred jittery washing-machine controllers and run them all together with one washing machine (such as by triggering a cycle whenever half of the controllers had agreed that it was indeed time to start up). This "averaging" of the times in the hundred controllers will improve the timing precision by a factor of ten: if an individual controller jitters over a range of one minute, the tandem arrangement of controllers will jitter over only one-tenth of a minute. Want a hundredth-of-a-minute accuracy? Just use 10,000 controllers.

Now in between those very special occasions when you're feeling paranoid and want to wash your most delicate sweaters for exactly the time it says on the instructions, you'd have ninety-nine extra controllers that weren't really needed for anything. Suppose the schemata they could manipulate included sensory schemata such as books, flowers, boats, and boots, that they could try stringing them together along with "wash" and "spin" to create novel scenarios. But that there was a "realistic or not" censor that commented "washing boats is a common practice, but washing books has seldom happened in your life so far." Still, even if the scenarios from ninety-five of the idle controllers proved unrealistic, four might yield realistic scenarios, though each with a different "quality" score. Suppose that you might just pick the one with the highest quality score for your next act? Is that imagination?

More candidate scenarios can make for more "clever" animals. That's the sort of situation that throwing might have set up, simply via selecting for individuals that happened to have extra sequence controllers capable of being hitched up in tandem on special throwing occasions. Is that why humans have more consciousness than dogs? Or is there something more to it?

Nature is extravagant, as witness all those bear cubs that die or the millions of mosquito eggs laid just to get one to grow up to lay more eggs. There is nothing easier than making a few more nerve cells, once the factory is working; indeed, they're overproduced during gestation and extra ones killed off. For any situation requiring precision, swamping it by assigning massive numbers of imprecise nerve cells is often a viable solution.

There is something wonderful in the idea that man's brain is the greatest machine of all, imitating within its tiny network events happening in the most distant stars, predicting their appearances with accuracy, and finding in this power of successful prediction and communication the ultimate feature of consciousness. . . . Our thought, then, has objective validity because it is not fundamentally different from objective reality but is specially suited for imitating it. . . .
The physiologist KENNETH J. W. CRAIK, *The Nature of Explanation,*
1943

□ □ □

I SUPPOSE THIS RATES AS A NIGHTMARE (I'm scribbling in the middle of the night again). I just dreamed that the washing machine repairman had been able to install a better clock, so that the hundred controllers weren't needed in parallel after all.

Then I dreamed that ape neurons were ten times better at timing accuracy than they really are. That would have eliminated the need for a hundred-fold increase in sequencers in the human brain—and with it, the big brain: apes could have been good throwers without it. No advanced consciousness emerging from redundant sequencers. While we'd have become fancy hunters, we'd still be no smarter than chimps, no more talkative, no better at planning. *Because it isn't so much the fancy timing that we need for language and imagining scenarios, it's all those extra sequencers that the tandem method encourages.* But only occasionally uses in tandem.

Thank goodness for noisy neurons. A little timing jitter was a good thing. There's a Noise Window in hominid evolution. No sidestep without enough noise. Not only are the more elaborate constructions of evolution based upon increased randomness via sex, but even the human brain may owe a recent debt to randomness. Subtitle: *How I learned to love noise.*

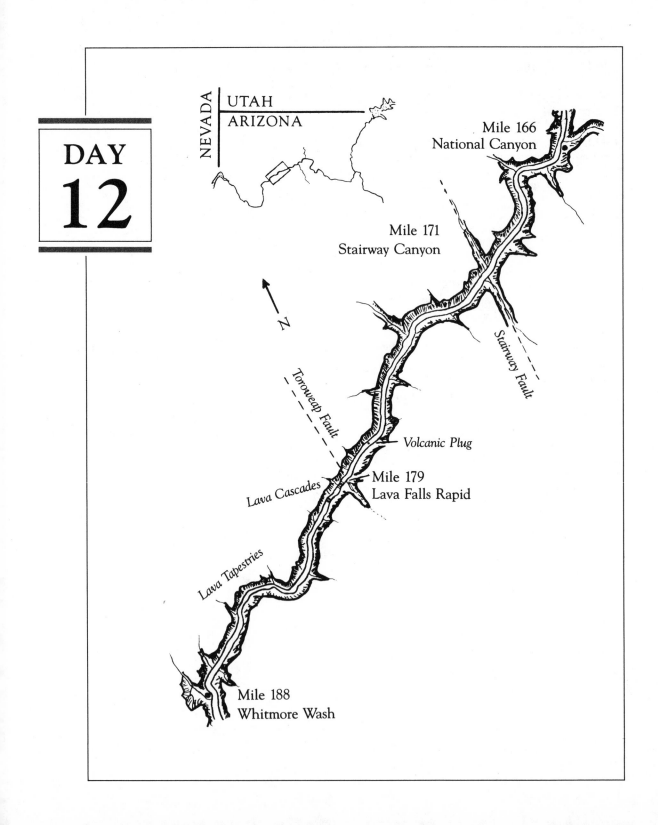

DAY

12

NEVADA | UTAH
| ARIZONA

N

Mile 166
National Canyon

Mile 171
Stairway Canyon

Stairway Fault

Toroweap Fault

Volcanic Plug

Mile 179
Lava Falls Rapid

Lava Cascades

Lava Tapestries

Mile 188
Whitmore Wash

IT'S A LITTLE EARLY for clouds. We're washing up before breakfast, and it is already overcast. Monsoon-type clouds don't usually build until afternoon, as the heat rising from the Canyon pushes up the moist ocean air arriving from the Pacific and Gulf of California. So these clouds must instead be a weather system. Grumble. But monsoons are another emergent property to add to the list—clouds emerge!

Perhaps we should add music to the emergent-properties list, as a sidestep from sequencing. And what was that other item from our first afternoon on the river? Ah, yes—humor. Can we explain that as another sidestep from sequencing? It does seem all tied up with our scenario-making consciousness—the surprise ending that plays on your expectations, and all that.

"But," asked Abby, who had originally posed that question, "what about laughter? I mean, it's almost involuntary, like a reflex. Why?"

We thought for a while as we were standing in the breakfast line. The best thing that we could suggest was that exhaling explosively might be related to the breathing control that we acquired for diving, perhaps in our aquatic phase. But why the link to mismatched expectations? We are stumped.

Maybe, suggested Ben, the outburst of laughter is related to literally "holding your breath" while awaiting the outcome of the joke!

AN UNEXPECTED SOCIAL CONSEQUENCE of the Law of Large Numbers surfaced after breakfast as we sat around avoiding the topic on everyone's mind, located downriver. This bit of sociology can be seen in the hiring of civil servants and, of particular concern to many of us, in the awarding of research grants. While our example is from the sociology of science, it's the same thing that happens in many committee decision-making processes, one with many implications for big corporations.

There is literally a priority list in most scientific fields: the funding agencies enforce the priorities seen by the established experts. Those scientific experts aren't narrow but the money available is thin. Of the applications their expert consultants select as worthy, the agencies can fund less than 20–30 percent (it used to be 50–65 percent). This inhibits re-checking the data collected by others ("That's been done before, so it's hardly top priority."), together with the pressure from animal protectionists and legislators who heap scorn upon "duplicated effort" as if basic scientists were defense contractors proposing to develop an existing airplane all over again from scratch.

But even more serious is that this top-of-the-pile-only funding unintentionally stifles diversity. Among the democratic ideals

MILE 166
National Canyon

Mathematical relationships tend to show a forever-surprising basic simplicity, as if implying that certain, relatively few fundamental laws, or their variants, underlie the infinite multitude of the observable detail that offers itself to our senses. To discover that the universe is structured, and moves, according to mathematical laws is to experience one of the most profound insights into the basic order of the cosmos.

The historian
THOMAS GOLDSTEIN
Dawn of Modern Science, 1980

that we Americans hold up, hoping for the rest of the world to copy, are the virtues of diverse political viewpoints and diverse businesses that compete for the consumer's approval. To these ends, we promote freedom of speech, diverse ownership of the press and media, capitalism without monopoly, states' rights, and the rights of the minority to hold a different view without being squelched by the majority (this civil liberty is largely what the U.S. Constitution's First Amendment is all about). School textbook adoptions are made by hundreds of different boards; there is no single approved promulgation. We encourage investors and small businesses to take risks. To our children, we hold up as heroes those who proved the experts wrong, the inventors who persevered and won.

Despite these ideals, we have created and allow to persist a system that forces scientists toward a mainstream. Our scientific heroes of the past, who followed the questions which most appealed to them, who saw it as a duty to duplicate the important results of others, who were independent—just like the medieval knights who went around doing good deeds, they too were usually men whose investments gave them the leisure and wherewithal to do things without first getting the approval of a committee and waiting several years after having the idea to start working on it. Most scientists today are paid less than garbage collectors. They often cannot afford to send their children to the universities from which they themselves graduated. In many cases, their tenure in their jobs lasts no longer than their current two- or three-year appointment or research grant. Completely dependent on the piecework grant system, they become cautious, careful not to antagonize others who might advise on whether their research grant will be renewed, aware from their friends' experiences that years of careful work can be "terminated" if their next renewal doesn't make it into the top 16 percent of worthy applications, scattering specially trained personnel to the winds while one tries again to find money. It's even worse than being the proprietor of a bankruptcy-prone small business, since there is no opportunity to recoup a funding loss in a good year.

The U.S. government channels money into basic research through mechanisms developed in the years just after World War II. They bear the stamp of a peculiar model of science fostered in legislators' minds by the Manhattan Project, in which physical scientists abandoned their academic surroundings to beat Hitler to the atomic bomb. It is an unrepresentative model for several reasons: it concerned physics and chemistry, not the full range of social, biological, and physical sciences. It was a technological rush job, not an investigation in basic science—even though the actors were mostly mathematics, chemistry, and physics professors, they were temporarily practicing applied technology, not the questing for unknown principles that characterizes true basic science (since the thirties, physicists had known the principles through which massive explosive power was available in the atom's nucleus; the 1942–1945 Manhattan Project was a great engineering endeavor to produce a portable bomb). Part of its legacy is the notion that group science is better than individual science—and that scientists be kept on a short financial leash.

The principles on which the U.S. National Science Foundation and the National Institutes of Health award research money seem (on the surface) more sensible than the one-person-decides principle on which the armed forces often award research funds (they are still an alternate source of money in some fields, if one can tolerate the potential censorship). Incredibly, though he or she may consult with advisors, a young military officer with a master's degree in engineering may make all funding decisions for wide areas of basic science. The civilian agencies make more use of "peer-review," literally a jury of one's scientific peers—though usually biased in membership towards the established, more senior scientists (they are not picked by the scientific community but by a bureaucrat). The civilian agency's scheme seems more "democratic," but it has some surprising, unwanted consequences—maybe the military has the better idea after all, many different pots, each tended by a different person every so often as officers rotate.

Rosalie said that she couldn't understand how twelve people—who, as individuals, were bright, inventive, broadly educated, delightful scientists—could, convened together into a peer-review committee, turn into twelve conservative scientists with limited horizons. What did the committee do to them, make them all into social conformists, so that they selected only "mainstream" people, and rarely those who prefer to explore opportunities off the beaten track? Perhaps. But there's another more likely explanation, that the Law of Large Numbers has struck again.

Everyone tends to look upon a selection committee as rank-ordering the best, the runner-ups, the also-rans, and the unworthy. Yet it isn't a horse race—it's more like comparing apples and oranges. Quality enters in, but preference often overrides. Fewer than 10 percent (often none) of the committee members are likely to be expert enough in the subfield of a particular proposal to judge it on any basis other than "attractiveness." So what do they wind up selecting?

The answer is that in attempting to select "the best," a com-

mittee merely selects the most widely acceptable, the most attractive to the members' diverse tastes. What else can it do?
The proposals selected may merely be in the middle of the diversity. The committee members may think that they are judging "quality" rather than consensus, but one person's expert
quality rating is often cancelled out by a less informed member's
attraction to another part of the diversity spectrum. Even if the
members are individually truly unbiased and quality-conscious
and representative and enlightened, such a committee process
can still result in the stifling of diversity—*when there is only
enough money to fund a small fraction of the worthy applications.*

Consider a diverse committee able to hire only two of a diverse
group of applicants (imagine, perhaps, a city council hiring civil
servants). Because consensus may be hard to reach on the others, only the applicants acceptable to a majority will be hired
(they may be no one's first priority or highest quality estimate).
The next time two jobs open up, the same thing happens again.
Take note: *the employees as a group will wind up being less diverse
than the committee that hired them.* Increasing the diversity of the
committee membership won't necessarily change the diversity
average, and so it's the middle-of-the-road which gets hired.

This isn't inevitable: there are some ways around this main-
streaming effect. If we have fifty jobs to fill at once rather than
two, we will be guaranteed some diversity. If the committee
members can trade votes, work out deals that result in alterna-
tion in hiring favorites, employee diversity might be somewhat
broadened. Some committees may be particularly enlightened
and strive to achieve some diversity—but the Law of Large
Numbers suggests that the typical committee is going to have a
natural tendency to select applicants which, as a group, are less
diverse in their interests than the committee itself. It's a result
completely contrary to the perceptions of the well-intentioned
committee members, each of whom is sure that quality counts.
But the whole is different than the sum of its parts, and a committee performance is not merely the sum of a dozen quality
judgments *when a spectrum of interests is also involved.*

When the money is thin, and the selection committee is
really more a one-time jury that is prohibited from bargaining
about reciprocation next time around (which are indeed the
rules in the peer-review of science research), it hires the middle-of-the-road—time after time after time. Now in science, the
average in diversity may be high in quality—and usually is, since
there is nothing mediocre about 95 percent of the applications
competing for funds.

The danger is that this system will breed much of the off-
center diversity out of the scientific population, just as animal

inbreeding eliminates useful-at-times traits in favor of one currently popular trait. In wild populations of animals, there is usually a wide range of diversity in the gene pool; whatever the climate dishes up next in the way of problems and opportunities, there will be some members of the species that have approximately the right set of insulating hair or sweat glands, of grazing or hunting instincts, of few-at-a-time or mass production in matters reproductive, of early or late breeding seasons. And the species survives. The inbred species, who may be uniformly great at turning grain into meat, may perish when the climate changes.

In science, we don't know where the future lies, where the revolutionary results may crop up (who'd have predicted that studying what happened to the dinosaurs would illuminate an unrecognized doomsday machine?). Try as we can, we cannot even predict the technological marvels of ten years ahead, much less the scientific ones. Diversity makes a lot more sense for institution-centered basic science than does emphasizing an artificial judgment of "the best." Spreading your bets means backing occasional losers, having pseudoscience occasionally get money that would—with hindsight—have been better spent elsewhere. Rather than the Congressional obsession with "wasted money" and auditing researchers' hourly efforts (they somehow think that our life's work can be treated as piecework in a repair shop), we need an audit for risk-taking: is an agency funding enough failures? When a good hospital reviews a surgeon's track-record, it looks for too many patients dying—but also for not enough dying. It isn't always variations in surgical operating skills that cause the high or low mortalities: variations in judgment and risk-taking play an important, though less obvious, role. A surgeon with no failures is a surgeon who plays it so safe as not to operate on a patient "who will probably die anyway." Some of those patients can be saved, but only by a surgeon willing to risk a personal failure. Researchers need to be able to gamble on long shots—but our present grant system penalizes that.

A committee with a small pie to divide up may be worse than no committee at all if the tight-money situation persists. If it is a sieve for the whole field, the fringes will be eliminated. Time after time after time. If we are to stand a chance of bailing ourselves out of the nuclear and ecological mess that our blind governments and juggernaut economies are creating, we are going to need both scientific depth and breadth to diagnose the problems, to propose cures and workarounds. We will indeed need to do what the Manhattan Project finally did: rather than trying to judge which manufacturing process was best for purifying the rare isotope of uranium, it tried all three known processes. At once. In parallel.

Of course we need more money. Research deserves its long overdue reinvestment of some of the profits already generated from the ideas and techniques that basic science has already donated to the marketplace (don't suppose that Hertz's family or university gets royalties for every radio manufactured, or Maxwell's, whose equations made it all possible). But we also need to protect the scientific minorities from the well-intentioned committee majorities. We cannot continue to filter all the money through one or two sieves in which only the middle-of-the-road proposals win. In a country that prides itself on protecting political minorities, it is hard to understand our drift in science toward center-take-all and winner-take-all.

MILE 170
Lake Lava

BOREDOM IS VERY IMPORTANT in an evolutionary perspective, we've decided. What is the use of a tendency to get bored with your food? Well, it promotes diversity of diet, so that one seeks out foods with vitamins and trace minerals. Boredom thus helps prevent deficiency diseases. Boredom of taste tends to be expressed by the changing of habitual behaviors, thus trying a different food-gathering strategy for a while—literally "doing something different."

Yet some animals achieve well-balanced diets with a monotonous food-gathering strategy: gorillas chewing their plants, dolphins catching their fish. The lack of boredom (those animals apparently don't need it to avoid deficiency diseases) may unfortunately spell an evolutionary dead-end for those species; since they're not stimulated to seek out infrequent foods using infrequent behaviors, they don't discover the virtues of new combinations of preexisting behaviors. Therefore, boredom could be an important stimulus to evolution among the animals, particularly omnivores.

And when one begins thinking about thought processes, one realizes that boredom is a critical parameter. Not enough boredom and you'll stay stuck in a rut. Too much boredom and you'll be hyperactive, constantly jumping around, failing to develop expertise in any one area. If we ever build a "thinking machine" in any true sense of that overused phrase, we'll have to adjust its "boredom factor" carefully so that it achieves breadth in coverage and occasional depth.

Common sense isn't faring very well on this trip. We seem to be collecting a paradoxical set of virtues: randomness, cowards, noisy nerve cells, even boredom. What's next, Cam quips: illness? And so we reminded him of the pathogen-escape hypothesis for the origins of sex, and thus our great evolutionary diversity.

AN INHERITED BRAIN DISORDER is a puzzle if you're a creationist, but more understandable—though it doesn't exactly achieve the status of a virtue—from an evolutionary viewpoint. It certainly shows that natural selection is imperfect, since brain disorders are far more common than even appendicitis. At least 1 percent of the population suffers from epilepsy, another 1 percent from schizophrenia (those are the underestimates—double them if you're a pessimist), and the figures for depression range from a few percent up to 15 percent, depending on how you define what you're counting. A sizeable fraction of the cases of each of these major brain disorders seem to be inherited, though only as a predisposition rather than a sure thing. How did they escape natural selection?

One possibility is that they're linked to traits that are useful, so that eliminating them would yield an overall reduction in fitness rather than an improvement. For example, boredom and schizophrenia are related in the sense that schizophrenics often cannot stick to a subject: thoughts intrude into their attempts at conversation, or they may hallucinate, hearing voices give a running commentary on their actions. It's as if the boredom mechanism had run wild, allowing subconscious thoughts such easy access to language consciousness that one becomes like a compulsive TV channel-changer flicking from one program to another after only a few seconds. I don't think for a moment that schizophrenia is as simple as a misadjusted boredom parameter, but there are aspects of it that could be interpreted this way.

Epilepsy in baboons has escaped natural selection: some subpopulations of *Papio papio* have photosensitive epilepsy, in which rapidly flickering lights trigger a seizure. A forest animal such as the typical monkey often experiences flickering lights, as it runs around through patches of sunlight and shadow; thus, photosensitive epilepsy in a diurnal forest animal would probably be selected out. But the baboon is a monkey adapted to the savannah, where the trees aren't densely packed: baboons simply aren't exposed to flickering lights very often, so that any epileptic tendencies that by chance develop in evolution are not promptly edited out.

In humans, some forms of epilepsy might be side effects of an improvement in neural machinery that has proven so successful that it hardly matters (to evolution, not the individuals affected) if 1 percent of the population has a problem. For ex-

Today's common sense is yesterday's science.

The physicist NEILS BOHR

ample, temporal-lobe epilepsy is a common form in humans, though no animals have been found to naturally exhibit it. We can often cure a patient with this form of epilepsy by simply removing the tip of the temporal lobe (a plum-sized chunk of brain tissue); surprisingly, no function disappears after the removal. Indeed, it is hard for observers to tell that anything is different about the patient (except that the seizures have been reduced or eliminated). The tip of the temporal lobe and the premotor regions of the inferior frontal lobe are, it so happens, the prime candidates for locations in which many of the brain's extra borrowable sequencers are located, augmenting precise timing via the tandem arrangement. Because those extra sequencers are not essential except when actually throwing (so my theory goes, at least), that might explain why removing the temporal tip seems to do so little to normal function. (Throwing accuracy, alas, is not usually examined by neurologists!)

And this also helps explain why the temporal lobe is so prone to epilepsy in the first place: seizures get started because a group of nerve cells go into a wild oscillation, rather like my washing machine at home when it gets to the spin cycle but all the towels are on one side of the drum, unbalancing the load. Timers are, of course, natural oscillators. A lot of them, particularly if hooked up to synchronize with one another (as I postulated for the "get set to throw" phase of throwing), would be a natural setup for a pacemaker that could drive the rest of the brain into a seizure. Correct or not, this little story illustrates the quandary in which evolution might sometimes be placed, where it has to take the bad with the good.

For such reasons, natural selection may be unable to act against seizures; the bad things are too closely linked to the good. There are other possibilities, too, such as a lack of enough time to select out the bad traits (if they'd developed recently in evolution). Or perhaps they're just not "exposed" to natural selection at a time when it will affect inheritance. And that's probably the key to why many kinds of depression have survived in evolution: depression often develops at an age when people have already had all their children. Initial hospitalizations for severe depression peak at age 55 (in contrast, for schizophrenia in males, the peak is at age 18 and for females at age 29, showing why one has to seek other explanations for schizophrenia escaping natural selection). While grandparents are quite useful in most human societies for both wisdom and babysitting, it's not the life-or-death usefulness of the parents, who forage for food and suckle the infant. And so late-appearing traits often escape natural selection—there is simply very little feedback into the gene pool when something goes wrong at age 55 or 70.

INDEED MUCH OF AGEING may be a similar problem of late-blossoming genes that have escaped natural selection over the generations. There are a lot of genes that are normally kept "repressed," their DNA sequence literally masked by a protein, so that RNA copies of them cannot be made. Only when certain conditions are met is the repressor removed so that the enzymes and other proteins can be manufactured from those genes. For example, there are DNA codes for several kinds of hemoglobin, one common in the fetus and the other a version that gradually replaces the early version; both carry oxygen just fine. The genes for fetal hemoglobin are still there, it's just that they're largely repressed with age, and the adult hemoglobin (repressed during gestation) is gradually expressed more and more during the changeover.

And similar transitions from one version of a gene product to a closely related form are probably common throughout life and in many body systems (the gene for making the enzyme that digests milk is repressed in some adults). Such gene repertoires, rather than wear and tear, may be responsible for most of the changes in body appearance by which we can estimate someone's age: the shape of the face and relative size of the head, compared to the rest of the body, are prime clues to the age of children, just as wrinkles and a broadened waistline are clues to whether someone is 20 or 50. In juvenilization among the primates, all life stages are slowed: not only are the periods of gestation, infancy, and childhood doubled, but adulthood is too. If a longer life span were really desirable, the logical way to achieve it would be to slow down the sexual and somatic clocks. It's likely they're what control the arrival of new versions of a gene.

One of the major hidden manifestations of ageing, seen from adolescence onward, is a decline in many of the neurotransmitter substances used by one nerve cell to signal an adjacent one. Since nearly all nerve cells are sensitive to the balance between plus and minus inputs rather than the absolute size of each, this decline may have no discernible effect on function; both plus and minus inputs might decline by half between ages 20 and 70, but that won't necessarily change a zero balance. Yet let one decline by a greater percentage than the other, and the system would somehow have to compensate in order to keep things running properly. In Parkinson's disease, the substantia nigra (an almond-sized collection of pigmented nerve cells below the thalamus) is affected—a viral infection might, for example, kill off half the nerve cells in that location at age 30, seemingly without consequences for function. But when the age-related loss of 5 to 7 percent of its nerve cells per decade adds

The secret to birthday happiness is learning to accept the ageing process as something as beautiful and natural as premenstrual tension.

up, and one gets down to only 20 percent remaining, then one starts getting symptoms of rigidity, tremor, and all the rest. Why won't the system run on just 20 percent? Maybe it's the Law of Large Numbers again, too much fluctuation about the same mean. Just too noisy.

Now, the "normal" 25 to 35 percent loss of neurons from the substantia nigra in adulthood is not the same in other brain areas; right next door in the reticular formation, the loss may be minuscule, with 98 percent of the original cells still there at age 70. What controls this loss rate? Probably gene expression, rather than exercise or virtuous living—but, in fact, nobody knows yet.

Depression, with its rising incidence with age, may be caused by genes that are expressed late enough in life that natural selection affects only the individual and not his descendants too. Those versions of the genes just haven't been improved for us by our ancestors. We owe our good health up to age 45 to our ancestors, but particularly to those would-be ancestors who dropped out because of natural selection before adding very many of their genes to the common pool. After age 45, it's a whole new ballgame, played with few evolutionary rules because natural selection has not operated on those particular combinations of expressed genes. Indeed, if there is a cutting edge of human evolution these days, it's in that post-reproductive age group that lives largely unrestrained (as well as unprotected) by the usual evolutionary constraints that have shaped our species.

RIVER CORRIDOR CROSS SECTION

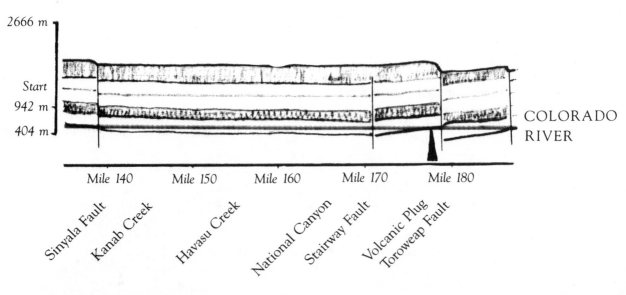

THE STAIRWAY-WILLOW SPRING FAULT cuts across the Canyon here so that we have two side canyons emptying into the river at this point. Like Badger Rapid back on the first day, that's a good setup for a major rapid—but Gateway Rapid is only rated 3 these days.

One can see that the two sides of Stairway Canyon are offset; the layers on the downriver side are jacked up nearly four stories higher than on the upriver side. I hear that we're going to see lots of fault lines later today and again tomorrow. The Colorado is now cutting into the Bright Angel Shale once again; I wonder if there are any more big landslides like the one that created Surprise Valley?

Up and down, but always different.

We're also seeing new plants now, such as the creosote bush. Cactus everywhere. Bighorn somewhere, it is claimed. But I'm still watching for rocks that move.

The clouds are still with us, but I think they're starting to clear. It'll probably be hot by the time we get to Lava Falls, and get cooled off in a big way. There's a lot of joking about Lava Falls this morning, gallows humor and the like. Someone's offering to make book on whether there is really a black hole there. Might as well bet on Clams Linguine.

There are clouds over some people's lives because they're "born wrong." We're all different, but there is a tendency to regard variations well away from the average as imperfections. We live in a world where variations suggest manufacturing defects, where people unable to learn to read suggest an "error" of development, an unfortunate gene, an unwelcome occurrence. But are they, perhaps, merely evidence of nature's method, of producing lots of variations and letting the marketplace decide? Once upon a time, a miswired visual cortex was probably better at color vision, and so those lucky monkeys that had it turned out to be better at spotting fruit among the leaves.

We may come to look upon much of mental illness this way, as the product of variants in the wiring of the brain much as reading disorders probably are. And some such variations are hard to get rid of, if they're late-blooming.

SPEAKING OF DEPRESSING SUBJECTS, how about pain? There are indeed some obvious relationships between pain and depression, between suffering and consciousness.

For what reason might the following collection of behaviors be appropriate? Lethargy, daytime sleepiness, loss of sexual drive, loss of appetite, and a tendency to not move around much? It matches up with how an injured deer behaves, when it holes up for a week without moving, to give healing a chance. And

---

MILE 171
Gateway Rapid

it isn't just deer—that's how most of us act in the days following an injury.

It is becoming evident that this behavioral syndrome can be
triggered in other ways, some inappropriate. Our pain system
really isn't very sophisticated: a toothache may, for example,
trigger the "holing up" behaviors, as may neuralgias—neither
of which will be helped by these behaviors.

Now this collection of behaviors constitutes a very characteristic part of the mental disorder we call depression. Does this
mean that depression is partly an inappropriate response to a
chronic pain of some sort? Certainly the converse is frequently
true: pain specialists have learned to try using the antidepres-
sant drugs to treat chronic-pain patients when aspirin fails, having found that these patients will often improve behaviorally—
and that their pain may also disappear at the same time. As
Rosalie pointed out, this suggests a research strategy that would
attempt to persuade the brain that a physical pain, or even a
psychological "pain" of the type we honor with such phrases as
"a pain in the neck," is not important, that it is inappropriate
to respond to it by holing up. One can see why treatments such
as psychotherapy might work.

Of course, depression is more than just holing up. Melan-
choly feelings are an important, though not essential, part of
the depression syndromes. And this brings up the distinction
between the phases of pain. We pain researchers (well, I guess
that I'm the only one on this trip) are finding out an increasing
amount about the specialized neural pathways for signaling and
evaluating sensations that may be associated with tissue damage. Those "fire-alarm" types of sensation are obviously useful;
you'd expect them to be about the same in a deer as in a human. But they don't always cause distress: 37 percent of the
emergency-room patients studied in a Montreal hospital didn't
report pain for hours after being injured, despite broken bones,
major abrasions, and other reasons why their sensory neurons
should have been carrying quite a lot of pain messages to the
brain. That's why neurophysiologists distinguish "nociception"
from "pain": pain is what one reports (sometimes) when noci-
ceptive messages arrive in the brain. It makes evolutionary sense
for sensation to be sufficient to tell you to get yourself out of
the situation—but you certainly wouldn't want the holing-up
phase to start right after the injury! And fortunately, the tenderness of an injured region doesn't develop immediately afterward but is instead delayed by hours.

In addition to nociception and pain, there's suffering. It is
greatly augmented by the predicting-the-future aspects of con-

sciousness; we can see what's coming, and so may be additionally distressed above and beyond anything caused by the current reports from our sensory nerves. We suffer less if we know that the sensations of pain will be short-lived (as in a dentist's chair) or innocuous (as in breaking in a new pair of shoes). But according to the scenario-spinning theory, human consciousness may be greatly enhanced over that of the deer, and that might enhance our suffering. Thus, even though the evolutionary perspective says we need not ascribe to animals quite the same extent of "suffering" that we would feel in a similar situation, the animal might feel more "pain" than we do in the short run, simply because it is unable to know that a pain is innocuous or will be short-lived. How these factors balance out in terms of distress produced is hard to predict; sometimes you just have to watch the animal's blood pressure for signs of alarm.

We are just starting to look at pain and suffering from a biological perspective, asking what role they really play in animals, asking what are the normal phases of response to an injury. So far, it looks as if the initial pain sensation (what most researchers study, what most physicians test, and what the analgesic drugs affect) is the least of the problems, as its function is merely to prevent further injury. It's the delayed tenderness and the prolonged holing-up syndrome that create most of our problems with pain (outside the neuralgias, which falsely report an injury when none exists)—and they may be related to some common types of depression. Beyond all that is suffering, and we don't know the extent to which animals share it with us.

Our brain and sensory nerves really aren't very good at reporting tissue damage accurately, either its exact location (can you tell exactly which tooth hurts?) or its magnitude. All sorts of errors occur, as when a heart attack is felt as a pain in the left arm instead of the chest. But maybe it just wasn't very important to know the exact location of a pain, in the days before doctors, when we were being shaped by evolution. If pain's first function is to change our activities so as to help stop the damage, it isn't critically dependent on accurate estimates of position and magnitude. "Good enough" engineering strikes again. In pain's second function—to aid healing during recuperation—an on-or-off type of tenderness report is again almost as useful as a detailed accounting of the damage. In evolution, one didn't need to know where an injury was exactly located in order to repair it—one's body does that automatically, without being consciously dispatched to the exact location of an injury.

When you get down to it, you realize that pain simply hasn't been exposed to a lot of selection pressures—except, perhaps, for distracting false-alarms. But malfunctions like neuralgias are again mainly confined to postreproductive phases of the life span and so have escaped selection.

This evolutionary analysis helps one to better appreciate the senseless, inhuman things such as cancer pain, in which there seems to be no natural way of turning the pain off after it has served a warning function. Evolution may have provided a cut-off switch for short-term pains such as those a tired athlete feels, so that they do not interfere with getting out of a threatening situation, but evolution hasn't provided any cutoff switch (so far as we've been able to discover) for the long-term pains of tenderness during repair attempts. After all, during most of evolution, a serious injury was life-threatening—either you got better or you died. And so humans have, until recent years, had to live with Seneca's sage advice: "Ignore pain. Either it will go away or you will."

Pain control is one of the most significant ways in which we can improve the quality of our lives; it is a far more humane goal than merely trying to extend the life span. We will be taking evolution into our own hands even more than usual in this area: nature hasn't done much, and our measures will strongly interact with whatever quality-of-life goals that we set for our society.

THIS LOWER SECTION OF THE GRAND CANYON is certainly starting to look different. There are lots of piles of land-slide debris, high up. But the Canyon walls are also studded with patches of green, the plants growing among the red rock. It's the way one can tell the difference between pictures of the lower Grand Canyon and of the same layers in the upper Canyon, at least if it has rained recently. We're at lower elevations here, with less severe winters, and the plant population is shifting over to a collection more like the Mojave Desert's.

In Jimmy's boat up ahead, someone is joking about us drifting toward our very own appointment with natural selection.

A gray day.

BLACK LAVA appears suddenly, but subtly, at Mile 177. There are a few boulders of lava disguised in a talus slope of ordinary rock coated with dark desert varnish. By geologic standards, this lava is quite recent compared to all other rock in the Canyon—such as the Cardenas lavas back at Furnace Flats from 1,200 million years ago. This lava is from the last several million years, which saw the ice ages and the threefold enlargement of the prehuman brain; it is left over from a giant lava flow that dammed up the Colorado River near here—and nearly filled up this part of the Canyon with muddy water. That lava up there at the 100-story level above the river is probably left over from that great lava dam. Influenced by Edward Abbey's vision of the end of the Glen Canyon Dam and Lake Dominy, we joke about what a sight it must have been when the lava dam broke. One of the boatmen wears a campaign button on his cap, reading: "*I Want to Run DOMINY FALLS, Glen Canyon.*"

A giant black rock about five stories tall sits in the right side of the river channel. Vulcan's Forge was once a volcano itself, which one day started to make the river boil. And then emerged in mid-river. Now it is a chunky remnant called a volcanic plug, a reminder of how fast things can come and go. We hear that there's some real marble hereabouts—contact metamorphism, just like what made that asbestos we peeled off the rock back at Deubendorff. Except this time it was limestone that got heated, and metamorphosed into marble rather than asbestos or schist.

This morning on the river has been very quiet. There have been no serious rapids, not one. Indeed, we've seen mostly riffles and whirlpools for almost 30 river miles. Now the Canyon is opening out, great flows of black lava sweeping down the right canyon wall to the river bank. The river is widening and slowing in anticipation of the biggest rapid on the river; the boatmen call this stretch of river "Lake Lava," and they row harder, getting warmed up for the big event.

Soon we faintly hear the low, continuous rumble of a distant thunderstorm. But the clouds are clearing, so it's probably Lava Falls announcing itself.

A black hole in Lava Falls? Surely they're joking. Ahah! I'll bet it's a hole surrounded by black lava rocks. That must be it. That, or maybe an allusion to another property ascribed to black holes: the tendency to not give back what they take in.

THE BOATS are all pulled up on the right shore, in the midst of a grove of seepwillows. Climbing upward along the black gritty trail through the lava, we are soon in the hot sun, the clouds having parted, the heat of midday approaching. The black rocks are too hot to touch, the lava too prickly for comfortable handholds anyway. But the trail is easy and leads up only far enough to give the boatmen a good vantage point from which to plan their run of the rapid.

We leave the boatmen to themselves, standing on their advanced perch discussing possible routes with much pointing and waving of hands. We stand back on the trail, engulfed by the heat beating down from above and rising up from the hot black

For days you have been hearing rumors about That Riffle-At-Mile–179.6. Lava Falls. This rapid offers the true test of a geologist's loyalty to his science. Will he, in the face of such an improbably violent rapid, be able to notice the cascades of black lava that once poured into the Grand Canyon and froze onto its walls? Will he examine this rock with its small olivine crystals, glassy matrix, and columnar joints, and conclude that it must have cooled quickly after flowing into the Canyon? Will he notice the cinder cones on the Canyon rims above? Will he remember that this rock is only a million years old, making it the youngest of all the Canyon's rocks? Probably not.

MICHAEL COLLIER
Grand Canyon Geology, 1980

MILE 179
Lava Falls Rapid

It is important to understand that you don't get splashed in Lava Falls; you get inundated. Eating a wall of solid water is one of the quintessential experiences of running this rapid. Not a few river runners have distinctly recalled being in a boat but completely underwater and unable, for a few tense seconds, to breathe. In one astonishing run a boat flipped over on one wave and back, right side up, on another. It required a film, taken from shore, to convince its occupants, who had never left their seats, that they went completely around.

Robert O. Collins and
Roderick Nash
The Big Drops, 1978

rocks beneath our feet. The pounding of the rapid is ceaseless, the loudest we've experienced—it is a low vibration that penetrates your body, from which there is no escape.

Lava Falls is well named: it looks more like a waterfall than any rapid we've encountered before. Crystal, the worst so far, dropped the river level by one and a half stories. Lava Falls drops three stories, almost four. And it doesn't take very long to do it, either: it looks like a short and harsh staircase, filled with boulders. There are a number of foaming holes scattered along its course, some to the left, others in mid-channel, others along the right. Black rocks dot the right side. All the holes seem surrounded by black rocks. There is one particularly large black rock just downstream of the last hole in the right channel, but there is no water going over it.

We evidently cannot go straight down the middle at this water level. One way or another, the boatmen will have to ferry sideways across the river: after passing to the right of the hole near the top, one would have to ferry left to avoid the big hole just ahead. But not too far left. I can spot no obvious safe path through the rapid. But then I'm not a pro. We amateurs trade proposed routes while waiting for the pros to finish doing the same thing. As we compare, I notice that the top left hole has changed, just in the 15 minutes since I first looked.

Though the boatmen still show no sign of finishing their planning—they're still spinning alternate scenarios—many people have gone back down to the boats. The view, together with the vibration, has convinced people that Lava Falls is not like other rapids, that maybe it deserves its reputation. I take a last picture and then head down myself. It's too hot and exposed up here, almost a lunar landscape. It is quieter and cooler at the boats, and they are comfortingly enclosed by shade-giving greenery. People are pretty quiet and certainly sober. One of the teenagers manages to look bored.

Without prompting, we are starting to tie down everything, tightening up on the nylon webbing that holds our ammo cans and bailer buckets in place. It is all too easy, after seeing Lava Falls, to believe the boatmens' cautions about securing everything.

Life vests are refitted, straps tightened far more than ever before. Most people lash their hats down to the raft somewhere, imagining the force of the heavy waves will be too much for their light brims. Perversely, I just tighten my chin strap and hope that my heavy hat brim will shield my face as it has before. I try to pull my knife out of its sheath and am surprised at how hard I must maneuver it before it comes free. First I tie the sheath more securely into the webbing of my life vest, so that I have something to pull against if I want to get the knife out. Then I brush off the sand adhering to the knife and sheath. I slide the knife in and out of the sheath numerous times, to loosen up the leather's grip, leaving it fitted just tight enough so that it won't fall out. Knives aren't on the official packing list, but some years ago a neurobiologist I knew, Donald Wilson, was drowned when he was held underwater by a rope in a white water accident in Idaho; he worked in the same subfield of neurophysiology as Dan Hartline and I, and we often discuss one of his last discoveries, about simple ways of generating rhythms, one of the first emergent properties discovered about neural committees.

Sandy reappears and the other boatmen can also be heard among the seepwillows, heading to their boats. I am glad to be riding with Sandy Heavenrich today. He is probably the strongest of all the boatmen, and that could make the difference in Lava Falls. I ask him what route he is taking. "Enter left, ride the lateral wave right, hook around that top right hole, ferry left to avoid the big hole at right bottom." Sober as ever, Sandy looks around, double-checking our preparations. He coils the mooring line, gives it a thump against the side of the boat to shake loose the sand, and swings onto his seat atop the freezer chest. Then he repeats the lecture on high-siding and what to do if you find yourself out in the river. And to please be sure to avoid foreign entanglements.

As we row out into the river, I surmise that we're to be the lead boat through Lava. We're the guinea pigs who get to test the currents. But the boatman who leads usually takes a conservative route—it's the boatmen further back in the order who get a chance to try the fancier routes, once they have someone downstream to catch them if they get into trouble. There are three boats in our group, but the other two are holding back, probably to see how we do before they start. Gary Casey is standing out on the rocks at the lip of the rapid, ready to watch us descend. He'll tell the two waiting boats what happens to us, as they won't be able to watch us.

The passengers from the other four boats will watch us from shore just as at Hermit's photo run, then come through afterward as we watch from shore downstream. As we row back upriver to position ourselves in the left-center of the channel, I see some temporarily-reprieved passengers from the remaining boats climbing back up the hot lava path carrying cameras with telephoto lenses.

Sandy leans over to check the spare oars, strapped to each

side of the boat. The straps are usually tied so that one pass of a knife can liberate an oar quickly. But Sandy has arranged them today so that pulling a simple shoelace knot is sufficient to free them up. He carefully instructs the rear passengers, Laura Sirota and me, to pull the knot only if he shouts at us to do so. I have heard that Lava frequently gets hold of an oar, snaps it out of the oarlock, and doesn't give it back. But Sandy doesn't mention that. He is strong, silent, and very competent.

We approach the lip of the rapid at left center, our stern pointing to the left shore slightly upstream—evidently Sandy is thinking ahead to the hard left turn he'll have to execute off the right shore after the lateral wave carries us to the right, past the top of the boulder with the hole. So Sandy is initially pushing on the oars to advance the bow of the boat to the right, a weaker stroke than the pull he'll need subsequently to make the U-turn off the wall—but Sandy's push stroke is as strong as many a boatman's pull stroke. Laura takes off her glasses, folds them hastily, and buttons them into a pocket. As we perch on the lip, I am surprised how far down the rapid I can see— this is really a steep gradient compared to earlier rapids. It's like looking from the second balcony down to the stage of a theatre. And then we take the first step—which is nothing like the gentle beginning of most rapids. Suddenly water seems everywhere around us, glittering in the sunlight. We are instantly soaked.

We are swept into the right lateral wave with a flourish of wake-up waves. Sandy immediately begins pushing hard and fast. He is trying to pick up additional rightward speed. And indeed we speed up. Another wave soaks us. Sandy is rowing faster than I've ever seen him row. But we are too slow and I see that we are being carried downriver toward the boulder faster than we are heading into the turn. That's not in the script. There's a hole below that boulder.

It's like seeing a skidding car heading toward you, one that you cannot evade, and just knowing there will be a collision. Like a crazy dream in slow motion, in which you're trapped, helpless. Nonsense—this can't happen to me. Yet the boulder is almost beneath us and the drop into the hole is imminent. Well, I always did wonder what it would be like.

Slowly we fall. The boat twists and arches its back. As we splash into the frothy hole, white water is everywhere—in the boat, outside the boat, soaring over our heads, scattering the sunlight. Our right oar is pushed back against the boulder, trapped between us and a hard place. It irresistibly pops loose from its oarlock, is torn out of Sandy's strong grip. The waterfall pours into the boat—I cannot see Laura anymore. She's under the waterfall. Then we spin around, and she reappears, shaking her head. Then I see the long oar flapping around alarmingly at the end of the short leash tying its shaft to the frame. I push Laura down; she is too close to grapple with it safely, even if she could see without her glasses. I reach across her stiffarmed in an attempt to fend off the oar or grab it. Sandy briefly makes an attempt to retrieve the flailing oar but soon leaves it to me, shifting both hands to the remaining oar, pulling hard each time, trying to get a bite on the frothy water.

The sunlight returns and I realize that we are out of the hole. Just like that. But we are still in the midst of Lava Falls, and the river below the hole seems only slightly less frothy than the hole. The oar still escapes me; I grab only water, repeatedly. I am still leaning across Laura; she must be wondering what is going on up above, what is taking me so long.

Swift currents again carry us downriver through smaller rocks, and Sandy is trying hard with his one oar to get us out of the right channel, back into the middle of the river somehow. And away from the big hole. But we are too slow again trying to ferry sideways, and are drawn back into the right channel.

Oh, no—not again! Haven't they ever heard of acquired immunity? It can't happen twice to me. But again we approach a precipice. The boat perches briefly atop the big boulder. And we twist and fall—a real drop of perhaps half a story—into the exploding waves, which batter us from all directions. At least we don't flip. By this time I have given up on the loose right oar and am again crouched down in my left rear corner, wedging myself in as tight as I can. Laura is still positioned with her head well down, and the loose oar is hard to see, what with all the airborne water. The boat is folding, filling with water, lashing around and spinning. We are bashed about, seemingly stuck in the hole, just like in the stories we've heard. With the lone oar, Sandy is valiantly trying to get a bite on some solid water with his two-armed pulls, but hits only froth. Again and again.

I remember the black hole story—once you're in, you can't get out again.

And there is no shape or form anywhere—I cannot see either Sandy or even where I'm holding on to the boat frame, there is so much white water everywhere. It might just as well be black for all the good the light does. But then there is even more water. And the light does begin to dim. I sputter as I try to breathe.

◻   ◻   ◻

I returned, and saw under the sun, that the race is not to the swift, nor the battle to the strong, neither yet bread to the wise, nor yet riches to men of understanding, nor yet favor to men of skill; but time and chance happeneth to them all.

BOOK OF ECCLESIASTES, about 200 B.C.

□   □ ~ □

AND THEN WE'RE LOOSE, who knows how. Maybe it just spit us out! We've been rejected! We come up for air and see real sunlight, snatches of riverbank scenery through the white water. Sandy now effortlessly grabs the loose oar and together we fit it into the oarlock. Laura is sputtering. After I stop leaning over her, she comes up wiping water away from her face, opening her eyes to see where we are. We are safe. The rapid isn't over yet, but we're safe. We start bailing out the thoroughly filled boat, though I must loosen my lifejacket corset straps to bend easily. My hat is still wedged on tight, and I push it back with relief, free at last.

Sandy rows us over to the right shore in the first quiet cove of swirling waters. Laura fishes her glasses out of her pocket, puts them on still wet, and looks around. We look back at the path we traveled and try to comprehend what we've been through. At least we missed all the holes in the left and center channels. We are looking up at three stories of white staircase and the two big holes that we survived. It seems quite absurd.

"I'd say we got kind of thrashed back there," opines Sandy with a big grin. "See them looking down at us?" He points upstream and then gives a prizefighter's victory wave to signal that we're okay.

Another boat is seen hovering at the top of Lava Falls, seemingly backpaddling. They couldn't see what happened to us. But presumably Gary, standing on the shore near the lip of the rapid, has shouted to the next boatman that the rightward lateral wave at the entry point is much slower than anyone guessed. Plans are probably being revised with much shouting back and forth.

Sandy has the other passengers disembark after we've finished bailing, and then prepares to play rescuer. He climbs up front and ties a long, medium-diameter rope into the D-ring of the boat's bow and tests the knot. Then he beckons me to come forward and hands the coiled rope to me. As we row back upriver and position ourselves behind a small boulder that affords some shelter from the swift currents, Sandy explains the different ways we might use this line. I can throw it to a swimmer (I haven't practiced with a lasso since childhood, however). But we have to be careful to keep the swimmer downriver of us—someone approaching from upriver will be carried under our boat by the current as we attempt to pull them out. Therefore, I should guide them around the bow to the downriver side before trying to haul them into the boat, says Sandy. We might also use the line to tow another boat.

I practice throwing the line sidearmed at a small rock in the river and, while overshooting less than I intended, do lay the line across the rock. I re-coil the wet rope with care, probably having exhausted my beginner's luck. I'm still annoyed with myself for failing to retrieve that oar, back between holes.

So, positioned behind our boulder by Sandy's regular push strokes, we watch the other boats come down Lava Falls. The next two make it look easy—though they ship a lot of water somewhere. They too take up rescue positions on the opposite shore, one opposite us and the other further downriver, each boat bailed dry in an intense flurry of activity by all passengers.

There is a long wait as the camera-laden passengers of the second group disappear from the trail's vantage point and get back to the four remaining boats. I am surprised that no one decides to walk around Lava—it's easy enough to do—after seeing our travail. We can no longer see them, but we imagine them rowing back upriver to position themselves in the center left of the river. Nothing happens for a long time. Sandy and I finally begin to joke about them rowing all the way back up to the volcanic plug—maybe even to Phantom Ranch! But then a boat appears on the horizon at the lip of the rapid and starts down the staircase, ferrying out of sight, then reappearing in the center channel.

It is not at all like the slow-motion of our ride down the rapid. In just a minute or so they zip past us—very wet but exhilarated. Soon they are bailing like crazy.

Indeed, all the boats make it without apparent incident, some taking a markedly different route than we'd planned, none following our white staircase, none needing our towing and pickup services.

The other two waiting boats take off, following the last boat through. But we're delayed, having to detour to shore to pick up our three happily stranded passengers with their cameras. We belatedly follow the other boats downriver, passing through Lower Lava Rapid alone. A mere 5. But enough so that we have to bail the boat again.

EVERYONE ELSE is clustered on a narrow Muav ledge on the left bank a mile below Lava Falls. It looks like an elevated stage filled with actors. Our late arrival is welcomed—we feel as if we're on stage. It appears that everyone has been talking about us, awaiting our delayed solo appearance.

We head for the lemonade. To hear the second group tell what they saw from shore, our trip was even more harrowing than we thought. We were out of sight in the holes and didn't reappear promptly, causing some concern. Sounds as if they were holding their breath from anxiety just as much as we were, to keep from breathing water. They saw our boat arch its back and then fold the other way, saw our oar flailing around at some point (Joanne Kerbavaz says she got a telephoto shot of us, just when we lost the oar in the first hole), saw us miss the middle channel and be swept back toward the second hole, sinking in it out of their sight. We, of course, are rather nonchalant, as if it were all in a day's work. Even the black hole. Our lemonade cups only shake because we are a trifle chilly from our soaking.

I can imagine the anxiety about going through Lava that our run must have triggered in the remaining six boats. But the only real casualty of Lava Falls was Ben, who had been thrown backward so hard by a wave that he got a bloody nose from a collision with the boatman's knee. Alan's knee looks unscathed.

Soon lunch is ready. Everyone is talking animatedly, the boatmen are exuberant. I think that the adrenaline is still running high. Lava Falls is past, it's history, it's done. Finished. I've never heard the group so lively.

And we are in no hurry to go anywhere for a while. Seconds on sandwiches become thirds. People keep dropping sandwich fillings because they're trying to gesture while they eat. Two ravens hang out nearby, offering to clean up if we'll just move. Sandy mixes up a second cooler of lemonade because the first one ran out. We exhaust the cookie supply, even the two buckets of oranges and apples.

And the flat, shaded ledges of water-sanded Muav limestone are comfortable. Some of us stretch out, nap for awhile.

A SNAKE PASSED ME BY. Larry Anderson awakened me, saying that a long, lovely snake had just zipped past my head. It is now hiding in a low, miniature cave nearby, formed by Muav layers just overhanging the stage on which we're spread out. He couldn't believe how fast that snake moved. That rather eliminates the possibility that it was a Canyon rattlesnake, since rapid locomotion is not one of its attributes. So I bend down on hands and knees and look in where Larry points. But I cannot see the snake for the longest time. Then it flicks its tongue twice and I see it in my peripheral vision. Snakes do that to sample the air—when the tongue arrives back home, it is inserted into the roof of the mouth and tasted. A funny way to

To the Primal Wonders . . . you shall win them yourself, in sweat, sun, laughter, in dust and rain, with only a few companions.

NANCY NEWHALL, 1960

smell, but it saves inhaling. The snake presumably smelled us that time.

What a lovely snake! It is khaki or perhaps a light reddish-brown, a perfect match for the Muav. It is also exactly the thickness of a limestone layer, so I have trouble following its body along the twists and turns of the staircased ledge on which it is stretched out inside the "cave." The snake looks like a little strip of color-matched molding clay tacked onto a lip of Muav. At one point, its body drops down to the next-lower ledge—looking just like a flexure in the rockbeds. Finally I locate its tail, after five false alarms. Superb camouflage. Snake and undulating ledge look like a rhythmical, subtle sculpture. Larry and I estimate its length at nearly 1.5 meters. If Larry hadn't seen it enter the low cave, we'd never have spotted it. Except for waving its tongue occasionally, it is in perfect repose.

I pick my way among the sleeping bodies to where Alan is sitting alone on his boat, and quietly describe the snake to him. "Probably a Red Racer," he says, showing absolutely no inclination to get up and come look. I think that the letdown has finally set in. Post-adrenaline lethargy. I see that another bucket of fruit has been put out, and help myself to an orange.

I get back and—once I finally relocate him, about an elbow's length from my face—find the snake still there, tasting the air again, blending in perfectly with the layers of limestone, waiting patiently for a lizard to walk past the entrance to his cave. Larry and I sit back at the river's edge so as not to scare away any foolish lizards. For a good half hour I stare, hoping to either see a lizard arrive or the snake leave. Nothing happens. The shadows change, the river rises a little, people stir.

People seem not to bother the Red Racer at all. People are temporary, lizards are forever.

Eventually we get ourselves together but, before casting off from our homely Muav ledge, Larry and I look inside the low cave once again. It takes a while to double-check all the possibilities, but it seems that the Red Racer has disappeared while we weren't looking. Larry says that at the speed it moved earlier, ignoring it for three seconds might have been enough. I am disappointed, having wanted to see its racing act for myself.

BUT THE BLACK HOLE OF LAVA FALLS wasn't really either of the holes we inadvertently explored, J.B. tells us as we get ready to start off downriver again. Appropriately enough for a black hole, we couldn't see the Great Black Hole of Lava Falls—though that's because it only exists at really high water, as during the Fool's Flood of 1983. That big black rock at the lower right, which we glimpsed downriver as we swirled around in the second hole, can have water pouring over its top when the river is really big.

The big black rock creates a monster hole and a giant back-eddy, that reaches downriver even farther than the spotter rocks that we hid behind while watching the other boats come down. Double the river's speed, as can happen at high water, and the size of an eddy may increase eight times. Order-from-fluctuation thermodynamics strikes again. Such a giant eddy is so strong that anything unlucky enough to be caught by it is inexorably carried back upriver, usually into the hole itself. And the high water also brings big lateral waves reaching halfway across the river, which similarly suck victims into the eddy. Sticks, even logs swept into the river by recent flash floods in side canyons, are trapped in the hole, which irregularly throws them upwards into the air, recapturing them as they fall, this stunning display of virility advertising, to all who watch, the unequaled strength and fury of this monster hole.

This last hole in the lower right channel, when it exists, is what deserves to be called a black hole. A boat swept into it would, the boatmen insist, have disappeared by having been torn to shreds (in 1983, the river companies often had passengers walk around Lava Falls while the boatmen took the lightened boats through alone). The Great Black Hole is surely the closest thing on the river to a Waring blender.

If Dante had seen a big eddy with a hole like Lava's, he would have had the perfect analogy for both Purgatory and Hell. The back-eddy tends to be a holding pattern, as one circles endlessly, only occasionally being swept back into the upstream hole. Once in the hole, one can't get out, and is really pounded.

My specialty is the time when man was changing into man. But, like a river that twists, evades, hesitates through slow miles, and then leaps violently down over a succession of cataracts, man can be called a crisis animal. Crisis is the most powerful element in his definition.

LOREN EISELEY
The Night Country, 1971

SOME RIVERS, such as the Middle Fork of the Salmon River up in Idaho where I first met Alan and Subie, are just plain downhill all the way, almost constant white water and a continual challenge. Others, such as the Colorado, are more of a staircase than a ramp. The impounded waters behind their rapids move slowly, then speed up as they shoot through the narrow and shallow confines of the rapids. Created by flash-flood debris from side canyons, the Colorado's rapids provide a regular challenge to the skills of the boatmen—but give them a breather between such stresses.

We're coming to see evolution as a lot like the Colorado. It used to be thought a gradual process, a ramp like the Middle Fork, that continually edited an organism's gene pool—whether bacterium, plant, or animal species—so that successive generations were better and better suited to the environment in which the organism found itself. While Darwinian gradualism does exist in the isolated subpopulations, it is easily reversed—it becomes unraveled, shall we say—and the big picture is now more like the Colorado's staircase. A long period of quiescence like Lake Lava, then a short period of stress where certain skills and snap judgments are all-important, then a high-siding period of swirling waters as the river seeks a new course and untangles its various currents, and finally another placid lake which gives time for the boatmen to compare notes, practice techniques, think about how they'll handle the situation better next time.

Their skills are thus in excess of what is needed most of the time, just because they're essential on occasion. We too have skills far in excess of our everyday challenges, simply because our ancestors needed them to get through the staircase of the ice ages.

The most common recurring challenge is, however, called "winter." Most species of both plants and animals live in the tropics, where they're never exposed to freezing weather. A week of freezing weather could wipe out many species of tropical plants—one of the things that makes the nuclear-winter scenario so scary. The plants that do survive freezing have learned to take the hints provided by cooling autumn weather and shortening periods of daylight, preparing themselves for the final onset of frost—although sudden, unheralded frosts can still kill them. Leafless, the dormant plants aren't very nutritious to eat—except for grass, accounting for the popularity of grazing. Many animals that live in winter-prone latitudes have developed behavioral strategies to get themselves through the winter. Some hibernate, living off their body fat. Some store food externally, like squirrels. A few depend on eating other animals that do one of these things, and so get grass and nuts secondhand, with fewer than 10 percent of the original calories left.

Thus, the tilt of the earth's axis of rotation has probably been the most regular contributor to the evolution of more complex animals. Many present-day tropical animals may have been though the winter editing process, skills such as extra cleverness in food-finding making them successful competitors against their ancestral species when they migrate back to the tropics. To see an animal in a tropical setting and assume that that's where it first evolved is probably one of the more common mistakes in biology.

While winter is the most common challenge to an animal that hasn't permanently moved to warmer climates, the decade-long fluctuations in climate surely hold second place. Even in the tropics, variations in the rainfall provided by monsoons can give rise to some hard years. The Anasazi of the Grand Canyon knew all about droughts. The years when Unkar Delta wasn't occupied match up with the decades that had poor rainfall, according to the tree rings.

A sustained dry period is usually blamed for the demise of the Anasazi, except those that took refuge near the present-day Pueblos. The Anasazi, who were flourishing in A.D. 1130 all the way from the humble habitations of the Grand Canyon to the great apartment complexes of Chaco Canyon, gradually disappeared over the next century or two as the rains kept failing. Much of the annual rainfall around here depends on the summer monsoons, the wet ocean air that drifts up over the land and releases its moisture in thundershowers each afternoon as warm air rises from the Colorado Plateau. But the thunderclouds are seen more often than their moisture is felt, because only small local areas—a canyon or two—actually get drenched. Unlike the frontal systems of winter which pass through, carpeting everything in their broad path with snow (although in the depths of the Canyon the snow often turns to rain or even evaporates before landing), the summer showers are hit-or-miss. In some decades, or even for some centuries, it was mostly miss.

On an even longer term basis, there are major ice age melts every 100,000 years, plus a lot of ups and downs in sea level. But that's a recent development, on the geological time scale. While there were briefly ice caps about 450 million years ago and again about 260 million years ago, the last 20 million years or so have again seen ice caps form as a prolonged cooling period has progressed. The ice ages occur when the ice caps become extensive, sometimes covering 30 percent of the land mass, but then the caps melt back every 100,000 years or so. This regular oscillation in the southern boundary of the northern ice cap has been pronounced only in the last 2 to 3 million years. Though it might be mere coincidence, that is also about the time that the hominid brain size began the enlargement that would carry it to 3.6 times the size of ape brains, more than three times enlarged over that of *Australopithecus afarensis* which existed 3 million years ago.

The ice age oscillation affected few, if any, other animals in the way that it seems to have affected hominids. For animals that live in the tropics, that's not too surprising, though there were surely climate changes in equatorial Africa as a result of the changes in ocean currents and therefore in weather patterns. One might be more likely to find changes in animals that lived in the temperate zones, but there again, no other known animal conveniently underwent a major enlargement of the brain.

And there is no evidence of hominids living in the middle

latitudes until *Homo erectus* took up residence in Europe about a million years ago, in the caves near Beijing about half a million years ago. That's after the brain size had already doubled. "No evidence" may, of course, be due to the spotty nature of the fossil record; for all we know, hominid species were forged on ice age frontiers, but then found the living easier in the tropics.

Where natural selection takes place, where the subsequent population boom occurs, and where the hominid fossils are most easily recovered may be three quite separate places—all may not have happened in the East African Rift Valley, as many anthropologists assume (and indeed may be forced to assume, in order to get on with testing hypotheses on the available material within their own lifetimes).

SO WHAT HAPPENS every 100,000 years? Does something throw another log on the fire, make the sun a little brighter? That seems unlikely from what is known about the sun. The sun has gotten brighter by about 30 percent since the earth went into business 4,600 million years ago. And while the energy released from the sun does fluctuate, the betting has always been on the amount of energy that actually reaches the surface of the earth.

Kepler realized that the earth's orbit was an ellipse rather than a circle. The change in distance from the sun causes the earth to receive about 7 percent less sunlight in some seasons than others. The ellipse changes, however, partly due to the attractions of Mars and Venus, so that the Earth's orbit varies from nearly circular (with no 7 percent annual fluctuation) to much more elliptical than at present, thus exaggerating the seasonal differences. Every so often, the ellipse stops flattening and heads back toward being circular. This was first realized in 1864 by geologist and physicist James Croll, long before the ice age rhythms themselves were known in any detail. But with the aid of integral calculus, Croll correctly predicted that the effect would be small when averaged around the annual cycle; over the eccentricity cycle, the annual energy in the total sunlight we receive at the top of the atmosphere should differ by no more than 0.3 percent (the modern estimate).

The period of this eccentricity change is, however, about 100,000 years (actually a combination of rhythms of 412,000, 95,000, and 123,000 years). We now know it to match up with the dominant period of the glacier meltoffs, and that it indeed has stayed right in phase with them for the last six ice-age cycles. But the yearly energy received varies so little over the centuries that most scientists have difficulty imagining how it could cause such a large effect. The suspicion, of course, is that there is something about how the earth accumulates and melts ice that has a natural cycle close enough to 100,000 years so that the slight change in annual energy reaching the earth is somehow amplified in its effect because of this resonance.

Ice builds up over the years because the winter's accumulation is not completely melted off the next summer. While the freezing and melting of ice seems like a symmetrical process when dealing with the heat exchange that affects a tray of ice cubes, there are some significant asymmetries in the exchange when dealing with polar ice caps of great thickness and extent. For example, in a cooling climate, the ice in a glacier just keeps building up layer after layer, while in a warming climate, melting water may eventually drain off underneath the ice sheet and lubricate it, so that it will slip along the ground. The mountain of ice may then begin to collapse, spreading out by several kilometers within a few months. As it breaks up, more surface area is exposed to the warm air, speeding further melting in a manner that has no analog in the accumulation of ice. Blocks of ice may be carried in rivers to the oceans, the ice subsequently melted in warmer latitudes than where it was laid down. The great ice shelves of the Antarctic, where glaciers fill up entire bays, are thought to be susceptible to collapse if the warmer ocean waters erode them from underneath. This would send whole icebergs adrift in the oceans, again exporting the job of melting ice to warmer places.

If all this isn't enough, there is also the problem of land sinking under the weight of mountains of ice, just as Hawaii seems to be sinking under the weight of the lava sent up through its volcanos. Although a slow process, the land sinking could aid ice breakup by lowering the land-glacier interface below sea level, promoting the undercutting of glaciers by runoff in warmer times and transforming the coastal land glaciers into a more vulnerable ice shelf. No one really knows how fast land sinks, but it does rebound once the weight is removed, and a part of Scandinavia covered by the glaciers of the last ice age is still rising, by about one story every 300 years.

IF SUMMERS BECOME HOTTER, even though winters simultaneously become equally colder, it won't average out because of that asymmetry in buildup and meltdown. There are several astronomical mechanisms that indeed produce such exaggerated summers. About half a century after James Croll analyzed our planet's orbital eccentricity, a Serbian mathematician was languishing in a jail during World War I, a prisoner-of-war held by the Austro-Hungarian Empire. He probably kept himself busy calculating the orbits of the planets, for in 1920, shortly after he was released from jail, Milutin Milankovitch published his calculations on the earth's orbit, showing how it had changed over many hundred of thousands of years due to the attractions of the other planets.

Not only does the eccentricity of the earth's orbit change, but so does the season in which the earth makes its closest approach to the sun (called perihelion). Currently we are closest to the sun on January 2 and about 3 percent farther away in July—which reduces our sunlight by about 7 percent. But the date of perihelion changes, getting later every year as the spinning earth precesses like a spinning top wandering around the floor (astronomers call this change in the season of perihelion the "precession of the equinoxes"). About 11,000 years ago, we were closest to the sun in June. The date of perihelion drifts later and later in the year; it takes anywhere from 13,000 to 25,000 years to complete a circuit. An average cycle is something like 22,000 years (actually, it is typically a combination of a 19,000- and a 23,700-year rhythm, giving different results each time around). When our closest approach is in June, we have hotter summers and colder winters in the northern hemisphere. Of course, it's vice versa in the southern hemisphere, but—another asymmetry—down south they don't have as much land mass at higher latitudes on which to house glaciers. Just look at a globe: in the southern half, there is little land between 50 and 70 degrees latitude, as compared to Alaska, Canada, southern Greenland, northern Europe, and the vast expanse of Siberia in the corresponding northern latitudes.

A change in the tilt of the earth's axis, over a cycle about 41,000 years long, exerts a second effect on the seasonal distribution of the yearly energy from the sun. At minimum tilt (22°), the sun comes about as far north of the equator as Isla de Pinos, off the south coast of Cuba. It currently makes it to 23.4°, just north of Havana. But at maximum, it stands overhead at noon in Key West, Florida (24.5°). This 2.5° difference in latitude is the same as that between New York City and Washington, D.C., between Edinburgh and Manchester, between Geneva and the Riviera. Such a 2.5° difference may not make much difference in Florida, but it amounts (because of the cosine of the angle changing more steeply) to a 10 percent difference in the noontime sunlight that reaches middle latitudes. The wobble cycle seems to repeat every 41,000 years, but it is again a complicated oscillation, involving major components from 39,700 years up to 53,600 years. When the tilt is maximum, the higher latitudes get a lot more sunlight than otherwise.

Because the advance of perihelion has a different cycle period than that of tilt, these two influences on summer heating in the northern latitudes are often out of phase (as they are now). But when the closest approach to the sun comes in early summer, and the tilt of the North Pole toward the sun is also near maximal, the conditions are optimal for melting glaciers: the daily sunlight reaching the North Pole in June is 28 percent greater than when conditions are worst for June sunlight there. This peak in June sunlight occurred 11,000 years ago, and 127,000 years ago, and 210,000 years ago, and 335,000 years back. This near-coincidence in the two rhythms might be called the "tilt-perihelion beat". It is this particularly successful melting of glaciers during hot summers at northern latitudes that may set the major ice age rhythm, not so much the sunlight during the rest of the climate cycle.

All of these rhythms can be seen in the climatic records of ice obtained from seafloor samples in which a long vertical core of sediment is taken for analysis. While most of the oxygen in water is the common isotope of oxygen that has an atomic weight of 16, about 0.2 percent has two extra neutrons, and H_2O made with it doesn't evaporate as well from the ocean surface. The ice is therefore built up preferentially with oxygen–16; the percentage of the heavier oxygen–18 in the ocean climbs slightly as the lighter isotope evaporates more than it returns via rainfall. By analyzing the ratio of the two isotopes in seafloor limestone, one can see that it changes over the millennia, reflecting ice building up and then melting. The sea-floor cores give much better evidence of the ice-age rhythms than does evidence from the land, since the evidence of one glaciation may be rearranged and ground up by the advance of the next one. Based on moraines and such, it was once said that there were only four ice ages, all in the last 800,000 years; now we know that there were several dozen spanning the last 3 million years.

The rhythms seen in the seafloor are complex, multiple frequencies building upon each other just as in the sound produced by a string quartet, but again there are identifiable components. The longest component identified is of about 413,000 years' duration, identical to the major component of the eccentricity change in the earth's elliptical orbit. The 105,000-year component in the cores matches up well with the other components of the eccentricity rhythm. The core shows that ice also fluctuates with a 41,000-year period, which matches up with the period of the earth's tilt change. Likewise, there are core rhythms of 24,000 and 19,500 years' duration, matching the two major components of the precessional period. There is even a minor 60,000-year rhythm in the cores that the Belgian astronomer André Berger predicted from an interaction of tilt and precession, and which Milankovitch missed. Everything contributes to the ice rhythms, but the switchover from accumulation to net melting may be the key factor because the melting goes faster than the accumulation.

TAPESTRIES OF LAVA adorn the right bank—billboard-sized walls composed of many vertical columns, the crystalline form that viscous lava takes when it quickly cools in place. The tall columns have six flat sides, and are formed via the cracks that develop as the lava shrinks during cooling. The packing principle strikes again: the array indeed looks like a fractured honeycomb, hexagons and all. Here and there a tall hexagonal column will be broken, the top remaining like a stalagmite, the exposed end being about the diameter of a bailer bucket. All together, it seems like a giant version of asbestos, the sun glistening on the polished dark bronze surfaces where the river has been at work.

The relief makes the honeycombs look like works of modern sculpture that might cover a whole wall of an art gallery. Someone ought to come down here and do some silicon impressions of them, make molds and cast bronze copies. That seems compatible with the spirit of the Park Service's nice rule for visitors: Leave only footprints, take only pictures. But don't step on the cryptogams!

One of the lava flows extends well below river level, we learn as Rosalie reads aloud from the geology guidebook. One wall shows that the river channel was once filled with lava, which caused the river to find a new path. This new channel was also partly filled with lava, though the river managed to cut through much of it. All this, one reads in the rocks. If one has a practiced eye.

GIVEN ALL THE CLOSE MATCHES, it seems clear that changes in the earth's orbit and spin axis drive the ice ages, though one still has to explain exactly how the accumulation and melting periods work. One model postulates that melting operates four times faster in warming climates than accumulation does in cooling climates; a melting rate of 63 percent in 10,600 years gives a close match to all the climate fluctuations in the last 100,000 years when driven by the precessional and tilt rhythms of the same period.

The last time that the climate was this warm was around 128,000 years back—and that warm "interglacial" lasted only 15,000 years before it had retreated halfway back to the glacial peak ice accumulation. Using the astronomical cycles and ice

Carried away, perhaps, by His matchless creation, the Garden of Eden, He forgot to mention that all He was giving us was an interglacial.

The playwright
ROBERT ARDREY, 1976

age models, one may predict that a similar half-back period may be only 3000 years in the future, though the peak glacial period is not predicted for another 114,000 years. We are probably 75 percent through our period of less-than-average ice. Indeed, there is a 5,000-year jitter—the ice sheets could have started anytime in the last 2,000 years, but haven't. Yet.

Of course all bets are off, because of the changes that our civilization has made in the atmosphere and in the plants during the last century. We may have to worry first about further melting from greenhouse-type warming, switching us out of the accumulation mode into the much faster melt mode.

Some people say, coastal cities aside, that a warmer global climate might be good for agricultural productivity because of both the warmth itself and the more CO_2 there would be in the atmosphere as raw material for the plants. It would, however, be a disaster for western states, let alone the river-runners: 2°C. of warming is predicted to reduce Colorado River runoff by 40 percent, the Rio Grande's by 75 percent. People conveniently forget that our best example of a warmer climate, the period about 8,000 to 4,000 years ago when even the Sahara Desert was growing grass and trees (this "climatic maximum" was due to tilt and perihelion effects peaking 11,000 years ago), also produced climate changes that created dust-bowl conditions and dried up the humid "corn belt" of North America (much of whose moisture comes up from the Gulf of Mexico). And while the Sahara, Arabia, and western Australia might temporarily get more rainfall for crops than would be lost in the American Midwest, the soils are poor in the subtropics; they are nothing like the superb soils of Europe and North America. Given that the American Midwest now feeds much more of the world than just North America, warming could cause mass starvation.

And paradoxical freezes often happen during melts, it would seem. For example, a sudden melt can dilute the salinity of the oceans, thus raising the freezing point of seawater. Easier freezing would cause the winter pack ice in the arctic latitudes to extend much farther south, its white surface reflecting light back into space that would otherwise be absorbed, and thus generally cooling things back down for a while. That's a lot of cold, just from a little warming. Five such quick reversals in a warming trend may have happened during the last ice age, brief cold periods taking hold within a century and usually aborted within a few more centuries (though one lasted 10,000 years).

It's not just paradoxical cold that would plague us during warming but also coastal flooding and the inundation of low islands. With only several stories' rise, Florida would be largely underwater. About 11,600 years ago, during the melting of the great North American ice sheet, part of that glacier may have surged forward into central Wisconsin due to all that lubrication beneath it. Then, so the interpretation goes, so much water poured down the Mississippi River that sea level rapidly rose. This date, it has been noted, corresponds to the date given by Plato's ancestor Solon, who said that Egyptian priests had told him that the deluge which destroyed Atlantis was 9,000 years before their time, putting it at about 11,500 years ago.

Whether the Wisconsin ice was responsible for a deluge or not, such nasty things can happen as ice sheets retreat. This is a matter which we worry about, because the greenhouse gases we release into the atmosphere might eventually warm things up enough to start Greenland and Antarctica melting. The usual concern is about "fossil" CO_2 from burning coal and oil—its atmospheric concentration has gone up 40 percent in the last hundred years. But there's also the refrigerator and spray-can gases; nitrous oxide from fertilizers; even such prosaic stuff as the smelly methane released as intestinal gases by humans and all the human-bred grazing animals (methane is increasing about one percent per year—and it's the most effective greenhouse gas known).

Since the last ice age melted off, agriculture has been remaking the face of the earth, allowing the hunter-gatherer population to expand a thousand-fold. Now we are busily engaged in insulting the earth in every possible way, cutting down the rain forests, polluting the oceans, burning up the fossil carbon deposited over hundreds of millions of years as coal and oil, acidifying the lakes downwind—and all in only a matter of a century or two. We should not expect the earth to be able to buffer these changes; the ecosystems just haven't experienced such insults in the past, there hasn't been time for resilient ecosystems to evolve.

> To keep every wheel and cog is the
> first precaution of intelligent tinkering.
> The ecologist ALDO LEOPOLD
> *The Sand County Almanac*, 1949

NO ONE HAS GONE HIKING. Unpleasant traces of civilization, such as the jeep trail up at the top of the cliff behind us, are too near at hand. Such as the hose hanging down a nearby cliff, once used to bring gasoline down to the river. Incredibly, the Park Service in 1960 permitted powerboats with giant engines to attempt to run upriver from Lake Mead as a stunt ("Jet-powered boats conquer the big rapids!" screamed the headlines). And they refueled here. Desert recovers slowly from

MILE 188
Whitmore Wash
Twelfth Campsite

insults. We instead go visit the Whitmore Wash art gallery.

No lava tapestries here, but up behind the sand dunes on the right bank is a flat rock face of sandstone about the size of two large outdoor billboards. Even from the river one can see that red symbols have been painted on it. There is an overhang that seems to have protected them from the rain for the millennium.

Upon closer inspection we see that they are reddish pictographs of typical Anasazi design. Some are high enough up that one wonders if the Anasazi used stepladders to reach them. The alternative, I suppose, is that ancient visitors eroded away the sandstone ledge in front of the rock face over the centuries, lowering the floor; this sandstone does easily revert to sand, I noticed, as an edge of the path crumbled away beneath my left foot. The trail climbs a little, and even more pictographs come into view. This must have been a very popular place. And the caves which form under some of the sandstone layers near the base of the trail look as if they would have made good places to live. Major Powell saw some wooden Paiute dwellings down here, but no trace of them remains.

There is seldom any realistic depiction in Anasazi pictographs, "modern art" having displaced realism even earlier than I'd thought. Except for some obvious sun symbols and a hand outlined by blown paint, one usually has trouble guessing what the pictographs are all about. Anasazi pictographs are more like modern trademarks and logos than like today's international information signs. Some may, like the pictographs we saw at the Hopi salt mines, simply be clan symbols. Pre-Columbian art in the Americas isn't big on the realistic depictions sometimes seen in the cave art that flourished at the height of the last ice age in Europe. Starting about 27,000 years ago, French and Spanish caves were decorated with hunting scenes, probably creating grottos in which young hunters were initiated into the mysteries of the big game hunts by the light of oil lamps.

Why did art start so late? Since modern-type *Homo sapiens* has been found in South Africa from as long as 100,000 years ago, our displacement of the Neanderthal type in Europe, between 41,000 and 33,000 years ago, hardly seems to herald the beginnings of a new, artistic human species.

□   □   □

Though man is originally tropical in his origins, the ice has played a great role in his unwritten history. At times it has constricted his movements, affecting the genetic selection that has created him. Again, ice has established conditions in which man has had to exert all his ingenuity in order to survive. By contrast, there have been other times when the ice has withdrawn farther than today and then, like a kind of sleepy dragon, has crept forth to harry man once

more. For something like [several] million years this strange and
alternating contest has continued between man and the ice.

Loren Eiseley, 1972

THE ADVANCE AND RETREAT of the glaciers surely affected our ancestors. Wherever they lived, the climate was
probably altered in some measure; even the hominids in Africa
could have seen glaciers on some of the tall mountains such as
Mount Kilimanjaro (both it and even Hawaii's Mauna Loa had
glaciers during the last ice age, as did—in synchrony with the
Northern Hemisphere glaciers—the mountains of New Zea-
land).

For the hominids trying to live in the temperate zones (dry
as it is, South Africa today has plenty of hailstorms, and snow
may be seen even in midsummer), it would have been a choice
of either retreating from the advancing glaciers or just moving
to the tropics. Migration is a sensible solution to winter, adopted
by many animals. But it depends on there being enough to eat
when one arrives at the warmer location. If others of the species live there year-round and have expanded their population
numbers to fully occupy the niche, there will be a lot of resistance to fair-weather migrants. And this "winter rule" surely
applies as well to ice-age changes in climate. Either the population will shrink, or the frontier inhabitants will just have to
learn to cope with the ice age. The Grand Canyon Anasazi
probably faced the same problem when the droughts forced them
out: the good land elsewhere was already taken.

And so the boom of population in interglacial times will create some incentives for those in temperate climates to stay put
and adapt to the situation as the climate worsens. They'd have
had to live at low density, much as the Inuits do today in the
Arctic. To get through the winters, they'd have had to either
learn to eat grass or an animal that did; living on a coastline
gives some additional opportunities, such as eating fish or fish-
eating seals and bears. Food storage is a fine idea, but it conflicts with the need to move around easily which hunting marginal areas tends to involve, as one depletes the game (or the
animals get wise to the hunters' tactics).

Hominids that were forced to hunt would have been edited
by natural selection for those with better brains for hunting.
Not all hunting involves throwing, but surely throwing skills
were under considerable selection pressure at some point, as
witness our skills compared to those of chimps and gorillas. Those
who interbred with the more tropical population wouldn't tend
to retain those features very well, because of the dilution. Those

tribes that were more isolated and inbred would tend to keep more of their hunting adaptations. Yet there are lots of hazards to inbreeding (reduced efficiency of the immune system, for example), not to mention the possibility of a small tribe being completely wiped out by a chance turn of events. The anthropologists suggest that a minimum tribe of 500 individuals is needed, probably composed of twenty bands of five families each, just in order for there to be a likely marriage partner available when an individual reaches the customary age.

Monogamy excepted, very similar arguments can be made for many species, especially omnivores. Why us? Why not other apes? Why not bears? What did we do differently so that such conditions selected for bigger brains? One answer, of course, is that perhaps the ice ages did affect other apes, but they didn't survive or conveniently fossilize where they could be found. When one is talking about a singular case, everything that happened along the way seems essential. That's why fast-track arguments are so important when sifting through probable brain-ballooning factors.

Throwing is a fast track, perhaps the fastest one. It is a skill important on the fringes, where natural selection is most severe, the dilution opportunities most restricted, and speciation most probable. It is crucial every year during the winter, when the alternatives to meat are poor. The regular improvement in the climate after each ice age would have led to a gradual population boom on the frontier—but not necessarily in the tropics, already pretty fully occupied. If the brain machinery for throwing is also useful for scenario-making and thus consciousness/cleverness/language, it might have led to frontier hominids that could occasionally displace the tropical population as advancing ice drove them south, even if throwing per se wasn't required to make a living there. Squeeze the center, but later expand the periphery. This ratchet for hunting ability would have been cranked another notch every now and then, thanks to the regular constriction and expansion of the frontier population by the ice ages.

Per aspera ad astra
("Through difficulties, to the stars")
LATIN MOTTO

ARE HUMANS STILL EVOLVING? The inevitable question comes up late in the evening. Darwinian gradualism did lead to the notion that evolution is always in progress, gradually changing us into something "better." The Colorado River Staircase (or, if you prefer, the punctuated equilibrium) view says that species don't change very much once they're established. Even though we interact with our environment and some fools falter, the large size of the human gene pool means that it is pretty hard to overcome the Law of Large Numbers. We're basically overqualified, at least in the environments in which most of the human population lives today, dying more by chance and disease and old age than from lack of relevant skills possessed by our neighbors. Even if the people living on the fringes, such as the Arctic Circle Inuits and the Kalahari San, were to be shaped by natural selection to have some inborn skills twice as good as other groups, the interbreeding possibilities are likely to dilute these skills. Travel being what it is today, the gene pool is getting stirred as never before. Natural selection doesn't do much to humans these days; while affecting individuals, the mean character of the human species probably doesn't change much. It probably hasn't since agriculture began.

Even if one of the traditional catastrophes were to happen (a meteor, volcano, or ice age), the sheer size of the human population makes it unlikely that much of a change would occur. If it did, it would be because of a fluke in the genome that created reproductive isolation for a small group under severe selection pressure. So forget about traditional natural selection when thinking about the human future; certainly, one cannot get any support from science for the notion that we shouldn't subsidize the unfortunate.

Besides, human evolution has been on a suprabiological track—called cultural evolution—for a long time. It's far faster than biological evolution, with a different set of rules. Consciousness, in combination with such cultural developments as writing and science, produces innovations almost unthinkable for biology. Cooperation, initially established by biology in ways seemingly counter to the popular conception of "competitive" Darwinism, has led to such cultural innovations as community child-care and banking. Plus other collectives as well, such as insurance companies, who take advantage of the Law of Large Numbers.

And we might also develop superhumans without actually causing speciation, merely by increasing the variability on the high end of the skills scale, so that there were more geniuses around than formerly. Just as genius currently winks on and off in the population, it might be quite random in nature, with bright parents being no guarantee of bright offspring. The most probable way, by far, to create more of these extraordinary people would be through education. Genius is basically a brain whose parts happen to work together extraordinarily well (not through any "genius gene" but through a particularly effective *combination* of many genes, education, and environment), and we might find some better ways of training for that kind of fine-tuning, rather than leaving it to the hit-or-miss of our present malnourished educational system.

Yet with all that said, human biological evolution may not be at an end. There are ways.

But it's late. There's a half-moon rising over the Canyon walls as we finally get up and head off to bed. Looking up at the Big Dipper, I estimate that it's after midnight. I've learned to use the pointer stars as a clock (the last two stars of the Big Dipper are in line with the North Star). In early summer, the pointer rotates around the North Star from about ten o'clock down to about six o'clock between dusk and dawn. I usually lay out my sleeping bag to face north so that I can easily check the time if I wake up in the middle of the night.

. . . Skinner wrote that "the contingencies responsible for unlearned behavior acted long ago" as though evolution of the mechanisms for generating endogenous behavior is somehow over, genetically set for ever, so that only ontogenic variants are now relevant. I submit that in every organism, including man, there are constant gene mutations affecting neurons, circuits, modulators, transmitters, and ion channels which result in genetically determined behavioral variation. Natural selection is acting on the resulting variants in behavior right now. The genetic changes may do no more than alter the time dependencies of a single ion channel, but they could change the world.

The neurobiologist
GRAHAM HOYLE (1923–1985)

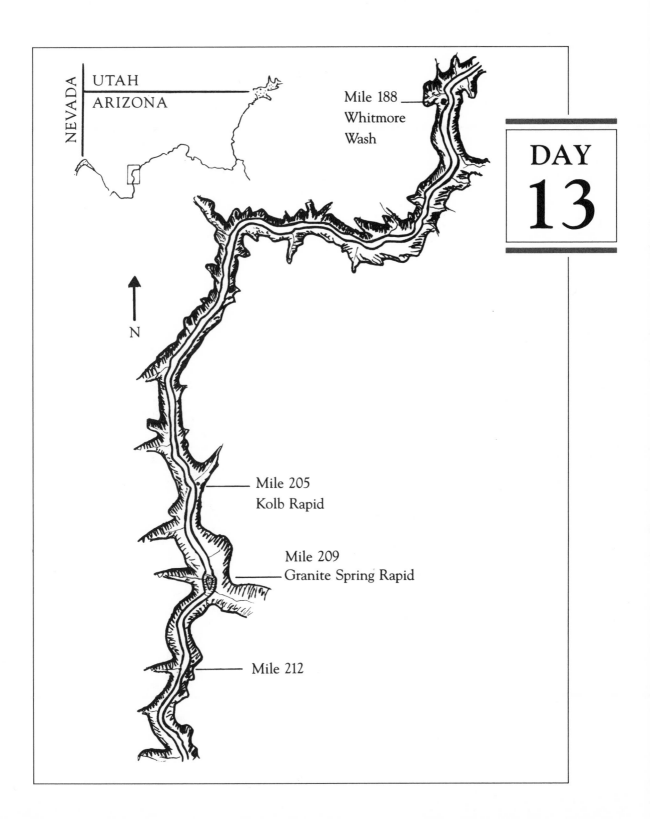

NEVADA

UTAH

ARIZONA

N

Mile 188
Whitmore
Wash

DAY
13

Mile 205
Kolb Rapid

Mile 209
Granite Spring Rapid

Mile 212

MILE 188
Whitmore Wash

Man's future is even more obscure than his beginnings. To venture to sound either depth is to enter an unknown, perhaps unknowable, realm, but it is characteristic of man that he constantly attempts these journeys.

LOREN EISELEY, 1967

It is possible to believe that all the past is but the beginning of a beginning, and all that is and has been is but the twilight of the dawn. . . . All this world's heavy with the promise of greater things, and a day will come, one day in the unending succession of days, when beings, beings who are now latent in our thoughts and hidden in our loins, shall stand upon this earth as one stands upon a footstool and laugh and reach out their hands amidst the stars.

H.G. WELLS, 1902

LATE FOR BREAKFAST AGAIN this morning, even without middle-of-the-night scribbling. I only woke up once. What's left of the sunrise is beautiful, lighting up some of the lava tapestries just downstream from here.

One thing that sure is different this morning, compared to previous mornings on the river—there is no Lava Falls awaiting us downstream. There are still many rapids, but no 10^+ waterfalls. I wouldn't be surprised if we've passed through most of our opportunities for natural selection to shape up the subspecies, *Homo sapiens riverrunnerus* L.

SO WHY AREN'T WE ALL MINIATURE PYGMIES? Abby asked that perfectly reasonable question as we discussed juvenilization. Just as the pygmy chimps presumably shrank in the transition from the full-sized chimps, so one would expect prehumans to have been repeatedly miniaturized if we went through repeated rounds of juvenilization on the road from our common ancestor with the chimps of 7 million years ago.

But we're about the same size as at least one tall specimen of *Homo erectus* from 1.6 million years ago, and the brain has enlarged a lot since then. Given all the prima facie (!) evidence of juvenilization having operated on us, that suggests that there was another selection pressure operating, one that enlarged the body size via a different mechanism whenever juvenilization reduced it.

Even in the marine molluscan species which stay around for 3 to 10 million years before being suddenly replaced by another species, there is a tendency for body size to creep upwards. There are various reasons why bigger is better: the "big mouth principle" which says that the bigger you are, the more choice you have in food and, of course, there are fewer predators that can successfully swallow you whole. While that's unlikely in the ape-to-human transition, there's the surface-to-volume ratio principle at work, most obviously in the area of regulating your body temperature: the bigger your body, the more slowly it changes temperature and so the longer you can tolerate extreme external temperatures before reaching a critical internal temperature. While warm-blooded animals have a variety of internal mechanisms for regulating temperature, extreme situations like blizzards will promote bigger bodies that survive better in some climates. While competition for mates can select for larger males, other conflicts within the species similarly promote bigger-is-better for both sexes.

So after a bout of juvenilization induced by a selection for more throwing accuracy (preserving those juvenile intracortical connections should aid tandem operation and timing accuracy), the body size might creep back up. The reduction in size would have come from selecting from the range of variations in the year of sexual maturity, but the creep back up would come from selecting from the range of variants in body size (of which juvenile status is only one factor). This would eventually yield individuals of the original body size while retaining the more juvenile features associated with early sexual maturity.

Not only is our present body size at variance with an unaugmented scenario of repeated juvenilization, but so is our doubling of life span phases: Juvenilization *by itself* suggests a shorter childhood, not a longer one. So is there a third ingredient in this alliance, a variation on the theme of body development rates (via, for example, the rate of release of growth hormone from the pituitary) and a third kind of natural selection for slowing?

It may be that the slowdown was all in aid of a bottleneck early in the developmental process. Perhaps fetal development was slowed, and the slowdown merely carried over into postnatal life phases as well. And there's a very important bottleneck at the end of fetal development: getting the head through the birth canal. Anything that selects for bigger heads is going to start killing mothers if they don't compensate in some way. And one way is to push out the fetus when only 60 percent complete (at least, by ape standards). That would solve the problem, provided parental care was capable of sustaining the premature infant.

So one has the prospect of a multifaceted solution to the repeated juvenilization problem: e.g., throwing's selection for more juvenile brain wiring, winter or competition selection for bigger adult bodies, and the birth canal's selection for slower developmental rates when faced with the other two facets' propensity of making bigger heads. It may be that there were actually oscillations in body size during *Homo erectus* and archaic *Homo sapiens* periods, distinct cycles which could show up in the fossil record some day to demonstrate that first one and then another of the facets came into play. But nothing in the theory so far would seem to prevent all three facets from proceeding in parallel within the modern range of human body size.

It's all rather sobering: While our relatively big heads might only be an epiphenomenon of retaining juvenile tandem wiring in the brain, they surely caused a lot of suffering and death during childbirth until a tendency towards slowed development solved the problem most of the time. Yet once development slowed down for the birth canal limit and incidentally moved menarche back out to the original year, the whole cycle could be repeated again. With suitable interleaving of the facets, it's a scenario for "juvenilization forever."

JUVENILIZATION FOREVER? Ah, yes. I seem to remember denying last night that natural selection could do much to Homo sap anymore. Individual Homo saps, yes, but generate a new species, no. But might there still be some possibilities for the biological evolution of humans? Were we, for example, to establish space colonies, and they became isolated, and were subjected to severe selection pressures, they might be small enough to evolve a different human species. Different, but who knows in what direction? But I can think of one way in which the juvenilization experiment of the last 34 million years of ape evolution could be continued.

No, I am not thinking of promoting marriage between the more baby-faced adults (I doubt that even the eugenics enthusiasts thought of that one). I am thinking of all the invisible selection that goes on *in utero*. If the meditating ovum somehow selects among many sperm, and if more than half of all pregnancies abort spontaneously, there is a lot of opportunity to influence the grounds for success. There may well be some cryptic selection that already goes on. And, given the much greater number of targets, prenatal selection pressures may well be as important as some of the postnatal ones on which we usually focus. If unseen natural or sexual selection goes on *in utero*, can artificial selection be far behind?

Suppose, for example, that proteins related to the genes that govern human developmental rate were expressed on the surface of the cells of the zygote/embryo, just as the immune system's genes are. Suppose that they affected the chances of successful implantation of the zygote in the wall of the uterus, or the chances of it being attacked by the mother's immune system, or the richness of the blood supply to the placenta, or some other such mechanism that might affect the usual poor survivability odds. Suppose that things were manipulated so that zygotes having the more juvenilized versions of those rate-governing proteins began having better luck than usual. This could shift the percentage of the more juvenilized individuals that survive to adulthood. They might grow up more slowly, might look more childlike as adults, and ageing might operate on a slower time scale as well. It would be the invertebrate-to-vertebrate, monkey-to-ape, and ape-to-human developmental trend, carried a little step further.

Whether they'd be smarter, or more musical, or better baseball pitchers is anybody's guess. It may be that juvenilization works only on the species level, not on the individual level—that there is little correlation between the more baby-faced and the more musical-or-whatever individuals across the population. I don't know. Nonetheless, this simple example does illustrate how the mix of surviving embryos could be changed—and thus the population characteristics of the species Homo sap—once we understand the rate genes and the *in utero* survival process better. Genetic engineering could operate in similar ways on the developmental-rate genes, though we might wish as a society to prevent couples who could afford it from "buying" a guaranteed-bright child in the way they're already engineering the desired sex in their next offspring. Leaving it to chance, as genius probably works now, does have its attractions from the standpoint of avoiding further exacerbation of the differences between the poor and the well-off.

This increased juvenilization would not be a superhuman species, of course, but only a broadened range of variability within the current mix of humans. It would affect the biological head-start that some individuals brought to the even more important educational process. I'm not recommending such an experiment, only pointing out that human biological evolution may not be at an end—and that we must recognize this possibility as we consider what kind of future society we want.

AUGMENTED HUMANS is the other way to go for superhumans. Rather than trying to evolve people with better memory performance, for example, we could simply try to augment the human memory with computer hardware. Use silicon rather than neurons, after finding some way of interfacing them. (Maybe by implanting a little computer behind the ear?)

No, any auxiliary brain will need to be bigger than that—it'll need a big memory.

Augmented humans? Implanted silicon? Bev Williams, Alan's mother, interjected that I really must tell the others about the nudists that we encountered up at Havasu the day before yesterday. Some of the nudists have preempted the future.

I didn't mention this, but we hiked up Havasu to Beaver Falls after lunch. Besides the confusion engendered by the numerous false trails, even the main trail was sometimes hard to follow. There is one section where the brush is so thick, despite the daily bushwacking by hikers, that you cannot see someone approaching from the opposite direction on this one-lane street. And you can't hear them coming either, because of the roar of the creek nearby. You can literally bump into a hiker coming downhill as you are going uphill, both of you jumping back with surprise, nose to nose in the wilderness.

And therein lies the tale. Bev and I were hiking downhill in the afternoon, starting back to the boats, bushwacking our way along through that section of the trail. We heard someone approaching from the rear, a rattling of necklaces accompanied by thudding footsteps. It was Dawn, surely the most spectacular of the nudists to whom we'd talked up at the waterfall, attired in hiking shoes. Uniformly brown, Dawn is an Amazon of a woman, heavier than most men but of distinctly feminine proportions, her extensive mammary development accentuated by the obligatory gold chain necklace augmented by a few noisier ones. We stood aside, since Dawn apparently hiked downhill like a cannonball, clearing the tracks ahead with the sounds of her approach. She sweetly said, "Oh, hello again" and whizzed past.

We resumed bushwacking, wondering how she made the willows and tall grasses stand aside for her, how her skin survived them without the protection of clothing. We faintly heard another "Oh, hello" a moment later, and wondered whom she had encountered this time. Silence. No reply, no comment, just silence.

We continued. And then we met a group of hikers coming uphill. They were three teen-aged Boy Scouts, fresh-faced, with blond crewcuts, carrying regulation canteens and official Boy Scout knapsacks. As Bev subsequently noted, they had a thoroughly innocent and sheltered look.

We stood aside to let them through. I'm not sure they saw us. Their eyes were focused somewhere far off. They didn't speak. They were automatically putting one foot in front of the other. They passed in stunned silence.

When they were out of sight and earshot, Bev and I both stopped and broke down laughing, sitting down weakly on a nearby rock and exchanging, "Did you see. . . ?"

It was all too easy to imagine what had happened to them as they trudged uphill under the hot sun, this naked Amazonian apparition suddenly appearing out of the brush ahead of them at high speed, all but bowling them over backwards like a string of pins, saying "Oh, hello" in the dulcet tones of a society matron, and then zipping on like a passing tornado, vanishing into the brush downhill before they could do a double take and see that she was at least wearing regulation hiking boots.

In their place, given my physiologist's training, I would have surely suspected a hallucination, perhaps an accidental ingestion of the Jimson Weed that grows wild there. Or maybe impending heat exhaustion, suggesting that I should cool off in the creek, quick—before getting trampled by the whole Follies chorus line. Scenes like that just don't happen in real life. I mean, a novelist couldn't insert something like those boys experienced into a story or you'd think it was too contrived, right? But Bev Williams is my witness, honest.

You may recall John DuBois noting earlier that human intelligence may someday come from a resident mix of biological and electronic circuitry, that in the future we may be "part Homo, part silicon." I've got news for him: The future is already here. A connoisseur of surgical scars told me later that a high percentage of the female nudists back at the waterfall had acquired double breast implants. Maybe the future is instead to make that silicon pad functional as well as decorative, a dual-purpose implant that simultaneously improves your thinking and your appearance. I should trademark it now: *Brain in a Breast*. I suppose a shoulder-pad version could be created for men? No, I've got it: *Brain in a Biceps*!

WHAT MIGHT A SILICON IMPLANT do to augment a human brain, now that we've solved the problem of where to house it? Personally, I'd sure like an improved memory of everything to which I'd paid careful attention. Not only are biological memories notoriously in error on occasion, but they lose things too readily. I don't really want a verbatim transcript of all my experiences because, as with a videotape library, it might take too long to locate what you want in the midst of all the unrefined junk. But I read a lot, and I'm always marking passages, and I'd sure like an auxiliary memory to hold all those key passages so I wouldn't waste hours searching through my file cabinets and bookshelves, trying to find the rest of some half-forgotten passage. I'd also like my supplementary memory to be portable, so I could store things in it while reading on the airplane, so I could retrieve things while walking along the beach. I'd like it to have an easy data-entry system, perhaps via a throat microphone so that it would pick up subaudible movements of the vocal cords as I read aloud softly to myself. I'd like it to have some natural form of query and retrieval. Perhaps I'd subaudibly speak a key word or phrase, and, in a high-speed scan, it would play back related sentence fragments from memory through an earphone until I commanded it to back up and repeat something at greater length. It would need a fair amount of programmed intelligence to know what was related and what wasn't, but it all seems possible.

I don't know about anyone else, but I'd find that consciousness-expanding. We naturally concoct "What-if" scenarios from remembered schemata, and this helper would allow me to load up my brain with more relevant information before thinking, allow me to check back against the facts, allow me

I have no doubt that in reality the future will be vastly more surprising than anything I can imagine. Now my own suspicion is that the universe is not only queerer than we suppose, but queerer than we can suppose.

The biologist
J. B. S. HALDANE, 1927

to store subspoken thoughts if I wanted to pursue them later.

In addition to supplementary memory, one might progress to supplementary scenario construction. Maybe I could set the silicon to work finding the possible ways in which one of my scenarios could be rearranged, or have somewhat different schemata substituted. Later I could play back my electronic ego's favorites and see how I liked them. I spend a lot of time trying to get a sentence just right, rearranging its elements in various ways to see which sounds best, which is shortest, which has the right connotations. Maybe I could put my supplementary scenario-maker to work on the more trivial problems while I did something else, then came back to review the possibilities. Such a silicon sub-brain would need a big vocabulary and would need to know a number of grammatical rules, but it might be a help if I were willing to wade through the nonsense it also turned up.

This sounds like an awesome programming task. *But if we ask how brains do similar tasks, we might find that, as in the case of a self-organizing system, a few simple rules might do wonders, that it was complicated only in its product.*

I suppose that one might also start building "quality scores" into this silicon supplement, so that it gradually built up a sense of what its owner had rejected over the years, and so modified its ranking of candidate scenarios. And maybe when it wasn't otherwise busy, I'd just let it free-run and see what it came up with. It might, in the limited sphere of reacting to word-codeable information, start thinking somewhat as I do.

Now once I'd trained it, I could always make a copy of the current program in my silicon supplement and trade it to my friends in exchange for a copy of their current program. Thus, I could temporarily switch my program to think in the way some expert had eventually trained her supplementary silicon to do. I'd look at a set of facts like a physiologist with my natural brain, then I'd see what my silicon thought about the matter—whether it had anything to add from its more reliable, but less complete, memory. Next I'd switch the silicon's program over so that it thought like the silicon supplement of an artist I admired, then like an experienced lawyer (I can just hear my father-in-law's program: "You'll notice that there are just two central issues that really control your decision in all that morass—all those other things are just peripheral issues that'll fall into place once you focus on how those two affect each other"), and then like a beginning student who still confused certain ideas, sometimes creatively. I'd still draw my own conclusions, but I'd have augmented not only my memory but my consciousness and creativity.

If I ever conceive any original idea, it will be because I have been abnormally prone to confuse ideas . . . and have thus found remote analogies and relations which others have not considered! Others rarely make these confusions, and proceed by precise analysis.

The physiologist
KENNETH J. W. CRAIK, 1943

ARTIFICIAL INTELLIGENCE is not particularly an endeavor of the brain researchers. It currently belongs to the computer scientists, and never comes across sounding like such a step-by-step improvement in a supplementary brain. Usually uninterested in neurobiology and evolutionary biology, which give one some ideas about how to build up from below with lots of parallel probabilistic elements and self-organizing system rules, the AI folk instead try to work from the top down using the kind of logical thinking required by computer programming. They try to get a machine to work through an Aristotelian series of logical propositions. It's a valid approach, one that is likely to result in some fascinating machines, but I doubt that these machines will interface very naturally with humans.

It is possible that a machine could be made that duplicated many human thought processes, did them faster and more accurately, was in some sense a superhuman without biology. As I mentioned, one of the challenges in tuning up such a thinking machine would be to adjust its "boredom" parameter, so that it didn't get stuck. So it occasionally got restless. Such computers might require vacations, even sabbatical leaves.

AI, and the computer sciences in general, are likely to provide brain researchers with some important analogies that will aid our research. Schemata are important in this business. Just because present-day digital computers are wired quite differently than biological brains doesn't mean that they may not have functional similarities. And we neurobiologists can use all the analogies that we can get, even if we do wind up discarding most of them as hopelessly inadequate. Search strategies for data banks, for example, help us to think about how the human brain might retrieve a series of related facts, even though the brain doesn't use reliable pigeonholes for information in the manner of computer memory (the brain overlays things, more like a hologram). Similarly, computer operating systems help us think about the executive functions of the brain, how we can modify our functional architecture when we switch from walking to talking to playing the piano. (Computers don't help us a bit in analyzing the stability of the brain; as Gerald Weinberg is fond of saying, if architects built buildings in the same way as programmers build software, the first woodpecker to come along would collapse civilization.)

There are real differences in goals between brain research and AI, not unlike the differences between science and technology. Computer "science" is out to extend the computer technology just as fast as it can push back the frontiers, seeing what it can do with each incremental advance in computer speed and memory size, just like the craftsmen who took us from the

Stone Age to the Bronze Age to the Iron Age. The neurobiologists want to understand natural brains, try to establish just what makes humans tick. We usually don't think about applications at all; but if we do, we naturally think in terms of working around parts of a damaged brain. And so we approach augmenting the human brain in gradual stages, with neurologically natural interfaces, not imitating part of the brain's logic via some largely unrelated creation.

To speak of a computer "brain" thinking is, in terms of today's approaches, truly a misnomer; the AI people often aren't even trying to imitate human problem-solving, and they are rarely trying to build a working model based on the real brain's circuitry principles.

My own assumption is that the real brain's way of thinking is more like: 1) take each of the elements of the problem and free-associate on it to find related schemata; 2) take this augmented collection of schemata and try arranging them into various scenarios, creating lots of permutations and combinations; 3) discard the absurd ones and then take a closer look at the possible ones; 4) grade those for quality using your accumulated experience (which may or may not involve some logical reasoning); and then 5) either implement the best one or just forget about it. Except that real thinking isn't that orderly, but rather all mixed up.

This "variations on a theme" basis for creativity sounds a lot like biological evolution itself, where gene-shuffling and sex create a large family of varied combinations, spontaneous abortion discards the absurd ones, and then natural selection grades the survivors according to how well each one's particular gene combination fits the environment in which it finds itself. It's not at all like the formal classification schemes and logical deductions on which philosophy (and now AI) focuses. Logic is important for humans, but it's probably only the icing on a shuffled cake. Our thinking is more of a back-and-forth fitting process, the way a carpenter hangs a door.

THE NOTION OF DESIGNING A COMPUTER that would get bored certainly stimulated conversation this morning. People had no trouble imagining the problems that could arise: the computer might act like a hyperactive child, always jumping from one thing to another with a short attention span (that does, Ben pointed out, sound just like time-sharing!). Or become set in its ways like a frontal lobe patient, who settles on one strategy and never changes it even when it no longer succeeds (rather like a computer trapped in a loop, its interrupts not working).

The brain of man is a device unlike any other on the planet, a device for the production of novelty, for drawing more from nature than meets the self-contained eye of a sunning lizard or a bird. The role of the brain is analogous in a distant way to the action of mutation in generating improbabilities in the organic realm.

LOREN EISELEY, 1967

Really we create nothing. We merely plagiarize nature.

JEAN BAITAILLON

And a sabbatical for a computer? "When am I going to get a sabbatical?" complained Rosalie. "No one in my department has ever taken a sabbatical. They seem to think that anyone who wants to take off for a year is a freak of some sort, not carrying their share of the load." Medical schools can be rather different from the rest of a university.

"The people who really need sabbaticals are typists and factory workers," Jackie said. "Just imagine doing the same thing every day. It just isn't natural. Life was probably a lot more interesting in the good old days."

Such specialization probably started with agriculture, not industry or the office. There is likely nothing more boring than walking behind a plow all day, unless it's stooping over to pick cotton while getting your brain baked. If they ever existed, the good old days were probably back before this current interglacial period started, before all this specialization began. Everyone had to be versatile; even if they developed some expertise in sewing or rock-flaking or basket-weaving, they still did some gathering and small-game hunting on the side, wandering around the countryside and observing. We've been under some natural selection to take an interest in what's new, to tinker and fiddle around, to get a change of scenery every so often—just as we've been under selection for protecting cuddly babies. To deny it is to breed unhappiness.

To be sentenced to doing one task all day is bad enough, but modern society tends to engineer things so that unchanging days become months and years; most jobs can be learned in a matter of days, after which the novelty is gone. The headlong rush into specialization ignores our evolutionary past, ignores the fact that we take pleasure in exercising our versatility, in developing new skills at our own speed. And so we see many people working without pleasure, just in order to earn the money to be able to do something more interesting on the weekends. Jobs that can be done by a computer should be done by a computer, just as cotton-picking should be done by a machine.

One of the things that becomes possible, once 10 percent of the population can feed all the rest, is for everyone to work only half as much. While we now tend to identify with our work, many people are coming to identify more with their hobby or sport. And if they can work half of the time on such things of their own choosing, they'll be a lot happier still. As productivity increases, so does the opportunity for individuals to live less restricted lives, to enjoy some of the things that evolution has made pleasurable for us.

"I see that work-in-order-to-play business in my neighborhood too," observed Rosalie, "but if you look around, you'll see that the first thing that more productivity brings is not sabbaticals but more children. And then the parents are trapped into working day and night to keep supporting them. To be able to have lots of children—that's the mark of success. Just look at Mexico or India or Egypt."

I am, somehow, less interested in the weight and convolutions of Einstein's brain than in the near certainty that people of equal talent have lived and died in cottonfields and sweatshops.

> The paleontologist STEPHEN JAY GOULD, 1980

Every prophet has to come from civilization, but every prophet has to go into the wilderness. He must have a strong impression of a complex society and all that it has to give, and then he must serve periods of isolation and meditation.

> WINSTON S. CHURCHILL, in a justification for sabbatical leave

□   □   □

MILE 205
Kolb Rapid

WE HAVE A BOAT CAUGHT IN A WHIRLPOOL, no less. Just after everyone successfully navigated our first big rapid of the day, rated a 7, the big eddy captured a boat. The baggage boat, rowed by Alan's brother, Ken Williams, is stuck in the middle of the eddy over on the right side of the river, where a cliff projects out into the river and creates a bay of sorts. This is Ken's first trip down the Colorado as an apprentice boatman (rowing the baggage boat without passengers is how one builds up Grand Canyon experience). Advice is shouted to him from the more experienced boatmen. Hard as he tries, Ken can't get

RIVER CORRIDOR CROSS SECTION

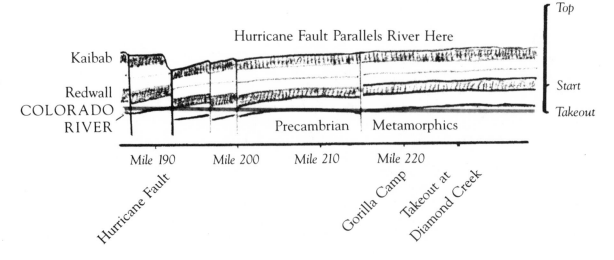

up enough speed to break out. And there being no passengers on the heavy boat, there is no extra musclepower.

J.B. allows as how all boatmen get caught occasionally. "You've got to always be wary or one of those mean eddies will just reach out and grab your boat," he explains to us. "And they can be hard to spot, especially when you're paying attention to getting through the rapid just upstream. See how quiet and peaceful it looks in that little bay? Doesn't look mean, now does it? But it's easy to get in, and hard to get out. You just turn slowly around and around."

After about ten minutes of watching Ken's attempts to extract his boat, we see Alan climbing the rocks along the shore, his boat tied up downstream. Pretty soon he is standing atop the three-story-high cliff overlooking the eddy. He tries spotting the right place in the swirling currents to break out, points it out to Ken. But Ken has no better luck there, and is soon back in the middle again, slowly turning around and around, and catching his breath. Trapped by one of those pesky emergent properties.

Now we see Alan tossing something down to the boat. Two things. His sandals? Apparently so, Alan is poised to jump off the cliff. I hear Bev mutter anxiously under her breath, "Don't dive head-first!" But not to worry. Alan leaps, using a cautious cannonball landing several lengths away from the boat. He swims over and climbs aboard, with a practiced heave.

There are now two boatmen to row, seated abreast, pulling together. It's the Williams Brothers Duo. They get up some speed, but are carried back around into the bay. Again they try and, to cheers, they break out.

Time for lunch. That was hard work, watching.

LOOKING AHEAD and doing a little planning, preferably with the aid of alternative scenarios, is one of the ways that we've improved on the chimpanzees. It's not infallible, as our passage through Lava Falls demonstrated yesterday, but it's nearly always better than plunging blindly in and taking whatever is dished out. Actually, looking ahead is one of the problems with being a boatman: like professional athletes, they can't run the river forever. The back gives out. Unlike the park rangers to whom they are otherwise akin, they have no pension plan, have to find other work for half of the year. As each season on the river comes to an end, they look into the future, trying to figure out a sensible course of action. But it's hard to leave this special place.

As Rosalie points out at lunch, planning ahead is one of the things that the brain's frontal lobes do for us. Planning ahead

How can I leave the river, what is the direction after downstream?

The boatman
LARRY STEVENS, 1981

for minutes, hours, even years. The famous Montreal neurosurgeon Wilder Penfield had a sister, Rosalie tells us, who was one of those cooks who could spend four hours preparing a five-course meal—and have everything turn out just right. Nothing got cold or overcooked, because it was always ready to come off the burner or out of the oven just when it was needed. Now that is truly a precision-timing scenario.

But Penfield's sister began to lose this ability. Over the course of several years, the holiday family dinners began to distress her because she couldn't get properly organized as she had used to. For ordinary dinners she was still a good cook. Most physicians would not have picked up on such subtle clues. But Penfield's clinical instincts told him that she might have a frontal lobe tumor. She did. He operated. She recovered.

Her kind of planning ability is, of course, highly valued in our world. It's what keeps factories from grinding to a halt because of parts shortages, what gets buildings built, what makes scientific experiments produce believable answers, what keeps airlines on time, what gets farms planted during the right week of the year. Executives in particular, besides organizing their day-to-day activities, also must project into the future, see which course to take. The typical trade-off between price and quantity means, for example, that the executive planner must try out alternate sales projections, see if a lower price will stimulate sales enough for the savings on a quantity purchase of supplies to bring in more profits.

Not too much of this can be farmed out by a busy executive. If the executive has an assistant do all the calculations, the executive doesn't wind up with a real feeling for where the figures are soft—what a projected savings in one place does to the costs or profits elsewhere in the budget. To see what a doubling in production will do to the budget, one has to increase the salary budget by one percentage, the supplies double but there are quantity savings, etc. The executive needs a feeling for how a budget reacts when pushed here or there, and that insight cannot be gained by a report from someone else. It's also hard to analyze someone else's budget proposal without working through it yourself in just such a way. To look into the future and assess risks and opportunities in any detailed way requires a lot of work.

And so no matter what printouts have been provided by the company's mainframe computer, many an executive has worked far into the night with a yellow pad of paper and an adding machine. My father, who was an insurance company executive, used to haul home an old mechanical calculator and work for an entire weekend on the budgets. This monster machine, the size of a portable sewing machine, was borrowed from his book-keeping department. It had hundreds of keys to press; because they were necessarily small, they seemed designed for a child's fingers (adults used a pencil eraser to push them). The monster made great whirling sounds, noisily stepped its carriage along kerchunk-kerchunk-kerchunk like a great mechanical toy, was guaranteed to attract children from around the neighborhood if the windows were open.

When it's so much trouble, one doesn't construct too many different budgets; there is a real limit to how many scenarios one can reasonably try out. Then a major executive tool came along, a computer program called the spreadsheet. When the first one, Visicalc, was introduced at a computer show in 1979, its creator, Dan Bricklin, sat alone and largely unvisited off in a side room. The experienced computer people still thought in terms of either word-processing or data-processing, routine things that executives hired specialists to do for them. Few of the experts could see who would want a spreadsheet program; it wasn't a proper accounting package, wasn't word-processing, and wasn't adapted from a program for a big computer, etc. And besides, how many executives would do their own typing? Who would explain how to work it to the secretary?

They underestimated the executives. It took Visicalc nearly a year to start moving. And soon imitators started appearing, with improvements. Within several years, microcomputers were being sold in great quantities, just so vice-presidents could prepare their own budgets more effectively. The spreadsheet software literally sold the hardware. And once the boss had his or her own desktop or portable computer, it became acceptable for everyone to have one. Before that, having a computer on your desk was a little like doing your own typing or becoming too closely identified as a data- or word-processing person rather than as a mainstream manager. And of course the boss' secretary had to have a compatible computer, so that the figures that the boss worked out on the airplane could be transferred from the portable computer to a letter or report. Once the executives' secretaries had computers, the other secretaries became less reluctant to give up their beloved typewriter for a microcomputer. The quantity savings from all the business purchases lowered the price enough so that even students began buying them for writing term papers; the micro began to replace the ubiquitous portable typewriter in college dormitories. One piece of software, and its many imitators and successors, caused an avalanche of microcomputer sales.

The history of the microcomputer era can, of course, be written to emphasize other aspects of these versatile machines, but this little parable has a purpose: If few people before 1980 could see why anyone would want spreadsheet software, how successful can anyone be at predicting the future course of technology? Our ability to look even a few years into the technological future and predict what will happen is, alas, poor. Spreadsheets allow step-by-step budget projections based on known variables, but they—and most peoples' imaginations—cannot take into account the sidesteps of cultural evolution, where something developed for one purpose suddenly becomes useful for something else, tripping an avalanche for yet another reason. There's no substitute for imagination.

□   □   □

Doubtless [Greek water clocks and sundials] were on occasion made to serve [a] practical end, but on the whole their design and intention seems to have been the aesthetic or religious satisfaction derived from making a device to simulate the heavens.

The science historian DEREK DE SOLLA PRICE, 1975

You may have seen in the grottoes and fountains which are in our royal gardens that the simple force with which water moves . . . is sufficient to put into motion various machines and even to set various instruments playing or to make them pronounce words according to the varied disposition of the tubes which convey the water. . . . [As they arrive, visitors] necessarily tread on certain tiles or plates, which are so disposed that if they approach a bathing Diana, they cause her to hide in the rosebushes, and if they try to follow her, they cause Neptune to come forward to meet them threatening them with his trident.

The philosopher RENÉ DESCARTES, 1634

ONE OF THE THINGS that you discover stepping through the various budget scenarios with spreadsheets is that pennypinching on capital investment or on research and development can produce big losses. If you don't make enough capital investment, growth saturates your production capacity and, by the time you expand your plant several years later, your disappointed customers have gone elsewhere, you lose the economies of scale, and you may even find yourself on a negative growth curve that makes the situation worse and worse. Pilots are familiar with this phenomenon: if one flies too slowly, speeding up the engines may only make the plane go slower still. It's called the "back side of the power curve," and the recommended solution for it is to build up speed by diving (instead of revving up the engine further). These days, one doesn't have to crash an airplane in order to discover this paradox; a computer simulation shows many of the factors that affect it, lets one try out schemes for recovery on the model, etc. And so too with economic models, models of how pollution affects the weather, models of electrical power grids, and so forth.

Rich Muller, the astrophysicist who shares the world's record for long-term predictions with the discoverers of the 28-million-year cycle of mass extinctions and meteor craters, also tells an interesting story about how small businesses fail even when seemingly successful. He says he finally figured out why so many good little restaurants in the San Francisco Bay Area fail after a year or so of operation, just when they seem successful. The paradox intrigued him: these restaurants were full of satisfied customers one night and closed down the next by creditors.

The restaurants do just fine, he says, as long as they continue to grow month after month; they get into trouble when growth flattens out. And that's because they've been subsidizing the customers by charging prices that are too low to cover their real costs—the meals have cost more than they were charging, but they never realized it until growth slowed down. That happens because customers pay cash, but suppliers are paid the following month—out of the following month's increased receipts. So, as long as there are additional customers each month, there is enough money to pay suppliers and all seems well. It's only when growth flattens out that it becomes apparent that the restaurant owner has been subsidizing the customers' food.

And that sounds familiar, because the same thing is likely happening on a larger scale too. Places like New York City already have too many people for the streets, sewers, and subways to handle, but the mayor and everyone else are madly promoting ever-bigger buildings, trying to attract big businesses to headquarter there, bringing even more people into the City. Because how are they going to pay last year's bills (all that needed maintenance on subways, for example) without new money? The businesses will move elsewhere if taxes are raised to reflect the true cost—so New York City tries to grow faster and faster, just to keep paying its bills with new money. At least governments that print money with which to pay bills don't consume resources and pollute their environment in the process.

And our whole civilization may be subject to Muller's Restaurant Rule: We too could go bankrupt just when seemingly successful. If we had to pay the true costs of a ton of steel that was extracted from junkyards rather than a strip mine (as we surely shall have to do before long), our economy might well stagger. The costs of pollution and overpopulation are rapidly catching up with us, yet suggestions that we slow growth are met with about the same apprehension that the powers-that-be in New York City greet the notion of a moratorium on construction that would put a ceiling on the number of people working in Manhattan.

One hopes that spreadsheets will help fledgling restaurant owners to avoid subsidizing their customers with insufficient prices. But those kinds of projections work well only when costs can be realistically estimated. It's hard to know what a mining operation for iron ore really costs; lately we've been discovering what it does to the health of miners, the health of the people living downwind of a smelter, and the health of ecosystems exposed to their acid rain. The owners of the iron works haven't paid those costs in the past; they've left it to future taxpayers. It's going to be a good trick to pull off a transition to no population growth, to full recycling of raw materials, to paying full costs; we'll need lots of computer modeling to figure out how.

Making working models of systems is nothing new. In some sense, the Greeks may have started it more than 2,300 years ago with the creation of clockwork machines that simulated the heavens. It may be that water clocks had little to do with telling time; rather, the motivation for their construction may have been to simulate the workings of the gods by making a model moon and planets wander through a model field of stars on the gods' own schedule.

Automata have long been a big thing; whether for prediction or just for show, they have stimulated the thinking of many people. Plato may have seen a machine that simulated the heavens; certainly by Roman times the Agora of Athens had a monumental water clock, the Tower of Winds, whose ticks were drips of water and which featured a working model of the moon and planets wandering through the backdrop of fixed stars. Descartes' notion of a mind separate from the body may stem from his contemplation of the Royal Gardens automata where cleverly utilized streams of water made the statues move, play musical instruments, and speak words. Descartes realized that the nerves might just be like pipes carrying water pressure to piston-like muscles, the whole thing orchestrated from the nervous system. Today we know that the signals are not hydraulic but electrical, that sliding filaments in the muscles make them contract, and that a separate mind isn't necessary—yet automata still stimulate our thinking about the higher functions of the brain.

Clever computer simulations of damaged nerves have suggested ways to work around some problems caused by disease or injury. Simulations of whole mosaics of nerve cells have, just like spreadsheets, given neurobiologists a sense of the possible, stimulated them to design experiments to see which scheme the brain actually utilizes. I got started doing this back in 1959, in my days as a physics undergraduate, making a model of the human retina based on the findings of Keffer Hartline and his followers. The only computer available to me then was an IBM 650, which even lacked a core memory. It had to get each instruction, one by one, from the equivalent of a disk drive (it was really a large revolving cylinder and it had an emergency shutoff switch in case—so the story went—the IBM serviceman got his necktie entangled in it). To get the amount of running time I needed, I came into the computer center (which was housed in an old astronomical observatory) at midnight and worked until dawn, no one else needing the computer at those hours. I didn't even have the company of astronomers, those traditional night owls, as the observatory was a bit obsolete for serious astronomy.

I promptly learned that the activity of retinal cells underwent wild oscillations unless the strengths of their interconnections were adjusted just right. And that there was a lot of missing information, forcing me to simply make guesses about how a component worked. Trying to figure out how to nail down such information from a real nerve cell is what led me into the experimental side of neurobiology for the next 20 years (I'm now back to making models again).

Computer network models have become much more sophisticated since those days. One of their best uses is to show us how a system can misbehave—in advance. When you've got a lot of actual data about a real system, you can sometimes make a quite detailed working model of it; this is quickly becoming the case with the weather. The atmosphere is represented by the computer-program equivalent of a giant three-dimensional stack of little cubes exchanging numbers representing wind, temperature, and moisture with their immediate neighbors according to the laws of physics. Operating on short time scales, one gets a weather forecast for the next week. Bigger models can show how major climate disturbances work, such as if ice sheets cover the northern latitudes to create the equivalent of mountain ranges that deflect jetstreams. And how a nuclear war could be devastating to the plants and animals all over the earth via the sudden disruption it would cause in climate.

THE COMPUTER SIMULATIONS of hawks-and-doves that the behavioral biologists have been running show a number of important properties about competing species in nature. Coexistence is possible if neither species can be wildly successful in matters reproductive. With exponential growth rates, one species can eventually win and displace the other. Should still another species get started that is sufficiently superior, however, it can eventually take over.

That's what we've always assumed about evolution, ever since Darwin. But there is a sobering note to the computer results: *if a species has a hyperbolic growth rate, it can kill off all competition permanently.*

Are there any species around with such threatening growth patterns? Alas. Since agriculture began, humans have had a hyperbolic growth rate, the time needed to double the population getting shorter and shorter. And we're coming to compete with many other species for food and space, causing animal species to go extinct at an alarming rate.

In a spatially limited environment, growth leads to saturation. There is a maximum limit for the total population. Individual subgroups, however, will display highly differentiated behavior in accordance with the particular law of growth affecting them:
1. coexistence (with linear growth or mutual stabilization)
2. competition and selection (with exponential growth)
3. once-and-for-all decision (with hyperbolic growth)

[Laws of growth between competing species sharing resources]:
1. Linear growth [creation rate is constant] always leads to coexistence and to population densities that are, on the average, determined by the ratio of the rates of formation and decomposition. ["coexistence" scenario]
2. Exponential [growth rate proportional to quantity currently present] and hyperbolic [faster-than-exponential, when doubling time progressively shortens in the manner of the human population] growth result in a clear selection of one species unless stabilizing interactions among different species enforce their coexistence. ["competition and selection" scenario]
3. In the case of exponential growth, "qualified" competitors (i.e., mutants with a clearly defined selective advantage) can establish themselves at any time. In hyperbolic growth this is practically impossible once a species has qualified and established itself ["once-and-for-all selection" scenario]
4. Rules 2 and 3 apply consistently only if there are no functional links between competitors. Links of this kind can lead to mutual stabilization of the partners involved or to a stiffening of competition between them or even to a total extinction of them all.
MANFRED EIGEN and RUTHILD WINKLER, *Laws of the Game,* 1976

□   □   □

EMERGENT PROPERTIES have certainly been accumulating during this trip. Compounded things really are much more than just the sum of their parts. Together with such evolutionary rules as punctuated equilibrium, they give one a much better picture of how life has evolved. But even with good imagination, predicting the future path of evolution can be problematic because of all the sidesteps and the occasional avalanches that follow them.

For human evolution, there is now the possibility that many of our more prized mental abilities, the ones that make us different from the apes, were initially sidesteps. Rather than primarily arising through a process of natural selection for planning ability, our higher consciousness may be a free gift whose powers we are still trying to fathom. Music certainly looks like a gift, its depths being so unlikely to have evolved by natural selection.

We're certainly more flexible than the remaining apes, able to shoehorn ourselves into living in all sorts of conditions that would have terrified our more distant ancestors (such as New York apartments and subways). They would have probably scorned our confined existence in buildings, most of us working at endlessly repetitive jobs, in just about the same way that we pity a chimpanzee inhumanely confined to a small zoo cage.

Emergent properties, such as back-eddies, can reach out and grab the unwary, trap them in a journey that goes nowhere. As the fieldhands and cycle-of-poverty people have been trapped, so humanity as a whole may be trapped by ecological snares. If we fail to put the brakes on population and pollution, we all may be trapped in one of the unhappy backwaters of the universe.

Or emergents can open up new vistas, as if they were a bonus for excellence in evolution. But we'll still bring pretty much the same biological makeup to whatever cultural setting we inhabit. That biology is mammalian, primate, ape, perhaps aquatic, African, certainly ice age. Our fears and pleasures will, however they may be refined by how we happen to grow up, still remain pretty much those that we have inherited from our biological background. Most of us will still like cuddly babies, campfires, foot races, natural settings, shellfish, meat, and fruit. We'll still like to sharpen our skills, to compare observations with others, to play the mating games that distinguish us from the apes. We have been selected to take pleasure in being interested in things, tinkering around with objects, and surely that will remain.

Some of those pleasures need to be restrained, rationed for the sake of our children's future. Just as we have limited some of our violent side with a system of laws, just as we have brought out our better side by developing a cultural system of ethics, so we may have to restrain some of our pleasures. Such as surrounding ourselves with big families. Such as indulging our taste for meat every day (the more systematic clearing of rain forests is, alas, for the purpose of growing grass to aid the export of cheap frozen meat—the conversion of Brazilian rain forest into junk food has been called the "hamburgerization of the Amazon").

And, if we want our children to be able to have an experience like our last two weeks away from civilization, we'll have to set aside from encroachment—firmly, with absolutely no exploitation or development even in bad economic times—many such natural areas. If the world keeps changing at as dizzying a pace as it is now, our children are occasionally going to want to stop and get off that artificial world, temporarily return to a more natural state to think things through, get some perspective, feel their roots. They'll need places such as this even more than we do.

MILE 212
Hangout Rock

SHADE IS SCARCE along this section of the river in the afternoon. The boatmen have a favorite stopping place on the left bank, where a high rock outcropping provides a bit of shade. And a platform from which to jump into a protected section of the river. The campsite down at Mile 220 is sunny at this hour; if we arrived there too early, we'd just be hot. The shade's here, so we stay here. Good planning is very useful in a desert. The desert has a way of being unkind to those who don't think ahead in matters relating to water and sunlight. At least the heat isn't as much of a problem for us as it is for the smaller desert animals—our large size slows down the temperature rise in our bodies.

One of the major lessons of biology is that size matters. We cannot simply double the size of something without considering the consequences, such as halving the rate at which it will gain or lose heat, and thus change temperature. And while surface-to-volume ratios have been obvious to architects and engineers for a long time, we may have some other limitations that are not so obvious. Can we further enlarge our cities without major breakdowns in the social fabric? Will human behaviors in matters reproductive—suited by evolution to the fluctuating climates of the ice ages and a scattered population of several million hunter-gatherers—remain safe when the world population reaches 5,000 million people?

What happens to human social behaviors, evolved in small bands of perhaps 25 people and their relatives among a larger tribe of perhaps 20 such bands (think of a small town, population 500), when a person has to cope daily with an impersonal society of strangers? When a person has to specialize in a manner that eliminates the pleasures of versatility and the great outdoors? It may be "economic sense" to build bigger and bigger skyscrapers and pack in people tighter and tighter, but is it humane? Temporarily tolerable, perhaps, but is that the sort of society we want, or are we simply abdicating decisions and going with the flow? Economic sense isn't everything.

There are consequences to not planning—people will die in famines if the population outstrips what food can be delivered to them in the bad years. People will die when resources are exhausted, unless we get back into balance with what nature produces. Even those who say that "it's their problem" must realize that hungry people topple governments, fail to pay back money owed and so topple international monetary systems, organize to invade neighbors with less densely packed land, and act in irrational, frustrated, irresponsible ways (including terrorism). Like the cute lion cubs who die when their parents stop feeding them, a large number of babies may be "natural" but it certainly isn't humane—and in the case of civilization, overpopulation and the destruction of ecological systems spell dangerous worldwide instabilities, not merely "localized failures."

We can learn to appreciate such things through science. We can project known growth processes (whether of population, pollution, or power supplies) into the future with working models, we can advise on the bad courses and identify good options (though science itself often cannot identify the appropriate values to emphasize). But none of that will change what happens unless the information is widely read—unless it creates an urgency to act to save a habitable world for our children. I'm afraid they're going to think that the twentieth century was holding one big irresponsible party, consuming everything as if there were no tomorrow. Leaving them the hangover and ruined land rather than their proper inheritance. As mindless as a plague of locusts.

After I be dead, others will follow. If people be killing killing, there will be no more buffalo, no rhino. If they be cutting cutting, there will be no more trees, no oxygen, no rain. Like a desert. What will my daughters think? They will come and there will be nothing. *Our father was stupid,* they will say.
                              RENATAS, a park ranger in Tanzania, 1985

It is true that mankind is in a more dangerous situation than ever before. But science has provided our culture with the tools to escape, at least potentially, the decline to which all previous high cultures have fallen victim. This is true *for the first time* in the history of the world.
                    The ethologist KONRAD LORENZ, 1973
                    □   □   □

MILE 220
Upper Gorilla Camp
Thirteenth Campsite

ACROSS THE RIVER from camp, there are alleged to be five bighorn sheep, browsing around on the hillside at various levels. Jim and Jeremy are insisting to a skeptical Marsha that there is also a gorilla over there above the sheep. Marsha asks Mike, busy unloading dinner from the depths of his boat, if there is really a gorilla over there. Mike, without even looking up, agrees that there is indeed a gorilla over there.

"But how do you know without looking?" Marsha asks suspiciously.

"I'd have noticed if he wasn't there anymore," is Mike's sage reply.

"And how do you know it isn't a she?" challenges Marsha.

"Sexual dimorphism is very prominent in gorillas," smiles Mike.

Suddenly Marsha sees the gorilla and runs off to tell Rosalie. And so I look more seriously myself. There are indeed five moving rocks, three of them clustered together. But a gorilla?

Ahah! The hilltop profile looks like the left rear profile of a big male gorilla. One sees the hump atop the head that anchors the big jaw-closing muscles that he uses to grind up the leafy plants of his dull diet. And the zygomatic arch coming around front below the temple, which ends in the big facial bone below the eye. Standing by the boats, I see the gorilla but complain that the hump on top is too exaggerated, even for a big silverback male. Mike says it's more persuasive when viewed from the middle of the camp. I walk back up to the tents to look, and he's right. A proper male gorilla, looking upriver into the gorge from which we emerged earlier. A giant sentinel.

I wave over Rosalie and Marsha, who also admire the improved view. We wonder what the Anasazi called it, not having a gorilla schema stored in their heads. Come to think of it, Major Powell and crew probably had never seen a gorilla either. Even in the nineteenth-century scientific journals, the description of the apes was somewhat confused; fairly rare even then, they were described later than most other primates. And they're even more rare now, their living space disappearing rapidly.

As we watch through binoculars, the three bighorns that were clustered disappear one after another. They just wander over the top of the ridgeline, literally dropping out of sight. Show's over.

Thoroughly relaxed, we wander down to the kitchen to see what's for dinner, now that the shadows are lengthening. Over the two weeks of our journey, the menu has gradually shifted from fresh to frozen to canned entrees.

Oh, no! As I should have suspected, for this last dinner we are actually having clams linguine. So help me, there is actually a big restaurant-sized can of the sauce propped atop the kitchen table, with its boldface label proclaiming **"CLAMS LIN-GUINE"** for all to see.

The boatmen just didn't say *when* we would enjoy the delicacy. No one took up J.B. on his bet (days ago, he offered cynics four-to-one odds that we'd have clams linguine for dinner). But the boatmen cheat, spreading the clam sauce over plain old spaghetti. Though I wouldn't be surprised if J.B. carries along a small package of real linguine, just in case he might lose a bet. Beware of making bets with boatmen!

SITTING AROUND THE CAMPFIRE is a reassuring old habit, one of those roots through which we evoke our pre-human days. Since collecting driftwood in the Canyon is prohibited in the summer, we had to make do with the charcoal left over from baking the cake for dessert, augmented by some of the flammable trash. This being our last night on the river, we're using up the rest of the charcoal supply that the boats have carried. Even a water-damaged paperback book fallen into a dozen pieces has been contributed to the fire. But the atmosphere feels right; it's hard for a campfire to feel ersatz. It's friendly, it focuses your attention.

"I'll bet," Rosalie said, "that most of you are sitting there thinking that preventing overpopulation and the rain forest scenario will surely be a matter of ecological education finally reaching the underdeveloped countries. That surely the prevention of the nuclear-winter scenario will be a matter of educating others about how dangerous it is.

"Maybe you added an afterthought," she continued, "hoping there's enough time to spare. You know—that the earth will be able to absorb the abuse for the time it takes to correct the situation through awareness."

She looked around for confirmation, her face etched by the flickering light of the campfire. "Or if you didn't think that, you probably thought that—just like the rationalizations of an addicted smoker—surely the scientific data isn't all in yet, that maybe-hopefully-somehow," she slowly drew out the word, "somehow all these dire predictions will turn out to be mistaken. Or maybe you hoped that science would invent some patch-up job in the meantime, to save us. Am I right?"

There were some embarrassed smiles this time, people distractedly drawing in the sand and nodding assent.

"Well, let me tell you a story. To comprehend such ecological danger places you and me in a very special situation. It sticks us with the responsibility to do something about it, just as the citizen happening upon a house fire has the unavoidable

Those who will not reason
Perish in the act;
Those who will not act
Perish for that reason.
W. H. AUDEN (1907–1973)

responsibility of warning the occupants and then calling the fire department. No matter what important errand he's involved with at the time.

"But special knowledge gives you and me an additional special responsibility that goes well beyond merely spreading the word about a fire. The Greeks said it very well, directed at the primary possessors of specialized knowledge of their day." She smiled. "I even memorized the ancient dictum for my medical school graduation ceremony:

'Life is short, the Art long, opportunity fleeting, experience treacherous, judgment difficult. The physician must be ready, not only to do his duty himself, but also to secure the cooperation of the patient, of the attendants and of externals.'

"That's Hippocrates. But the basic bind hasn't changed in the last 2,500 years for situations in which knowledge is fragmentary and time is short. The nature of the patient has just enlarged to include the whole human race. And maybe more."

After that sank in, she continued. "It says that even though the data are incomplete, you have to act—opportunity is fleeting, judgment always difficult.

"And the last part of that Hippocratic quote pointedly reminds you of one of the most difficult nonscientific aspects of the problem. You've got to be able to persuade others to do things that are in the best interests of the patient, even though they lack your special knowledge of why those things must be done—'secure the cooperation' says you've also got to stage-manage the whole damn treatment just as surely as if it were a Greek drama."

She paused and then repeated, "It isn't enough to act as a specialist, but you've got to play stage manager too."

Rosalie leaned forward and looked around at us, her face again brightened by its closeness to the campfire. "Don't let those words 'physician' and 'patient' fool you—a physician and a scientist and a philosopher were much the same back then, all wrapped up in one person. So that Greek admonition out of the past applies to us all, to all educated persons, not just today's specialized doc who is licensed to gamble one-on-one with another person's life. And with the whole human race—the whole earth—being the patient in this case, we're not just talking physicians here, we're talking about everyone who understands the problem, even a little. Every one of you understands more ecology today than Greek philosopher-physicians understood about physiology back then. And they still had to act.

"Life is still pretty short. Experience still isn't a reliable guide. The time window in which you have an opportunity to act effectively is certainly fleeting. Judgment's still difficult—and yet you've still got to act and not postpone. You can't just do your duty yourself, in the sense of calling attention to the situation and educating the next generation when you get the opportunity. Not everyone, certainly not in the hungry developing countries, can afford to study the subject long enough to gain your understanding of the interdependencies of ecology. Awareness isn't going to solve this problem. You've got to go out and secure the cooperation of the patient and stage-manage the situation."

She counted on her fingers. "It is imperative that countries act quickly—One, to stop the population growth that can cancel out all our gains and waste the resources that a future generation will need for recovery. Two, to stop cutting down the tropical forests and causing the wholesale extinction of other species. Three, to force the superpowers to stop their macho nuclear posturings that could trigger a living nightmare. Four, to see that no temporarily insane nation of the future acquires the power to endanger humanity. Five, to recognize that us-and-them won't do anymore, that we're all in this together, all one people.

"We've got to stage-manage it all. And it's not just ecologists or physicians. If the people who half-understand the situation don't get started, we're lost."

THE BIG DIPPER has now moved down a quarter-turn around the North Star since sunset. Six hours by my celestial clock. That makes it the middle of the night; morning will come in several hours. Sleep does not come easily. Everyone within earshot seems to be tossing and turning and sitting up and lying down.

That was some ancient pea planted under our mattresses. By starlight, I've seen two people pacing the beach, one upstream and another downstream. The moon will rise soon and the Milky Way will fade. At least we don't have to save the universe from itself, only our earth.

We've been soothed too long by the folklore of wishful thinking. But there are no guarantees. Even evolution did not fit us to our present world. We're winging it. We're probably alone, and we'd better start looking after ourselves.

We may not be suited to the task, but here we are. We need to engineer a new emergent property that converts hunter-gatherer mentalities into responsible world citizens with ever-expanding niches, and to do it in short order. Improbable? So what? The whole world's improbable. Yet it exists. And we'd like to see it stay in business.

True art . . . clarifies life, establishes models of human action, casts nets towards the future, carefully judges our right and wrong directions, celebrates and mourns. It does not rant. It does not sneer or giggle in the face of death, it invents prayers and weapons. It designs visions worthy of trying to make fact. It does not whimper or cower or throw up its hands and bat its lashes. It does not make hope contingent on acceptance of some religious theory. It strikes like lightning, or *is* lightning; whichever.

The novelist JOHN GARDNER (1933–1982)

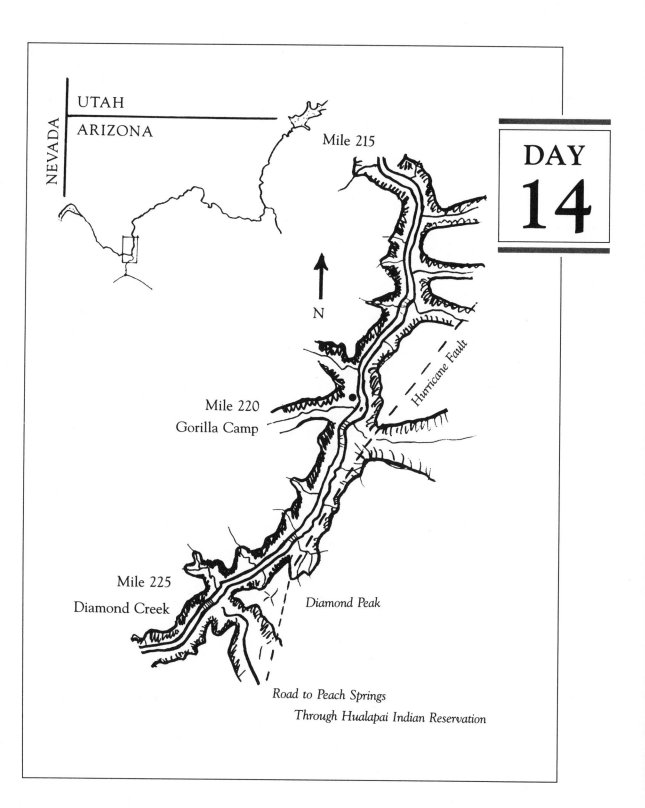

NEVADA

UTAH

ARIZONA

Mile 215

DAY
14

N

Hurricane Fault

Mile 220
Gorilla Camp

Mile 225
Diamond Creek

Diamond Peak

Road to Peach Springs
Through Hualapai Indian Reservation

MILE 220
Upper Gorilla Camp

THE BOATMEN who row the Colorado River often seem exuberant, but they leave the Grand Canyon on the final day in a reverent way. They believe in silence. We got up two hours before dawn, in the light of a recently risen half-moon in the east and fading stars in the west. We silently stumbled our way across the rocky campsite to gather near the boats. Without speaking, we quietly loaded the boats with our black waterproof river bags, muffling the usual clang of metal cups and waterproof storage boxes. Gestures seen in the moonlight substituted for speech.

No breakfast, not even tea or coffee to announce the new day. We just packed up and, the phrase suddenly meaningful, silently stole away from the camp, starting the float down our river in the predawn darkness.

The Colorado River is now colorless, as is all of the surrounding moonlit Canyon, but the river's surface glistens in the windless night air. I am in the first boat and, looking back, see ghostly silhouettes of the other six boats strung out behind us on the river. I cannot identify either boats or people; the sun is coming our way from back east, but it is still night here. We are each alone in a pervasive black and gray stillness, as if this were a continuation of a private nighttime dream.

All is in profile on the land; all on the water is swirling motion as the moonlight reflects on the waves. The loudest sounds are the talking ripples beneath our bow, except when a more sustained breeze drums up a beat.

Looking around at the hilltops, dark against the milky sky, I imagine that I see a large bighorn sheep watching us. Perhaps he is one of the five that we saw last evening. But the shape eventually reveals itself. It is only an oddly shaped ocotillo shrub on the skyline. The only animals that I see for sure are the bats, still busy catching flying insects over the river, flipping and dipping and gliding near our boats, their clicking sonar vaguely heard.

> To see a World in a Grain of Sand,
> And a Heaven in a Wild Flower,
> Hold Infinity in the palm of your hand,
> And Eternity in an hour.
> WILLIAM BLAKE (1757–1827)

WHAT LIES AHEAD? On the river itself, new sights, new rapids, the experiences of a new day. Thinking ahead, one wonders what news will await us after we end our isolation on the river. The abrupt intrusion of the outside world at Phantom Ranch last week is only too fresh in our minds.

But for ourselves, as lone humans on a blue-green planet circling a minor star in a middling segment of the Milky Way galaxy, member of the Local Group of the Universe—in this larger sense, we wonder what lies ahead for the human species. What will be the next thrust of evolution? Which of our present skills and institutions will inadvertently provide the foundation for something really new? In what new way might we take flight? Can we only look back, try to understand the terrain over which we have traveled to get where we are? Or can we guess ahead, just as we try to look at the canyon ahead for the telltale side canyons which foretell the next rapid?

The stars are fading in the western sky. To those not used to being up at this hour, the stars not the familiar ones of the evening. Only a few of the brightest can still be seen. And I now begin to think about sidesteps in evolution rather than mere "progress." What is really striking, about both biological and cultural evolution, are the unexpected sidesteps, not the commonplace straight-line improvements in locomotion or cleverness.

At some point, there were enough forelimb feathers for a novel, unexpected property to emerge—flight. I keep coming back to that, somehow. There is nothing in the theory of thermodynamics that predicts gliding or soaring, yet unexpected properties of feathers gave rise to a whole new class of vertebrates, the birds, that would dominate the air surrounding the earth until their basic aerodynamics were finally mimicked successfully by twentieth-century humans, who built a flying machine with the technical knowledge their forebears had accumulated over the centuries.

There is similarly nothing in the Newtonian physics governing a thrown stone or spear that predicts a blossoming of brain size and consciousness and language. Yet such sidesteps—more insulating feathers or more timing neurons having unexpected properties—are the really dramatic stuff of biological evolution over the millennia. And, on a time scale of only a generation or less, of cultural evolution too. They're the waterfalls of the uphill river.

A RAPID INTERRUPTS. It, certainly, is no dream. The river water is as cold a shower as one might imagine, and some of us probably needed it to wake up on this particular day. This is my first rapid without sunglasses and hat brim shielding my face, and so my face gets thoroughly washed by the modicum of river that unexpectedly sails in over the bow. My face cold and dripping, I somehow feel that I can see more clearly now. I could hear the rapid better too—you notice the sounds of the individual splashes over the roar while you're in the middle of it. Reassigning brainpower, you hear better when you can't see.

Besides our half of a moon, we have a single morning star—the planet Venus, low in the eastern sky just above the canyon wall. And the dawn light is now strong enough so that the highest of the Redwall cliffs has taken on a chocolate-orange hue. But the rest of the canyon below is in monochrome. Even the orange lifejackets on the other boats are only part of the ghostly dark silhouettes following us down the river. The dawn comes an hour later in the depths of the Canyon than on the rim, so the twilight period is pleasantly prolonged.

The shapes of the eroded rock formations are sometimes suggestive of human architecture. Especially when you see only profiles and not details, they stir up many schemata in one's imaginative brain. It is easy to imagine that a predawn journey down the Nile through Luxor would reveal similar shapes of temples and monuments hugging the riverbanks. A triangular pyramid is even seen downriver: Diamond Peak, with the dimly illuminated rock strata tilted along its side to look like a winding road up to the top. We had seen a false Diamond Peak last night, one of its several look-alikes, spotlighted by the changing clouds after the threatened storm, framed by a great rainbow, complete with a secondary set of outrider stripes. This morning, there is little suggestion of color in the predawn light illuminating the real Diamond Peak, looking like a rough caret of the Redwall mounted in a striped setting.

Though the right bank has normal layering, the left shore has been strangely featureless for a long stretch. But now there is a huge, squarish block of dark lava sitting atop the slopes, a recent addition of the last million years during the final uplift of the Colorado Plateau and its volcanos. The dim light, presumably concealing a honeycomb tapestry, belies what must have been the original appearance of the lava: the orange-hot hue of freshly emerged magma, flowing slowly in high mounds, stiffly pushing and filling until it jells to its dark, blocky presence, the hexagonal columns snapping into place as it cools.

REMEMBERING A GEOLOGY GUIDEBOOK, I now realize that the path that the river is currently following must be the Hurricane Fault. If we could see it beyond the low, eroded hills, the Redwall on the left bank would be elevated. Indeed, by as much as one-third the total depth of the Canyon—just as if the ground under a building in a downtown canyon were uplifted until the sidewalks were at the 120th floor of the skyscraper across the street. Slowly one realizes the extraordinary magnitude of this, that all the underlying metamorphic rock has been

For now we see through a glass darkly; but then face to face.

FIRST EPISTLE OF PAUL TO THE CORINTHIANS, 1800 years ago

pushed up out of the hot depths of the earth's crust by some ancient, earth-shaking event.

Our orderly, layered world seems turned on end, thrown awry. We seem split between two ancient worlds—we are drifting, ever so casually and innocently, along a great and powerful crack in the earth's crust. A fault that still occasionally quakes.

And the shadowy boats behind continue to follow us. Do they realize where we are?

But our unspoken injunction against speaking inhibits me from calling out to the other boats. They just blindly follow us down the great crack. For a moment, I am reminded of our playful reenactment of Ingmar Bergman's figure of Death leading away a long serpentine chain of his victims along the moonlit skyline, our frolic that night shortly before the moon entered the earth's shadow to be eclipsed.

That image now merges in my head with another figure of myth. That of Charon, the boatman on the River Styx remembered from Michelangelo's ceiling in the Sistine Chapel. And from Greek mythology, if I remember correctly. Charon, he who ferried silent passengers on their one-way journey to Hell.

I shudder—but only, I tell myself, because there is no sun to warm my soaked clothing.

LOOKING BACKWARD as we first emerge from a minor rapid, the other boats seem to be embedded in the mirror-smooth surface of the river just before the lip of the rapid. Then each one slips into the turbulence, pitches up and down the standing waves, and finally emerges into the swirl of currents downriver from the rapid.

The water mills about, little whirls appearing and disappearing, before settling on a new path. Much of the surface water reverses course, flowing back up toward the rapid in a back-eddy. Like backsliding in evolution. We pick our way down a line of foam that marks the narrow fence of sheer currents separating the left- and right-handed back-eddies, so as to avoid the backwaters that entrap. The boatmen only row enough to steer us down this ever-changing channel, the creak of the oarlocks the only sound other than the songs of the birds awakening, now that we are past the rapid.

Emerging from the monochrome, the eastern sky now has pastel shades, and the orange of our lifejackets can now be dimly seen. Even a hummingbird has come over to inspect them, but it rejects the strange, oversized flower. The wet sand along the shore has taken on a purple pastel hue, one that I have never seen in sand before. Nor seen captured in a painting. Another, larger bird makes a sudden pass at me, almost hitting my head, going "cheep-cheep" as it flies away disappointed.

I keep hearing music run through my head. It's Beethoven. The Ninth Symphony, I think, the Choral. Not the whole thing, fortunately—just part of the final movement. It's appropriate, anyway. At least it's not Mozart's *Requiem* which he wrote in his dying days. At age thirty-seven.

THE AIR IS VERY CLEAR, and we can see for many miles when the walls of the inner canyon permit. The high limestone cliffs appear white. The cicadas begin to take note of the approaching dawn, adding a chorus to the fluting sounds of the water passing over some minor rocks in the river, the pattering sounds of the occasional light windwaves against the bottom of the boat, perhaps even the distant roar of another rapid.

Two large ravens fly by overhead, maintaining an orderly formation amidst the random motions of the cruising bats—as if they were the king's messengers striding purposefully to an important downriver appointment. I wonder where they're going?

There are a few patches of red downriver among the white cliffs, looking like partially applied makeup. But the first real sign of sunrise is glowing in the clouds overhead, the fluffy cumulonimbus left over from last night's threatened thunderstorm. These scattered clouds look dark and pregnant against the eastern sky, but their undersides are tinged with pink. Below them, the sky passes from deep blue to purple and violet, then almost to pink before reaching the reddish mauve of the rocky rim of the canyon. Rainbows were never like this.

I look around to see who my fellow passengers are on this final morning, now that there is enough light. We are all unrelated: a woman from New York, a man from Alaska, a woman from Switzerland, and our head boatman, Gary Casey. By common consent, we are each alone with our thoughts, but passing through this moment in time together.

We turn a corner and the next rapid announces itself with a subdued roar. We can see the water splashing randomly above the surface of our mirror-like river. The course of our lives, even our progress to more complex evolutionary stages, is not unlike the river's progress. We too have our quiet moments when time passes uneventfully, as well as our passages through uncertainties and turbulence, our moments of finding a new course once the froth has quieted down. But the swirls still abound, pulling us one way and then another.

But the cold water of the real rapid is no metaphor.

THE DESCENT down the energy gradient somehow creates a self-organizing ascent, almost a river that flows uphill. From descent to ascent: How? How did the existentialists' world of chaos become our orderly universe? Good old irreversible thermodynamics and stratified stability is the short answer. But when it comes to biology, a principle is no substitute for the major details—because there is nothing inevitable about the directions taken. History is everything.

Like the dozens of rapids on the Colorado that cause notable descents, we've been jacked up through dozens of major ascents during our evolutionary history. From quantum radiation to quarks to matter. From elementary particles to simple atoms like hydrogen and helium. Jacked up via supernovae into heavier elements such as carbon and oxygen. Jacked up via the volcanos and rainfall of a fortunately situated planet, simply because the resulting rivers created an assortment of particle sizes. Ascending via the clay, catalyzing more complex molecules by providing the right framework. And then the big step to self-replicating molecules.

They're all big self-organization steps, but some are more revolutionary than others. Self-replication is the key step to life as we know it—it set in motion a fundamentally different line of evolution because it allowed small effects to accumulate. Before, both time and change had occurred—now history happened.

The cell itself was another big step—the self-replicating machinery enclosed in an envelope. The little bacteria that eventually evolved 3,500 million years ago captured sunlight themselves and turned it into even more bacteria, filled up the oceans with life. Supercell was another great step, the success of the committee building on the success of the envelope, where the sum of the symbiotic parts produced a cell with the capability to evolve far fancier life forms.

Gene duplication, followed by diversification, was another super-sidestep—another metaptation. As was sex—because sex institutionalized randomness, and so made more inheritable variants on which natural selection could operate.

And multicellularity was a step that engendered another super-sidestep: nerve cells and then nervous systems and then brains. And while brains were handy for coordinating defense against predators, the super-sidestep aspect came from the brain's ability to combine unlike behaviors to yield some totally new behavior. And that institutionalized rapid innovation.

The Cambrian explosion of life forms might be considered a big step—we're riding along the Great Unconformity again—but it's not really a sidestep. There's nothing to keep a mollusk from evolving into something as fancy as higher primates—just look at how far the octopus has come. But there's something about mammals, and particularly the primate lineage, that seems to lend itself to juvenilization, so that the proportionately larger brain and the juvenile behaviors like curiosity and play have been repeatedly enhanced, jacking up complexity once again. Step back to leap, get caught by stratified stability at a new level. All the way up to the point of our elaborate form of consciousness, weaving scenarios about the past and future, with ourselves at the intersection of several possible futures—surely that ability marks another major point of departure, another metaptation.

And cultural evolution must be seen as a super-sidestep, another inverted waterfall: While not peculiarly human, in the context of the human brain it makes possible additional sidesteps such as language. Such as writing. Written history. Science. Such as building a computer with some brain-like properties—a sidestep of evolution that may turn out to be the next super-sidestep.

Now all we have to do is figure out which imminent steps are really back-eddies in disguise, paths that lead nowhere. And entrap us.

NOW THERE IS DIRECT SUNLIGHT falling on the topmost layers of the canyon walls to the west, looking like pink frosting on a chocolate cake. The half-moon is crisp, with its flat plains clearly to be seen, suspended on a blue backdrop of morning sky. The Canyon behind our boat is still in deep shadow.

An early morning freshening breeze begins drifting upriver, rippling the glossy surface of the water and bringing new smells to our nostrils. A canyon wren sings its distinctive song of eight notes descending the scale, as if warming up for a voice lesson, competing with the sounds of riffles. We are now passing through upturned slabs of granite, foliated and pointing upriver as great slabs. The river narrows here, thanks to the granite on both riverbanks, and the flow speeds up, squeezed through the narrower space carved through the harder rock. Rows of ocotillo line the nearby hilltops, like a row of regularly spaced sentinels flanking an approach. As we look back upstream, not only does the water glisten but the riverbank granite shines in the early morning light where it has been polished by the river in centuries past. Our other boats eventually float silently past these marbled gates. The creaking turn of the oarlocks is the only sound of our progress.

Our silent boatmen aside, none of us really knows which bend in the river will bring us to our takeout beach, none of us knows which rapid will be the last one for us. And none of us knows what news awaits, back in civilization when we intrude on the resident lizards at a lonely desert telephone booth.

A whole new section of sunlit canyon is now revealed, emerging from behind a shadowed profile of nearby cliff, with more red and white layers coming into view with each creak of the oars. Layer-cake geology, being slowly colored in, layer-by-layer, from the top with a broad brush.

A CRASH IS HEARD, shattering our silence. It is like the "ker-plunk" made by a large rock being dropped in the river. I instantly surmise that we are witnessing another rare episode in the Canyon's slow erosion, a repeat performance of that first evening on the river. But I can neither see nor hear other small rocks trailing behind in usual rockfall fashion.

I keep looking around, puzzled. "Ker-plunk." Again we are startled by the same singular crashing sound, even closer to us this time.

Gary points silently and then I see it: we have a beaver swimming off our bow. Sleek and domineering, he is trying to scare us away, using great flips of his flat tail. He wasn't merely giving an alarm, announcing our arrival—he's trying to herd us, threatening us with that tail flip.

Beware, all ye that enter here. Go back, stay away. The beaver dives after each resounding tail flip, to emerge many seconds later, to challenge us again.

The beaver is cruising ahead of us downstream, swimming through what appears to us as an orange pool of water. I look up. The orange is the reflected sunlight from high cliffs downstream that the dawn has reached. The beaver keeps pace with us but occasionally turns to face us, as if a sheep dog trying to turn us aside, warning us to come no further. He then crashes his tail into the orange water, emphatically telling us that this is his territory. I hope that, like some car-chasing dogs I've known, he doesn't snap at the passing rubber—those teeth might puncture a pontoon, giving the poor beaver a rude surprise.

There is no sign of his toothwork among the willows and tamarisk lining the shore—perhaps he has just eaten all of the fallen trees, having failed to dam the great river. This river would be enough to frustrate a thousand beavers—except, unfortunately, the busy kind that pours concrete. Finally, after another great crash of his tail, our beaver doesn't reappear.

The river seems lonely without him. Beaver are actually common all along the river corridor but, because of their nocturnal habits, we haven't been out at the right hour to run into one.

I'm beginning to miss his companionship, aggrieved though it was. Then we hear him again, more distantly this time. We look back. And there he is, repeating his unheeded warnings to the second boat in our silent string. He is determined, that beaver. We continue onwards, forewarned trespassers.

TO ADD EMPHASIS to our sense of being on the threshold of some forbidden gateway, the left riverbank changes. Great up-tilted slabs of Vishnu Schist rise skyward, cathedral-like spires ascending from bases along the shore, laced with veins of granite.

The river has also reached a dead-end against the steep canyon wall up ahead. It just ends, right there.

This has happened before. We have learned by now that this is an illusion caused by the river taking a sharp turn. But which direction? We've made a game of it, each person on a boat offering their considered judgment. Today, I guess silently to myself. To the left, I predict, concentrating on the dead-end and comparing its left corner to the right one, unable to see details in this light.

And then I see, in the right corner, that the morning sun now shines directly like a spotlight on—well, I'd swear it's a polished black marble-like pillar standing alone, out in the river. That's crazy. But it casts a long morning reflection out onto the river's swirling surface. . . .

What is it? It stands alone in the water, spotlit. The next thing to happen, I tell myself, is that I'll be hearing the Strauss *Also Sprach Zarathustra* music from the opening score of the film *2001*. Did Arthur C. Clarke ever take this river trip? Now that we're closer, I see the others staring at the prominent black pillar too, wondering.

Our boat slowly emerges into the small sunlit section of river, and we see the sunrise peeking out from behind a cliff to our rear. Soon it disappears as we float a little further and are in shadow again. One thinks of the ancient Anasazi, faithful observers of the rising and setting sun, who waited each morning for such a first glimpse of the new day, atop a chosen hilltop in the Canyon.

We begin turning left, the view ahead no longer seeming to be a dead-end but opening up to the left, into the dogleg of the trench carved by the river. After we pass the enigmatic black pillar and look back on it, we see that it is not as regular and polished as it earlier appeared from the distance. It is only a rectangular slab of rock several stories tall that stands on the shore in front of the regular schist wall of tilted vertical slabs. It has been polished somewhat by the spring floods of the untamed river. Liquid sandpaper. With no more silt-laden spring floods, little more sculpting will occur until the dam's demise.

The Strauss music fades. But the mood is still expectant, pregnant with mixed emotions.

AGAIN COMES the familiar sound of a major rapid, though we cannot see it. Indeed, a major side canyon can now be seen downriver on the left. Is this Diamond Creek, with its connection to the Hurricane Fault? The fault that is now followed by a rough road up the canyon walls, through the Hualapai Indian reservation to Peach Springs? Is this brightly lit section of Canyon heralding our return to civilization?

I turn and look away—up at our half-moon and our spotlit pyramid, back up-canyon to our indignant beaver and our silent boats, to the warm and rich colors of dawn in the Grand Canyon.

But downriver, when I finally look again, there are some concrete picnic tables relentlessly emerging from behind the greenery on a broad sandy beach. We haven't seen picnic tables since Lee's Ferry, where our journey began outside the wilderness. I'd happily do without them forever.

And then a sturdy blue truck can be seen, if one dares to look. Unmistakable, unavoidable clues that we are about to leave our wilderness. But inscrutable ones. We drift closer and closer to the left riverbank.

As we near the shore, I drop off the side of the boat into the river and wade in to the sandy beach, my hands kept occupied by the coiled mooring line. I am reluctantly the first person ashore from the first boat. I turn my back on the signs of civilization, and try to heave the stern of the boat up onto the sand, looking back all the while at the river and its passengers. I see the faces of my fellow travelers as their six boats also slowly approach the takeout beach, one by one.

It is an enigmatic procession, one whose creaking oarlocks sound a counterpoint to the intermittent cicada chorus from the trees, to the morning calls of the birds, to the unending roar of the rapid heard downriver.

We are all—without exception—silent, somber, and reflective. As in a sanctuary.

Perhaps. I look into more faces as I move along the beach, pull another boat in. Somehow, the faces express sorrow. Almost, but not quite, disbelief. Where, on so many faces together, where have I seen that look before?

I keep surveying faces as more boats approach.

Our eyes focus at a great distance, our jaws hang slack. . . .

As, I now remember, we appeared at the funeral of a young graduate student who died suddenly.

Unexpectedly. His was an untimely death, even earlier than Mozart's. That's the way we look.

No one wants our journey to end, this flowing interlude in a life that is too brief.

The creaking oarlocks have fallen silent. The pounding roar of the rapid continues just downstream. But we shall not pass through this one.

Time is a river which sweeps me along,
    but I am the river;
it is a tiger which mangles me,
    but I am the tiger;
it is a fire which consumes me,
    but I am the fire.
                  JORGE LUIS BORGES
                  A New Refutation of Time

Decay is inherent in all compounded things.
Strive on with diligence.
        THE BUDDHA's last words

Postscript

> The test of a book (to a writer) is if it makes a space in which, quite naturally, you can say what you want to say.
>
> Virginia Woolf

While this is a work of nonfiction, some incidents have become a collage for rhetorical purposes, some characters have become chimeras, some material imported from off the river, and certainly four Colorado River trips have been amalgamated into one. I hope that the Canyon boatmen will forgive me if I have inadvertently put someone's favorite Canyon story into the mouth of another. The boatmen are people like those that John Maynard Keynes had in mind when he said:

We shall once more . . . prefer the good to the useful. We shall honour those who teach us how to pluck the hour and the day virtuously and well, the delightful people who are capable of taking direct enjoyment in things.

And I must thank them all. My friends Alan R. Fisk-Williams and Susan P. Bassett, two professional boatmen from whom I learned much about the Canyon, were of great help with an early draft of this book; I hope that no errors regarding the river have crept in since they last annotated the manuscript. My wife, Katherine Graubard, periodically gave me the benefit of her thinking, including several useful metaphors. Two skillful volunteer editors have aided me far beyond any call of duty: Blanche Kazon Graubard and Kathryn Moen Braeman. Everyone should be so lucky. Among the readers of the first draft, particularly helpful comments were made by Beatrice Bruteau, John DuBois, Michelle DuBois, Seymour Graubard, Dan Hartline, Christine Phillips,

Dan Richard, and Beverly Williams. Students in my undergraduate honors course on brains and evolution were influential in helping me decide what subject matter could be included for general readers; Ajit Limaye and Laurel Brown later undertook to red-pencil the professor's writing efforts and were most helpful. The author Michael Talbot, together with my literary agent John Brockman, wisely persuaded me to abandon my early plans for writing the book in fictional format. The careful editing by Charles Levine and Robert Nieweg at Macmillan considerably improved almost every page of the manuscript. The Grand Canyon anthropologist Robert C. Euler extended many kindnesses to me; Barbara Isaac, the late Glynn Isaac, Terry Deacon, and their anthropology students at Harvard University greatly aided my knowledge of African archaeology. My University of Washington colleagues John Edwards, Joan Lockard, John Loeser, George Ojemann, John Palka, Robert Pinter, Wayne Potts, and Dennis Willows have steered me in the right direction on many occasions; the Quaternary Research Center's lecture series arranged by Stephen Porter was invaluable. The neurobiologist David G. King stimulated my thinking on evolutionary biology and sidesteps. I am most grateful to all of them.

I feel a special gratitude toward brains, evolution, and the Grand Canyon. Writers sometimes feel as if they have been taken over by a book: it develops a life of its own, proclaims its own imperatives, almost writes itself once the framework is established; one has to somehow live up to its expectations. When I ran across Virginia Woolf's comment, it reinforced what I had long felt: that the present combination of subject and setting was an unparalleled opportunity to say what many scientists would like to convey about science to their nonscientist friends. On the first trip that I took down the Colorado River in 1975, half of the passengers were neurobiologists. And half were nonscientists who, on balance, reminded me of what someone once described as the old lawyer who courteously probes for the facts but who expects to draw his own conclusions. It was that trip which made me aware of how an easier dialogue between scientists and nonscientists could develop.

But this book is not that 1975 trip except in inspiration. Nor is it the eclipse trip, though connoisseurs of the *Nautical Almanac* will find that the movements of the sun and moon match those of the first half of July 1982. The book's two weeks are, rather, a medley of events which took more than three years to write and rewrite. The facts and interpretations are almost entirely part of the published scientific literature; only a few (such as my parking-garage metaphor, my squeeze-the-center, expand-the-periphery ice age ratchet, and the juvenilization-then-slowing cycle) make their first appearance here. Particularly outside neurobiology, many of the interpretations are adapted from someone else's lecture or popular article. But most of the *speculations*—such as those about archaeoastronomy, post-aquatic monogamy, cryptic selection, big brains, consciousness, music, and auxiliary memories—can be assigned to me.

I still haven't figured out how to describe going through a rapid, except as seen through my own eyes; were I a properly trained writer,

I wouldn't have had to use the first person. And it does present some problems to a scientist. I found myself "switching hats" constantly: sometimes authoritatively describing science, sometimes speculating and attempting to convey less assurance, sometimes participating in the exaggerated overstatement that replaces careful understatement as getting-away-from-it-all sets in. Even serious scientists become silly. In attempting to capture some of the feel of a river trip, I have not always adequately qualified statements, both scientific (beaver and bird behavior are more complex than presented; see the end notes) and nonscientific (surely Phoenix, Las Vegas, and the Glen Canyon Dam have some good points; inquire at the appropriate Chamber of Commerce). The end notes cannot fully counterbalance textual omissions, but in them I have tried to point to more complete treatments, at least for scientific topics.

In the case of the big-brain problem, I attempted to discuss appropriate criteria for an explanation, give a balanced view of alternative proposals for both how the biology varies and how/where/when selection might operate upon those variants, and then—hopefully having armed the reader with a basis for making one's own evaluation—present my favorite hypothesis for consideration. The reader should be aware that many other topics in this book could be similarly qualified but—because of the river-diary format and space limitations—the full pros-and-cons treatment has had to be reduced down to my favorite story. This book, I hope, makes no pretense of being an unbiased digest of respectable anthropological and biological opinion; it's a personal view and not a general consensus.

The extensive bibliography in my 1983 essay book, *The Throwing Madonna*, may be of more use to the serious student than the present end notes; that book was written as a warmup for this river book, and has a more complete discussion of some of the behavioral and neurophysiological topics, especially throwing per se and its implications for language. My ideas about self-organizing systems, the implications of throwing machinery for consciousness and music, the oscillating ice-age frontier (pumping up brain size by compressing the central population but then expanding the more versatile frontier population), and the appalling debt we owe to would-be mothers, have largely developed since that book was written.

The river stories, such as the "freeze-dried tadpoles" or the passenger who swore so creatively while swimming a rapid (yes, she really did say that), have sometimes been modified to help make a scientific point. I have even embroidered a few: for example, to Alan's tadpoles, I added the dehydrated C-Minor cicadas. The genetic-code necklace is pure invention; however, the scene that would be another logical candidate for a contrived story for didactic purposes, the scientist who got news of his father's unusual stroke while at the lone outpost of civilization, and then hiked out of the mile-deep Canyon, is unfortunately true; it was my father. I like to think that he would have enjoyed this book. He would certainly have loved the river trip and all the science.

W.H.C.
Friday Harbor
Summer 1986

End Notes and Bibliography

The River

John Blaustein, Edward Abbey, and Martin Litton, *The Hidden Canyon: A River Journey*, Viking, New York (1977; 1978 Penguin softcover edition). A superb collection of river pictures by boatman-photographer John Blaustein, with a river diary by Ed Abbey and introduction by Martin Litton.

Robert O. Collins and Roderick Nash, with photographs by John Blaustein, *The Big Drops: Ten Legendary Rapids*, Sierra Club Books, San Francisco (1978).

W. Kenneth Hamblin and J. Keith Rigby, *Guidebook to the Colorado River*, parts 1 and 2, Brigham Young University Geology Studies, Provo, Utah (1968). This is the mile-by-mile description of the Grand Canyon geological features seen from the river.

François Leydet, *Time and the River Flowing: Grand Canyon*, Sierra Club/Ballantine abridged edition (1968).

John Wesley Powell (1869 diary) and Eliot Porter (1969 photographs), *Down the Colorado*, Promontory Press (1969).

Larry Stevens, *The Colorado River in Grand Canyon: A Comprehensive Guide to its Natural and Human History*, Red Lake Books, P.O. Box 1315, Flagstaff, Arizona 86002 (Second Edition, 1984). The best of the river guidebooks, a work of love by a biologist-boatman.

The Canyon

Harvey Butchart, *Grand Canyon Treks*, La Siesta Press, Glendale (1976). Together with *Treks II and III*, the major resource for off-the-beaten-path hiking and climbing routes in the Canyon.

Michael Collier, *An Introduction to Grand Canyon Geology*, Grand Canyon Natural History Association, Grand Canyon (1980). Another beautiful publication in the boatman tradition, this time by a geologist-boatman ("Boatmen will do anything for one more trip—even graduate geology research").

Robert C. Euler and Frank Tikalsky, eds., *The Grand Canyon: Up Close and Personal*, Western Montana College Foundation (1980). A lovely collection of photographs and essays by experts on Canyon ecology, anthropology, geology, biology, river-running, and hiking. Available by mail (as are most other regional books listed here) from the bookstore of the Museum of Northern Arizona, Route 4, Box 720, Flagstaff, Arizona 86001, or Ken Sleight Books, Box 1270, Moab, Utah 84532.

Paul F. Geerlings, *Down the Grand Staircase*, Grand Canyon Publications, Salt Lake City (1978).

Ron Redfern, *Corridors of Time*, Times Books, New York (1980).

Postdamnation

Steven W. Carothers and Robert Dolan, "Dam changes on the Colorado River," *Natural History* 91(1):74–83 (1982).

Robert Dolan, A. Howard, and A. Gallenson, "Man's impact on the Colorado River in the Grand Canyon," *American Scientist* 62:392–401 (1974).

Phillip L. Fradkin, *A River No More: The Colorado River and the West*, New York: Alfred A. Knopf, New York (1981). For a briefer and more pictorial treatment, see John Boslough's "Rationing a river," *SCIENCE 81* 2(5):26–37 (June 1981).

Donald Worster, *Rivers of Empire: Water, Aridity, and the Growth of the American West*, Pantheon, New York (1986). "Total power, total possession was the program," he writes. "Nature in the West could not be allowed to defy it, nor could human cussedness."

"Water on the Plateau" is a special issue of *Plateau*, the publication of the Museum of Northern Arizona (Summer, 1981).

The Anasazi

J. Richard Ambler, *The Anasazi*, Museum of Northern Arizona Press, Flagstaff (1977). ". . .the Anasazi . . . were slightly shorter than the average today, had straight black hair and spoke in tongues unintelligible to the western ear. They were people worried about their crops and children, remembering the past and wondering about the future."

Don D. Fowler, Robert C. Euler, and Catherine S. Fowler, "John Wesley Powell and the anthropology of the canyon country," Geological Survey professional paper 670, U.S. Geological Survey, Washington D.C. (1969). This summarizes the Anasazi ruins along the river corridor.

Alfonso Ortiz, ed., *Handbook of North American Indians*, volume 9, *Southwest*. Smithsonian Institution, Washington, D.C. (1979). Many chapters on both archaeology and present-day Pueblo Indians.

End Notes

PREFACE

Owen J. Flanagan, Jr., *The Science of the Mind*, MIT Press, Cambridge (1984), p.19.

"Neurophysiologists": Terminology describing brain researchers can be confusing; I recommend that the reader ignore it. But for those trying to figure out the specialties, here goes. A *neuroscientist* is a brain researcher; this includes neurobiologists but also research neurologists, psychiatrists, neurosurgeons, and neuropathologists. A *neurobiologist* is typically a neuroscientist outside the clinical areas, often with a biology or psychology background rather than a medical school one, typically with a Ph.D. degree rather than an M.D. (though psychiatrists doing research on invertebrates are usually also called neurobiologists). Within neurobiology, there are subdivisions by interests and methodological expertise. I am a *neurophysiologist*, more concerned with function than anatomy (vice versa for a *neuroanatomist*); in particular, I do theoretical work (making mathematical models, doing computer simulations, trying to piece together the big picture), though in the past I have primarily been known as an experimental neurophysiologist (studying the electrical properties of nerve cells, and how these cells encode and decode information). There are, of course, neuropsychologists, neurochemists, specialists in development, and many others within the neurosciences. None of these names should be taken too

seriously, since many individual scientists are involved in several specialties. For example, since leaving physics, I have done comparative primate anatomy, comparative behavior, membrane biophysics of stochastic processes, comparative vertebrate and invertebrate neurophysiology, clinical neurophysiology on single human nerve cells in patients with epilepsy or pain problems; mathematical modeling at the membrane, whole-cell, circuit, and perceptual levels; and modeling of evolutionary processes related to brain size within prehuman evolution—yet I still think of myself primarily as a neurophysiologist with a biophysical bent (probably because my Ph.D. was in physiology and biophysics). A similarly diverse story could be told for many neurobiologists—though, I might add, most of the advances come from people who narrowly specialize, painstakingly developing the techniques that allow them to force the nervous system to yield unequivocal answers to precisely phrased questions.

Those who admire holistic approaches will find some examples in this book, but let me venture a caution: *Holism is very hard to practice without reductionism, either your own or someone else's.* If one is to see the forest for the trees, it helps to know that a tree is the appropriate building block out of which forests are constructed (blades of grass are not the biological units of a lawn, for example). For the forest of the brain, we're still trying to figure out the individual units of action and of information storage; see W. H. Calvin and K. Graubard, "Styles of neuronal computation." In *The Neurosciences, Fourth Study Program*, edited by F. O. Schmitt and F. G. Worden (MIT Press, 1979), chapter 29.

PROLOGUE

"Mile-high ice," see Jonathan Weiner, "The Grimsel glacier," *The Sciences* (New York Academy of Sciences) 25(2):22–29 (March 1985).

An excellent illustration of the Marble Platform and Grand Canyon is in Redfern's *Corridors of Time* on pp.38–39 (the Marble Platform is unlabeled, but the Marble Canyon cuts through it). *I will periodically note the pages in the various picture books to which the determined reader can refer for a color illustration of various views of the Grand Canyon.*

Glynn Llywelyn Isaac, "Aspects of human evolution." In *Essays on Evolution: A Darwin Centenary Volume* (Cambridge University Press, 1983). His obituary appears in *Nature* 319:15 (2 January 1986).

DAY 1

MILE 1

Front and back, bow and stern aren't so obvious when a boat is symmetrical. In rowboat terminology the boatman faces the stern because the pull stroke is more powerful than the push. I prefer symmetrical ferryboat terminology, where the end that the captain faces is defined as the "bow"; ever since Nathaniel T. Galloway developed the technique in 1897, the Canyon boatmen have run rapids looking where they're going, and using a push stroke to steer. In our boats, the luggage is piled in a big canvas bag in the front floor, creating additional ballast for crashing through waves with the bow. The rear has the mooring line and the bigger of the bailing buckets.

MILE 4

S. W. Janes, "The apparent use of rocks by a raven in nest defense," *Condor* 78:409 (1976).

Vultures bombing eggs: Jane Goodall, "Tool-using in primates and other vertebrates," *Advances in the Study of Behaviour* 3:195–249 (1970).

MILE 5

For a discussion of the origins of flight, see S. J. Gould, "Not necessarily a wing," *Natural History* 94:12 (October 1985); J. G. Kingsolver and M. A. R. Koehl, "Aerodynamics, thermoregulation, and the evolution of insect wings: Differential scaling and evolutionary change," *Evolution* 39:488–504. John S. Edwards would assign the origins of flight to insects taking a flying leap to escape predators such as spiders (all known flying insects launch themselves with such a jump); see "Predator evasion and the origin of insect flight: an exercise in evolutionary ethology," *Society for Neuroscience Abstracts* 152.10 (1985). For the phylogeny of birds and their origins in the dinosaurs ("The dinosaurs aren't extinct—we just call them birds"), see J. H. Ostrom, "The origin of birds," *Annual Review of Earth and Planetary Sciences* 3:55–77 (1975).

The gliding snake is *Chrysopelea*; See p.100 in

David Attenborough's *The Living Planet*, Little Brown, Boston (1984).

Behavior first, anatomy follows: The idea goes back to Lamarck (see S. J. Gould, *The Flamingo's Smile*, p. 36). Another formulation is that of R. F. Ewer: "Behaviour will tend to be always one jump ahead of structure and so play a decisive role in the evolutionary process." See Alister C. Hardy, *The Living Stream; a Restatement of Evolution Theory*, Collins, London (1965).

MILE 8

Badger Rapid photos 10,11 in Blaustein; facing p.152 in Collins et al.

MILE 10

Actually, there are proposed evolutionary scenarios for laughter, most of which see it (as did Freud) as a form of aggression. See the review in Irenäus Eibl-Eibesfeldt, *Krieg und Frieden*, R. Piper Verlag, Munich (1975) (translated as *The Biology of War and Peace*, Viking Penguin, New York, 1979). My interpretation is given on Day 12.

MILE 12

David Barash, *The Whisperings Within: Evolution and the Origin of Human Nature*, Harper and Row, New York (1979). "Foresight" paragraph paraphrased from C. Pittendrigh.

MILE 17

Glen Canyon references: See photos in Leydet, pp. 151–160; Powell and Porter, and in Eliot Porter, *The Place No One Knew: Glen Canyon on the Colorado* (1963).

MILE 18

E. J. Kollar and C. Fisher, "Tooth induction in chick epithelium: Expression of quiescent genes for enamel synthesis," *Science* 207:993–995 (1980). Fossil footprints, see Mile 136 notes.

MILE 21

The *Ursa major* constellation usually known as the Big Dipper in North America is called the Casserole in France, the Plough in England, the Celestial Bureaucrat in China, and Revolving Male by the Navajo. See pp.46–47 in Carl Sagan's *Cosmos*, Random House, New York (1980).

Timothy Ferris, *The Red Limit*, William Morrow and Co., New York (1977). An excellent history of cosmology with a glossary of terms.

Eric Chaisson, *Cosmic Dawn: The Origins and Matter and Life*, Atlantic Monthly Press, Boston (1981).

Paul S. Henry, "A simple description of the 3°K cosmic microwave background," *Science* 207:939–942 (29 February 1980). For a history of the fossil photon discovery, see Jeremy Bernstein, "Three degrees above zero," *New Yorker*, pp. 42–70 (20 August 1984), or James S. Trefil, *The Moment of Creation*, Scribner's, New York (1983).

John McPhee, *The Curve of Binding Energy*, Farrar, Straus, and Giroux, New York (1974).

Don Mathewson, "The clouds of Magellan," *Scientific American* 252(4):107–114 (April 1985).

Building heavier elements: Hans Bethe and Gerald Brown, "How a supernova explodes," *Scientific American* 252(5):60 (May 1985).

One recent, though tentative, estimate of the age of the universe is 13 billion years, the Hubble constant calibrated using the double image (produced by a gravitational lens effect) of a distant quasar with an 18-month lag between the two images because of different path lengths. See John Gribbin's news article, "A new way to date the universe," *New Scientist*, p.24 (7 March 1985).

The expansion of the universe after the Big Bang has always presented theorists with difficulties in accounting for the uniform directions of arrival of the fossil photons, but also for the nearly uniform distribution of matter in the universe. Notwithstanding the "empty space" between the Local Group and the Virgo Cluster, the universe is far too uniform on a larger scale to have arisen from a simple explosion scattering matter from a point source (like light intensity, the mass density would fall off). For a recent summary of theory, see Alan H. Guth and Paul J. Steinhardt, "The inflationary universe," *Scientific American* 250(5):116 (May 1984), and Andrei Linde, "The universe: Inflation out of chaos," *New Scientist*, p.14 (7 March 1985). John P. Huchra, Margaret J. Geller, and Valérie de Lapparent (in the 1 March 1986 *Astrophysical Journal Letters*) note that galactic clusters lie at the intersections of large "bubbles" of empty space; in 1981, Jeremiah P. Ostriker and Lennox L. Cowie theorized that a bubble structure for the universe might have arisen from the shock waves of a series of supernovae explosions.

DAY 2

MILE 21

North Canyon pool, photo 17 in Blaustein.

MILE 23

Layers of rock are illustrated in Redfern, pp. 36–37, 66.

MILE 26

Desert varnish can be dated to provide indications of human modifiction of rocks: See Ronald I. Dorn et al., "Cation-ratio and accelerator radiocarbon dating of rock varnish on Mojave artifacts and landforms," *Science* 231:830–833 (21 February 1986).

MILE 29

Silver Grotto first pool is shown following p.63 in Powell and Porter (but is misidentified).

MILE 30

The DDT story with the parachuting cats is in the late William T. Keeton's excellent text, *Biological Science*, Third Edition, W. W. Norton, New York (1980), p.854. While there are many good college biology texts, Keeton is also one of the best for reference purposes; the 4th edition will be edited by James L. Gould.

MILE 31

South Canyon petroglyphs are shown in photos 27 and 28 of Blaustein; "Sun Dagger" spirals, see notes for Mile 71.

The average visitor to Grand Canyon National Park is said to stay only 3 hours—2½ of which are spent in the gift shops. *The New York Times* (24 May 1986).

For references on blood groups and dating, see J. S. Jones and S. Rouhani, "How small was the bottleneck?," *Nature* 319:449–450 (6 February 1986).

Peter Farb, *Man's Rise to Civilization: The Cultural Ascent of the Indians of North America*, Second Edition, Dutton, New York (1978). The genetics is from W. F. Bodmer and L. L. Cavalli-Sforza, *Genetics, Evolution, and Man*, Freeman, San Francisco (1976).

Tom D. Dillehay, "Ice-age settlement in southern Chile," *Scientific American* 251(4):106 (October 1984).

Bering Strait not a barrier even at high sea levels, corridor open 13–14,000 years ago when grizzly bears came south: Lecture by R. Dale Guthrie, "Ice age mammals and early man in Alaska," at the University of Washington, Seattle, 15 May 1984.

Taos epigram: Jeannette Henry, Vine Deloria, Jr., M. Scott Momaday, Bea Medicine, and Alfonzo Ortiz, eds., *Indian Voices: The First Convocation of American Indian Scholars*, The Indian Historical Press, San Francisco, p.35 (1970).

DAY 3

Mile 32

Ancient condors, see Steven D. Emslie, "Canyon echos of the condor," *Natural History* 95(4):10–14 (April 1986).

Mile 33

Vasey's Paradise, Redwall Cavern photos 19–21 in Blaustein. Euler and Tikalsky (p.37) and Redfern (p.152) show a split-twig figurine.

Aspirin and willows: See Gerald Weissman's column in *Discover*, pp.78–79 (February 1986). The Indians are said to have strapped mashed willow bark to their foreheads to combat headaches: See *New Scientist*, p. 19 (27 March 1986).

Peter Molnar, "The geological history and structure of the Himalaya," *American Scientist* 74(2):144–154 (March–April 1986).

Mile 35

River corridor near Nautiloid Canyon is shown in photo 22 of Blaustein. For an evolutionary tree of the nautiloids, see p.254 of G. L. Stebbins, *Darwin to DNA, Molecules to Humanity*, Freeman, San Francisco (1982).

Mile 39

John McPhee, *Encounters with the Archdruid*, Farrar, Straus, and Giroux, New York (1971). For more on Colorado River dam building, see Fradkin (1981). For the salt stories, see Janet Raloff's articles in *Science News* 126:289, 298, 305, 314 (1984).

For more on beaver behavior, see L. Wilsson, *My Beaver Colony*, Doubleday, New York (1968), and Victor B. Scheffer, *Spires of Form: Glimpses of Evolution*, University of Washington Press, Seattle (1983), pp.33–35. The noise of running water was analyzed by L. Wilsson, "Observations and experiments on the ethology of the European beaver

(*Castor fiber* L.), a study in the development of phylogenetically adapted behavior in a highly specialized mammal," *Viltrevy, Swedish Wildlife* 8:117–266 (1971). Since beavers do build dams in slowly flowing quiet water, it isn't just the noise of running water that stimulates them to build dams. As Scheffer notes, even more impressive is the beavers' ability to construct canals for barging in construction materials.

Eric Seaborg, "The battle for Hetch Hetchy," *Sierra Club Bulletin* 66(5):61 (November-December 1981).

Mile 41

Royal Arches, photo in Leydet, p.47.

Mile 47

Smart animals: See Euan M. Macphail, *Brain and Intelligence in Vertebrates*, Clarendon Press, Oxford (1982).

Mile 52

View from Nankoweap granary trail is shown in photo 29 of Blaustein. Granary is Blaustein's #26, Redfern pp.156–157. Euler and Tikalsky (p.38) show the interior of a similar food cache.

Columbus discovering "Indians": Daniel J. Boorstin, *The Discoverers*, Random House, New York (1983), reviews the surprisingly accurate (15 percent high) estimate of the Earth's circumference by Erastosthenes (276?–195? B.C.), the errors of Ptolemy (A.D. 90–168) in adopting a circumference 25 percent low and in greatly exaggerating the size of Asia, and how Ptolemy's map that shrank the unknown part of the world was adopted by the Europeans. Carl Sagan in *Cosmos*, Random House, New York (1980), pp.15–17, notes that Christopher Columbus in 1492 also cheated on his calculations of the distance sailing westward to India through the unknown portion of the earth, thereby minimizing the estimated distance to both his sponsors and those who risked their lives for his venture. This sales technique has since been adopted by the military-industrial complex, who now systematically underestimate the costs of their projected ventures (e.g., in the U.S. Navy in 1985, the *average* cost of a new ship was 63 percent higher than estimated).

Anasazi as astronomers: See John A. Eddy, "Archaeoastronomy in North America: Cliffs, mounds, and medicine wheels," chapter 4, *In Search of Ancient Astronomies*, edited by E. C. Krupp (Doubleday, New York, 1978); and Ray A. Williamson, *Living the Sky: The Cosmos of the American Indian*, Houghton Mifflin, Boston (1984).

J. C. Brandt, S. P. Maran, R. Williamson, R. S. Harrington, C. Cochran, M. Kennedy, W. J. Kennedy, and V. D. Chamberlain, "Possible rock art records of the Crab nebula supernova in the western United States." In: *Archaeoastronomy in Pre-Columbian America*, edited by A. F. Aveni, pp. 45–58, University of Texas Press, Austin (1975). Sagan's *Cosmos* has a photograph of the Chaco Canyon pictograph on p.232.

William C. Miller, "Two possible astronomical pictographs found in northern Arizona," *Plateau* 27(4):6–13 (1955).

David H. Clark and F. Richard Stephenson, *The Historical Supernovae*, Pergamon, Oxford (1977). Chapter 8 is on the Crab Nebula supernova of A.D. 1054. The Anasazi elders may well have been sensitized to supernovae in their youth by the A.D. 1006 supernova, the brightest and most long-lasting one in recorded history. It reached three times the size of Venus and provided as much illumination at night as when the moon is one-third full. It disappeared from the daytime sky after three months. On current supernovae prospects, see Ellen Fried's "The ungentle death of a giant star," SCIENCE 86, pp.60–64 (January-February 1986).

DAY 4

Mile 56

East Kaibab Monocline: See Redfern, p.42.

Stephen Trimble, *The Bright Edge: A Guide to the National Parks of the Colorado Plateau*, Museum of Northern Arizona Press, Flagstaff, Arizona (1979), p.7.

Mile 61

The gray matter is gray due to alterations by preservatives. Few books contain pictures of freshly removed human brains with some of the original "Colorado" color left intact, but see p.276 of Carl Sagan's *Cosmos* (1980); it is the underlying warm reddish-brown to which I refer (best seen in the right side of the bottom picture), not the obvious red of the fine surface blood vessels.

Steven M. Stanley, "Mass extinction in the ocean," *Scientific American* 250(6):64–72 (June 1984). He notes that the dinosaurs went extinct over a period spanning several million years; this would be consistent with the time spanned by the meteor "shower" and multiple impacts on Earth disrupting the climate.

P. Ward, "The extinction of ammonites," *Scientific American* 249(4):136–147 (October 1983). Martin A. Buzas and Stephen J. Culver, "Species duration and evolution: benthic foraminifera on the Atlantic continental margin of North America," *Science* 225:829–830 (24 August 1984).

The comet mass-extinction proposals are in the 19 April 1984 issue of *Nature*. See also Stephen Jay Gould, "The cosmic dance of Siva," *Natural History* 93(8):14–19 (August 1984), and the last chapter in *The Flamingo's Smile*, W. W. Norton, New York (1985). The scientific excitement generated by this important theory is not always appreciated by the media; on 2 April 1985, the *New York Times* pronounced its disapproval. Such "speculation" about extraterrestrial effects on earthly life, it said in what many scientists viewed as an incredible anti-science and anti-intellectual editorial, should be left to the astrologers!

David M. Raup and J. John Sepkoski, Jr., "Periodic extinction of families and genera," *Science* 231:833–836 (21 February 1986). See also the forthcoming *Patterns and Processes in the History of Life*, edited by David Jablonski and David M. Raup, Springer Verlag, New York (1986), and Steve Gould's *Flamingo's Smile*, ch. 15.

Meteor Crater dating: Stephen R. Sutton, letter, *Nature* 309:203 (17 May 1984).

Mile 64

Fred B. Eiseman, Jr., "The Hopi salt trail," *Plateau* (Museum of Northern Arizona) 32:25–32 (1959).

Mile 65

Furnace Flats shown in Powell and Porter (facing p.69); shows Desert View Tower and Tanner Trail.

B. Bloeser, J. W. Schopf, R. J. Horodyski, and W. J. Breed, "Chitinozoans from the late precambrian Chuar group of the Grand Canyon," *Science* 195:676–679 (1977). They date these unicellular zooplankton to 750 million years ago. Chuar Butte, its layers tilted at dramatic angles, is between Miles 61–64 on the western bank up Carbon Creek.

Stromatolite formation: See pp. 30–31 of William Day, *Genesis on Planet Earth*, Second Edition, Yale University Press, New Haven (1984), and Stefi Weisbund, "The microbes that loved the sun," *Science News* 129:108–110 (15 February 1986). Stevens' "blue bible" guidebook shows a picture of Subie sitting atop a large stromatolite. Early dates: See Gary L. Byerly, Donald R. Lower, and Maud M. Walsh, "Stromatolites from the 3,300–3,500-Myr Swaziland Supergroup, Barberton Mountain Land, South Africa," *Nature* 319:489–491 (6 February 1986).

Mile 71

Cardenas Creek and Unkar Delta are shown in Geerlings' p.100 (hilltop ruin in very center of tricuspid of ridgelines, campsite lower center, delta at upper left center, rapids obscured), p.130 (delta only, cliffs on left). The photo on p.100 is mislabeled; it is an aerial photo taken from above Mile 70, not from Desert View Tower. Redfern's large foldout on pp.15–18 shows Unkar Creek coming down from the North Rim. The photo on p.67 shows Unkar Delta and the cliffs above the rapid; the hilltop ruin is about 3 mm left of the dark cloud shadow in the upper middle of the picture (a close-up appears in Euler and Tikalsky, p.51). Also see photo 7 in Blaustein.

Douglas W. Schwartz, Richard C. Chapman, and Jane Kepp, *Archaeology of the Grand Canyon: Unkar Delta*, School of American Research Press, Santa Fe, NM, volume 2 (1981).

Robert C. Euler, George J. Gumerman, Thor N. V. Karlstrom, Jeffrey S. Dean, and Richard H. Hevly, "The Colorado plateau: Cultural dynamics and paleoenvironment," *Science* 205:1089–1101 (14 September 1979).

The Chaco Canyon "Sun Dagger" story is summarized by Anna Sofaer, Rolf M. Sinclair, and L. E. Doggett, "Lunar markings on Fajada Butte, Chaco Canyon, New Mexico," in *Archaeoastronomy in the New World*, edited by A. F. Aveni, pp.169–181, Cambridge University Press, Cambridge (1982); the sun-only part of the story may be found in A. Sofaer, V. Zinser, and R. M. Sinclair, "A unique solar marking construct," *Science* 206:283–291 (1979). See Williamson (1984) for a commentary and contrast to another Anasazi "Sun Dagger" at Hovenweap. Some doubts about the Sofaer et al. interpretation are expressed by M. Zeilik, *Science* 228:1311–1313 (1985) and J. E. Reyman, *Science* 229:817 (1985).

Other astronomical pictographs: the Preston's discoveries are illustrated in *Arizona Highways Magazine*, pp. 22–25 (February 1983).

The lunar eclipse may perhaps be best appreciated by reading while listening to the musical composition of Alan Hovanhess, "On the Long Total Eclipse of the Moon, July 6, 1982." That eclipse was also the basis for this section of the book (see notes for Day 14).

Thomas Goldstein, *Dawn of Modern Science*, Houghton Mifflin, Boston (1980).

Lunar calendars and corrections: The early Romans had a very complicated and inaccurate moon-based calendar. Voltaire once quipped that the Roman generals always triumphed, but never knew what day it was when the victory occurred!

Horizon calendars: See Williamson (1984) and Stephen C. McCluskey, "Historical archaeoastronomy: The Hopi example," in *Archaeoastronomy in the New World*, edited by A. F. Aveni, pp.31–57, Cambridge University Press, Cambridge (1982).

Possible biological basis of religion: See Lionel Tiger's book review in *The Sciences* (New York Academy of Sciences), 25(2):61–63 (March 1985).

DAY 5

Mile 71

Much of the population ecology in this section is based on Paul Colinvaux, *The Fates of Nations: A Biological Theory of History*. Simon and Schuster, New York (1980). A short version is Paul Colinvaux, "Towards a theory of history: fitness, niche, and clutch of *Homo sapiens* L." *Journal of Ecology* (1982). (Reprinted in the 1984 Penguin paperback edition of Colinvaux' 1980 book, as an appendix). The conclusions expressed are, however, mine.

The lemming population booms are caused by a mechanism reminiscent of the "Groundhog Day" story about late winter weather; see Paul Colinvaux, *Why Big Fierce Animals Are Rare*, Princeton University Press, Princeton (1980), ch. 6.

Ecosystems provide many examples of simple rules with complex results: see A. K. Dewdney in *Scientific American* 251(6):14–22 (December 1984) for a computer simulation mimicking the boom-and-bust population cycles of the lynx and hare at Hudson's Bay.

Daniel R. Vining, Jr., "The growth of core regions of the third world," *Scientific American* 252(4):42–49 (April 1985).

The hormonal influences on birth spacing are summarized by Melvin Konner, "The nursing knot," *The Sciences* (New York Academy of Sciences), 25(6):10–12 (December 1985).

Spontaneous abortion estimates are from C. J. Roberts and C. R. Lowe, "Where have all the conceptions gone?," *Lancet* i:498 (1975), and Paul S. Weatherbee, "Early reproductive loss and the factors that influence its occurrence," *Journal of Reproductive Medicine* 25:315–318 (1980).

Constance Holden, "Population studies age prematurely," *Science* 225:1003 (7 September 1984). News article reporting on a Ford Foundation study by Jack and Pat Caldwell.

Climatic cycles in Africa: See news article by Richard A. Kerr, "Fifteen years of African drought," *Science* 227:1452–5 (22 March 1985), and articles in *Science News* 127:282–285 (4 May 1985).

MILE 76

Hance Rapid: See photos near p.153 in Collins et al., Geerlings' pp. 105,106. Redfern pp.36–37 shows the transition from Furnace Flats (Unkar Delta at right center) to the inner gorge near Hance Rapid (at left center).

Ilya Prigogine, *Order Out of Chaos*, Bantam, New York (1984).

MILE 84

Fluted granite and schist photographs in Powell and Porter, facing p.80; Geerlings, p.3; Leydet, p.90.

Prebiotic evolution and the genetic code: See William Day, *Genesis on Planet Earth: The Search for Life's Beginnings*, 2d ed., Yale University Press, New Haven (1984).

MILE 88

Redfern, pp.176–177, shows the view from the South Rim down to Phantom Ranch; this is about all that most Grand Canyon visitors see of the Colorado River, and only if they look carefully from the right spot.

Alexia is described by W. H. Calvin and G. A. Ojemann, *Inside the Brain*, NAL (1980), p. 32. For more such tales, see Oliver Sacks, *The Man Who Mistook His Wife for a Hat (and other clinical tales)*, Simon and Schuster, New York (1985).

MILE 93

Monument Creek camp, photo in Leydet, p.123; Blaustein photo 46.

George E. Simpson, *Melville J. Herskovits*, Columbia University Press, New York (1973). Herskovits (1895–1963) was virtually the founder, in the United States, of African studies and Afro-American studies. In 1936 he said, "the debt we owe the society that supports us must be made in terms of longtime payments, in our fundamental contributions toward an understanding of the nature and processes of culture, and through this, to the solution of some of our own basic problems."

Hit-or-miss toolmaking: See Mile 137 notes. Genetic code, see any modern biology text; Day's book (Mile 84) is particularly thoughtful.

Delimiting the enkephalin gene is, in practice, more complicated than just identifying the traditional start and stop codes used for this necklace. The RNA string is copied from a DNA sequence that is much longer, and includes the DNA instructions for making the stress hormone ACTH; a special code precedes the ACTH and enkephalin instructions. If there are lots of corticosteroids circulating in the bloodstream, the RNA copy is made from the enkephalin instructions; if few corticosteroids are in circulation, the ACTH instructions are copied instead. And so the circulating corticosteroids are used to determine whether ACTH is manufactured (thus producing more corticosteroids in the adrenal glands) or more enkephalin is produced.

DAY 6

MILE 95

Hermit Rapid standing waves, photo in Geerlings, p.106.

Multiple sensory maps: Michael M. Merzenich and Jon H. Kaas, "Reorganization of mammalian somatosensory cortex following peripheral nerve injury." *Trends in Neurosciences*, pp.434–436 (December 1982). A useful summary is the news article by Jeffrey L. Fox, "Research News: The brain's dynamic way of keeping in touch." *Science* 225:820–1 (24 August 1984).

Templates: See "receptive fields" in any neurobiology or physiology text, or Chapter 11 in William H. Calvin and George A. Ojemann, *Inside the Brain*, New American Library, New York (1980).

The computational building blocks of the brain are discussed by William H. Calvin and Katherine Graubard, "Styles of neuronal computation," in: *The Neurosciences, Fourth Study Program*, edited by F.O. Schmitt and F.G. Worden, MIT Press, Cambridge (1979), p.503.

MILE 97

The Park Service itself gave up power boats some time ago; the superb and dedicated park rangers who patrol the river corridor now use oar-powered boats much the same as ours.

Visual 4 cells for color and depth perception: See M. Zeki, "Cells responding to changing image size and disparity in the cortex of the rhesus monkey," *Journal of Physiology* 242:827–841 (1974).

Gene duplication, crossing-over, etc.: Tim Hunkapiller et al, "The impact of modern genetics on evolutionary theory," ch.10 in *Perspectives on Evolution*, edited by Roger Milkman, Sinauer, Sunderland MA (1982).

MILE 99

Crystal Rapid photos in Blaustein et al, Collins et al, and Redfern.

Thomas J. Wolf, *High Country News* (12 December 1983) tells the story of how Glen Canyon Dam was nearly lost. The 1983 flood story is documented in a clipping file maintained by the River Committee of the Sierra Club. For a summary, see James R. Udall, "After the flood: Grand Canyon 1983." *Sierra Club Bulletin*, pp.28–32 (November 1983).

MILE 104

Martin Seligman and Joanne Hager, *Biological Boundaries of Learning*. Meredith, New York (1972). Discusses taste avoidance one-trail learning.

Birds and hawks: See Irenäus Eibl-Eibesfeldt, *Ethology*, Holt, Rinehart, & Winston, New York (1975), pp.87–88.

Bee learning: See James L. Gould and Carol Grant Gould, "The Instinct to Learn," *SCIENCE 81* 2(4):44–50 (May 1981).

MILE 106

Hermann Weyl, *Symmetry*, Princeton University Press (1952).

Science advisor to television program, quoted by Gerry Wheeler in *The Sciences*, pp.8–9 (September 1980).

Victor H. Denenberg, "Hemispheric laterality in animals and the effects of early experience," *Behavioral and Brain Sciences* 4:1–50 (March 1981).

A useful collection of reviews on human brain asymmetries can be found in *Cerebral Dominance*, edited by the late Norman Geschwind and by Albert M. Galaburda, Harvard University Press, Cambridge (1984).

Brain asymmetries can be seen in the freshly removed human brain pictured on p.276 of Carl Sagan's *Cosmos*. Note that the brain's right hemisphere is much larger than its left, that the right frontal pole (lower left in top picture on p.276) and left occipital pole (upper right in picture) extend beyond their neighbors. Its "skew" is typical of most human brains; its left-right volume difference is somewhat greater than most brains show.

MILE 109

Horace B. Barlow, *Nature* 304:209 (21 July 1983).

Victor Weisskopf, quoted in K. C. Cole's *Sympathetic Vibrations: Reflections on Physics as a Way of Life* (Bantam, 1985).

Stephen Jay Gould, "The meaning of punctuated equilibrium and its role in validating a hierarchical approach to macroevolution," ch. 5 in *Perspectives on Evolution*, edited by Roger Milkman, Sinauer, Sunderland, Massachusetts (1982).

Steven M. Stanley, *The New Evolutionary Timetable: Fossils, Genes, and the Origins of Species*, Basic Books, New York (1981).

Ernst Mayr, *The Growth of Biological Thought*, Harvard University Press, Cambridge (1982). Gulick, Hagedoorn, and Sewell Wright earlier emphasized the importance of small populations for evolution; Mayr then showed in the 1940s how some kinds of evolution are not possible in large populations, such as those resulting from sustained inbreeding.

An excellent undergraduate text on evolution is G. L. Stebbins, *Darwin and DNA: Molecules to Humanity*, Freeman, San Francisco (1982).

DAY 7

MILE 109

Powell Plateau, seen from the river, is shown in Euler and Tikalsky (p.73).

Richard W. Effland, Jr., A. Trinkle Jones, and Robert C. Euler, *The Archaeology of Powell Plateau: Regional Interaction at Grand Canyon*, Grand Canyon Natural History Association Monograph 3 (1981).

Mile 111

An excellent introduction to speciation and isolation mechanisms is Keeton's chapter 18. For the breeding seasons of Abert and Kaibab squirrels, see Donald F. Hoffmeister, *Mammals of Grand Canyon*, University of Illinois Press, Urbana (1971). They have a diet-influenced mating season which only lasts about 18 hours per year—and not every year! D. F. Hoffmeister and V. E. Diersing, "Review of the tassel-eared squirrels of the subgenus *Otoscuirus*," *Journal of Mammalogy* 59:402–413 (1978).

Dog ancestry: See Konrad Lorenz, *King Solomon's Ring*, Methuen, London (1952), pp.134–5. "The northern wolf (*Canis lupus*) only figures in the ancestry of our present dog breeds through having been crossed with already-domesticated Aureus [jackal] dogs. Contrary to the widespread opinion that the wolf plays an essential role in the ancestry of the larger dog breeds, comparative research in behaviour has revealed the fact that all European dogs . . . are pure Aureus and contain, at the most, a minute amount of wolf's blood. The purest wolf-dogs that exist are certain breeds of Arctic America, particularly the so-called malemuts, huskies, etc." He also discusses juvenilization in dog domestication on p.136. His 1953 book *Man Meets Dog* continues the story.

Mile 115

The unmatched XY chromosomes are only found in males, but that's only true among the mammals. The birds have it backwards, the female having XY and the male XX. What really defines male/female is gamete dimorphism: small sperm, large egg. The development of this anisogamy (it is argued that once any slight size differences developed, it would have been unstable and immediately gone to extremes, the "sperm" carrying no nutrition for the zygote) a billion years ago was the beginnings of sex, together with crossing-over and outcrossing. An argument can be made that the latter originate from genetic repair mechanisms and genetic complementation—and that variation arises as a by-product: H. Bernstein et al., "Genetic damage, mutation, and the evolution of sex," *Science* 229:1277–1281 (20 September 1985).

Mile 116

Gregory E. Vink, W. Jason Morgan, and Peter R. Vogt, "The earth's hot spots," *Scientific American* 252(4):50–57 (April 1985).

Harold T. Stearns, *Road Guide to Points of Geologic Interest in the Hawaiian Islands*, 2d edition. Pacific Books, Palo Alto (1978).

Roger Lewin, "Hawaiian Drosophila: Young Islands, Old Flies," *Science* 229:1072–4 (13 September 1985).

Plate tectonics are illustrated by Redfern (p.23); Preston Cloud's "Beyond Plate Tectonics," *American Scientist* 68:381–387 (July 1980) is a useful introduction. For a review of North American fragments, see Richard A. Kerr, "The bits and pieces of plate tectonics," *Science* 207:1059–1061 (7 March 1980). The Colorado Plateau uplift is complex: See D. I. Gough, "Mantle upflow under North America and plate dynamics," *Nature* 311:428–433 (4 October 1984).

John McPhee's geology books are *Basin and Range* (1981), and *In Suspect Terrain* (1983), Farrar-Straus-Giroux, New York. His series on the uplift of the Rocky Mountains starts in the *New Yorker* of 24 February 1986.

John W. Harrington, *Dance of the Continents: Adventures with Rocks and Time*, Houghton Mifflin, Boston (1983).

Elves Chasm photos are Blaustein (#56), Porter (facing p.126), Leydet (p.104).

Mile 118

George Gaylord Simpson, "The concept of progress in organic evolution," *Social Research* 41(1):51 (1974).

Romer's rule, as rephrased by C. F. Hockett and R. Ascher, "The Human Revolution," *American Scientist* 52:72 (1964).

William V. Mayer (professor emeritus of biology, University of Colorado), "The arrogance of ignorance—ignoring the ubiquitous," *American Zoologist* 24:423 (1984). For a description of the intellectual climate surrounding American science textbooks' treatment of evolution, see Thomas H. Jukes, "The fight for science textbooks," *Nature* 319:367–368 (30 January 1986).

For a description of Edward Blyth's statement of natural selection (about the same time that Darwin stumbled upon it), see Loren Eiseley's posthumous book *Darwin and the Mysterious Mr. X*, Dutton, New York (1979). While Blyth provided one early description of natural selection, he saw its role in conserving species characters (so-called convergent selection, indeed the most common role of natural selection) but not its creative role. It was Darwin, and later Wallace, who appreciated the divergent uses of natural selection that can create new species. See also *Flamingo's Smile*, pp. 335 ff. For a history of evolutionary thought, see Peter J. Bowler, *Evolution: The History of an Idea*, University of California Press, Berkeley (1984).

Jacques Monod, *Chance and Necessity*, Alfred A. Knopf, New York, 1971.

Ralph Estling, "The trouble with thinking backwards," *New Scientist* pp.619–621 (2 June 1983). Spontaneous abortion estimates, see Mile 71 notes.

My treatment of spontaneous abortion in the "natural scheme of things" will hopefully contribute to a much-needed discussion of when legal "personhood" starts; obviously, I don't think it starts with conception. I personally don't know where to draw the line for either legal or moral purposes; certainly, I find it repugnant for a pregnant woman to endanger a potential person with alcohol and smoking, but I also consider it immoral (as a form of slavery) to attempt to force a woman to continue an unwanted pregnancy. And because nine-month fetuses are only about 60 percent as developed as are other primates at birth, I tend to think there is nothing special about birth per se in starting legal protection, and believe that the parents who will bear the responsibility for raising an infant should be allowed considerable latitude in deciding what to do about an infant with a poor prognosis. There has been an immense amount of simpleminded sloganeering about fetuses, to the neglect of real problems such as endangering fetuses by smoking and alcohol, endangering young children by failure to protect them from injury in car accidents, and the scandalous malnourishment of many of our children, both literally and through the nonchalant attitude toward their medical care and education. In a world with real problems, we don't need to invent more.

MILE 119

Cell death as sculptor during development: See ch. 6 in Dale Purves and Jeff Lichtman, *Principles of Neural Development*, Sinauer, Sunderland, Massachusetts (1985). For a brief overview of neural development, see Hilary Anderson, John S. Edwards, and John Palka, "Developmental neurobiology of invertebrates," *Annual Reviews of Neuroscience* 3:97–139 (1980). For some relationships between neontology (development) and paleontology (species evolution), see Wallace Arthur, *Mechanisms of Morphological Evolution: A combined genetic, developmental and ecological approach*, Wiley-Interscience (1984).

Donald O. Hebb, in "Alice in Wonderland, or Psychology among the biological sciences." From *Biological and Biochemical Basis of Behavior*, edited by H. F. Harlow and C. N. Woolsey, University of Wisconsin Press, Madison (1958).

MILE 120

Besides Peter Medewar's dictum, there is another old saying about what happens to new ideas: At first, it's merely wrong. Then it is characterized as being against religion. Finally, it is said to be something that everyone knew all along, and so what's the fuss about? Punctuated equilibrium is now said to have entered the third phase: See Roger Lewin, "Punctuated equilibrium is now old hat," *Science* 231:672–673 (14 February 1986).

Glenn Hausfater and Sarah Blaffer Hrdy, eds., *Infanticide: Comparative and Evolutionary Perspectives*, Aldine, New York (1984). See also *Current Anthropology* 25:500–501 (1984). The journal *Ethology and Sociobiology* is also a source; in its first issue (1979), Sarah Hrdy's analysis of infanticide in terms of natural selection was an important landmark in such research.

Barbara Burke, "Infanticide," *SCIENCE 84* 5(4):26–31 (May 1984).

Richard Dawkins, *The Extended Phenotype*, Freeman, San Francisco (1982).

Michael Ruse and Edward O. Wilson, "The evolution of ethics," *New Scientist*, pp.50–51 (17 October 1985).

Melvin Konner, *The Tangled Wing: Biological Constraints on the Human Spirit*, Holt Rinehart Winston, New York (1982).

Stephen Jay Gould, *The Mismeasure of Man*,

W. W. Norton, New York (1981). A sobering story of biological "determinism" but also of the scientific search for a correlate to bigger brains.

Robert Trivers, *Social Evolution*, Benjamin/Cummings, Palo Alto (1985).

Philip Kitcher, *Vaulting Ambition: Sociobiology and the Quest for Human Nature*, MIT Press (1985). See also the review of it by John Maynard Smith, *Nature* 318:121–122 (14 November 1985).

Theodosius Dobzhansky, *Genetic Diversity and Human Equality*, Basic Books, New York (1973).

Brain specializations for cooperation: detecting lies is one function of right temporal lobe. For its application to pitches made by actor-politicians, see pp. 77–79 of Oliver Sacks, *The Man Who Mistook His Wife for a Hat (and Other Clinical Tales)*, Simon and Schuster, New York (1985).

DAY 8

Mile 120

Francis H. C. Crick, "Thinking about the brain," *Scientific American* 241 (September 1979).

Virgin births prediction: See *New Scientist* (18 December 1980).

John Maynard Smith, "Game theory and the evolution of behaviour," *Behavioral and Brain Sciences* 7(1):95–126 (March 1984).

Robert Axelrod, *The Evolution of Cooperation*, Basic Books, New York (1984). The classic paper of the same name is by Robert Axelrod and William D. Hamilton, *Science* 211:1190–1196 (1981). For a history and discussion, see Douglas Hofstadter's columns in *Scientific American* (May and June, 1983), reprinted as chapters 29–30 in *Metamagical Themas*, Basic Books, New York (1985).

Mile 127

Eve, then Adam: See Jeremy Cherfas and John Gribbin, *The Redundant Male*, Pantheon, New York (1985).

Arms race between plants and insects: lecture by May Berenbaum, "Chemical ecology synergisms," at the University of Ottawa (19 January 1985). The arms race concept in ecology was originally developed—another example, presumably, of how technology has occasionally stimulated theoretical thinking in biology—by Paul R. Ehrlich and Peter H. Raven, "Butterflies and plants: a study in co-evolution," *Evolution* 18:586–608 (1964). See also Lawrence E. Gilbert and Peter H. Raven, eds., *Coevolution of Animals and Plants*, University of Texas Press, Austin, revised ed. (1980).

A. Rosenfeld, "When man becomes as God: the biological prospect," *Saturday Review* 5:15–20 (1977).

Asian flu hypercycle discussed by Erich Jantsch, *The Self-Organizing Universe*, Pergamon, New York (1980) at p.191.

Immune system self-organization: See Manfred Eigen and Ruthild Winkler, *Laws of the Game: How the Principles of Nature Govern Chance*. Harper, New York (German edition 1976, English translation 1981). They summarize the model of locks and keys on the same defender cell and self-organization for diversity and self-recognition. The extension of the idea to a restricted setup period in early development using the sterile male strategy is, so far as I know, mine (but I may have reinvented the wheel). My what-if description of antigens and antibodies is over-simplified: See Niels K. Jerne, "The generative grammar of the immune system," *Science* 229:1057–1059 (13 September 1985).

Mile 132

Stone Creek photo in Powell and Porter (facing p.91). Redfern (pp.28–29) illustrates a time line.

Evolution of neural mechanisms: for a discussion of the evolution of the protein that controls the sodium channel in neural and muscle membranes, see the last chapter of Bertil Hille's *Ionic Channels of Excitable Membranes*, Sinauer, Sunderland, Massachusetts (1984).

William H. Calvin and Daniel K. Hartline, "Retrograde invasion of lobster stretch receptor somata in the control of firing rate and extra spike patterning," *Journal of Neurophysiology* 40:106–118 (January 1977). For signal code comparisons, see W. H. Calvin, "Normal repetitive firing and its pathophysiology," in *Epilepsy: A Window to Brain Mechanisms*, edited by Joan S. Lockard and Arthur A. Ward, Jr., Raven Press (1980), pp. 97–121.

Calcium entry in Paramecium: See Roger Ekert and David Randall, *Animal Physiology: Mechanisms and Adaptations*, 2d edition, Freeman, San Francisco (1983), p.324, p.401.

For an example of self-organization principles

applied to neural circuits for sensory templates ("schemata"), see: George N. Reeke, Jr., and Gerald M. Edelman, "Selective networks and recognition automata," *Annals of the New York Academy of Sciences* 426:181–201 (1984). See also Gerald M. Edelman and Vernon B. Mountcastle, *The Mindful Brain*, MIT Press, Cambridge (1978).

MILE 134

Tapeats Canyon atop Bright Angel is shown in Blaustein's photo 60, Colorado River near campsite in photo 63. Tapeats Creek near river is shown facing page 102 in Powell and Porter. Thunder Springs in shown in Blaustein's photo 61 and in Powell and Porter facing page 104.

R. C. Euler epigram, in Fowler et al. (1969) cited at Mile 52.

Ann Trinkle Jones and Robert C. Euler, *A Sketch of Grand Canyon Prehistory*, Grand Canyon Natural History Association, Grand Canyon (1979).

Mount St. Helens landslide: The mark of the great wave can be seen by driving to Windy Ridge at the end of the forest road about 40 km south of Randle, Washington.

Tropical soils: See Paul Colinvaux, *Why Big Fierce Animals Are Rare*, Princeton University Press, Princeton (1978).

Daniel Simberloff, book review in *The Sciences* (New York Academy of Sciences), 25(1):54 (January 1985). E. O. Wilson, *Biophilia*, Harvard University Press, Cambridge (1984).

Norman Myers, *The Primary Source: Tropical Forests and Our Future*, W. W. Norton, New York (1984).

Catherine Caufield, *In the Rainforest*, Alfred A. Knopf, New York (1985).

Stephen H. Schneider and Randi Londer, *The Coevolution of Climate and Life*, Sierra Club Books, San Francisco (1984).

Mick Kelly, "Not with a bang but a winter," *New Scientist*, pp. 33–36 (13 September 1984).

The TTAPS paper and the biologists' assessment are in *Science* 222(4630):1283–1300 (23 December 1983); they are reprinted as an appendix in Paul R. Ehrlich, Carl Sagan, Donald Kennedy, and Walter Orr Roberts, *The Cold and the Dark: The World after Nuclear War*, W. W. Norton, New York (1984). See also: National Academy of Sciences (U.S.), *The Effects on the Atmosphere of a Major*

Nuclear Exchange, National Academy Press, Washington, D.C. (1985).

The Cruetzen story is reported by Dennis Overbye, "Prophet of the cold and dark," *Discover*, pp. 24–32 (January 1985). The Alvarez discovery is related by Richard A. Muller, "An adventure in science," *New York Times Magazine*, pp. 34–50 (24 March 1985).

Valmore C. LaMarche, Jr., and Katherine K. Hirschboeck (1984). "Frost rings in trees as records of major volcanic eruptions," *Nature* 307:121–126 (12 January 1984).

Stephen H. Schneider, "Atmospheric double exposure," *Natural History* 93(4):98–101 (April 1984).

DAY 9

MILE 134

Ringtails: See Donald F. Hoffmeister, *Mammals of Grand Canyon*. University of Illinois Press, Urbana (1971).

DNA dates: See Charles G. Sibley and Jon E. Ahlquist, "The phylogeny of the hominoid primates, as indicated by DNA-DNA hybridization," *Journal of Molecular Evolution* 20:2–15 (1984).

Steven M. Stanley, *The New Evolutionary Timetable: Fossils, Genes, and the Origin of Species*, Basic Books, New York (1981).

Stephen Jay Gould, "The cosmic dance of Siva," *Natural History* 93(8):14–19 (1984).

John A. O'Keefe, "The terminal Eocene event: formation of a ring system around the Earth?" *Nature* 285:309–311 (1980). Also see *New Scientist*, p.13 (21 March 1985) for suggestions of a lunar volcanic origin of the tektites.

MILE 136

Deer Creek lower falls is shown in Geerlings on page 120, in Blaustein's photo 67. The entrance to the hidden valley is shown in Powell and Porter, facing page 113, looking back towards the river to where the trail emerges. Facing page 118 is a view of the cataracts. Leydet, page 139, has a view of the trail above the cataracts leading in to the valley; page 141 shows the "restricted" view of upper Deer Creek Falls which begins the cataract.

Alister C. Hardy, "Was man more aquatic in the past?" *New Scientist* 7:642–645 (1960).

Elaine Morgan, *The Descent of Woman*, Stein

and Day, New York (1972), and *The Aquatic Ape: A Theory of Human Evolution*, Stein and Day, New York (1982). Her 1982 appendix reprints much of Leon LaLumiere's article, together with Alister Hardy's articles. Recent *New Scientist* updates are 12 April 1984 (p.11, on salt regulation) and 21 March 1985 (p.27, on sweating and tearing), and 6 March 1986 (pp. 62–63, on the evolution of the larynx). For the "water on the face" effect, see Masaud Mukhtar and John Patrick, *Journal of Physiology* (London) 370:13 (1986). For a bibliography, see Marc J. B. Verhaegen, "The aquatic ape theory: Evidence and a possible scenario," *Medical Hypotheses* 16:17–33 (1985).

For a recent summary of what's happening geologically in the old Danakil Straits, see P. Choukroune, et al., "Tectonics of the westernmost Gulf of Aden and the Gulf of Tadjoura from submersible observations," *Nature* 319:396–399 (30 January 1986).

Shlomo Cohen, *Red Sea Diver's Guide*, Red Sea Publications, Tel Aviv, Israel (1975). After Israel returned the Sinai to Egypt in 1982, Egyptian fishing boats returned to the Sinai waters, throwing dynamite overboard to kill fish, collecting what floated—and destroying numerous million-year-old coral reefs in the process.

Randall Susman's observations of pygmy chimps wading in water and catching fish are reported by Paul Raeburn, "An uncommon chimp," *SCIENCE 83* 4(5):40–48 (June 1983).

Adrienne L. Zihlman, John E. Cronin, Douglas L. Cramer, and Vincent M. Sarich, "Pygmy chimpanzee as a possible prototype for the common ancestor of humans, chimpanzees, and gorillas," *Nature* 275:744–746 (1978).

John Emsley, "There is no substitute for salt," *New Scientist* 1433:28–32 (6 December 1984). An encyclopedic treatment is by Derek Denton, *The Hunger for Salt*, Springer Verlag, New York (1982).

Jane Goodall, *In the Shadow of Man*, Houghton Mifflin, Boston (1971).

Jane Goodall, "Continuities between chimpanzee and human behavior," In *Human Origins: Louis Leakey and the East African Evidence*, volume 3 of *Perspectives on Human Evolution*. Edited by Glynn Ll. Isaac and Elizabeth R. McCown, pp. 81–96. W. A. Benjamin, Menlo Park, California (1976).

Jane Goodall, "The behaviour of free-living chimpanzees in the Gombe Stream Preserve," *Animal Behaviour Monographs* 1(3):161–311 (1968). See p.203 for throwing data.

Geza Teleki, "The omnivorous chimp," *Scientific American* 228(1):32–42 (1973).

Frans de Waal, *Chimpanzee Politics: Power and Sex Among Apes*, Harper and Row, New York (1983).

Dian Fossey, *Gorillas in the Mist*, Houghton Mifflin, Boston (1983). Her life work (she was murdered in late 1985) makes it possible to compare gorillas with chimps in their natural settings; the differing diet and mating systems help one construct a possible composite picture of our ancestor 10 million years back.

Lewis R. Binford, *In Pursuit of the Past: Decoding the Archaeological Record*, Thames and Hudson, New York (1983).

Robin Dunbar, "The ecology of monogamy," *New Scientist* 103:12–15 (30 August 1984).

Nancy Makepeace Tanner, *On Becoming Human*. Cambridge University Press, New York (1981). The food sharing that does occur among chimps is seen when dividing up a kill of a small animal, such as a young bushpig or monkey.

Consort relationships in primates: for baboons, see Shirley C. Strum, "Baboons may be smarter than people," *Animal Kingdom* (New York Zoological Society) 88(2):12–25 (April 1985). For chimpanzees, see de Waal and Goodall.

David R. Carrier, "The energetic paradox of human running and hominid evolution," *Current Anthropology* (August 1984).

Eric Delson, "Oreopithecus is a cercopithecoid after all." *American Journal of Physical Anthropology* 50(3):431–432 (1979).

Concealed ovulation: See Richard D. Alexander and Katherine N. Noonan, "Concealment of ovulation, parental care, and human social evolution," pp. 436–453 in *Evolutionary Biology and Human Social Behavior: An Anthropological Perspective*, edited by N. A. Chagnon and W. G. Irons, Duxbury Press, North Sciuate, Massachusetts (1979). Summarized in R. D. Alexander, *Darwinism and Human Affairs*, University of Washington Press, Seattle (1979).

C. Owen Lovejoy, "The natural detective," *Natural History* 93(10):24–28 (October 1984). For a modern savannah theory, see C. Owen Lovejoy,

"The origin of man," *Science* 211:341–350 (23 January 1981). His reproductive strategy arguments are reported by Donald Johanson and Maitland Edey, *Lucy: The Beginnings of Humankind*, Simon and Schuster, New York (1981).

Richard B. Lee, "What hunters do for a living or, how to make out on scarce resources." In: *Man the Hunter*, edited by R. B. Lee and I. DeVore, pp. 30–48. Aldine, Chicago (1968).

Sarah Blaffer Hrdy, *The Woman That Never Evolved*, Harvard University Press, Cambridge (1981).

Lucy and family are reviewed by Donald C. Johanson and Tim D. White, "A systematic assessment of early African hominids," *Science* 203:321–330 (1979) and in the popular book by Donald Johanson and Maitland Edey, *Lucy: The Beginnings of Humankind*, Simon and Schuster, New York (1981). The Afarensis aficionado should see *Journal of Physical Anthropology*, 57:373–724 (1982). The dating of upright posture is covered by Richard L. Hay and Mary D. Leakey, "The fossil footprints of Laetoli," *Scientific American* 246:50–57 (1982).

Mile 137

Everett J. Bassett, Margaret S. Keith, George J. Armelagos, Debra L. Martin, and Antonio R. Villanueva, "Tetracycline-labeled human bone from ancient Sudanese Nubia (A.D. 350)," *Science* 209:1532–34 (26 September 1980).

Richard Potts, "Home bases and early hominids." *American Scientist* 72:338–347 (July-August 1984). Cautions that the early sites may be butchery sites, not habitations. Existing hunter-gatherers don't reoccupy exact site as before when they move back to an area, since ants and such have been attracted to the old garbage dump. It might have been best for hominids to nest in trees like other apes, and not butcher nearby.

Cave-dwelling and fire in Peking Man: See some cautions by Lewis Binford and Chuan Kun Ho in *Current Anthropology* 26:413 (1985).

Glynn Ll. Isaac and Diana C. Crader, "To what extent were early hominids carnivorous? An archeological perspective," chapter 3 in *Omnivorous Primates: Gathering and Hunting in Human Evolution.* Edited by Robert S. O. Harding and Geza Teleki, Columbia University Press, New York (1981).

Eileen M. O'Brien, "What was the Acheulean hand ax?," *Natural History* 93:20–23 (July 1984).

Eileen M. O'Brien, "The projectile capabilities of an Acheulian handaxe from Olorgesailie," *Current Anthropology* 22:76–79 (February 1981).

M. D. W. Jeffreys, "The Handbolt," *Man* 65:153–154 (1965).

Acheulean hand axes are of two main types: those with one heavier end, and those that are ovoidshaped, with their center of gravity in the middle and which are trimmed to a thin edge on their whole circumference. See p.46 in *Flint Implements* from the British Museum, Third Edition (1968). "Often even the butt of a pointed hand-axe is so much sharpened by trimming that it is difficult to believe it was held in the hand, while the point is often so delicate as to seem too fragile for any use which the comparatively massive butt would suit. . . . The possibility that the ovates were thrown at the prey cannot of course be dismissed."

Because of aerodynamic lift, the discus will travel farther when thrown *into* the wind, which surely aided hunters trying to stay downwind of their prey. See Peter J. Brancazio, *Sport Science: Physical Laws and Optimum Performance*, Simon and Schuster, New York (1984), p. 367.

My term "stochastic toolmaking" is a description of the brute force, hit-or-miss fracturing of potato-sized rocks (see Day 5, Mile 93). The late Harvard archaeologist Glynn Ll. Isaac demonstrated the method in a lecture at the University of Washington on 31 January 1984, entitled "Early hominids: evolution and environmental settings, technological and social initiatives." The Berkeley archaeologist Nicholas Toth details his experiments with toolmaking techniques in "The Oldowan reassessed: a closer look at early stone artifacts," *Journal of Archaeological Sciences* 12:101 (1985), and "Archeological evidence for preferential right-handedness in the lower and middle Pleistocene, and its possible implications," *Journal of Human Evolution* 14:607 (1985); related issues are reviewed by Sarah Bunney, "The origins of manual dexterity," *New Scientist*, p.24 (28 November 1985), and Roger Lewin, "When stones can be deceptive," *Science* 231:113–115 (10 January 1986).

Glynn Llewelyn Isaac, "Aspects of human evolution," in *Essays on Evolution: A Darwin Centenary Volume* (Cambridge University Press, 1983).

For a brief history of the IBM PC and the 1985

demise of IBM's independent Florida offshoot, see Dennis Kneale, "IBM will move headquarters of PC division," *Wall Street Journal*, p.2 (14 June 1985). It "began in 1981 as an autonomous 'independent business unit' with a handful of employees working outside IBM's close corporate oversight. The unit developed a PC prototype in only three months and brought the machine to market less than a year later by breaking IBM's usually rigid rules against relying on outside suppliers for many parts."

Of course, the energy economics of the food chain mean that 90 percent of the calories are wasted by each intermediate stage. Some animals favored by farmers are more efficient than 1/10, at least in turning corn into meat: 1/8 for beef, 1/4 for pork, 1/2 for poultry (at best). Half of the grain in the world is now consumed by animals in aid of providing meat on the plates of the Western world, rather than the grain itself. E. J. Kahn, Jr., "Profiles (Corn)," *New Yorker* (18 June 1984), p.49.; see also his *Staffs of Life*, Little, Brown, Boston (1985).

DAY 10

MILE 137

Brain size in *Homo erectus*: G. Philip Rightmire, lecture entitled "Early hominids in southeast Asia" at the University of Washington, 6 March 1984. The argument of changing brain size within the 1.5 million years of *Homo erectus* is made by Milford H. Wolpoff in *Paleobiology* (Fall 1984).

Wu Rukang and Lin Shenglong, "Peking Man," *Scientific American* 248:86–94 (June 1983).

Erik Trinkaus and William W. Howells, "The Neanderthals," *Scientific American* 241(6):118–133, December 1979.

A summary of primate behavior and hominid data is John E. Pfeiffer's *The Emergence of Humankind*, Harper and Row, New York (1985).

The African origins of anatomically-modern *Homo sapiens sapiens* about 100,000 years ago, and the population explosion by the relatively small numbers who spread out of Africa, are discussed by J. S. Wainscoat et al., "Evolutionary relationships of human populations from an analysis of nuclear DNA polymorphisms," *Nature* 319:491–493 (6 February 1986).

MILE 143

Randall L. Susman, ed., *The Pygmy Chimpanzee*, Plenum, New York (1984). Gavin de Beer, *Embryos and Ancestors*, Oxford University Press (1958).

Stephen Jay Gould, *Ontogeny and Phylogeny*, Harvard University Press, Cambridge (1977).

Ashley Montagu, *Growing Young*, McGraw-Hill, New York (1981).

Raymond P. Coppinger and C. Kay Smith, book review in *The Sciences* (New York Academy of Sciences), 23(3):50–54 (May/June 1983).

Lloyd D. Partridge, "The good enough calculi of evolving control systems: Evolution is not engineering," *American Journal of Physiology* 242:R173-R177 (1982).

The "explosive speciation" of cichlid fish in East African lakes: see P. H. Greenwood, *Bulletin of the British Museum (Natural History), Zoology Supplement* 6:1–13 (1974). The many new species are, however, being eliminated by the thoughtless importation of fish-eating fish species into African lakes; the introduction of Nile perch into Lake Victoria has been a disaster; the indigenous fishes of commercial importance have not merely declined but have virtually disappeared. See C. D. N. Barel et al., "Destruction of fisheries in Africa's lakes," *Nature* 315:19–20 (2 May 1985).

Mosaic selection oversold: The primary "challenge" to Darwinism these days is not from creationists but from evolutionists who believe in Darwinism but think that random variations and natural selection aren't everything, that developmental processes and self-organization properties of matter keep the variations from being truly random. See Mae-Wan Ho, Peter Saunders, and Sidney Fox, "A new paradigm for evolution," *New Scientist* 1497:41–43 (27 February 1986).

MILE 145

A comprehensive physical anthropology textbook is Bernard Campbell's *Human Evolution*, Third Edition, Aldine, New York (1985). See also Fred H. Smith and Frank Spencer, eds., *The Origins of Modern Humans*, Liss, New York (1984).

Head size in proportion to rest of body at various developmental stages: See fig. 17.17 in W. T. Keeton's text, *Biological Science*, 3d ed. (1980), and W. M. Krogman, "Growth changes in the skull, face, jaws, and teeth of the chimpanzee," in *The*

Chimpanzee: Anatomy, Behavior, and Diseases, edited by G. H. Bourne, pp. 104–164, Karger, Basel (1969).

For comparison of brain size among primates: See Richard Passingham's fine undergraduate text, *The Human Primate*, Freeman, San Francisco (1982), at p.112. Note that Passingham, an expert on primate brain/body ratios, manages to avoid juvenilization-neoteny-paedomorphosis as a topic relevant to hominid evolution; the anthropologists are, alas, not alone in this predilection. Many biology texts, e.g., Keeton, also omit juvenilization as a topic.

Length of gestation, age at weaning, age at menarche, and lifespan (data are for preagricultural societies). Similar data for many primate species are tabulated by P. H. Harvey and T. H. Clutton-Brock, "Life history variation in primates," *Evolution* 39:559–581 (May 1985).

	Gestation	Weaning	Menarche	Lifespan
Lemur	0.36	0.3	2.0	30 years
Rhesus	0.46	1.0	4.0	30
Baboon	0.50	1.2	3.8	35
Gibbon	0.57	2.0	8.0	31
Orangutan	0.71	3.0	7.0	50
Gorilla	0.70	4.3	6.5	39
Chimpanzee	0.62	4.0	10.0	45
Homo sap	(0.73)	6.0	16.5	70

While chimpanzee gestation is about 8 months, human gestation would be double that (1.3 years) if we were born as mature as other apes are (judging developmental landmarks, such as the ability to sit upright and closure of skull sutures). See J. M. Tanner, *Foetus into Man: Physical Growth from Conception to Maturity*, Harvard University Press, Cambridge (1978). The first half-year or so after birth is, in a sense, extrauterine gestation, 40 percent of the total (fetal head size is, of course, the major reason for the "premature" birth). It is something akin to what happens with kangaroos, but without a pocket. Stephen Jay Gould discusses this in relation to *Homo erectus* in an essay in *Discover* (December 1985), pp. 53–58. Thus, most life phases approximately double in going from chimp to human, suggesting a halving of developmental clock rates.

Masao Kawai, "Newly acquired precultural behavior of the natural troop of Japanese monkeys on Koshima islet," *Primates* 6:1–30 (1965).

Toolmaking by the orangutan: R. V. S. Wright's research is shown in Passingham, pp.135–7.

For a more general treatment of brain size in vertebrates, see Paul H. Harvey et al., "Brain size and ecology in small animals and primates," *Proceedings of the National Academy of Sciences* (U.S.) 77:4387–4389 (1980).

MILE 148

Matkatamiba is shown in Blaustein's photos 73–75, Powell and Porter facing page 77, and Redfern p.154.

"We do not think because our brain is big. . . .": Robert Ardrey, *The Hunting Hypothesis*, Atheneum, New York (1976), p. 106. Stephen Jay Gould (as usual) said it well in *The Flamingo's Smile*, p. 401: "Always be suspicious of conclusions that reinforce uncritical hope and follow comforting traditions of Western thought."

"Reliable recipe for rapid ratcheting." You'll notice that mutation rates do not play a prominent role in this recipe for speeding up evolution; permutation is assumed to be quite sufficient, thanks to sex. But there are some cycles that might increase cosmic rays, and thus point mutations: the earth's magnetic field has reversed a few times during the last 2 million years; during such reversals, the Van Allen belts, which normally trap some of the incoming particles out in space, are temporarily eliminated. Just how important these reversals are is unknown; they could operate either by increasing mutations or simply by making natural selection more severe, messing up the food supply. The field hasn't reversed since 0.73 million years ago, although if its strength keeps decreasing as fast as it has since about 1950, we could see another reversal 250 years from now.

Scavenging arguments: See Pat Shipman, "The ancestor that wasn't," *The Sciences*, 25(2):43–48 (March 1985) and the news article by Bruce Bower, "Hunting ancient scavengers," *Science News* 127:155–157 (9 March 1985). Relying on a rare top predator as a middleman makes quantitative energetic arguments quite important, though this obvious food-chain-niche-size limitation usually goes unmentioned; scavenging is a good example of a limited growth curve.

William H. Calvin, "A stone's throw and its launch window: Timing precision and its implications for language and hominid brains," *Journal of Theoretical Biology* 104:121–135 (September 1983).

William H. Calvin, *The Throwing Madonna: Essays on the Brain*, McGraw-Hill, New York (1983). An appendix reprints my 1982 article from *Ethology and Sociobiology*; its proposals for how prehumans got started throwing have been largely superceded by the present ones involving threat throwing by scavengers, unaimed handaxe throwing into waterhole herds, developing into aimed throwing at smaller solitary targets. I thank my colleague Joan Lockard for having called threat throwing to my attention. For a modern discussion of the origins of handedness, see Peter F. MacNeilage, Michael G. Studdert-Kennedy, and Björn Lindblom, "Primate handedness reconsidered," *Behavioral and Brain Sciences* (1987).

William H. Calvin and Charles F. Stevens, "Synaptic noise and other sources of randomness in motoneuron interspike intervals," *Journal of Neurophysiology* 31:574–587 (July 1968).

Philip J. Darlington, Jr., *Evolution for Naturalists*. Wiley, New York (1980). One of the first champions of throwing in evolution.

Jane Goodall, *In the Shadow of Man*, Houghton Mifflin, Boston (1971).

Darwin, recognizing that variation around the average, rather than the average type itself, was the motive force for evolution: See Richard C. Lewontin, "Darwin's revolution," *New York Review of Books* (16 June 1983).

Sven O. E. Ebbesson, "Evolution and ontogeny of neural circuits," *Behavioral and Brain Sciences* 7(3):321–331 (September 1984). My commentary "Precision timing requirements suggest wider brain connections, not more restricted ones" appears in the same issue at p.334. Retaining more widespread corticocortial connections: this is only a neuroanatomical example of the widespread biological principle of progenesis, backing up from an overspecialized body form to regain a more generalized one.

Scientists use the Law of Large Numbers all the time, because of its application to statistics (it's why one strives for a large number of separate measurements, so that random sources of error will average out); to halve your measurement error, take four times as many samples. But we tend not to think in terms of the Law of Large Numbers when it comes to nature. That's because something has to do the adding and subtracting and dividing: when doing a scientific experiment, we do that with paper and pencil. And that's so artificial that we don't imagine nature doing the same thing. But nature sometimes does, as when the heart cells pool their irregular electrical currents to make the beat more rhythmic. *THINK STOCHASTIC!*

MILE 150

Female scenarios for evolution of hammering and throwing: See ch. 1 and ch. 3 in William H. Calvin, *The Throwing Madonna: Essays on the Brain*, McGraw-Hill, New York (1983). Hunting by women is discussed by Agnes Estioko-Griffin, "Daughters of the forest," *Natural History* 95(5):36–43 (May 1986).

William McGrew, "Evolutionary implications of sex differences in chimpanzee predation and tool use." In *The Great Apes*, volume 5 of *Perspectives on Human Evolution*. Edited by David A. Hamburg and Elizabeth R. McCown, pp. 441–464, Benjamin/Cummings, Menlo Park, California (1979).

Christophe Boesch and Hedwige Boesch, "Sex differences in the use of natural hammers by wild chimpanzees: A preliminary report," *Journal of Human Evolution* 10:585–593 (1981).

Jane Goodall, "Tool-using in Primates and Other Vertebrates," *Advances in the Study of Behaviour* 3:195–249 (1970).

Frances Dahlberg, ed., *Woman the Gatherer*, Yale University Press, New Haven (1981). Includes a discussion of the Agta of the Philippines, where the women hunt systematically.

MILE 153

I hope that there are no Catholics who are offended by my choice of illustrative example ("Hail Mary," etc.); it actually did happen, just as I present it, and the woman was as Catholic as years in a convent-run school make one. As I hope the evening's discussion about word-order language vs. emotional language eventually makes clear: If it hadn't happened, I would have had to invent something rather like it to serve as a teaching example. Similarly, at Mile 136, when discussing the barnyard model for human sexual behavior: It is, of course, the contrast between the Catholic Church's views on nonreproductive sex and its oft-expressed concern with the integrity of the family that makes it an instructive example of how a misunderstanding of reproductive sociobiology can detract from a humanitarian goal. Living as I do in a country where a quarter of all children live in poverty, often because of a one-parent family, where the divorce rate is twice that of the runner-up country, one can only wish that everyone took raising children as seriously as the Catholic Church.

MILE 155

William H. Calvin and George A. Ojemann, *Inside the Brain: Mapping the Cortex, Exploring the Neuron*, New American Library, New York (Mentor paperback, 1980). Pre-throwing-theory, this supplementary text illustrates brain maps and is especially good as an introduction to the language specializations. For an advanced treatment, see George A. Ojemann, "Brain organization for language from the perspective of electrical stimulation mapping," *Behavioral and Brain Sciences* 6(2):189–230 (June 1983).

Doreen Kimura, "Neuromotor mechanisms in the evolution of human communication." In *Neurobiology of Social Communication in Primates*, edited by H. D. Steklis and M. J. Raleigh, Academic Press, New York, pp. 197–219 (1979).

Ashley Montagu, "Toolmaking, hunting, and the origin of language." *Annals of the New York Academy of Sciences* 280:266–274 (1976).

Phoneme-order at the level of words, and word-order at the level of sentences, both keep separate the representation of signals and meaning, a feature that is called duality of patterning. See C. F. Hockett, "The origin of speech," *Scientific American*, 203:88–108 (1960).

Ovid J. L. Tzeng and William S.-Y. Wang, "Search for a common neurocognitive mechanism for language and movements," *American Journal of Physiology* 246:R904-R911 (1984). Sequencing as the neural predecessor of language.

Antecedents of word-order rules in primate behavior patterns: See Rom Harre and Vernon Reynolds, eds., *The Meaning of Primate Signals*, Cambridge University Press (1984).

Sue Taylor Parker and Kathleen Rita Gibson, "A developmental model for the evolution of language and intelligence in early hominids," *Behavioral and Brain Sciences* 2:367–408 (1979). Also see follow-up comments in June 1982 issue.

Dwight Sutton, "Mechanisms underlying vocal control in nonhuman primates." In: *Neurobiology of Social Communication in Primates*, edited by H. D. Steklis and M. J. Raleigh, Academic Press, New York, pp. 45–68 (1979).

J. L. Bradshaw and N. C. Nettleton, "The nature of hemispheric specialization in man," *Behavioral and Brain Sciences* 4:51–92 (March 1981).

Neighbors of language cortex: the premotor cortex, while classically related to things such as planning sequential motor acts (and there are extensive connections to the wrist part of the motor cortex), also serves as a language area in humans (see Ojemann's maps). Stephen P. Wise, "The primate premotor cortex," *Annual Reviews of Neuroscience* 8:1–19 (1985); K. F. Muakassa and Peter L. Strick, "Frontal lobe inputs to primate motor cortex: Evidence for four somatotopically organized 'premotor' areas," *Brain Research*, 177:176–182 (1979); Gary Goldberg, "Supplementary motor area structure and function: Review and hypotheses," *Behavioral and Brain Sciences* 8(4):567–616 (December 1985).

The descent of the larynx: See Jeffrey T. Laitman, "The anatomy of human speech," *Natural History* 93(8):20–27 (August 1984).

For an overview of language biology: See William S. Y. Wang's collection of *Scientific American* pieces entitled *Human Communication: Language and its Psychobiological Bases*, Freeman, San Francisco (1982). And see Philip Lieberman's *The Biology and Evolution of Language*, Harvard University Press, Cambridge (1984). As he correctly points out, neoteny cannot explain the descent of the larynx in anatomically-modern *Homo sapiens sapiens*; this hardly "refutes neoteny" as being a major factor in hominid evolution but only provides another example of how it cannot explain every feature. Neoteny cannot explain the shape of our nose either, and that's not subtle and hidden (Elaine Morgan suggests that our nose shape is an aquatic adaptation).

Nonverbal communication: See Alison Jolly, "The evolution of primate behavior," *American Scientist* 73:230–239 (1985); and Joan S. Lockard, ed., *Evolution of Human Social Behavior*, Elsevier, Amsterdam (1980).

Elizabeth Bates, "Bioprograms and the innateness hypothesis," *Behavioral and Brain Sciences* 7:188–189 (1984).

Theodore Holmes Bullock, "Comparative neuroscience holds promise for quiet revolutions," *Science* 225:473–478 (3 August 1984).

Joan Didion, *Michigan Quarterly Review*, 18(4):521–534 (Autumn 1979).

DAY 11

MILE 155

Manfred Clynes, ed., *Music, Mind, and Brain*, Plenum, New York (1982).

MILE 157

Havasu Canyon is shown in Blaustein's photos 76,77; Geerlings pages 124–128. For a history of the Indians who now live in the Grand Canyon, see "The Havasupai," *Plateau* (Museum of Northern Arizona) 56(4) (1986).

Loren Eiseley, "Man and novelty," in *Time and Stratigraphy in the Evolution of Man*, U.S. National Academy of Sciences, publ. 1469 (1967), pp.65–79.

Melatonin, the hormone from the pineal, is not related to melanin, the skin pigment. It was, however, named after it because melatonin causes melanin to cluster in frog skin.

Melatonin-pineal: See the symposium volume "The Medical and Biological Effects of Light," *Annals of the New York Academy of Sciences* 453 (1985). See also Bruce Fellman, "A clockwork gland," *SCIENCE 85* 6(4):76–81 (May 1985).

Awareness as consciousness: Neurologists tell of examples of brain damage where the patient will deny seeing a light—but can point to it accurately if asked to guess. It's called blindsight.

The classic reference on how the common sense view of consciousness leads to absurdities is Gilbert Ryle, *The Concept of Mind*, Barnes and Noble, New York (1949); Arthur Koestler's *The Ghost in the Machine* (London, 1967) may also be of interest. The serial ordering of concepts as a key aspect of consciousness was elaborated by G. Humphrey, *Thinking*, Menthuen, London (1951) and K. S. Lashley, "Cerebral organization in behavior" in L. A. Jeffress (editor), *Cerebral Mechanisms in Behavior*, Wiley, New York (1951), pp.112–146.

Kathryn Morton, "The Story-Telling Animal," *New York Times Book Review*, pp.1–2 (23 December 1984).

Peter Brooks, *Reading for the Plot*, Vintage (1985).

Walter J. Freeman, "A physiological hypothesis of perception," *Perspectives in Biology and Medicine*, (Summer 1981), pp.561–592.

Edward O. Wilson, *On Human Nature*, Harvard University Press, Cambridge (1978).

Richard D. Alexander, *Darwinism and Human Affairs*, University of Washington Press, Seattle (1979).

Random elements essential to thought: see Gregory Bateson, *Mind and Nature*, E. P. Dutton, New York (1979).

W.H. Auden, in *The New Yorker* (1970), quoted by Loren Eiseley in *The Star Thrower*, p.20.

Elizabeth Loftus, *Memory*, Addison-Wesley, Boston (1980).

Canals on Mars: See Arthur C. Clarke, *1984: Spring, A Choice of Futures*, Ballantine Books, New York (1984).

Julian Jaynes, lecture "The Self" at New York Academy of Sciences, 9'December 1985, and *The Origin of Consciousness in the Breakdown of the Bicameral Mind*, Houghton Mifflin, Boston (1976). His book's first section is a good summary of what consciousness isn't. One will not find my present view of consciousness (the narrator arising from temporarily-independent sequencing circuits playing games with schemata, the "most reasonable" then funneled through the language serial bottleneck) expressed in more detail elsewhere; most of the following references are to classical views.

For willed intentions starting before one is aware of it, see Benjamin Libet et al., "Subjective referral of the timing for a conscious sensory experience," *Brain* 102 (March 1979) and the various critiques in *Behavioral and Brain Sciences* 8(4):529–566 (December 1985).

Donald R. Griffin, *Animal Thinking*, Harvard University Press, Cambridge (1984). A view of animal consciousness, though lacking in any comparison of sequential planning skills amongst animals.

A common view of consciousness is expressed in the tendency to attribute to animals much of our human awareness, e.g., to see a monkey using a tool, say "isn't that clever?" and attribute to them the kind of insight and planning of which humans are sometimes capable. Ethology and behavioral psychology tend to take a narrower view, looking for antecedents of the tool use and studying the ways in which tool use arises in a naive population. Cebus monkeys (Capuchin and organ-grinder's monkey are some common names) are among the most clever tool-users outside of the apes; still, the discovery of how to probe for hidden syrup down a hole using a broken branch seems not so much a "eureka" phenomenon as a gradual piecing together of the elements of the puzzle by some trial-and-error, with the finished concept then spread by observation learning, and elaborated into making the appropriate tool. Talk at the University of Washington by Professor Doree Fragaszy on 28 May 1985 entitled "Capuchin monkeys making and using tools: How do they measure up to chimps?"

Francis H. C. Crick, "Thinking about the brain," *Scientific American* 241 (September 1979).

The various positions that neuroscientists have taken on the mind-brain problem are usefully summarized by Ronald Chase in "The mentalist hypothesis and invertebrate neurobiology," *Perspectives in Biology and Medicine*, pp.103–117 (Autumn 1979). See also Gordon Rattray Taylor, *The Natural History of the Mind*, Dutton, New York (1979). Particularly notable are the books of the neurophysiologist John C. Eccles [e.g., *The Human Mystery* (1979) and *The Human Psyche* (1980) from Springer Verlag]; among the best-informed and most accomplished of neurophysiologists, his skillful—but, I think, increasingly unsuccessful—efforts to fit our knowledge of the brain into a classical philosophical framework convince me that the questions are simply posed wrong in classical thinking, and that for heuristic reasons if none other, we must seek new ways of thinking about the mind-body problem.

My model of sentence formulation, based on quality judgments made about many random permutations of schemata which come to mind, may provide a parallel mechanistic model for Noam Chomsky's proposal to permit syntax to overgenerate profusely and then to provide most of the significant reduction in the form of a system of filters and constraints on logical form. This is the starting point of what is called trace theory in linguistics: See *Binding and Filtering*, edited by Frank Heny, MIT Press, Cambridge (1982).

Selective attention: See S. Hochstein and J. H. R. Maunsell, "Dimensional attention effects in the responses of V4 neurons of the macaque monkey," *Society for Neuroscience Abstracts* 364.6 (1985). Swamping precision problems with large numbers of neurons: Besides throwing, I have extended the theory to fine sensory discriminations such as depth perception. See William H. Calvin, "Fine discrimination as an emergent property of parallel neural circuits," *Society for Neuroscience Abstracts* 10(2):756 (1984); the same principle also applies to color discriminations as well.

Shawn Carlson, "A double-blind test of astrology," *Nature* 318:419–425 (5 December 1985).

Mile 163

The Thomas Traherne epigram comes from R. Miller, *Meaning and Consciousness in the Intact Brain*, Clarendon Press, Oxford (1981).

Mile 166

National Canyon "chute" is shown in Powell and Porter facing page 142.

Peter K. Stevens, *Patterns in Nature*, Little Brown, Boston (1974). The classic is D'Arcy Thompson, *On Growth and Form*, Cambridge University Press (1917, abridged edition 1971); the bighorn's corkscrew is among its many examples.

Emergent patterns from simple component parts: Stephen Wolfram, "Cellular automata as models of complexity," *Nature* 311:419–424 (4 October 1984). Unfortunately, the inverse problem is more difficult: What rules and initial conditions tend to give self-organizing patterns?

Erwin Schrödinger, *What is Life?*, Cambridge University Press, Cambridge (1944).

Conway game of life: See Eigen and Winkler (1976) or William Poundstone's *The Recursive Universe*, Morrow, New York (1984).

David G. King, "Metaptation: The product of selection at the second tier." Submitted to *Paleobiology* (1985). See also Elizabeth Vrba and Niles Eldredge, "Individuals, hierarchies, and processes: towards a more complete evolutionary theory," *Paleobiology* 10:146–171 (1984).

Knut Schmidt-Nielsen, *Scaling: Why is animal size so important?*, Cambridge University Press (1984).

Jumps into hyperspace: At least that's how it worked on the first such computer game, Spacewar, which I used to play on the PDP–1 computer at M.I.T. in 1961. For a description of those heady days, see ch. 3 of Steven Levy's *Hackers*, Doubleday, New York (1984). It omits an important aspect of microcomputer history. See W. H. Calvin, "The Missing LINC," *Byte* 7(4):20 (April 1982).

J. B. S. Haldane, *On Being the Right Size (and Other Essays)*, Oxford University Press (1985).

Theodosius Dobzhansky, *The Biology of Ultimate Concern*, Rapp and Whiting, London (1969).

DAY 12

MILE 166

Loren Eiseley, "Man and novelty," in *Time and Stratigraphy in the Evolution of Man*, U.S. National Academy of Sciences, publ. 1469 (1967), pp.65–79.

Historical research has shown that if one identifies a series of advances in science, the key research that opened up the advance was considered at the time so remote from the area eventually illuminated as to be essentially irrelevant. See the book by the medical physiologist Julius Comroe, *Retrospectroscope: Insights into Medical Discovery*, Von Gohr Press (1977). A short version is in *Science* 192:105–111 (1976). A similar analysis for the physical sciences is by Leon M. Lederman, "The value of fundamental science," *Scientific American* 251(5):40 (November 1984).

MILE 170

Parkinson's disease cell-death percentages, summarized by J. W. Langston, "The case of the tainted heroin," *The Sciences* (New York Academy of Sciences) 25(1):40 (January 1985).

Selection evolutionarily ineffective after menopause except for rearing existing offspring: I can think of one major exception to this. Because of juvenilization-plus-slowing doubling the duration of life span phases, our age 45 may be age 22 in our ape-like ancestor; chimps may be reproductive for a decade after that (e.g., "Flo" at Gombe), corresponding to our age 65. Thus, our ape ancestors might have been under some selection for our kind of longevity, even though more recent hominids are not. We could owe some of our post-menopause life span to our long-lived ape ancestors rather than more recent long-lived hominid ancestors.

Ronald Melzack and Patrick D. Wall, *The Challenge of Pain*, Basic Books (1984).

MILE 177

Vulcan's Forge and lava dam: See Redfern, pp.108–110.

MILE 179

Lava Falls photos in Blaustein et al., Collins et al., and Redfern pp.104–105, 190–191.

I have thus far spared readers a description of my 1984 trip through Lava Falls. It was less daunting than the 1982 run described in the text, but appalling in another way. There was a yellow hel-

icopter (registration N93MI) at Lava, making repeated passes over the rapid so that a TV camera could follow a little one-person boat going through the waves, then picking up the boat and ferrying it back upriver so that still another run could be photographed. It was all for a cigarette commercial for German television. As we ate lunch on the ledge below Lava, we were buzzed a half-dozen times by the helicopter, engaged in its ignoble mission of promoting a drug addiction by persuading gullible viewers that real outdoors people smoked cigarettes. Of the several dozen "outdoors types" in our group (largely nonscientists that trip), there was only one regular smoker (a seventeen-year-old, exactly the age group at which such commercials are aimed); none of the boatmen were smokers.

Besides the ubiquitous tourist overflights, we were buzzed in 1980 by an F-15 at 50 m altitude; later at Mile 220, we were buzzed four times at dusk by a small plane flying at 10 m altitude above the river in the narrow canyon. It was trying to drop ice cream to a "super deluxe" motor tour group camped downstream of us. In 1985, a helicopter crashed into the Colorado River at Mile 4, killing two, while filming a movie. In midday, the virtually unregulated air traffic is audible more than half of the time at many places in the Canyon; the governor of Arizona compares the noise to Phoenix at rush hour. The U.S. Secretary of the Interior (who is responsible for the national parks) was quoted in August 1985 as saying that the mounting complaints about air traffic over the Grand Canyon were unimportant. I don't mind small planes (I have a private pilot's license myself) but their routine use in wilderness areas and national parks is clearly incompatible with the reasons for which we set such areas aside. See Dennis Brownridge, "Dogfight over Grand Canyon Continues," *High Country News*, p. 26 (26 May 1986).

MILE 182

Hexagonal basalt "tapestries" are shown in Blaustein's photos 88,91.

Loren Eiseley, *The Star Thrower*, p.202 (1978).

Stephen H. Schneider and Randi Londer, *The Coevolution of Climate and Life*, Sierra Club Books, San Francisco (1984).

John Imbrie and K. P. Imbrie, *Ice Ages: Solving the Problem*, Enslow, Short Hills, N.J. (1979).

John Imbrie and J. Z. Imbrie, "Modeling the

climatic response to orbital variations," *Science* 207:943–953 (1980).

John Gribbin, "New statistics tie climate theories together," *New Scientist*, p.20 (7 February 1985).

Rainfall changes due to CO_2 warming: See Gina Maranto, "Are we close to the road's end?," *Discover*, pp.28–50 (January 1986).

Methane is the most effective of the Greenhouse gases; See the editorial in *Science* 231:1233 (14 March 1986).

G. Kukla, A. Berger, R. Lotti, and J. Brown, "Orbital signature of interglacials." *Nature* 290:295–300 (26 March 1981).

André Berger, "Support for the astronomical theory of climatic change," *Nature* 269:44–45 (1 September 1977).

Aldo Leopold, *Sand County Almanac*, Oxford University Press, Oxford (1949), p.190.

MILE 186

William F. Ruddiman, lecture entitled "CLI-MAP reconstruction of the last interglaciation," 7 May 1985, at the University of Washington.

Ice sheet data for the last glacial period are summarized by Wallace S. Broecker, Dorothy M. Peteet, and David Rind, "Does the ocean-atmosphere system have more than one stable mode of operation?," *Nature* 315:21–26 (2 May 1985). In their figure 2, note the many brief "spikes" of intensified cold lasting many hundreds of years; these occurred during the period between 32,000 and 10,000 years ago in Greenland (but not Antarctica). The most intense event, a cold snap lasting from 11,000 to 10,200 years ago during the end of the last ice age, was recorded in the flora of Europe but not North America (it is known as the Younger Dryas). These spikes are seen in ice cores but not deep-sea cores (worms churning the ocean floor serve to smooth the rapid fluctuations; this was discovered when the surface layers of the ocean floor gave radiometric dates of 3000 years old! The worms serve to average the last 6000 years. Having done pioneer studies of soil churning by worms, Charles Darwin presumably would have been amused.)

MILE 188

Cave art: See John E. Pfeiffer, *The Creative Explosion*, Harper and Row, New York (1982).

Immunological hazards of inbreeding are evident in the cheetah; all living individuals seem closely related, as if the present population sprang from only a few ancestors because of a bottleneck. See S. J. O'Brien et al., "Genetic basis for species vulnerability in the cheetah," *Science* 227:1428–1434 (22 March 1985).

Graham Hoyle, "Behavior in the light of identified neurons," *Behavioral and Brain Sciences* 7:690–691 (December 1984).

DAY 13

MILE 188

Whitmore Wash photo in Leydet, page 118.

Juvenilization: Note that shifts in the overall range may be misleading. The improved diet which has reduced the age of menarche about 25 percent during the last three centuries has produced some change in juvenilization, just as it has also increased adult height, but that didn't bias our gene pool. Now if something had eliminated those individuals with less juvenilization (e.g., poor hunting success in a winter climate), then the gene pool would have been changed. "Size," of course, means volume (proportional to weight), not mere height; think of a heavyset Eskimo, not an East African.

Loren Eiseley, "Man and novelty," in *Time and Stratigraphy in the Evolution of Man*, U.S. National Academy of Sciences, publ. 1469 (1967), pp.65–79.

H. G. Wells, "The discovery of the future," *Nature* 65:326 (1902).

Further slowing of developmental clock rates for further juvenilization, see lemur-chimp-human comparison in notes for Mile 145. If a doubling of human life span were desirable, halving the clock rates again would seem one possibility. See, however, Aldous Huxley's cautionary novel, *After Many a Summer Dies the Swan*, Harper, New York (1939); it is briefly summarized by Ashley Montagu in *Growing Young* on pp.243–244.

Creative thinking via variations on existing schemata: See Kenneth Craik, *The Nature of Explanation*, Cambridge University Press (1943), and Douglas R. Hofstadter, "Variations on a theme as the crux of creativity," in his *Metamagical Themas*, Basic Books, New York (1985).

MILE 200

Stephen Jay Gould, *The Mismeasure of Man*, W. W. Norton, New York (1981).

Loren Eiseley, "Man and novelty," in *Time and Stratigraphy in the Evolution of Man*, U.S. National Academy of Sciences, publ. 1469 (1967), pp.65–79.

Parallel processing by the brain: See Dana H. Ballard, "Cortical connections and parallel processing: Structure and function," *Behavioral and Brain Sciences* 9(1):67–120 (1986).

MILE 205

Larry Stevens, "A boatman's lessons," *Plateau* 53(3):24–28 (Summer 1981).

Penfield's sister: Adopted, with some liberties taken, from a lecture by Brenda Milner, Society for Neuroscience meeting, 1981. For a survey of frontal lobe research, see *Trends in Neurosciences* (November 1984).

Richard A. Muller, remarks in New York City, 4 December 1985.

Derek de Solla Price, *Science since Babylon*, Yale University Press (1975).

Damaged nerve computer simulations reviewed by W. H. Calvin, "To spike or not to spike? Controlling the neuron's rhythm, preventing the ectopic beat." In *Abnormal Nerves and Muscles as Impulse Generators*, edited by W. J. Culp and J. Ochoa pp. 295–321, Oxford University Press, New York (1982).

MILE 212

Tanzanian native quoted by Bunny McBride, "If people be killing killing. . . ." *Sierra Club Bulletin* 70(2):67 (March 1985). Many languages intensify the verb by repeating it.

Lorenz epigram: This is the translation from the German provided in Eigen and Winkler's 1981 American edition, which I prefer to the inelegant translation of the same concluding passage in the American edition of Lorenz's book, *Behind the Mirror*, Harcourt Brace Jovanovich, New York (1977).

MILE 220

Hippocrates. This is not from the Hippocratic Oath but from the aphorisms of his school.

John Gardner, *On Moral Fiction*, Basic Books, New York (1978).

For an ecologist's agenda, see Paul R. Ehrlich, *The Machinery of Nature*, Simon and Schuster, New York (1986).

DAY 14

MILE 222

Purple sand, etc. Some of the dawn colors described here may not be repeated regularly, as my notes were taken in July 1982. Sunrise colors were affected by the El Chichón volcanic eruption in Mexico three months earlier, once the cloud had been around the world. Unusually brilliant and prolonged sunrises and sunsets were reported in Arizona beginning a month after the eruption; for some time, the sky was a whitish blue instead of its normal bright blue. Following such eruptions which inject aerosols into the upper atmosphere, sunsets typically begin with a lavender glow that appears high over the horizon and changes gradually to yellow and orange. After the sun sets, there is often a strong red afterglow (Day 8 sunset) that shades into purple higher above the horizon. See Michael R. Rampino and Stephen Self, "The atmospheric effects of El Chichón," *Scientific American* 250(1):56 (January 1984).

POSTSCRIPT

John Maynard Keynes, *Essays in Persuasion*. Harcourt, New York (1932), pp.371–373.

Index